Animals

compiled by
Sarah Johnson

Themes in Environmental History, 4

'Themes in Environmental History' is a series of readers for students and researchers. Each volume aims to cover a prominent subject in the discipline, combining theoretical chapters and case studies. All chapters have been previously published in the White Horse Press journals *Environment and History* and *Environmental Values*.

1. *Bioinvaders* (2010) ISBN 978-1-874267-55-3
2. *Landscapes* (2010) ISBN 978-1-874267-60-7
3. *Indigenous Knowledge* (2012) ISBN 978-1-874267-68-3
4. *Animals* (2014) ISBN 978-1-874267-80-5

Copyright © The White Horse Press 2014
First published 2014 by
The White Horse Press, 10 High Street, Knapwell, Cambridge, CB23 4NR, UK

Set in 10 point Times

All rights reserved. Except for the quotation of short passages for the purpose of criticism or review, no part of this book may be reprinted or reproduced or utilised in any form or by any electronic, mechanical or other means, including photocopying or recording, or in any information storage or retrieval system, without permission from the publishers.

British Library Cataloguing in Publication Data
A catalogue record for this book is available from the British Library

ISBN   978-1-874267-80-5 (PB)

Contents

Publisher's Introduction
Sarah Johnson   v

An Animal: What is it?
Keekok Lee   1

USING ANIMALS: POPULATIONS AND EXPLOITATION

Livestock

Bodies on the Beach: Domesticates and Disasters
in the Spanish Philippines 1750–1898
Greg Bankoff   21

Goats, Marginality and the 'Dangerous Other'
David Siddle   42

Hunting

Three Centuries of Whaling and Walrus Hunting in Svalbard
and its Impact on the Arctic Ecosystem
Louwrens Hacquebord   58

A 'Sportsman's Paradise':
The Effects of Hunting on the Avifauna of the Gippsland Lakes
Coral Dow   74

Environmental History of Marine Mammal Exploitation in
Trinidad and Tobago, W.I., and its Ecological Impact
*Aldemaro Romero, Ruth Baker, Joel E. Cresswell, Anuradha Singh,
Annabelle McKie and Michael Manna*   93

ANIMAL CONSERVATION: HISTORY AND THEORY

Conservation and Individual Worth
Gill Aitken   115

Preservation and protection

The Grey Seal in Britain: A Twentieth Century History of
a Nature Conservation Success
Robert A. Lambert   131

For the 'Preservation of Friends' and the 'Destruction of Enemies':
Studying and Protecting Birds in Late Imperial Russia
Brian Bonhomme   156

Population management: past realities and future strategies

Wolves in the Early Nineteenth-Century County of Jönköping, Sweden
Örjan Kardell and Anna Dahlström   185

De-Domestication: Ethics at the Intersection of
Landscape Restoration and Animal Welfare
*Christian Gamborg, Bart Gremmen, Stine B. Christiansen
and Peter Sandøe*   215

WHERE CULTURE MEETS CREATURE

Conservation as negotiation

'The Common Cormorant or Shag Lays Eggs Inside a Paper Bag'.
A Cultural Ecology of Fish-eating Birds in Western Australia
Joanna Sassoon   237

A Cultural History of Crocodiles in the Philippines:
Towards a New Peace Pact?
Jan van der Ploeg, Merlijn van Weerd and Gerard A. Persoon   258

Wild displays

Demonstration Wildlife: Negotiating the Animal Landscape
of Vancouver's Stanley Park, 1888–1996
Sean Kheraj   293

Hunting Narratives of the Age of Empire:
A Gender Reading of Their Iconography
Karen Wonders   323

Publisher's Introduction

Sarah Johnson

WHAT IS AN ANIMAL (AND WHY DOES IT MATTER)?

Fascination with animals is one of a child's earliest impulses and, to that child, there is no problem of definition – a dog is a dog, be it Great Dane or bichon-frise. There are no clouding questions of taxonomy, no quandaries of ethics. Innately, it seems, we recognise members of another species as different from humans and similar to each other, and value them for it. The child does not appreciate the boundary-bending of the bryophytes, thallophytes and cholorophytes cited by Keekok Lee in this volume's opening essay, and is often bemused by the human-animal hybridity of such mythical beasts as the centaur or mermaid (though not, interestingly, with the talking, clothed bears and wolves of fairytale). Species boundaries seem to be instinctively understood, but in the child's mind that does not preclude relational urges that might be defined as anthropomorphism.

As with the infant, 'lay consciousness' of animals is, Lee observes, dominated by household, garden and farmyard 'friends' and 'charismatic' species confined in zoos or seen on television. Lee points out that, of some 1,032,000 species known to science, mammals and birds account for only 4,000 and 8,600 species respectively. The well-loved dog, cat, cow, elephant, tiger, budgerigar, chicken and robin are statistically almost irrelevant. Of Lee's posited four approaches to defining animals – those of (a) scientists as zoologists, (b) the ordinary person in the street, (c) philosophers or writers concerned with animal liberation and/or animal rights, (d) apologists for zoos – she argues that only the zoological account, with its focus on genetics and species, properly considers the full range of creatures that may taxonomically be defined as animals. Zoology also provides the (normally) clear-cut genetic distinctness of 'species' as a framework for consideration of individual animals:

> No amount of training, pumping steroid, eating large helpings of steak or taking ginseng by the mouthful could lead a human to perform in the same way a cheetah does. The difference can only be satisfactorily understood and explained in terms of their species characteristics.

Thus far, the zoological view accords with the commonsensical. Though human societies down the ages have, hopefully or fearfully, fabulated about, say, centaurs or selkies – hybrids possessing qualities of other animals that we desire – such things belong to a realm 'outside over there'; experientially we recognise *essential* dissimilarities between species. However, where the zoological view diverges from the lay perception is in an insistence on contextualisation: Lee argues that zoologists think not of individual creatures but of 'members of species which themselves are historical lineages, having evolved and continue to evolve (if not made extinct) within their particular habitats and ecosystems'. Here she crystallises a crucial 'polarisation' in thought about animals – individualism versus holism. Should we consider animals as individual selves, or insofar as they belong to evolving species that, in turn, is part of a wider ecosystem? These questions are central to many conservation debates.

As Lee outlines, animal rights philosophers, lay people and the zoo industry consider and (re)present animals in ways that emphasise their individuality, their relationality, their degree of likeness to us. Such focus on the individual can motivate highly laudable feelings and actions – animal philosophers think about animals and attempt to prescribe how we treat them in relation to their ability to experience suffering or to engage in mental activity (both traits which stir human empathy); whereas the 'pure' zoologist only allows that an animal 'is capable of metabolism, growth, adaptibility, irritability and interaction with the environment' (Lee). And yet, human relations with and thought about animals – the stuff of animal environmental history – are inextricably rooted in 'the roles they play in human lives', their 'religious/cultural, culinary, economic or personal significance for the social group or individual in question' (Lee). To limit the conception of the animal to cells and genes is artificially to sideline the cultural factors that direct intellectual inquiry in the first place.

As part of the series 'Themes in Environmental History', this volume is concerned with the cultural: what an animal innately *is* is of less importance here than the tracing of overlapping, contradictory, changing conceptions of animals, in different times and different cultures – from 'the beast within' to the object of everyday use to cases where human beings, by design or otherwise, influence the futures of entire populations and species. Like the infant with whom I began, we shall, by and large, be happy to accept that a dog is a dog (and that, as Kardell and Dahlström explore, a wolf is something quite other, culturally and zoologically). This volume seeks to elucidate how human societies have used, abused, thought about and represented animals. That is not to say that Lee's trenchant questioning of the societal tendency to sloppy definition is irrelevant: while none of the essays here looks beyond the mammals and birds she reminds us form only a tiny proportion of the Earth's biota, her emphasis on viewing animals in the contexts of species and of ecology is vital to the 'management' debates informing the essays by Lambert, Aitken, Kardell and Dahlström and Gamborg et al.; while the forces of sentiment, curiosity and utilitarianism that for her inflect all definitions except the zoological play out in almost every essay. For historians, it is essential to remain conscious that the ways in which data and ideas on any subject are generated, transmitted and interpreted are culturally shaped. Historians are not interested in animals just as organisms with metabolism: the utility, sentiment, wonder and repulsion they have held

Introduction

for human societies throughout history, the *relationships* of humans and animals at various levels, are the basis of the historical animal studies.

USING ANIMALS

As Bankoff observes at the close of his analysis of the impacts of natural disaster on domestic animals in the Philippines, human–animal relations may be reciprocal, but, almost always, the 'terms of exchange favour humans over animals much as they do in any patron-client relationship'. In terms of the natural hazards of flooding and volcanoes investigated by Bankoff, the animal death-tolls (where they were deemed worthy of recording at all) were undoubtedly increased because humans, by domesticating – by concentrating animals 'in large numbers often in hazardous locations such as on floodplains or in close proximity to active volcanoes' and by breeding out features geared towards survival – made animals more vulnerable. The human desire to extract use from animals – milk, eggs, meat, labour – not only directly led to animal mortality (by means of slaughter), but increased accidental mortality as animals perished alongside their owners and 'as people abandoned their homes and belongings and precipitately took sanctuary on higher ground ... were often left to fend for themselves'. Even if animals survived initial disaster impacts, the loss of food supplies in the aftermath meant casualties would rise as humans saved themselves rather than their beasts. That such deaths were frequently recorded in the annals Bankoff investigated, however, indicates the significance these domesticated animals had for the human population: the 'bodies on the beach' represented loss of livelihood and food supply for humans and, as such, animal and human vulnerability were mutually constitutive.[1]

More usually, animal mortality is the desired outcome to fulfil human wants. Animals have long been used for food – in earliest times by hunting and later by domestication, provision of products such as eggs and milk and eventual slaughter. Siddle, for example, argues the importance of goats in providing 'a measure of subsistence security' for economically marginal populations in pre-Industrial Mediterranean lands. Animal bodies have not only aided human subsistence but have been (and continue to be) valuable trade commodities, as two essays on sea mammal hunting by Hacquebord (whales and walruses in Svalbard) and Romero et al. (whales and manatees in Trinidad and Tobago) demonstrate. Romero et al. offer a visceral portrait of the realities of small-boat whaling on the Caribbean island, where whale products were restricted to (but important for some years in) the local economy:

---

1. On the responsibilities associated with domestication, Bankoff's historical study intersects interestingly with Gamborg's exploration of the ethics of de-domestication, discussed below.

Introduction

These boats were at the Bay, and when a whale was sighted a horn would be blown, signalling the crew, who all lived at the Bay, to run down the hill to man the boats, and push them off. When a cow was spotted with its calf, the whaler aimed at wounding the calf with the least possible injury in order to ensure that the mother could be easily approached and harpooned. A flag was stuck in the whale, the mouth was sewn up so it would not take in water and sink, and it was towed into the station. Local personnel worked for up to 24 hours at a time flensing the animal, as near to the shore as possible, and the slices of blubber were carried to the sugar coppers, for boiling to extract the oil.

It seems from their analysis that, though whaling here was a 'rudimentary' and 'uncoordinated' local operation, an annex to a thriving vegetable oil industry, powered by slaves, populations of sea mammals, never enormous, were relatively quickly wiped out. Hacquebord's account, by contrast, is of a large-scale and long-duration whaling industry conducted by crews who travelled vast distances to the Arctic and dwelled there for many months, processing their catch at shore-based industrial and living facilities whose middens offer archaeological treasure trove to researchers. Hacquebord calculates from the extensive records maintained by whaling crews ('Very often the place, the moment and the circumstances under which a whale was killed were noted in official notarial statements') that 46,000 Greenland right whales and 25,000 walruses were removed from the local ecosystem from the seventeenth to nineteenth centuries. His paper offers a fascinating insight into the long-term effects that this removal of predators from the ecosystem (and concomitant releasing of prey for consumption by other species, primarily eider duck and little auk) appears to have had. The pair of whaling papers offers a locally-specific case-study focused largely on cultural practice and an extensive analysis of historical seabird population dynamics based on statistical analysis of bones found in middens and sizes of present-day seabird colonies. Both are stories of unremitting drives to extinction but Hacquebord's piece shows how one species' misfortune may be another's opportunity.

Dow investigates historical impacts of fowling on the Gippsland Lakes of south-eastern Australia during the late nineteenth and early twentieth centuries. While some of this activity was undertaken by 'pot-shooters' or professionals with 'punt guns' shooting large numbers of birds for sale, Dow's focus is on the dramatic population impacts of sport shooting. The diaries of individual sportsmen reveal shooting as a colonial manifestation of British culture, with hunters seeking out the species that most resembled familiar gamebirds from the Old Country. Despite their adherence to 'gentlemanly' sporting practice (if the target species, e.g. snipe, could not be found they would not shoot just anything) 'unrestrained slaughter of their favourite species' was the norm, with few birds actually being eaten. In one season alone, one of Dow's case-studies recorded shooting 783 snipe. Dow believes her research partly overturns a common stereotype about colonial treatment of native fauna: 'settlers' lack of emotional

Introduction

engagement with a new environment' is traditionally linked to indiscriminate killing of local wildlife, but Dow points out that those 'Australian avifaunal species more alien to the Old World, birds such as parrots and honeyeaters ... survived the initial colonial conquest' and 'more familiar species', 'more reminiscent of the Old World', suffered from the recreational slaughter carried out by 'gentlemen'. These hunters were 'ignorant of the ecology of their target species' (in her essay, Sassoon makes a similar observation about the ecological blindness of game laws) and their hunting practices seem to have contributed substantially to species decline in a period for which there is little reliable data about waterfowl populations. Habitat modification in the twentieth century was indeed a major cause of species decline, but, using records such as sporting diaries, Dow aims to piece together 'the "first chapter" in the story of species decline', whereby fowl unfortunate enough to resemble old world species were assigned 'a position at the top of the hunting taxonomy, and that position placed them under considerable pressure in the period before major habitat modification'.

CONSERVATION – ITS UNDERLYING VALUES, ASPIRATIONS AND OUTCOMES

In Dow's case-study, that which was valued most, paradoxically, experienced the worst outcomes. Lee ruminates on how human attitudes to animals – decisions, for example, as to which have 'rights' and which should be exhibited or preserved in zoos – are essentially value judgments, based on charisma, utility and familiarity. As Bonhomme outlines, early conservation efforts in Russia (the point stands in many societies) were founded largely on game-laws (so a desire to preserve viable, huntable populations) or on other considerations about value to humans: species' fate could be determined by

> debate about [their] being 'useful' or 'harmful' to agriculture, forestry and the human economy in general ... Although significant debate existed about which 'side' a given species was on, and while some were occasionally reassigned ([sparrows], for example), in general there does not seem to have been much doubt across and beyond Europe in the viability of the categories themselves.

Later, though, these and associated categories have increasingly been called into question. Aitken's essay, which introduces the conservation section of this volume, addresses how problems of valuation arise in human efforts to 'conserve' certain species or habitats.

She cites red deer culling in Scotland as an exemplar of conservationists' potentially misguided concern for 'whole' ecosystems, which has in this case led to their vilifying the red deer as an 'unwanted part', somehow jeopardising its environment. Conservationists, she argues, tend to value wholes – species, ecosystems – and to discount concern for individuals (for example rehabilitating injured or otherwise disadvantaged animals) as somehow naïve and anthropocentric. In the norms of conservation, culling of certain individual deer is deemed to be of benefit to the wider population (due to competition for resources) and the ecosystem (vegetation is threatened by too many deer) and, thus, the loss of individual lives is acceptable collateral damage. However, Aitken argues that this is doubly wrong, on animal rights grounds (among other evidence, she cites the trauma inflicted on a whole herd by the sudden, violent death of one member) and on its own 'scientific' terms: the cherished notion of holism is challenged in creating a hierarchy of parts within the ecosystem (and indeed species) and defining some as valuable and some not. Extending the argument, she quotes Deakin's articulation of a typical conservation dilemma – hedgerows compromise the open spaces needed by lapwings, a declining species, but 'uprooting hedgerows is like taking an India rubber to the history that is written into the landscape ... Of course, saltmarshes and wetlands are valuable habitats – and beautiful places – but who is to say that a dunlin is more "valuable" than a dunnock?'. Altering habitats in the name of conservation may serve nothing so much as human bias.[2] Aitken's essay incisively questions some of the underlying assumptions of conservation about the value of individuals, species and whole ecosystems, demonstrating that the basic human drive to protect is, in practice, complicated and sometimes uncomfortably allied with the equally basic drive to kill.

While – as Dow, Bonhomme and Siddle attest for their different places and eras – the protection of game populations to be hunted by the wealthy was the predominant early driver of conservation, many early preservation drives were based less on deliberate population modification than on what modern conservation scientists might dismiss as Romantic, sentimental and religiously-rooted notions of protecting the vulnerable (the same urges that inform rehabilitation) and of 'good stewardship'. However, Bonhomme's essay interestingly notes that all peoples in all places do not experience these impulses equally: the Russian peasantry of the late nineteenth century were much less amenable to the 'feathered friends' rhetoric that more economically developed populations had begun to promulgate about birds; and Bonhomme speculates that lack of popular pressure was one reason for Russia's not signing up to the 1902 Paris Convention on bird protection. When the drive towards bird conservation began in Russia, its twin poles were utilitarianism (the idea that encouraging insect eating birds would limit damage to crops) and nationalism: 'Many calls for bird protection between 1870 and 1914 were couched in nationalist tones, emphasis-

---

2. Siddle argues that similar prejudice about the desirability of certain species and vegetations over others (in this case a preference for enclosed and intensive farming over traditional extensive models) contributes to the conception of the goat as ravager of dryland ecosystems: 'in the official mind and in popular consciousness the goat has been the bête noire of dry farming areas. It has been damned as one cause of the encroachment of desert margins in Africa, the degradation of Mediterranean and Middle Eastern hillsides and the general decline of fertility'.

Introduction

ing the notion that a nation or state would be judged by how it treats its wildlife' as well as the uniqueness of Russia, geographically and biologically as well as culturally, which made conservation strategies adopted by other countries seem irrelevant. Later, in the 1880s, the RISPCA (Russian Imperial Society for the Prevention of Cruelty to Animals) campaigned to ban the plumage trade, emphasising the 'ennobling' effect on the 'the human spirit [of] more ethical and moral approaches toward non-human creation'.

Lee points out that philosophers traditionally framed conceptions of animal rights and suffering in terms of the human experience of 'humaneness': 'infliction of cruelty upon animals could dispose us to be callous towards fellow human beings' or simply to fail to attain the nobility of spirit that ought to be our aspiration. In a sense, though modern philosophy as developed, say, by Peter Singer, has striven to be more animal-centric, the lay conception of animal protection and conservation owes much to this idea: we frame who we are, in part, by how well we feel our deeds reflect upon us and this works at the societal level too. Lambert's essay on British grey seals and the high profile public campaigns to stop their culling in the 1960s and 1970s, after mid-century protection measures proved rather *too* successful for some fishermen, reflects on what he describes as 'the emergence of sentiment and emotion as a key factor in wildlife management'. In the 'totemic' cases of seals and whales – both of which were freely hunted into late twentieth century in many countries – the creatures are embraced as symbols of the eco-awareness that we like to feel we possess as a (post)modern society. Seals have become iconic in 'the way that we have constructed nature around us', our concern at species level being strengthened by an emotional engagement with the 'individual plight of an orphan seal pup or stranded whale', examples from which we construct a lovable, huggable version of Nature.

Lambert says – though Aitken's essay partly undermines his point – that, by contrast, 'there has been little protest about the culling of red deer in Scotland ... the public seem to accept this as a necessary evil and accept the advice of science'. Lambert argues that scientific evidence showed in the 1960s and 1970s that, as well as competing with fishing interests, seals were falling victim to their own success (the UK population bounced back from as few as 2,000 to 123,000 during the twentieth century) and that overpopulation was at times a serious welfare issue in colonies. The same argument is used of deer populations in the Highlands, though Aitken challenges the assumption that, in either case, the 'holistic' scientific view is the only one with validity. Either way, though, it is curious how, 'On issues of wildlife management, public opinion has become strangely variable. Sometimes it tolerates traditional pest control, other times it seems to demand absolute protection for certain iconic animals' (Lambert).

Kardell and Dahlström realise that this can only create more problems in the future: in Sweden the government has committed to protect wolves, whose populations are slowly growing and spreading, while much of the public feels 'fear and hatred' towards the creatures, believing they pose risks to humans, livestock, game and hunting dogs, and would favour culling 'under certain circumstances'. Kardell and Dahlström analyse historical data about wolf territories and about the quantities of livestock consumed by the predators in eighteenth and early nineteenth century Jönköping county; and investigate the effects of bounty-hunting on wolf populations in the period. In general, their essay attempts to reconstruct past realities, as distinct from the (persistent) folkloric view of the wolf as 'hålehund' (hell-hound), child-slayer and ravager of herds. In the past bounty-hunting was highly successful in exterminating populations, not just because of the prizes offered but because 'Christian dogma ... branded the wolf as inherently evil, a fact which ... made wolf control a worthy cause in its own right'. Even as wolf numbers dwindled to levels at which they were deemed in need of national protection, 'popular myths and legends' preserved deep-seated 'apprehensions about wolves' that persist to this day in the face of re-establishment measures. Kardell and Dahlström consider what the effects of increased wolf populations might be in the twenty-first century, when livestock numbers are much lower but wild game has greatly increased: since game is not guarded in the same way as livestock was in the early nineteenth-century, they extrapolate that, compared to the 'nearly negligible' proportion of total livestock consumed by wolves historically, 'a larger proportion of the population would end up as wolf feed if the county was recolonised by *Canis lupus*'. They explore what the necessary physical, territorial preconditions for population re-establishment might be, but it seems that there is also considerable work to be done in winning hearts and minds. As with seals, the conservationist approach must straddle uneasily the indications of science and the unstable, often vicious, vagaries of public feeling.

If re-introduction of previously persecuted species is one aspect of the drive toward 'rewilding', Gamborg et al. explore the practicalities and ethics of another – de-domestication, or 'the deliberate establishment of a population of domesticated animals or plants in the wild' such that, 'in time, the population should be able to reproduce, becoming self-sustainable and incorporating "wild" animals'. De-domestication is a facet of more holistic 'rewilding' projects whereby, for example, ancient breeds of cattle and horse (Heck and Konik in Gamborg et al.'s Netherlands case) are put to graze pasture to begin a process of habitat restoration that should end with 'wild animals living in open land'. The general idea is seductive – a habitat will be allowed to revert to a prehistoric state (modeled on Vera's view of ancient Europe as a grazed savannah) and the animals who do the grazing will have to 'toughen up' and revert genetically to resemble their extinct ancestors. But, as Gamborg et al. explores, there are serious ethical questions: in animal husbandry it is assumed that humans have a duty of care to livestock in terms of feeding, veterinary care, etc. Such duties are not generally assumed to pertain to wild herds, where the focus tends to be on the whole population, not individual animals. Indeed, Gamborg et al. points

Introduction

out that the difference shadows the individualism / holism debate already considered by Lee and Aitken: it is that between 'animal welfare, with a focus on the well-being of each individual animal, and ... wildlife management, with a focus on the well-being of population and/or species'. If domestic animals are released into the wild, without supplementary feeding or veterinary care, high mortality rates inevitably ensue. Some therefore regard de-domestication as cruelty and, if a level of support is given at the outset to avoid this consequence,

> when, if at all, should we cease to regard the animals, individually, as domestic animals (with the associated right to be treated in accordance with the welfare legislation covering animals in our care)? When should we begin to regard the populations of which those same animals are members as wild populations?

Gamborg et al.'s essay challenges any idyllic view of rewilding and illuminates its potential for contradiction and dilemma, as 'a practice caught between two sets of norms governing animals and nature', a blurring of boundaries that forces us to think about whether 'it [is] reasonable to try to differentiate wild animals and animals in our care?' Indeed, we might ask whether 're-wilding is really possible, or whether it is just a matter of changed breeding goals and methods which, ultimately, represent a novel variety of domestication'. As with the dilemma between the hedgerow and the saltmarsh, human attempts to rewrite ecosystems and animal populations are open to scrutiny and charges of self-indulgence and bias.

The intentions behind human interference are legion: different groups of human beings, in different places and at different times, make different choices (some more deliberate than others) about whether and how to alter animal populations and ecosystems. Sassoon's essay about cormorants in Western Australia traces effects, negative and positive, on populations during the twentieth century, when they were bounty-hunted because of the belief that they consumed fish wanted by humans; then protected as it was realised they actually 'ate fish and crustacea that were predators on commercial species, and that eradicating the cormorants served ultimately to reduce fish stocks'; and still later suffered from habitat reduction during river reclamation projects; finally, the establishment of wildlife sanctuaries led to further increases in the bird population, but in areas specifically delimited from the urban. Whereas previously the Swan River foreshore in Perth was part of the birds' habitat – albeit one where they were in conflict with fishermen and with local pleasure-boat owners who objected to their guano – now the birds are gone and the Esplanade is decorated by lamp-posts in the shape of cormorants: 'situated on land reclaimed from what was once biologically rich shallows that formed their predecessors' feeding grounds, they stand as mute and immobile monuments'. Sassoon's essay, like Lambert's and Kardell and Dahlström's, reminds us that human relationships with certain species are fluid, over time and also in terms of the acceptability or otherwise of animal presence in given locations: creatures may be iconic

Introduction

in one place and unwelcome in another. Her study, with its urban locus, looks forward too to Kheraj's essay on Vancouver's Stanley Park, another case of uneasy co-existence in an environment where animals are expected to respect human-made boundaries.

Van der Ploeg et al. explore the notion of shared space and cultural strategies developed to deal with it in their essay on crocodiles in rural areas of the Philippines. Official conservation efforts tend to assume that local populations will be hostile to a creature they regard and indeed experience – attacks on humans do occur – as dangerous; thus, the argument goes, in order to encourage indigenous populations to assist in crocodile conservation measures, economic incentives are needed. The Philippine government has thus taken the route in crocodile conservation of promoting 'sustainable' ranching or farming for skins which, it is argued, will profit local communities. In fact, Van der Ploeg et al. argue, 'conventional conservation strategies that focus narrowly on economic values' may be misguided. The 'negative attitudes of rural communities' that are deemed to obstruct crocodile conservation attempts are far from universal: in speaking to rural Kalinga and Agta people, the authors found a rich cultural imaginary of crocodiles, with rules of engagement underpinned by longstanding myths. There are bonds between crocodiles and faith healers, for example, and one must never attack a crocodile for it will remember and seek vengeance: of an attack on a boy in the northern Sierra Madre in 1967, several of those interviewed still believed that

> Crocodiles never forget and always take revenge. Arnel cut the tail of a small crocodile and threw stones at it. After a few years he was bitten in his legs by the same crocodile. A crocodile will always remember you.

If one abides by the rules, though, humans and crocodiles can live peacefully together. Though the Kalinga people interviewed took pains to insist that *they* no longer believed crocodile myths, these form the cultural background to strategies of co-existence that mean that, even without active conservation measures, crocodiles survive in these areas: 'the peace pact is still honoured'. In the Philippines more widely, crocodiles get bad press – corrupt politicians are likened to them and people think them evil and dangerous – but these beliefs are most prevalent in areas without surviving crocodiles: 'the fear of the beast paradoxically increased as crocodiles disappeared from the landscape'. Van der Ploeg et al. show that Catholic missionaries recast the traditionally-venerated crocodile as a symbol of evil: overturning its traditional alignment with a creator-god and role as instrument of moral arbitration (crocodile attacks were seen as ancestor-spirits 'aveng[ing] the transgression of taboos') Catholic priests taught that it was an enemy that stood for sin and evil. Van der Ploeg et al. suggest that the culture of a few upland communities where crocodiles remain associated with 'ancestors, fertility and mystic power', could be a fruitful route to encouraging crocodile conservation; the crocodile could be recast as 'rare and

Introduction

iconic', exploiting the remnants of a much-older tradition of veneration and a predisposition in crocodiles' favour:

> Philippine history and culture provide a conservation ethic entrenched in society and history and adaptive to local circumstances ... Here people know crocodiles from their own experience and treat them with respect. These are not archaic remnants of a forgotten past, irrelevant to modern life. On the contrary, the worldviews and ecological knowledge of the Kalinga and Agta offer pragmatic solutions for living with crocodiles.

CULTURED CREATURES

Crocodiles in the Philippines were identified by Catholic friars with forces of evil, presumably at least in part because the missionaries saw in ancient practices of crocodile veneration an obstacle to adoption of the new religion and to the cultural control that this would grant the colonisers. Siddle outlines a similar process at work in representations of the goat, which is lambasted in Medieval and Early Modern sources as a 'Bête Noire', redolent of 'rampant sexuality and evil', witchcraft and satanic forces. From Dionysian associations in classical mythology to a darker 'Goat-Man-Beast-Satan' complex of images, goats have attracted a morass of superstition and prejudice, linked to their inhabiting of 'peripheries: woods and forests. For those who lived in the towns and villages of the lowlands, such areas were always dangerously "other"'. Such prejudices, Siddle argues, naturally extended to the keepers of goats who, like their charges, were branded 'smelly, bad breathed, lying and cheating subversives' and the whole negative complex gave rhetorical weight to 'serious charges of ecological degradation': goats and their herds were bad characters requiring the severest control to stop them from destroying vulnerable environments. Siddle argues that wealthy interests wished to exclude goats and goatherds from high quality pastures that might support more profitable sheep – so their destructiveness was exacerbated by their being confined to marginal and vulnerable ecosystems – and, further, that the wrecking of such ecosystems mattered to the privileged goat-detractors because these were the habitats of game species whose preservation was necessary for a favoured leisure pursuit of the wealthy: hunting. While the goat was 'a provider of good things to poor people', it trespassed on two areas of interest to the better-off and Siddle argues that this led to its being 'smeared' throughout the Medieval and Early Modern periods: the established iconography of the goat was exploited by those who wished to promote 'an ideology of command and control'. Siddle claims that, instead of merely restricting goat numbers and enforcing control measures such as tethering, landowners used draconian goat bans as a means of controlling the most anarchic elements of the population, a means to ease the path to commercial woollen enterprise and a means of improving timber supplies for the navy. Bans also better preserved the hunting grounds for hawk and hound. In such circumstances the poor manbeast, the Caliban of the periphery, stood no chance.

Though Siddle's case is ungeneralisable, the class struggle he perceives in historical goat control measures is an interesting extension of several other authors' observation that conservation and the preservation of game stocks for the wealthy were closely linked throughout history: as Bonhomme observes 'Game laws were designed to protect aristocratic privilege and the social exclusivity of the hunt'. A modern analogy might be perceived links between conservation and profitable leisure / amenity value – seal-watching boat trips being privileged over fishermen's calls for seal culling or nature reserve land being withdrawn from community use. The battle-lines here are drawn not around class as such but certainly around social divisions – for example 'townies' versus rural people – but animals remain important signifiers in social conflicts.

Kheraj shows how the decision to devote Stanley Park in Vancouver to animals as display and leisure objects – with a zoo and fly-fishing lake and even occasional hunting (of crows) for sport – and to exclude 'consumptive' uses, such as grazing domestic animals and shooting for the pot, led to conflict similar to that Karl Jacoby perceived in late nineteenth century US conservation schemes: 'previous legitimate uses of animals through hunting, trapping, and fishing were suddenly outlawed with the creation of national parks and reserves ... [transforming] subsistence practices into delinquent behaviour'. The Stanley Park Case study illuminates tension between the legislators of permitted types of use and the public at large but also that between the 'wild' and the urban.

The Park zoo was originally intended as a showcase for the same Canadian wildlife that made Vancouver residents feel most uncomfortable if it appeared on the city streets: Kheraj cites Patricia Partnow's 'argument that the urban view of wildlife is rooted in a territorial separation of humans and wild animals'. But animals do not know or care that they are supposed to respect such boundaries – consider urban foxes in England, raccoons and bears in the US, monkeys in India – and, moreover, the new Park seemed an irresistible opportunity to some animals that were not supposed to be there: 'Human modifications to the park environment opened niches for opportunist animal species to exert their autonomy and occupy the park ... to elude park policy and operate beyond the purview of human control'. The case of the Stanley Park cougar was a particularly dramatic example (thrilling and unsettling in equal measure to Vancouver residents) of animal autonomy and boundary transgression: a wild cougar took up residence, finding the zoo's collection of animals an irresistible feeding ground, and it took a team of hunters several weeks to track down and shoot it. Though some Vancouverites were sympathetic to the cougar, its fate was sealed. But lesser debates about animal management have had direct effects on the evolu-

Introduction

tion of the Stanley Park biota, from concerns about the annual crow hunt and the recreational fishery to changing opinions about the zoo itself which, after a public referendum in 1993, was eventually disbanded. Kheraj quotes Nigel Rothfels saying that, as 'at their most basic level zoos are for people and not for animals' and, in the end, the people of Vancouver no longer wanted the zoo that had, over the twentieth century, expanded from a Canadian collection to an assemblage of international exhibits, not all suited to the Canadian climate or the conditions of their captivity.

In Stanley Park, no less than in the Sierra Madre investigated by Van der Ploeg et al., people and animals interacted in a shared environment and their identities were to an extent mutually constitutive. Though, as Kheraj points out, animals are an integral part of the Canadian identity (down to the beaver that adorns the five cent coin) the self-image of the people of Vancouver no longer had room for a zoo collection of exotica. Animals and our treatment of them, beyond any use value, shape human identities – from Dow's Australian shooters, yearning to replicate the fowling experience of the Old Country, to the public adoption outlined by Lambert of seal and whale as icons of (self-conscious) environmental awareness. How we perceive and present animals tells back the preoccupations of our culture: as Lee argues, the modern zoo with its homilies on ecosystems, extinctions and climate change is not less anthropocentric in its founding impulse than the old-fashioned chimps' tea-party, though the story it constructs is more edifying to modern tastes. Examining the iconography of hunting narratives of the late nineteenth and early twentieth century Rocky Mountains, Wonders' essay weaves together these issues of display, discourse and identity. Game hunting and colonialism are often aligned as discourses of conquest, but Wonders' main agenda is a prevalent story about gender. Game hunters in the Rockies, she argues, undertook hunts (in difficult locations, for fearsome animals), and subsequently had themselves portrayed in positions, that emphasised their great masculinity in taking on such formidable adversaries. Wonders uncovers a variety of representational conventions that foreground the masculinity of the conquering hunters.

> The game species most valued were represented as having those qualities most admired as exhibiting human male virtues such as aggressive displays of dominance and courage in battle, determined upon victory or death.

The great horns of a wapiti, for example, most prominent during the aggressive, sex-driven rutting season and signifiers of its animal masculinity and strength, were pictured so as to imply comparable qualities in the human hunter, by what Wonders calls a 'conflation of victor-and-vanquished'. The hunter has both conquered the beast and assumed aspects of its identity.

The overlapping tropes contained in Wonders' phrase might be extended to a wider meditation on human–animal relations. We simultaneously exercise domination over them, very often to the point of cruelty, and admire them for powers that we can never possess; we want to control their actions, environments and eco-system positions, but also promote and idealise their freedom; we regard them as 'other' but seek to cross the divide with an armoury of anthropomorphic discourses. The histories collected here demonstrate that we can never stand back from animals.

NOTE

The selected articles represent the views held by the authors at the time of original publication and the state of scholarship at that time.

An Animal: What is it?

Keekok Lee

I.

The title of this article may at first sight seem either silly or rhetorical, as it is surely obvious what an animal is. But is it? Closer examination of the matter shows that there are different implicit answers to the question depending on the type of enquiry and the kind of preoccupation, whether theoretical or practical, in which the answers are embedded. At least four different accounts may be identified, that given by (a) scientists as zoologists, (b) the ordinary person in the street, (c) philosophers or writers concerned with animal liberation and/or animal rights, (d) apologists for zoos.

This article attempts to (i) explore more fully each of these accounts, (ii) bring out the overlapping concerns and relationships, if any, between them, (iii) make clear, whenever relevant, their respective hidden agenda and assumptions, and (iv) discuss what an adequate answer to the question might be in the light of certain crucial issues in environmental philosophy, such as maintaining biodiversity and the polarised controversy involving individualism and holism (or biocentrism and ecocentrism).

II.

Zoology is commonly understood as the scientific study of animals; one of the Greek words composing the term itself – *zoon* – is usually translated to mean 'animal', although it has a wider denotation referring to living things.[1] Of course, zoology in turn is part of biology, the study of life itself – the Greek word *bios* means life.

So how does zoology answer the question 'what is an animal?' It will soon be obvious that as far as it is concerned, there is no simple and quick reply. Any systematic answer, no matter how schematic, starts with the by no means easy problem of first distinguishing between life and nonlife. Although both the living and the nonliving are subject to the same laws of physics and chemistry as well as the law of the conservation of energy, the crucial differences between them lie in the fact that the former is very differently organised and structured from the latter – unlike the latter, it is capable of metabolism, growth, adaptability, irritability and interaction with the environment.

But how in turn is animal life to be distinguished from plant life? As the terms 'zoology' and 'botany' themselves indicate, we, lay people, take for granted that there are two recognisable kingdoms to which all organisms are said to belong: plant or animal. We instinctively know to classify mosses, ferns, and trees as plants on the one hand and mammals, birds and fishes as animals on the other. Yet this time-honoured Aristotelian schema may be said to have outlived its usefulness in the light of more up to date understanding of the various forms of life on Earth. Complexities appear straightaway. The central point to grasp is that, unfortunately, no single criterion exists which can serve to distinguish all animals from all plants. Take the presence or absence of chlorophyll as an obvious distinguishing mark. Chlorophyll is a necessary condition for photosynthesis to take place. We unhesitatingly associate chlorophyll with plants but not with animals; an oak has it but not a hedgehog. Under photosynthesis, green plants produce organic compounds from sunlight and atmospheric carbon dioxide and, at the same time, restore free energy to the biosphere. These photoautotrophic organisms in converting inorganic substances into organic materials not only sustain their own functioning integrity but also provide food for heterotrophic organisms, mainly animals, which live on them as these themselves lack the capability for photosynthesis. Yet some organisms, for example, *Euglena*, display photosynthesis under some conditions but not others – in the light, it functions like a plant, in the dark, like an animal. So is it an animal or a plant? They are considered to be animals by zoologists and plants by phycologists. Another borderline group is the slime moulds – zoologists call them Mycetozoa and botanists Myxomycophyta. Furthermore, not all plants possess chlorophyll – the higher parasitic plants and a large plant group, Fungi, also do not have it. So the presence of chlorophyll cannot identify and include all plants; neither does its absence identify all animals.

Another distinguishing mark may be said to be motility. We commonsensically believe that animals have the ability to move about in their environment (and some even travel between very different environments depending on the season) at some stage in their life history, whereas plants are stationary. Yet movement is not restricted solely to animals – a good many of the thallophytes such as Oscillatoria, several bacteria and colonial chlorophytes are quite motile.

In biology today, scientists, as we have seen, no longer regard the two kingdom schema to be all that illuminating; instead, they attach greater significance to the procaryote/eucaryote distinction. 'Procaryote' literally means 'before the nucleus'. The genetic material of such organisms is not enclosed in a well-defined nucleus, but located in a nuclear region (nucleoid). In contrast, the genetic material of eucaryotes is contained within a well-defined cell nucleus with a protein coat. However, besides this crucial difference, there are others. All living organisms, except viruses, bacteria and blue-green algae (cyanobacteria) are eucaryotic.

The problems mentioned above, amongst others, led to a proposal in 1969 for a five-kingdom system which incorporates the procaryote-eucaryote distinc-

An Animal: What Is It?

tion. The procaryotes are assigned to the kingdom Monera while the eucaryotes are divided into four kingdoms. The kingdom Protista includes the unicellular eucaryotic organisms (protozoa and unicellular eucaryotic algae). The multicellular eucaryotic organisms are in turn organised into three kingdoms according to their mode of nutrition and other significant organisational differences. The kingdom Plantae contains multicellular photosynthesing organisms, higher plants and multicellular algae. The kingdom Fungi includes yeast, moulds and fungi that get their food through absorption. Finally, the kingdom Animalia comprises the invertebrates (except the protozoa) and the vertebrates.

Traditionally, the animal kingdom has included the unicellular protozoa, but the new schema excludes them. Yet they share many characteristics with so-called animals, such as ingestion of food, advanced locomotory systems, sexual reproduction, etc. For this reason, books on zoology regard the protozoa as animals and have a chapter on them.

To sum up a very complex set of issues, it may be fair to say, that zoologists today clearly identify all invertebrates and vertebrates as animals while agreeing that the protozoa, too, be considered as such.

One should also be reminded that the consensus which emerges takes place against a background of theoretical ideas and assumptions which have developed since the nineteenth century, of which the most salient are (a) the Darwinian theory of evolution in terms of natural selection, (b) the Mendelian theory of particulate inheritance and the gene/chromosome theory, (c) developments in cell theory, (d) DNA genetics and molecular biology, (e) animal ecology, (f) ethology.

The larger framework is still basically neo-Darwinian. As such, it necessarily excludes as bogus contenders either so-called Creation-Science or Vitalism. A further point which is more germane to our purpose here, is that it is mainly informed by the theory of natural selection as the mechanism of evolution. Its primary object of study is, therefore, animals in the wild, to understand their ancestry, how they come to have the characteristics they do possess through certain fundamental concepts and principles that govern the understanding of organic life in general and animal life in particular. This basic orientation, as we shall see later, presupposes an ecocentric philosophy which focuses on the survival of animal species rather than of individual animals, irrespective of whether or not they are charismatic, exotic, capable of suffering pain or of mental activity.

III.

Ordinary people are very concerned with animals, but their preoccupation is obviously quite different from that of the zoologists. So one expects their conception of an animal to be also different. By and large, they stick to a commonsensical understanding of the traditional two-kingdom schema and would have no difficulty classifying squirrels as animals and conifers as plants. They would not have heard of protozoa and if asked whether bacteria or fungi are plants or animals, they would have no opinion because of their total ignorance about such matters.

In general, society's interest in certain animals was/is dictated by the roles they play in human lives – these animals have either religious/cultural, culinary, economic or personal significance for the social group or individual in question. For instance, some groups have chosen even rats (vertebrate) and snakes (invertebrate) as objects of religious worship. Some cherish the bald eagle as a symbol of national (tribal) virility, others the lion. Which animals are good to eat and which are not, clearly, vary according to culture and to historical period. Dogs are good to eat for the Dayaks while cows, for Hindus, are not for eating at all. Tigers, rhinoceroses and some whales, today, are in danger of being hunted to extinction for economic reasons.

Beyond identifying animals which belong to these main categories of concern, people remain in ignorance of those not encompassed. 'Animals', as a generality, is not all that pertinent to their lives. Particular types of animals may, outside these categories, catch their attention because they are exotic (in which case they go to the zoo to see them or watch them in a television programme), charismatic like the lion, or cuddly like the panda. As far as lay people are concerned, birds seem to be the only class which commands a sizeable minority of followers dedicated to watching and studying them; and amongst ornithologists, knowledge of them can be thorough and comprehensive.

As most societies have long left the hunter/gatherer stage of existence behind, the only animals which enter their immediate experience and consciousness are domesticated animals – cows, pigs, sheep, goats, chickens (which are good to eat), horses, bullocks, camels (which are, in general, good for traction and transportation) and dogs and cats (which are good for companionship, guarding the house or catching mice). Except for chickens, ducks and latterly turkeys which are birds, the rest are mammals. In other words, the word 'animal' would, in the context of utility derived from domestication, typically conjure up either of these two classes of the phylum chordata. In some cultures, some species of fish have been domesticated and increasingly today, salmon and trout are also being cultivated. However, domestication throughout world history has been confined to only a few species of these vertebrate classes.

In contemporary consciousness, the image or idea of what an animal is has become even more circumscribed, as increasingly in urban contexts domesticated animals are not directly confronted with. Some children even have difficulty associating pork with an animal called the pig, or milk with the cow, as pork and milk are just packaged items the family purchases from the supermarket. This means that animals as domestic pets occupy centre stage, especially in developed countries, cats and dogs being the most prevalent. Children, increasingly, are taught to identify animals via these as exemplars. For them, the denotation as well as the connotation of the term 'animal' is paradigmatically

An Animal: What Is It?

given and determined by the varieties of dogs and cats they find in households. If asked whether they share their homes with animals, they will confidently say no provided they keep no cats, dogs, budgerigars, goldfish or hamsters. If reminded that most homes, and therefore, theirs would have a mouse or two, they would feel justifiably shocked. But to them, if compelled to acknowledge their presence, mice are not animals in the way pets are animals – they are at best animals only in some technical sense. To them they are just pests. And if told that mites live in the detritus of their scalp or upon their skin or in their carpets, they would be horrified; but unlike mice or rats, they would even have difficulty accepting or understanding these as animals at all.

To sum up, increasingly, the lay consciousness is confined to grasping animals in terms of a few domesticated species of mammals which are regarded as friends to humans or a few exotic and/or charismatic animals which they see in zoos occasionally. The latter, we shall see, are themselves, in the main not caught from the wild to live in captivity but merely the descendants of such animals, often a few generations removed. This means that domestication in one form or another looms large in the animals people are likely to experience at first hand. At least one clear difference then has emerged between the account of what is an animal as understood by zoologists and that as understood by ordinary people in general – the former are primarily interested in natural evolution and, therefore, in all species of animals in the wild (the number of known species are said to be just over a million and those unkown, several millions more, even on a conservative estimate), whereas the latter are essentially preoccupied with a relatively small number (probably a few dozens at best) of domesticated species of animals whether encountered at first hand frequently in the home or occasionally at the zoo.[2]

IV.

The defence of animals against human cruelty is a protest against the ways in which they are (a) kept and then slaughtered for food, (b) used in scientific research and experimentation whether for the serious purpose of saving human lives or the trivial one of improving the appearance of human bodies, (c) hunted, hounded or killed for human pleasure.

This defence is capable of being grounded in two very different types of philosophical perspectives:

1. The more traditional justification, derived from philosophers like Kant, is that the duty not to be cruel to animals is in reality an indirect duty to humans, as the infliction of cruelty upon animals could dispose us to be callous towards fellow human beings. But of late, this highly anthropocentric standpoint has been powerfully challenged by two contemporary philosophers – Peter Singer and Tom Regan – who, in spite of the obviously different philosophical stances each has

adopted, nevertheless, are united in repudiating the dominant humanist tradition of Kant and the Enlightenment, at least regarding the treatment of animals.

2A. A minimalist reconstruction of Singer's philosophy of animal liberation includes the following:

(a) the hedonic postulate – pleasure and pain as mental states are respectively intrinsically good and evil;

(b) the consequentialist/utilitarian postulate – one ought always to maximise pleasure and minimise pain in one's actions;

(c) the boundaries of sentience postulate – (a) and (b) are 'blind' to the kind of being which is capable of feeling pleasure and pain. Humans clearly are sentient but empirically it can be shown that humans are not the only sentient beings. Other mammals, too, clearly are sentient. Birds are as well. Erring on the side of caution and charity, the boundary should then be drawn somewhere around shrimps and, possibly, lobsters; and

(d) the consistency postulate – as we, today, believe that we have a moral duty not to keep and eat fellow humans for food, to perform vivisection on them with or without their consent, to hunt, maim or slaughter fellow humans for entertainment, then equally, we have a moral duty not to do likewise to fellow sentient beings.

2B. A minimalist reconstruction of Regan's philosophy of animal rights includes the following:

(a) the rights postulate – (i) an entity is intrinsically (or inherently, in Regan's terminology) valuable if and only if it is capable of being a subject of a life, that is to say, possessing memory, beliefs and desires as well as other mental states, and (ii) an entity is a rights holder if and only if the entity is capable of being a subject of a life;

(b) the conceptual postulate – to be a subject of a life, to experience mental states like beliefs and desires, conceptually speaking, it is not necessary to possess language at all or human language as we understand it to be;

(c) the boundaries of subject-of-a-life postulates – (a) and (b) are 'blind' to the kind of entity which can satisfy the criterion of being subject of a life, Humans (or at least the majority of them) are clear candidates, but empirically it can be shown (once (b) has been conceded) that mammals, too, are candidates. Erring on the side of caution and charity, the boundary of eligibility should then be drawn at birds; and

(d) the consistency postulate – as we, today, hold the view that human beings have a right not to be kept and eaten by fellow humans, to have vivisection performed on them with or without their consent, to be hunted, maimed or

An Animal: What Is It?

slaughtered by fellow humans for entertainment, then equally, other mammals (and possibly birds) have a right not to be treated likewise by us humans.

In spite of the obvious difference in the philosophical foundations provided by Singer and Regan and the debate which ensues between them – one anchored in moral duties understood in the context of hedonic consquentialism, the other in moral rights deontologically understood in the context of certain characteristics of mental life in humans and closely related mammalian others – the two do have certain things in common, apart from their agreed common goal to end cruelty and suffering to animals. Their respective implicit conceptions of what is an animal are given by the criterion they each have chosen as the most fundamental postulate of their philosophy of animal liberation – the hedonic postulate in the case of Singer and the rights postulate in the case of Regan.

In either, the paradigmatic animal is the human animal. Although Bentham, as a founding father of modern utilitarianism, had acknowledged that certain nonhuman animals also come within the purview of his fundamental postulate, nevertheless, utilitarianism as propagated and inspired by him has chosen to concentrate on humans as the paradigmatic sentient beings. Similarly, the concept of rights – either understood as natural or as contractual rights – has long been conducted, until very recently, within an exclusively human domain.

Singer himself uses the image of the expanding (moral) circle, in order to draw certain other beings, so far excluded by Western philosophy, into its orbit. Regan endorses this implicitly. However, both proceed on the assumption that there is a limit to which this circle may be enlarged – Singer's fundamental postulate allows him to redraw it with a somewhat wider radius than Regan's. But in the centre of their circles is the human. The further a being is from that centre, the more difficult it would be to make a case for extending moral considerability to it. The human is, of course, a mammal. Hence, extending moral duties or rights to other fellow mammals is their most obvious target. This has prompted some commentators to say, especially of Regan's account, that it is really about mammalian rights.

In general, it might not be too unfair to say that both philosophies are underpinned by an overarching postulate, namely, the search for similarities and likenesses between humans and certain animal others. As such, the more an animal resembles humans in certain specified ways, the easier it is to admit them into the moral circle. Of the mammals, the Great Apes come closest to us – indeed, this class is held to consist of the gorillas, the orang-utangs, the chimpanzees and then ourselves as the long missing fourth Great Ape.

While those animals within the pale are accorded a dignity befitting their newly acquired status of being morally considerable, those outside, as a result, are dealt a double blow – first, they are owed no moral duties or denied moral rights, and second, the term 'animal liberation' or 'animal rights' itself goes even further and serves implicitly to deny them the status of animality itself. In other words, only those beings which qualify to be the bearers of rights or to be the object of our moral duties are 'proper' or 'true' animals. The denotation and connotation of the word 'animal' has surreptitiously and subtly been revised so that even on Singer's more hospitable expansion of the moral circle, worms, molluscs and many more are debarred. The similarities postulate has forcefully challenged human chauvinism, the view which sets humans apart from other animals, assigning to themselves a superior status of privilege and domination. It attempts to force human consciousness to concede that humans, as mammals, are really fellow animals. They (together with those others admitted into the expanded circle) and us are all owed duties not to be tortured or held to enjoy rights to life, etc. Strictly speaking, in Singer's moral/political philosophy, a single hedonic consquentialist theory is postulated to embrace all sentient beings, from mammals down the evolutionary scale to possibly some crustaceans like lobsters, just as in Regan's moral/political philosophy, a single unified theory of rights is postulated, covering all mammals and possibly birds. But the price for this revision is the construction of a new demarcation line between the in-group and the out-group. Members of the latter are pariahs because they are unlike us in the crucial respects and, therefore, cannot be animals, a category to which we, ourselves, now belong. But a hierarchical or class system remains in place – the franchised and the privileged against the nonfranchised and the disadvantaged – it is just that the former now includes not simply us but those beings which are like ourselves in certain selected aspects. Human chauvinism may have been vanquished but its spirit has not been challenged by either Singer or Regan and remains unexorcised in their respective philosophies.

V.

Zoos are said to exist for the following reasons:

(a) to entertain and amuse the public;

(b) to educate the public;

(c) to advance scientific knowledge;

(d) to save endangered animal species from extinction.

It will be shown, all things considered, that the goal of entertainment is fundamental and every zoo has to bear it in mind if it is to survive. Chimpanzees may no longer take part in tea-parties, a practice which London Zoo, a zoo noted for its claim to advance science rather than entertainment, only ended in 1972. But it remains true that animals in many zoos today are still expected to perform strenuously to earn their keep, and even the most highly regarded zoos in the world indulge this demand to some extent. Animals may not be expected to do it relentlessly the whole day; instead, they are carefully trained and managed to

An Animal: What Is It?

do it in shifts as in Happy Valley Zoo in Minnesota. In any case, families would not want to visit zoos, as a day out, unless they can see animals doing something, be it eating, grooming one another, swinging from post to post, etc. Visitors do not, as a matter of course, find dozing or snoozing animals really fascinating or compelling. Zoos keep civilised office hours, but their inmates do not. For instance, bats which are nocturnal animals would not be active during zoo visiting times unless their nights are artificially turned into days and *vice versa*.

From the educational point of view, zoos, in one respect are obviously deficient; traditionally, they have not stocked and still do not, in the main, stock domesticated animals. It is simply assumed that the public by and large have either first hand experience of them or know about them already and so are not interested in seeing them. But as we saw in section III, this assumption increasingly holds less and less except for cats and dogs which are kept in the home as pets. Perhaps, zoos in the near future may come to stock other domesticated animals, like horses, cows and goats, as the urbanised population comes to find these unfamiliar and, therefore, 'exotic'. But in any case, not all zoos take the educational purpose over seriously. Furthermore, not many members of the public are over eager to be properly educated about the animals they look at beyond observing them feed their young perhaps, or playing with one another, and occasionally retaining one or two facts about their place of origin or their mating habits. More crucially, to stand any chance of being put across at all the educational message has to be packaged as part of entertainment or the public will be turned off.

As for advancing scientific research, not many zoos are equipped or even pretend to aspire to such a goal. But in so far as it is pursued, its studies fall into two principal areas – animal anatomy and pathology on the one hand and animal behaviour on the other. The latter is particularly controversial, with some critics claiming that observing the behaviour of captive animals is an irrelevancy as far as behaviour of animals in the wild is concerned. At best, it would be a kind of laboratory for observing their behaviour when crucial factors like predation have been suspended and controlled. Some zoos, however, are also in a position to make contributions to veterinary science.[3]

But of late, another *raison d'être* has been added to the scientific justification, namely, to prevent the extinction of endangered species. Advocates are keen to emphasise that their first priority is still to save the habitats of endangered species. But living in the real world, they claim that such an ideal is not often achievable. As a fall back and a second best, they favour using zoos to undertake breeding programmes in captivity (but with the ultimate aim of returning them to the wild if and when suitable habitats can be found for them). Such a programme is feasible given, it is said, the recent advances in scientific understanding in disciplines like DNA genetics, population genetics, and engineering possibilities like building and maintaining cryotoria, etc.

However, the whole breeding programme is regarded by its critics to be problematic in spite of the seemingly strong arguments normally advanced in its favour. One of the most crucial reservations lies in the potentiality of domestication in generating such animals. (However, there is no room here to pursue this critique in great detail.) But in any case, only very few zoos in the world have the resources, financial, intellectual and political, to undertake such a complex task, which requires a very long term commitment.

The first justification, namely, that zoos are in the business of entertainment and amusement, is the most anthropocentric in orientation whilst the fourth is the most nonanthropocentric. However, the seemingly most lowly of human motives and the most noble motive, namely, to save the species for their own sakes not for our own pleasure, agree on this – their implicit conception of what an animal is.

It is a conception which is also shared by the person in the street in all respects except one, namely, that it excludes domesticated animals, while the lay public includes them. In the words of one prominent apologist for zoos, particularly advocating their use to implement captive breeding programmes, zoos deal in the main with animals like 'the rhinos, the tigers, leopards, primates, parrots, ... the Asian elephants, many an antelope, many a bird of prey, various cranes and so on; all the creatures of our childhood; what most people mean by the word "animal"' (Tudge, *Last Animals at the Zoo*, p. 46). In other words, various exotic birds and several large charismatic (land) mammals.

The zoo image, then, powerfully reinforces the lay image of what counts as an animal. As one of the purposes of zoos is to educate the public, such a goal, in so far as it is achieved, is at best partial as necessarily it has nothing to say about those organisms and their species which the public does not mean by the word 'animal' and which *ipso facto* are not zoo residents.[4] Furthermore, zoos, as already commented on, also claim to advance scientific research. But again, in so far as this is achieved, the objects of study are entirely confined to the favoured and the selected which are necessarily few in number. As for the fourth justification – zoos saving endangered species – Colin Tudge is quite happy to admit, as we have seen, that what zoos ultimately can save may turn out to be no more and no less than those animals which zoos have, in the main, always kept to 'pull the punters in through the gates'. To put the point in a slightly different way, it seems fair to say that zoos, at the end of the day, are sustained and maintained by what the public wants to see for their entertainment and amusement.

What ordinary people and zoos mean by the word 'animal' and the species the animals belong to, refers then to a minuscule fraction of the total animal species known today to science; that number stands at 1,032,000 species, of which insects account for nearly three quarters, standing at 751,000 species. Mammalian species only total 4,000, with birds slightly more than double that at 8,600 species.

An Animal: What Is It?

Conservation biologists estimate that about 2,000 species of land vertebrate would need captive breeding in the next 200 years if they are to be saved from extinction. But according to estimates about what zoos could do in this rescue programme, there are about 1,000 or so zoos in the world considered suitable for the task, which, between them, could take care of 800 species. The breakdown is as follows: 100 or so out of the 900 species of bats, all the 35 living dogs including wolves and foxes, 60 out of 72 cats, the 2 living elephants, all 4 of the sirenians, the manatees and dugongs, 100 of the 172 even-toed ungulates including antelopes, deer and giraffes, all 15 species of odd-toed ungulates including the rhinoceroses, horses and tapirs and all 160 species of living primate including the apes, monkeys, lemurs and their relatives. The animals targeted for saving are mammals, or land mammals to be precise, as it is not envisaged that sea mammals like whales and dolphins could be saved at all through captive breeding in watery equivalents of zoos. Yet given this severe limitation, Colin Tudge's recent scientifically serious, though popular book, *Last Animals at the Zoo* has for its subtitle: *How mass extinction can be stopped,* which is highly misleading and scientifically, totally, inaccurate.

It appears that for the lay person, for animal liberationists, for zoo apologists in general, animals as mammals feature crucially, even if not exclusively. The further down the (historical) evolutionary scale an animal or species is, the less it is perceived to be an animal. Today, the pride of place traditionally occupied by humans has been challenged, but mammals have been installed centre stage instead. The rest of the animal kingdom (or at least what counts as belonging to it according to scientific consensus today), deemed neither to be interesting nor charismatic, but infinitely far more numerous, remains unenfranchised; indeed, not even perceived as animals, and certainly owning no rights to be claimed against humans and owed no duties by humans towards them.

VI.

Today's philosophical sensibility is not hospitable even to the posing of the very question 'what is an animal?' as it seems to imply a static essentialist answer. However, the object of this paper is not so much to indulge in arid verbal definitions passing off as essences, but (a) to clarify how various groups of people who have interests of one sort or another in animals themselves explicitly or implicitly understand what they mean by the term 'animal'; (b) to see how adequate such meanings might or might not be when judged against a much more comprehensive conception given by the community of zoologists; and (c) to explore the zoological framework a bit more fully in order to work out if its implicit account of what an animal is will be of help in elucidating certain issues which are the common preoccupations of environmental philosophy and conservation biology, such as concern with biodiversity and the saving of endangered animals. The earlier sections of the paper have looked at (a) and (b); this section is concerned with (c).

At the end of section II, it is briefly mentioned that the study of zoology (indeed of biology in general) is carried out within a larger framework which is basically neo-Darwinian in orientation, the main components of which include the theory of evolution resting on natural selection as the mechanism to account for change, classical gene/chromosome theory which of late has been reinforced by DNA genetics and DNA biology, population genetics, cell theory, ecology and ethology.

Once upon a time, nearly four billion years ago, Earth was more or less devoid of life. When life did appear, it was first in water as microbial mats. The first organisms were procaryotic and single-celled. Then the 'higher' eucaryotic organisms appeared about 1.8 billion years ago, at first as single-celled, later as multi-cellular. It was not until the Cambrian explosion, 540 to 500 million years ago, that macroscopic animals appeared in abundance to give rise to the types which still exist today. Apart from the protozoans, as already observed in section II, the Kingdom Animalia comprises the vertebrates and the invertebrates, dating largely from the Cambrian period.

However, this historical fact of evolution hides two very different types of phenomena which ought to be distinguished – vertical evolution where there is change but without speciation and vertical evolution which involves speciation. According to E. O. Wilson, Darwin was primarily concerned with the former, not the latter – for instance, a genetic mutation in a population of white moths which happens to bestow survival advantage could end up by being one with predominantly black moths. There has been change but no speciation; you start and end with one species.

Furthermore, Darwin is often cited by theorists sympathetic to the philosophy of animal liberation or animal rights as a scientist who held that only individual animals exist and are real, but not species – James Rachels is a prominent holder of such a view. But to understand biodiversity, as it stood historically and as it stands today, scientists are interested primarily in evolution leading to speciation – for instance, a single species of wasps which came to Hawaii 100,000 years ago has given rise to hundreds of species as the members of the original colonising population spread out, changed and evolved in response to the distinctive environments they found themselves, which were peculiar to a particular island, mountain ridge or valley. As such, the scientists are interested, not so much in the individual animal (or organism) but in the species and in the mechanisms of speciation, namely, how changes in a population of individual organisms lead eventually to the emergence of two or more populations which no longer exchange genetic material with one another. To make empirical and conceptual sense of this kind of phenomenon, their work requires the so-called biological-species concept[5] which may briefly be defined as follows: 'a species

An Animal: What Is It?

is a population whose members are able to interbreed freely under natural conditions' (Wilson, 1992, p. 36).

This has fed into a polarisation in environmental philosophy between those who endorse an individualist framework based on the individual animal (organism) and those who argue for the centrality of the species, and in turn of the habitat and ecosystems of which species are a part (a view often referred to as holism). However, this paper is not concerned with evaluating the arguments and counter arguments which constitute this controversy; rather it will focus on an aspect of it which is not usually commented upon, namely, the by and large ahistorical decontextualised character of the individualist perspective and the implicit historical contextualised character of the holist approach.

The former appears to be involved primarily with the individual animal as it is confronted; its implicit account of what is an animal is governed by this outlook. For want of a better term, one could call this kind of individualist approach 'the phenomenalist account' or less solemnly, 'the what you see is what it is' account. Singer's sentientism could be interpreted in this light – mammals, in particular, could be observed to exhibit pain behaviour when they find themselves in certain situations, such as when their legs are caught and mangled by traps. From their behavioural symptoms, we infer that they feel pain and are in pain, just as in the case of humans who are fellow sentient beings, one similarly infers from the behavioural symptoms that other humans also feel pain and are in pain. Their sentience, therefore, constitutes their saliency if not their essence and gives the ground for their moral considerability. Regan's subject-of-a-life criterion could likewise be interpreted. Mammals could be observed reacting in the way humans do in certain situations – for instance, a cat would scratch at its owner's legs and/or miaow loudly until its owner opens the door to let it out, just as someone might persistently knock on the window until the person within hears the knocking and opens the door for one to come in. In the case of humans, the persistent knocking is taken to be the acting out of, and upon, certain desires and beliefs. Analogously, the cat is held, too, to be acting out of, and upon, certain desires and beliefs, the only difference – though deemed not to be relevant – is that while human desires and beliefs can be linguistically expressed, those of mammals are not and can not be thus expressed. The display of mental activity constitutes their only saliency and the grounds for their moral considerability.

Such an approach takes no account of any other aspect of animal existence including even the numerous obvious differences between all those that are identified and classified as animals according to the respective criterion of animality endorsed by Singer or Regan. Take any two animals, a cheetah and a human. A cheetah can run at a top speed of 70mph, but a human, at best, can run a mile between 3 and 4 minutes. Yet this salient difference cannot be accounted for in terms of the individual animals concerned. No amount of training, pumping steroid, eating large helpings of steak or taking ginseng by the mouthful could lead a human to perform in the same way a cheetah does. The difference can only be satisfactorily understood and explained in terms of their species characteristics.

In other words, behind the individual animal stands the species. What one observes of individual animals cannot be properly comprehended except in relationship with their species, whether one is thinking of cases which are inter species or intra species. The cheetah/human example is an illustration of the former. But consider the following intra species instance: a human suffers from severe brain damage because of an accident at birth and, so, leads a so-called vegetable existence. We lament this and regard it as a tragedy. Conceptually speaking, a sense of the tragic is only appropriate because the individual in question had the potential to speak, although that potentiality was never realised because of the accident. But the potential can only meaningfully be invoked because the individual is a member of the human species, one of its species attributes being the power of speech. It is not meaningful to say it is tragic that a cheetah or a lion cannot speak, no more than it is meaningful to say it is tragic that a human cannot sprint as fast as a cheetah.

An individual is but a very transient member of a species.[6] A species, as Rolston puts it, is a historical lineage. It comes to possess the characteristics it does as the outcome of an extended period of evolution which sometimes spans several thousand years. Hence an individual animal properly understood against the background of its species is not an ahistorical being – it is the product and an embodiment of evolutionary history itself. In other words, in observing a particular animal, one is not merely observing an individual being displaying whatever characteristics it does possess, but through it, one grasps the whole historical dimension of its evolutionary past. This aspect of public education, as earlier intimated, is impossible, not merely extremely difficult, to achieve in the context of a zoo; zoos, by their very nature, decontextualise the animal, having deliberately excluded it from that very context which embodies its evolutionary past, substituting for it an environment, so different from its original, that its evolutionary future may also be said to be more or less doomed.[7]

Evolution of species means that a population responds not merely to genetic variations but to such variations in the context of specific environments. Over time, variations which prove to be adaptive may ultimately lead to the emergence of two or more species, as we know. This means that ecology in general, and habitats and ecosystems in particular, play a vital part both in the emergence and the maintenance of a species. Going back to the Hawaiian example, the original colonising population of wasps would not have diverged and diversified into hundreds of different species thousands of years later if there had not been obvious or subtle, but in either case importantly different environments as provided by the numerous islands in the archipelago, the numerous valleys and mountain ridges on each particular island.

An Animal: What Is It?

The philosophy of animal rights and animal welfare is also necessarily blind to the historical and evolutionary dimensions of the animals it is interested in. Furthermore, this is hardly surprising given its failure to distinguish between domesticated and wild animals; whereas as far as zoology is concerned, its very object of study is wild animals and the context they imply. A concern with biological diversity is also in the main a concern with species diversity in the wild. To save species (in the wild) from threatened extinction is necessarily to save not only individual members of the endangered species, but the species themselves, together with the habitats and the ecosystems of which the species are members. To save the tiger is not to capture a few individual tigers and put them in a zoo or a secure enclosure of some kind – it is to save the tigers-in-the forests. But one is told that this is unrealistic and instead to rely on zoos to engage in captive breeding programmes of some 800 mammals for the next 200 years while waiting for an opportunity to return them to the wild. However, to believe this may turn out to be unrealistic, or at least, just as unrealistic as it is to aspire here and now to save the numerous identified endangered species *in situ,* for the following reasons:

(a) The major cause of species extinction today is habitat destruction and fragmentation caused by humans. It is assumed that (i) the impetus behind such destruction is pressure of human population, and (ii) in time to come, within the next 200 years or so, the human species would have come to control its population growth and indeed, drastically to reduce its numbers in global terms, releasing back to the captive animals the space now denied them. But these assumptions may be ill founded – (ii) may be no more than a pious hope and a declaration of faith, while (i) may be a misdiagnosis of the human impulse to destroy the habitats of fauna (and flora). It is true that human numbers as such put great pressure and stress on the natural environment; but one should not ignore another extremely powerful motivation at work which is altogether independent of the numbers of humans around as well as of the aspiration to increase human welfare and comfort. This is the urge and tendency to make over Earth according to the human image, which is greatly enhanced and encouraged in modern times through our ever- increasingly powerful technology. By such means, *homo faber* sets out systematically to transform the natural to become the artefactual.

(b) It assumes that 200 years of suspending natural evolution and the processes at work which sustain such evolution is not really equivalent to deliberate domestication. Although the genetic composition of the group of animals may be carefully monitored, so that an analogue of the genetic pattern and structure of a population in the wild could be replicated, no remotely plausible simulation of the habitat and ecosystem of the endangered species could be mounted under captive conditions.

(c) Nor is there any real guarantee that in 200 years time, when optimistically space is once more made available to return such animals to the wild, the new habitat would resemble in crucial ways the original of which their wild ancestors were a part. To assume otherwise is to subscribe to what may be called the additive/subtractive notion of causation[8] – consider a watch which has stopped working, but which upon examination shows up a defective spring. Remove the broken part, and replace it with a new functioning substitute. Wind up the watch and it should continue working exactly as it had done before. The stoppage brought about by the malfunctioning part, its removal and its subsequent replacement at any later moment in time makes no relevant ostensible difference to the watch whatsoever. A habitat or an ecosystem is not like a watch – the removal of a component (not even necessarily a keystone species) may lead to very significant new changes so that after a period of time, it is no longer in crucial respects the same habitat or ecosystem.

In the light of the discussion above, it seems fair to conclude that the dichotomy between individualism and holism may be misleading in one respect, namely, that a proper characterisation of the individual animal has to go beyond what I have called the phenomenalist approach to the species of which the individual is a member, and in turn to the evolutionary past which has produced the species as well as the present habitat and ecosystem which sustain the species and its continuing evolution by sustaining the individual members which live their lives within it. The individual animal is the nexus in which all these strands cohere for a limited period of time. To ignore this larger, 'holistic', historical background is to distort the nature of the individual animal by decontextualising it.

VII.

By looking behind the respective accounts of what is an animal implicitly given by the four different groups which have an interest in animals, this paper has arrived at the following conclusions:

1. The characterisation endorsed by three of these groups – namely, that of the lay public, the philosophy of animal liberation and animal rights, and zoos, is partial at best, and therefore, inadequate and misleading.

2. The characterisation given by the community of zoologists is more comprehensive and goes beyond what human sentiments alone see fit to identify and classify as animals. Furthermore, when suitably teased out, it is seen to endorse a view of animals which does not decontextualise them; through presenting them, not as mere individuals which happen to possess certain attributes, but as members of species which themselves are historical lineages, having evolved

and continue to evolve (if not made extinct) within their particular habitats and ecosystems.

3. This, in turn, has certain implications, both philosophical and practical. In particular, it reveals the philosophical drawbacks (i) of the kind of individualism upheld by the exponents of animal rights and animal welfare, (ii) of the captive breeding programmes undertaken or urged upon zoos, which seem to give undue prominence to DNA differences between individual animals whilst de-emphasising the larger, 'holistic' and historical dimensions against which they must be understood. As for the practical implications, it follows that (a) the policy of captive breeding to save (some selected) endangered species may be just as unrealistic as trying to save them in situ, (b) any attempt to save biodiversity must begin with educating the public about the issues raised by the question 'what is an animal?', weaning them from their untutored assumptions of identification and classification, (c) that zoos, by their very nature, are not necessarily the right institutions for this public education, given that their primary goal is entertainment and amusement.

NOTES

[1] I owe this point to Mary Midgley who has also made other suggestions for improvement, for all of which I am most grateful.
[2] This sense of domestication regarding animals in zoos will be defended later in section VI.
[3] The limited number of zoos in the world which participate in the captive breeding programme do engage in scientific research which goes beyond what has just been mentioned. But this work is directly bound up with their recently acquired goal of conserving species threatened with extinction.
[4] However, to my knowledge one zoo director has agonised about this matter. See David Hancocks' paper 'Lions, Tigers and Bears, Oh No!' in Norton (1995).
[5] This is not to say, however, that the concept is without difficulties. For instance, it is not applicable to organisms (mainly plants) which reproduce asexually.
[6] This should not be taken to imply that species are immortal. A mammalian species lasts, on average, a million years.
[7] The point made here about the educational limitation of zoos is not that zoos cannot provide information by way of videos, lectures, notices and pamphlets about the evolutionary history and habitat of the species which has led to that history, but that this is done, necessarily, in a decontextualised fashion, as zoos, no matter how 'naturalistic' the settings in which most of their animals (especially the larger ones) are exhibited, can only simulate their natural habitats.
[8] For a fuller account, see Lee, *Social Philosophy and Ecological Scarcity*, pp. 58-70.

REFERENCES AND SELECTED BIBLIOGRAPHY

Clark, Stephen R. L. 1977. *The Moral Status of Animals*. Oxford: Clarendon Press.

Hickman, Cleveland, Jr., Larry S. Roberts and Frances M. Hickman, 1984 (seventh edition). *Integrated Principles of Zoology. St.* Louis, Toronto and Santa Clara: Times Mirror/Mosby College Publishing.

Jamieson, Dale, 1985. 'Against Zoos', in *In Defense of Animals,* edited by Peter Singer. New York: Harper and Row.

Lee, Keekok, 1989. *Social Philosophy and Ecological Scarcity*. London: Routledge.

Midgley, Mary, 1979. *Beast and Man: The Roots of Human Nature*. Hassocks: Harvester.

Midgley, Mary, 1983. *Animals and Why They Matter*. Harmondsworth: Penguin.

Norton, Bryan et al. (eds), 1995. *Ethics on the Ark: Zoos, Animal Welfare and Wildlife Conservation*. Washington and London: Smithsonian Institution Press.

Rachels, James, 1991. *Created from Animals: The Moral Implications of Darwinism*. Oxford and New York: Oxford University Press.

Regan, Tom, 1983. *The Case for Animal Rights*. Los Angeles: University of California Press.

Rolston, Holmes, III, 1988. *Environmental Ethics: Duties to and Values in the Natural World*. Philadelphia: Temple University Press.

Singer, Peter, 1976. *Animal Liberation: Towards an End of Man's Inhumanity to Animals*. London: Jonathan Cape.

Tudge, Colin, 1992. *Last Animals At The Zoo: How Mass Extinction Can Be Stopped*. Oxford: Oxford University Press.

Wilson, Edward O., 1994. *The Diversity of Life*. London: Penguin Books.

Using Animals: Populations and Exploitation

Bodies on the Beach: Domesticates and Disasters in the Spanish Philippines 1750–1898

Greg Bankoff

Disasters are simply a fact of life in the Philippines; natural hazards such as earthquakes, volcanic eruptions, typhoons, floods, droughts, landslides, tsunamis and the like occur with such relentless intensity that they can be regarded as 'frequent life events'.[1] While these phenomena have historically been the source of much privation and suffering in the archipelago, their impact has largely been chronicled only in so far as it affects human society. Their severity is usually only assessed in terms of human deaths, injuries and missing persons and the damage caused to human property, principally dwellings, fields, orchards, roads, bridges and the like. Domestic animals are sometimes enumerated in this latter category but surprisingly rarely and then mainly in very unspecific terms. Yet animals were also very much adversely affected by natural hazards especially the floods caused by the torrential rainfall that frequently accompanied the passage of typhoons. In particular, domestic animals such as carabaos, horses, cattle, pigs, goats, sheep, ducks and chickens, often concentrated in large numbers as a result of their utility to human communities, were exposed to harm and sudden death.[2]

Attempts to describe and assess the impact of hazards upon human communities have more recently become the subject of serious scholarly debate but little if any attention has been paid to the plight of animals.[3] Even detailed studies on the history of human-animal relationships rarely make mention of hazards other than disease or human predation.[4] This neglect is all the more remarkable given the dire outcomes the loss of livestock in the form of work animals, beasts of burden, and sources of protein had for rural populations in the past or indeed still have in the present. Quite apart from the distress inflicted on the animals, loss of livestock and poultry was a major factor, along with crop spoliation and damage to cultivated fields, that adversely impacted upon the immediate livelihood of farmers and also upon their long-term agricultural viability.[5]

The historical records that detail the disasters that overtook human communities in the Philippines are also peppered with accounts of how other species fared under such circumstances. Making use of such material and a more detailed case study from a community in Central Luzon struck by a typhoon in 1831, this paper attempts to assess the extent of domestic livestock loss occasioned by natural hazard especially flood as well as the impact their deaths had on human communities. In particular, it applies the concept of vulnerability or whether the same factors that determine human exposure to risk on an individual or group basis pertain also to animals. Was the vulnerability of domesticates exacerbated by enforced location in large numbers at sites decided upon by humans and were the relative levels of risk between and even within species different? Answering such questions about such actors in such a time and place, however, is fraught with difficulties consequent upon fragmentary data and 'unscientific' accounts that make statistical estimations unreliable and that preclude definitive statements. Nevertheless, the data are sufficient, even in an Asian colonial society whose history is little known outside the archipelago, to reach some suggestive conclusions.

THE NATURE OF HAZARD

According to any criteria, the Philippines are an extremely dangerous place to inhabit. One of the most comprehensive records on the occurrence of recent natural hazards even advised that the archipelago has experienced more disasters than any other country in the world since 1900.[6] However, modern databases are always limited by their inability to provide a more extensive historical overview. Archival sources, on the other hand, have a greater temporal span and Spanish chroniclers have left an incomplete but suggestive record of hazard that stretches back to the beginnings of European settlement in the mid-sixteenth century.

Situated at the convergence of several tectonic plates, the islands are a place of extreme seismic activity. There have been at least 74 major earthquakes since records first began in 1599 as well as countless smaller ones. Saderra Masó's study of the last two decades of the nineteenth century recorded an average of 53.4 earthquake days a year or 4.5 per month. Extremely destructive earthquakes have occurred in all major regions as well as in the capital, Manila, most notably in 1645, 1658, 1863 and 1880, when large parts of the city were laid to ruin.[7] There are also 220 volcanoes, 21 or 22 of which are classified as active, and there have been at least 41 eruptions described as destructive between 1572 and 1993, an average of one major event every decade.[8] Aside from the seismic activity, however, the Philippines is also prone to climate-related hazards especially in the form of powerful typhoons that sweep across the archipelago from the Southwest Pacific, mainly during the months between June and November. On average, over 20 typhoons each year, some with wind speeds in excess of 200 kilometres an hour, enter what is termed the Philippine Area of Responsibility and regularly devastate low-lying areas particularly of the eastern seaboard. There are a surprising number of historical sources on typhoons, known locally as *baguios*, testifying to their frequency and their impact on communities. These sorts of statistics, however, give little real impression of what the actual historical experience meant to a person in the past. Local histories, on the other hand, provide a much better insight into what people were subjected to and how communities fared under such circumstances. Thus the residents of southern Luzon were likely to face a major typhoon once every five to six years in the eighteenth century and once every four to five years in the nineteenth century.[9]

Bodies on the Beach

Along with the baguios, however, came rain, lots of it falling over a short period of time. While the meteorological phenomenon of repeated tropical cyclones makes a significant and necessary contribution to total precipitation levels, it is also partly responsible for the frequency and intensity of flooding throughout the islands. The 'furious typhoon' that struck the province of Capiz on 19 November 1835 was 'accompanied by a dense and cold rain that lasted from daybreak till seven o'clock at night with equal intensity'. Floods have historically been the

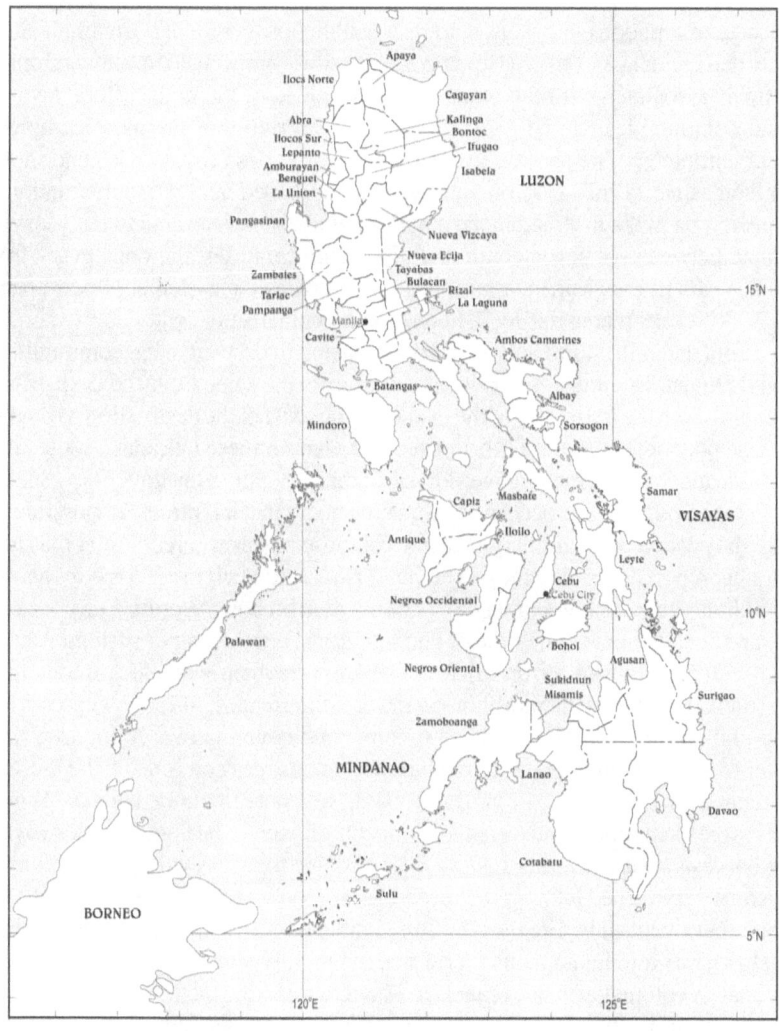

FIGURE 1. Map of Philippine Provinces in 1900

source of much privation and suffering and were often more to be feared than the high winds. 'Almost always during typhoons', an official in Pangasinan noted in 1854, 'the floods are more terrible and destructive than the winds of the storm'.[10] Again, local accounts testify to the frequency of such hazards. A list drawn up from such sources found in the Archive of the Manila Observatory constitutes a record of major floods that occurred between 1691 and 1900. While almost certainly incomplete, it does provide an indication of the primary causes, geographical predisposition and even the frequency of such events in specific areas. Moreover, local histories regularly refer to flooding in connection to the passage of typhoons that were held responsible for over 56 per cent of all such recorded incidences. Otherwise, floods were simply attributed to heavy rainfall, at times associated with the monsoons. Some idea of the impact flood had on local communities can be gauged by a closer scrutiny of the more complete local chronicles. The records for Nabua in Camarines (1691–1856) and those for Pangasinan (1768–1872) suggest how regularly people faced such situations. A person on average experienced a major inundation every nine to ten years in Nabua between the seventeenth and nineteenth centuries and once every five to six years in Pangasinan, a province that includes the extremely flood-prone Agno River delta area during the eighteen and nineteenth centuries.[11]

Wind and rain, storm and water, typhoon and flood were what communities could expect. Document after document repeats the same litany of despair bemoaning both the frequency of the event and the scale of the destruction wrought. 'These phenomena are so unfortunately frequent in these latitudes', writes the Alcalde mayor (provincial governor) of Camarines Sur to the governor-general in October 1882, 'some occurring so unexpectedly that it is almost impossible to take the needed precautionary measures at those places where it might matter'. Another report describing the rise of the Abra river to a height of 25 metres above its ordinary level in September 1867 commented on how: 'Hardly a province of the archipelago, but at one time or another, has heard the roar of rushing waters and seen the flight of terror-stricken man'. So frequent were such floods that they actually shaped the morphology of local landscapes, filling in depressions and obliterating *esteros* (canals or streams) and covering everything in a rich layer of silt that might go far to explain why such areas continued to be the site of repeated human occupation. But flooding was not always beneficial: 'When they were exceptional and lasted too long, they covered the fields and destroyed the harvests, causing losses that were impossible to assess with any certainty'. Streams were turned into raging torrents in moments and rivers became walls of water that swept all before them causing immense destruction and transforming the lowlands into an aqueous world where the only sure means of transit was by boat. A colonial official, Francisco Plana, wrote how the towns and villages under his jurisdiction had literally been 'effaced from the map of this District'. Watercourses broke their banks within minutes and what had been but 'yesterday fertile fields and roads' were 'today converted into one immense lake'. In

Bodies on the Beach

such circumstances, there was but one thing for people to do – fly. Take to the nearest high ground or hill at once 'abandoning everything'.[12]

The tally of destruction was immense. The local history of San Nicolas in Ilocos Norte describes a violent storm and flood that destroyed half the town in 1798. That of Pagsanjan in Laguna gives details of the overflowing of the Balanoc and Bumbungan rivers on a number of occasions: flooding the town with enormous loss to both life and property on 22 October 1831, rising to over half a metre along the Calle Real in October 1840, and again inundating the town in 1882. In the town of Caibiran on Leyte, a big flood in 1876 washed away 'most of the houses, and even the church and bell tower'. The already described rising of the Abra River between 25 and 27 September 1867 caused the deaths of over 1,800 people, while the typhoon and flood that hit Bulacan in October 1882 left more than 15,000 people 'without shelter'. The entire town of Caoayan in Ilocos Sur was said to have disappeared beneath the waters.[13] The most obvious flood-prone areas in the archipelago and those hardest hit were the ancient channels of river systems filled with Quaternary alluvial deposits. As these are also among the flattest, most fertile and easiest to irrigate landscapes, they have also been the richest centres of agriculture and the sites of intensive human settlement. They were also the location where large numbers of domesticated animals were concentrated.

BODIES ON THE BEACH

Archival sources make frequent reference to the dead thrown up by the sea, of bodies on the beach as those caught by the swiftly-flowing current or trapped by suddenly rising water levels were washed off shore only to de deposited on land again by the incoming tide. Closer reading through the documentary record though reveals that most of these corpses were not human but animal. Despite the much greater amount of ink expended on the enumeration of human losses, by far the greater number of casualties were domestic animals, those either unable to flee or forgotten in the sudden flight and simply abandoned to their fates. 'With respect to the animals', writes José García, the commander of a schooner to the military governor of Mindanao in 1891, 'the greater part of them have been killed some drowned by the waters, and the others by the multitude of fallen trees'. Animals were literally dragged off their feet by the force of water and 'thrown into the sea'. So strong was the flow that a horse and rider found it impossible to negotiate a passage through even quite shallow waters. There was the too often repeated 'spectre' of the Cagayan river 'tumbling northward' bearing with it 'a grim cargo of dead carabaos'. Sometimes, these bodies were not swept away but were trapped in situ so that: 'Many animals were to be seen lying around dead in the fields and within the town proper'. The local chronicler of Nueva Caceres reported an extensive flood of the Bicol river in October 1872 that left the plain of Naga a 'tide-less sea' that stretched from Pili to Pamplona on whose surface floated: 'Corpses, carcasses, carabaos, sewage, filth ... rotting in the sun, spreading pestilence in every direction'.[14]

A great number of animals were lost in this way. There are repeated references to 'many animals', 'a multitude of animals', 'considerable numbers', 'hundreds of head' or 'a total past reckoning' being drowned or otherwise lost.[15] Other accounts, however, try to be more exact and give some idea of the extent of the loss. There are mentions of the number of livestock lost by communities: 39 head of cattle in Pili drowned during a typhoon on 7–8 November 1865; or 72 head in San Isidro and more than 100 in Santa Cruz from the typhoon that hit Zambales between 19 and 20 October 1881. Collectively, these totals mounted up. The governor of Abra reported that besides the 600 souls and at least 950 houses carried away by the rushing waters of the river during the terrible flood of 1867 that as many as 6,500 animals had also drowned. The typhoon and subsequent flood that struck Isabela de Luzon on 7 October 1879 caused the death of a reported 8,160 domestic animals.[16]

As people abandoned their homes and belongings and precipitately took sanctuary on higher ground, animals were often left to fend for themselves. The strength of the current posed their most immediate threat, compounded by the debris – objects that had come away from buildings or the whole structure itself and uprooted trees or sawn logs – that might inflict mortal blows on those they struck. Other animals were left stranded on any patches of higher ground that became small islands of dry land but without food or escape.[17] One official, Jesús Mellados, graphically described what he had seen in the aftermath of the typhoon that hit Leyte on 12 October 1897:

> ... And there were the remains of all kinds of animals around that presented a fearful portrait of the titanic struggle they had sustained in their grim tussle for life in which they were finally overcome after suffering horrendous injuries to limb and body.[18]

On another occasion, the provincial governor of Camarines Sur, touring the damages caused by the typhoon of 7–8 November, witnessed animals still swimming aimlessly among the houses though he noted that many had already drowned. Some animals, though, were able to find safety on their own account. The same official noted how in Milaor: 'There was little water in the atrium of the Convento [priest's house] and there many animals had taken refuge'.[19]

In the aftermath of typhoon and flood, the carcasses of many of these animals found their way onto the beaches of the 7,100 odd islands that comprise the Philippines archipelago where they lay under a tropical sun 'in a state of corruption'. Disease was a major concern for officials. It was 'a matter of the utmost urgency', continued Jesús Mellados, to clear away this putrefying matter from both shore and dwellings and to rid the place of the 'poisonous and disagreeable odours'. Strict laws were also passed on the sale and consumption of

Bodies on the Beach

meat derived from dead or infirm animals or flesh 'whose provenance could not be completely guaranteed without the slightest doubt'. However, it appears that such regulations were not always complied with and the injunctions had to be repeated on numerous occasions. Large numbers of bloated and decomposing animal bodies were gathered together into mounds and burnt 'as a precautionary sanitation measure', their stench adding to the already heavy reek exuded by the sodden landscape.[20] Even for many of the animals who survived the rushing waters, the total loss of provender and farmland rendered infertile by a thick layer of sand and stone often meant that a slower death through starvation awaited.[21]

Flood, of course, was not the only cause of death though more animals perished in this manner than from any other natural hazard. Volcanic eruptions, though perhaps more deadly within a given locality only affected a limited area. Historical data on Taal, one of the most active volcanoes (erupting at least 34 times since 1572) and situated only 50 kilometres south of Manila (and so the best documented site) gives some idea of the devastation that could be wrought. Father Buencuchillo, an eyewitness of the terrible eruption of November 1754 – the most devastating in the recorded history of the archieplago – concluded that: 'All the animals of whatever kind have perished'. An exceptional feature of Taal is its location in the middle of a lake so that eruptions are frequently accompanied by a tsunami-like wave that devastates the surrounding shoreline, drowning human and animal populations alike. Much the same kinds of observations were made about subsequent major eruptions on 19 July 1874 and 30 January 1911. Mr Martin, who witnessed the latter event, was absolutely certain that no animal life could have lived through it. Dean Worcester, an American colonial official, noted in this respect that a particularly 'distressing feature of this calamity was that crops and grasses were killed over immense areas within which no other very serious damage was done, with the result that a large number of domestic animals starved to death'.[22] Domestic animals also undoubtedly died in many other natural hazards such as earthquakes and landslides but not evidently in sufficient numbers to make it a matter of historical note and so the extent of their demise is unknown. As a matter of perspective, however, all these death tolls pale in comparison to the animal fatalities caused by disease. The outbreak of rinderpest among carabaos and surra among horses in the 1880s and 1890s drastically reduced herds, killing up to 90 per cent of livestock in some regions. Nearly 60 per cent of equine deaths from all causes (including those in slaughter houses) were still caused by disease in 1918.[23]

Data on how non-domesticates fared during natural hazards is even more difficult to reconstruct and there is only the occasional inadvertent or otherwise chance remark on their fate. An added peril during floods was poisonous snakes flushed out of their lairs by the rushing waters or taking refuge in abandoned homes especially above door-lintels and liable to bite anything they encountered under these circumstances. Of course, such incidents were only occasionally recorded when the victims were human but the same fate befell livestock. Somewhat more frequent are the references to unusual animal behaviour during such phenomena: how birds disappeared during a flood or how wild animals fled their forest homes at the first sign of an earthquake. Antonio Mendoza, an eyewitness to the 1911 eruption of Taal volcano, remembered certain signs that preceded the event in an interview he gave in 1977. He noted how *pugo* (quails) and *labuyo* (wild chickens) came down from the mountainside and sought shelter among the domesticated chickens and ducks under the stilt houses and how his sister had even been able to easily catch a wild 'batu-batu' bird because it had become so tame.[24] The idea that animal behaviour was somehow portentous of an impending disaster seems deep-rooted among Filipino folk culture. In D. Santiago Patero's *Reglas Practicas para Librarse de los Huracanes en el Archipiélago Filipino*, he recounts how the sight of a large wild bird common to Mindoro that suddenly became tame and 'almost seemed to want to come and hide itself among us' was sufficient to persuade the commander of the boat he was travelling on to forgo the pleasures of a dance that evening and immediately board the craft 'so as to prepare ourselves properly to survive [the impending storm]'.[25]

Nor were terrestrial animals the only victims of natural hazard as marine creatures were also sometimes affected though not always adversely. According to one Pedro Andres de Castro y Amadeo, the lake waters during the eruption of Taal in 1754 'threw up dead alligators and fish, including sharks'. Fishponds where milkfish or *bangus* (*Chanos chanos*) were raised from fingerlings were frequently damaged by floodwaters and their stock 'lost'. On the other hand, the destruction caused by typhoons and floods to marine gear and tackle severely restricted subsequent fishing activities and may have offered a temporary respite especially to demersal fisheries. The many fish corrals known as *baklad* that dotted the shoreline were especially vulnerable to storms, tidal surges and floods. A number of reports note their 'total ruin' and 'complete disappearance' from certain areas recently affected by flooding. The unwary fisherman who went down to the sea too soon to recovery his corral risked drowning. Floodwaters may also have had an effect on marine fisheries by depriving fishermen of their boats either 'smashing them to pieces' or simply bearing them away without trace.[26]

DOMESTICATION AND VULNERABILITY

The documentary evidence overwhelmingly shows that domesticated animals in the Philippines were at risk from natural hazards and died in large numbers during the nineteenth century especially as a result of floods. While all animals were threatened in one way or another by such events, were domesticates more exposed than other animals because of the intense nature of their relationship with human society and did this vulnerability increase over the period? The process of domestication has always been viewed more from an anthropocentric perspective as one conferring, on the one hand, great benefits through increased

Bodies on the Beach

speed, strength, utility and productivity balanced, on the other hand, by increased morbidity through the mutation across species of a new set of contagious diseases such as smallpox, measles and influenza incubated among livestock, pets and poultry.[27] Viewed from the animal standpoint however, domestication entailed among many other factors, both positive and negative, concentration in large numbers often in hazardous locations such as on floodplains or in close proximity to active volcanoes. That is to say, domesticated animals were rendered more vulnerable to natural hazards through their association with humans than were their feral or wild counterparts.[28]

The concept of vulnerability assesses exposure to hazards in terms of what renders people unsafe, a condition that depends primarily on a society's social order and the relative position of advantage or disadvantage that a particular group occupies within it. Vulnerable populations are those at risk not simply because they are exposed to hazard but as a result of a particular form of marginality that is usually determined by a combination of variables such as class, gender, age, ethnicity and disability, among others.[29] The emphasis is on historical process, the combination of factors that come together at a particular time and place to expose some individuals, groups, communities or societies to the effect of hazard. Of course, this notion has only been applied to humans but its application to animals may add to a deeper understanding of the nature of the relationship between the two.

Going back to the documentary record with this concept in mind does reveal more about the impact of hazards and their influence on particular animal populations throughout the archipelago. It is clear that in some instances all domestic animals were reported either to have drowned or have been lost so that 'in some places there did not remain either a working carabao, or a cow or a horse [as] all had been washed away'. On Leyte, the flood that swept through Mauyog (Mayorga?) on 12 December 1879 totally destroyed the harvest and, again, was said to have killed all domestic animals. The same was true of domestic animals in Lupon in what is now the province of Davao Oriental where all of them apparently perished as well. Calibrating monetarily, the civil governor of Zambales estimated that the value of the animals drowned or disappeared amounted to 400 pesos, a considerable sum.[30]

This devastation was seemingly only localised, however, when it comes to equating losses against total populations. Such comparisons can only be very rough estimates given the paucity of extant statistics, their reliability and the nature of the politico-administrative boundaries on which they are based but occasionally they are rather suggestive. Thus the 188 cows and horses specified as lost in Isablea de Luzon during the typhoon of 7 October 1879 only represented 2.4 per cent of the province's 7,973 recorded head of these species in 1891.[31] Another comparison using data from a typhoon in October 1890 in the Batanes Islands and the animal populations there in 1911 yields similar results for cows and pigs but suggests that the loss of goats and sheep was very much more significant and could have been as high as 12.5 per cent of the total (Table 1).

TABLE 1. Batanes livestock lost October 1890 as per cent of population in 1911.[32]

Animals	Cows	Pigs	Goats & Sheep
1890 deaths	60	123	152
1911 population	5358	2560	1220
Per cent	1.1%	4.8%	12.5%

All domestic animals were vulnerable to hazard but perhaps some were more vulnerable than others. It is difficult to calculate whether some domesticates were more at risk: larger animals such as carabaos, cattle and horses often figure more prominently in the documentary record but this may simply be a matter of their greater respective value and therefore the magnitude of their consequent loss. Thus 1,343 cattle, 842 horses and 761 carabaos are listed as having perished in the sudden rising of the Abra river in 1871 but only a 'numberless' amount of hogs. The town of Calabanga and its outlying *visitas* (dependent settlements) in Camarines Sur lost 170 carabaos, 30 horses and 15 cattle in November 1885. After the floodwaters that swept through the district of Principe on 12 November 1892 had retreated, the bodies of 22 carabaos and 19 horses were recovered but these figures did not include the more than 80 other head that had simply disappeared.[33] But when it comes to smaller and lower value livestock and poultry, there are frequent references to the 'many pigs and chickens', 'the great number of pigs' or the 'great number of roosters and hens' that had been drowned or lost. In the case of the municipalities of Baganga and Quimablang in Surigao, the loss of pigs, ducks and chickens in this manner was apparently total.[34] Where the statistics are more comprehensive, less large domesticates constitute a higher percentage of all losses. A total of 715 animals perished as a result of the typhoon that hit the Batanes Islands, the most northerly point in the Philippines between 11 and 12 October 1890 of which 60 were cattle (9 per cent), 123 pigs (17 per cent), 152 goats and sheep (21 per cent) and 380 pets and poultry (53 per cent). Pigs represented fully 48 per cent of the 3,216 animals listed as lost in La Unión during the passage of three successive typhoons in 1859.[35]

TABLE 2. Per cent of Domestic Animals Lost 22 October 1831 in Bacoor, Cavite.[36]

Animals	Carabaos	Horses	Pigs	Chickens	Total
Loss	47	11	221	1722	2001
Per cent	2.4%	0.6%	11%	86%	100%

Bodies on the Beach

More detailed data on how a 'community' of domestic animals fared during such a hazard is extant for the pueblo of Bacoor in Cavite where information on loss is listed by household. Bacoor is a pueblo south of Manila but close to the capital that was hit by a strong typhoon and subsequent flood on 22 October 1831. There are 450 households mentioned as having suffered damage of one description or another during the storm of which 326 or 72 per cent reported the loss of domestic animals of some description.[37] Again the data corroborate that smaller domestic animals accounted for the majority of fatalities with pigs amounting to 11 per cent and poultry for fully 86 per cent of all losses. The number of deaths among larger livestock is much less though still significant particularly in the case of the 47 carabao that were drowned (Table 2). An interesting feature of the data on Bacoor, however, is the much fuller picture it presents of the extensive damage to fish farming and fisheries. Here both fish ponds and fish pens (corrals) are mentioned as well as the undefined 'fisheries' with 73 such operations identified as destroyed (Table 3). Information is also provided on fishing boats with the loss of 27 craft reported, most described as small (22 or 81 per cent).

TABLE 3. Per cent of Fisheries Lost 22 October 1831 in Bacoor, Cavite.[38]

Fish	Ponds	Small Ponds	Pens	Small Pens	Fisheries	Total
Loss	45	12	8	1	7	73
Per cent	62%	16%	11%	1%	10%	100%

While the data provides a snapshot of how a community of domestic animals fared during a flood, the evidence suggests that smaller animals might be more vulnerable under such circumstances than larger ones. Thus some 1,708 hens (and an additional 14 pullets) perished on 22 October but this number does not include the 11 other occasions when mention is made to the loss of 'many hens' nor the 22 references to the demise of chicks. Greater detail is provided for swine though this reinforces the idea that smaller, younger and perhaps feeding mothers were more particularly at risk. Suckling pigs and piglets accounted for 83 or 38 per cent of all losses not including the respective 11 further entries that mention the death of an undefined number of such animals. In addition, 21 suckling sows were also specifically listed as having perished. None of these conclusions, however, can be more than tentative given the nature of the evidence, especially the absence of data on the total population of each species in a community prior to the hazard striking.

Nor did the vulnerability of domesticates remain the same over the nineteenth century as human activity shaped and reshaped the landscape with an intensity and purpose hitherto unknown in the archipelago. Rural areas experienced profound changes during the nineteenth century partly due to the unprecedented increase in human population and partly as a result of the growth of commercial agriculture both of which had environmental consequences. The sheer number of people rose from just over two and a half million in 1818 to just under eight million by the end of the century, an annual rate of increase of slightly over 1.4 per cent.[39] Population density across the islands also rose accordingly on average from 8.8 to 26.8 per square kilometre. Migration, still predominantly between rural areas and not as yet primarily a rural-urban phenomenon, ensured that some regions grew faster than others and an 'inland frontier' emerged during the course of the century primarily in the central plain of Luzon but also on some islands, notably Negros and more latterly on Mindanao. Agriculture, too, for the first time was subjected to international market forces with the result that increasingly large swathes of land were devoted to the planting of export crops such as sugar, abaca and tobacco in place of the staple, rice. The demand for arable land quickened and its value rose as capitalist agriculture came to dominate certain sectors of the economy.[40] Much land was cleared and forest cover declined rapidly in some provinces to little more than six to seven per cent on Cebu and 11 per cent on Bohol. Overall, as much as 50 per cent of those areas under effective Spanish colonial rule may have been deforested by the end of the nineteenth century.[41] As human settlement spread more intensively over the full extent of the Philippines, the environment, too, was subjected to new pressures that were reflected in the greater frequency and intensity of droughts and floods though the evidence is somewhat inconclusive given the islands' exposure to the full brunt of the El Niño-La Niña weather pattern, or ENSO. These changes affected domesticates as well. In particular, great stock farms were established by the religious orders as early as the seventeenth and eighteenth centuries with animals brought mainly from China and Japan. The Jesuit *estancia* at Zamboanga, for instance, reportedly had over 2,100 livestock (horses and cattle) by 1768.[42] Such concentrations increased animals' vulnerability to disease and forced them to live under conditions more exposed to extreme climatic events.

Moreover, the relationship between humans and domestic animals is always a complex one that is never easily understood on just one level or basis of exchange. Just as the association is a multi-reciprocal one in terms of benefits, it is also one characterised by a compounded sense of vulnerability. Animals may have been more exposed to hazard because of their domestication but their loss in large numbers, in turn, made human communities that much more vulnerable. In a sense, the immediate hazard was only half the story – or only half the pain. The *principales* (leading citizens) of a small group of islands off Palawan complained how floodwaters 'carried away the fields already sown with rice leaving us without seed to sow anew', uprooted fruit trees, coconut palms and banana groves and deprived [us] of 'precisely the only resources ... from which the people depend upon for subsidence'. But not only did natural hazard deprive people of their crops and their seeds, it also left them without the animals they needed to work the fields. The great flood of September 1867 in Abra destroyed the harvest and 'left hardly a single work animal' so that there was a 'scarcity of the means of sustenance caused both by the loss of provisions and animals'. The result was that famine often followed hard upon the retreating waters, 'a great hunger' that caused 'incalculable hardship to the poor' as 'people were threatened with the misery caused by the lack of even the most basic necessities of life'. Memories of such events evidently stayed fresh in the minds of local communities. In the 1950s, the inhabitants of Barrio Bantog in Victoria, Tarlac still recalled a big flood that had occurred at the beginning of the nineteenth century when the Tarlac and Guimba rivers had overflowed their banks and washed away most of the fertile soil, the crops and many of the draft and domestic animals. 'Since the last disastrous flood to the present time', wrote down the elders in their local history, 'the place [has] remained generally low'.[43]

'TOGETHER YET APART'

The human toll in disasters is always a matter of record but animal deaths rarely warrant a mention. Yet many more animals usually die in such events than do people. Not only are animals vulnerable to hazard but the fact of their domestication and the changes wrought by human activity on the environment may actually increase their exposure and place them more at risk. In tropical climates without extensive grazing lands, domesticated animals are concentrated in large numbers at sites that are more often situated to take advantage of good soil conditions and proximity to market rather than from any awareness of their vulnerability to seismic or meteorological conditions. These settlements are frequently located on floodplains, near active volcanoes or besides waterways, all areas that are more likely to create the conditions for a disaster to occur. Just as a disaster is not the product of natural hazard alone but is the result of an extreme event in association with a particular social, economic, political and cultural system, so it is also with animals. Animals are not just vulnerable but are made so by a range of factors, one of which is their domestication.

Domestication, however, is too broad a categorisation to be anything more useful than a means of differentiating broad groups of animals from one another and from humans. Vulnerability may have varied among domesticates as well. As the evidence from the nineteenth century Philippines shows large numbers of pigs, goats, sheep and especially poultry died as a result of hazards, especially floods. There is even a suggestion that these domesticates were more at risk than larger livestock such as carabaos, cattle and horses. Due to the inconclusive and fragmentary nature of the data, however, further research needs to be conducted to ascertain whether this was true and why it might be the case. Was it simply a matter of greater mass, better ability to swim or some other factor such as weight of sodden fleece? Also, there is next to no information on domestic pets and their fates during such occurrences; these animals are almost completely absent from the extant historical accounts when contemporary studies show their importance as a consideration in modern emergency management.[44] On the other hand, the more detailed data does suggest that even within species there were differences and that the young and suckling mothers were more at risk than their fellows. But vulnerability is rarely a matter of simply assessing one group in isolation from another but is more often a matter of compounded exposure. Just as animals were more at risk from their domestication so human societies that depended upon them for labour and nourishment were rendered more vulnerable by their sudden demise.

Animals, of course, have their own histories quite apart from that of humans though their narratives have run along parallel and converging lines particularly over the last five thousand years or so in the case of domesticates. There is no denying the centrality of this relationship but neither should it obscure the separateness of their histories. On the one hand, this history is about reciprocal partnership though one where the terms of exchange favour humans over animals much as they do in any patron-client relationship. On the other hand, it is also about mutual vulnerability, where the nature of the dependent relationship compounds the risks to which both are exposed. Animals may have increasingly begun to figure in historiography. As Harriet Ritvo argues, they are an integral part of 'our grand narrative' about the way in which humanity has come to terms with its environment both literally and symbolically. Yet, in a very real sense, they are still often ignored as in the case of natural hazards or represented in such a manner that they are 'absent yet present' in history.[45] Perhaps the challenge now is how to express the symbiotic nature of their histories in such a way that animals and humans are depicted as 'together yet apart'.

NOTES

[1] Greg Bankoff, *Cultures of Disaster: Society and Natural Hazard in the Philippines* (London: RoutledgeCurzon, 2003): 179–83.

[2] Humans are animals as well but the differentiation between humans and non-human animals seems somewhat contrived in the context of this discussion. The carabao or Asian water buffalo (*Bubalus bubalis*) is the principal draft animal employed in the archipelago due to its ability to work in thick mud or the flooded conditions characteristic of rice paddies.

[3] For example, Gilbert White's seminal study of the impact of flooding in the USA published in 1945 only deals peripherally with livestock under the general heading of 'agricultural losses', an approach that largely holds true till the present. Gilbert White, *Human Adjustments to Floods: A Geographical Approach to the Flood Problem in the United States* (Chicago: Department of Geography, Research Paper No. 29, 1945): 78. A notable exception, however, is Sebastian Heath, *Animal Management in Disasters* (St. Louis: Mosby, 1999). On the effects of natural hazards on human populations, especially the concept of vulnerability, see among others: Kenneth Hewitt, 'The Idea of Calamity

Bodies on the Beach

in a Technocratic Age', in *Interpretations of Calamity from the Viewpoint of Human Ecology*, ed. Kenneth Hewitt (Boston: Allen and Unwin, 1983): 3–32; Ben Wisner, 'Disaster Vulnerability: Scale, Power and Daily Life', *GeoJournal* 30, 2 (1993): 127–40; Terry Cannon, 'Vulnerability Analysis and the Explanation of "Natural" Disasters', in *Disasters, Development and Environment*, ed. Ann Varley (Chichester, New York, Brisbane, Toronto and Singapore: John Wiley & Sons, 1994): 13–29; Kenneth Hewitt, 'Sustainable Disasters? Perspectives and Power in the Discourse of Calamity', in *Power of Development* ed. Jonathan Crush (London and New York: Routledge, 1995): 115–28. See also Amartya Sen, *Poverty and Famines: An Essay on Entitlement and Deprivation* (Oxford: Oxford University Press, 1981).

[4] James Serpell, *In the Company of Animals: A Study of Human-Animal Relationships* (Oxford, New York: Basil Blackwell, 1986); Harriet Ritvo, *The Animal Estate: The English and Other Creatures in the Victorian Age* (Cambridge: Harvard University Press, 1987); Elinor Melville, *A Plague of Sheep: Environmental Consequences of the Conquest of Mexico* (Cambridge: Cambridge University Press, 1994). See also in this respect the more recent study by Virginia Anderson, *Creatures of Empire: How Domestic Animals Transformed Early America* (Oxford: Oxford University Press, 2004).

[5] Juliet Clutton-Brock, *A Natural History of Domesticated Mammals* (Cambridge: Cambridge University Press, 1987); Juliet Clutton-Brock ed., *The Walking Larder: Patterns of Domestication, Pastoralism, and Predation* (London, Boston, Sydney, Wellington: Unwin Hyman, 1989); Sebastian Heath, Simon Kenyon and Cristobal Zepeda Sein, 'Emergency Management of Disasters Involving Livestock in Developing Countries', *Revue Scientifique et Technique* 18, 1 (1999): 256–71. Land usage shrank from 21 to 6.4 per cent in the areas affected by the massive tidal bore that devastated parts of coastal Bangladesh in November 1970 killing on average between 60–80 per cent of all draft animals. Alfred Sommer and Wiley Mosley, 'East Bengal Cyclone of November 1970: Epidemiological Approach to Disaster Assessment', *The Lancet* 13 May (1972): 1029–36. See also Amartya Sen and M. Chander, 'Disaster Management in India: The Case of Livestock and Poultry', *Revue Scientifique et Technique* 22, 3 (2003): 915–30.

[6] Centre for Research on the Epidemiology of Disasters, Université Catholique de Louvain, Brussels (hereafter CRED) EM-DAT: The OFDA/CRED International Disaster Database. Between 1900 and 2001, there were 612 disasters – earthquakes, volcanic eruptions, typhoons, floods, droughts, landslides, epidemics and wild fires – an average of six a year, causing 87,922 human deaths and affecting a staggering 214,518,635 persons. The totals do not include extreme temperatures, tidal waves/surges or insect infestations. CRED defines a disaster as an event requiring international assistance, or causing ten deaths or affecting more than 100 persons.

[7] Emelina Almario ed., *Disasters: The Philippine Experience* (Quezon City: Citizens' Disaster Response Center, 1992): 63; Raymundo Punongbayan, 'Natural Hazards in the Philippines', in *Natural Disaster Mitigation in the Philippines: Proceedings of National Conference on Natural Disaster Mitigation 19–21 October 1994* (Quezon City: DOST-PHIVOLCS, 1994): 5. Bailey Willis documents 17 earthquakes as destroying entire towns and devastating whole districts between 1600 and 1900 and categorises another 36 as capable of causing buildings to topple and fall. Bailey Willis, 'Philippine Earthquakes and Structure', *Bulletin of the Seismological Society of America* 34, 2 (1944): 79–81. Major earthquakes occurred: on Mindanao in 1879, 1885, 1897 and 1924; in the Visayas in 1608, 1743, 1877 and 1948; in southern Luzon in 1877 and again in 1897; in northern

and central Luzon in 1627 and 1892. Masó, 'Volcanoes and Seismic Centers', vol. 1, 208, 216, 219, 227, 245–46, 248; William Repetti, 'Catalogue of Philippine Earthquakes, 1589–1899', *Bulletin of the Seismological Society of America* 36, 3 (1946): 143–53, 155–7, 187–90, 236–7, 243–6, 249–54, 273, 314–7). The frequency of earthquakes in the capital reflects Manila's proximity to a seismic fault line that links it to one of the most active volcanoes in the archipelago, Taal, as well as the supposedly extinct cones of Maquiling, Banájao and Aráyat. 'Volcanoes', in *Report of the Philippine Commission to the President* (Washington: Government Printing Office, 1901): vol. 3, 147.

[8] Giovanni Rantucci, *Geological Disasters in the Philippines: The July 1990 Earthquake and the June 1991 Eruption of Mount Pinatubo* (Rome: Dipartimento Per L'Informazione E L'Editoria, 1994): 25–6. As the historical record does not extend much beyond 400 years, there will undoubtedly be a future reclassification of some volcanoes from inactive to active. Mylene Martinez, 'Volcanoes, Volcanic Hazards and Hazards Mapping in Mindanao, Philippines', in *Natural Disaster Mitigation in the Philippines: Proceedings of National Conference on Natural Disaster Mitigation 19–21 October 1994* (Quezon City: DOST-PHIVOLCS, 1994): 107.

[9] Rantucci, *Geological Disasters in the Philippines*, 27; Archive of the Manila Observatory, Manila (hereafter AMO): List of Typhoons Box 9-35.

[10] AMO, Manila: Miguel Duran to Governor and Captain General, Panitan, 20 November 1835 Box 4, 11; AMO, Manila: Miguel Selga, El Baguio del 4 de Octubre de 1854 en Pangasinan Box 10-36/10. A study undertaken by PAGASA (Philippine Atmospheric, Geophysical and Astronomical Services Administration) attributes 38 per cent of annual average rainfall from 1951–1997 to the passage of tropical cyclones. *Documentation on the Impacts of and Responses to Extreme Climate Events: Food and Agricultural Sector* (Quezon City: Bureau of Agricultural Statistics, 2001): 9.

[11] AMO, Manila: Floods in the Philippines 1691–1911 Box 10-37.

[12] AMO, Floods in the Philippines, 2, 5; Philippine National Archive, Manila (hereafter PNA): Francisco Plana to Coronel Gobernador Político Militar de Mindanao, Surigao 2 July 1862 Calamidades Publicas, Baguios y Huracanes, Bundle 3; PNA, Manila: Parte Producido por el Jefe de 3er Distrito de Esta Ysla, Dando Cuenta de los Estragos Causados por un Baguio en los Pueblos del Sur del Mismo en el Mes de Diciembre de 1868, Comandante Militar de Bislig, Surigao 1 February 1869 Calamidades Publicas, Baguios y Huracanes, Bundle 1; PNA, Manila: Alcalde Mayor de Bulacan to Governor-general, Bulacan, 6 March 1872 Calamidades Publicas, Baguios y Huracanes, Bundle 2; PNA, Manila: Noticia Reasumida de las Perdidas y Daños Causados en Varios Pueblos de Esta Provincia por Consecuencia del Baguio Sufrido del 19 al 20 de Dicho Mes, Yba, 28 October 1881 Calamidades Publicas, Baguios y Huracanes, Bundle 2; PNA, Manila: Alcalde Mayor de Camarines Sur to Governor-general, Nueva Caceres, 30 October 1882 Calamidades Publicas, Baguios y Huracanes, Bundle 1; PNA, Manila: Francisco Gómez to Governor-general, Bacalor, 25 September 1887 Calamidades Publicas, Baguios y Huracanes, Bundle 2.

[13] AMO, List of Typhoons; AMO, Floods in the Philippines; PNA, Manila: Alcalde Major de Bulacan to Governor-general, Bulacan 21 October 1882 Calamidades Publicas, Baguios y Huracanes, Bundle 2.

[14] AMO, Floods in the Philippines, 5, 16; PNA, Manila: Gerónimo Vida to Director General of Civil Administration, Masbate 29 November 1879 Calamidades Publicas, Baguios y Huracanes, Bundle 1; PNA, Manila: Diego Zayas to Governor-general, Tayabas, 7

Bodies on the Beach

December 1882 Calamidades Publicas, Baguios y Huracanes, Bundle 2; PNA, Manila: Expediente sobre la Inversión de los $1000 Concedidos para Socorrer a los Habitantes del Distrito del Príncipe que Sufrieron Perdidas a Consecuencia del Huracán de 7 de Noviembre, Misión de Mangaran, 16 November 1886 Calamidades Publicas, Baguios y Huracanes, Bundle 2; PNA, Manila: José García, Capitán de Goleta to Gobernador Militar de Mindanao, 14 May 1891 Calamidades Publicas, Baguios y Huracanes, Bundle 1. The Cagayan river was reported in flood in October 1845, November 1870, October 1871, September 1874, August 1881, October 1908, October 1909, October 1924 and December 1937.

[15] AMO, Manila: Pedro Antonio Salazar to Secretario de Estado, Manila, 2 January 1836 Box 4-11; AMO, Manila: Marisco Clavería to Secretario de Estado, Manila, 5 December 1844 Box 4-11; AMO, List of Typhoons; AMO, Floods in the Philippines, 4; PNA, Manila: Noticia Reasumida de las Perdidas y Daños Causados en Varios Pueblos de Esta Provincia por Consecuencia del Baguio Sufrido del 19 al 20 de Dicho Mes, Yba, 28 October 1881 Calamidades Publicas, Baguios y Huracanes, Bundle 2.

[16] AMO, Floods in the Philippines; PNA, Manila: Participando el Baguio Sufrido en Dicha Provincia el 8 de Noviembre y Disposiciones Adoptadas en su Consecuencia por el Jefe de la Misma y Junta de Socorros Nombradas al Efecto, Nueva Caceres, 10 November 1865 Calamidades Publicas, Baguios y Huracanes, Bundle 2; PNA, Manila: Provincia de la Ylsabela de Luzon, Estado por Pueblos que Manifiesta las Perdidas Habidas en la Citada a Consecuencia del Vaguio que Tuvo Luga[r] la Noche del 7 del Actual [October 1879] Calamidades Publicas, Baguios y Huracanes, Bundle 1; PNA, Noticia Reasumida ... 28 October 1881.

[17] On the perils of livestock experience during floods, see Heath, *Animal Management in Disasters*, 65–6.

[18] PNA, Manila: Jesús Mellados to Inspector General de Beneficiaria y Sanidad, Tacloban, 29 October 1897 Calamidades Publicas, Baguios y Huracanes, Bundle 2.

[19] PNA, Participando el Baguio Sufrido en Dicha Provincia...10 November 1865.

[20] PNA, José García, Capitán de Goleta ... 14 May 1891; PNA, Manila: Espediente sobre Petición de Recursos para Atender a los Necesidades Producidas por la Inundación Ocurrida en 12 Noviembre 1892 en el Distrito del Principe, Principe, 12 November 1892 Calamidades Publicas, Baguios y Huracanes, Bundle 1; PNA, Jesús Mellados to Inspector General ... 29 October 1897.

[21] PNA, Manila: Report of Colector de Abra 30 September, Administración de Colecciones y Labores de Tabaco de Filipinas to Governor-general, Manila 15 October 1867 Langostas, Inundación, Terremotos; PNA, Expediente sobre la Inversión de los $1000 ... 16 November 1886. Prolonged inundation not only kills vegetation and reduces the nutritional value of the pasturage that remains but also removes organic matter from the soil, diminishing its water-retaining capacity and rendering the soil much more susceptible to drought. Previously flooded pasture cannot support the same density of livestock, often leading to a vicious cycle of overgrazing and soil erosion. Heath, *Animal Management in Disasters*, 65–6.

[22] Dean Worcester, 'Taal Volcano and Its Recent Destructive Eruption', *The National Geographic Magazine* 23, 4 (1912): 327–8, 353, 355. Apart from the actual eruption, the blanket of ash that covers the ground to a greater or lesser extent depending on the prevailing winds, preventing grazing and inducing toxaemia, posed the principal danger to animals. On Taal volcano, see Thomas Hargrove, *The Mysteries of Taal: A Philippine*

Volcano and the Lake, Her Sea Life and Lost Towns (Manila: Bookmark Publishing, 1991).
[23] Marshall McLennan, *The Central Luzon Plain: Land and Society on the Inland Frontier* (Quezon City: Alemar-Phoenix Publishing House, 1980): 169; Reynaldo Ileto, 'Hunger in Southern Tagalog, 1897–1898', in *Filipinos and their Revolution: Event, Discourse, and Historiography*, ed. Reynaldo Ileto (Quezon City: Ateneo de Manila Press, 1998): 113–15; Greg Bankoff, '*Bestia Incognita*: The Horse and Its History in the Philippines 1880–1930', *Anthrozoös* 17, 1 (2004): 5–9; Greg Bankoff, 'Horsing Around: The Life and Times of the Horse in the Philippines at the Turn of the Twentieth Century', in *Smallholders and Stockbreeders: Histories of Foodcrop and Livestock Farming in Southeast Asia*, ed. Peter Boomgaard and David Henley (Leiden: KITLV Press, 2004): 233–55.
[24] PNA, Manila: Alcalde Major de Ilocos Sur to Governor-general, Vigan, 9 October 1881 Calamidades Publicas, Baguios y Huracanes, Bundle 2; PNA, Manila: José Marina to Governor-general, Cottabato, 12 November 1894 Calamidades Publicas, Baguios y Huracanes, Bundle 1; Paul Incamina, 'No Sign of Eruption Yet, Taal Folk Say', *Philippine Daily Express* October 17 (1977); Heath, *Animal Management in Disasters*, 64–5.
[25] D. Santiago Patero, *Reglas Practicas para Librarse de los Huracanes en el Archipiélago Filipino* (Madrid: Imprenta de Miguel Ginesta, 1873): 38–9. The bird is not named by the author but is described as large with striking markings on the wings and having an open-scissor-like tail. It might have been the Mindoro Imperial Pigeon (*Ducula mindorensis*), a shy bird now almost extinct but still common in the nineteenth century.
[26] AMO, Floods in the Philippines, 21; PNA, Manila: Relación de los Perjuicios Ocasionados en los Pueblos de este Distrito por Consecuencia del Temporal Habidos en la Noche del 19 al 20 del Actual y Mañana de Este [1879] Calamidades Publicas, Baguios y Huracanes, Bundle 1; PNA, Manila: Alcalde Major to Governor-general, Bulacan 26 October 1882 Calamidades Publicas, Baguios y Huracanes, Bundle 2; PNA, Manila: Enrile Moul to Governor-general, Moroni 10 November 1882 Calamidades Publicas, Baguios y Huracanes, Bundle 1; PNA, Manila: Gobernar Político Militar de Negros to Director General de Administración, Bacolod, 18 October 1886 Calamidades Publicas, Baguios y Huracanes, Bundle 1; PNA, Manila: Bernardo Echalues, Governor PM of Carolinas Occidentales to Director-general of Civil Administration, Manila 26 March 1895 Calamidades Publicas, Baguios y Huracanes, Bundle 2; Thomas Hargrove, 'Submerged Spanish Era Towns in Lake Taal, Philippines: An Underwater and Archival Investigation of a Legend', *The International Journal of Nautical Archaeology and Underwater Exploration* 15, 4 (1986): 334. These corrals consisted of split bamboo barriers that blocked the movement of fish and then guided them through a series of successively smaller chambers until they could be easily netted. John Butcher, *The Closing of the Frontier: A History of the Marine Fisheries of Southeast Asia c.1850–2000* (Leiden: KITLV Press, 2004): 41–2. Demersal fisheries refer to those fish found living near or at the sea floor.
[27] On the transmission of diseases between humans and animals, see Lise Wilkinson, *Animals and Disease: An Introduction to the History of Comparative Medicine* (Cambridge: Cambridge University Press, 1992) and Joanna Swabe, *Animals, Disease and Human Society: Human-Animal Relations and the Rise of Veterinary Medicine* (London: Routledge, 1999).
[28] On domesticates in the Philippines in general, see Dan Doeppers, *Feeding Manila 1850–1945: Provisioning and National Integration* (forthcoming). On the origins of the horse, see Greg Bankoff, 'A Question of Breeding: Zootechny and Colonial Attitudes towards the Tropical Environment in Late Nineteenth Century Philippines', *Journal of*

Asian Studies 60, 2 (2001): 413–37. The history of animal domestication and introduction in the Philippines has still largely to be researched and is often quite apocryphal or conjectural. Take the native duck (*Anas domestic Linnaeus*) as an example. It is popularly believed to have been introduced by Chinese traders who settled in a place outside Manila prior to the Spanish conquest in 1565 that was subsequently called Pateros, a name derived from the Spanish word for duck 'pato' and so literally means 'duckers'. Perdro Manalao, *Duck-raising in the Philippines* (Manila: Department of Agriculture and Natural Resources, Popular Bulletin 38, Bureau of Printing, 1953): 4.

[29] Michael Watts, 'Hunger, Famine and the Space of Vulnerability', *GeoJournal* 30, 2 (1993): 118–20; Wisner, 'Disaster Vulnerability', 131–3; Kenneth Hewitt, *Regions of Revolt: A Geographical Introduction to Disasters* (Edinburgh: Longman, 1997): 141.

[30] PNA, Parte Producido por el Jefe de 3er Distrito ... 1 February 1869; PNA, Manila: Estado Demostrativo de los Destrozos Causados en los Pueblos de Esta Provincia a Consecuencia del Baguio del día 11 al 12 de Diciembre del Presente Año [1879] Calamidades Publicas, Baguios y Huracanes, Bundle 1; PNA, Manila: Alcalde Major de La Laguna to Governor-general, Santa Cruz, 6 November 1882 Calamidades Publicas, Baguios y Huracanes, Bundle 2; PNA, Manila: Gobernador Civil de Zambales to Governor-general, Iba 15 October 1894 Calamidades Publicas, Baguios y Huracanes, Bundle 2.

[31] PNA, Provincia de la Ylsabela de Luzon ... [October 1879]; *Census of the Philippine Islands, 1903* (Washington: United States Bureau of the Census, 1905): vol. 4, 235.

[32] Sources: PNA, Manila: Francisco Paulino, Gobernador Político Militar de Batanes to Governor-general, Santo Domingo de Basco, 20 December 1890 Calamidades Publicas, Baguios y Huracanes, Bundle 2; 'Number of Horses, Cattle, Carabaos, Hogs, Goats and Sheep in the Philippine Islands, by Province, at the Beginning of the Fiscal Year 1911', *Philippine Agricultural Review* 4, 7 (1911): 373.

[33] AMO, Floods in the Philippines, 15; PNA, Manila: Expediente sobre Concesión de $1500 del Fondo de Calamidades Publicas y Franquicia para la Corta de Maderas hasta el 30 de Abril de 1886 a los Habitantes de la Provincia de Camarines Sur que Hayan Sufrido en el Huracán de los 6 y 7 de Noviembre, Nueva Caceres, 16 November 1885 Calamidades Publicas, Baguios y Huracanes, Bundle 1; PNA, José García, Capitán de Goleta ... 14 May 1891; PNA, Manila: Espediente sobre Petición de Recursos...12 November 1892.

[34] PNA, Parte Producido por el Jefe de 3er Distrito ... 1 February 1869; PNA, Manila: Estado Demostrativo de los Perjuicios Ocasionados por los Baguios Acaecidos en las Días 25 y 31 de Diciembre del Ano Próximo Pasado [1874] en los Pueblos que a Continuación se Expresen Según se Desprende de los Partes Recibidos de los Mismos Calamidades Publicas, Baguios y Huracanes, Bundle 1; PNA, Manila: Estado Detallado de los Perdidas Ocurridas por el Baguio del 25 del Actual en los Pueblos que a Continuación se Expresen, Surigao 2 January 1877 Calamidades Publicas, Baguios y Huracanes, Bundle 1; PNA, Manila: Espediente sobre Petición de Recursos ... 12 November 1892.

[35] AMO, Manila: Miguel Selga, Tres Baguios en La Unión en 1859 Box 10-36/15; PNA, Manila: Francisco Paulino ... 20 December 1890. Some animals are simply denominated as 'wool-bearing', presumably sheep and goats but the number of the former in the Philippines was limited and the Batanes is atypical in this respect to most other areas of the archipelago.

[36] Source: Archdiocesan Archives of Manila, Manila (hereafter AAM): Baguios, Incendios y Terremotos 1831 40.D.10 Folders 1–3.

[37] The population census of 1885 lists Bacoor as having a population of 12,300 inhabitants

or, using the accepted factor of five people per family, a total of 2,460 households. *Estado General de los Pueblos del Arzobispado de Manila y de los Obispados Sufráganos de Nueva Cáceres, Nueva Segovia, Cebú y Jaro* (Manila: Establecimiento Tipográfico de Ramirez y Giraudier, 1886). As there is no definition of what constitutes an extended group of domestic animals of different species living together in an area greater than a farm, it seems reasonable to use the term 'community' based on the human politico-administrative divisions that are responsible for their congregation in the first place.

[38] Source: AAM, Baguios, Incendios y Terremotos.

[39] The actual figures are 2,593,000 in 1818 and 7,928,384 in 1898. Ildefonso de Aragon, *Población de las Islas Filipinas con Algunas Noticias Curiosas de su Producciones* (Manila, 1817); Onofre Corpuz, *Education and Socio-Economic Change in The Philippines, 1870–1960's* (Quezon City, University of the Philippines, 1967).

[40] McLennan, *The Central Luzon Plain*; Camille Lataillade, Alexandre Dumontier and Nicolas Grondard *L'Agriculture des Philippines: La Plaine Centrale Histoire et Perspectives* (Paris: Les Indies Savantes, 2002); Benito Legarda, *After the Galleons: Foreign Trade, Economic Change and Entrepreneurship in the Nineteenth-Century Philippines* (Madison: Center for Southeast Asian Studies, University of Wisconsin-Madison, Monograph No. 18, 1999). Land was either acquired by outright purchase (*venta real*), by royal grant, by legal or illegal methods of seizure or by settlement. Land tenure patterns are discussed in detail in a number of works. See: Leslie Bauzon, 'Rural History, Land Tenure and the Negros Hacienda Complex: Some Preliminary Notes', *PSSC Social Science Information* January (1974): 5–7, 21, 23; Nicholas Cushner, *Landed Estates in the Colonial Philippines* (New Haven: Yale University Southeast Asian Studies Monograph Series No.20, 1976); Dennis Roth, *The Friar Estates of the Philippines* (Albuquerque: University of New Mexico Press, 1977); as well as McLennan, *The Central Luzon Plain*.

[41] Sebastián Vidal y Soler, *Memoria de la Colección de Productos Forestales Presentada por la Inspección General de Montes de Filipinas en la Exposición Universal de Filadelfia* (Manila: Imprenta de la Revista Mercantil de J. Loyzaga y Ca., 1875); Greg Bankoff, 'One Island Too Many: Reappraising the Extent of Deforestation in the Philippines Prior to 1946', *Journal of Historical Geography* 33, 2 (2007): 314–34. Spanish dominion was only nominal over large areas of Mindanao and Palawan.

[42] Pedro Chirino, Pedro, 'Relación de las Islas Filipinas, 1604', in *The Philippine Islands, 1493–1898*, eds. Emma Blair and Alexander Robertson (Mandaluyong: Cachos Hermanos, 1973): vol. 12, 191; 'Expulsion of the Jesuits, 1768–69', in *The Philippine Islands, 1493–1898*, eds. Emma Blair and Alexander Robertson (Mandaluyong: Cachos Hermanos, 1973): vol. 50, 304. ENSO (El Niño Southern Oscillation) is a weather phenomenon that gives rise to particular anomalies in rainfall, wind and temperature on a cyclical basis throughout the Pacific Basin as well as having more global implications. Alternating droughts and floods are connected to corresponding 'warm' and 'cold' episodes of ENSO and are the regular climatic sequence to be expected in the Philippines.

[43] PNA, Report of Colector de Abra…Manila 15 October 1867; PNA, Manila: Asimismo se han Perdido Muchísimos Sembrados Hallándose los Naturales Amenazados de Miseria por Falta de los Primeros Artículos de Necesidad, Adolfo Avilo[?] to Governor-general, Cebu 16 January 1883 Calamidades Publicas, Baguios y Huracanes, Bundle 1; PNA, Manila: Gobernar Político Militar de las Islas Visayas to Governor-general, 25 May 1883 Calamidades Publicas, Baguios y Huracanes, Bundle 1; PNA, Manila: Principales de Calamianes to Governor-general, Cabecera de Calamianes, 16 May 1896 Calamidades Publicas, Baguios

y Huracanes, Bundle 2; Historical Data Papers, Manila: Historical Data of the Town of Victoria, Tarlac, Barrio of Bantog Reel 72: 7–8.

[44] Sebastian Heath, Susan Voeks and Larry Glickman, 'A Study of Pet Rescue in Two Disasters, *International Journal of Mass Emergencies and Disasters* 18, 3 (2000): 361–81; Sebastian Heath, Philip Kaas, Alan Beck and Larry Glickman, 'Human and Pet-related Risk Factors for Household Evacuation Failure During A Natural Disaster', *American Journal of Epidemiology* 153, 7 (2001): 659–65. On the history of pets during the nineteenth century, see Ritvo, *The Animal Estate*, 82–121 and Kathleen Kete, *The Beast in the Boudoir: Petkeeping in Nineteenth Century Paris* (Berkeley and Los Angeles: University of California Press, 1994).

[45] Harriet Ritvo, 'Animal Planet', *Environmental History* 9, 2 (2004): 204; Erica Fudge, *Perceiving Animals: Humans and Beasts in Early Modern English Culture* (Basingstoke: Macmillan Press, 2000): 3.

Goats, Marginality and the 'Dangerous Other'

David Siddle

> ... the billy goats and their flocks are the most serious enemy of viticulture, woodland management, olive groves, and orchards and above all for all those who are not especially diligent, of the kitchen gardens. They are nasty, odious, bad tempered, noisy, beasts distinguished particularly by the stink of their bad breath. From the times of antiquity until our present era people have been of the same opinion ...[1]

Recent events both in Greece and in California present environmental historians with what is fast becoming a truism: that in the hottest and driest summers of this warming planet, huge tracts of the coastal regions of Mediterranean climate are at risk from fire. What were once localised outbreaks, now become rapidly expanding infernos, as summer land/sea breezes sweep the flames rapidly from one hillside to another consuming valuable properties and threatening life. While some of these fires are started by accident others are clearly the work of arsonists.[2] If global warming is a major factor in causing an increase in the number and severity of such catastrophes, there are ecologists who argue that the main reason is the breakdown of the natural controlling mechanisms which were, at least in southern Europe and the Middle East, a by product of the traditional pastoral economies. Managed extensively under régimes of open evergreen woodland, these landscapes used to have a balanced biodiversity.[3] Grazing by both sheep and goats was an essential part of this structure and there is evidence from at least medieval times that controlled firing was one of the mechanisms used by shepherds to improve pastures.[4]

As rural populations in the Mediterranean declined, so sheep and more particularly goat populations were also reduced. By the late nineteenth century, what was called the *garrigue* in the Alpes Maritimes, (the long-term product of controlled grazing), became the *maquis:* poor scrubland readily abandoned by farmers anxious to enrich themselves by lucrative land sales. This new wilderness of under-utilised land is on slopes increasingly valued by property developments for their sea views and their distance from the cluttered coastal zone. So land, which was economically marginal for any other use than rough grazing, escalated in development value. Thus fire- susceptible abandoned land abutted directly on new property.[5]

The answer sought by conservationists and developers alike turned them back to the most effective of all vegetation controls in this region, sheep and goats.[6] Alongside recognition of the importance of the animal to subsistence societies and its recent adoption as an icon for charitable donations, for the goat this is a

Goats, Marginality and the 'Dangerous Other'

considerable change of opinion. In the official mind and in popular consciousness the goat has been the *bête noire* of dry farming areas. It has been damned as one cause of the encroachment of desert margins in Africa, the degradation of Mediterranean and Middle Eastern hillsides and the general decline of fertility. Nor is this aspect of their reputation newly acquired – indeed until very recently goats seem to have almost always had a bad press from the authorities.

My own acquaintance with this topic extended out of a search of parish documents in the mayoral archive of a perched village in the Alpes Maritimes.[7] The commune of Cipières is situated above the Loup valley on a bench below the extensive plateau of Calern. It extends over forty square kilometres of slope, bench, terrace and limestone plateau. Here there is no doubting of the scale of woodland removal. Indeed many of the upper surfaces, now denuded of all but scrub vegetation, were almost certain to have been covered by deciduous woodland in the period when topographical features and fields were named, perhaps over a millennium ago. This grazing and foraging environment supported over 20,000 sheep and goats during much of the last thousand years.[8] In the medieval period of rapid expansion in the market for wool, the region as a whole 'groaned under the weight of sheep flocks'[9] in particular and this expansion was managed with some difficulty. The pressure this placed on resources is evidenced by the number of times attempts were made to manage the animal population either by taxation, in the case of sheep, or by restrictions on herd size and eventually by total banning orders, in the case of goats.

There is clear evidence of restriction on goat numbers, even as early as the fourteenth century.[10] Nor was this purely a local phenomenon. Indeed one finds injunctions to ban goats or to restrict the areas open to them for grazing in the official documents to survive from many areas in southern France.[11] Sometimes the problem was deemed to be so severe that only one goat per flock of sheep could be kept, as in Seyne in 1363[12] and references appear in the surviving village council deliberations in Cipières through succeeding centuries. In the seventeenth century, for example goat numbers were limited at first to five per family and gradually raised to nine by the end of the century as subsistence pressures increased through rising population.[13] Most of the direct evidence of disapproval comes, however, from the total bans on goat keeping in the eighteenth and nineteenth centuries both in Languedoc and Provence.[14] The longest ban in Provence lasted for almost forty years, from the time of the court banning order on the 21 of January 1731.[15] Evidence of such legislation can be found in the records of both state parliaments and village council minutes at intervals through the eighteenth and nineteenth centuries for both Mediterranean upland areas of France and further north in the pre-alps of Dauphine, Savoie and elsewhere.[16]

The question that one must ask is do these actions demonstrate a very early and persistent ecological awareness and sense of official environmental responsibility, or are there other forces at work? It is possible to relate these bans and restrictions on herd size to periods of population expansion both in the period before the Black Death in the fourteenth century and in the eighteenth century: precisely when one might expect the most serious ecological damage through population pressure. But were goats really so bad that they needed to be so comprehensively and universally banned when a tight restriction on numbers per family and on tethering, (tactics deployed in the fourteenth and fifteenth centuries),[17] should surely have been sufficient? What at first appears as an entirely laudable, almost, response to environmental pressure becomes, on closer inspection an attitude with rather different over-tones. Indeed as Kolars[18] and Forbes and Koster[19] suggest the case against goats per se is nowhere as strong as it might appear.[20] In the first place, goats have been herded as an integrated part of the Mediterranean rural economy for over seven thousand years.[21] Archaeological evidence yields no reliable indication that they were the cause of environmental deterioration. Kolars draws attention to the way in which, away from the coast, forest and goat management existed side by side in upland Turkey for at least 500 years without any appreciable degradation. Indeed Forbes[22] has made a very good case for rejecting the goat as a major factor in removal of vegetation in the Eastern Mediterranean region. Both Kolars and Forbes point to the place of other demands made by populations on their vegetation resources. Timber and brushwood have been removed for centuries, first for building and then for heating. As the economy expanded, ship-building, charcoal-burning and lime production increased the range of these demands.[23] In fact the main agent of environmental destruction seems rather to have been the search for profit rather than subsistence. It is here we come to a crux in the case that begins to develop in defence of the goat.

For the poorest in the rural populations of the Mediterranean region, the goat held the same position on the subsistence economy as the cow held in northern and Western Europe. It provided a measure of subsistence security. For the majority, who had no access to the forage or the shelter capacity necessary to maintain even a small flock of sheep, keeping a few goats, even when they were restricted to pastures on village wastelands at the margins or on otherwise unused roadside verges, was a considerable subsistence asset. Goats represented a source not only of meat, milk and high protein cheeses but also a wide range of other uses. These varied from the purely practical such as the safe transport of liquids (water, wine, oil) in their skins to the recreational and ceremonial uses of skins and horns for bagpipes and for drums and horns. For a subsistence pastoral economy in a dry upland environment, the food-tolerant goat may be seen as much more valuable than sheep and certainly than the demanding bovines. Indeed, as a recent NGO campaign testified, a goat represents the best possible investment for a poor family. For a very small outlay a goat could yield between fifteen and thirty per cent more value than a sheep. With no break in fertility after gestation, one pair can produce a hundred offspring in five years.[24] This is three times as many as for a pair of sheep and ten times more than cattle.[25] Moreover, goats are much better adapted to eating the woody forage of the margins of the used spaces of a community and need less to sustain life than either sheep or cattle. They are also able to eat almost anything and have the agility to cope with the most severe slopes. Here lay the root of the problem for the hapless animal. Goats were not only a cheap and valuable subsistence asset, they were also perfectly adjusted to ravage those parts of the environment most vulnerable to erosion.[26] This was perfectly well understood by a poor peasantry always trying to guarantee subsistence. When this perception was challenged by authorities seeking to improve woodland for maritime timber, or for hunting, bans and restrictions were introduced and peasants were more than willing to subvert laws which aimed to restrict numbers.[27]

So just as the goat became crucial to the earliest subsistence economy of the Mediterranean, when the base of the mediaeval economy shifted towards the commercial production and trade in wool, the goat was increasingly marginalised. It remained above all an animal of the subsistence economy: popularly characterised 'the poor man's cow.'[28] On the other hand sheep became the creatures of emergent merchant capitalism. So the practice of grazing sheep and goats together was replaced by their separation into different flocks. As far as possible goats were restricted to those areas which could not sustain the best sheep pastures. But as both urban populations and commerce increased, the demands made upon the grazing environment also grew. The poor man's goat came increasingly in competition more directly with richer man's sheep. So the early restrictions on goat numbers were probably a manifestation of this conflict rather than a deep concern for the environment. Throughout the long history of bans and relaxations of control, the clear line of conflict was between the goat-keeper, who persistently tried to avoid control, and the increasingly differentiated flock masters and their sponsors, who competed with them for resources. Even if the restrictions were contravened the net effect was always to push the goat towards the more environmentally fragile land and in this way to make them even less popular with those in authority.

But having been restricted to the maquis and more marginal areas of woodland least suitable for sheep, the goat came into conflict with an even more formidable enemy. If the aristocracy shared in the profits of sheep farming, and supported the restrictions elicited by emergent commerce, their passion was for hunting. It was a focal part of a lifestyle of leisure. The habitats of game (deer, wild boar, stag, and partridge) were precisely those under threat from an increasing goat population. It is clearly possible to argue that the goat herder was caught in the pincers formed by emergent merchant capital on the one hand and feudal lifestyle and power on the other. Clearly as time went on commercial interests assumed increasing importance. Consequently, towards the end of the *ancien régime*, the restrictions of earlier periods were replaced by much more stringent banning orders. By this time of rising population and following centuries of environmental deterioration, the pleas for restoring the rights to pasture goats were much more specifically cast in terms of the relief of poverty.[29]

We can now open the door on a more intriguing mystery: why did the virulent persecution of the goat provoke so very little in the way of peasant response, especially in the eighteenth century? The level of docility in the face of this supposedly severe threat to subsistence does not accord with experience of rural dissent in other areas of peasant Europe.[30] Perhaps it was because the very nature of goat keeping removed them from the eyes of the authorities? Goats were probably as invisible as smugglers to those who did not know the environments in which they lived. Where minor skirmishes between the forces of law and order and peasant goat-keepers have been reported the agile goats and their keepers seem to have found it fairly easy to avoid the penalties of confiscation and avoidances meant that enforcements took time and considerable effort if they were to be effective.[31]

Before the ban in 1730 in Cipières, the 3,500 goats were part of the subsistence economy in the seventeenth and early eighteenth century. By the time of the troop occupations [32] of the War of the Austrian Succession (1742–1747) they had disappeared. This was at a time of crisis that, together with a series of drought years (1739–1743), totally depleted the local rural economy and left the people to face three serious crises of subsistence, in 1747, 1750 and 1764.[33] As a product of this distress the goat ban was lifted in 1770, albeit after a careful survey and within strict limits of both numbers and in terms of designated grazing areas.[34] But it was not lifted as the result of violent protest, a confrontation with a desperate population following a post-war famine, which had removed two whole generations of young children from the village population. It seems to have been the product of quiet diplomacy by literate council members (all goat owners) on behalf of poorer villagers. Fresh bans were introduced by local government in the 1820s.but raised again in 1838, after a similarly polite exchange in the village council.[35] The question we must ask is how did such draconian measures, which had such drastic effects on the life of the poorest, pass with so little response? This is remarkable enough in the uneasy last decades of the Ancien Régime, let alone after the Revolution.

In this paper I argue that an explanation for this phenomenon may best be sought by examining the attitudes that had developed in the previous four centuries or more. From this longer perspective what seems to be happening is an over-layering of deeply embedded attitudes and prejudices. Restrictions on goat numbers, it can be argued, were part of a well-established and perfectly well accepted rural frame of reference, aiming to preserve the crops and pastures. But those who would ban goats altogether in the eighteenth century and those who complied with such regulation, were responding to a new ethos. Do we see a clear manifestation of the Age of Reason and the command and control mechanisms of the emergent nation state? Although quite specific in his points of reference, my reading of Foucault suggests that the changes which took place in effectiveness of control through the institutions of an emergent bureaucracy depended on new attitudes towards reasonable behaviour.[36] He draws attention

Goats, Marginality and the 'Dangerous Other'

to the way that these new discourses were privileged through refinements of prohibition and the introduction of new virtues of orderliness and acceptability. Best known is his identification of the ways in which attitudes to curtailment and confinement changed as the mediaeval concepts of madness as 'non being' or 'bedazzlement' were replaced by the notion of 'unreasonable behaviour'. Within this new structure of meaning, the mad, the bad and the 'self inflicting' poor were all confined together in one institution. (The *Hôpital Général* founded in Paris in 1666). Foucault argues that it was through manipulation of such changes by the organs of the state that the exercise of power became much more effective in the eighteenth century.

What I am suggesting is that real insight into the behaviour of powerful interest groups, in the pre-industrial past as much as the modern period, can come from such an interpretation of the way in which first restriction and then prohibition could be accepted. I want to argue that such docility is made possible by the often-subliminal subversion of alternative views, the product not of a sudden change of emphasis but a much longer and persistent ideological subjection of the poorest elements of the rural population. But I also wish to extend this explanatory framework to serve a longer time period: to suggest that Foucault's epistemological cut-off point, dividing pre and post Enlightenment, is too harshly drawn. While admitting that extension of mechanisms of state power became much more pervasive in the Age of Reason, one might argue that compliance was an instrument of power relations well before the opening of the *Hôpital Général*. The changing attitude to the goat may well have been in part a by-product of the raw psychological power of religious prejudice. In the periods before the Age of Reason the command and control mechanisms of cultural subversion were controlled by the Church.[37] In all its manifestations, the church drew on a subtle blend of fear and superstition to evolve powerful mechanisms of control over the majority. It consolidated its power through the violence of the prejudice it fuelled. First it was against Islam through the late mediaeval Crusades and then through the assault on protesting 'heresies' and 'blasphemies' of all kinds, from the Cathars and Waldenesians in the twelfth and thirteenth centuries to the witch trials of the sixteenth and seventeenth centuries.[38] The linking thread is the powerful manipulation of a sub-literate and ill-educated majority by a literate minority, which included a small religious elite. They used not so much the written word but a mix of iconography and rumour to engage compliance. If this argument is valid then nowhere is it better illustrated than in the case of the goat.

I would argue that an exploration of the subtle mix of myth, prejudice, fear and superstition which the more powerful had at their disposal in the case of the restrictions placed on goat keeping, takes one to some deep dark places of the collective cultural subconscious. Even from classical times the goat has occupied a curious place in our most basic perceptions. It is the way in which these perceptions were made manifest which allowed the goat and his keepers to be so easily marginalised. Endorsement of such policies came from a common acceptance of a set of mores that extended across all levels of society. The goat quickly came to represent beastliness in which the 'beast without' 'the dangerous other', quickly became 'the beast within'. From the earliest phase of our cultural heritage the goat, creature of mountain and forest, has been associated with fear of peripheries: woods and forests. For those who lived in the towns and villages of the lowlands, such areas were always dangerously 'other'.

In exploring the origins of what we might call the myth of 'goatism' it is possible to envisage two powerful re-enforcing cultural strands of polite disapproval: a Graeco-Roman cultist strand, and a Hebraic-Christian strand.[39] These strands fuse in the apostolic and patristic period because the gospel was born and developed within a world of Hellenistic thought and Roman power. This, I would suggest, fed through to the Renaissance and into modern times, both in polite and popular culture.

If the early pastoral nomads of the Greek peninsula saw the goat as a benign creature, for those who followed them, working in the cleared spaces to establish agricultural order, the world of woodlands and hills came to represent the terrifying alternative universe of the unpredictable. Poorer peasants, who inhabited such regions where goats were common, spoke strange languages, wore strange clothes, often made from goatskins, and had weird and eventually 'heretical' practices. Already marginalised in the mythology of a settled Greek agricultural population as a creature of the magical periphery, the goat became a natural component of woodland Dionysian cults,[40] deified as the spirit of the mountains and woods. Even at this time it also came to be feared as a dangerous manifestation of male sexuality and unpredictability. For the lowland farmers and town dwellers the Beast and the Man were soon overlapping images, which were reflected in mythology and iconography. The wildest and most fearsome wood sprites in ancient Greece served the god Pan. It was the over-endowed Pan that represented the wildest and most sexually dangerous aspect of the dangers which lurked in the hills and forests spending much of his priapic time roaming the wildscape, consorting with satyrs (who were similarly inclined) seducing or raping nymphs and entertaining fauns. It is easy to see how even an innocent goat keeper in a skin jacket and carrying pan-pipes 'pan-icked' urban travelers already seeing mythological creatures behind every rock. Indeed, this basic separation between the earthy and sensual and the ethereal and intellectual is deeply embedded in Hellenistic thought particularly after Plato. The two overlapping images, once they had been reflected in the iconography of a culture, became very deeply rooted. There is wide ranging evidence that the Goat-Man-Beast-Devil was to persist, as a strand of associations to be taken through classical literature, repeated on endless pots, the subject of songs and charades in an image which survives to our own times. The place of the goat within the parallel Hebraic Christian cultural tradition of western civilisation complements the set of images referred to above. For the Jews and early Christians the goat was the

Goats, Marginality and the 'Dangerous Other'

repository of sin – the 'scapegoat' – a creature to be cast into outer darkness, a representative of evil to be divided from the lambs of God, and the Bible is rich in references to goats and their symbolic association with sinfulness

If the increasingly valuable wool economy could easily be linked with the rich Christian symbolism of the gentle shepherd and his safely grazing flock, it was different for the sinful goat. Given the many references to the dichotomy between the good sheep and the bad goat in both biblical testaments, the demonisation of the goat in western culture becomes less than surprising.[41]

Already identified with sin and the devil, fear and danger, in both cultural traditions, it was an easy incorporation. These powerful currents of ideology were reinforced by the natural suspicion which continued to develop between ways of life that increasingly divided, as settled agriculture marginalised the pastoral, turning it into a contrast between the 'good' open field and terraces near settlements with their 'fields full of folk' and the wild, forested and mountainous peripheries – places of danger anarchy, fear and evil.[42] Put both of these strands of cultural awareness together and they were likely to fester in the dark corners of the collective soul. Even before the spin that was put on common prejudices by the Christian attitudes to sin, chastity and the development of heresies, the isolated grazing and foraging spaces of hills and woodlands could become the psychological black holes which represented the primitive, the lustful and the impure: a process by which two parallel literate discourses of the Hebraic Christian and Graeco-Roman classical iconography were brought into service and aligned with a sub literate culture of superstition and fear.

Within our own West European culture, the stories of evil and corruption attached to mountains and forests pass down to us as folklore and nursery stories. Many were written down quite early. Animals of the periphery became symbols of evil. The beast 'without' became the 'beast within'. The mixing of the two images became a powerful tool in the hands of those seeking out corruption and heresy. This was made easier because for the illiterate and superstitious rural populations, which were the subject of these restrictions on their subsistence, the tools of subjugation were iconographic and verbal rather than en-scripted. What emerges from the evidence is that the goat was a formidable iconographic weapon in the development of an ideology of command and control, which extended to the environments in which these animals grazed. The rest of this paper explores the justification for proposing an agenda, which identifies the goat as a powerful and persistent mechanism of subversion of the weak by the strong.

As public order increased in the nascent power structures of Western Europe, goats and their keepers were increasingly more likely to be seen as up to no good. Mountain areas, by their nature often close to borders, were nest-beds of contraband, anarchy and brigandage. So on their excursions to towns and into lowlands, mountain people were already identified as potential brigands, preying on lonely travellers and sexually assaulting urban women either in mind or in deed. Like their goats they were likely to be seen as smelly, bad breathed, lying and cheating subversives. The specific associations remain buried. All that one can say is that for polite or even relatively polite elements in society, the Goat-Man-Beast-Satan could not have been in a position to develop a worse reputation. At the very lowest level of disapproval it is possible to produce a list of anthropomorphised unpleasantness which extends from lascivious (horny) sexual proclivities, unpleasant noise, halitosis, anarchic deviousness to serious charges of ecological degradation.

In such a discourse the goat becomes a powerful symbol. Such fears become explicit as the economy expands in the phase of population growth during the early feudal period. As population pressed closer to the margins of cultivation in the twelfth and thirteenth centuries, upland areas were further opened up for pastoralism and transhumance. The different behaviour of the anarchic pastoral groups which managed the increasingly large flocks and herds led to ever increasing apprehension among lowland or settled agricultural peoples.

The first recorded relationship between the devil and a man/goat dressed (or naturally covered) in animal hair dates from the period just before the Black Death. From this time the picture of Satan formed in the popular mind. Frequently, though admittedly not invariably the animal form he took was the goat. A population terrified by the traumas of the plagues and disasters of the fourteenth century and harassed by the Inquisition developed a paranoia, which led eventually to the witchcraft purges of the sixteenth and seventeenth centuries. Here the goat became a crucial figure in manifestations. Like the cat, the goat is a creature of natural agility. It was easy to associate them with the behaviour of witches and their festivals, to which they flew through the air. So various forms of perversion associated with bestiality focused on this set of conjunctions between pastoralism, witchcraft and Satanism. It was an easy association in which the frequently anarchic lifestyles and heretical beliefs of shepherds were linked to the animals with whom strange people kept lonely company.

For a culturally powerful mediaeval priesthood, tortured by sexual repression, the whole context lay within the mind set in which maleness was all too easily seen as beastliness, the whole scene was too close to the dark world of the senses for comfort. It is not surprising that, fed by the prejudices and fears of both cultural streams, Satan was often perceived to take the shape of this the wildest of domestic animals in such a region. Attached to all the other roots of cultural disapproval the Judeo Christian iconography of the scapegoat represented similar murky and deep sexually dangerous relationships with the outer edge, the periphery, the unknown.

So by the mid-fourteenth century when natural disasters of drought and flood culminating in the Black Death had a deep impact on powerful opinions, those in charge became all too willing to believe in the intervention of dark forces. When the great heresies of the Waldenesians and Cathar shepherds spread through the mountain peripheries of the Pyrenees and the Alps in the wake of the Black Death, they were signaled by the upsurge in witchcraft accusations

Goats, Marginality and the 'Dangerous Other'

which linked the fear of the unknown and the dangerous periphery with the whole psycho-sexual drama of fear and repression: of devil worship, the devil's kiss, of witches Sabbaths, of eating babies, of wild Dionysic orgies of dancing and depravity in secret woodland glades.

After the production of a kind of guidebook for the study of witchcraft for the literate minority *Malleus Malleficarum* in 1486 (running to fourteen reprints by 1520),[43] the great period of hysteria was unleashed. The witch hunting in Renaissance Europe extended over two centuries and resulted in the persecution and death of over perhaps 100,000 people many of them poor, old, or mentally ill widow women.[44] Indeed much of this fantasy was underpinned by the crude overtones of misogyny driven by fear of female sexuality and the cult of virginity.

The place of the goat in the symbolism of witchcraft was very well defined. If witches sometimes rode on rams they were much more often seen in the close company of the 'Bête Noire' and the association of goats with rampant sexuality and evil was a potent source of satanic imagery. It is here I make my major point. I would suggest that the continued presence of the goat in the developing iconography of evil created precisely the circumstances in which the medieval bans could be pursued. For most, the parade of bad qualities outlined above, re-enforced a deep seated if not overt association in the minds of poor goat owners, with a rich tapestry of bad associations. The commercial implications of this prejudice were certainly convenient for those who would use the goat as a scapegoat for their own greedy appropriation of the product of the natural environment. At the very least, the comprehensive curtailments were validated by the whole portfolio of fears.

So in many respects it may be possible to position this animal as one of the clearest symbols of class division in preindustrial rural society. For the authorities and better off peasants the goat became a surrogate for the anarchic intemperance and strangeness of the upland poor, sharing their most dangerous or unpleasant attributes. In fact one might be hard put to distinguish some descriptions of the peasant poor from those of the goats they relied on. Both were renowned for their unpredictability and their deceitful deviousness. Both poor peasants and goats were dangerously numerous and therefore deemed to be sexually profligate and anarchic. At the margins of acceptable society, they were easily assumed to be in league with the devil. The opinion of goats in both popular as well as the official mind became, increasingly, directly related to one's position in the economic and social hierarchy. Even in the great age of classification in the nineteenth century goats remained difficult to place in emerging lexicons. [45]

Cultural historians have been at pains to point out that there has often been a clear distinction to be made between the frames of reference of polite as opposed to popular culture. In the case of goats it would seem that there is an increasingly confused divide between polite, official views and popular opinion. If goats defined the divides, not only between lord and peasant but also between rich and poor in peasant society, the tensions the bans might have engendered were blurred by the subversive influence of cultural reputation, which reinforced the goatish, dark and threatening unpredictability of the periphery. These attitudes persist to this day and are still evident in cartoons, cinema and many cultural references.[46]

So the goat has three separate images, the first as a provider of good things to poor people, the second as a ravager of land and crops, the third as a manifestation of unpleasant habits and behaviour both on their own account and as surrogates for those semi-savages who tended them. Out of the derogative aspects of the animal's place in mediaeval and Renaissance and early modern cosmology and mythology, it is primarily represented to all as the animal closest in nature to the Great Satan. How easy it became to ban the *bête noire*, framed for disapproval by a millennium of developing fear and distaste. Goat bans were, at the same time, a means of controlling the most anarchic elements of the population, a means to ease the path to commercial woollen enterprise and a means of improving timber supplies for the navy. Bans also better preserved the hunting grounds for hawk and hound. In such circumstances the poor man-beast, the Caliban of the periphery, stood no chance.

In more recent times the images have begun to shift. Goat numbers have increased around the world by sixty per cent and even in high income countries by twenty per cent.[47] Not only is the goat now seen as a provider for poor families in Africa but as a producer of specialist dairy products, part of the agro tourist industry in high-income countries.[48] An active International Goat Association, founded in 1982, promotes scholarship through the journal *Small Ruminant Research*.[49] Goat management is also beginning to be regarded as a part of a package of strategies for reducing fire risks in California.[50]

Nonetheless, while this repositioning continues, recent calamities suggest that there is still a long way to go if the animal is to shed its deeply embedded images and goat farming is to become a fully integrated part of environmental management systems in all scrublands, and especially those close to areas of settlement.

NOTES

I would like to thank colleagues David Chester, Noel Castree and John Dickinson who provided helpful comments on early versions of this paper.

[1] Segui 1946, 11.

[2] Estimates of this effect in the Bouche de Rhône in south-eastern France in 1972 indicated that thirty per cent of fires were deliberate. The rest are the product of negligence. See Houerou 1981, 487.

[3] Pinto-Correia 1993.

[4] Timbal 1969.

Goats, Marginality and the 'Dangerous Other'

[5] Naveh and Liebermann 1993; Rundel et al. 1997.
[6] Lejaruen 1976, 44–55; Charlet and Lejaruen 1976; Naveh and Whittaker 1979; Naveh 1982, Etienne 1997; Di Castri et al. 1981, 327, 333.
[7] Archives Communale de Cipières, hereinafter ACC.
[8] Archives de Bouches de Rhone 1609 B1326, f225.
[9] Duby 1968, 147: Sclafert 1959, 61.
[10] Archives de Bouches de Rhône, Novembre 1334: 396 E17 and 18; Samaran 1957, 67.
[11] Sclafert 1934, 131 et seq.; Solakian 1988, 33–6.
[12] Archives Basses Alpes: E 64 bis
[13] ACC: *Deliberations* 1657–1695 folio 37; ACC Del 1657 f.351; ACC Del 1671; ACC Del 1695.
[14] Archives de Bouches de Rhône 1730 C287 *Inquete concerrnant les chèvres*; Arret Prefectoriale de Provence 22.2. 1827; ACC: *Deliberations* 1827. The final ban was 'absolu'! See ACC *Deliberations* 3.5. 1841 f.33.
[15] Segui 1946. The state legislature of Languedoc banned goats in 1725.
[16] Delano Smith 1979, 225–6; Bonnin 1984, 275.
[17] Archives Basses Alpes E, 1484, Barcelonnette, 3 -5bis; Sclafert 1934, 132.
[18] Kolars 1966.
[19] Forbes and Koster 1976.
[20] A recent paper by Melinda Zeder of the American Museum of Natural History to the American Association for the Advancement of Science claimed that goats were domesticated well before sheep and confirmed the view that their bad reputation was not justified.
[21] McNeill 1992; Boyazoglu et al. 2005.
[22] Forbes 1982, 162–3, 165–6, 223–5, 298–302, 388–9.
[23] A similar point is made by Sclafert 1934, 134–5.
[24] One reason why goat populations expanded so rapidly after bans were lifted.
[25] Lejaruen 1976, 500–502.
[26] Barry 1960.
[27] Segui 1946.
[28] Delano Smith 1979, 225; Chevallier 1956, 309; Hatziminaoglou, and Boyazoglu 2004.
[29] Chevalier 1956, 305: ACC, Del. 1769; Sclafert 1934, 134–5.
[30] Hobsbawm 1959; 1969; King 1975.
[31] Segui 1946, 31.
[32] ACC Armée, 1742–1747. Cipières catered for a total of 22,000 troops from six different armies during this period.
[33] ACC Vital Event registers 1692–1772; Siddle 1996.
[34] ACC Del 1769.
[35] ACC Del 1838.
[36] Foucault 1965.
[37] Cragg 1961.
[38] Trevor-Roper 1969; Cohn 1972; Kors and Peters 1972.
[39] Kolars, 1966.
[40] Stanislawski 1975; Gerschen 2005.

[41] Schwager 1987. There are 150 Old Testament references to goats: 13% are concerned with sinfulness, and the use of a sacrificial scapegoat for carrying human sin into the wilderness. See, for example Leviticus, Chapter 16, verse 9 ('and Aaron shall lay both hands upon the head of the live goat and confess over him all the iniquities of the people of Israel, and send him away into the wilderness'). The New Testament is equally clear on this point. Though it may not be easy to tell them apart from a distance, Jesus, the Lamb of God, leaves us in no doubt as to the symbolic difference between sheep and goats.

[42] Fuller in Cosgrove and Daniels, 22–3; Cooper 1992; Chevalier and Gheerbrant 1982, 237–8.

[43] Sprenger and Kramer 1968 edn. This was the work of two Dominican inquisitors, Jacobus Sprenger and Heinrich Kramer. But there were other similar works by Lutheran divines.

[44] Trevor-Roper 1969, 88; Levack 1987; Russell 1972, 182, 185, 237, 243, 245, 247, 255; Russell 1977, 20, 72, 127, 215.

[45] Ritvo 1997, 58. She refers to the 'barbarous assemblage of names, as if to describe all the mongrels in creation', with which the Zoological Society of London labelled a single wild goat in 1830.

[46] In 1995 the *Oxford Book of Creatures* describes the animal like this: 'the goat with amber devious eye, the blasé lecher, inquisitive as sin, the nothing-like-him goat ...' Adcock and Simms 1995, 363.

[47] Morand Fehr et al. 2004.

[48] Dubeuf et al. 2004

[49] Sinapis et al. 2000; Boyazoglu and Morand Fehr 2001; Boyazoglu 2005.

[50] Woods 2006.

BIBLIOGRAPHY

Adcock, F. and J. Simms (eds.) 1995. *The Oxford Book of Creatures*. Oxford: Oxford University Press.

Ankarloo, B. and G. Henningsen (eds.) 1990. *Early Modem European Witchcraft: Centres and Peripheries*. Oxford: Clarendon Press.

Barry, J.P. 1960. 'Contribution – 1'étude de la vegetation de la région de Nimes' *Annàles Biologie*, Sdr. 3. 36: 309–530.

Bonnin, B. 1984. 'L'élevage dans les hautes terres dauphinoises aux Xlle – XVIIIe siècles', in *L'Elevage et la vie pastorale dans les montagnes de lEurope au moyen age et l'époque moderne* (Clermont Ferrand), 263–281.

Boyazoglu, J. and P. Morand-Fehr 2001. 'Mediterranean dairy sheep and goat products and their quality. A critical review' *Small Ruminant Research* 40, 1: 1–11.

Boyazoglu, J., I. Hatziminaoglou and P. Morand-Fehr 2005. 'The role of the goat in society: past, present and perspectives for the future', *Small Ruminant Research* 60, 1–2: 13–23.

Charlet, P. and P.J. Lejaruen 1976. 'Populations caprines du bassin mediterranéen: aptitudes et devolution', *Options Meditérranien* 35: 44–55.

Chevalier, J. and A. Gheerbrant 1982. *Dictionnaire des Symboles*, Paris: Robert Laffont.

Chevalier, M. 1956. *La Vie Humaine dans les Pyrénées Arigoises*. Paris: Genin.

Cohn, N. 1972. *Europe's Inner Demons: An Inquiry Inspired by the Great Witch Hunt* Chatto, Sussex: Heinemann.

Cooper, J.C. 1992. 'The mythological and symbolic significance of goats', in *Symbolic and Mythological Animals* (Wellingborough: The Aquarian Press).

Cragg ,G.R. 1961. *The Church in the Age of Reason 1648–1749*. Harmondsworth: Penguin Books.

Delano Smith, C. 1979. *Western Mediterranean Europe: An Historical Geography of Italy, Spain and Southern France*. London: Academic Press.

di Castri,N., D. Goodall and W.R.L. Specht (eds.) 1981. *Ecosystems of the World 11. Mediterranean Type Shrublands*. Amsterdam: Elsevier Scientific Publishing Company.

Dubuef, J-P. et al. 2004. 'Situation changes and future of goat industry around the world', *Small Ruminant Research* 51:165–73.

Duby, G. 1968. *Rural Economy and Country life in the Medieval West*, trans. Cynthia Postan. New York: Columbia.

Etienne, J. et al. 1997. 'Abandoned land and land use conflicts in southern France', in P.W. Rundel et al. (eds.), *Landscape Disturbance and Biodiversity in Mediterranean Type Ecosystems* (Berlin: Springer-Verlag).

Forbes, H.A. 1982. *Strategies and Soils*. Ann Arbor Michigan and London: University Microfilms International.

Forbes, H.A. and P. Koster 1976. 'Fire, Axe, Plow: human influence on local plant communities in southern Argolid', *Annals of the New York Academy of Sciences* 268: 109–126.

Foucault, M. 1965. *Madness and Civilisation: A History of Insanity in the Age of Reason*, trans. R. Howard. London: Tavistock Press.

Fuller, P. 1988. 'The geography of mother nature', in D.E. Cosgrove (ed.), *Iconography of Landscape: Essays on Symbolic Representation, Design and Use of Past Environments* (Cambridge: Cambridge University Press), 22–3.

Gershen, B.V. 2005. 'Goats,satyrs and fauns', *Maryland Med* 6, 1: 35–6.

Hatziminaoglou, Y. and J. Boyazoglu 2004. 'The goat in ancient civilizations: from the fertile crescent the the Aegean Sea', *Small Ruminant Research* 51: 123–9.

Hobsbawm, E.J. 1959. *Primitive Rebels*. Manchester: Manchester University Press.

Hobsbawm, E.J. 1969. *Bandits*. London: Weidenfeld and Nicholson.

Houerou, H.N. 1981. 'The impact of man and animals on Mediterranean Vegetation', in N. di Castri et al. (eds.), *Ecosystems of the World 11. Mediterranean Type Shrublands* (Amsterdam: Elsevier Scientific Publishing Company), Chapter 3.

King, R. 1975. *Sardinia*. London: David and Charles.

Kolars, J. 1966. 'Locational aspects of cultural ecology: the case of the goat in non-western agriculture', *Geographical Review* 56: 577–84.

Kors,A.C. and E. Peters 1972. *Witchcraft in Europe, 1100–1700: A Documentary History*. Philadelphia: University of Pennsylvania.

Lejaruen, C. 1976. 'Populations caprines du basin méditeranéen: aptitudes et evolution', *Options Méditeranéen*, 3544.

Levack, B.P. 1987. *The Witch Hunt in Early Modem Europe*. London: Longmans 1987.

McNeill, J.R. 1992. *The Mountains of the Mediterranean World: An Environmental History*. Cambridge: Cambridge University Press.

Morand Fehr, P. et al. 2004. 'Strategy for goat farming in the 21st Century', *Small Ruminant Research* 51: 145–53.
Naveh, Z. and A.S. Lieberman 1993. *Landscape Ecology: Theory and Applications*. NewYork: SpringerVerlag.
Naveh, Z. and R.H. Whittaker 1979. 'Structural and floristic diversity of shrublands and woodlands in northern Israel and other Mediterranean areas', *Vegetation* 41: 171–219.
Naveh, Z. 1982. 'Mediterranean landscape evolution and degradation as multivariate biofunctions: theoretical and practical implications', *Landscape Planning* 9: 125–46.
Pinto-Correia, T. 1993. 'Threatened landscapes in Alentejo Portugal: the montado and other agr-silvo-pastoral systems', *Landscape and Urban Planning* 24: 43–8.
Ritvo, H. 1997. *The Platypus and the Mermaid and other Figments of the Classifying Imagination*. Cambridge: Harvard University Press.
Rubino, R. 2002. 'La Rôle des chèvres dans le sud de l'Italie', *Ethnozootechnie* 70: 29–34.
Rundel, P.W. et al. (eds.) 1997. *Landscape Disturbance and Biodiversity in Mediterranean Type Ecosystems*. Berlin: Springer-Verlag.
Russell, J.B. 1972. *Witchcraft in the Middle Ages*. Ithaca, NewYork: Cornell University Press.
Russell, J.B. 1977. *The Devil: Perceptions of Evil from Antiquity to Primitive Christianity*. Ithaca, New York: Cornell University Press.
Samaran, C. 1957. 'Etude sur la vie en Haute Provence Orientale', Masters Thesis, University of Aix en Provence.
Schwager, R. 1987. *Must there be scapegoats? Violence and Redemption in the Bible*. San Francisco: Harper and Row.
Sclafert, T. 1934. 'A Propos du Déboisement des Alpes du Sud: le rôle des troupeaux', *Annàles de Geographie* (Paris) LXIII: 126–145.
Sclafert, T. 1959. *Cultures en Haute Provence: déboisement et paturages au Moyen Age*. Paris: SEVPEN.
Segui, E. 1946. 'La Guerre aux Chèvres sous l'Ancien Régime'*Cahiers d'histoire et d'archaéologue* (Nimes) Nouvelle serie. 1: 11–21.
Siddle, D.J. 1996. 'Cipières et la guerre de la sucession d'autrich: les repercussions démographiques', *Actes des 8ieme journées d'étude de l'éspace, Provencale* (Mouans Sartoux: Centre Régional de Documentation Occitans), 11–21.
Sinapis, E. et al. 2000. 'Transfert de technologies vers un élevage caprin en voie de reconstruction', *Proceedings of the Seventh International Conference on Goats*. (Tours: International Goat Association), 15–17.
Solakian, D. 1988. 'De la question des chèvres en France au XVIII siècle', *Ethnozootechnie* 41: 33–46.
Sprenger, J. and H. Kramer 1968. *Malleus Maleficarum* [1486], trans. M. Summers. Bungay: Chaucer Press, for the Folio Society.
Stanislawski, J. 1975. 'Dionysia westward – early religion and the economic geography of wine' *Geographical Review* 65: 427–44.
Timbal, P.C. 1969. *La Vie en Provence aux 14ième et 15iéme siècles*. Paris: Presses Universitaire de France.
Trevor-Roper, H.R. 1969. *The European Witch Craze in the Sixteenth and Seventeenth Centuries*. London: MacMillan.

Vidler, A.R. 1961. *The Church in the Age of Revolution*. London: Pelican Books.
Woods, D.B. 2006. 'How to keep fires down in California scrub: chew it', *Christian Science Monitor*, 18 September.

Three Centuries of Whaling and Walrus Hunting in Svalbard and its Impact on the Arctic Ecosystem

Louwrens Hacquebord

INTRODUCTION

Four centuries ago England and the Netherlands started walrus hunting and whaling in the waters around Spitsbergen.[1] The whaling trade began in 1611 and lasted about three hundred years (Figure 1). Its success was very dependent on ice and weather conditions.[2] By around 1850, whaling in Spitsbergen had led to a complete removal of the Greenland right whale or bowhead (*Balaena mysticetus*) from the marine ecosystem.[3] Atlantic walruses (*Odobaenus rosmarus rosmarus*) were hunted first by English and Dutch whalers and later by Russian and Norwegian fur hunters (Figure 2). The walrus hunt started in 1604 on Bear Island and lasted till the end of the nineteenth century when the species was depleted in Svalbard. The extermination of the whale and the walrus are good examples of the impact of a historical long-distance fishery or trade on natural local ecosystems, in this case the marine ecosystem of Svalbard.

During twenty years of archaeological field research on Spitsbergen many traces have been found from the whaling period. Remains of whaling stations were discovered and studied on the beaches of the west coast of Spitsbergen. On almost every suitable place along the west coast, the seventeenth-century European whalers had built stations to boil the blubber of the whales into oil.[4] At these places many bones and sometimes even complete skeletons of Greenland right whales have been found.[5] The many remains indicate an intensive hunt of the whales in the coastal waters of Spitsbergen. It also proves the existence of a large whale stock in this area before the European whaling period started. Nowadays, between the islands of Franz Jozef Land Greenland right whales are sometimes sighted.[6] In the waters of Spitsbergen sightings of Greenland right whales have been very rare ever since the nineteenth century.[7]

Remains of walrus haul-outs of the same period were also found on many places along the coasts of Svabard. Many bones and sometimes even complete skeletons of walruses were found. These places indicate an intensive walrus hunt that led to a complete elimination of the Atlantic walrus from the marine ecosystem around 1870. This lasted till 1970 before the Atlantic walrus reappeared in Svalbard coming from Franz Josef Land. Today close to 1,000 animals can be observed.[8]

Three Centuries of Whaling

FIGURE 1. Hunting of the Greenland right whale by Dutch and Basque whalers in the seventeenth century. Detail of an oil painting by Cornelis Claesz. Van Wieringen (ca. 1620). Courtesy Kendall Whaling Museum, Sharon, Mass., USA.

FIGURE 2. Walruses on the beach at Moffen, north of Spitsbergen.
Photo: Ben Bekooi

This article will focus on the following questions: what impact did whaling and walrus hunting in Svalbard have on the local ecosystem, what happened to the large quantities of plankton which became available for the other organisms in the ecosystem, and which competitors took advantage of the removal of the Greenland right whale and the Atlantic walrus from the local ecosystem?

SOURCES AND METHODS

This multidisciplinary research was set up to find answers to the questions formulated in the introduction. The sources of information were: archaeological sources such as excavations of settlements and their houses, working platforms, ovens, middens and graveyards; historical sources such as ships' logs, itineraries, notarial acts and catch records; biological sources such as excavated animal bones and recent zoological inventories and pedological sources such as soil samples.

Archaeological excavations were carried out on several locations along the west coast of Spitsbergen: Amsterdam Island (1979–1981, 1983, 1986 and 1987) and Ytre Norsk Island (1980) in the north and Lægerneset in the Recherchefjord (1998) and Midterhuken between Van Mijenfjord and Van Keulenfjord (1999) in the south (Figure 3). Archaeological structures and material culture were studied to improve knowledge of whaling on Spitsbergen. The animal bones excavated in the middens were studied to increase our knowledge of the natural environment of the stations. In this way the avifauna around the seventeenth-century whaling stations was reconstructed. The same was done with soil samples around the settlements. Pollen analysis of these samples gave information of developments in the vegetation and the impact of whaling activities on the vegetation around the settlements.[9]

Written sources were used to reconstruct the whaling history and to collect more information of the ecology of the Greenland right whale, its early habitat and its former migration route. The historical-biological information is compared with the results of recent biological research north of Alaska in the Bering Sea.[10] In this way it is possible to study the life of the Greenland right whale in the North Atlantic Ocean although the species no longer exists there today.

The catch records inform us about the number of whales killed per voyage and per ship from 1669 to 1800. Several lists are preserved and comparison of these lists made it clear that the figures on the different lists do agree with each other rather well. We used these lists to calculate the number of Greenland right whales before exploitation and to assess the impact of whaling on the stock. Beside ship logs and catch records other written sources also provided information about whaling. Very often the place, the moment and the circumstances under which a whale was killed were noted in official notarial statements. These documents could be used to reconstruct the distribution of whales in the hunt-

Three Centuries of Whaling

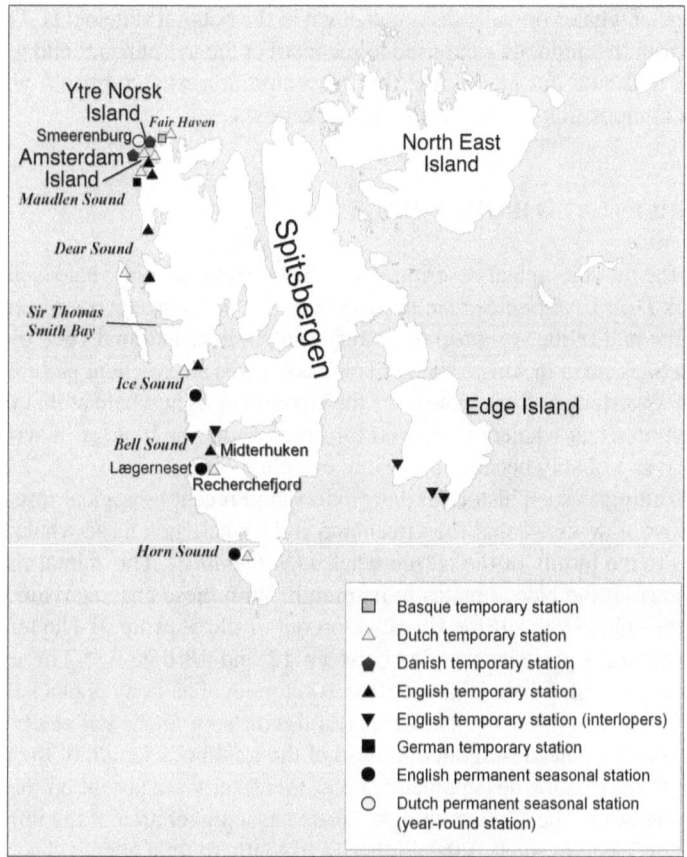

FIGURE 3. Remains of seventeenth-century whaling stations on Spitsbergen. Drawing: F. Steenhuisen

ing area. Surviving trade correspondence and newspapers provided additional information about the economic aspects of whaling.

Although several historical documents exist, walrus hunting is not as well documented as whaling.[11] For Western European countries it was very often an adjunct to whaling and for the Russian and Norwegian fur hunters one of their many activities. Some incidental records are preserved but serial information about catches is not available for the walrus hunt. This makes it difficult to calculate the number of Atlantic walruses before exploitation and to assess the impact of the hunt on the Atlantic walrus stock.

Bones on the beaches were used to study the distribution of these sea mammals around the Arctic islands and this information was compared with the sightings of whales or walruses noted down in the notarial statements. The bird bones from the middens were used to reconstruct the avifauna around whaling stations and haul-out places and this reconstruction was compared with the species composition of the recent bird rookeries.

THE GREENLAND RIGHT WHALE

One of the first biological descriptions of the Greenland right whale is given in the book *Drie Voyagien gedaen na Groenlandt...* which was written sometime in the first half of the seventeenth century and published around 1668 by Gillis Joosten Saeghman in Amsterdam.[12] This book gives an excellent picture of the level of knowledge of the biology of the Greenland right whale at that time. It demonstrates that whalers were well informed about the biology of whales in those days, probably because they were excellent observers.

According to such historical descriptions and recent biological research in Alaska we now know that the Greenland right whale is a large whale which belongs to the family of the baleen whales (*Balaenidae*). The animal received its name from the baleen plates in its mouth. With these characteristic baleen plates the animal can sift the zooplankton out of the seawater.[13] The length of the Greenland right whale varies between 12 and 18 metres.[14] The average weight of an adult whale is about 50 to 100 tonnes. The body is black and the whale has a white spot on its chin and a lighter spot on its tail stock and/or fluke plates. The head is about one-third of the total body length of the animal and the bonnet callosities characteristic of this family are absent on the upper part of the head. The Greenland right whale has a higher arch of the upper jaw than related species, such as the northern and southern right whales. The widely separated blowholes cause a double blow, the V-shape of which is characteristic of the Greenland right whale. The eyes are placed quite low on the side of the head about 30 cm above the corner of the mouth.[15]

Greenland right whales are endemic to Arctic and sub-Arctic waters. They are usually not seen south of 68° N. In the (sub-)Arctic, the whales spend a great part of their life close to the edge of the pack ice in the waters near Arctic and sub-Arctic islands.[16] From historical sources, it appears that the 200-m depth contour is of great significance to them.[17]

Migration of the Greenland right whale

Historical sources in combination with the results of recent biological research in the Bering Sea have made it possible to reconstruct the life and migration of Greenland right whales in the Atlantic Arctic.[18] The Greenland right whales wintered along the edge of the pack ice east and southeast of Greenland and migrated to the north in the springtime following the ice edge. In 1634, the seven Dutch sailors who wintered on Jan Mayen observed the first whales on 28 March.[19] Because of upwelling the Greenland Sea between Jan Mayen and Spitsbergen is rich in nutrients. This availability of nutrients and the general ice thickness determines both the growth of phyto- and zooplankton. This growth of plankton shows a seasonal rhythm, with the peak coming later with increasing latitude. In the northern direction the number of species of zooplankton decreases as well. The Greenland right whale migrates to the north to feed on this zooplankton and returns south in autumn after the feeding season.[20]

The whale probably had its calving area near Jan Mayen. Pregnant females were caught and many female and young whales were seen near Jan Mayen in the first half of the seventeenth century. Male and non-pregnant female whales migrated directly to the feeding grounds northwest and north of Spitsbergen.[21] Under certain ice conditions – for instance when the pack ice was closed and the edge near the coast of Spitsbergen – many whales were concentrated there, making this a productive hunting area. Sometimes it was so crowded with whales that the whalers called it the Whalebay (Table 1).

Year	Observer	Place	Observation	Source
1607: 14 July	Henry Hudson	Kingsbay, Spitsbergen	'many whales'	Conway 1906: 25
1610: 16 June	Jonas Poole	Kingsbay, Spitsbergen	'I saw great store of whales'	Purchas 1906 XIV, ch. IV:14
1612: 29 June	Jonas Poole	Kingsbay, Spitsbergen	'great store of whales'	Purchas 1906, XIV ch. IV: 42, 43
1619	Matthys Jansz Hoepstock	Hoepstockbaai, Jan Mayen	'44 whales killed'	GAR ONA* invnr. 91, fol. 191
1634: March/ April	Journal of the winterers	Noorderbaai, Jan Mayen	many whales	L'Honoré Naber 1930: 62e
1648	Christian Müller	Magdalenabaai, Spitsbergen	more than 1000 whales	Oesau 1955: 20
ca. 1660	Lancelott Anderson	Bell Sound, Spitsbergen	'many young ones with the olds...'	Conway 1900: 630

TABLE 1. Records of large concentrations of whales in the bays of Spitsbergen and Jan Mayen.

* GAR ONA: Rotterdam Municipal Archive, Old Notarial archive.

The logbook of the seven winterers on Amsterdam Island (1633/1634) mentioned the first whale sighting on April 27.[22] Other written sources name the end of May or the beginning of June as the date the whales arrived in the fjords of Spitsbergen.[23] Later in the season, female and young whales were seen feeding in the fjords of Spitsbergen. In this period whales were also seen in the eastern part of Svalbard and even in the Barents Sea. Remains of whaling stations on some islands south of Edge Island demonstrate the former presence of whales in these waters.[24]

THE ATLANTIC WALRUS

Hessel Gerritsz (1613) in his *l'Histoire du Pays nommé Spitsberghe*[25] was one of the first authors to give a description and a drawing of the Atlantic walrus. Later, Gerritsz' very rough description was completed by Martens (1710) and Zorgdrager (1720). Recent biological research has produced much more information.[26] The Atlantic walrus belongs to the family *Odobenidae*. It received its Latin name from the 80 cm tusks in its upper jaw which are sometimes used to help the animal move about – literally the name means tooth-walker.[27] Nowadays walruses occur only in cold temperate, sub-Arctic and Arctic regions. The migratory behaviour of Atlantic walruses is poorly understood, and some local populations are non-migratory.[28] This is probably the case with the Atlantic walrus in Svalbard. There they appear to be very tied to places like Moffen and Andretangen.

The Atlantic walrus feed on benthic organisms such as large bivalves and decapod crustaceans[29] and its daily food consumption is approximately 5.7 per cent of its body mass, or about 57 kg. Adult male Atlantic walruses are, on average, 3 metres long and weigh 1,000 kg: large females 2.4 metres and weigh 800 kg. Young animals are usually 1.4 metres long and weight less than 85 kg at birth. Walrus skin is extremely thick, up to 6 cm on an adult male's neck. The body colour varies from grey to reddish brown.[30]

Unlike the whale stock it is very hard to calculate the walrus stock in Svalbard before human exploitation. Weslawski et al.[31] calculated this at 25,000 by assuming that the initial walrus stock in Franz Josef Land was 6,000–12,500 animals,[32] taking into account that Svalbard is much larger in area and had more haul-outs (Figure 4). From historical sources we know that the original population on Bear Island numbered at least 3,000 animals and that the population in Svalbard still numbered about 10,000 animals after two hundred years of walrus hunting. After 1870 however, the Atlantic walrus was absent from Svalbard. In 1970 the Atlantic walrus reappeared in Spitsbergen from Franz Josef Land and today there are again about 1,000 animals in the waters of Svalbard.[33]

Three Centuries of Whaling

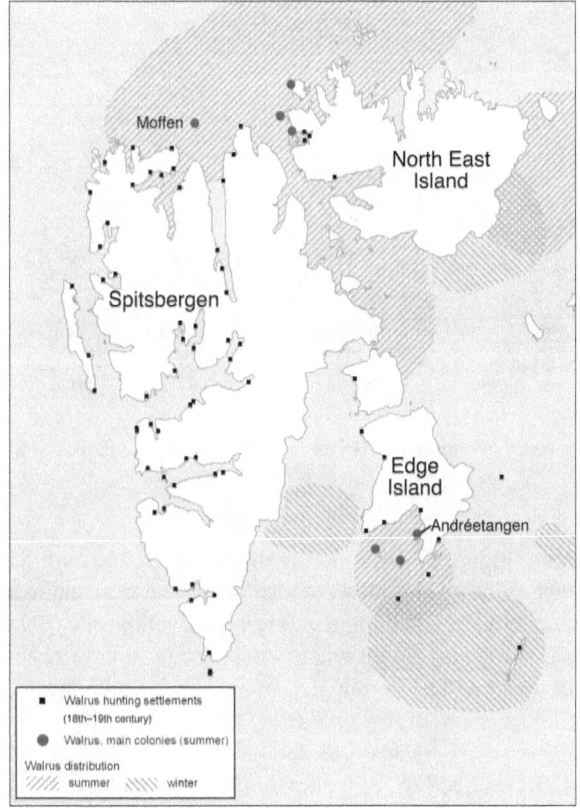

FIGURE 4. Remains of eighteenth- and nineteenth-century walrus hunting stations and recent walrus colonies on Svalbard. Drawing: F. Steenhuisen.

IMPACT OF WHALING AND WALRUS HUNTING

Many scholars have tried to estimate stock sizes prior to commercial whaling.[34] With help of these estimates and many newly collected catch records it proved to be possible to estimate the stock size before exploitation. There is only one difficulty, and that is the fact that the catch records from the first period (1610–1669) of the Spitsbergen whaling trade are not continuous. Only from some years has information been preserved. Based on this incidental information the total catch can be estimated at 15,000 whales in this first period. We are much better informed of the catch in the next period. From 1669 onwards the whalers kept catch records on a yearly base. From 1669 to 1800, 86,644 whales were killed by English, Dutch and German whalers in the seas between Jan Mayen

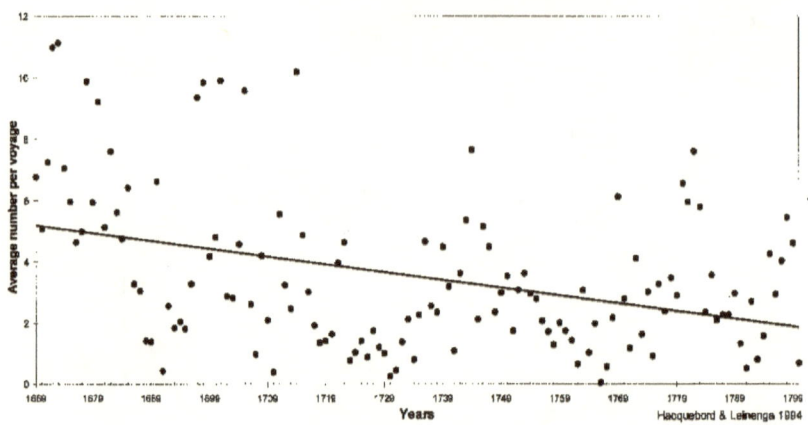

FIGURE 5. Average number of Greenland right whale caught in the Spitsbergen waters 1669–1800.

and Spitsbergen (Figure 5). Considering these records and taking into account that 20 per cent of the whales hit were lost[35] we come to a total record of about 122,000 whales killed. Assuming a yearly reproduction rate of 2 per cent the pre-exploitation Greenland right whale stock size must have been 46,000.[36]

This stock was totally exterminated by whaling, which means that 46,000 whales were taken out of the original ecosystem, thus making 3.5 million tons of food available yearly for seabirds and fish feeding on plankton. Since little auks (*Alle alle*), polar cod (*Boreogadus saida*) and capelin (*Mallotus villosus*) feed on the same food as the Greenland right whale they would be the first organisms that would benefit from the extermination of the Greenland right whale. Increasing populations of polar cod and capelin then stimulated the increase of fish eating birds like Brünnich's and common guillemots (*Uria lomvia* and *Cepphus grylle*) as well as Greenland seals (*Phoca groenlandica*) and minke whales (*Balaenoptera acutorostrata*).[37] The same happened with the Atlantic walrus stock: 25,000 walruses were taken out of the original ecosystem, making 0.5 millions tonnes of food available yearly for bearded seals (*Erignathus barbatus*) and diving ducks as eiders (*Somateria mollissima*).[38]

In this connection it is fascinating that research in Antarctica has shown that three of the most abundant bird species almost totally dependent on Antarctic krill – (*Euphausia superba*): Chinstrap (*Pygoscelis antarctica*), Adelie (*Pygoscelis adeliae*) and Macaroni (*Eudyptes chrysolophus*) penguins – have increased 5 to 10 per cent in population after the modern whaling period.[39] The same research made clear that after the increase of the number of penguins the minke whale, crabeater seal (*Lobodon carcinophagus*) and even the Antarctic fur seal (*Arctocephalus gazella*) increased in number too.[40] If the same happened in the Arctic after the Greenland right whale hunt, plankton-feeding birds and

Three Centuries of Whaling

fish will have increased, and subsequently birds and sea mammals feeding on these fish. Recent sea bird observations have shown a high (31 per cent) representation of kittiwake (*Rissa tridactyla*) and little auk (34.7 per cent) on the west coast of Spitsbergen. Nowadays these two species account for almost 65 per cent of the total seabirds there[41] (Table 2).

	Smeerenburg		Lægerneset		Midterhuken		Recent	
	no.	%	no.	%	no.	%	no.	%
Fulmar	3,290	79.7	43	5.4	42	11.0	383	10.3
Kittiwake	333	8.1	16	2.0	21	5.5	1,151	31.0
Glaucous gull	114	2.8	25	3.1	15	3.9	138	3.7
Brünnich's guillemot	179	4.3	635	79.1	283	74.3	600	16.2
Black guillemot	51	1.2	9	1.1	2	0.5	65	1.8
Little auk	23	0.6					1,289	34.7
Common guillemot							3	0.1
Puffin							82	2.2
Eider	134	3.2	1	0.1				
Goose	2	0.1	5	0.6	2	0.5		
Other (various)			69	8.6	16	4.2		
	4,126	*100.0*	**803**	*100.0*	**381**	*99.9*	**3,711**	*100.0*

TABLE 2. Number of bird bones from excavations of Smeerenburg (1979–1984), Lægerneset (1998) and Midterhuken (1999) on the west coast of Spitsbergen compared with recent bird inventories (1991).
Sources: van Wijngaarden-Bakker (1987); Joiris (1996); Prummel (1998 and 1999).

Historical and archaeological sources however, give another picture. The birds mentioned in one of the surviving wintering logbooks (1633/1634) are kittiwake, fulmar (*Fulmarus glacialis*), Brünnich's guillemot, black guillemot (*Cepphus grylle*), glaucous gull (*Larus hyperboreus*) and eider (*Somateria mollissima*). Black guillemot and glaucous gull are mentioned most in the wintering logbook (Table 3). The archaeological excavations of the middens at the sites nearby the rookeries contain bones of fulmar, kittiwake, glaucous gull, Brünnich's guillemot, black guillemot, little auk, eider and barnacle goose (*Branta leucopsis*) (Table 2). In Smeerenburg fulmar bones (79.7 per cent) were most frequently found but this probably was because the flensing took place on the beach instead of alongside the ship in the fjord. On the beach the carcass of the whale would have attracted many of these birds. Beside the fulmar, kittiwake (8.1 per cent)

Bird Species	Abundance 1633/4*	Abundance Recent	Ease of catching	Taste	Quotation from F. Martens, Voyage to Spitzbergen, 1671**
Kittiwake	+++	+++	++	0	There is but little meat upon them. We eat but the legs and the breast, for the wings are nothing but skin and bone
Glaucous gull	+	+	++	0	
Brünnich's guillemot	+	++	0	0	The old ones are full of flesh, but it is very dry and tough and therefore unpleasant to eat. They boil them like the pigeons and scum off the fat when they boil, then they fry them in batter.
Black guillemot	+++	+	0	+	Their flesh is good to eat when the fat is taken away from it, if afterwards it be fryed in butter.
Little auk	0	+++	++	++	They are very good food, and the best next the Strandrunner; are fleshy and fattish; we boyl and then roast them.
Common guillemot	0	+	0	0	
Puffin	0	+	0	++	He hath more flesh upon him than the diving pigeon and is very good to eat
Fulmar	+	+++	++	0	His breast and legs are only to be eaten; they are tough and taste strong of train oyl.
Eider	+++	+++	+	+	These ducks have a very good flesh. We boyl'd and roasted them as we did the other birds, but the fat of them we flung away for it tasted of train-oyl (and made us vomit).

TABLE 3. Bird information from written historical sources.

+++ very good   ++ good   + fair   0 poor

* Recorded in the wintering logbook of 1633/4 (l'Honoré Naber 1930).
** Adam White 1855.

and Brünnich's guillemot (4.3 per cent) were well represented in the middens of Smeerenburg. Not so many fulmar bones (11.3 per cent) were found in the middens of Lægerneset. In the middens at this site in the Rercherchefjord near Bell Sound most were Brünnich's guillemots (79.1 per cent) and the same pattern was found in the middens at Midterhuken, a whaling station on a spit of land between Van Mijenfjord and Van Keulenfjord with 74.3 per cent Brünnich's guillemot. The middens of Smeerenburg contained only a few bones of the little auk (0.6 per cent) and those of Lægerneset and Midterhuken did not contain any bone of the little auk at all, whereas this bird is very well represented today in a neighbouring bird cliff. According to the written sources the little auk was eaten by the whalers as much as any other species, so it certainly is not because of the taste that the bones of this bird are almost absent from the middens. It was probably more a question of rarity. The same is true for the eider duck. This bird is found in the middens of Smeerenburg (3.2 per cent) but is almost absent from the middens of Lægerneset (0.1 per cent) and Midterhuken (0 per cent), whereas many eiders are found in this region nowadays.

CONCLUSIONS

This study demonstrates that with the help of historical, archaeological and biological sources it is possible to reconstruct the ecology of animals that were exterminated more than 100 years ago in the North Atlantic. Using surviving catch records, it is possible to calculate the number of Greenland right whales before and during the first years of exploitation as about 46,000. Although more difficult and less certain, an estimate of the original Atlantic walrus stock was possible, at about 25,000. Both animals were eliminated from the marine ecosystem of Svalbard, which made large quantities of zooplankton available for other organism in the system. This surplus of pelagic zooplankton is now almost certainly consumed by planktonivorous seabirds like the little auk and by fish, while eiders and probably also bearded seal benefited from the extinction of the Atlantic walrus. Archaeological and historical research show an enormous increase of little auk and eider since the elimination of the whale and the walrus from the ecosystem. The increased amount of pelagic fish in turn provided food for piscivorous alcids and gulls. In this way whaling and walrus hunting may have caused the great increase of present-day seabird colonies on the west coast of Spitsbergen.

NOTES

[1] Conway 1906, de Jong 1983, Lono 1972, Jackson 1978, Hacquebord 1984a, Stora 1987, Bruijn 1988.

[2] Hacquebord 1984b.
[3] Hacquebord and Leinenga 1994.
[4] Hacquebord 1984a, Hacquebord 1988a.
[5] Hacquebord 1987.
[6] Moore and Reeves 1993, de Korte and Belikov 1994.
[7] Moore and Reeves 1993.
[8] Gjertz and Wiig 1994, Born et al. 1995.
[9] Van der Knaap 1985.
[10] Hazard and Lowry 1984, Everitt and Krogman 1979, Nerini et al. 1984, Leatherwood and Reeves 1983, Burns et al. 1993.
[11] Conway 1906, Lono 1972, Stora 1987.
[12] l'Honoré Naber 1930.
[13] Leatherwood and Reeves 1983.
[14] Haldiman and Tarpley 1993.
[15] Ibid.
[16] Scoresby 1820.
[17] Hacquebord 1984a.
[18] Hacquebord and Leinenga 1994.
[19] l' Honoré Naber 1930.
[20] Moore and Reeves 1993.
[21] Hacquebord 1987.
[22] l'Honoré Naber 1930.
[23] Hacquebord and Leinenga 1994.
[24] Hacquebord 1988b.
[25] l'Honoré Naber 1924.
[26] Reeves et al. 1992, Gjertz and Wiig 1992, Gjertz and Wiig 1994.
[27] Reeves et al. 1992.
[28] Ibid.
[29] Fay et al. 1977, Gjertz and Wiig 1992.
[30] Reeves et al. 1992.
[31] Weslawski et al. 2000.
[32] Gjertz and Wiig 1998.
[33] Gjertz and Wiig 1994, Born et al. 1995.
[34] IWC report 1978, Gambell 1983, Leatherwood and Reeves 1983, Mitchell 1977, Mitchell and Reeves 1981, Hacquebord 1984a, 1987, Woodby and Botkin 1993, Hacquebord and Leinenga 1994.
[35] Kugler 1984.
[36] Hacquebord and Leinenga 1994.
[37] Mehlum and Gabrielsen 1993, Weslawski et al. 2000.
[38] Weslawski et al. 2000.
[39] Croxall and Prince 1979, Croxall 1984, Laws 1985, Croxall et al. 1988.
[40] Laws 1985.
[41] Joiris 1996.

REFERENCES

Bruijn, J.R. 1988. 'De ontplooiing van een nieuwe bedrijfstak' in: L. Hacquebord and W.H. Vroom, eds., *Walvisvaart in de Gouden Eeuw. Opgravingen op Spitsbergen* (Amsterdam) 16–29.

Born, E.W., I. Gjertz and R.R. Reeves, 1995. 'Population assessment of the Atlantic walrus', *Meddelelser Norsk Polarinstitutt* 138, 1–100.

Burns, J.J., J.J. Montague and C.J. Cowles, (eds) 1993. *The Bowhead Whale*. Special Publication Number 2 (Lawrence).

Conway, M. 1900. Some unpublished Spitsbergen MSS. *The Geographical Journal* 15, 628–635.

Conway, M. 1906. *No Man's land. A history of Spitsbergen from its discovery in 1596 to the beginning of the scientific exploration of the country* (Cambridge).

Croxall, J.P. 1984. 'Seabirds', in R.M. Laws (ed.) *Antarctic Ecology*, 533–616.

Croxall, J.P. and P.A. Prince 1979. 'Antarctic seabirds and seal monitoring studies', *Polar Record* 19(123), 573–595.

Croxall, J.P., T.C. Mc Cann, P.A. Prince, and P. Rothery, 1988. 'Reproductive performance of seabirds and seals at South Georgia and Signy Island, South Orkney Islands, 1976–1987: Implications for Southern Ocean Monitoring Studies', in D. Sahrhage (ed.), *Antarctic Ocean and Resources variability* (Berlin/Heidelberg) 261–285.

Everitt. R.D. and B.D. Krogman 1979. 'Sexual behavior of the bowhead whales observed off the north coast of Alaska', *Arctic* 32, 277–280.

Fay, F.H., H.M. Feder and S.W. Stoker 1977. *An estimation of the impact of pacific walrus population on its food resources in the Bering Sea*, Marine Mammals Committee Reports, MMC-75/06, 74/03.

Gambell, R. 1983. 'Bowhead whales and Alaskan Eskimos: a problem of survival', *Polar Record* 21, 467–473.

Gjertz, I. and O. Wiig 1992. 'Feeding of walrus *Odobaenus rosmarus* in Svalbard', *Polar Record* 28, 57–59.

Gjertz, I. and O. Wiig 1994. 'Past and present distribution of walruses in Svalbard', *Arctic* 47, 34–42.

Gjertz, I. and O. Wiig 1998. 'Back-calculation of original population size for walruses Odobaenus rosmarus in Franz Josef Land', *Wildlife Biology* 4, 223–230.

Hacquebord, L. 1984a. *Smeerenburg. Het verblijf van Nederlandse walvisvaarders op de westkust van Spitsbergen in de zeventiende eeuw*. PhD Thesis, (Amsterdam/Groningen).

Hacquebord, L. 1984b. 'The history of early Dutch whaling: a study from the historical angle', in H.K. s' Jacob, K. Snoeijing and R. Vaughan (eds), *Arctic Whaling. Works of the Arctic Centre* 8 (Groningen) 135–148.

Hacquebord, L. 1987. 'Migratie, levenspatroon en habitat van de Groenlandse walvis *Balaena mysticetus L.*, 1758 in de Atlantische Arctis in de 17de eeuw', *Lutra* 30, 123–141.

Hacquebord, L. 1988a. 'Traankokerijen op de kusten van Spitsbergen; wat de historische-archeologie ons ervan leert', in L. Hacquebord, and W.H. Vroom (eds), *Walvisvaart in de Gouden Eeuw. Opgravingen op Spitsbergen* (Amsterdam) 49–65.

Hacquebord, L. 1988b. 'Three 17the century whaling stations in southeastern Svalbard:

an archaeological missing link', *Polar Record* 24, 125–128.

Hacquebord, L. and J.R. Leinenga 1994. 'De ecologie van de Groenlandse walvis in relatie tot walvisvaart en klimaatsveranderingen in de zeventiende en achttiende eeuw', *Tijdschrift voor Geschiedenis* 107(3), 415–438.

Haldiman, J.T. and R.J. Tarpley 1993. 'Anatomy and physiology', in J.J. Burns, J.J. Montague and C.J. Cowles, *The Bowhead Whale*. Special Publication Number 2 (Lawrence).

Hazard, K.W. and L.F. Lowry 1984. 'Benthic prey in a bowhead whale from the northern Bering Sea', *Arctic* 37, 166–168.

l'Honoré Naber S.P. 1924. *Hessel Gerritsz, Beschrijvinghe van der Samoyeden Landt en Histoire du Pays Nommé Spitsberghe*. Werken uitgegeven door de Linschoten-Vereeniging XXIII ('s Gravenhage).

l'Honoré Naber S.P. 1930. *Walvischvaarten, overwinteringen en jachtbedrijven in het hooge noorden 1633–1635* (Utrecht).

IWC 1978. 'Reports of the Scientific Committee', in *Report of the IWC* 28, 38–89.

Jackson, G. 1978. *The British Whaling Trade* (London).

Jong, C. de, 1983. 'The hunt of the greenland whale: a short history and statistical sources', in *Reports International Whaling Commission*, Special Issue 5 , 83–101.

Joiris, C.R. 1996. 'At-sea distribution of seabirds and marine mammals around Svalbard, summer 1991', *Polar Biology* 16, 423–429.

Knaap, W.O. van der 1985. 'Human influence on natural arctic vegetation in the 17th century and climate changes since A.D. 1600 in Northwest Spitsbergen: a paleobotanical study', *Arctic and Alpine research* 17, 371–387.

Korte, J. de and S.E. Belikov 1994. 'Observations of Green whales (*Balaena mysticetus*), Zemlya Frantsa Iosifa' *Polar Record* 30(173), 135–136.

Kugler, R.C. 1984. 'Historical survey of foreign whaling: North America', in H.K. s' Jacob, K. Snoeijing and R. Vaughan (eds), *Arctic whaling*, Works of the Arctic Centre 8 (Groningen).

Laws, R.M. 1985. 'The ecology of the Southern Ocean', *American Scientist* 73, 26–40.

Leatherwood, S. and R.R. Reeves 1983. *The Sierra Club handbook of whales and dolphins* (San Francisco).

Lono O. 1972. 'The catch of walrus *Odobaenus rosmarus* in the areas of Svalbard, Novaya Zemlya and Franz Josef Land', *Norsk Polarinstitutt Årbok 1970* , 199–212.

Martens, F. 1710. *Nauwkeurige beschrijvinge van Groenland of Spitsbergen (etc.)*, (Amsterdam).

Mehlum, F. and G.W. Gabrielsen 1993. 'The diet of high-arctic seabirds in coastal and ice-covered, pelagic areas near the Svalbard archipelago', *Polar research* 12, 1–20.

Mitchell, E. 1977. *Initial population size of bowhead whale (Balaena mysticetus) stocks: cumulative catch estimates*. Unpublished IWC report (Cambridge).

Mitchell, E. and R.R. Reeves 1981. 'Catch history and cumulative catch estimates of initial population size of cetaceans in the eastern Canadian Arctic', in *Report of the International Whaling Commission* 31, 645–682.

Moore, S.E. and R.R. Reeves 1993. 'Distribution and Movement', in J.J. Burns, J.J. Montague and C.J. Cowles, *The Bowhead Whale*. Special Publication Number 2 (Lawrence).

Nerini, M.K., H.W. Braham, W.M. Marquette and D.J. Rugh 1984. 'Life history of the bowhead whale, *Balaena mysticetus* (Mammalia: Cetacea)', *Journal of Zoology* 204, 443–468.

Oesau, W. 1955. *Hamburgs Grönlandfahrt auf Walfischfang und Robbenschlag von 17–19 Jahrhundert* (Hamburg).

Prummel, W. 1998. *Faunal remains of Lægerneset, Spitsbergen*. Internal report GIA, (Groningen).

Prummel, W. 1999. *Faunal remains of Midterhuken, Spitsbergen*. Internal report GIA, (Groningen).

Purchas, S. 1906. *Hakluytus Posthumus or Purchas His Pilgrimes*, Vol. XIII and XIV. (Glasgow).

Reeves, R.R., B.S. Stewart, and S. Leatherwood 1992. *The Sierra Club Handbook of Seals and Sirenians* (San Francisco).

Scoresby JR., W. 1820. *An account of the Arctic regions, with a history and description of the northern whale-fishery*. Two volumes. (Edinburgh).

Stora, N. 1987. 'Russian walrus hunting in Spitsbergen', *Etudes Inuit Studies* 11, 117–138.

Weslawski, J.M., L. Hacquebord, L. Stempniewicz and M. Malinga 2000. 'Greenland whales and walruses in the Svalbard food web before and after exploitation', *Oceanologia* 42(1), 37–56.

White, A. (ed.) 1855. *A collection of documents on Spitzbergen and Greenland*, The Hakluyt Society. First Series 18. (New York).

Wijngaarden-Bakker, L.H. 1987. 'Zooarchaeological research at Smeerenburg', in *Smeerenburg Seminar. Report from a symposium presenting results from research into seventeenth century whaling in Spitsbergen*. Norsk Polar Institutt Rapport serie, 38 (Oslo), 55–66.

Woodby D.A. and D.B. Botkin 1993. 'Stock sizes prior to commercial whaling', in J.J. Burns, J.J. Montague and C.J. Cowles, *The Bowhead Whale*. Special Publication Number 2 (Lawrence).

Zorgdrager, C.G. 1720. *Bloeyende Opkomst der Aloude en Hedendaagsche Groenlandsche Visschery* (Amsterdam).

A 'Sportsman's Paradise':
The Effects of Hunting on the Avifauna of the Gippsland Lakes

Coral Dow

INTRODUCTION

The Gippsland Lakes form an extensive lake system in the state of Victoria in south-eastern Australia. The Gippsland Lakes system is fed by rivers draining south from the Australian Alps. Until the engineered opening of a permanent entrance to the sea in 1889 they were predominantly a freshwater system with lake margins regularly inundated by floodwaters forming extensive wetlands locally known as morasses. Historical sources document an environment of avifaunal abundance, particularly of waterfowl, which declined rapidly by the early twentieth century. This paper examines hunting in the colonial era and attempts to evaluate its role in avifaunal decline on the Gippsland Lakes. Hunting was part of British imperial expansion and is well documented in colonial Africa, Asia and North America.[1] However, the Australian context of colonial hunting has received little scholarly attention. Using historical sources including ethnographic records, diaries, contemporary observations and records it is possible to bring together indigenous, social and natural history in an understanding of hunting in a local narrative with national significance. A synthesis of these sources shows that it is possible to avoid the generally held assumption that the 'records of hunting are incomplete' that 'we will never know its full effects' or that we are unable to 'reconstruct the original population structure of most bird communities'.[2]

COLONIAL SPORT

Tourism arrived with the railway to Sale, Gippsland, just in time for the Easter holiday of 1878. Some tourists who boarded steamers and sailed the Lakes sought the picturesque. Others on that first crowded train carried guns or rods and were accompanied by 'sports dogs' seeking the conquest of nature not its contemplation.[3] The environment was not generally regarded as picturesque: swamps, known locally as morasses, surrounded Sale and the shores of the Gippsland Lakes. *Argus* journalist 'Vagabond' pondered what tempted 'a leading Melbourne barrister to spend long hot summer days in the morasses on the Thomson and

A 'Sportsman's Paradise'

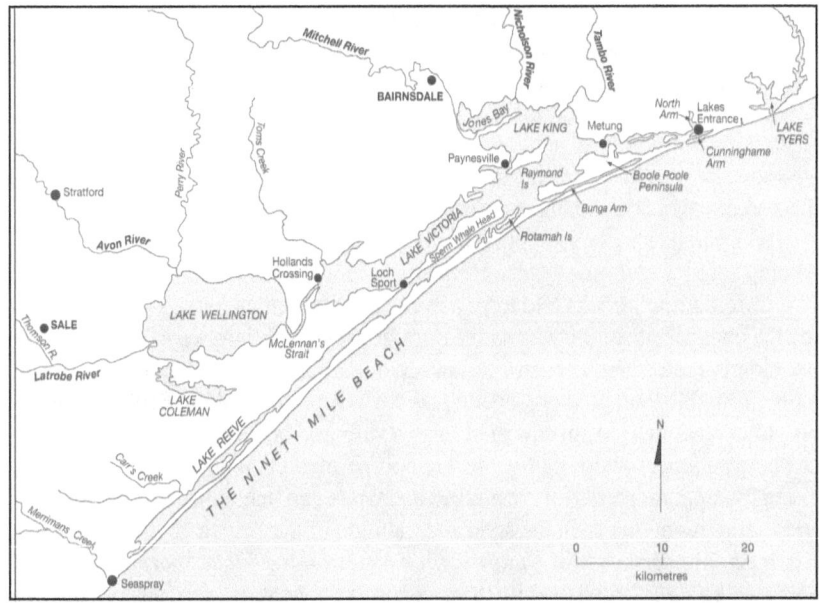

FIGURE 1. The Gippsland Lakes system.

Latrobe, going through an amount of physical exertion which would knock up half the swagmen in the country'?[4] Such labour, ordinarily deemed inappropriate for a Victorian gentleman, was in this case laudable because the barrister was indulging his passion for 'sport'. Hunting was a colonial manifestation of British culture and the best sport was on the swamps and their margins where species that most resembled Britain's pheasant, partridge, grouse and quail were found.

Hunting in the Australian colonies was at first confined to subsistence: indigenous species supplemented European food supplies. Professional hunter, Horace Wheelwright, noted nearly every immigrant arrived with a 'first rate gun' and, without the old game laws of Britain, they were free to sample the local fauna.[5] A young Alfred Howitt found living off the land was easy: 'a person can travel through the country for days with tea, sugar, some biscuits and a gun'. In 1854 he joined naturalist William Blandowski on a museum collecting trip to the Mornington Peninsula, near Melbourne where he not only skinned and preserved bird specimens but also ate them, trying 'parrots, parroquets, miners, magpies and quail', preferring the first and last.[6] His was a common colonial experience. As Penny Olsen points out, James Cook's 1770 expedition began a 'long history of parrot eating' by Europeans in this 'land of parrots'.[7] Settlers sampled species to establish acceptable substitutes for domestic fowl and European game species. There was agreement on the delicacy of Pacific Black Duck (*Anas superciliosa*), Chestnut Teal (*Anas castanea*), snipe, quail species, pigeon species, and the Australian Bustard (then known as Native Turkey). Opinion was mixed on Magpie Goose (*Anseranas semipalmate*) and Black Swan (*Cygnus atratus*) but swans' down was found to be an excellent substitute for eider down and their epicurean contribution came via their eggs, which were in high demand by colonial cooks. Australian ornithological publications, such as the work of the Polish artist Gracius Broinowski, provided not only scientific descriptions and aids for species identification but also notes on their desirability for 'the table'.[8]

Professional shooters supplied Melburnians with a huge range of species, including small waders such as the Hooded Plover (*Thinornis rubricollis*). In 1853, when Melbourne's cooks had to pay twenty-four shillings for a pair of domestic fowl, a cheaper substitute was native duck at twelve shillings a pair. At such rates one elderly man who had been a gamekeeper in England found hunting easier and more profitable than gold prospecting, and was reported making £1000 a year by his gun.[9] Wheelwright, an educated Englishman and lawyer by profession, wrote of his experiences shooting for the Melbourne market. Wheelwright earned his living by supplying birds for the market, and wrote as a 'naturalist' and 'sportsman' addressing his audience in the style and tradition of the British gentleman hunter. His *Bush Wanderings of a Naturalist; or Notes on the Field Sports and Fauna of Australia Felix,* published in 1861, elevated the colonial versions of the 'Old World' species for their ability to provide the best sport, to test a sportsman's skills, equipment and dogs. In it he wrote:

> For small game, I do not think this country can be surpassed; and ducks, pigeon, quail and snipe, may be killed in almost any quantities, at the proper seasons, in those districts where they have not been shot out ... a man can always make sure of a better day's sport here than at home ... without the expense of a certificate, and with no fear of a bullying gamekeeper before his eyes.[10]

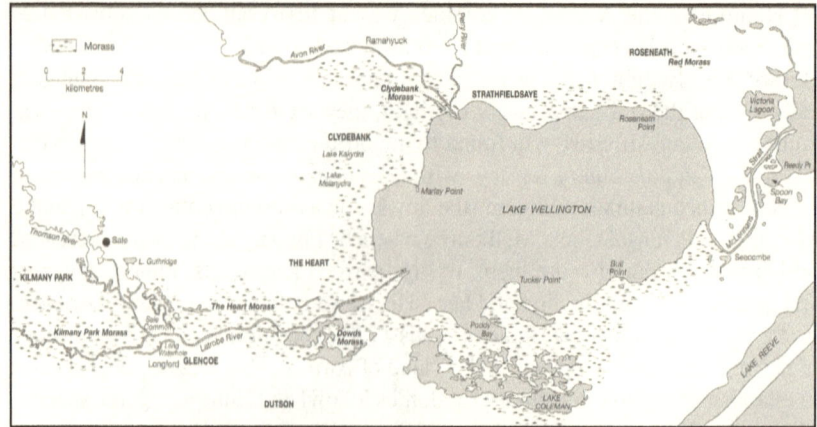

FIGURE 2. Lake Wellington and its surrounding morasses.

A 'Sportsman's Paradise'

'Old World' species passed both the taste and the sporting test and consequently graduated into a small desirable class within a fauna that was fascinating and beautiful to some settlers but generally dismissed as 'useless' or 'vermin'.[11] Before the arrival of the railway, the Gippsland Lakes were too distant to supply Melbourne's market, leaving them the preserve of the Indigenous people and local sportsmen. In 1849 Isaac Buchanan of Roseneath on Lake Wellington invited a 'party of gentleman' to spend Christmas on the Lakes where they were promised some 'scenery quite equal to the lovely watered landscapes of Tasmania'. The six men, provisioned with 'everything required for camping out, and plenty of ammunition', sailed a whaleboat through the Lakes to the Boole Poole Peninsula near the entrance to the Lakes and camped and hunted for a fortnight.[12]

THE GENTLEMAN HUNTER

In 1851 a young Englishman, William Henry Foster, about to enter Oxford University, was instead banished from England by his father after William's practical joke brought disgrace to the Foster family. He arrived in Melbourne in 1852 with a letter to an influential relative, Governor La Trobe, through whom he obtained a position in the Mounted Police Corps. He was promoted to gold-fields warden at Omeo and in 1865 to police magistrate in Sale, a position he held until 1878. His position and background provided an entrée into the small Sale elite. He purchased a substantial property, 'Mowbray Park', as the family home and a yacht, *The Ripple*, to compete in the regattas on Lake Wellington and to holiday on the Lakes.[13] Despite being disgraced at home, in the colonies, William Foster was regarded as a respectable gentleman from a well-to-do English family who indulged in a sport worthy of his class.

Foster was well grounded in the British hunting tradition. His diary, which also acted as his game-book, displayed similarities to that of English sportsman Colonel Peter Hawker and suggests Foster may have read Hawker's influential *Instructions to Young Sportsmen* which guided gentlemen hunters, including Royalty.[14] The diary is a remarkable legacy because of the meticulous records Foster kept and the insights it provides to his zealous attitude. It recorded the dates, places and numbers of birds he and his companions bagged.[15] His shooting companions were the Sale pastoralists, in particular William Boyd Cunninghame; the legal fraternity, especially Judge Bindon; and local police officers Palmer, Freeley and Sadlier. Foster was always on the lookout for new shooting grounds and keen to finish court early in order to get in an afternoon's sport. A dedicated shooter, he was prepared to wade morasses, row the Avon River, rise early for three hours' sport before breakfast or shoot until after midnight, if conditions were suitable. Keen to perform well, he practised trap shooting with Magpies and noted in his diary when he shot well, which meant a high kill rate per shot.

The species Foster most desired was Australian Snipe, now called Latham's Snipe (*Gallinago hardwickii*).[16] Wheelwright regarded it as 'the finest small-game bird in Victoria' and naturalist G. J. Broinowski considered it 'one of the few examples we have of true game and is prized accordingly by sportsmen who have been trained to field sports by English associations'.[17] Like English Snipe, Latham's Snipe is 'cryptic and retiring' and this increased its appeal to sporting shooters, the challenge coming from its habit of bursting in a fast twisting flight when flushed and then dropping for cover.[18] Ignoring the heat, flies and the call of a Kookaburra or cockatoo, snipe shooters could almost believe they were back shooting in the old country. Foster waited eagerly for the snipe's arrival in spring. On 27 August 1869 he and Judge Bindon finished court early, heading for Glencoe on the Latrobe River and the first afternoon of snipe shooting of the season. Foster's records reflect the migratory habit of the species, with only a few birds shot as they arrived in early September and again when they departed in February. In 1866–7, despite losing a month's shooting through breaking his collarbone, Foster and his companions bagged 783 snipe.[19] They shot as many birds as possible in the time available, such as in three hours at Nambrok and The Ridge when 98 were killed. On 2 November 1867 Foster and William Boyd Cunninghame went to Murdering Hut on The Heart, to shoot snipe. They 'found 15 in a small swamp – shot all but one, neither of us missing a shot'.[20]

What happened to the kill? Foster made no entry of how, or even if, he carried such large numbers out of the swamps but some did grace the pastoralists' dining tables. Foster's sister-in-law, Elizabeth Montgomery, remembered 'the splendid game brought in by the shooting parties'. William Foster 'was a good sportsman and kept our table well supplied with small game ... wild turkeys and many braces of wild duck, teal and pigeon'.[21] But not all got to the table. Wheelwright blamed the Australian climate and the ferocity of the flies for the loss of many bagged birds and one suspects Foster, shooting for sport rather than profit, left many where they fell in the swamps.

In March when the snipe returned to Japan, Foster turned to quail shooting, which also brought back memories of England for quail was regarded as the 'Australian partridge'. Wheelwright described quail shooting as:

> The least laborious and pleasantest of all field sports out here. It reminds the sportsman of September at home, for it is fair open sport, and a man can have the pleasure of seeing his dogs work in the old style.[22]

Foster did not distinguish the species but I assume it was the more common Stubble Quail (*Coturnix novaezealandiae*) that he shot, although Brown Quail (*Coturnix australis*), which prefer the margins of swamps, were also present.[23] Ornithologist A.J. Campbell said all quail species were 'esteemed especial favourites by the sportsman, the naturalist and the epicure,' whilst the Stubble Quail's 'gamey little body is excellent for the table'.[24] Quail appeared in Gippsland in January and nested during their stay which coincided with the summer and Easter holiday influx of tourists, resulting in many being shot during their breeding season. Nesting did not deter Foster either, he shot 608 in 1867 and 567 in 1868, but these were not unusually high figures. Wheelwright recorded one hunter near Melbourne who shot 1,500 brace (or 3,000 birds) in one season. Like snipe, little was known of their movements or breeding habits until the 1890s.

Foster was at his most enthusiastic when there were snipe and quail to shoot. He was more restrained when shooting duck, possibly because he regarded them as easy targets. One of his shooting companions, Police Officer Sadlier, recalled 'the abundance of game in Gippsland – Snipe, Quail and Black Duck – was far beyond one's wildest dreams'. Sadlier described shooting Pacific Black Duck which rested during the day in 'countless numbers' on the Lakes but left in the afternoon for nearby lagoons. In passing over an old riverbed on The Heart Station 'they could be seen far in the distance coming in twos and threes quicker than one could reload'.[25]

Foster's shooting parties did not subscribe to the 'if it moves shoot it' philosophy. On the rare occasions when they had 'no luck' bagging their target species, they were never tempted to shoot 'undesirable species' for such actions would have been unsporting and uncivilised. But in their adherence to British sporting tradition they indulged in unrestrained slaughter of their favourite species. The Britain they had left behind was changing. Such unrestrained shooting at home where 'notable shooting houses vied for the highest number of kills of specific species in particular seasons' had depleted target species.[26] By 1860 British estate owners were forced to return parts of their agricultural land to 'wilderness' as private reserves where grouse, partridge and pheasants could breed in sufficient numbers for the winter shoot. Pheasant eggs were incubated and the birds were hand-reared for their release on the day of the shooting party. No longer did shooters have to walk the fields, moors or swamps to flush their prey; instead the released birds were driven towards the shooters by an army of gamekeepers, beaters and servants. Such methods allowed even greater numbers of kills. By 1900 the Prince of Wales's Sandringham estate in Norfolk was rearing 12,000 pheasants a year and he and his guests were shooting 1,000 birds a day.[27]

Such kills, although controlled and orchestrated, reinforced the acceptance and the respectability in competition to kill the most numbers of birds. Hunting was sport and sport meant competition, not just between shooters but between hunter and the birds and their environment. Hunting pitted skills, knowledge and equipment against all that evolution had provided their prey. The wanton and gratuitous destruction of Australian flora and fauna has been explained by settlers' lack of emotional engagement with a new environment, resulting in melancholia and alienation.[28] However, those Australian avifaunal species more alien to the Old World, birds such as parrots and honeyeaters, although hunted for the pot, survived the initial colonial conquest.[29] It was the familiar species that were pursued and in environments most reminiscent of the Old World.

Hunting's cultural values were replenished by a steady stream of British aristocrats appointed as Governors to Victoria. W. H. Foster hosted Lord Canterbury to a day's shooting when they bagged 217 ducks.[30] Sir George Bowen went kangaroo hunting and Lord Hopetoun's wife, Lady Hopetoun, a keen angler and a crack shot, spent her holidays snipe shooting in Western Victoria and fishing at Lake Tyers.[31] The highest seal of approval came when the Duke of York, with an entourage of dignitaries, came for a day's shooting at Kilmany Park, near Sale. The Duke arrived in Melbourne in May 1901 to open the Commonwealth Parliament, and, as a respite from his official schedule, requested a day of sport. Victoria had nothing to match the Royal Sandringham estate with 1,000 hand reared birds ready for a day's shoot, so instead an old style shooting party was organised with sport dependent on nature's provision. Kilmany Park, William Pearson's estate near Sale, was chosen as the estate with the best chance of good bags of quail. The colony's best dogs, guns and gamekeepers were brought in for the shoot and Pearson must have been greatly relieved to see plenty of quail in the tussocky paddocks unaware of their impending 'Royal execution'. Three hundred and sixteen Stubble Quail were bagged and the Duke finished the day shooting 'parrots' in the orchard. Colonial sportsmen must have felt pride and honour at such Royal approval, but one brave field naturalist dared to question the Duke's actions. Field naturalists were lobbying for protection of birds through improved game laws and more realistic closed seasons for quail species. Although the Duke's shooting party gave them the opportunity to voice their concerns and to highlight the need for protection, they regretted the encouragement his day at Kilmany Park gave to shooters.[32]

The gentlemen shooters may have been discriminating in their choice of targets, but others were not. At the popular local summer camp of Prospect on the Ninety Mile Beach, every man and boy seemed to have a gun and there was ample opportunity for honing shooting skills.[33] A favourite time was on dusk when 'a continuous firing of guns may be heard'. If ducks were hard to get, shooters went for swans, 'an easy prey to the breechloader'.[34] Rarity was no protection, in fact it may have been an added incentive to those shooters who descended on Sale's Eastern Lagoon in May 1865 when a flock of large egrets had appeared, a species not seen in the district before. Egrets were not a game species, for they were easy prey, hunted when in breeding for their plumage, but in this case the motive seems to have been pure pleasure. Shooters converged on the swamp and shot them all.[35] It was hardly 'sporting' and brought criticism from at least one Sale 'naturalist' who sought to simply enjoy the observation of such rare birds. This was early criticism, at a time when Victoria's first Game Act of 1862 largely protected introduced species and a few indigenous game species in the breeding season. Snipe and quail were not protected by the Act. There was some support for their protection but Dr Hedley, the local Member of Parliament, recognised that they were the most desirable species in his electorate, which included the Lakes. He argued against regulation claiming

A 'Sportsman's Paradise'

'it would prevent quail and snipe shooting altogether'.[36] In the next forty years there was a discernible shift in attitude such that Sale's 'naturalist' was not alone. Appropriate protection of indigenous species, not only game species, was intensely debated and paralleled the increased intensity of hunting by professional and tourist shooters on the Lakes.

TOURISTS AND PROFESSIONALS

The opening of the railway to Sale made professional hunting on the Lakes more attractive, and at the same time transported hundreds of sporting shooters to the district.[37] The Lakes were promoted as a 'sportsman's paradise' where an unlimited bounty awaited the shooter. Tourist guides quoted examples of successful shooters such as 'the gentleman from Daylesford who had almost a boatload of wildfowl from two days shooting with one gun'.[38] The *Gippsland Times* urged tourists to employ local guides with expert knowledge and to camp out 'inland' close to swamps where some of the best shooting existed.[39] Many, however, preferred to stay in comfort, even if the shooting conditions were uncomfortable. The English cricket team spent their 1897 Christmas break at Metung, staying in the Kalimna Hotel. They spent a day in 'scorching hot sun, pockets loaded with cartridges, skin being eaten alive by flies but not getting in a single shot or even seeing one flight of duck'. The next day they resorted to shooting cormorants, coots and swans. At Lake Tyers on Christmas Eve they were more successful, bagging forty brace of snipe, a heron and Wonga Pigeon (*Leucosarcia melanoleuca*).[40] They were typical sporting tourists, supplied with guns, ammunition and information by their hotel. They were prepared to endure the discomforts in order to obtain favoured species of snipe, duck and pigeons but when those species were unavailable they sought some 'sport' by shooting common easy-target waterbirds.

Competition to local and visitor sporting shooters came from professional hunters who shot as many birds as possible, for profit, not sport. They were treated with disdain by sporting shooters largely because they used a crude but effective weapon: the punt or swivel gun. Such guns, mounted on a swivel on a small boat, enabled them to kill great numbers of birds quickly, cheaply, and with as little effort as possible. Punt guns were murderous weapons with a long muzzle-loading barrel and were loaded with a variety of ammunition including broken glass, shot, gravel and pieces of scrap iron.[41] In a few days at Port Albert in 1866 one was used to shoot 800 snipe, duck and Black Swan.[42] But only when the use of punt guns on the Lakes threatened the tourist industry was there an outcry from the local press.[43] On the Lakes, public opinion supported the protection of birds if it protected the tourist industry. However, when legislation worked against tourism, such as in 1891 when the opening of the duck season was moved to the end of February, a time when most tourists had returned to Melbourne, it was opposed. One aggrieved shooter ventured to claim the opening date should suit the shooter not the birds.[44] The tourist industry set Gippsland apart; elsewhere game laws were debated largely on class lines. Opponents of Victoria's first Game Preservation Bill in 1862, introduced to protect imported game species, argued that it 'was not preserving game but keeping the people off the squatter's run'.[45] Similarly debate on the prohibition of swivel guns was largely between the sporting shooters who criticised swivel guns as 'unmanly' and 'unsportsmanlike' and those advocating the rights of the working class to earn a living by supplying Melbourne households with plentiful and reasonably priced native game.[46] Sporting shooters lobbied through the Acclimatisation Society and thought they had won when the Game Protection Act of 1884 prohibited the use of the swivel gun. Swivel guns continued to be used due to loopholes in the legislation. Some shooters escaped prosecution by proving that they could lift the gun to their shoulder, others by freezing birds, such as in 1897 when 7,655 'teal and other ducks' were found in Melbourne freezers waiting to be sold at the end of the closed season.[47] In 1884 it was estimated 200 professional shooters were using swivel guns throughout Victoria. How many were operating on the Lakes is unknown but the campaign against swivel guns on the Lakes continued. In 1890, the *Gippsland Mercury* claimed the unrestrained and indiscriminate shooting by professionals was having a significant impact: 'in a short time duck shooting in Gippsland will be a thing of the past'.[48]

THE COLLECTOR

There was another type of hunter in the colonial era: the collector. Some leading naturalists were also collectors and hunters. Two distinguished newspaper columnists, Donald Macdonald and A.J. Campbell, wrote of their delight in hunting. Macdonald found nothing 'to equal the fascination of sitting over a pool at night waiting for duck to come'.[49] Both learnt about birds from hunting and by visits to Melbourne game shops that Macdonald described as 'amazing museums of dead game'.[50] Related to Gippsland's pioneer Campbell family, A.J. Campbell spent summers at Metung where he took nests, eggs and shot specimens for his collection.[51] Like many naturalists of the nineteenth century Campbell and Macdonald were not opposed to hunting but they were against what Macdonald called outrageous, illogical and 'overpowered sportsmanship', preferring instead regulation and closed season shooting.[52] As Tom Griffiths has shown, the study of nature and the culture of hunting were closely aligned in the nineteenth century. Hunting and collecting were respectable and often synonymous.[53] Melbourne's National Museum of Victoria, founded in 1854, collected and exhibited colonial nature, while in Gippsland the gentleman hunter, Judge Bindon, was responsible for establishing the Sale Mechanics Institute Museum in 1874.[54] Collecting was a respectable pastime of the educated and wealthy who were prepared to pay for specimens. On the Gippsland Lakes, Cyril Stafford who had begun his hunting career as Horace Wheelwright's mate supplying the Melbourne markets with game, later earned his living shooting birds for collectors.[55] Stafford moved to Metung and lived in a hut overlooking the Lakes. Stafford, who died in 1902, was remembered as 'an interesting and well educated man, engaged in capturing bird specimens for museums all over the world'.[56] His target species were the exotic for European collectors and the rare for museums. Between 1873 and 1885 he supplied the Museum of Victoria with many specimens including the first record of a Scarlet Honeyeater (*Myzomela sanguinolenta*) in Victoria which he shot at Lakes Entrance.[57] In 1899 Cyril Stafford sold 28 skins, including 'some very rare ones' to Metung shooter Arthur Morduant Hunter who sent them 'home' to English collector Gracie Ulterson.[58] The extent of Stafford's hunting is unclear but it is evident that to meet the demands of collectors and collections throughout the world, rarities were targeted.

Hunting culture in all its manifestations – the gentleman shooter, the sporting tourist, the pot shooter, the professional and the collector – seem to pervade the historical record of human interaction with nature on the Lakes. Was there any man who did not shoot? And could any shooter show restraint? One man not averse to shooting and eating birds, but who was not a hunter, was Foster's work colleague, Bairnsdale's police magistrate, A.W. Howitt. Howitt and Foster were a similar age, both left England in 1852 and worked in positions in the goldfields before their appointments as police magistrates, Foster in Sale in 1865 and Howitt in Bairnsdale in 1866. Both used the court rounds to be out in the field and to indulge their passions for hunting, but Howitt was interested not in shooting but in collecting, a type of collecting that filled notebooks not display cabinets. While his prime interests were geology and the emerging discipline of anthropology, he had more than a passing interest in the biological fields of botany, zoology and entomology.[59] His letters to his family in England display a sensibility to his environment not evident in Foster's diary. In April 1869 while Foster was out shooting 130 ducks, Howitt wrote to his sister describing a recent trip to the Boole Poole Peninsula on the southern shores of the Lakes:

> We rounded some low promontories and turned towards our destination for the night, a place called 'Boul Boul'. It was beautiful to see the gradual changes in effect as night came in – how the distant shore of the lakes seemed to recede as they became dim and the distant mountains drew dense curtains of clouds round their summits and vanished in the grey of the evening. The bay at the end of which lay Boul Boul was covered with waterfowl – and as we pulled along they got up before us in a half circle of countless swans, ducks, coots and in fact all kinds of birds – their wings flapping the water as they rose and echoing against the forest shores like no other sound I ever heard; when Palmer fired a shot the thundering echoes and the din of the fowl was deafening.[60]

Police Officer Palmer, a regular shooting companion with Foster, was there with Howitt. He was more restrained on this trip, shooting just three waterhens, which they roasted for breakfast.

Another group of men hunted with restraints imposed by a different culture and under differing laws. Victoria's Aborigines were exempt from the provisions of the Game Acts, but at Ramahyuck Mission on Lake Wellington hunting rights were regulated by the missionary the Rev. Friedrich Hagenauer, who rewarded well-behaved residents with permission to hunt on Saturdays or to act as beaters for visiting shooters. Visiting shooters were offered some good sport on Ramahyuck's 1500 acres and adjacent morasses on the Avon River and they benefited from Aboriginal skills and local knowledge.[61] Hunting alongside Gippsland's Kŭrnai brought sharp contrasts between the two hunting cultures, not so much in technology and methods but in attitudes. European hunters were surprised at the number of kangaroos on Ramahyuck. Their culture suggested that such abundance should have been reduced by an enthusiastic sporting effort. Instead they learnt that Ramahyuck residents held great respect for kangaroos and were therefore restrained in their hunting.[62]

ESTIMATING AND EXPLAINING CHANGE

What effect did this nineteenth century hunting culture have on bird numbers on the Lakes? Environmental historian Keith Hancock in *Discovering Monaro: A Study of Man's Impact on his Environment* recognised the difficulties of explaining faunal changes. He concluded that 'to explore these swings of population is a task that an ecologist and a historian might profitably tackle in partnership, provided they had a few years to spare'.[63] Such collaborative work has rarely taken place. Scientists who have undertaken historical research have restricted their conclusions to establishing the existence of species rather than explaining population change, and most of this work has been undertaken on the mammalian rather than ornithological record.[64] The latter emphasis might be explained by the greater number of mammal extinctions and by the difficulty of interpreting data on birds because they move greater distances.

Two fundamental problems exist in such historical research: establishing the number and density of species at the time of European settlement and explaining population change, particularly population decline. Scientists have argued the data does not exist and have evaluated change from more recent data, leaving what wildlife researcher H.J. Frith calls 'chapter one' of Australia's wildlife history unwritten. Frith, an ecologist and a contemporary of Hancock, believed that the greatest sin of European settlers was not their exploitative practices but their lack of collecting and documentation. According to Frith, 'it is one of the tragedies of early settlement of New South Wales that people did not record the wildlife ... The first chapter of the story is missing, we only know the second chapter'.[65]

A 'Sportsman's Paradise'

Can this missing chapter be told? Frith was generalising but in some regions, including the Lakes, it can be told. It is possible to at least compile a species list and make general conclusions about densities and changes in the period before major habitat modification occurred.

One of the most overlooked historical sources is the ethnographic record of the Tatungalung people that lived on the Lakes. I deliberately use the word lived on, rather than beside or around the lakes, because their cultural focus was the water and its resources rather than the land or sea. *Bung Yaarnda*, the name for Lake Tyers, encapsulates this emphasis. It contains the word *yaarnda* for water, and the word *bung* for camp or sometimes canoe. It is glossed as 'home on water' but is better expressed as 'water country'. Tatungalung plant and animal food sources came largely from the Lakes and all were named. However, unlike some areas where word lists collected by Europeans are too general, for example with reference to ducks but not duck species, Gippsland's ethnographic record is rich, largely a legacy of the scientific knowledge of A.W. Howitt. His word lists have notes and asides, sometimes even scientific names, which aid the compilation of flora and fauna lists to species level. In the case of the Anatidae family, consisting of swans, geese and ducks, ten species can be identified from the word lists collected between the 1840s and 1880s. The two teal, Chestnut Teal (*Anas castanea*) and Grey Teal (*Anas gibberifrons*), are indistinguishable due to the shortcomings of the collector and the Hardhead (*Aythya australis*) is most likely the bird on Howitt's word list described as 'a duck with a white ring round the eyes'.[66] Therefore thirteen of the nineteen species of Australian waterfowl were present on the largely fresh water lakes and adjacent wetlands of the Gippsland Lakes.

Establishing the status of these species – their numbers, how common they were and if they were residents or migrants – is more difficult. What were their numbers and did they fluctuate during the year or in particular climatic conditions? Such questions may have been answered by Aboriginal ecological knowledge based on observation and cultural tradition, but Europeans appropriated scraps of knowledge that assisted their own hunting, leaving the body of ecological knowledge unrecorded. Establishing the status of species at and after European settlement is left to an analysis of the European record, which scientists assume to be vague and unreliable. However, hidden in a range of historical sources exists sufficient detail to provide some insight into their numbers. The first European record of the Lakes' avifauna is from Angus McMillan who arrived at Lake Victoria in January 1840 and found it 'covered with wild ducks, swans and pelicans'.[67] In 1842 pastoralist W.A. Brodribb reached Lake Wellington where he observed 'thousands of black swans and ducks [which] almost darkened the air'.[68] McMillan and Brodribb, pastoralists in search of grazing country, had some contextual knowledge from their experience in New South Wales and reported significant numbers of waterfowl. In May 1844, Protector of Aborigines, G.A. Robinson visited Eagle Point on Lake King where he observed innumerable 'swans, geese, ducks and other birds are on these lakes'.[69] In November 1846 the deputy leader of the expedition in search of the white woman, James Warman, observed that on Lake Reeve 'all sorts of wildfowl are in the greatest abundance, but as for ducks they are innumerable'.[70] Like McMillan and Brodribb, Robinson and Warman were well-travelled, careful observers and acceptable witnesses. Forty years later scientists Baldwin Spencer and French on a trip through the Lakes could do little better at quantifying the Black Swan on Lake Wellington. They resorted to agricultural terms: 'counted by the acre'.[71] These records suggest that on the four lakes that comprise the Gippsland Lakes, waterfowl existed in greater densities than they do today. Did nineteenth century hunting contribute to declining numbers, or did the status of avifaunal species remain stable until more recent habitat modification?

Australian scientists have stressed habitat loss as the most significant factor in species decline. Even A.J. 'Jock' Marshall in *The Great Extermination: a Guide to Anglo-Australian Cupidity, Wickedness and Waste*, a chronicle of hunting, egg collecting and extinctions, argued 'habitat destruction does the worst damage'.[72] However, there is evidence that suggests hunting had a significant impact. When the Field Naturalists' Club of Victoria was formed in 1880 members displayed growing concern for the destruction of birds and the inadequacy of their protection. Ornithologist A.J. Campbell, whose knowledge came from earlier collecting expeditions, was by 1890 an advocate of protection, raising awareness through his column in the *Australasian* and in the *Victorian Naturalist* and later the ornithological journal *Emu*, of which he was an editor.[73] Unlike the more regulated fishing industry, the records of professional hunting are patchy, but thousands of birds were sold at the markets and many destroyed that never made it to market. In 1938 ornithologist George Mack met one man on the Lakes who, in the 1880s, 'commonly shot as many as eighty pairs of ducks per day for the Melbourne market'.[74] This man alone may have accounted for 15,000 birds per annum. In 1897 Campbell said that restaurants always sold White-eyed Duck (now Hardhead) and that on the Gippsland Lakes they 'are, *or were*, exceedingly numerous'.[75]

One species, the Magpie Goose (*Anseranas semipalmata*), declined to such an extent that it was locally extinct by 1900. It was probably the goose mentioned by Robinson on Lake King in 1844. In the 1850s, surveyor John Pettit wrote to his father in England from the Mitchell River. Listing the available sport, he promised his father: 'I could manage to give you always Kangaroo, Swan, Goose, Turkey, Duck, Quail, Pigeon and Wallaby shooting – or should you prefer it an evening of Wallaby or Wildcat hunting'.[76] The emphasis on 'always' implies that these species were common, but forty years later the Magpie Goose, turkey (Australian Bustard) and one of the native cats were locally extinct. In 1885, *The Argus* correspondent 'Vagabond', reported Sale's Lake Guthridge as a refuge and breeding place for waterfowl including Magpie Geese where they were protected within the municipal boundaries from shooters.[77] However, such a small refuge was not sufficient. In the same year, naturalist and artist, G.J. Broinowski, reported 'great numbers of

A 'Sportsman's Paradise'

Magpie Geese are consumed in Melbourne, where the birds are obtained fresh from Gippsland by railway, and can be bought at the low price of half a crown apiece'. He went on:

> When the Gippsland Lakes and rivers are high and the extensive flats in the vicinity of Sale are submerged, the surface waters are literally covered with Wild Geese and Black Swans ... the destruction of these birds carried on by means of swivel guns, which generally wound twice the number they secure, and by the nets which drown great numbers that are never recovered, besides those which fall to the more legitimate sportsman is simply wholesale.[78]

Further records are patchy and unreliable. In 1887 'geese' were present on Lake Reeve and the last Gippsland record may be that of 'wild geese heard' at Sale in July 1894. However, both records could possibly refer to the Cape Barren Goose.[79] It is considered the Magpie Goose was extinct, not only in Gippsland, but also throughout Victoria by 1911 and south-eastern Australia by the 1920s.[80] Recent analysis indicates that as in Gippsland hunting was a significant factor in the early decline of the species.[81] Magpie Geese are a traditional food supply of the Northern Territory Mak Mak people. They are hunted in the wet season until it is observed that they are no longer feeding on *Eleocharis dulcis* (spike rush) bulbs. This is a sign that the birds are under stress and hunting stops.[82] Gippsland does not have an equivalent wet and dry season, but similar signs may have existed, particularly in dry years, but went unnoticed by Europeans intent on uncontrolled harvesting to meet market demands.

It is certain that hunters were ignorant of the ecology of their target species. They knew little about bird migration and breeding habits. Hunters were unfamiliar with the nomadic habits of Australian waterfowl and quail, and their ability to respond to irregular climatic prompts instead of predictable seasons. With few localised and sedentary species, hunters had minimal ability to ascertain any changes at the local level because nomadic populations replenished or replaced birds that were shot. Such factors misled hunters into a sense of complacency and clouded the historic record.

Such ignorance is best exemplified in W.H. Foster's favourite target, Latham's Snipe. Hunters knew snipe appeared in August and departed in March but speculated as to where they spent the winter and where they bred. Wheelwright had heard 'that they breed on the high ranges at the head of the Yarra'.[83] Not until the 1890s did ornithologists establish they breed in Japan and then migrate to the wetlands of eastern Australia for the Australian summer.[84] As late as 1946 ornithologist Neville Cayley wrote 'little is known of its habits while in Australia'.[85] A real understanding of the snipe's migratory habits was finally gained when Elliott McClure surveyed and banded migrating birds along 'the East Asian flyway' between 1963 and 1971.[86] Near Melbourne, snipe were hunted to such an extent that Wheelwright declared 'no bird has been driven from this district more than the snipe, and to get a good day's shooting a man must now go a long way afield'.[87] Increasingly Sale became the destination for those shooters who believed it provided 'the best snipe shooting in the colonies'.[88] In the 1980s the wetlands of the Latrobe River were still regarded as suitable habitat where snipe might be found in 'large numbers': defined as 100 birds recorded in a day on a single wetland.[89] The significance of Foster's data becomes apparent, when he recorded shooting that number in one day. Shooters in Gippsland may have made a significant impact by the 1880s. Foster's contemporaries, Elizabeth Montgomery and Police Officer Sadlier, suggest hunting had some impact on bird numbers. In 1913 Sadlier claimed 'the sport as it existed in Gippsland in those days has ceased for ever;' and Foster's sister-in-law, Elizabeth Montgomery, observed in 1916 'nothing like the bags [of teal, duck and pigeon] are to be had now'.[90]

In 1973, North American zoologist, Ian McTaggart Cowan, using Australian research data, argued that over-exploitation of waterfowl had contributed to their declining numbers to a greater extent than previously accepted by Australian scientists.[91] The degree of wetland modification on the Gippsland Lakes is significant. In 1980 scientists Corrick and Norman estimated since European settlement seven per cent of wetlands in the Snowy River and Gippsland Lakes catchment had been eliminated and a further 29 per cent greatly modified by drainage and flood control works.[92] However, the effects of significant habitat changes such as the permanent opening of the entrance to the Lakes, drainage of the morasses, river modification, dam construction, and salinity and pollution of wetlands were largely felt in the twentieth century. The 'first chapter' in the story of species decline is set in the nineteenth century. Despite a depleted scientific record, the first chapter is not missing. It can be written from ethnographic and other historical sources. It shows the Lakes held an abundance of birds, that a hunting culture elevated those species reminiscent of old world species to a position at the top of the hunting taxonomy, and that position placed them under considerable pressure in the period before major habitat modification.

NOTES

[1] John M. MacKenzie, *The Empire of Nature: Hunting, Conservation and British Imperialism* (Manchester: Manchester University Press, 1988).

[2] See for example: I. McAllan, 'The Legacy of Hunting', *Wingspan* 17,1 (2007): 34–9.

[3] *Gippsland Mercury*, 23 April 1878.

[4] 'Vagabond', *The Argus*, 26 December 1886.

[5] H.W. Wheelwright, *Bush Wanderings of a Naturalist; or Notes on the Field Sports and Fauna of Australia Felix* (London: Routledge, Warne and Routledge, 1861), 185.

[6] A.W. Howitt to his father. Quoted in Mary Howitt Walker, *Come Wind, Come Weather: a Biography of Alfred Howitt* (Melbourne: Melbourne University Press, 1971), 76–7.

[7] P. Olsen, 'A Penchant for Parrot', *National Library News* 16,9 (2006): 7–9. See also Bruce Boehrer, who argues that in Europe, despite a source of plentiful supply of par-

rots from the Americas, parrots were regarded as 'pets and as zoological marvels and annoyances, but seldom as dinner'. B. Boehrer, 'The Parrot Eaters: Psittacophagy in the Renaissance and Beyond', *Gastronimca* 4,3 (2004): 46–59, doi: 10.1525/gfc.2004.4.3.46.

[8] Gracius J. Broinowski, *Birds of Australia* (Melbourne: Charles Stuart, 1890–91); Gracius J. Broinowski, *Birds and Mammals of Australia* (Sydney: Murray, 1885).

[9] J. D'Ewes, *Sporting in Both Hemispheres* (London: Routledge and Co., 1858), 323.

[10] Wheelwright, *Bush Wanderings of a Naturalist*, xi–xii.

[11] J.M. Powell, 'Conservation and Resource Management in Australia 1788–1860', in *Australian Space and Time: Geographical Perspectives*, ed. J.M. Powell and M. Williams (Melbourne: Oxford University Press, 1975), 18–60.

[12] *Gippsland Times*, 28 May 1879.

[13] Dorothy La Trobe Leopold, *With a Letter to Mr La Trobe: Life of W. H. Foster, 1852–1894* (Melbourne: Dorothy Leopold, 1988).

[14] Peter Hawker (1786–1853) published his *Instructions to Young Sportsmen* in 1830 and it was revised a number of times. See also Peter Hawker, *The Diary of Colonel Peter Hawker* (Richmond: Publishing Co., 1971).

[15] W.H. Foster, Diaries 1862–1870, Royal Historical Society of Victoria, MS 000980 (hereafter Foster Diary). Foster's diaries for the years 1871–1878 remain in a private collection and have not been consulted.

[16] Latham's Snipe is also known as Japanese Snipe, Common Snipe, Jack Snipe, Bleater, Longbill. Its Kŭrnai name is Klik.

[17] Wheelwright, *Bush Wanderings*, 96–100; Broinowski, *Birds of Australia*, Vol. 2.

[18] See Graham Pizzey, *A Field Guide to the Birds of Australia* (Sydney: Collins, 1980), 126.

[19] In 1865–6 Foster and his companions shot 511 snipe (401 by Foster). In 1866–7, 783 (420 by Foster). 1867–8 and 1868–9 were poor seasons, followed by 1869–70 when 683 snipe were shot (385 by Foster).

[20] Foster, Diary, 2 November 1867.

[21] Leslie and Cowie, *The Wind Still Blows*, 101–2.

[22] Wheelwright, *Bush Wanderings*, 103.

[23] Stubble Quail is also known as Grey Quail. The Brown Quail is also known as Swamp Quail, Silver Quail and Partridge Quail.

[24] A. J. Campbell, *Australasian*, 14 March 1896.

[25] John Sadlier, *Recollections of a Victorian Police Officer* (Melbourne: George Robertson, 1913), 141–2.

[26] MacKenzie, *Empire of Nature*, 19.

[27] Jonathon Garnier Ruffer, *The Big Shots: Edwardian Shooting Parties* (London: Debrett's Peerage, 1984). MacKenzie, *Empire of Nature*, 19–21, discusses the creation of private estates as reserves.

[28] This view has been challenged. See Tim Bonyhady, *The Colonial Earth*, (Melbourne: Melbourne University Press, 2000).

[29] P. Olsen, 'A Penchant for Parrot',

[30] Leopold, *With a Letter to Mr. La Trobe*,

[31] *Gippsland Mercury*, 17 December 1878; *Table Talk*, 30 September 1892, 15; Marguerite Hancock, *Colonial Consorts: The Wives of Victoria's Governors 1839–1900* (Melbourne: Melbourne University Press, 2001), 212.

[32] *The Australasian*, 18 May 1901; *Gippsland Times*, 16 May 1901, 10 June 1901; 'Quails in Victoria', *Emu* 12 (1913). 202–3; A.J. Campbell, 'The Protection of Native Birds', *Emu* 2 (1903): 187–94; J.R. Kinghorn, 'Economic Value of the Stubble Quail', *Emu* 25 (1926): 112–19.

[33] *Gippsland Times*, 10 February 1890.

[34] *Gippsland Times*, 7 February 1887.

[35] *Gippsland Times*, 10 May 1865.

[36] Victorian Parliamentary Debates, 1862, 876.

[37] *Gippsland Times*, 28 December 1877.

[38] 'Tanjil', *Our Trip to Gippsland Lakes and Rivers* (Melbourne: M.L. Hutchinson, 1882), 38.

[39] *Gippsland Times*, 5 October 1881.

[40] Frank Keating, 'Way Back When', *The Guardian (London)*, 22 December 1997, 6.

[41] C. McGuiness, *Gippsland Memories* (Moe: Star Newspaper, 1948[?]). 11.

[42] *Gippsland Times*, 24 April 1866, 2 December 1881.

[43] *Gippsland Mercury*, 24 April 1879; *Gippsland Times*, 9 June 1879, 2 June 1880.

[44] *Gippsland Times*, 29 July 1891.

[45] Victorian Parliamentary Debates 1861-2, 231–2 and .415–18. For discussion of Victoria's game laws see M.C. Downes, 'Early Wildlife Legislation in Victoria', *Fur, Feathers and Fins* 50 (May 1962): 13–18; A. Dunbavin Butcher, 'Attitudes to Wildlife', *Victoria's Resources* 5, no. 1 (March–May 1963): 2–3; F.I. Norman and A.D. Young, 'Short-sighted and Doubly Short-sighted are They: A Brief Examination of the Game Laws of Victoria, 1858–1958', *Journal of Australian Studies* 7 (November 1980): 3–24.

[46] Victorian Parliamentary Debates 1884, 2220-24.

[47] *Australasian*, 16 October 1897.

[48] *Gippsland Mercury*, 2 December 1890.

[49] Donald Macdonald, 'The Wild-Fowlers', in Donald Macdonald, *The Brooks of Morning: Nature and Reflective Essays* (Sydney: Angus and Robertson, 1933), 108–13.

[50] Macdonald, 'The Wild-Fowlers', 109.

[51] From 1893 to 1900 A.J. Campbell wrote 'Some Australian Birds', a column for *The Australasian*. His notes on collecting and correspondence with readers were used in A.J. Campbell, *Nests and Eggs of Australian Birds: Including the Geographical Distribution of the Species and Popular Observations Thereon* (Sheffield: A.J. Campbell, 1900).

[52] Macdonald, 'The Wild-Fowlers', 108; see for example A.J. Campbell, 'The Protection of Our Native Birds', *Victorian Naturalist* 1 (1885): 161–6; A.J. Campbell, 'The Protection of Native Birds', *Emu* 2 (1903): 187–94.

[53] Tom Griffiths, *Hunters and Collectors: The Antiquarian Imagination in Australia* (Melbourne: Cambridge University Press, 1996), 12–21; Tom Griffiths, *Forests of Ash: An Environmental History* (Cambridge: Cambridge University Press, 2001), 102–14.

[54] Peter Synan, *Three Cheers for the Commonwealth of Australia: George Henry Wise – Federationist* (Bairnsdale: Kapana Press, 2001), 27.

[55] Wheelwright wrote of 'his mate' but did not name him. H.M. Whittell identified Stafford as 'the mate' who camped at Mordialloc with Wheelwright from 1853 to 1858. See H.M. Whittell, *The Literature of Australian Birds: A History and a Bibliography of Australian Ornithology* (Perth: Paterson Brokensha, 1954).

A 'Sportsman's Paradise'

[56] Gay Halstead, *Whispers Over Wildwood, 1066–2003* (Metung: Nungurner Press, 2003), 35.

[57] Whittell, *The Literature of Australian Birds;* Campbell, *Nests and Eggs of Australian Birds,* 353.

[58] Arthur Morduant Hunter, Diary 10 May 1899; see also a similar entry on 24 April 1895 when Hunter sent parrot skins to Ulterson. Royal Historical Society of Victoria, MS 000888.

[59] Howitt's scientific endeavours and the connections between his geology and anthropology is discussed by Ian Keen, 'The Anthropologist as Geologist: Howitt in Colonial Gippsland', *The Australian Journal of Anthropology* 11,1 (2000): 78–97.

[60] W. H. Foster, Diary, 20 April 1869; A.W. Howitt to Anna Mary Watts, 18 April 1869. Howitt Papers, State Library of Victoria, Box 1046/3b (9).

[61] Aborigines were exempt under Clause 13 of *An Act to Protect Game, 1867*; Ramahyuck Visitors Book, 18 February 1882, 27 July 1895; 'Vagabond', *Argus,* 2 January 1886; Franz Barfus, 'A Visit to the Mission Station Ramahyuck, at Lake Wellington, Gippsland (Victoria), [1881]' Monash University Churchill, Centre for Gippsland Studies Collection, 3063.

[62] *Gippsland Times,* 19 January 1891.

[63] Keith Hancock, *Discovering Monaro: A Study of Man's Impact on his Environment* (Cambridge: Cambridge University Press, 1972), 65.

[64] For the collaborative work on Gippsland see the 1970s research undertaken by the Arthur Rylah Institute. For example: K.C. Norris et al., *Vertebrate Fauna of the Gippsland Lakes Catchment Victoria,* Occasional Paper Series No. 1. (Melbourne: Ministry for Conservation. Fisheries and Wildlife Division, June 1983); A.H. Corrick and F.I. Norman, 'Wetlands and Waterbirds of the Snowy River and Gippsland Lakes Catchment', *Proceedings. Royal Society of Victoria* 91 part 1 (1980): 1–15; I.M. Mansergh et al., 'An Annotated Bibliography of the Avifauna of the Gippsland Lakes Catchment and Hinterland', *Memoirs of the National Museum of Victoria* 40 (1979): 201–28. For examples of mammalian research, see Daniel Lunney and Tanya Leary, 'The Impact on Native Mammals of Land-Use Changes and Exotic Species in the Bega District, New South Wales, Since Settlement', *Australian Journal of Ecology* 13 (1988): 67–92, doi: 10.1111/j.1442-9993.1988.tb01417.x; J.H. Seebeck, 'Terrestrial Mammals in Victoria: A History of Discovery', *Proceedings. Royal Society of Victoria* 107, no. 1 (1995): 11–23.

[65] H.J. Frith, Evidence to the Commonwealth Parliament. House of Representatives Select Committee on Wildlife Conservation, 1 September 1970. Unpublished typescript, Commonwealth Parliamentary Library. See also similar views in H. J. Frith, *Wildlife Conservation* (Sydney: Angus and Robertson, 1973).

[66] I.M. Mansergh and L.A. Hercus, 'An Aboriginal Vocabulary of the Fauna of Gippsland', *Memoirs of the National Museum of Victoria* 42 (1981): 107–22; see also Howitt Papers, Australian Institute of Aboriginal and Torres Strait Islander Studies Library.

[67] McMillan in *Letters from Victorian Pioneers,* ed. Thomas Francis Bride (Melbourne: Currey O'Neil, 1983), 205.

[68] W.A. Brodribb, *Recollections of an Australian Squatter 1835–1883* (Sydney: John Ferguson, 1978), 40.

[69] G. A. Robinson, Journal, 24 May 1844. Mitchell Library, A 7040.

[70] Warman, Diary, 8 November 1846, *Port Phillip Herald,* 23 February 1847.

[71] Baldwin Spencer and C. French, 'Trip to Croajingolong', *Victorian Naturalist* 6, (1889): 1–38.

[72] A.J. Marshall, *The Great Extermination: A Guide to Anglo-Australian Cupidity, Wickedness and Waste* (London: Panther, 1968), 44.

[73] A.J. Campbell, *Oology of Australian Birds* (Melbourne: Campbell, 1883).

[74] George Mack, 'Cormorants and the Gippsland Lakes Fishing Industry', *Memoirs of the National Museum Victoria* 12 (1941): 95–117.

[75] *The Australasian*, 20 November 1897.

[76] John Pettit, letter to his father from camp on the Mitchell and Macarthur River, [No date, ca 1857]. Mitchell Library MS B 1418.

[77] *The Argus*, 15 December 1885.

[78] Broinowski, *Birds and Mammals of Australia,* no pagination.

[79] *Gippsland Times*, 7 February 1887; *Gippsland Mercury*, 13 July 1894.

[80] H.J. Frith, W*aterfowl in Australia* (Sydney: A.H. and A.W. Reed, 1977), 44–63; E.R. Nye, C.R. Dickman and R.T. Kingsford, 'A Wild Goose Chase: Temporal and Spatial Variation in the Distribution of the Magpie Goose (*Anseranus semipalmata*) in Australia', *Emu* 107 (2007): 28–37, doi: 10.1071/MU05012.

[81] Nye et al., 'A Wild Goose Chase'

[82] Deborah Bird Rose, *Country of the Heart: An Indigenous Australian Homeland* (Canberra: AIATSIS, 2002), 88.

[83] Wheelwright, *Bush Wanderings*, .98.

[84] A.J. Campbell *The Australasian*, 29 July 1893. See also A.J. Campbell, *Nests and Eggs of Australian Birds: Including the Geographical Distribution of the Species and Popular Observations Thereon* (Sheffield: A.J. Campbell, 1900), 823.

[85] Neville Cayley, *What Bird is That? A Guide to the Birds of Australia* 11th edn (Sydney: Angus and Robertson, 1946).

[86] See: Libby Robin, *The Flight of the Emu: A Hundred Years of Australian Ornithology 1901–2001* (Melbourne: Melbourne University Press, 2001), 246–7.

[87] Wheelwright, *Bush Wanderings,* 100.

[88] *Gippsland Times*, 23 January 1875; *The Argus*, 26 December 1885.

[89] Brett A. Lane, *Shorebirds in Australia* (Melbourne: Thomas Nelson, 1987), 110–11; M. Blakers, S.J.J.F. Davies and P.N. Reilly, *The Atlas of Australian Birds* (Melbourne: Melbourne University Press, 1984).

[90] Sadlier, *Recollections of a Victorian Police Officer,* 142; Leslie and Cowie, *The Wind Still Blows,* 101; *The Australasian*, 20 November 1897.

[91] Ian McTaggart Cowan, *The Conservation of Australian Waterfowl* (Canberra: Australian Government Publishing Service, 1973).

[92] A.H. Corrick and F.I. Norman, 'Wetlands and Waterbirds of the Snowy River and Gippsland Lakes Catchment', *Proceedings of the Royal Society of Victoria* 91, part 1 (1980): 1–15.

Environmental History of Marine Mammal Exploitation in Trinidad and Tobago, W.I., and its Ecological Impact

Aldemaro Romero[1], Ruth Baker, Joel E. Creswell, Anuradha Singh, Annabelle Mckie and Michael Manna

INTRODUCTION

In order to better understand ecological modifications at large temporal scales we need to apply a historical perspective.[2] That means that increasingly we have to use palaeoecological, archaeological and historical data in order to extend ecological records back long enough to understand changes on natural resources through time.[3] This approach has already been successfully employed for reconstructing the pre-Columbian conditions of coastal ecosystems for the northern Caribbean[4] and for specific resources such as pearl-oyster beds along the northern coasts of South America.[5] Also, the incorporation of environmental background when interpreting history is becoming more commonplace.[6]

The arrival of Europeans on the American continent offers a good opportunity to analyse neoextinctions. Post-Columbian extinctions are not only more recent in time but also much better documented from a historical perspective, providing us with the opportunity to understand the interplay of social and ecological factors. For example, the history of marine mammal (cetaceans, seals, and manatees) exploitation for many parts of the Caribbean is poorly known. West Indian manatee (*Trichecus manatus manatus*) exploitation has taken place since pre-Columbian times and most populations have been extirpated by now.[7] Organised commercial whaling and dolphin fisheries have existed in the southern and eastern Caribbean for at least two centuries.[8] From a recent review of published literature on marine mammals for the Caribbean,[9] it can be concluded that the islands of Trinidad and Tobago are probably among the least known for their marine mammal diversity and utilisation in that part of the world. Despite the fact that a number of whaling operations took place during the nineteenth century, the information is scant, especially when dealing with the exploitation of small species of marine mammals. Further, in recent years, an increasing number of Caribbean countries have joined the International Whaling Commission and have stated their intention to resume whaling and/or support the return to commercial whaling by other nations.[10] Thus, more comprehensive and up-to-date information is needed regarding marine mammals utilisation for this area.

Aldemaro Romero et al.

The aim of this article is to document the past and present of both the exploitation practices and the conservation status of marine mammals in Trinidad and Tobago. This is part of a long-term study on the distribution and conservation status of cetaceans in the Caribbean. Studies for Venezuela and Grenada have been completed and published.[11] Here we provide all available historical records of marine mammal utilisation for Trinidad and Tobago and then analyse this information within its own historical context.

METHODS

This paper is largely based on field and archival studies carried out between the 8 and 20 January 2000 and 12 and 24 March 2001. We explored all known land-based whaling sites, all of them located in the north-western area ('Bocas')

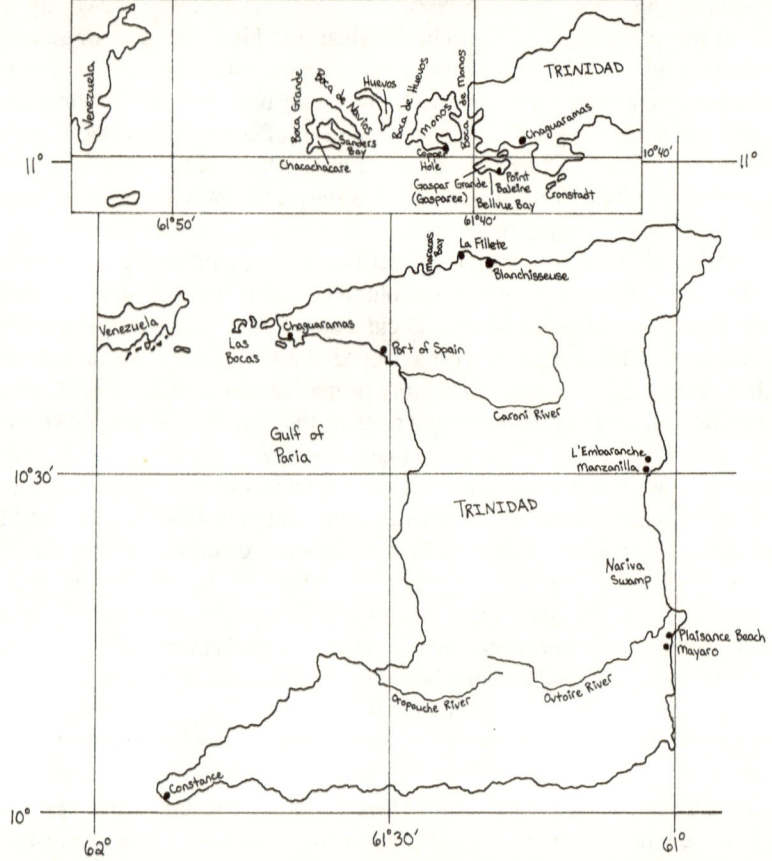

FIGURE 1. Map of Trinidad, including the localities mentioned in the text.

Marine Mammal Exploitation

of Trinidad (Figure 1), where we examined all possible remains of whaling operations. Any indication of whaling activity in the area was photographed and/or videotaped. We also visited the National Library, National Archives, the National Museum at Port-of-Spain, the West Indiana Library Collection at the University of the West Indies in St. Augustine, the Biology Seminar Library of the same university, the Library of the Institute of Marine Affairs, and the archives of the Wildlife Division and the Fisheries Division. There, we examined every available publication, record or remain related to marine mammals. All pertinent documentation was photocopied, scanned and electronically stored, photographed, and/or video taped.

We also visited the following fishing towns: Maracas Bay, La Filette, and Blanchisseuse (in Trinidad) and Castara Bay, Speyside, and Charlottesville (in Tobago) (Figures 1 and 2). We interviewed the fishers from those localities about past and present marine mammal utilisation.[12] We visited the Nariva Swamp where has been reported the last remaining population of manatees for Trinidad.[13] Toponyms were used based on official Trinidadian maps: Directorate of Overseas Surveys for the Government of Trinidad and Tobago Sheets 4, 11, 12, 36, 46, at a scale 1:25,000.

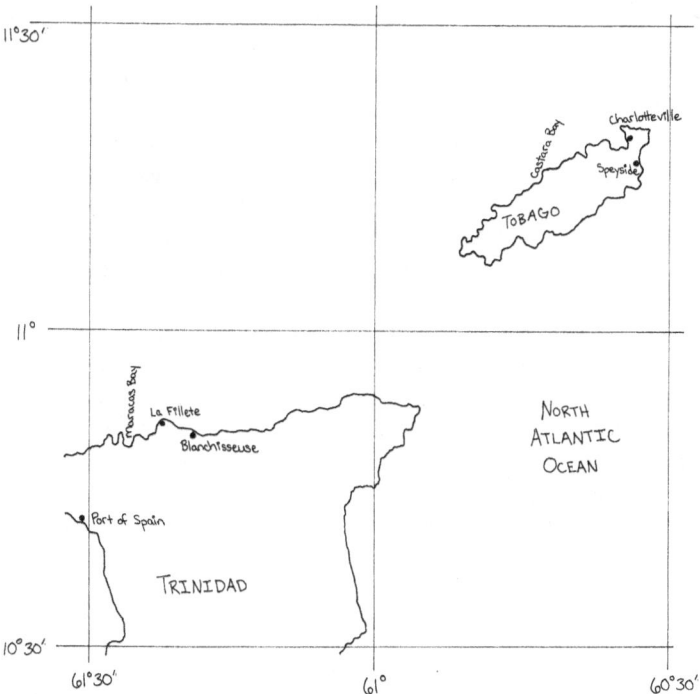

FIGURE 2. Map of Tobago, including the localities mentioned in the text.

RESULTS AND DISCUSSION

Historical Account
Pre-Columbian Era

There is only one piece of evidence of possible utilisation of cetaceans by pre-Columbian inhabitants of Trinidad: remains of an unidentified cetacean from St. Joseph (the first Spanish capital of Trinidad) on a branch of the Caroni river on the south side of the North Range.[14] There is no indication on the type of capture.

Land-Based Commercial Whaling

European knowledge about cetaceans in the waters of Trinidad and Tobago is presumed to have begun with Christopher Columbus naming the Gulf of Paria as 'Golfo de la Ballena' (Whale's Gulf), although from reading his diary it is not clear whether or not he saw whales in those waters.[15]

Equally unclear is when commercial whaling began in the area. According to a display at the National Museum at Port-of-Spain, 'Whaling was one of the earliest industries of Trinidad. A whaling station existed at Bulmera Bay, Chaguaramas in 1775. The whales were sighted at Bob Rocks, which was named after the female slave, Bolo, a whale watcher who gave the signal of a sighting by blowing a conch shell.' This reference does not seem reliable for a number of reasons. First, in 1775 Trinidad was still under Spanish rule and there is no historical record of the Spaniards ever been involved in whaling in the American continent other than through Basque whaling along the eastern coasts of North America. Second, we examined a map of Chaguaramas dated 1792[16] deposited at the U.S. Library of Congress and could not find any indication of a whaling station in that locality. Third, we could not find the author or the source of this display. Finally, none of the sources consulted for this paper mentioned in any way such an operation.[17]

Commercial whaling most likely began around 1826. In that year, C.A. White, a retired sea Captain from Bermuda, bought 17 *quarrees* (55 acres) of land on the flat westernmost tip of Gasparee (Gaspar Grande), from a Trinidadian, Mr. de Percin. This land later came to be known as Pointe Baleine (Whale Point) and in May 1827, White petitioned the Cabildo (Port-of-Spain Council) for permission to open a subscription list to establish a whaling industry.[18] The Cabildo granted his request, since they felt it would not interfere with their sale of coconut oil from Manzanilla on eastern Trinidad; the 2,400 gallons they produced each year could not satisfy local demand for lamp oil. White appointed Charles Hugon as his sales agent.[19] A 15 March 1826 article describes the first whaling operation as follows:

> Sometime ago we noticed the introduction of the Whale Fishery in this Gulph;[20] and we have much pleasure in stating that the commencement of the undertaking

Marine Mammal Exploitation

affords every prospect of success and profit to the enterprising speculators. In the beginning of last week the arrangements were completed, boiling houses & c. having been erected of the west end of the Island of Gasparee: and the sloop Mary & Lucy Ann and two whale boats commenced the fishing on Thursday last, and in a short time two large whales were struck but owing to delay on the part of the boats, both made their escape. On the same day, however, a small one was struck and taken; and on Monday morning the boats took two large whales to the works. On Saturday and Sunday a number of residents of Port-of-Spain visited the works, which with the rest of the apparatus, we are informed are very complete.[21]

Shortly after this notice, local newspapers published a series of advertisements for 'Whale oil the produce of the Trinidad Whale Fishery' for sale as well as 'Spermaceti candles'.[22] To accommodate these activities, a ferry service was introduced in the late 1820s, with the S.S. Woodford facilitating movement of produce and people between the islands and the mainland.[23] In 1830 between 14 and 15 whales were killed using one boat and Trinidadian whale oil was priced at half the international market price[24] while importation of whale oil dropped sharply by that year. Most oil was used for burning in lamps and (mixed with honey) as flu remedy. Although most oil was locally consumed, some was exported (mostly to British colonies) and whalebone was also sent to London.[25] All land-based whaling took place in the island of Trinidad and there is no indication that such operations ever took place in Tobago.

These operations must have required extensive local investment, given that from the beginning we find the names of upper-class Trinidadian families involved in this business. By the 1830s, the whole whaling industry had expanded into four stations: two on the north coast of Gasparee Island or Gaspar Grande (10°40'00" N, 61°39'55" W), one being at Point Baleine, mentioned earlier, owned and managed by White and the other presumably at the present Belle Vue Bay owned by the Tardieu family.[26] The third was located at Copperhole (or Jenny Point) at Monos Islands (10°40'30" N, 61°41'00" W) owned and managed by the Gerold family,[27] and a fourth was established at Chacachacare Island (probably in what is today Sanders Bay at 10°40'15" N, 61°45'00" W), operated by members of the Gerold family and Friederich Urich who had formed a partnership in 1834,[28] but originally established by the Carige family.[29] All of these were merchant and planter families. The Urichs had been involved in the coconut oil production and sales; therefore, they saw in the whale oil a way to expand their business.[30] The development of commercial whale fisheries in Trinidad coincided with bad economic times for the island and with a decline in the local population between 1827 and 1833.[31]

The whale hunting method was very primitive, as were the whaling stations.[32] They used 'pirougues' (wooden skiffs made of a hard, heavy wood, locally known as balata or poui, *Tabebuia* spp.) led by a captain at the stern, six stalwart oarsmen, and a harpooner in the bow. These boats were at the Bay, and when a whale was sighted a horn would be blown, signalling the crew, who all lived at the Bay, to run down the hill to man the boats, and push them off. When a cow was spotted with its calf, the whaler aimed at wounding the calf with the least possible injury in order to ensure that the mother could be easily approached and harpooned. A flag was stuck in the whale, the mouth was sewn up so it would not take in water and sink, and it was towed into the station. Local personnel worked for up to 24 hours at a time flensing the animal, as near to the shore as possible, and the slices of blubber were carried to the sugar coppers, for boiling to extract the oil. During this period, numerous sharks showed up to take bites out of the remains of the whales. Apparently they were so numerous that the whaling company had to employ men to kill them with harpoons and hatchets. The whaling season was between January and May. Between 1830 and 1862, the number of whales caught annually was between 20 and 35, the oil (about 20,000 gallons on average) was taken to Port of Spain, for export or local use as lamp oil or medicine-whale oil, and the meat was locally consumed.[33]

These whaling techniques may have been introduced by 'Old Abraham' a Bermudan whaler.[34] In 1834, the Gerolds brought a professional harpooner from Germany and that same year asked the Governor Sir George Hill to refuse authorisation for the American Schooner *Harmony*, out of Nantucket, to whale in the Gulf.[35]

Kenny and Bacon (1981) say that the species exploited was 'pilot whales, *Globicephala*, although occasional sperm whales were taken', yet, the description of the whales in the contemporary records as well as the name used to identify them at that time[36] lead us to believe that they were humpback whales, *Megaptera novaeangliae*. This is consistent with the fact that the whaling season coincided with the migration season of humpback whales into those waters. Further, pilot whales are not as productive in terms of blubber as humpbacks are.

Whaling operations continued until at least 1865 although there is some mention of operations as late as the 1870s.[37] We and others[38] have checked contemporary documents but have failed to find any evidence of commercial whaling after 1865. From the 1870s, on, there was an overproduction of whale oil which, together with kerosene being used for lamps fuel, brought prices down.[39] Even if the local whale population had survived, its hunting would probably not have been commercially feasible.

Today there is little left of these whaling operations. We found and videotaped three coppers and one container submerged just a few metres from the former Copperhole station, which had been thrown there when the station was converted into a Sea Scouts facility.[40]

Yankee Whaling

Activities by Yankee whaling ships for Trinidad and Tobago have been summarised elsewhere.[41] All indications are that there was never much interaction between Yankee and land-based whalers. Yankee whaling in the area did not

Marine Mammal Exploitation

start until the 1830s, when their Trinidadian counterparts were already fully engaged in whale hunting. If anything, Yankee whaling may have furthered the whale population decline.

Current Utilisation

Whaling is no longer practised in the waters of Trinidad and Tobago. Baleen whales no longer frequent Trinidadian waters and are only seen in very small numbers around Tobago. We hypothesise that humpback whales have become extinct in the waters of Trinidad, particularly in the Gulf of Paria. This conclusion is supported by a number of facts: 1) With the exception of a possible, but unconfirmed, 1922 record[42] of what appears to be a humpback whale (*M. novaeangliae*) which, according to the caption, was washed up on the beach, there are no records of humpbacks or any large whale for the Gulf of Paria in the twentieth century; 2) our extensive interviews with local fishers revealed that none of them have ever seen or heard of any large whale being seen in the Gulf of Paria; 3) a visual and acoustic survey in March 2000 in the Gulf of Paria failed to produce any record of any large whale in that area.[43]

Based on the evidence presented in this paper and elsewhere,[44] there is little question that humpbacks were very common in the Gulf of Paria during the nineteenth century. We also know that until 1926 they were common in the neighbouring island of Grenada.[45] Therefore, it is worthwhile to speculate on the possible causes for their local extinction. A common hypothesis we have heard and read is that their local extinction was prompted by pollution.[46] However, such disturbances are relatively new (post Second World War) and do not explain why they have not been seen since late last century.

The data presented in this paper is consistent with our hypothesis that these whales were driven into local extinction by the whaling operations described in this paper. Similar exploitation patterns were also responsible for the extinction of local populations of the same species in Grenada.[47] Figure 3 shows the levels of whale captures. Despite the lack of information for some years, confirmed reports point to at least 500 whales being killed between 1826 and 1865. To that we need to add catches by Yankee whalers. In the neighbouring island of Grenada in 1925 and 1926, 102 and 72 humpbacks were taken respectively and that drove the local population to almost complete extinction, to the point that they are now very rare in those waters.[48] Therefore, the number of 500+ catches over a 40-year period is not an unreasonable foundation supporting our premises. Because of this lack of whales, whale-watching in the waters of Trinidad and Tobago is not a very likely activity.

Although official documents that we had the opportunity to review at the Wildlife Section casually mention that 'all cetaceans (are to be considered) endangered', the fact of the matter is that they lack legal protection under either the Fisheries Act (1980) or Conservation Wildlife Act (1980). Japan has requested

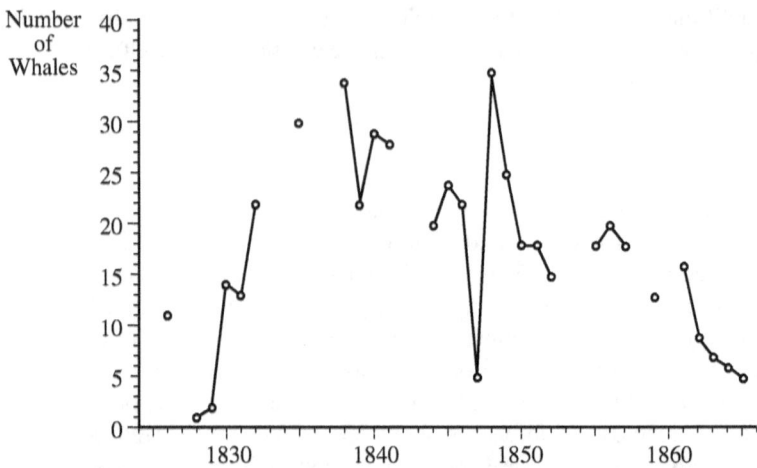

FIGURE 3. Confirmed whale catches for Trinidad based on Reeves et al. 2001. The solid line represents variations among consecutive years.

the government of Trinidad and Tobago to join the IWC and to oppose the ban on commercial whaling.[49] To date, the Trinidadian government has done neither.

Dolphin Fisheries

Dolphin fisheries have always been rare in Trinidad and Tobago waters. Reports of these activities are scant and most are related to accidental nettings. Earlier reports are from the beginning of this century[50] and they relate to some occasional harpooning of 'porpoises'. There are also some more recent reports of 'porpoises' being occasionally harpooned in Tobago.[51] Our interviews with the local fishers have convinced us that active dolphin fisheries do not take place and have not taken place for many decades in Trinidad and Tobago in any significant way. The only place in which fishers were not totally forthcoming to us was in Charlottesville, Tobago, probably due to bad publicity regarding an incidental netting in the past.[52]

In general, dolphin fisheries in Trinidad and Tobago consist of incidental takings. Most animals that are captured are caught in Italian seines and sometimes in gill nets, at various locations. They are usually *Stenella* spp. and *Tursiops truncatus*. When captured, they are usually sold in the wholesale market, and may be seen occasionally offered on the roadsides on the north coast.[53] They are sometimes labelled as 'shark' and sold as such but they are easy to distinguish from the latter because of their dark red, fatty and chewy meat. The dolphins are already dead when the nets are retrieved, but if still alive, they are killed.[54] The largest animal ever taken in this way was an orca, *Orcinus orca*. That took

Marine Mammal Exploitation

place on 10 July 1987. It was a 4.5 m female landed at the small boats jetty at Chaguaramas. The fisher reported that the whale had become entangled in his drift gill net as it was being hauled in. At the time he was out in the Gulf of Paria between Cronstadt and Gaspar Grande islands, in six-seven metres of water. The animal was a member of a pod numbering about 15.[55]

On 16 October 1989, a local inhabitant of Mayaro, on the east coast of Trinidad, reported to the authorities that nine days earlier a '15 foot long dark brown whale came up in semi-drowned condition with harpoon hole about 4 feet from head. It came up at Plaisance Beach and was helpless. The villagers cut it up and utilised the meat and oil. It was apparently harpooned offshore'.[56]

Another noted incident of opportunistic use of cetaceans took place on 1 May 1987, when a pod of 15 adults and two calves of short-finned pilot whales (*Globicephala macrorhynchus*) stranded at La Filette on the North Coast. All were returned to the sea except the two calves and one adult. The dead animals were taken to a fish market for sale. On 23 January 1987, an unidentified 'whale' (probably a pilot) was slaughtered by fishers and towed inland to Chaguaramas and its meat was placed on sale in the area. These reports exemplify the paucity and utilisation of marine mammals off the coasts of Trinidad.

Finally, we learned of a 'Dolphin Watch' operation at Charlottesville, Tobago. The owner of the boat told us that he had been doing it for three years taking people out to see what he identifies as bottlenose dolphins (*T. truncatus*). We could not ascertain the success of this operation which seems to be based on occasional presence of these animals in those waters.

Manatee Exploitation

Archaeological remains indicate that the West Indian manatee, *Trichechus manatus manatus*, was distributed along the Lesser Antilles and that they were used by the indigenous people inhabiting those islands.[57] Historical accounts also support the contention that manatees were hunted, using harpoons, by the local inhabitants of that and neighbouring islands up to Colonial times.[58]

There are numerous reports of manatees being harpooned for their meat, oil, and hide from Colonial times until relatively recently[59] (Figures 4 and 5). Today the only remaining area with manatees in Trinidad is the Nariva Swamp; a 1997 survey revealed the presence of at least 18 individuals.[60] This number is down from an estimation of 25–30 made in 1991.[61] Records have also been made of unconfirmed reports by other fishermen from other east coast rivers, the Ortoire, south of the Nariva Swamp, and through the north, the North Oropouche River.[62] In 1990 a manatee sighted at the L'Embaranche River was accidentally caught in a fishing net and butchered.[63]

The manatee in Trinidad and Tobago is offered protection directly under the Conservation of Wildlife Act, Chapter 61:01. Under the provisions of this act, the manatee is considered a 'protected animal' and thus cannot be hunted at any

FIGURE 4. Picture of a manatee after being hunted around the turn of the century. Exact place and time of the picture are unknown. Picture found at the Library of the University of the West Indies in St. Augustine, Trinidad.

time. Protection of the habitat and indirectly the manatee is also provided under the Forest Act Chapter 66: 01, with the Nariva Swamp dedicated as a Prohibited Area in April 1993. Although the manatee is offered protection under these two pieces of legislation, it is still threatened with extinction. The enforcement arm of the wildlife section cannot provide the required manpower to enforce laws. Therefore, poaching, squatting, incompatible agriculture practices, indiscriminate harvesting of mangroves and mining continue at an alarming rate. Accession to international treaties/conventions has been another management tool used to afford manatee protection. The Nariva swamp was named as a Ramsar site in 1993.[64]

Marine Mammal Exploitation

FIGURE 5. Picture of manatee hides hanging on a boat. This picture, taken around the turn of the century, shows that manatee hunting was more than and artisanal practice. Exact place and time of the picture are unknown. Picture found at the Library of the University of the West Indies in St. Augustine, Trinidad.

CONCLUSIONS

Marine mammal exploitation in Trinidad and Tobago is different from in neighbouring countries such as Venezuela, Grenada, and St. Vincent and the Grenadines. Table 1 compares the nature of such activities in those countries. Marine mammal exploitation in Venezuela has been largely restricted to dolphin fisheries. This activity was carried out for centuries and became a large scale operation beginning in the 1960s when vessels from Japan, South Korea, and Taiwan were given docking rights and subsidised fuel. Fishers from those countries extended this practice and the locals increased their dolphin capturing practices. They mostly used harpoons for capturing the animals and the most important product was meat for human consumption. Whaling in Venezuelan waters was practised only by Yankee whalers and only in occasional fashion.[65] Marine mammal exploitation in Grenada was almost exclusively confined to whaling operations between 1925 and 1927 and was carried out by Norwegians who employed locals only in the processing of whaling products. Thus that country never developed a local culture of utilisation of these animals.[66] Marine mammal exploitation for St. Vincent and the Grenadines commenced even before it did in Trinidad and continues to this day, although it was always very moderate in intensity. It has a wider range of species though since it has included both large whales and dolphin fisheries. They have mostly used harpoons regardless of the target species. While being heavily influenced by Yankee whalers in terms of the way boats were crewed and the type of harpoon used, it has almost always been carried out by local shore-based fishers.[67]

Trinidad and Tobago is particularly unique by the fact that whaling was developed essentially by local elites that employed slaves first and then labourers later to do the manual part of the job. Those elites were essentially planters, some of whom were already involved in the production of vegetable oil. By all accounts it was extremely rudimentary from a technological viewpoint, making it wasteful and uncoordinated. They also lacked the support of foreign investments. As in Grenada, exploitation ended when the local populations of humpback whales became either extinct or almost completely depleted. All that took place even before the prices for whale oil sank in the 1880s. Unlike Venezuela, dolphin fisheries in Trinidad and Tobago have always been marginal and largely confined to opportunistic utilisation as a result of by-catches.

The only common pattern we have found among Venezuelan, Trinidarian, and Grenadian marine mammal exploitation has been the hunting of manatees. Manatee exploitation was practised in these three areas before the arrival of Columbus and the increase in human population accelerated their decline. Manatee hunting was carried out easily in all these countries using mostly harpoons and the meat, oil, and hide were almost always used. In a small island like Grenada, the local manatee population became extinct by the eighteenth century while the populations of this species became extremely depleted in both Venezuela and Trinidad. Manatees in Trinidad, although still present, seem to be in a very critical situation, confined to a small population in a very small area threatened by habitat destruction.

It is interesting to see how four neighbouring countries that share essentially the same marine mammal species[68] developed different exploitation practices at different periods of time (Table 1). This strongly suggests that local culture shaped by history, more than anything else, was the main factor in the development of the type of marine mammal exploitation for each one of these countries.

NOTES

[1] Corresponding author.
[2] Meine 1999.
[3] Jackson, 2001.
[4] Jackson, 1997.
[5] Romero et al. 1999.
[6] See, for example, Ponting 1991, Sale 1991, Pastor Bodmer 1992, Simon 1997.

Marine Mammal Exploitation

TABLE 1. Modes of exploitation of marine mammals in the southeastern Caribbean. Information for Venezuela is based on Romero et al. 1997 and Romero et al. 2001; for Trinidad and Tobago this paper; for Grenada based on Romero and Hayford 2001; for St. Vincent and the Grenadines on Rack 1952, Adams 1971, Adams 1973 and Beck 1986.

	Venezuela	Trinidad and Tobago	Grenada	St. Vincent and the Grenadines
Whaling				
Nature	Locally absent	Intense shore-based	Intense shore-based	Moderate shore-based
Period	n/a	1826–1865	1925–1927	1860s–present
Induced by	n/a	Local planters (elites)	Norwegians	Local fishers
Yankee whaling?	Very marginal 1850s–1870s	Moderate 1820s–1870s	Moderate 1860s–1880s	Moderate 1830s–1880s
Species	Humpbacks	Almost all humpbacks	Almost all humpbacks	Mostly humpbacks, some sperm
Usage	Oil	Oil, meat, whalebone	Oil, meat, manure	Oil, meat
Intensity	Minor	Significant	Significant	Significant
Ecological effects	Very little (?)	Total depletion	Total depletion	Partial depletion
Dolphin fisheries				
Nature	Intense	Marginal	Absent	Significant
Period	Mostly 1960s–present	n/a	n/a	1920s–present
Induced by	Local and Far-east fishers	Local fishers	n/a	Local fishers
Species	Common, Bottlenose			Pilot, killer, Risso's, *Stenella* spp.
Capture method	Harpooning, nets, guns	Harpooning nets		Harpooning, nets
Usage	Meat, oil, artisanal	Meat		Meat, oil
Ecological effects	Population depletion	No noticeable effects	n/a	?
Manatee exploitation				
Nature	Opportunistic	Opportunistic	Opportunistic	Absent
Period	Pre-Columbian –present	Pre-Columbian –present	Pre-Columbian –18th century	
Practised by	Locals	Locals	Locals	n/a
Capture method	Harpooning	Harpooning	Harpooning	n/a
Usage	Meat, oil	Meat, oil	Meat and oil (?)	n/a
Ecological effects	Largely depleted	Largely depleted	Extinction	n/a

[7] McKillop 1985, Marsh and Lefebvre1994.

[8] Caldwell and Caldwell 1971, Mitchell 1975, Gaskin and Smith 1977, Perrin 1985, Price 1985, Reeves 1988, Romero and Hayford 2000, Romero et al. 1997.

[9] Romero et al. 2001.

[10] IWC 1997.

[11] Romero et al. 1997, Romero and Hayford 2000, Romero et al. 2001.

[12] We used an abbreviated form of a questionnaire similar to the one described in Dolar et al. 1994.

[13] We want to thank the following people for their field assistance and information provided during our work in Trinidad and Tobago: Gary Aboud, Anthony de Verteuil, Kyla T. Hayford, Barry Higman, Mary Alkins Koo, Floyd Lucas, Joseph Mitchell, Gupti Lutchmedial, Kathleen Helense Paul, Mike Rogers, David Rooks, and Donna Spencer. Steven L. Swartz provided us with the galley proofs of the Reeves et al. (2001) article. Anna Payden drew the maps of Fig. 1 and 2. Field work for this research was supported by a Wallace Research Grant to A. Romero. We thank the personnel at the Department of Life Sciences of the University of the West Indies (St. Augustine) for logistical support. The Wildlife Section of the Forestry Division of the Government of Trinidad and Tobago granted the research permit. Hanne Eastwood and two anonymous reviewers read the MS and made valuable suggestions.

[14] Wing 1962.

[15] Columbus 1498/1986. He also gave the name of *El Delfín* (the dolphin) to the twin islands today known today as *Huevos* (Eggs), but not because of any dolphin or porpoise but because when seen from the westward it is very like a dolphin fish (*Coryphaena* spp.). See Sauer 1966.

[16] Anonymous 1792.

[17] For example, Borde (1876) who wrote the most comprehensive history of Trinidad under the Spanish government (until 1797), says nothing about that operation despite the fact that on page 3, he mentions the *Golfo de la Ballena* where 'it abounds with fish, and every year whales come to feed on the sea plants which grow there in abundance'. But then he adds ' These whales furnish a thick oil which is greatly priced'. Whether it is a general comments about whales or a tangential reference to whaling in Trinidad is unclear. According to Joseph (1838), the first whale fishery established in Trinidad was 'by a Mr. R. [Richard] Joell', but no date is cited. Joell is mentioned in some sources (*Trinidad Guardian* 20 June 1828) as selling whale oil. He would have been involved in hiring whale catchers for the operation at Gasparee Island (Point Baleine) (*Port-of-Spain Gazette* 24 Dec. 1833). All this may have led Joseph to believe that Joell was the initiator of commercial whaling in Trinidad.

[18] City Council Records 1827.

[19] *Port-of-Spain Gazette* 3 and 14 Mar. 1827.

[20] *Port-of-Spain Gazette* 3 and 14 Mar. 1827.

[21] *Port-of-Spain Gazette*, No. 51, Vol. 1, p. 2.

[22] E.g., The *Port-of-Spain Gazette* for Saturday, 18 Mar. 1826 No. 52, Vol. 1, p. 2.

[23] Costelloe 1998.

[24] *Port-of-Spain Gazette*. 5 May 1830. Whole # 481. Vol 5, number 36.

[25] Reeves et al. 2001.

[26] Mostly Charles and Jean Baptiste, A. de Verteuil 1993.
[27] Jenny Point-Chaguaramas Assessment Roll 1884, Besson 1985, p. 122, includes picture.
[28] Carmichael 1961, de Verteuil 1994.
[29] A. de Verteuil 1986.
[30] A. de Verteuil 1994.
[31] A. de Verteuil 1975.
[32] See Trollope 1859 for the only contemporary account of the stations themselves.
[33] L.A.A. de Verteuil 1858, Ottley 1974, L. Fraser unpublished MS cited in de Verteuil 2000.
[34] de Verteuil 1986, de Verteuil 2000.
[35] Request to Governor-Trinidad Duplicated Despatches 1834.
[36] 'razor backs', Joseph 1838.
[37] A. de Verteuil 1993, de Verteuil 2000.
[38] Swartz et al. 2001.
[39] Archer 1881.
[40] Pers. comm. provided by local fishers.
[41] Reeves et al. 2001.
[42] A picture of four ribs and three vertebrae at Constance in the southwestern tip of Trinidad, ca. 10°03' N, 61°55' W, de Verteuil 2000.
[43] Swartz et al. 2001.
[44] Romero et al. 2001.
[45] Romero and Hayford 2000.
[46] Swartz et al. (2001) hypothesised that the abandonment of the Gulf of Paria by humpbacks 'could be attributable to disturbance from extensive oil and gas development and production that occurs off the southeastern end of Trinidad and in the southern Gulf of Paria, along with shipping traffic into and out of the Port of Spain harbor.'
[47] Romero and Hayford 2000.
[48] Romero and Hayford 2000.
[49] Araujo 1986.
[50] For example, Vincent (1910) mentions that 'Sharks, sword-fish, saw-fish, and two kinds of porpoise locally called "marsouen blanc" (the small one) and "marsouen canal," weighing about three quarters of a ton, are plentiful, so the harpooner with a stout pirogue and four good oars can get plenty of fun'. This activity took place at the Bocas.
[51] Mendes 1932, Mendes 1937, Turpin 1978, Lee 1980.
[52] Turpin 1978.
[53] Kenny and Bacon 1981, pers. comm. by local fishers at La Blanchisseuse.
[54] Lee 1980, Gary Aboud, pers. comm.
[55] Ottley et al. 1994.
[56] Typewritten report at the Wildlife Section office, headed 'Harpooned whale. Date: 89-10-16. Report received from Winsie Ali of Mayaro.'
[57] Ray 1960, Wing et al. 1968, Watters et al. 1984, Levebvre et al. 1989, Wing and Wing 1995.
[58] Du Tertre 1667, Dapper 1673, Labat 1742, Bullen 1964; Wing and Wing 1995; for additional citations on pre- and post-Columbus use of manatees in the Caribbean see McKillop 1985.

[59] M'Callum (1805) mentions the presence of this species on the coastal rivers in which they were captured by Indians and blacks using harpoons for meat consumption. L.A.A. de Verteuil (1884) cites this species as 'scarce' but being hunted for its meat. Kingsley (1871) and Collens (1892), both recorded the manatee in the Mitan (Nariva river). Collens (1892) mentions its capture not only for meat consumption but also for its oil which 'is very abundant in quantity, and in quality is not unlike cod liver oil'. Mole (1925) also indicated that the manatee was hunted as a source of food by the local population. Vincent (1910) mentions the use of manatee skin. An article published in the *Port-of-Spain Gazette* (6 Sept. 1925) cites the use of manatee skin to tie rafters in the early nineteenth century. As late as 1980 Trinidadian officials reported illegal hunting of these animals in the Nariva swamp (Lee 1980).

[60] Gupti Latchmedial, pers. comm.

[61] Boyle and Khan 1993.

[62] Amour 1993.

[63] Armour 1993.

[64] The Ramsar Convention on Wetlands of International Importance Especially in Waterfowl Habitat. Armour 1993.

[65] Romero et al. 1997.

[66] Romero and Hayford 2000.

[67] See Rack 1952, Adams 1971, Adams 1973, and Beck 1986.

[68] See Romero et al. 2001 for a comparison of cetacean species distribution among Caribbean countries.

REFERENCES

Adams, J. E. 1971. Historical geography of whaling in Bequia Island, West Indies. *Caribbean Studies*, **11**: 55–74.

Adams, J. E. 1973. Shore whaling in St, Vincent island, West Indies. *Caribbean Quarterly*, **19**: 42–50.

Anonymous. 1792. *Plano geométrico de la Boca de Monos y puertos de Charguaramas y Carenero en la Ya. de Trinidad* (unpublished map, at the Library of Congress, G5149.C53 1792).

Amour, K.1993. *Status of the West Indian Manatee (Trichechus manatus) in Trinidad and Tobago*. Trinidad and Tobago: Forester I Wildlife Section, Forestry Division. Ministry of Agriculture, Land and Marine Resources. 14 September 1993.

Araujo, A. 1986. *The problems associated with the international whaling industry and Trinidad and Tobago's involvement with the International Whaling Commission* (unpublished report).

Archer, A.S. 1881. Sea-fishing in Barbadoes. *The Field, The Country Gentleman's Newspaper* (1054) (22 Oct.):592.

Besson, G. 1985. *A Photographic Album of Trinidad at the Turn of the Nineteenth Century*. Port-of-Spain, Trinidad: Paria.

Beck, H.P. 1986. "Bleows" The Whaling Complex in Bequia. *Folklife Annual*, **1986**: 42–61.

Borde, P. G. L. 1876 (1982). *The History of the Island of Trinidad under the Spanish*

Government. 2 vols. Paris: Maisonneuve et Cie.

Boyle, C. and Khan, J. 1993. *National Report of the status of the West Indian manatee in Trinidad and Tobago* (unpublished). Manatee subcommittee, Trinidad Field Naturalist Club.

Bullen, R.P. 1964. The Archaeology of Grenada, West Indies. *Contributions of the Florida State Museum,* **11**: 1–67.

Caldwell, D.K. and Caldwell, M.C. 1971. Porpoise Fisheries in the Southern Caribbean- Present Utilizations and Future Potentials. In J. B. Higman (ed) *Proceedings of the 23rd Annual Session of the Gulf and Caribbean Fisheries Institute,* pp 195–206. Coral Gables, FL: University of Miami, Rosenstiel School of Marine and Atmospheric Sciences.

Carmichael, G. 1961. *The History of the West Indian Islands of Trinidad and Tobago 1498–1900.* London: Alvin Redman.

Collens, J. H. 1892. The Trinidad Manatee. *Journal of the Field Naturalist Club,* **1**: 170–2.

Columbus, C. 1498 (1986). *Colón y el Viaje Tercero.* Madrid: Pando Ediciones.

Costelloe, S. 1998. *Scotland Bay – 1875 to the 1960s A family perspective* (unpublished manuscript).

Dapper, O. 1673. *Die unbekante neue Welt, oder Beschreibung des Welt-Teils Amerika, und des Sud-Landes.* Amsterdam: J. von Meurs.

de Verteuil, A. 1973. *Sir Louis de Verteuil. His Life and Times. Trinidad 1800–1900.* Trinidad: Columbus Publishers.

de Verteuil, A. 1975. *The Years Before.* Port-of-Spain: Caribbean Ltd. Publishers.

de Verteuil, A. 1986. *Sylvester Devenish and the Irish in Nineteenth Century Trinidad.* Port-of-Spain: Paria Publishing Co. Ltd.

de Verteuil, A. 1993. *Scientific Sorties.* Port-of-Spain: The Litho Press.

de Verteuil, A. 1994. *The Germans in Trinidad.* Port-of-Spain: The Litho Press.

de Verteuil, A. 2000. *Great Estates of Trinidad.* Port-of-Spain: The Litho Press.

de Verteuil, L. A. A 1858. *Trinidad: Its Geography, Natural Resources, Administration, Present Condition, and Prospects.* London: Ward and Lock.

de Verteuil, L.A.A.G. 1884. *Trinidad: Its Geography, Natural Resources, Administration, Present Condition, and Prospects.* London: Cassell & Co. Ltd..

Dolar, M.L., Leatherwood, S.J., Wood, C.J., Alava, M. N. R., Hill, C. L., and Aragones, L.V. 1994. Directed Fisheries for cetaceans in the Phillipines. *Reports of the International Whaling Commission,* **44**: 439–49.

Du Tertre, J.B. 1667. *Histoire générale des Antilles habitées par les François,* 4 volumes. Paris: T. Jolly.

Gaskin, D.E. and Smith, G.J.D. 1977. The Small Whale Fishery of St. Lucia, W. I. *Reports of the International Whaling Commission,* **27**: 493.

IWC. 1997. *Forty-Seventh Report of the International Whaling Commission.* Cambridge, UK: International Whaling Commission.

Jackson, J.B.C. 1997. Reefs since Columbus. *Coral Reefs,* **16** (Suppl.):S23–S32.

Jackson, J.B.C. 2001. What was natural in the coastal oceans? *Proceedings of the National Academy of Sciences (USA),* **98**: 5411–18.

Joseph, E L. 1838 (1970). *History of Trinidad.* London: Frank Cass & Co. Ltd.

Kenny, J. S. and Bacon, P.R. 1981. Aquatic Resources. In G. C. Cooper and P. R. Bacon (eds) *The natural resources of Trinidad and Tobago*, pp 112–201. London: Edward Arnold.

Kingsley, C. 1871. *At Last, A Christmas in the West Indies*. London: MacMillan & Co.

Labat, P. 1742. *Nouveau Voyage aux Isles de l'Amerique*. 4 volumes, Paris: Chez Theodore le Gras.

Lee, Z.C.Y. 1980. Water dwelling mammals. *Trinidad Naturalist*, **3**:3.

Lefebvre, L.W., O'Shea,T.J., Rathbun, G.B. and Best, R.C. 1989. Distribution, status, and biogeography of the West Indian manatee. In C.A. Woods (ed) *Biogeography of the West Indies. Past, Present, and Future*, pp 567–609. Gainesville, FL.: Sandhill Crane Press.

Marsh, H. and Lefebvre, L.W. 1994. Sirenian status and conservation efforts. *Aquatic Mammals* **20**: 155–70.

M'Callum, P. F. 1805. *Travels Trinidad during the months of February, March, and April in a series of letters*. Liverpool: W. Jones.

McKillop, H. I. 1985. Prehistoric exploitation of the manatee in the Maya and circum-Caribbean areas. *World Archaeology*, **16**: 337–53.

Meine, C. 1999. It's about time: Conservation biology and history. *Conservation Biology*, **13**: 1–3.

Mendes, A.L. 1932. Around Trinidad with rod, line and harpoon. *Canada West Indies Magazine*, **22**: 18–21.

Mendes, A.L. 1937. Fisherman's paradise. *The Canada-West Indies Magazine*, **26**: 21–4.

Mitchell, E.D. 1975. *Porpoise, dolphin and small whale fisheries of the world*. IUCN. Monograph No. 3 Morges, Switzerland: IUCN.

Mole, R.R. 1925. Lamantin in Port of Spain Gazette. Sept. 6, 1925. Vol. 48, (13698), p. 6.

Ottley, C.R. 1974. *Slavery Days in Trinidad. A social history of the island from 1797–1838*. Trinidad: Published by the author.

Ottley, T.; Henry, C.; Khan, A.; Siung-Chang, A. and Sturm, M. 1994. Incidents involving Whales in Trinidad waters during 1987. From the compilation: Regional Management Plan for the West Indian Manatee (*Trichecus manatus*). Regional Workshop on the Conservation of the West Indian Manatee in the Wider Caribbean Region. Kingston, Jamaica, 1–4 March, 1994 (reprinted in Living World. Journal of the Trinidad and Tobago Field Naturalists' Club 1987–88).

Pastor Bodmer, B. 1992. *The armature of conquest. Spanish accounts of the discovery of America, 1492–1589*. Stanford: Stanford University Press.

Perrin, W.F., 1985. The Former Dolphin Fishery at St Helena. *Reports of the International Whaling Commission*, **35**: 423–8.

Ponting, C. 1991. *A green history of the world. The environment and the collapse of great Civilizations*. New York: Penguin Books.

Price, W.S., 1985. Whaling in the Caribbean: Historical Perspective and Update. *Reports of the International Whaling Commission*, **35**: 413–20.

Rack, R.S., 1952. *Fisheries in the Caribbean. Report of the Fisheries Conference held at Kent House, Trinidad, March 24–28, 1952*. Port-of-Spain, Trinidad.

Ray, C.E. 1960. The Manatee in the Lesser Antilles. *Journal of Mammalogy*, **41**: 412–13.

Reeves, R.R. 1988. Exploitation of Cetaceans in St. Lucia, Lesser Antilles, January 1987. *Reports of the International Whaling Commission*, **38**: 445–7.

Reeves, R.R., Khan, J. A., Olsen, R.R., Swartz, S. L. and Smith,T.D. 2001. History of whaling in Trinidad and Tobago. *Journal of Cetacean Research and Management*, **3**: 45–54.

Romero, A; Agudo, A.I. and Green, S.M. 1997. Exploitation of cetaceans in Venezuela. *Reports of the International Whaling Commission*, **47**: 735–46.

Romero, A., Agudo, A.I., Green, S.M. and Notarbartolo di Sciara, G. 2001. Cetaceans of Venezuela: Their distribution and conservation status. *NOAA Technical Reports NMFS*, **151**: 1–60.

Romero, A., S. Chilbert, & M. G. Eisenhart. 1999. Cubagua's Pearl-Oyster Beds: The First Depletion of a Natural Resource Caused by Europeans in the American Continent. *Journal of Political Ecology*, **6**: 57–78.

Romero, A. and Hayford, K.T. 2000. Past and present utilisation of marine mammals in Grenada, West Indies. *Journal of Cetacean Research and Management*, **2**: 223–6.

Sale, K. 1991. *The conquest of paradise. Christopher Columbus and the Columbian legacy*. New York: Alfred A. Knop.

Sauer, C. O. 1966. *The Early Spanish Main*. Berkeley and Los Angeles: University of California Press.

Simon, J. 1997. Prophecy, plague, and plunder. *The Amicus Journal*, **1997**: 28–33.

Swartz, S.L., Martinez, A., Cole, T., Clapham, P.J., McDonald, M.A., Hildebrand, J.A., Oleson, E.M., Burks, C. and Barlow, J. 2001. Visual and acoustic survey of humpback whales (*Megaptera novaeangliae*) in the Eastern and Southern Caribbean Sea: Preliminary Findings. *NOAA Technical Memorandum NMFS-SEFSC*, **456** 1–37.

Trollope, A. 1859. *The West Indies and the Spanish Main*. London: Chapman & Hall.

Turpin, E.C.S. 1978. A factual account of an incident involving porpoises. *Journal of the Trinidad and Tobago Field Naturalist Club*, **1978**: 28–29.

Vincent, H. 1910. *The Sea Fish of Trinidad. Port of Spain*. New York: Press of J. J. Little & Ives co.

Watters, D.R., Reitz, E.J., Steadman, D.W. and Pregill,G.K. 1984. Vertebrates from Archaeological sites on Barbuda, West Indies. *Annals of the Carnegie Museum*, **53**: 383–412.

Wing, E. S. 1962. Succession of Mammalian Faunas on Trinidad, West Indies. *Unpublished doctoral dissertation*. University of Florida.

Wing, E.S., Hoffman, C.A. and Ray, C.E. 1968. Vertebrate remains from Indian Sites on Antigua, West Indies. *Caribbean Journal of Science*, **8**:123–39.

Wing, E.S. and Wing, S.R. 1995. Prehistoric ceramic age adaptation to varying diversity of animal resources along the West Indian Archipelago. Journal of Ethnobiology **15**: 119–48.

Animal Conservation: History and Theory

Conservation and Individual Worth

Gill Aitken

INTRODUCTION

Conservation is widely held to be properly concerned with groups or 'wholes' that make up the natural world. These groups may consist in populations, species, habitats, ecosystems, and other such assemblages. Such concern tends to eclipse any potential consideration for individuals, indeed it is very often at the expense of individuals. Holistic thinking is not merely theoretical: it permeates practical conservation. Perhaps the clearest example is to be found in the conservation practice of culling: grey squirrels and red deer are culled in order to prevent damage to woodland; the Royal Society for the Protection of Birds (RSPB) and Wildfowl and Wetlands Trust proposed a cull of the ruddy duck,[1] as a rare species – the white-headed duck – is said to be threatened by interbreeding with the former;[2] foxes, crows, stoats and other predatory animals are culled in their thousands for the conservation aim of protecting 'game' bird species such as grouse, which are thought to be an important constituent of moorland habitat.[3] In the light of conservation's neglect of consideration for individuals, it may be supposed that any practice that prioritises individuals – as exemplified by wildlife rehabilitation – would at best have no conservation value, and at worst, compromise conservation. Furthermore, wildlife rehabilitation has been accused of compromising the conservation values of 'natural selection' and 'fitness'. For example, in the aftermath of oil spills, the clean-up operation commonly includes the rescue, washing and rehabilitation of oiled birds. While widely recognised as a humanitarian exercise, it has been severely criticised by some as not only a waste of potential conservation resources (it is costly and labour-intensive) but, more seriously, as potentially damaging to populations.[4] Are these criticisms justified?

PLACING WILDLIFE REHABILITATION

Wildlife rehabilitation may be described as 'the rescue of incapacitated wild animals that are considered unable to survive in the wild without human intervention, their care and subsequent release'. While this description is a good starting point, it leaves us unclear as to what, precisely, would *count* as rehabilitation.

For example, in order for an action to be considered as rehabilitation, an individual must receive direct help. That is, rehabilitation consists in specific action for a specific individual. Indirect, or incidental help will not do. In treating and releasing a lactating fox, it could not be said that her offspring – though clearly saved by this action – have been rehabilitated. In addition to this, it is necessary for a problem to first be identified before rehabilitation can take place. Putting food out for the birds over winter as an 'insurance policy' against their starvation cannot be considered to be rehabilitation. However, should one of these birds be found huddled in a corner one morning, it is a candidate for rehabilitation. Rehabilitation is embarked upon when, with respect to its wild existence, an animal is disadvantaged.

The notion of 'disadvantage' requires clarification. It refers to those animals that are suspected of being in imminent danger of dying, those whose lives are apparently under threat, or those whose quality of life in the wild is seriously compromised. There are five categories of 'disadvantage': illness; injury; incapacity (e.g. oiling); dispossession (e.g. disturbance from hibernation) and orphaning. Though categories are useful methods of clarification, clearly some cases will straddle more than one category.

The degree of human intervention in the process of rehabilitation varies greatly, and can be categorised in the following way:

(i) De-training[5] and/or re-training.[6]

(ii) Rearing, including hand-feeding.[7]

(iii) Treatment, of varying intensity and duration.

(iv) Sometimes, all that is required to set a disadvantaged wild animal on its way again is intervention of the most minimal kind. Grounded swifts are a fairly frequent summer casualty at rehabilitation centres (Fenter 1990: 55). All that is needed is for the bird to be held aloft on an open hand, thereby allowing it to take off – an action the swift, with its long wings, is unable to do from the ground.

Although widely differing degrees of human intervention are to be found within rehabilitation practice, what is common to all is some kind of correction procedure, a procedure that changes the expected course of the animal's life, thereby allowing it to resume its earlier mode of being (wild survival).

DOES WILDLIFE REHABILITATION UNDERMINE EVOLUTIONARY FITNESS?

Conservationists value natural processes in which natural selection plays a pivotal role. Natural selection, it is believed, ensures the 'survival of the fittest', and this, some critics say, is seriously undermined by the sort of human intervention typical of wildlife rehabilitation. Kirkwood (1993: 237), for instance, has written that '[t]reating compromised individuals and therefore giving the less fit

Conservation And Individual Worth

a second chance represents an interference with natural selection'. Elsewhere, Kirkwood & Sainsbury (1996: 239) expand on this:

> Wild animals have always fought their own battles with competitors, parasites, infections, and with the rigours of the environment and are as they are – anatomically, physiologically, behaviourally and immunologically – entirely because of this. The treatment of compromised individuals and thus giving the evolutionarily 'less fit' (which, by definition is what wild animals that are sick or injured through natural causes are) a second chance, is no less an interference than shooting the fit.

There are serious problems with this criticism. To begin with, the authors claim that wild animals that are sick or injured through natural causes are, *by definition*, evolutionarily less fit. Here, however, they conflate evolutionary fitness (a hereditary concept) with the popular notion of fitness as 'vigour' or 'health'. Elsewhere, while discussing the vital part played by the release process in rehabilitation, they reinforce this confusion: '[t]he fitness of the animal and the timing, location and other circumstances of the release must be carefully considered'.[8] This is clearly a reference to fitness as a quality that can be assessed and thus something akin to vigour. Since frequently, part of conservation-based criticisms of wildlife rehabilitation rely upon a misuse of the term 'fitness' they are undeniably weakened.

Kirkwood and Sainsbury's claim is further inaccurate in suggesting that the less fit are those individuals *that become sick or injured*. This, however, is quite wrong. Fitness ought to be judged, not merely on the basis of *succumbing* to one or another ailment, but also on the basis of the ability to recover. Evolutionary fitness may be understood in one of two senses. In one understanding it is synonymous with 'survival' – that is to say, those individuals that are fit are those that survive (Darwin's 'survival of the fittest' is seen to be tautological[9]). With this reading of 'fitness' an individual can only be deemed unfit if it does not survive, and so clearly recovery (from disease x, for example) is just as relevant as is resistance to disease x. Alternatively, fitness may be understood as meaning 'good design' – a quality that an animal passes on to its offspring but which cannot be predicted in advance: animals with a thick coat may turn out to be better designed for survival than those without such coats, should the climate turn colder.[10] As with the previous reading of fitness, an animal's good design is as reliant upon 'ability to recover from x' every bit as much as it is upon 'resistance to x'. This is so, not only because the ability to fight against adversity is a sign of good design. Many debilitated animals have succumbed, not because of a flaw in their design, but because they have simply met with misfortune; they have been *unlucky*. Very often, debilitated animals have been in the wrong place at the wrong time; the victims of an oil spill, for example. Darwin himself said that such individuals may be every bit as fit as other members of the species; misfortune is unrelated to evolutionary fitness. Thus, it is clear that, however 'fitness' is understood, the idea that individuals earmarked for rehabilitation can be identified as 'less fit' is ill-conceived.

However, wildlife rehabilitation is still open to the challenge that if an animal requires *help* in order to recover, this must indicate that it was, after all, 'less fit'. The treatment of debilitated individual animals may mask the fact that they are 'less fit'. Treatment may mask one of two things: either the animal's poor design (which was responsible for it succumbing in the first place) or, assuming it to be unlucky to have succumbed, its lack of fitness in terms of ability to recover on its own. Either way, natural selection would appear to be compromised.

Whilst it is important to recognise the help that rehabilitation offers debilitated wildlife, such help does not promote the survival of less fit individuals. Rehabilitation in itself requires a certain capability for coping. There is no doubt that it can be a stressful process as Kirkwood and Sainsbury (1996: 238) note:

> the stresses of capture from the wild, hospitalisation, treatment and subsequent release are hard to assess but may be substantial. For example, Rebar *et al*.... considered that confinement and handling may have contributed to deaths due to shock in oiled sea otters at rehabilitation centres.[11]

Thus, if an animal is to survive not only its disability but rehabilitation too, it must be an animal that is well-designed for survival. A likely objection will be that fitness, as a product of *natural* selection, demands a selection procedure devoid of human influence. Alongside this may be found the related objection that an animal's capability to survive rehabilitation procedures is not a relevant capability; it is of little value in nature. The way Kirkwood and Sainsbury state their case gives weight to these objections. Whereas natural selection is usually contrasted with artificial selection (which involves human-determined reproductive outcomes – as in domestication) the contrast Kirkwood and Sainsbury are making is of a more rigorous kind, in which natural selection is taken to mean selection devoid of any human influence. Quite apart from the question of whether, given the all-pervading nature of human influence upon the natural world, it makes sense to make such a rigorous distinction,[12] natural selection is rarely understood in this way. Kirkwood and Sainsbury themselves make the implicit assumption that individual animals that do not succumb to debility (or indeed, recover on their own) are 'fit', thereby legitimising the human-influenced environment as one in which it makes sense to talk of fitness. Indeed, to do otherwise, is to invoke some kind of mythical selection procedure in which human influence does not feature. An animal's good design must relate to a real context not an illusory one, and it is a fact that wild animals' environments include humans and human hazards.

It is a separate question as to whether wild animals can become well-designed in a human-influenced environment, for we are uniquely random in our actions: we oscillate between destruction and protection in a most haphazard way, and it may be that species require consistent pressures in order to become adapted.[13]

Conservation And Individual Worth

Irrespective of this, given our ubiquitous presence and widespread impact on natural selection, it would be quite wrong to single out rehabilitation as guilty of compromising natural selection and undermining Darwinian fitness. If rehabilitation is guilty, then so too, are all our activities, including conservation – be it the management of a wood or the reintroduction of a species. It is not clear that there is a difference in kind between the conservation practice of re-establishing a threatened species (which is losing the battle in the face of human hazards) and the rehabilitation practice of aiding the recovery of a compromised individual animal. Nor is it clear that there is any important difference (in terms of 'fitness') between providing red squirrels with food-hoppers (or managing a woodland for them) and rehabilitation. Indeed, in that rehabilitated animals have survived debility and the process of rehabilitation, they may be argued to have survived not (as may be said of red squirrels whose competitors, the greys, are controlled) by the *removal* of challenge, but rather, by the *replacement* of challenge. And as we have seen, the challenge presented by rehabilitation is no more different, or less relevant to wild survival than a plethora of other challenges faced by wild animals. Getting by in the face of direct and indirect challenges from humans is the lot of today's wild animals.

Though wildlife rehabilitation is merely one of a whole range of human influences upon natural selection, the different influences require differing evaluation. Rehabilitation is, in common with aspects of conservation practice, of a particular kind of human influence: it is reparational in nature, it is in the business of making amends. This is in contrast with many other human activities that are indifferent to, or even antagonistic towards all concerns other than human ones. Kirkwood and Sainsbury (1996: 239) are quite wrong, for instance, in claiming that '[t]he treatment of compromised individuals ... is no less an interference than shooting the fit', if their intention is – as it would seem to be – to suggest that they ought to be evaluated in the same way. Their claim has to be rejected immediately on pragmatic grounds, since evolutionary fitness is not a quality that we can predict or even recognise. Shooting the fit would be an impossible task. However, putting aside this practical difficulty, there are other factors that illustrate the difference in nature between helping the less fit and shooting the fit.

An important point of distinction between the two approaches is the degree to which they are amenable to human control. Help can never dictate a desired outcome, it can merely facilitate one. Shooting, on the other hand, has a far more certain outcome. Furthermore, unlike shooting, rehabilitation requires an input from the animal itself – it is reliant upon the animal's coping mechanisms. Although an animal will sometimes manage to avoid being shot, more often, the animal's wiles and the gun are grossly mis-matched.[14] Shooting, therefore, generally works against the animal (in that it leaves little or no room for drawing upon survival strategies) whereas help in the form of rehabilitation works *with* the animal. In this respect, rehabilitation is shown to be much closer to Kirkwood and Sainsbury's ideal of wild animals as having 'always fought their own battles' than is shooting – which leaves little room for a battle at all. So, although the criticism that rehabilitation compromises natural selection has immediate – and popular – appeal, it does not stand up to scrutiny. There is no evidence to suggest that wildlife rehabilitation works against the conservation values of 'natural selection' and 'fitness' which might lead to an undermining of conservation. At least this one example of prioritising the individual is compatible – in the terms discussed – with the practice of conservation.

There is, nevertheless, no room for complacency. If concern for the individual does not compromise the particular conservation values of natural selection and fitness, there would appear to be little room for this sentiment within the holistic philosophy adopted – and practised – by conservationists.

CONSERVATION, CULLING AND PRIORITISING INDIVIDUALS

The culling of individual animals is a holistically-driven conservation strategy. For example, in order to promote the revival, in Scotland, of the capercaillie species, the RSPB has undertaken extensive culling of foxes and crows.[15] The culling of red deer in parts of Scotland is believed to be an ecological necessity, the deer population having apparently increased to the point at which they are 'out of control' and an ecological liability.[16]

The conservationist's pro-culling holistic argument contains three premises. The first is that conservation value is placed on the 'whole'; individuals are mere members or parts of the 'whole'. The second premise is that conservationists ought to promote the good of the 'whole', be this species, habitat or ecosystem. Given the third premise – that selective culling is good for the 'whole' – conservationists conclude that selective culling is desirable for the sake of conservation.

(i) *Conservation value is placed upon the 'whole'*

If the protection of 'wholes' is of paramount importance to conservation, it is curious that culling, by its very nature, is a form of *compartmentalising* nature. To advocate culling is to differentiate, to segregate, to divide nature into parts according to perceived worth. In the case of red deer culling, the red deer species is isolated from the wider environment which it inhabits, in its identification as an unwanted 'part'. And further, the process of culling involves differentiating between those groups of deer to be targeted and those to be left alone. The culling of red deer, for instance, is achieved by targeting hinds of particular age and condition.[17] If conservationists' 'wholes' (themselves, of course, only parts) are to be holistic concepts at all, then they ought to be seen as being *whole* 'wholes', that is, complete in themselves and part of the wider picture. The notion of culling seems to be anathema to a coherent approach to the protection of 'wholes'.

Conservation And Individual Worth

The conservation supremacy of the 'whole' must be questioned further. In advocating the sacrificing of individuals for the sake of the 'whole', conservationists usually (thankfully) exclude human individuals. They cannot, therefore, be taken literally when they argue that the 'whole' is always of greatest value. This must be seen for what it is: mere 'conservation-speak', a rough shorthand that suggests where their priorities tend to lie. Humans, after all, are the worst offenders of environmental damage. It behoves the conservationist to explain why the taking of non-human life is to be so very differently regarded to the taking of human life. Yet even assuming a convincing argument could be made, the conservationist will still surely find it difficult to justify the taking of non-human lives for the sake of 'wholes'. For the fact is that the value of these 'wholes' is not only usurped by the value of human lives, but also by very much more trivial things to do with human comfort, amusement and convenience. Though individual conservationists may spurn certain conveniences, conservationists do not, as a body, boycott cars, meat-eating, or houses without cavity-wall insulation, all of which contribute to the degradation of the environment. Nature's 'wholes' may be worthy of protection but there are clear limits to the costs involved. These limits cannot merely be assumed by conservationists to include the culling of non-human individuals. Indeed, the difficulty is in understanding how conservationists can justify culling. Furthermore, for conservationists to argue that humans ought to be afforded special treatment because they are not part of nature is neither in tune with a holistic philosophy nor does it sit entirely comfortably with the conservationist's championing of nature.

In the conservation clamour to protect 'wholes', not only is the necessity for particular measures often taken for granted, but so too may the true nature of such measures be masked. Such is the case with culling. It should not be forgotten that the term 'culling' is a euphemism for 'killing'. Too easily a subconscious connection is forged between conservation and culling, as if they somehow belonged together, facilitated, no doubt, by the apparent innocuousness of the term 'culling'. It has become sanitised killing – part of the great conservation quest. But the act of killing de-humanises us and takes its toll, even on the most hardened of killers. Wigan (1993: 96), in discussing a particular red deer cull in Scotland in which the population is regularly reduced by 35 per cent writes:

> Something that is seldom taken into account is the emotional stress to stalkers having to shoot animals in these numbers, piled upon the physical stress. Only those who have done it, who have followed up an unmothered calf, hanging round its suddenly-deceased parent, yet somehow awkward to get a sure shot at, will understand the stress I am talking about ... No one normal enjoys shooting dependent calves, or a slaughter of hinds. A large estate cull in east Sutherland had to be interrupted for a week while stalkers recharged their psychological batteries before continuing.

Lacy (1995: 118) makes culling sound more acceptable by characterising it thus: 'Culling is the termination of the life of an animal before it would have died from unavoidable disease or failures of organ systems (old age or natural causes).' It is as if culling is merely the end-result that comes about anyway. However, such consequentialist thinking misses a vitally important point. To view killing in this way is to ignore the importance of process: the process of life and the process of death. Thus, neither the wonder of life nor the way in which death comes about is seen worthy of mention. Yet for those conservationists (such as Lacy) who adhere to an evolutionary biological approach to conservation, process clearly does matter. And if process is of relevance to conservation, then it is not self-evident that the processes surrounding individual lives are of less importance than the processes connected with species. Indeed, to dismiss the former is to impoverish conservation: the wonder of *lived* lives provides most of the motivation and energy that is required for the uphill task of conservation. Deer-watching, for instance, inspires many, and in Scotland, the red deer has become a national symbol.[18] A recognition of the value – to conservation – of the processes connected with individual lives prompts a quite different perception of culling.

(ii) *Conservationists ought to promote the good of the 'whole'*

In order for conservationists to promote the good of the 'whole' they must first recognise which 'wholes' are worthy of this help and how to assess their relative value. In any one area there will be a number of 'wholes' that might be considered worth protecting (a variety of habitats, species, subspecies or populations). With no objective decision-making process, judgements are made according to the particular perspective of the conservationist in charge. For example, Deakin (1997: 70) points out that '[t]he designation of an SSSI often dictates a tunnel vision of the habitat, skewed towards the debatable selection of what is deemed "scientifically interesting"'. Discussing the Countryside Council for Wales' decision to remove more than 900m of hedgerow in North Wales in order to encourage waders to feed there, he writes of the terrible dilemma between the uprooting of fast-disappearing hedgerow and the creation of open space in which declining lapwing thrive:

> Uprooting hedgerows is like taking an India rubber to the history that is written into the landscape. It also silences what Richard Mabey memorably calls 'the rich harvest of bird song'. Of course, saltmarshes and wetlands are valuable habitats – and beautiful places – but who is to say that a dunlin is more 'valuable' than a dunnock?

Even within a single organisation, the task of prioritising is problematic. Wigan (1993: 77) tells of the confusion over the Nature Conservancy Council for Scotland's management of SSSI's: 'It often seemed to the ordinary farmer, crofter or

Conservation And Individual Worth

landowner that within the conservancy one hand did not know what the other was doing. The peat-bog specialist would arrive in nesting-time to trample over a site just descried as vital for rare nesting birds'.

In parts of Scotland, red deer populations are considered to be too large and culling seen to be a necessity for two distinct but interconnected reasons: the requirement for the regeneration of past habitats and the desire for protection from degradation of existing valued habitats (in both cases, usually woodland). It is supposed, usually without critical discussion, that tree regeneration is a laudable conservation objective. However, it is not obvious that the forested hillside has greater conservation value than the treeless hillside. Each habitat has its own combination of plant and animal species, its own ecological interest and attractions.

To justify woodland regeneration conservationists often adopt the argument of historical precedence. However, this argument is every bit as susceptible to bias as is the evaluation of different 'wholes'. There is no objective way of deciding which period from the past should be emulated. Although evidence from the pollen record informs us that most of Britain was covered with forest around 7,500 years ago,[19] the fortunes of forests have varied considerably over time.[20] Earlier, from at least 70,000 to 9,000 years ago tundra conditions prevailed throughout Britain,[21] while later, forest cover waxed and waned according to climate, human activity and disease.[22] From about 5,000 years ago 'the representation of tree pollens becomes, erratically but inexorably, less and less [with the] minimal ... reached around 300 BP' followed by evidence of replanting.[23]

Conservationists may argue that there is no bias involved, for by removing deer they are simply allowing the land to do what it does best in the present climate – which is growing trees. The problem with this argument is that it relies upon an assumption that the appropriate circumstances for allowing the land to do what it is good at call for an absence of deer. Yet it is not clear why this should be so. There seems no reason – other than bias – why the presence of deer ought to be any less acceptable a circumstance than the absence of deer. Perhaps, though, the conservationist equates large deer populations with human interference and thus with circumstances that run contrary to a conservation rationale. Such reasoning would, however, be difficult to sustain. Not only is human influence all-pervading,[24] so that it is unreasonable to characterise conservation as separate from it, but conservation makes use of human intervention for its own ends. Consider, for instance, the re-introduction of species, the re-flooding of wetlands, and the use of grazing animals to maintain certain habitats. Human impact, as such, may be viewed positively or negatively by conservationists. A clear example of negative impact is the destruction of a habitat (such as has recently occurred with the building of another runway at Manchester Airport). However, when a habitat is changed from one type to another, there is no obvious sense of conservation damage and it may simply be bias that dictates the acceptability of one but not the other.

If the arguments of historical precedence or of allowing the land to do what it does best cannot convince us that tree-covered hillsides are of greater conservation value than deer-covered hillsides, the argument for biodiversity does little better. The conservation call to maximise biodiversity is a call for maximising representatives of as many different 'wholes' as possible. But as we have seen, there are no satisfactory answers to the question of how to compare or evaluate different 'wholes'. While wooded hillsides carry representatives of different species of tree and support, for example, red squirrel, goshawk, redpoll, capercaillie and Scottish crossbill, open hillside will be covered in plants such as heather and grasses, and support species such as golden eagle, merlin, short-eared owl, ptarmigan, meadow pipit and mountain hare. As Wigan (1993: 95) has observed, under-grazing can disadvantage moorland wildlife.

Some conservationists would object, though, that the change from woodland habitat to moorland or grassland habitat is an example of habitat *degradation*. However, even if it were agreed that permanent disappearance represented either loss or degradation, the impact that deer have upon woodland could not be so described. Wigan (1993: 80-81), for instance, in a discussion of one man's rigorous deer culling policy, notes that as soon as the grazing deer had gone, saplings sprouted up vigorously, '[p]roof, perhaps, that the notorious degradation of habitat is an over-simplification, or a misrepresentation'.

(iii) *Selective culling is good for the 'whole'*

It may be argued that the claim that any habitat is as good as any other is too extreme. There may, sometimes, be good reasons for wishing to conserve particular habitats, and in order to achieve this, culling particular species may seem a reasonable strategy. However, even when a specific end-goal is desired – let us say, the protection of a forested hillside in the Scottish Highlands – the value of culling is not as clear-cut as might be supposed.

Let us accept – for it seems to be true – that in deer populated areas, without intervention of some kind, woodland regeneration will not occur. Accepting, for the sake of argument, that woodland has greater conservation value than moor or grassland, it would appear sensible to reduce deer numbers through culling. There are two problems with this apparently simple solution.

The first problem is that it fails to take into account the fact that deer population is just one factor out of many[25] that dictate the fate of a habitat. Of particular note is the effect of sheep grazing on habitats. Though aerial photographs have provided evidence 'that Scotland's vegetation profile is changing', the causes have never been established. The stark fact is that 'sheep effects were never separated out from those of deer or climate', and the '[d]eer population reduction has seldom been talked of in the only sensible way – in conjunction with reduction in sheep numbers ... [r]educing one and not the other will merely lead to increased fertility, bodily condition and productivity in the other'.[26]

Thus, where habitat protection is sought, deer culling is not the panacea it is often supposed to be.

The second problem with taking the simplistic deer-culling line is that in order to achieve woodland regeneration, deer need to be virtually (or actually) eliminated.[27] However, when a deer populated area has all of its deer removed, there occurs the 'sump effect', 'whereby deer are sucked in to ungrazed ground by the more succulent feeding it offers'.[28] Wigan notes that the East Grampians Deer Management Group 'submitted that to create a deer-free zone on an area of 50,000 hectares of open hill would require a reduction in numbers over an area ten times that size'. It seems, in fact, that '[i]t will never be possible to kill out deer in a localised way and expect the gap to remain empty'.

The upshot of the problem with creating grazed-free zones is that if woodland regeneration is a serious aim, there is no alternative but to employ fencing. Trying to achieve natural regeneration without fencing is, in deer expert Ronnie Rose's opinion like 'making a circle in the sea and trying to stop the water coming in'.[29] Though fencing can be effective in allowing regeneration to occur,[30] some conservationists object on the grounds of artificiality.[31] The absurdity of this complaint coming from the same conservationists who advocate culling is quite profound. And further, if fencing is rejected in favour of culling alone, in order to control the deer, it will be necessary to create artificial clearings.[32] Thus, to insist on culling but not fencing on the grounds of artificiality is perverse. At the moment, culling is employed alongside fencing and it may be that fencing on its own would not achieve the desired results. However, given that fencing is, as it were, the active ingredient in the recipe for regeneration it would not be surprising if, with a little thought and ingenuity, it could be effective without the need to cull.

There are, then, problems with all three of the conservationist's premises which lead to the conclusion that selective culling is desirable for the sake of conservation. We can therefore legitimately reject the conclusion. However, one final worry remains: culling will sometimes be advocated for the sake of the individual animals. Perhaps wildlife rehabilitators – who have the welfare of the individuals at heart – should view culling favourably, as it prevents slow death through starvation in those cases where numbers have escalated. Furthermore, in such circumstances, wildlife rehabilitation would seem to be contra-indicated.

CULLING AND INDIVIDUAL WELFARE

In the wake of escalating deer numbers, concern for animal welfare has prompted responses such as this one:

> The effect of over population on the animals themselves is, by any standards, unacceptable. Red Deer on the open Scottish hills are, even under good management, stunted specimens of their race. The lack of winter fodder that results from

year-round heavy grazing can reduce them to starvation in the late winter and
early spring, or at least bring them to a state of malnutrition that inflicts lengthy
suffering and leaves the animals highly vulnerable to the stress of hard weather.[33]

It cannot be denied that some years, large numbers of deer die from starvation.
Wigan (1993: 100) himself admits this. Talking of the winter of 1992-3 – at
the time of his writing – he says that when the records are collated, deaths are
certain to be high. However, the reason for the high mortality, Wigan claims, is
climatic. A lack of rain in May 1992 produced little summer grass for fattening.
Summer was followed by prolonged, inhospitable rain through to January 1993.
He goes on to say:

> Those who hasten to attribute deer deaths in 1992-3 to overpopulation should
> think again: deer deaths were as numerous in lowly-populated areas as in dense-
> ly-populated ones. The explanation lies in the weather cycle. Nor is it simply
> to do with the fact of rain. It is when the rain falls, or fails to fall, that matters.
> The December/January Highland rains, which can be heavy, do not affect deer
> unduly. But if they enter the winter in poor condition it is a long time to wait
> until first grass in April or May from which to build up recovery.[34]

Talking of the many deer deaths in the winter of 1989-90, the pertinent point
revealed by Wigan is this: 'deaths had occurred in places where there was no
perceptible population problem [such that] [i]t is now accepted that the relationship between population and winter death is not simple'.[35] Indeed, work
by scientists on Rum's deer populations has shown that 'even heavily culled
populations will not always affect the proportional number of winter deaths'.[36]
The grounds, therefore, 'for reducing deer numbers for humane reasons, to
prevent them dying in bad winters, have weakened'.

The argument for culling as a humane measure is not only flawed because
winter mortality is such a complex matter, it is also questionable in its assumption that it is preferable – from a deer's point of view – to die by the gun than
to die of natural causes. A strong case for the greater acceptability of a natural
death over death through culling has been put for the elephant (Guthrie 1992).
According to Kiley-Worthington,[37] elephant culling cannot be achieved humanely.
And with any social species (which includes red deer), the distress caused to
other members of the group when an individual is killed, can be considerable.

We may be mistaken in assuming that it is kinder to kill a deer quickly by
shooting than to let it die more slowly of cold or hunger. Two zoologists, Chris
Barnard and Jane Hurst, both of Nottingham University, have recently put forward
a new theory of animal suffering. They claim that suffering is triggered 'when
the world frustrates an animal's adaptive drives' (Vines 1997: 31). If evolution
has designed an animal to deal with a certain condition, then despite the way
it may look to us, the animal may not be suffering, or at least may be suffering
less than we imagine. Although this cannot be supported as a way of defining
suffering,[38] it seems to add important vision to the animal welfare debate. Ac-

cording to this theory, the stag suffers so excessively in being hunted by hounds because it has not evolved to cope with a prolonged chase. This thinking would be in accord with the work on deer stress, set out in the Bateson Report[39] which has found that red deer are, in fact, sedentary and relatively unfit. It is not only that British red deer have no current predator (other than humans), it is, more importantly, that there was no ancestral predator that subjected them to a lengthy chase (a wolf chase, for instance, was brief).

Given this way of understanding suffering, it is no longer safe to assume that it is kinder to kill a deer quickly than to allow it to die of natural causes. It is part of the deer's long history to have been faced with inclement weather and starvation: it is possible that because these factors are part of the deer's evolution, they cause individuals less suffering than is supposed. Indeed, if Barnard and Hurst are right, an animal will suffer if it is deprived of making its own evolutionary-based choices – whether these are beneficial or harmful. As Vines[40] reports, Barnard claims that the paradoxical implication of the theory is 'that cost itself may not have welfare significance, but frustrating the animal's ability to incur a cost may have'. It might thus be ventured that – as it has been suggested is the case with elephants – a natural death is a better option for the deer than is culling, which involves the instant break-up of social groups, a certain number of injuries which result in painful, protracted death,[41] and the depriving of any opportunity for evolutionary choice. Assessment of the suffering experienced by other creatures will no doubt always be a thorny issue.[42] It is fair to say, though, that there is some evidence for the belief that, for the deer, death by natural causes may be preferable to death by shooting. Certainly, there is no clear evidence that even if deer mortality were proportionally related to population size (which, it has been argued, is not the case) deer culling would be a welfare requirement. There is nothing, then, to suggest that the wildlife rehabilitator need view culling in a favourable light. The worry that it may be necessary to impose limits on rehabilitation practice in order to safeguard deer welfare can be dismissed.

CONCLUSION

The popular criticism that wildlife rehabilitation works against the conservation values of natural selection and evolutionary fitness is unfounded. Furthermore, each of the conservationists' premises which lead to the conclusion that selective culling is desirable for the sake of the 'whole' have been found wanting. Within the limits of our discussion, then, there is no obvious clash between the individualistic stance of wildlife rehabilitation and conservation practice. Only some of the possible arguments relating to their compatibility have been considered. Wildlife rehabilitation and conservation practice cannot be assumed to be entirely compatible. Nevertheless, it seems fair to say that there is very little standing in the way of the conservationist's acceptance of the practice of wildlife rehabilitation. Concern for the individual need not, it seems, compromise conservation.

NOTES

I am grateful to Alan Holland and Kate Rawles for comments on an earlier draft of this paper.

[1] Although the cull was cancelled due to 'unobliging' land owners and public protest (see Anon 1997, p. 9), the relevant conservation bodies are still keen to go ahead with it.
[2] Anon 1996a, p. 62.
[3] Anon 1996b, p. 8.
[4] See, for example, Sharp 1996, and Schmidt 1997.
[5] This is more commonly required in reintroduction procedures (see, for example, De Blieu's 1993 description of the red wolf reintroduction project). But it may also be required in rehabilitation with, for example, ex-performing dolphins (see Johnson 1990, p. 8).
[6] Re-training examples include the 'hacking back' and flying of raptors.
[7] Rearing usually takes place on rehabilitation premises. However, it has been advocated, for example by Robertson & Harris (1991), that orphan (weaned) fox cubs be reared at the earth in preference to captive rearing.
[8] Kirkwood and Sainsbury 1996, p. 236.
[9] Arguments in support of this claim can be found in Shimony (1989) and Ollason (1991).
[10] This example has been taken from Gould (1977: 42) who is a proponent of the 'good-design' theory.
[11] Kirkwood and Sainsbury 1996, p. 236. See also Schmidt (1997).
[12] See Aitken, forthcoming.
[13] Ibid.
[14] Even where animals escape with injury, the type of injuries inflicted by the gun often preclude the possibility of recovery.
[15] Linklater 1997, p. 7.
[16] Scott 1991, p. 848.
[17] See Wigan 1993, pp. 27; 137.
[18] See Scott 1991, p. 848.
[19] Yalden 1982, p. 10.
[20] Ibid., see pollen diagram, p. 6.
[21] Dyer 1990, p. 23.
[22] Ibid., pp. 24-63; 92-118.
[23] Yalden 1982, pp. 9-10.
[24] Aitken, forthcoming.
[25] Other factors include climate, human impact, and the effects of other grazers such as rabbits.
[26] Wigan 1993, p. 142.
[27] Ibid., p. 143.
[28] Ibid., p. 82.
[29] Ibid., p. 76.

[30] Tickell 1995, p. 27.
[31] Wigan 1993, p. 85.
[32] Ibid., p. 76.
[33] Watson 1989
[34] Wigan 1993, p. 101.
[35] Ibid., p. 93.
[36] Ibid., p. 17.
[37] Kiley-Worthington 1997.
[38] See for example, the objections put forward by Manser (Vines, 1997: 33).
[39] Bateson 1997.
[40] Vines 1997, p. 33.
[41] Bateson 1997.
[42] For a thorough analysis of the problem see Mason and Mendle 1993.

REFERENCES

Aitken, Gill forthcoming 'Extinction', *Biology & Philosophy*.
Anon, 1996a. 'Duck Politics', *BBC Wildlife* **14**(4), April.
Anon, 1996b. 'Grouse shooters to seek Euro subsidy?', *Wildlife Guardian* (Journal of the League Against Cruel Sports) **35**, Autumn.
Anon, 1997. 'Ruddy duck cull cancelled', *Wildlife Guardian* (Journal of the League Against Cruel Sports) **37**, Summer.
Bateson, Patrick 1997. 'The Behavioural & Physiological Effects of Culling Red Deer', Executive Summary of Report to the Council of the National Trust.
Deakin, R. 1997. 'Questions', *BBC Wildlife* **15**(4), April.
De Blieu, J. 1993. *Meant to be Wild; The Struggle to Save Endangered Species Through Captive Breeding*. Colorado: Fulcrum Press.
Dyer, James 1990. *Ancient Britain*. London: B.T. Batsford Ltd.
Fenter, D. 1990. 'The Practicalities Involved in the Release of Wild Birds after Treatment'. In *The Proceedings of the Third Symposium of The British Wildlife Rehabilitation Council*, edited by Tim Thomas. British Rehabilitation Council.
Gould, S. J. 1977. *Ever Since Darwin*. London: Penguin.
Guthrie, B. 1992. (Ed.) 'Keepers of the Kingdom' Wallchart, Anglia Television, produced from Anglia *Survival Special*, ITV (21 August).
Johnson, William 1990. 'Whales and Dolphins in Captivity', *International Whale Bulletin* **6** (Summer): 8.
Kiley-Worthington, Marthe 1997. Philosophy Department Seminar, Lancaster University: 1 February.
Kirkwood, J. 1993. 'Intervention for wildlife health, conservation and welfare', *The Veterinary Record* **132** (March 6): 235-238.
Kirkwood, J. K., and Sainsbury A. W. 1996. 'Ethics of Interventions for the Welfare of Free-Living Wild Animals', *Animal Welfare* **5**: 235-243.
Lacy, R. 1995. 'Culling Surplus Animals for Population Management'. In *Ethics on the Ark; Zoos, Animal Welfare, and Conservation*, edited by Bryan Norton. London:

Smithsonian Institute Press.

Linklater, Magnus 1997. ' RSPB takes risk on capercaillie's survival', *The Times*, May 10.

Mason, G. and Mendle, M. 1993. 'Why Is There No Simple Way of Measuring Animal Welfare?' *Animal Welfare* **2:** 301-319.

Ollason, J. G. 1991. 'What Is This Stuff Called Fitness?', *Biology & Philosophy* **6**: 81-92.

Robertson, C. and Harris, S. 1991. 'Rehabilitation of Orphaned Fox Cubs Summary Report', W-7/91.

Schmidt, K. 1997. 'A drop in the ocean', *New Scientist* (3 May): 41-44.

Scott, Michael 1991. 'Cull to be kind', *BBC Wildlife* **9**(12), December.

Sharp, B. 1996. 'Post-release survival of oiled, cleaned seabirds in North America', *IBIS* **138**: 222-228.

Shimony, A. 1989. 'The Non-Existence Of the Principle of Natural Selection', *Biology & Philosophy* **4**.

Tickell, O. 1995. 'Return to the Wild', *Geographical* (February).

Vines, G. 1997. 'Who's suffering now?', *New Scientist* (22 March): 30-33.

Watson, D. 1989. 'Red Deer in Scotland – A Resource out of Control', *ECOS* **10**(3).

Wigan, M. 1993. *Stag at Bay: The Scottish Red Deer Crisis*. Shrewsbury: Swan Hill Press.

Yalden, D. W. 1982. 'When did the mammal fauna of the British Isles arrive?', *Mammal Review* **12** (1), March.

The Grey Seal in Britain: A Twentieth Century History of a Nature Conservation Success

Robert A. Lambert

INTRODUCTION

We often lament the failures of nature conservation, but rarely, if ever, do we address the historical roots and current problems of nature conservation successes. The Atlantic grey seal *Halichoerus grypus* is the most obvious and extreme example of the problems associated with a nature conservation success in Britain in the twentieth century. Such successes may well prove more and more important as a pressing environmental issue over the course of the twenty-first century. Although this essay is, in part, based on a study of the archives of the National Trust (NT) in London and relates to their management experiences with the grey seals on the Farne Islands off Northumberland in north-east England, it uses other public and private archives to examine the culls in Scotland, illustrating the historical value of a range of environmental archival sources, most obviously those of voluntary conservation or animal welfare bodies.

There are broader lessons to be confronted. Such an investigation can shed light on the wider question of the changing nature of our complex relationship to the natural world, which has been overlooked in twentieth-century historical writing.[1] A dominant theme has been the explosion of our use of natural resources.[2] One neglected but important theme is our rising anxiety about the preservation of nature and how we treat other animals. This has its roots in the nineteenth century, with the establishment of the Society for the Prevention of Cruelty to Animals in 1824 (obtained its royal charter in 1840, and thus RSPCA),[3] and the Society for the Protection of Birds in 1889 (obtained its royal charter in 1904, and thus RSPB).[4] The rise of these animal welfare and protection bodies is an important part of modern British social history and environmental geography that has not been looked at in great detail yet, although John Sheail has published on the political and scientific history of the British nature conservation movement.[5]

If this essay is an attempt to use a case study to put a current environmental problem in historical context and thus demonstrate the practical value of environmental history, it will also show how the grey seal over the twentieth century became a mammal of interest to politicians, fishermen, scientists, conservationists, animal welfare groups, and overwhelmingly, the general public. The grey seal passed from being a source of folklore, a resource for hunters and a sporting trophy in the nineteenth century, to being a curious but valued part of our natural heritage in the first half of the twentieth century. By the 1950s, due to one aspect of its behaviour, a sector of the population (certain fishermen) saw it as a real pest, and urged government to make it an object of scientific inquiry. From the 1960s, especially in the years of the biggest seal culls in Scotland (Orkney) and the Farne Islands, the public took up the grey seal as a domestic environmental cause in a far more popular crusade than the naturalists who had first sought its protection in the second decade of the century. On the international scene, the 1970s and 1980s alliance of Greenpeace, the International Fund for Animal Welfare (IFAW), RSPCA, the media and Brigitte Bardot (she visited Newfoundland in March 1977), took up the photogenic cause of harp seal *Pagophilus groenlandicus* pups bludgeoned to death on the Canadian pack-ice. Television reports on the seal hunt, with the ice dyed red with blood, provided some of the most compelling images ever broadcast of our mastery over and use of Nature.[6]

STATUTORY PROTECTION

The grey seal was the first mammal protected by Parliament, under the Grey Seals (Protection) Act 1914, which established a close season from October 1 to December 15 each year when the seals were reproducing.[7] This came about after a small group of concerned sportsmen put pressure on a handful of MPs and the Secretary of State for Scotland, worried that this 'quite harmless and interesting beast' then numbered less than 500 individuals in the UK.[8] Biologists now suspect that this figure was likely to be somewhere between 2,000 to 4,000 animals,[9] but the Act halted centuries of subsistence and commercial exploitation of the grey seal at its known breeding colonies,[10] although it was difficult to police. The grey seal could still be shot or poisoned (strychnine was put in a salmon bait at nets) outside of the close season. In much of Scotland a bounty was offered by Fishery Boards for the tail of any 'rogue' seal seen near fixed nets. Further parliamentary protection came with the Grey Seals (Protection) Act of 1932 which extended the close season, and gave year-round protection to the grey seals resident on Haskeir in the Outer Hebrides where many of the most bloody seal raids had taken place in the nineteenth and early twentieth century. However, this Act also gave government the power to order the suspension of protection at a site or to alter close season dates.[11]

A Conservation of Seals Act in 1970 gave protection to the common seal *Phoca vitulina* after public protests about the hunting of this species in the Wash in the 1960s, and scientific concern about the impact of hunting in Shetland which was removing virtually every common seal pup born there. The Act was seen as an important compromise between the interests of conservationists and fishing communities. This new legislation urged conservation through good management, rather than blind protection.[12] However, complete protection post-

The Grey Seal in Britain

FIGURE 1. Blind cow grey seal and pup. This photograph is held in the archives of J. Morton Boyd (former Director Scotland, Nature Conservancy Council 1970–1985), in the University of St. Andrews Library. The photograph was taken on the island of Tiree, Inner Hebrides, some time between 1953 and 1957 and is referenced ms389/Box 1/1.11. By kind permission of the University of St Andrews Photographic Collection.

1914 during the vital breeding season was one influential factor in allowing the British grey seal population to rise to about 9,000 by the mid-1930s, to 34,000 by the mid-1960s, and it has been increasing at 6 per cent *per annum* since then. In 1999, the British population was almost 123,000 animals.[13] Around 40 per cent of the world population now breeds in Britain, giving the UK government international responsibility for the species.

NATURE SANCTUARIES

The Farne Islands, comprising 28 islands and rocks at low water and 15 at high water, lie around two to five miles off the Northumberland coast from Bamburgh and Seahouses. For the first half of the nineteenth century the Farnes were held by tenants of the Ecclesiastical Commissioners for England, but in 1861 Inner Farne was purchased by Archdeacon Charles Thorp of Durham. Outer Farne was bought by Lord Armstrong in 1894. Over the last two decades of the nineteenth century the Farnes became an unofficial nature reserve with protection bolstered

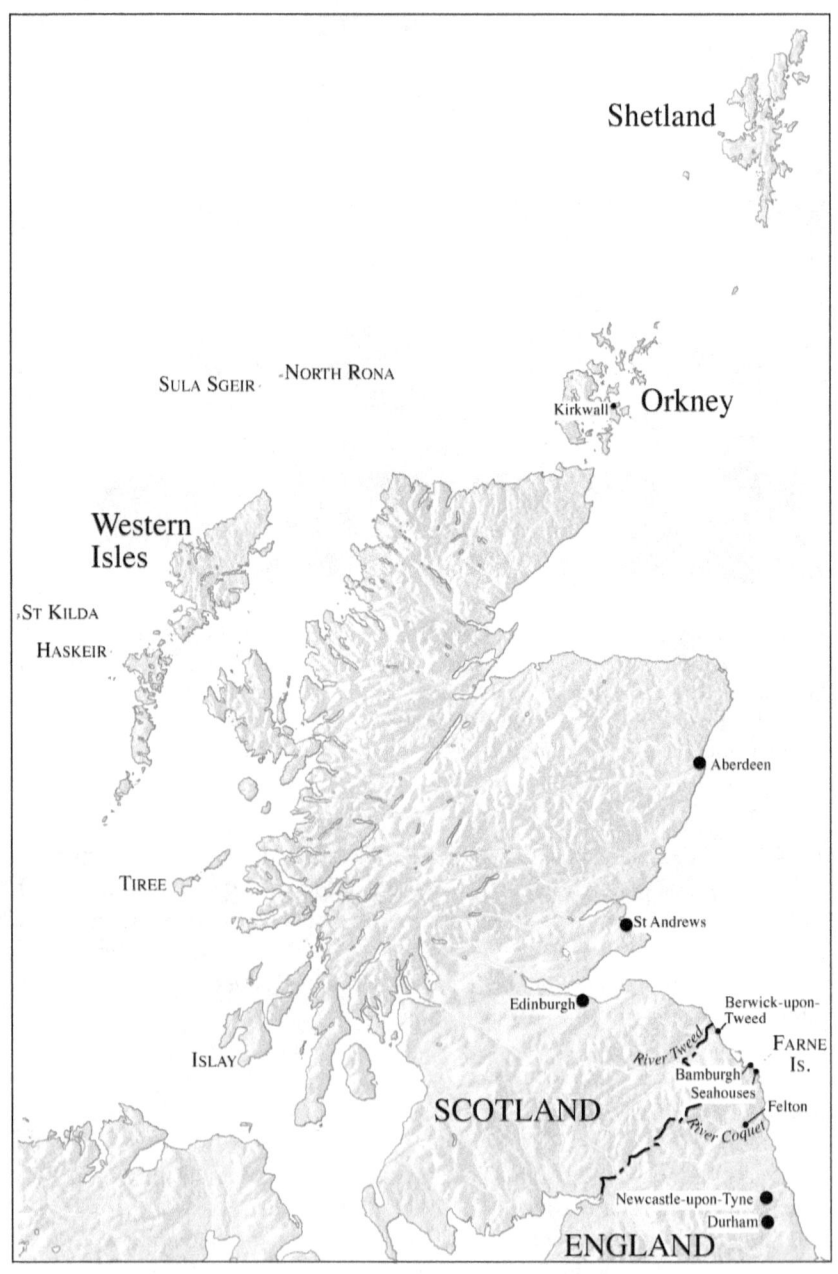

FIGURE 2. Map showing principal places mentioned in the text

by the employment of wardens on Inner Farne after 1881, and the establishment of the Farne Islands Association (FIA) in the same year on the instigation of concerned local naturalists. Stricter protection measures were put in place in 1888 after egg-collectors had seriously disturbed the 1887 seabird nesting season.[14] By 1900, the Farnes suffered little human disturbance or scientific oology and were an early example of a British wildlife sanctuary built on the goodwill of local proprietors and the hard work of the FIA. This private ownership continued until October 1922, when the Thorp family proposed that the Farnes be given to the National Trust, which had been established in 1895. The Thorps were no doubt comforted (in their search for more organised protection for the Farnes) by the knowledge that under the National Trust Act 1907, the NT had the right to declare its property inalienable, meaning it could never be taken away from the NT without the express will of Parliament. In January 1923, an appeal was launched by the NT under the chairmanship of the statesman and birdwatcher, Viscount Grey of Fallodon, to purchase Inner and Outer Farne together for £2,200. After press coverage and with anonymous donations, the money was raised by February 1924. The NT took full legal possession of the Farnes in August 1925.[15] The London headquarters of the NT felt that although the FIA had an intimate working knowledge of the Islands and could form a core membership of a new NT local management committee (appointed on 5 June 1924), ultimate control must rest with London.[16] Only in April 1946 did the FIA agree to change its name to become the Farne Islands Local Committee of the NT.[17]

The grey seal population of the Farne Islands probably held steady at around 100 animals from 1850 to 1920. By the 1930s, the Newcastle naturalist T. Russell Goddard believed the population to be around 150/200 strong. Information about the seals at this time is scanty and unsubstantiated. A trend does appear though. Local naturalists often gave a low figure to make the animal appear still rare and the population fragile, whilst Fishery Board estimates were always high to give the appearance of a growing seal menace. The naturalist Frank Fraser Darling mistakenly under-estimated the population to be 300 in 1939, whereas local naturalist Grace Hickling, Honorary Secretary of the Natural History Society of Northumberland, Durham and Newcastle-upon-Tyne, thought the colony could be at least 600 to 1,000 strong by the late 1930s. By 1950, Hickling estimated the colony size as between 1,500 and 2,000. Despite the lack of real figures it is apparent, as Hickling concludes, that almost 90 years of both unofficial (under the Thorps and FIA) and official protection (under the NT since 1924/5) had 'resulted in a very marked increase in the size of the colony'.[18]

One reason for the lack of rigorous scientific investigation into the grey seals on the Farnes, is the obsessive personal protective stance that the Thorp family had taken since 1861. In particular, Collingwood Thorp (nephew of the Archdeacon) 'ruled' the Farnes and the NT Local Committee from the 1920s to his death in December 1955, and emphatically refused all access to the islands for photographers, university science departments and government bodies. No visitors or even FIA committee members were allowed to land on Brownsman Island, save for Thorp himself. In a letter in August 1943, the Chief Agent of the NT in London expressed how the Farnes Local Management Committee no longer represented the national interest in the site and that few realised what the NT had to contend with in its dealings with Collingwood Thorp, later adding: 'I venture to think that there would be general rejoicing at his departure, not only on the part of scientific associations who have been baulked at every approach by his attitude, but also among local people'. The frustration caused by Thorp's distrust of science and scientists is amply revealed by the urgency of the application made by the Nature Conservancy (NC) to the NT on 8 November 1955 to send a research team to investigate the seal population, as Thorp lay on his death bed.[19]

THE WIDER ENVIRONMENT

The first complaints about the impact of the grey seals of the Farnes on local fisheries came from the River Tweed Commissioners, who asked the River Coquet Fishery Board meeting in November 1933 if they would join with the Northumberland Sea Fisheries Committee in making an application to the Ministry of Agriculture and Fisheries (MAF) for the destruction of some local seals. Collingwood Thorp wrote to the Secretary of the National Trust in London, urging that all be told that 'the islands belong to the National Trust and the seals are protected by them during the whole and not only during the close season'.[20] The NT pressed the Ministry to protect the grey seals, especially as there was such contradictory evidence presented at the meeting of the Coquet Board in Felton. Some net fishermen sought to blame both the grey seal and the common seal for diminished Atlantic salmon *Salmo salar* and sea trout *Salmo trutta* catches, whilst Herbert Wright representing the Northumberland Anglers' Federation took the contrary view that all seals drove the salmon into shallow water and were thus good for his sport. The Coquet Board suggested they would not act, as they did not have sufficient evidence about seal damage at nets or in rivers.[21]

By 1937, the Tweed Commissioners were pushing for action again, claiming they were being thwarted by fishermen in Seahouses who wanted to see grey seals prosper as they were good for local boat tourism. Indeed, the seals had been providing additional tourist income for boatmen since the 1920s, and probably back to the late nineteenth century. Collingwood Thorp, perhaps sensing that the distant NT hierarchy in London might bend to concerted pressure from fishing interests, kept up a constant barrage of letters to the Trust, enclosing newspaper cuttings and passing on hearsay. In September 1937 he warned, 'there is a movement afoot to attack the seals where they breed. I hope you will be able to do something to prevent this – no one has any right to land there to molest them'.[22]

The first conference to address the possible deleterious impact of grey seals on fisheries met in Newcastle on 12 April 1938, attended by the NT, FIA, the Northern Sea Fisheries Committee, the Tweed and Coquet Conservancy Boards, MAF, three local fishermen, and T. Russell Goddard of the Hancock Museum in the city as the recognised regional expert on seals. Fishing representatives called for some reduction in the local grey seal population because of damage to white fishing, salmon and trout fishing, and net fishing in rivers. Russell Goddard spoke in passionate defence of 'the interesting and rare grey seal', asking if the Fishery Boards were truly confident that they could identify which seal species was really to blame, and could a few 'rogue' seals not be heaping blame on the whole population? Although these were the first tentative shots of a war that is still going on today, the tone of the meeting was remarkably conciliatory with the fishermen agreeing that it would be 'unreasonable to ask for any action to be taken until some more conclusive evidence had been produced', and that they 'might have been mistaken' to blame the grey seal so quickly.[23]

There was a difference of opinion developing in the 1940s and 1950s between the fishermen of Seahouses local to the Farnes who obviously felt a sense of affection and attachment (albeit primarily financial) to the seals, and the net fishermen of the River Tweed, 20 miles to the north, who suffered all the seal damage. At a meeting of the FIA at Bamburgh in April 1946, boatman William Shiel spoke for the Seahouses fishermen, arguing that they had no objection to the presence of the grey seals, and found their mournful cries a useful guide in foggy autumn weather. Shiel would later write in anger to the NT in London fearing the utter destruction of 'our Atlantic grey seals' in 1958, and the subsequent loss of tourism and opportunities for scientific study.[24]

Grace Hickling and Ian Telfer began their pioneering seal tagging experiments around the Farnes in 1951, but were already keenly aware of the significant growth of the seal population. In November 1950 they had counted at least 900 adults and 454 pups. Hickling consistently hoped this increase was just temporary, a natural upward fluctuation, and would be adjusted in future years. At this stage, the issue was how to keep this statistical information from fishing interests, and thus stave off any demands for culling. Hickling thought the only way was to keep quiet and 'emulate Brer Rabbit and hope for the best', but H.J.F. Smith, Chief Agent of the NT, sensed the approaching storm. He thought the time would come when the NT could no longer sit on this problem and would have to make a gesture of sorts: 'Before the Tweed Commissioners start a Hullabaloo, I think we would be well advised to consider possible steps to be taken, although in conformity with Brer Rabbit tradition, we must do so *sub rosa*'. Shooting might be necessary he warned, but could the NT make any money in selling surplus pups to zoos?[25]

In the early 1950s there was no real indication that the Ministry of Agriculture, Fisheries and Food (MAFF) would act on this issue. They claimed no firm evidence had been submitted to them that the increase had any adverse affect on the salmon fishery and believed the advice of naturalists that the population could crash just as easily and unpredictably as it had grown. They did, however, agree that the situation needed watching, and sought the advice of Capt. Cyril Diver, first Director-General of the Nature Conservancy (NC).[26] Diver had no great affection for grey seals, having described them once in committee as 'tiresome organisms', that failed to grasp the difference between land and sea, Scotland and England. Indeed, there is a sense early on that the fledgling NC (created in 1949) failed to fully resolve the issue of their responsibility for British seals, and how that responsibility might change when the seals were in or out of the water, on or offshore from a nature reserve. They did rally in 1950/51 to protect breeding seals on North Rona, St Kilda's stacs and Sula Sgeir from Air Ministry and Admiralty plans to use these islands for live bombing exercises.[27] However, Diver and E. Max Nicholson (Director General of the NC 1952–1966), even at one stage considered dissipating the seal problem and boosting world stock by transportation, musing that surplus UK grey seals could be sold for profit to Norway, Iceland, USA and Canada.[28] There was no plan made on how to stop the seals swimming back!

EXPERT ASSESSMENT

What turned the situation around was a report in May 1955 to the Tweed Commissioners (who had been silent on this issue for a while) by a retired naval officer, Commander H.C. Courtney Clarke. He had lived by the River Tweed since 1933, and set about trying to gather definitive financial information on the actual damage that seals did. He calculated a total annual loss to the Tweed salmon industry of £5,700, divided thus: £1,300 loss in revenue on sale of damaged fish; £3,000 lost in fish eaten by seals from nets; £800 physical damage to nets, and £600 depreciation loss to rod fishings. The report contained submissions by local companies and concerned individuals. Clarke had some sympathy for 'the seal lovers', but argued that few of them had ever seen 'the same seals hunting and harrying the unfortunate salmon and killing and maiming so many'. He urged his report be publicised widely to the press, MPs and government departments.[29] The Tweed Commissioners now had the evidence they had been searching for since the early 1930s, and so put pressure on MAFF to act. MAFF turned to the NC scientists, who despatched J.D. Lockie (NC Scientific Officer) to Berwick in September 1955 to investigate the problem.

The Nature Conservancy report of March 1956 concluded that as only a small proportion of the Farnes' grey seals were raiding the Tweed, efficient control measures should be employed at the salmon fishing grounds, not at the breeding colonies. It suggested that although the grey seal should remain under the protection of the law, full-time marksmen should be used by the Tweed Commissioners at the nets, more evidence of damage should be gathered, seal tagging and marking experiments on the Farnes must continue, and the situation be reviewed every two years.[30] The NT Nature Conservation Sub-Committee, chaired by the plant ecologist Sir Edward Salisbury, accepted this report, but urged caution and sought further evidence before any cull should take place on the Farnes, although importantly, they did advise the Trust that such a cull could be on the horizon.

The Executive Committee of the NT, and their Local Committee were at this time (indeed, until the early 1970s) overwhelmingly wedded to the sanctuary ethos. Salisbury, however, was a keen advocate of controlling 'the unrestricted increase of any plant or animal', once biological knowledge had a thorough understanding of the species concerned. His work on weeds and agricultural pests had taught him that confronting the problems generated by an artificial condition created by man was a fundamental principle of modern nature conservation. He wrote to the NT in 1957, that they must accept that the establishment of a protected area for the seals had not meant an equal degree of protection to predators or parasites that controlled seal populations. He warned: 'I do feel most strongly that we shall place ourselves in a false position if we do not make it clear that we do not belong to the band of those, and there are many, who think conservation consists in leaving things severely alone. We should not give substance to those who claim that nature lovers are quite prepared to allow organisms they protect to increase beyond reason and disclaim all responsibility for permitting them to get out of hand. Such critics can only be silenced if it is manifest that conservation accepts the responsibilities that accompany its benefits'.[31]

A Nature Conservancy memo to the NT of February 1957 (in response to the Scottish Home Department's request for action to be taken against Farne Islands' seals that were marauding across the national border), suggested their willingness for 'control on a limited and experimental basis', as it was now felt advisable to control the seal numbers for biological reasons, and because it was 'not proved but virtually certain' that they were damaging local fisheries.[32] In response the NT Nature Conservation Sub-Committee thought it wise to show some willingness to prevent any increase in the growth of the colony, whilst being aware of the Local Committee's implacable opposition to any interference with the colony, and their fear that unauthorised raids on the colony might take place once a green light had been given. At the same time they urged that no costs should be borne by the NT in this culling, and that MAFF had to come forward and make a formal request for action to take place.[33]

Certainly there was a feeling in Spring 1957 amongst some of the prominent administrative staff of the NT that some culling of seals was more than likely, although there were differing viewpoints within the organisation. Grace Hickling and the Council of the Natural History Society of Northumberland publicly remained much against any culling, citing welfare and scientific research reasons. In February 1957 Hickling predicted, 'a storm of protest from animal lovers', should any control measures be taken. Worse, there was great anger in the Northumberland Natural History Society over the NC's suggestion of a cull of 300 seals, when Max Nicholson privately admitted to local naturalist Eric Ennion that this was a purely arbitrary figure without any scientific justification at all. Hickling wrote to the NT that 'the Council were horrified at this attitude...they considered it an absolute disgrace that a figure with such a basis should be published as the official recommendation of a supposedly scientific government department'.[34]

January 1958 saw the first national and regional press reports that a seal cull might take place on the Farnes, with suitably dramatic headlines as 'Murder in the Nursery' ('The friendly grey seals who sing happily on the Farne Islands are in trouble. Murder is planned in their nursery'), and 'What harm would I do?', accompanying emotive pictures of grey seal pups.[35] Various chapters of the Northern Naturalists' Union came out against any cull in March 1958 in a letter to the north-east regional press.

The Executive Committee of the NT considered the advice of the NC and their own staff and advisers, and privately drafted a conciliatory press release that spoke of there being 'no sufficient reason to justify an operation which would be unwelcome to many nature lovers, particularly on a sanctuary of such long-standing and international repute', nor would the killing be effective at stopping marauding seals in the Tweed. The Trust would, however, if pushed, not stand in the way of a MAFF-led cull 'in the national interest',[36] if a specific order was made under the 1932 Protection Act. The pressure was mounting on the NT and government. In April 1957, the Salmon Net Fishing Association of Scotland presented a memorandum to the Scottish Home Department drawing attention to the seal damage caused on all sections of the Scottish coast, citing marauding seals from the Farnes in some cases, and calling for an investigation and then action to be taken.[37] In May 1958 a suspension of close season order was made to allow experimental culling by MAFF on the Farne Islands in November. In July 1959 a similar order was made to allow experimental culls in Scotland in December 1959 and October 1960.[38]

THE CULLS AND POPULAR PROTEST

The Farne Islands, England

The first experimental cull of grey seal pups on the Farnes in 1958 was eventually called off, because local boatmen refused to help in the killing expeditions, the local press came out against it, and the NT put pressure on MAFF after receiving a gruesome report from Grace Hickling about inefficient culling methods employed.[39] But the pressure to cull was great. MAFF urged the NT to step aside, accusing them of 'harbouring on their property a stock of seals which is damaging the property and interfering with the commercial livelihood of fishermen'.[40] Culling began again in December 1963 to reduce the Farnes population to 750 breeding females, and continued until 1965/66.

The issue was first brought into the wider public domain in 1963/64, with coverage of the culls in the media, and the vocal opposition of Grace Hickling, animal welfare groups and local natural history societies. The NT Council's decision reluctantly to allow regulated culling saw them estranged from their local management committee who in general opposed the culls and called for more scientific research to be done. The issue was first put to NT membership at the November 1964 AGM in Cardiff, when a vote (63 to 23) fought off a resolution (from 3 members in south-east England) condemning the NT culling policy. There was discernible anger within the NT membership. By February 1964, there were 73 letters of complaint, 14 requests for information, 13 resignations, 9 threatened resignations, and a Co. Durham petition of 150 names against culling.[41] But this was easily absorbed in a national membership of 151,000. In 1964, when R. Bloom of Flamingo Zoo raided the Farnes and rescued six pups, he was hailed as a 'seal saviour' in the press and public's eyes.[42] The RSPCA were initially very against the culls, but later accepted them (angering some of their membership) as long as they could have an observer and vet on site to oversee animal welfare issues.[43] Over the 1960s and 1970s, the World Wildlife Fund (WWF), University Fund for Animal Welfare (UFAW), Beauty without Cruelty, and the Seal Preservation Group (with links to the hunt saboteur movement) emerged as vocal campaigners against the culls and accomplished manipulators of public opinion. They argued that fresh financial assessments of seal damage to salmon, of £50,000 to £100,000 each year, were controversial and unsubstantiated.[44] The public outcry worked, as the NT refused to grant permission to cull after 1966 (by which time almost 1,000 pups had been killed, almost all of them females), hiding behind a call for more scientific evidence.

More importantly, these mid-1960s seal culls saw the emergence of a new coalition of middle class protestors in Britain, which comprised three strands of interest. First, wildlife enthusiasts, who would go on in the 1980s and 1990s to protest about fox *Vulpes vulpes* hunting, government-sponsored badger *Meles meles* culls, and stag hunting on National Trust land. Second, animal welfare supporters who would later protest about vivisection, call for wider animal rights and the humane transport of veal calves. And finally, the group we often underestimate, people who on a weekend walk at the beach hope to see a seal, or just want to know that seals are out there doing well. This last group now visit sea-life centres and seal rescue centres,[45] and pay for recreational seal-watching trips.

Press and television coverage of the culls hurt the image of the NT most, a November 1964 letter in the Newcastle *Evening Chronicle*, pouring scorn on 'the National Trust myth', which 'had exploded with a blood red plop'. 'Never again can anyone interested in wildlife regard the National Trust as anything but a bitter joke', it ended.[46] This criticism was more relevant after February 1971, when the NT eventually produced a management plan for islands they had owned for 46 years. There had been growing NT concern from the late 1960s about seal and human damage to vegetation and puffin *Fratercula arctica* burrows. This, and subsequent plans in 1975 and 1981, indicated that the fragile ecosystem of the Farnes was under threat from seal overcrowding, and so turned the NT from being reluctant cullers in the 1960s, into 'gung-ho' cullers in the 1970s, the aim being the reduction of the breeding female population to 1,000.[47] This was a real shift in attitude for the NT, that they justified to their members as being done in the interests of the islands and their wildlife, and not for fisheries.

The Trust took a pro-active role in the 1970s, probably because they wanted to be seen to be in control of the situation themselves, especially as the new Conservation of Seals Act now gave government the right, if they wished, to enter private land to cull seals for the national good. However, some NT staff actually felt it was better to let government take full control, the Assistant Secretary asking in 1971, 'why don't we sit tight and let HMG, now they have assumed all the powers, take on the odium and the cost also?'[48] The NT also began their own control measures against rabbits *Oryctolagus cuniculus*, gulls *Larus spp* and weeds, but nobody protested about that. In 1979/80 they even fell out with the government's Sea Mammal Research Unit (SMRU) who had asked for a halt to the culls, to provide the undisturbed opportunity for the study of colony population dynamics.[49]

There were still letters of protest to the NT in the 1970s and 1980s, usually about 10 per year, and seal preservation groups even hatched a plan to parachute the comedian Spike Milligan onto the Farnes to stop the culls in 1972 and 1975![50] Protest letters rose to 43 in 1983/84 when the Sea Shepherd Fund campaigned against the culling. These protest letters were more aggressive, and promised more direct action, than those of the mid-1960s, showing how the more modern radical wing of the animal rights movement was now influencing the public debate.[51] In the long run, all subsequent culls and public outcries in Britain were in character shaped by events on the Farnes, but would have the added potency of enduring media hype, the animal rights movement, IFAW and Greenpeace.

Orkney, Scotland

In Scotland the first culls took place on Orkney. The experimental culls by Aberdeen Marine Laboratory tested various killing methods in 1959: shooting, clubbing and injections of nicotine pellets.[52] In 1960, Bennet Rae published his Department of Agriculture and Fisheries for Scotland (DAFS) report *Seals and Scottish Fisheries*, which showed graphic photographs of seal-marked salmon, presented evidence of damage to nets and spoke of concerns over the propagation of the sealworm *Pseudoterranova decipiens* by seals.[53] Rae believed that possibly 15 per cent of the total annual British catch of all kinds of fish from home waters fell victim to seal predation, concluding that 'seal stocks must be reduced and thereafter maintained at a level which will not interfere unduly with commercial fisheries'.⁵⁴ This gave the Scottish Office their *raison d'être* for future action against the seals.

The first complaints against the culling were raised in 1960 by Jo Grimond, the Orkney MP, who pressed DAFS over the evidence they had for the specific guilt of Orcadian grey seals. In 1962, Grimond was joined in his protests by the Orkney and Shetland Scottish Society for the Prevention of Cruelty to Animals (SSPCA) branches, some local people, and the Orkney Field Club. The debate pitted local seal enthusiasts against local fishermen. However, some of the disquiet in Orkney at this time was not based on protection, rather that local people were not being given culling permits to make the business of 'some economic advantage to the islands'. British marine mammal expert, H.R. Hewer of the University of London,⁵⁵ urged DAFS to involve local people: 'this co-operation and understanding is absolutely essential for the successful carrying out of research of this character over a number of years, leading to the control of populations of animals'.⁵⁶ Local permits were introduced. In October 1963, 974 seals were killed, including an overkill of 224 by over-enthusiastic local hunters, causing DAFS to believe their local representative was losing control of the situation.⁵⁷

At this time events in Orkney were geographically distant from the bulk of the British population, but by the mid-1960s the more public culls on the Farnes were beginning to have a knock-on effect in the far north. In Scotland, the Nature Conservancy sought to distance themselves from the culling in April 1964, worried about the PR implications for their conservation work across the UK, concerned about over-zealous culling, and irritated that the MAFF publicity office insisted on directing all queries to them. Internal DAFS memos show that they were keenly aware of a gathering storm of bad publicity rolling north from the Farnes brought on by a one-sided 'Tonight' TV programme and press photos of pups being killed. DAFS civil servants suggested that perhaps the naturalist Peter Scott might be persuaded to broadcast to the nation on the problems of seal overcrowding and damage to fisheries, though it subsequently transpired that he was against the culling. In Orkney, the police expressed concerns over their lack of officers to deal with a protest, should it come, and suggested the involvement of Coastguard and Customs officers if necessary.⁵⁸ The Orkney culls continued over the 1960s, with the aim of reducing the breeding population there by 25 per cent, as urged in the findings of the 1959 NC Consultative Committee, published in 1963 as *Grey Seals and Fisheries*.⁵⁹

The 30 year rule prevents much of the Scottish story past 1970 being told; indeed, some of the government files are closed for 50 years most probably because of political sensitivities and domestic security issues generated by the culls in the 1970s. However, oral history has yielded some information. In 1977, DAFS introduced a six-year plan to reduce the Scottish grey seal population by 15,000 to its mid-1960s level of around 35,000. The 1977 cull on the Western Isles went ahead with little local opposition to it, but was hindered by bad weather.⁶⁰ However, in concert with growing international protest in Canada going back to the mid-1960s, growing British protest disrupted the 1977 culls in Orkney. Then Greenpeace with the support of much of the British public, forced an abandonment of the 1978 cull. The Scottish Office no longer felt that the proposed culling of 900 adults and 4,000 moulted pups in Orkney and North Rona in the west, would be successful or safe.

Sir William Fraser, Parliamentary Under Secretary in the Scottish Office, recalls that the Secretary of State for Scotland, Bruce Millan, saw the seal culls as a huge political issue, and despite a compelling economic case from DAFS urging him to authorise further culls, thought it 'politically disastrous and would have none of it'. Fraser recalls the 1978 furore as a clash between economic logic (depleted fisheries) and political reality (men with clubs killing baby seals). He also considers that the normally tough Millan backed down because of huge media interest in the killing, and because the Scottish populace was heading towards the March 1979 referendum on independence under the Scotland Act of 1978. The Scottish Office came under pressure at home and overseas. A petition with 42,000 names against the culling was delivered in October 1978, as the Greenpeace boat *Rainbow Warrior* lay in Kirkwall harbour. Internationally, the European Parliament, and later the International Union for the Conservation of Nature and Natural Resources (IUCN) meeting in USSR, asked for an immediate halt to the killing.[61] Newspapers carried headlines such as 'Fight on the Beaches', and 'Battle Lines Set in Seal War'; The *Sunday Mirror* appealed direct to the Prime Minister with an editorial saying, 'Come on Jim: Stop it'.[62] On 12 October 1978 there were angry clashes between protestors and government officials on Kirkwall quay, and a later bomb scare on the Norwegian cullers' vessel gave the protest a sinister angle. Clearly Millan ignored his scientists and made a political decision; as Fraser noted, it was simply 'best to avoid all controversy; do not incur the wrath of the bulk of the population'.[63]

On the morning of 17 October 1978 every national newspaper had the end to the cull as its main headline, proclaiming 'Greenpeace Victorious'. With the important support of local conservation groups and people, they had used their international protest experiences gained in Canada to ensure that their campaign in Orkney was so effective. Now holding the political and moral ascendancy, a group of wildlife conservation and animal welfare groups opposed to the culls formed the Council for Nature's Grey Seals Group in 1979 and kept the issue in the public eye (calling for more scientific evidence before more political gestures were made), as did the local groups across Britain that emerged from Animal Welfare Year 1976/77.[64] The emergence of sentiment and emotion as a key factor in wildlife management, and a corresponding public lack of respect for science, angered biologist Charles Summers, who penned a stinging attack in the *New Scientist* on ill-informed animal welfare groups and conservation bodies, blaming them for truly putting the 'con in conservation'.[65]

KINDNESS KILLS

In the modern British environmental movement, the naturalist Frank Fraser Darling is seen as something of a mid-century prophet in the wilderness, a British Aldo Leopold.[66] He was particularly interested in grey seals, having studied them on North Rona in 1938, sensing overcrowding already at this colony and estimating that 15 per cent of pups died because of this.[67] In August 1939 he had been employed on the Tweed to ascertain the impact of seals on the fishery, and although his investigations were never finished because of the war, he openly predicted that there was a problem developing. At this stage in his career, Darling was striving to make the conservation establishment wake up to the doctrine of utilitarian conservation, American President Teddy Roosevelt's dictum of 'conservation through wise use'. Darling wrote in January 1951 to Grace Hickling: 'The lesson of conservation appears more and more insistently to be that absolute protection should be a temporary and local measure, not an inflexible rule'. By the early 1950s, he was pushing for 'an overall carefully controlled annual toll of the Atlantic grey seals', thus both conserving the species and cutting out criticism from fishery interests. Such a new policy, he reasoned, 'would be better for the seals because they would be valued as a continuing natural resource rather than purely sentimentally'. Sentiment was a dangerous foundation for conservation policy, he warned Hickling, for the seals would be in grave danger as, 'government departments are fickle bodies who can be rushed by well organised vested interests. The seals are extremely efficient gatherers of energy which the nation should not neglect at present'.[68] They could yield fat, protein and leather. Darling wrote along similar lines in a open letter to the Scottish Committee of the Nature Conservancy (NC) in December 1950,[69] but this vision found little favour among those firmly wedded to the concept of species protection through representative habitat nature reserves.

By the mid-1960s, although serving as Vice-President and Director of the Conservation Foundation in the USA, Darling remained passionate about the challenges and problems of nature conservation in his homeland. In a 1964 draft press article 'Kindness Kills', he returned to the grey seals of the Farnes and his experiences on the River Tweed.[70] An organised seal cull was necessary, 'but it would be harder work and harder on our feelings' than just blindly protecting the seal through mere sentiment in a designated sanctuary. Darling was the first to recognise that the grey seal issue was a scientific, technical and ethical problem: 'it would be cowardly to ignore it and deceive ourselves by holding inflexibly to the idea of sanctuary'. If Americans had accepted 'after an emotional battle' that elk *Cervus elaphus* needed to be culled in National Parks to reduce damage to aspen trees and bring the population in line with the carrying capacity of the habitat,[71] then in Britain we should steel ourselves for a similar policy with the grey seal. People had to be made to realise, he argued, 'that the welfare of the species is more important than the survival of individuals'.[72]

Darling was supported by other influential commentators with international experience. The President of IUCN, Dr Francois Bourliere, wrote in a 1964 bulletin of the evolution of the concept of nature protection, and the dangers of the now outdated nineteenth century preservation movement that simply put habitats and species 'under a bell-glass'. He argued that the long-term survival of all life on earth depended on conservation through wise management where tough choices would have to be made. Overpopulation, brought about by absolute protection or the removal of predators, could only be dealt with by regulated culling, or else it would radically alter the structure of existing fragile biological communities. It was no longer good enough to take a *laissez-faire* attitude to wildlife protection. In many instances, active environmental management was necessary. To this end the International Union for the Preservation of Nature (IUPN) created in 1946 at Fontainebleau had recognised this development, with a name change to IUCN in 1956 at the Edinburgh General Assembly.[73] The scientific community in Britain did not unequivocally agree that the grey seal was a pest to fishing interests. Government took the line that before a change in the legislation was needed, there had to be better knowledge of the biology and feeding behaviour of the animal, and founded the Natural Environment Research Council's (NERC) SMRU in December 1977 at Cambridge, by amalgamating the Seals Research Division and Whale Research Unit, hitherto part of the Institute for Marine Environmental Research. SMRU have never agreed that there is enough scientific data to justify a grey seal cull in the last twenty years, and in the absence of hard evidence and knowing the strength of popular resistance in the 1960s and 1970s, British governments have dodged calls for a return to organised official culling.

Grey seals have not been culled on the Farne Islands since 1985. Instead, human disturbance and aggressive wardening are used to keep the seals away from Inner Farne, so important for its breeding seabird populations. Each year a very small number of seals may be shot for welfare reasons, usually ill health or serious injury.[74] The National Trust has ultimately heeded the advice of a civil servant in the Scottish Office, who when asked in December 1961 if Orkney MP Jo Grimond should be kept abreast of the culling in the Northern Isles, suggested: 'No, it might just encourage him to raise the whole thing again. Better to let sleeping pups lie!'[75]

SEALS AND POPULAR CULTURE

Before the late nineteenth century there was no real sense of people taking delight in seals in Britain, save for a few enlightened proprietors who offered some limited and unofficial protection to the animals at places as diverse as Haskeir in the Outer Hebrides, the Farnes off Northumberland, and the Isles of Scilly off Cornwall (SW England).[76] Also important is the delight we can extract from the seal's role in literature, and Gaelic folklore as the 'selkie'.[77] Our most traditional response to grey seals was to use them as a resource for food, for their oil and for sealskins made into waistcoats, sporrans and fashionable motoring jackets. Over the course of the twentieth century humans voluntarily removed ourselves from our position as top predator of the grey seal after naturalists and sportsmen informed us that it was rare, and we then embraced it first as a treasured part of our natural heritage worthy of protection, and later (post 1960) as an environmental icon, a potent eco-symbol.

The rise of the totemic status of both seals and whales is one of the great post-war changes in the way that we have constructed nature around us. We now not only show great concern for the welfare of some species, but focus in our thousands on the individual plight of an orphan seal pup or stranded whale. The British countryside writer and broadcaster, Richard Mabey, sees this popular totemism as worthy, but unpredictable and volatile: 'underneath there are more fundamental and less easily resolved conflicts of values – about who can legitimately be said to own natural resources, about the rights of humans and animals, about the relative importance of present livelihoods and past traditions – conflicts which involve deeply held personal beliefs and meanings'.[78] The last 30 years have seen a dramatic rise in the popularity of mass recreational seal watching around British coasts, from Scotland to Northumberland, Norfolk to Cornwall. To an angry fisherman whose livelihood is threatened, this must be little more than 'city folk gawping at vermin',[79] reflecting the social and economic conflicts between the bulk of the British public and hard-pressed fishing communities.

In Scotland, the political debate over a return to culling has recently been resurrected by the Scottish National Party (SNP), who are strongly supported in remoter rural regions. In 2000, the Atlantic Salmon Trust (founded in 1967), called for action to reduce the effect of predation on salmon by seals, cormorants *Phalacrocorax carbo* and goosanders *Mergus merganser* to be taken on a local or regional basis, rather than attempting any wide-ranging national control.[80] This proposal perhaps represents a possible 'middle ground' solution, but would it be acceptable to all interests?

The growth and popularity of coastal seal-rescue centres reflects our continued fascination with marine mammals and our wider cultural need to establish contact with an accessible, and with what we construct as a benevolent and sympathetic nature. We search for something human in the animals we watch, and the grey seal pup cloaked in white fur is a potent symbol of baby-like innocence, with eyes that shed tears, an ability to sing, and a dog-like face. This enables us to construct it as a sensate creature and accept it as most like ourselves. In effect, we have in Britain established a 'special relationship' with the grey seal. As Fraser Darling observed in 1939, 'there is no creature born, even among the greater apes, which more resembles a human baby in its ways and its cries than a baby grey seal'.[81] This British popular attitude to seals is seen as rather eccentric in Norway, where seals are still seen in a utilitarian light, and sealing is seen as inherently traditional. Grey seals have always been seen as vermin in Ireland. In 1924, Charles Green, Minister of Fisheries in Dublin, wrote to George Hogarth of the Fisheries Board for Scotland, 'while you have been cherishing the brutes, we have been offering rewards for their destruction!'[82]

CONCLUDING REMARKS

In 1982 the European Parliament announced a ban on 'baby seal' skin exports from Canada to Europe, which had a dramatic effect as catches fell from 200,000 in 1982 to a minimum of 45,000 in 1985. By 1987, under massive international pressure, the Canadian government had banned commercial hunting of harp seal pups under 3 weeks old.[83] Of course, this is in part the product of the cultural change that has altered the way we think about animals since 1800, the implications of which are enormous for those who are charged with the management of animal species, especially those species that were once endangered but are now regarded as a pest in some aspect of their behaviour. It also reflects the rise of environmentalism and animal rights issues post 1960, and the power of mass membership environmental NGOs when allied with the media. Grey seals are the extreme case of this cultural shift in Britain, but increasing populations of African elephants *Elephas africanus* in parts of sub-Saharan Africa post-1960 (especially South Africa, Botswana and Zimbabwe), and even tigers *Felis tigris* in reserves bordering parts of rural India, show people/wildlife conflicts to be an international policy problem.[84]

There has been little protest about the culling of red deer in Scotland over the last thirty years,[85] where the public seem to accept this as a necessary evil and accept the advice of science, but this is not necessarily paralleled in responses to the culling of roe *Capreolus capreolus* and muntjac *Muntiacus reevesi* deer in England. One concern expressed in Scotland is that deer will not be shot from helicopters as is practised in New Zealand wildlife management. The culling of barnacle geese *Branta leucopsis* and Greenland white-fronted geese *Anser albifrons flavirostris* by farmers on the Hebridean island of Islay, where the huge flocks damage crops, was halted recently in a lawsuit by WWF and RSPB quoting wider European bird legislation. On issues of wildlife management, public opinion has become strangely variable. Sometimes it tolerates traditional pest control, other times it seems to demand absolute protection for certain iconic animals.

The Atlantic grey seal has proved to be an exceptionally challenging mammal to manage in Britain over the twentieth century. It inhabits both the land and the sea, and therefore cuts across the institutional and administrative land/sea divide. It is also a difficult animal for scientists to study in the wild, and we need a far deeper understanding, gained from further research, of such issues as grey seal demographics, biology, diet, seasonal movements, behavioural traits, and the extent to which it poses a threat to domestic fisheries. The grey seal story also challenges us to think hard about the strengths and weaknesses of the three key approaches to nature conservation practice here in the UK, namely protection through legislation, the designation of nature reserves as sanctuaries from uncontrolled human disturbance, and the dissemination of environmental education and information in its broadest sense. Given the diverse range of political and social perceptions and environmental and economic impacts of the grey seal, it has been far from easy to co-ordinate policies here in Britain (in England and Scotland), and indeed, within the wider North Atlantic. The exceptional thing about the grey seal is that the bulk of the British public (and, indeed, the public in Europe and North America), not just the voluntary conservation bodies (as is the case with geese on Islay, and hen harriers *Circus cyaneus* on grouse moors) are up in arms about the thought of government-sponsored seal culls. This attitude has not really changed for at least 50 years now. Thus, those responsible for the management of this nature conservation success, or any other controversial species population in the modern era, will have to take into account not only scientific and biological opinion, but also the relative contemporary (and historical) political and popular strength of the animal's human friends and enemies. Although this essay has focused on the British experience of coping with the grey seal and its varied interactions with both the natural and more explicitly human environments, the themes developed are common to many international situations where there is conflict between conservationists and other user-interests as to the optimal management of a species.

The trial of wildlife management by public opinion is here to stay. When it came to culling in the 1960s and 1970s in Britain many organisations, including nature conservation bodies like the Scottish Wildlife Trust (founded in 1964),[86] were taken genuinely by surprise over the weight of public opinion to halt the culls immediately. The RSPCA 'seal rally' held around Trafalgar Square on 10 March 1979 was a huge British propaganda and publicity success, as staff dressed as seal pups were 'clubbed' on busy London shopping streets by RSPCA Chief Inspector Frank Franzmann (dressed as a sealer with a baseball bat).[87] Remember, those of us who take great delight in seals, do so without any economic loss.

ACKNOWLEDGEMENTS

The author was previously Senior Research Fellow, Centre for Environmental History and Policy (CEHP), University of St Andrews, Fife, Scotland, KY16 9QW. This paper was written with the support of a Leverhulme Special Research Fellowship, and I am grateful to the Leverhulme Trust for the intellectual stimulation and challenge the fellowship gave me. I would like to thank the National Trust (London), RSPCA (Horsham, West Sussex) and SSPCA (Edinburgh) for granting me access to their private archives, and the staff of the National Archives of Scotland (NAS) in Edinburgh. I offer warm thanks to Professor T.C. Smout CBE who commented on drafts of this paper, and to my colleagues at the University of St. Andrews, Jill Payne and Dr Jodie Thorne, who have also commented on drafts. Professor John Harwood of SMRU kindly supplied pertinent biological information. Dr John Harvey, Assistant Head of Estates and Head of Nature Conservation at the National Trust, offered useful conservation policy insights. Two anonymous referees provided constructive and supportive comments.

NOTES

[1] Exceptions are: Keith Thomas, *Man and the Natural World: Changing Attitudes in England 1500–1800* (London: Penguin, 1984). Peter Coates, *Nature: Western Attitudes since Ancient Times* (Cambridge: Polity, 1998). T.C. Smout, *Nature Contested: Environmental History in Scotland and Northern England since 1600* (Edinburgh: Edinburgh University Press, 2000).

[2] See especially, John McNeill, *Something New Under the Sun* (London: Allen Lane, 2000). B.W. Clapp, *An Environmental History of Britain since the Industrial Revolution* (Harlow: Longman, 1994). Ian Simmons, *An Environmental History of Great Britain* (Edinburgh: Edinburgh University Press, 2001). John Sheail, *An Environmental History of Twentieth Century Britain* (Basingstoke: Palgrave, 2002).

[3] John Harrison, 'Animals and the state in nineteenth century England', *English Historical Review*, LXXVIII (October 1973) :786–820. The RSPCA is driven entirely by welfare issues (RSPCA officers are contractually obliged to care for any injured animal).

[4] Tony Samstag, *For the Love of Birds: The Story of the RSPB* (Sandy: RSPB, 1988). The RSPB concerns itself with the protection of birds and their habitats from a wide range of threats.

[5] John Sheail, *Nature in Trust* (London: Blackie, 1976); John Sheail, *Seventy-five Years in Ecology: The British Ecological Society* (Oxford, Blackwell, 1987); John Sheail, *Natural Environment Research Council: A History* (Swindon: NERC, 1992); John Sheail, *Nature Conservation in Britain: The Formative Years* (London: TSO, 1998).

[6] The Gulf of St. Lawrence and Front (off Labrador) harp seal herds have been exploited commercially since the 1760s, with the Norwegians taking a major part in the hunt from 1937. During the 1960s the Norwegians took up to 100,000 harp seals a year for commercial reasons. See especially, Briton Cooper Busch, *The War against the Seals: A History of the North American Seal Fishery* (Kingston: McGill-Queen's University Press, 1985); Farley Mowat, *Sea of Slaughter* (Toronto: Seal Books, 1997); Paul Watson, *Sea Shepherd* (New York: W.W. Norton, 1982). The Royal Society for the Prevention of Cruelty to Animals (RSPCA) archives, Horsham, West Sussex, are illuminating on this issue.

[7] *Grey Seals (Protection) Act 1914*, 4 & 5 George V, Chapter 3.

[8] National Archives of Scotland (NAS) AF56/1443. See letters from Charles Lyell MP, draft bill and minutes by naturalists and Fishery Board civil servants.

[9] Conversations between author and staff of the Sea Mammal Research Unit (SMRU), University of St. Andrews.

[10] Mary Bones, 'The Slaughter of Selchis: Notes on Seal Hunting in the Outer Hebrides', *Hebridean Naturalist*, 10 (1990): 7–16.

[11] *Grey Seals (Protection) Act 1932*, 22 & 23 George V, Chapter 23.

[12] *Conservation of Seals Act 1970*, 18 & 19 Elizabeth II, Chapter 30. W.N. Bonner,

'Legislation on the Seals in the British Isles', *The Salmon Net*, 7 (1971): 30–33; Robert A. Lambert, 'Grey Seals:To Cull or not to Cull', *History Today*, 51, 6, (2001): 30–32.

[13] Michael B. Usher, 'Minimum Viable Population Size, Maximum Tolerable Population Size, or the Dilemma of Conservation Success,' in B. Gopal, P.S. Pathak, K.G. Saxena (eds) *Ecology Today: An Anthology of Contemporary Ecological Research* (New Delhi: International Scientific Publications, 1998). Figures kindly supplied by Professor John Harwood of the Sea Mammal Research Unit (SMRU).

[14] Grace Hickling, 'Islands of the Wanderers: the Farne Islands Nature Reserve', in G. Jackson Stops (ed.) *National Trust Studies 1981* (London: NT, 1981).

[15] The islands actually passed to the NT on 13 March 1924.

[16] National Trust (NT) archives, File 208/2, Extract from the Farne Islands Association Report for the year 1922 by Collingwood F. Thorp; cutting from *Times*, 6 February 1924; NT Executive Committee and Council Minutes for meetings 17 October 1922, 9 April 1923, 18 June 1923, 11 February 1924, 5 June 1924.

[17] An interesting sub-plot of this study is that it provides a window on the history of the NT itself, especially in the *ad hoc* way it dealt with its regional members and local management committees, and more importantly, in the often strained relationships it had with donors of properties.

[18] Grace Hickling, *Grey Seals and the Farne Islands* (London: Routledge and Kegan Paul, 1962). It is important to document what these numbers refer to. There is some confusion. In some cases the figures given are the numbers of pups born on the islands, in others they are the maximum number of seals counted at the Farnes at any time of the year, and some are simply best estimates of the total number of seals associated with the islands.

[19] NT archives, File series 208, Letter from E. Max Nicholson, NC London, to H.F. Smith, NT London, 8 November 1955.

[20] NT archives, File series 208, Letter from Collingwood Thorp, Alnwick to S.H. Hamer, Secretary NT, London, 10 November 1933. The more pressing concern for the NT at this time was the control of human visitors to the Farnes.

[21] NT archives, File series 208, cutting from *Newcastle Daily Journal*, 6 November 1933.

[22] NT archives, File series 208, Letter from Collingwood Thorp to D. McLeod Matheson, Secretary NT, London, 9 September 1937.

[23] NT archives, File series 208, Report of 'Conference convened by the Farne Islands Association to discuss the question of the Grey Seal', by R.E. Hale, April 1938, 18pp.

[24] NT archives, File series 208, Minutes of meeting of the Farnes Islands Association Committee, Bamburgh Castle Hotel, 8 April 1946. Letter from William Shiel, Seahouses to NT London, 2 February 1958.

[25] NT archives, File series 208, Letter from H.J.F. Smith, NT London, to Grace Hickling, 10 January 1951.

[26] NT archives, File series 208, Letter from T.S. Leach, Chief Inspector of Fisheries, MAFF London to Capt. Cyril Diver, NC London, 29 May 1951.

[27] NAS, SNH1-1, Minutes of meetings of the NC Scottish Committee, Edinburgh, 2 November 1950 and 25 January 1951.

[28] NAS, AF62/929/14. Letter from Cyril Diver, NC London to T.S. Leach, MAFF London, 12 February 1951; Letter from John Berry, NC Edinburgh to A.J. Aglen, Scottish Home Dept, 16 February 1951.

[29] NT archives, File series 208, 'Report by H.C. Courtney Clarke on the damage done by

seals to the Tweed Salmon Industry', Clint Lodge, St. Boswells, 9 May 1955.

[30] NT archives, File series 208, 'Report on the Grey Seals and Damage to Salmon Fisheries on the Northumberland and Berwickshire Coast', by NC, distributed by MAFF on 3 March 1956.

[31] NT archives, File series 208, Letters from E.J.K. Salisbury, Felpham, West Sussex, to Hubert Smith, NT London, 31 December 1957 and 4 January 1958.

[32] NT archives, File series 208, NC memo 'Grey Seals: Question of Control on the Farne Islands', 13 February 1957.

[33] NT archives, File series 208, Minutes of the meeting of the NT Nature Conservation Sub-Committee, London, 25 February 1957.

[34] NT archives, File series 208, Letter from Grace Hickling, Hancock Museum, Newcastle to Hubert Smith, NT London, 16 January 1958.

[35] NT archives, press cuttings files. *The Sunday Sun*, 5 January 1958; *The Newcastle Journal*, 16 January 1958.

[36] NT archives, File series 208, Press release 'Farne Islands: Grey Seals', 28 February 1958.

[37] NAS, AF62/4201, Memo from Salmon Net Fishing Association to P.R.C. Macfarlane, Inspector of Salmon Fisheries, Scottish Home Department. The seal menace was 'a matter of national importance'.

[38] See NT archives, File series 208; NAS AF62/3927.

[39] NT archives, File series 208.

[40] NT archives, File series 208. Letter from C.F. Huntly, MAFF London, to H.J.F. Smith, NT London, 2 March 1959. See Sheail, *Nature Conservation in Britain*, 76–82.

[41] NT archives, File series 208. Memo from C.J. Gibbs, NT Chief Agent, 7 May 1964.

[42] NT archives, File series 208. Report on 1965 cull by Grace Hickling, February 1966. The NT received many letters from individuals and organisations asking could they come to the Farnes and rescue seal pups from the culls, to keep as pets or donate to zoos and wildlife parks.

[43] RSPCA archives, IF/29/4 Policy 'Culling of Farne Islands Seals'. NT archives, File series 208. Letter from Mrs M. Hamilton, Stockton, to *Newcastle Journal*, 19 September 1958: 'Is it humane to rain blows on the head of a grey seal pup in view of its mother? I am heavily ashamed to identify myself with the RSPCA who, in my opinion, steer a middle course in various subjects'.

[44] NT archives, File series 208, WWF statement by British National Appeal on Grey Seals, 27 November 1964: 'It is a sad reflection that these culls should happen in a country which leads the world in conservation; which rallied to the cause of saving the Leonardo da Vinci cartoon, but which puts commercial profit above the saving of one of God's treasures'.

[45] Ken Jones, *Seal Doctor* (Glasgow: Fontana, 1978). Orphan seal pups can be viewed at 17 Sea Life Centres around the UK coast, at places such as St. Andrews, Scarborough, Hunstanton, Weymouth, Newquay etc. The National Seal Sanctuary is at Gweek in Cornwall. There is a Seal Rehabilitation and Research Centre at Pieterburen in the Netherlands.

[46] NT archives, File series 208, extract from Newcastle *Evening Chronicle*, 24 November 1964.

[47] NT archives, 208/2/PF, W. Nigel Bonner and Grace Hickling, 'Grey Seals at the Farne Islands: A Management Plan', February 1971.

[48] NT archives, 208/2, memo from S.H.E. Burley, Assistant Secretary NT, London, to Chief Agent NT, 7 April 1971.

[49] NT archives, 208/2, Letters between SMRU Cambridge, and NT London.

[50] Letters from Frank and Mavis Strudwick, held in archives of Sea Mammal Research Unit (SMRU), University of St. Andrews. The Strudwicks now live on Orkney. These 1970s Farnes culls were carried out by Norwegians, as was the 1977 cull in the Outer Hebrides, and the aborted 1978 cull in Orkney.

[51] NT archives, File series 208, protest letters 1983/84.

[52] NAS, AF62/3927.

[53] This worm was originally known as the codworm *Porrocaecum decipiens*, although it parasitises many other fish species in addition to cod. Seals are the definitive host of this parasite.

[54] Bennet Rae/DAFS, *Seals and Scottish Fisheries* (Edinburgh: HMSO, 1960) Marine Research 2.

[55] H.R. Hewer, *British Seals* (London: Collins, 1974). H.R. Hewer, *Grey Seals* (London: Sunday Times Books, 1962).

[56] NAS, AF62/2329, Letter from H.R. Hewer, University of London, to J.R. Gordon, DAFS, Edinburgh, 19 September 1961.

[57] NAS, AF62/2327. Internal report on 1963 culls.

[58] NAS, AF62/2327.

[59] NC, *Grey Seals and Fisheries* (London: HMSO, 1963); E.B. Worthington, 'Grey Seals and Fisheries', *Nature*, 203 (11 July 1964): 116–118. The Consultative Committee on Grey Seals and Fisheries was set up in 1959 by the Nature Conservancy and the Development Commission, with the zoologist E.A. Smith appointed as special research officer based in Edinburgh.

[60] Letter to author from John P. Grundy, Senior Inspector SSPCA, Portree, Isle of Skye, dated 21 September 2001. Grundy was the Scottish Society for the Prevention of Cruelty to Animals (SSPCA) representative at the 1977 culls on the Western Isles and the 1978 cull on Orkney. He makes the observation, supported by evidence in the SSPCA archives (Edinburgh), that the SSPCA were placed in a difficult position in 1978 as their sister organisation in England and Wales, the RSPCA, had come out on the side of Greenpeace. Grundy notes that the SSPCA were, 'neither pro- nor anti-cull, our position being that the cull was a legally licensed act authorised by the Secretary of State for Scotland and our sole role was to ensure that the legal cull was carried out humanely'.

[61] W.N. Bonner, *The Natural History of Seals* (London: Christopher Helm, 1989). W.N. Bonner, *Seals and Man: A Study of Interactions* (Seattle: Washington Sea Grant, 1982).

[62] John Lister-Kaye, *Seal Cull* (Harmondsworth: Penguin, 1979): 42.

[63] Sir William Fraser, Edinburgh, letter to author 22 December 1999, and telephone conversation.

[64] NT archives, File 208/2, 'A summary of the report presented to the Secretary of State for Scotland by the Council for Nature's Grey Seals Group, 27 September 1979'. A Scottish Grey Seal Group was formed in Edinburgh in April 1981. See Sheail, *An Environmental history of twentieth century Britain*, 148–150.

[65] Charles Summers, 'Grey Seals: the 'Con' in Conservation', *New Scientist* (30 November 1978): 694–695.

[66] Frank Fraser Darling delivered the 1969 Reith Lectures, which were later published

as *Wilderness and Plenty* (London: Ballantine, 1971). Aldo Leopold (1887–1948) was first a professional forester in the US Forest Service from 1909, who turned to wildlife management, restoration ecology and wilderness preservation, proposing that society embrace a 'Land Ethic' including the natural world within its ethical structure. See especially, Leopold, *A Sand County Almanac* (Oxford: OUP, 1949); J. Baird Callicott (ed.), *A Companion to a Sand County Almanac* (Madison: University of Wisconsin Press, 1987); Peter Coates, *In Nature's Defence: Americans and Conservation* (Keele: BAACS Pamphlet 26, 1993).

[67] F. Fraser Darling, *A Naturalist on Rona: Essays of a Biologist in Isolation* (Oxford: Clarendon, 1939).

[68] NT archives, File series 208, Letter from Frank Fraser Darling to Grace Hickling, 15 January 1951.

[69] NAS, AF62/929/14, copy of Fraser Darling's open letter to Scottish Committee of NC, 28 December 1950, where he declared: 'My ultimate aim is to see the British stocks of the Atlantic grey seal valued as a natural resource, conserved as such and regularly used'.

[70] This was published in *The Guardian*, 13 January 1964.

[71] See Stephen Budiansky, *Nature's Keepers: The New Science of Nature Management* (London: Phoenix, 1996) for the USA National Park Service's failure to keep to a culling policy in the face of public outcry. The culling of northern elk in Yellowstone NP ended in 1967.

[72] NT archives, File series 208, transcript of lecture 'Kindness Kills: The Ethical and Technical Problems of the Conservation of Wildlife', by F. Fraser Darling, 13 January 1964. But Darling was wrong. The welfare of the grey seal has never really been threatened. This belief came from his misreading of the North Rona situation in the late 1930s.

[73] NT archives, File series 208, *IUCN Bulletin*, New Series No.10, January/March 1964.

[74] Dr H.J. Harvey, Assistant Director of Estates and Head of Nature Conservation, National Trust, Cirencester, *pers.comm*.

[75] NAS, AF62/3927, Department of Agriculture and Fisheries for Scotland memo, Gilmour Leburn to J.B. Godber of MAFF, 14 December 1961.

[76] Robert A. Lambert, 'Grey Seals on Scilly', in ISBG (ed) *Isles of Scilly Bird and Natural History Review 2000* (2001): 186–187.

[77] John M. MacAulay, *Seal-Folk and Ocean Paddlers* (Cambridge: White Horse Press, 1998); L.A. Knight, *The Morlo* (London: Gryphon Books, 1956); Rowena Farre, *Seal Morning* (London: Hutchinson, 1957); Monk Gibbon, *The Seals* (London: Jonathan Cape, 1935); R.M. Lockley, *The Seals and the Curragh* (London: J.M.Dent, 1954); H.G.Hurrell, *Atlanta – My Seal* (London: William Kimber, 1963); R.H. Pearson, *A Seal Flies By* (London: Rupert Hart-Davis, 1959); Nina Warner Hooke, *The Seal Summer* (London: Arthur Barker, 1964); Frank Stuart, *A Seal's World* (London: George Harrap, 1954); L. Harrison Matthews, *The Seals and the Scientists* (London: Peter Owen, 1979); Victor B. Scheffer, *The Year of the Seal* (New York: Charles Scribners, 1970); R.M. Lockley, *Grey Seal, Common Seal* (London: White Lion/Survival, 1977); Alison Johnson, *Islands in the Sound* (London: Gollancz, 1989).

[78] Richard Mabey, *The Common Ground* (London: J.M. Dent, 1993).

[79] This phrase was used by an actor playing an irate local fisherman in an episode (screened 1 September 2000) of the popular BBC1 drama 'Badger' about the life and loves of a Northumberland Police Wildlife Liaison Officer.

[80] Letter to author, from Jeremy Read, Director, Atlantic Salmon Trust, Pitlochry, 10 July 2000.

[81] Darling, *A Naturalist on Rona*, 76–90; J.W. Kempster, *Our Rivers* (Oxford: OUP, 1948): 24.

[82] NAS, AF62/929/2 Letter from Charles Green, Minister of Fisheries, Dublin, to George Hogarth, Fishery Board for Scotland, Edinburgh, 19 December 1924.

[83] Interestingly, the seal hunt seems to no longer be an issue of mass public concern, as total annual catches of harp and hooded seals in Canada and Greenland have now climbed to over 350,000: the highest levels for thirty years. The resurgent seal hunt has been able to continue uninterrupted because the Canadians have found new markets for different seal products (like seal penises for their supposed aphrodisiac properties for Eastern traditional medicine, and seal oil to reduce human cholesterol levels in the Western world), which are much less susceptible to the market disruptions that were so successful in the 1970s and 1980s. Although white-coated seal pups are no longer killed, and no animals are clubbed, IFAW still raises a good percentage of its income through campaigns to end the harp seal hunt.

[84] See John Knight (ed.), *Natural Enemies: People-Wildlife conflicts in Anthropological Perspective* (London: Routledge, 2000). Richard Carrington, *Elephants* (Harmondsworth: Penguin, 1962). Peter Boomgaard, *Frontiers of Fear: Tigers and People in the Malay World, 1600–1950* (New Haven, Yale University Press, 2001).

[85] Some estateowners in the Scottish Highlands are very much opposed to any cull of red deer hinds, though they will accept the culling of young stags in the belief this makes for better quality older deer with magnificent antler racks. These 'monarchs of the glen' bring in good money in the stalking season, especially from overseas clients. From a purely nature conservation perspective, a large cull of hinds is needed to bring the population of red deer in Scotland down to levels that would allow for the regeneration of the native Caledonian pine forest.

[86] See SWT, *Scottish Wildlife*, Volumes 14, 15, 1978–1979.

[87] RSPCA archives, File IF/7/10 'Wild Animals – Seals'. See also RSPCA (Horsham, West Sussex) photographs of this demonstration.

ARCHIVAL SOURCES

The archives of the National Trust for Places of Historic Interest or Natural Beauty (England and Wales) are privately held at 36 Queen Anne's Gate, London SW1H 9AS.

The archives of the Royal Society for the Prevention of Cruelty to Animals (RSPCA) are privately held at RSPCA Headquarters, Wilberforce Way, Oakhurst Business Park, Southwater, Horsham, West Sussesx RH13 7WN.

The archives of the Scottish Society for the Prevention of Cruelty to Animals (SSPCA) are privately held at Braehead Mains, 603 Queensferry Road, Edinburgh EH4 6EA.

The archives of the Department of Agriculture and Fisheries for Scotland are held in the National Archives of Scotland (NAS), West Register House, Charlotte Square, Edinburgh EH2 4DF at ref: AF.

The archives of the Scottish Committee of the Nature Conservancy/Nature Conservancy Council are held in the National Archives of Scotland (NAS), West Register House, Charlotte Square, Edinburgh EH2 4DF at ref: SNH.

For the 'Preservation of Friends' and the 'Destruction of Enemies': Studying and Protecting Birds in Late Imperial Russia

Brian Bonhomme

INTRODUCTION[1]

This paper surveys major developments in the Imperial Russian history of wild bird protection and related contextual issues of ornithology during the century or so up to 1917. It is conceived as an interdisciplinary essay, in dialogue with recent research in both Environmental and Russian History. Primarily, it explores Russian input into a history whose main lines are usually traced in continental Western Europe and (especially) the Anglo-American world – exploring the diverse eighteenth- and nineteenth-century strands from which were woven the whole cloth of modern wild bird protection: its assumptions and priorities, organisations, procedures and laws. In this western context, a large literature now exists chronicling and analysing the development of professional and amateur natural history and ornithology; the organisation of opposition to animal cruelty and the plumage trade; the establishment and history of key entities (such as the RSPB, Audubon Society and so on); landmark legislation (including Britain's 1869 Sea Bird Protection Act); and the various social groups and cultural forces behind these.[2] This paper treats analogous developments in the Russian Empire and their relationship to foreign trends.

Because most of the ornithologists and bird-protection advocates surveyed here were Russian[3] (including non-nationals who lived and worked in the Russian Empire), this paper is inevitably also a case study of Russian national identity – its construction, peculiarities and evolution – during the Imperial period (1689–1917). Much has been written describing a widespread sense among part of the Russian elite, especially in the nineteenth century, that in a great many fields their country was behind or inferior to its most advanced western neighbours. This inferiority complex has recently been explored through the lens of Russian nature and landscape painting by Christopher Ely, who describes painters' successful efforts to overcome it by creating distinctive, iconic and truly *Russian* national landscapes and scenery – images designed to compete with, rather than just to follow, European models.[4] In their modest ways, as will be seen, Russian ornithologists and bird-protection advocates worked from the same perspective on a similar project. Like their national peers in other fields they too were often self-critical in the light of developments abroad, and strove to catch up with them, in some cases with moderate success. However, like their artistic compatriots, Russians did not simply chase foreign leads. They also developed their own ideas about bird study and, particularly, bird protection. By the late nineteenth century many of them were coming to understand Russia as in some ways a unique case, noting on the one hand, the peculiarities of its avifauna, climate and geography, and on the other, the distinctive characteristics of relevant Russian public habits and culture. In this sense, this article chronicles something akin to the 'coming of age' of bird study and protection in the Russian Empire after about 1870. Particular emphasis will be given to two related outcomes, both of which set the Russian Empire somewhat apart from many of its western neighbours: the country's refusal to sign a landmark international treaty on cross-border bird protection (the 1902 Paris Convention, see below), and the fact that it did not pass any significant domestic legislation dedicated to wild bird protection.

STUDYING BIRDS IN EIGHTEENTH- AND NINETEENTH-CENTURY RUSSIA

Generally speaking – and compared with Britain, Germany and the USA – through 1917 and across the Russian Empire, broad-based popular knowledge, interest or advocacy regarding birds remained at a low level – an important circumstance. The situation began to change only very slowly, and slightly, after about mid-century. Consequently, almost the only people talking or writing much about birds up to then were professional and academic ornithologists. Yet even here, Russian contributions were held in relatively low regard (even among the Russians themselves). The indirect assessment of British naturalist Hugh Strickland was typical. In his famous 'Report on the Recent Progress and Present State of Ornithology' presented at the 1844 meeting of the British Association for the Advancement of Science, Strickland counted no Russians among the 'central core of internationally-recognised ornithologists' and noted no Russian-sponsored expeditions or studies, though he did include Moscow in a list of cities wherein operated scientific societies 'whose publications included ornithological details'. Strickland was silent on the Russian Empire when noting journals, collections, congresses and other ornithological apparatus, focusing instead on Britain, the USA and Western Europe.[5]

In at least one regard, however, the Russian Empire deserved more credit than this, having by Strickland's time already carried out a century or so of significant work in basic ornithological reconnaissance (including specimen collecting) – in the European parts of the Russian Empire (from Karelia south to the Crimea), in Siberia and in the Pacific Northwest. During 1768-74, for example, the Swedish-born naturalist Johann Peter Falck travelled across Siberia to the Chinese border on a Russian state-sponsored expedition led by Peter Simon

Pallas, a Russian-based German-born naturalist. Falck's pioneering ornithological observations were subsequently gathered in volume 3 of his *Contribution to an Understanding of the Topography of the Russian Empire* (1786), covering 222 species of birds in eighty-four pages along with plates of some of these.[6] Falck also collected bird specimens later deposited with the St. Petersburg Zoological Museum, founded in 1832.[7] Probably at the behest of Pallas, an ornithological mission was included among the tasks set a few years later by Empress Catherine II to Joseph Billings who in 1785 was sent to seek out and survey the Northeast Passage along Russia's Arctic coast: 'To collect birds [and their eggs] and cause to be stuffed or otherwise preserved all extraordinary birds observing as closely as possible their habits, food, propagation, sounds, migrations and habitations, as well as mode of catching them ...'[8] Expedition naturalist Carl Heinrich Merck carried out these orders.[9] By Strickland's time the Russian government had organised and sponsored many important Siberian-oriented natural historical expeditions besides these. Significant ornithological descriptions, notes or plates that resulted can be found in works by I.I. Lepekhin,[10] Johan Anton Güldenstädt,[11] Samuel Gottlieb Gmelin,[12] and Simon Peter Pallas.[13]

Particularly important Russian contributions were made during the eighteenth and early nineteenth centuries still further east in the North Pacific, a virtual *terra incognita* at the time. Surveying specifically the ornithological writings of early Russian, British, American, Spanish and French explorers up to 1830, one modern writer has asserted with justification that Russia 'contributed more than any other country to the early knowledge of the resources' of this region.[14] The massive Great Northern Expedition of 1733–42[15] (also known as the Second Kamchatka Expedition) yielded huge ornithological dividends. G.W. Steller, ship's naturalist on Vitus Bering's journey of 1741–42 in search of Alaska, was first to describe (and thus named) the Steller's Jay, Steller's Sea Eagle and Steller's Eider.[16] One chapter in his general *History of Kamchatka* is dedicated to 'land birds'.[17] His journal (published in two parts in 1781 and 1793) contains further ornithological work on species found across the waters, islands and shores of Kamchatka, Alaska and the many islands in between. His paper on birds' nests and eggs in Siberia appeared earlier, in 1758. Of Steller's many other natural history writings – several on birds – some have been lost, while others, apparently, have yet to be published.[18]

The same set of travels also yielded Stepan Petrovich Krasheninnikov's *History of Kamchatka and the Kurile Islands with Countries Adjacent*. Published in St. Petersburg in 1754[19] – before any of Steller's works – this was perhaps the 'first book to deal with [Kamchatka's] history and resources scientifically'.[20] It included copious descriptive ornithology in chapters dedicated to 'Sea Fowls', 'Birds which haunt ... about the fresh Water', and 'Land Fowls'.[21] Other ornithological observations carried out by this expedition appeared in larger natural history works or more general descriptive travel narratives.[22] And a major Russian publication, Pallas's *Russo-Asiatic Zoogeography*, vols. 1-3

(1811-13) synthesised and summarised discoveries from the above and other expeditions. Thereafter, Russians also helped pioneer the ornithology of Antartica, the expedition of Faddei Faddeevich Bellingshausen in 1819–21 yielding specimens and important new written materials.[23]

It is worth noting, when considering how to assess 'Russian' contributions of this time, that many of the expeditions noted above, though they were organised by Russian institutions, relied heavily for their leadership on imported experts – including the Germans Gmelin, Pallas and Steller, and the Swede Falck. In this regard ornithology simply conformed to the prevailing trend in all fields of Russian science and technology at the time, stemming from the westernisation policies of Tsar Peter the Great.

As the century progressed, however, at least in ornithology this trend began to turn. In 1853, for example, A.F. von Middendorf, a Russian-born naturalist of Baltic German ancestry, published an account of his observations and collections made in Siberia's frigid Taimyr peninsular during 1843–44.[24] This proved to be a major publishing event, catalysing a great amount of further study of the Russian east, by native- and foreign-born specialists alike.[25] It also provides a stepping stone to the 1870s, by which decade a truly Russian ornithology was clearly emerging. Two developments stand out in this regard. First, in much the same way that Germans had organised and led much of the basic reconnaissance of Russian and Siberian avifauna, so did subjects of the Russian Empire begin to do the same in Central Asia (often referred to at the time as 'Turkestan') and China.[26] Only a few of the most important expeditions can be mentioned here. Best-known, perhaps, are the four journeys of Captain Nikolai Mikhailovich Przheval'skii through Mongolia, northern China and Tibet (1871–73, 1876–77, 1879–80, 1883–85). Aimed primarily at reaching the forbidden Tibetan city of Lhasa, these also yielded (in addition to the discovery of the famous Przheval'skii's wild horse[27]) thousands of bird specimens, including at least twenty previously unknown to science, such as the Black-necked Crane (*Grus nigricollis*) and Severtsov's Grouse (*Tetrastes sewerzowi*). Przheval'skii was accompanied on his third expedition by the naturalist V.I. Roborovskii and on his fourth and final one by Roborovskii again and P.K. Kozlov. All were Russians. Following Przhevalskii's death in 1888, his planned fifth expedition went out during 1889–91 under the Russian Colonel M.V. Pevtsov, again with Kozlov and Roborovskii, both of whom scored further important bird discoveries and specimens, many from the then little-studied plateau of Chang Tang. Kozlov proved particularly influential in the study of western Chinese avifauna, journeying there three more times from 1893 to 1909.

Less well-known than Przheval'skii, but even more important for Russian ornithology were the nine expeditions made by the Russian N.A. Zarudnyi: five to Transcaspia during 1879–92 and four to various parts of Persia in 1892–1906, after which he based himself and his studies permanently in Tashkent. His publications on the birds of these regions are extensive. The Russian explorer-zoologist N.A. Severtsov spent more than two decades in various parts of Central Asia between 1857 and 1879, eventually producing perhaps the first comprehensive account of Central Asian flora and fauna. His ornithological collection surpassed 12,000 specimens. Other noteworthy and truly Russian expeditions of the time to Central Asia and China include those of the botanist G.N. Potanin and M. Berezovskii to Kansu, eastern Tsinghai and Szechwan in 1884–86; and of the brothers Grum(m)-Grzhimailo to Sinkiang and Kansu in 1889–90. Travels in the region during 1902 by the botanist-geographer V.V. Sapozhnikov provided further specimens and helped establish the Central Asian collection at Tomsk University.

The second way in which the Russian Empire began now to assert its ornithological identity was in producing its own world-class ornithologists, who in turn made significant contributions to theory. Notable here is the work of the aforementioned N.A. Severtsov and M.A. Menzbir who, during the 1870s and 1880s, worked out a system of ornithogeographic zonal distribution for the birds of the palearctic region, albeit drawing on models developed in the 1850s by the Englishman P. Sclater.[28]

Menzbir in particular stands as perhaps the first great Russian ornithologist. Based at Moscow University, he was well regarded among his peers internationally, travelled widely, and worked on collections and in museums in Vienna, Leiden, Brussels, Paris and several places in Britain during a long career. He held honorary or corresponding member status in zoological and ornithological societies in France, the USA, Germany and Britain and was elected a candidate member of the Russian Academy of Sciences in 1896 (he became a full member in 1929). He was also a long-time member (and president after 1915) of the Russian Society of Nature Enthusiasts (*Obshchestvo liubetelei prirody*). Menzbir relentlessly collected specimens. As of 1912 he owned 12,545 examples covering more than 900 species, mostly of Russian imperial provenance.[29] But his foremost achievement was his monumental *Birds of Russia* (*Ptitsy Rossii*), published in three significantly revised and expanded editions between 1893 and 1918. In the prefaces to each edition, he identified and lamented major problems plaguing Russian ornithology at the time: the absence of a comprehensive published field-guide; existing Russian books that were out of date, out of print or filled with errors; ill-advised innovations in nomenclature; and a paucity of information on distribution and behaviour.[30] And he called for action: Writing in 1895 in tones that mixed scientific objectivity and Russian patriotism, he asserted that the absence of a systematic, comprehensive domestic guide to Russian avifauna promoted reliance on German and English works that were based not on fieldwork but primarily on collections held in Western Europe. Consequently, as guides for Russia and Eastern Europe they were 'fragmentary, distorted' and 'incomplete'. Given such realities, he added, Russian ornithology still 'lagged terribly' behind western developments.[31] (Menzbir did not note another problem frequently cited by Russian ornithologists and conservationists

– the paucity of funding available compared with abroad.[32]) Menzbir intended *The Birds of Russia* as an effort to address some of these problems. A recent Russian-language historical assessment considers it 'the first ... synthesis of all [then-current] knowledge on the systematics, distribution and biology of the birds of [Russia]', one of the 'more important events in [Russian] zoology' of the period. Although it did not cover all areas of Russia's vast empire, still it had 'a decisive influence on the development of ornithology' in that country and was for 'several decades ... the [standard] desk reference for all Russian ornithologists'.[33]

Menzbir's most important Russian successor was S.A. Buturlin (1872–1938).[34] Buturlin, some of whose career highlights came during the Soviet period, was not exclusively an ornithologist, but rather an incredibly productive polymath with interests in the hunting economy (he is credited with pioneering scientific approaches to hunting in Russia and also wrote some Soviet hunting legislation), Russian far north affairs, and other matters. Another pioneer in ornithological systematics, he 'laid the foundations for describing sub-speciation among the avifauna of the Russian Empire'[35] and mapped in detail the geographical distribution of birds in most parts of Northeast Siberia. He is credited in Russian sources to this day with having solved in 1906 questions by then a century old regarding where and how Rosy Gulls nested.[36] His pre-war collection of ornithological specimens, begun as a youth in the 1880s, had 2,000 birds (plus a separate egg collection). It contained 'almost all known Russian species and subspecies of the time' and constituted 'one of the fundamental collections [anywhere in the world] for the study of Russian avifauna'. Its significance is indicated by the British Museum of Natural History's offer, made at some point before 1909 via Ernst Hartert, to purchase it for a sum recently calculated as equivalent now to one million US dollars.[37] Sadly, Buturlin's original materials for a comprehensive guide to the birds of the entire Russian Empire, almost ready for publication around 1917, were lost forever during the chaos of the First World War, forcing him to begin over. Finally emerging in 1934 as the five-volume *Guide to the Birds of Soviet Union*, it is considered his greatest achievement and the first truly comprehensive work on the birds of what by then had become the Soviet Union.[38] With the general trend of Russian ornithology at the turn of the century, Buturlin was well known and connected internationally. For several years during the early 1900s he was a frequent contributor to *The Ibis* – journal of the British Ornithologists' Union (founded 1858).

By the outbreak of the First World War, the Russian Empire had also developed a solid ornithological infrastructure in several academic settings, including the Department of Ornithology of the Russian Academy of Sciences' Zoological Institute in St. Petersburg, at Moscow University (where Menzbir was based), and in the Department of Ornithology of the Imperial Russian Society for the Acclimatisation of Animals and Plants. Before 1910, Russian ornithologists lacked a dedicated specialised journal. Consequently, most of them published in domestic hunting or more general zoological journals or in foreign ornithological publications. In 1910, however, this lack too was addressed as publication of *The Ornithological Herald (Ornitologicheskii vestnik)* began at Moscow University. This appeared four times a year until just after the Bolshevik Revolution.

THE EMERGENCE OF BIRD PROTECTION AGENDAS IN EUROPE AND RUSSIA

The cause of wild bird protection in the Russian Empire also lagged behind western developments, though more in terms of results than of dialogue. Russians did indeed *call* for protection, especially during the second half of the nineteenth century, but as noted, and unlike in Britain, the USA and elsewhere, the Russian Empire neither produced nor signed onto any major, dedicated wild bird protection laws. This does not mean, however, that in Russia there was no *interest* in legislation. One should also avoid the temptation to assess these outcomes as failures. As will be seen, Russians worked within somewhat different political, social and environmental-geographical contexts compared with, say, the British. Consequently, they sometimes chose to focus their energies differently: on working bird protection into existing game law rather than pioneering (as many of their European counterparts were doing) a separate tradition of wild bird protection legislation, or on expanding popular education and participation in voluntary bird protection initiatives.

Like other European states, by the nineteenth century the Russian Empire already had a long-standing tradition of offering legal protections to some birds via the game laws. The earliest of these are eleventh-century statutes protecting falcons – used by princes and nobles for hunting. Between then and the late nineteenth century there were innumerable alterations and additions to this corpus of law. Whether in Russia or elsewhere, however, game law typically protected only a very few, mostly food-species (typically pheasants, grouse and the like), and did so for a small set of specific reasons quite different from those behind the later bird protection agendas with which this paper is concerned. Game laws were designed to protect aristocratic privilege and the social exclusivity of the hunt[39] (the birds themselves were largely incidental); or to protect private property (a noble's personal hunting-falcons, for example). By contrast, the sort of wild bird protection that began to flourish across Western Europe and the USA during the second half of the nineteenth century was conceived in a very different context; and it filtered and combined different concerns, often at odds with the game laws.[40] Especially in Darwin's wake, secular- and scientifically minded persons increasingly saw nature as a vast network of interdependency, complexity and fragility, and they concerned themselves with the role of birds therein. This inspired others – of a more utilitarian bent – to think about the practical uses of certain categories of birds and in particular of insectivores as destroyers of insects harmful to crops. Others emphasised the evils of animal cruelty, seen both as demeaning the perpetrator and causing needless suffering to the victim. Still others noted the Christian duty toward good stewardship of nature. Typically, not just a few game species, but many – in some cases, all – birds (and animals) were of concern here. In this context, the legislative and organisational bases for these new trends – dedicated wild bird protection laws, and groups such as Britain's Royal Society for the Protection of Birds (RSPB) – began to emerge and achieve critical mass across much of the West particularly during the 1860s, '70s and '80s. Most of these trends were in evidence also in the Russian Empire, though with some unique twists.

BIRD PROTECTION IN THE RUSSIAN EMPIRE: DEBATES, CONCERNS, GROUPS

Although the subject certainly has a longer pre-history, serious and sustained interest among Russians in encouraging, organising and legislating wild bird protection dates from about 1870. Several distinct, but overlapping, concerns began to be articulated around this time, all in one way or another echoing similar developments in the West. It will be useful to approach these in turn.

1. Utility

Some of the most frequently and clearly articulated voices in favour of wild bird protection emphasised issues of utility – especially the useful services provided to agriculture by insectivorous birds. The issue acquired early momentum in 1871 at a general session of the Russian Imperial Free Economic Society (*Imperaterskoe vol'noe ekonomicheskoe obshchestvo*; hereafter RIFES[41]) and was immediately pursued further in two related committees.[42] A statement made to the second of these by the Russian animal welfare advocate V.E. Iverson summed up much of the debate then and subsequently:

> It is a known fact that caterpillars and maggots, as well as the birds that eat them, consume in a day a quantity of food about equal to their own body weight. Thus ... 100 birds, weighing about twenty pounds ... over the course of ninety summer days would preserve about 1,800 pounds of vegetable matter [that would otherwise have been consumed by insects].

Citing German research, Iverson estimated the total financial loss to Russian agriculture caused by insects at 1.2 billion rubles (over what period is not noted). Insectivorous birds could help cut this loss, he argued, adding that birds' uses went even beyond this, since their droppings also fertilised the soil and helped control fungal diseases. These startling realities, he claimed, went shamefully unacknowledged, both in law and in popular attitudes towards birds:

> 'In [our] hunting laws – both current and projected – only game birds are discussed. There is not even any mention of the types of [insectivorous] species we are talking about here. Of course in one part [of current hunting law] it does say that during a certain time of year it is forbidden to hunt game and indeed any kind of useful birds; but first, there is no clear indication of which kinds of birds are considered useful; and second, banning hunting of certain birds *only* for [the close-season] means allowing fully their destruction over the rest of the year.'[43]

(In this particular case, Iverson did not indicate which species he considered useful.)

The Committee ended up making strong statements in favour not only of protection, but of *increasing* populations of insectivorous (and some rodent-eating) birds. Suggested actions focused on three areas. The first was education, where propositions included organising public lectures and exhibits, publishing and distributing brochures and wall-charts, making relevant curriculum reform in village and rural schools, providing outreach to peasant communes, and even establishing a special museum – all designed to promote recognition and better treatment of 'useful' birds and other animals. The second suggestion was for new legislation. Noting that Russia's hunting laws were currently under review by the government, the Commission drew up several draft clauses outlawing the trapping, hunting, killing and other destruction of all birds, eggs and nests – other than those explicitly identified as 'pests' or 'harmful' – at all times of the year. The third proposal was for practical measures – including planting particular tree species and hanging nest boxes – designed to attract insectivorous birds to agricultural areas. Efforts were also urged to lobby and coordinate efforts with the Forest Department and the Ministries of the Interior and Education.[44] Here, indeed, was much of the agenda Russian bird protection advocates would pursue for the remainder of the Imperial era.

As Iverson's citation of German research indicates, Russians were not the only ones interested in the agricultural benefits of protecting insectivores. Besides the Germans, British ornithologists too had already raised the issue, and the British Parliament explicitly considered it in discussions leading to the passage of that country's 1869 'Sea Birds Preservation Act'.[45] In Britain the benefits of protecting such birds were cited more forcefully in debates leading up to passage of the 'Wild Birds Protection Act' of 1872, the year *following* Iverson's comments. In France the idea of protecting insectivorous (and reptile-eating) birds for the benefits of agriculture had been discussed in some depth at least as early as 1854.[46] Russians thus appear to have been joining rather than pioneering this debate. At this time, across nations, there was also great similarity in the species most often noted: swallows, nightingales and blackbirds – all softbills – were perennial and secure favourites; while larks and finches – hardbills whose diets combined seed and insects – invoked mixed sentiments. In Britain and the US, for example, and during the second half of the nineteenth century, sparrows went from being considered friends of agriculture to its enemies.[47] Russian debate, as will be seen, would eventually pursue a slightly different course.

2. Animal Welfare and Anti-Cruelty

The cause of bird protection was advanced also by the founding in 1865 of the Russian Imperial Society for the Prevention of Cruelty to Animals (*Rossiiskoe obshchestvo pokrovitel'stva zhivotnym*, hereafter, RISPCA).[48] Modelled closely on similar foreign societies (especially the British RSPCA) the RISPCA focused first and foremost on domestic animals – ensuring they received basic food, water, shelter; were generally kept and transported without undue cruelty; were not used for tasks beyond their strength or abilities; and were slaughtered humanely.[49] The RISPCA committed from the start to achieve these goals by 'assisting, advising, and issuing edicts'[50]; by establishing animal hospitals and slaughter houses; encouraging 'primarily among the simple folk [*prostoi narod*] a sympathy for animals by means of the publication and free distribution of books', 'instruction via the clergy', awards for those who set a good example and efforts to bring punishment upon the worst offenders under existing anti-cruelty laws.[51] (The Society's first successful prosecution was brought in February 1870 against a St. Petersburg merchant who was eventually fined 20 rubles for organising cock-fighting.[52])

The RISPCA quickly expanded its purview from poultry to include caged and wild birds. During 1870–71 it lobbied the Ministry of Internal Affairs to consider a ban on selling small birds on the street and convinced the St. Petersburg Chief of Police (*Ober-Politsiemeister*) to approve turning over to local courts (*mirovye sudi*) individuals accused of such trade.[53] The RISPCA was also an early advocate for protecting insectivorous birds. Interestingly, in this endeavour cruelty arguments were rarely mentioned. Instead the Society emphasised the same themes of utility and agriculture already outlined, for example in 1871 at a highly successful public lecture that attracted an audience of 360.[54] Similarly, in 1874 the Society published a call from N. Vil'kins, one of its most active leading members, to 'turn the attention of the local authorities to the significance of migratory birds for our grain-cultivation and for our forests, point out the importance of protecting them from destruction and the necessity of strict adherence to the [Society's] existing [draft] laws in this regard'. In this particular case Vil'kins cited research by the Paris Entomological Society showing that, in the Dieppe region of France, fees collected from hunting licenses (10,000 Francs profit) were massively outweighed by the loss to agriculture (17,000,000 francs!) caused by insects. For Vil'kin's the connection between these two facts was simple and direct: 'This ... clearly shows what significance the protection of insectivorous birds has for Russia – a country of grain-farms and forests.' The RISPCA, he continued, must 'boldly defend these small but strong ... allies of mankind'.[55]

Starting in the 1880s, the Society also began opposing the plumage trade. Here, although birds were portrayed as the direct victims of unwarranted cruelty, the Society also pointed out the demoralising effects of the trade on the people involved: from the cruelty of the trapper and trader to the vanity of the mostly female consumers of hats and other feathery accoutrements. Stamping out the trade was construed as an effort toward 'ennobling' the human spirit through more ethical and moral approaches toward non-human creation.

Little success came of the Society's lobbying and public education efforts, however. For example, whereas in the 1860s the total number of exported birds – mostly but not exclusively dead – numbered 'two or three thousand specimens worth three or four thousand rubles', by 1889 the figure had skyrocketed by one contemporary estimate to '3 million *pud*s valued at one-and-a-half million rubles'.[56] A quarter-century later, in 1915, the figure was put at 'millions of pairs' annually sold both on the domestic and export markets.[57] Though these figures describe 'game birds', it seems clear from contemporary anecdotal evidence that the term was used generically and actually included a very large number of birds killed in the Russian Empire for their feathers as well as their meat and then sold into the international plumage trade – often, interestingly, to Western European countries that had already depleted bird populations from other sources, passed their own bird protection legislation, or signed onto international protection measures.[58]

3. National Image

Many calls for bird protection between 1870 and 1914 were couched in nationalist tones, emphasising the notion that a nation or state would be judged by how it treats its wildlife. (This was also the case in Britain at the same time, and almost certainly in many other places, too.) A good example is provided again by N. Vil'kins, this time in his capacity as Russian delegate to the 1875 International Congress of Societies for the Prevention of Cruelty to Animals, held in London. Vil'kins took Britain's efforts toward more humane treatment of animals as *prima facie* evidence of that country's 'civilised' nature, holding England up as a 'model' for the world. Even though Vil'kins was aware of the persistence in Britain of 'barbarism towards animals', the fact that the country had organised and legislated efforts against this was enough for him to write off such cruelties as reflecting only on 'individuals' not the nation as a whole.[59] Laws, here, were a reflection of national culture.

Vil'kins was far less complimentary or indulgent, however, regarding 'Southern European countries'. Spain was 'cruel', he opined, noting that 'the Spaniard goes [to a bullfight] not to watch the fight, not to compare the strength of the combatants, quite the opposite, [he goes] simply to watch the dying agonies of the animal; he is ready to thrust a dagger into anyone who dares to defend the animal from his torture'. Vil'kins was unwilling to excuse Spanish cruelties merely as the acts of certain individuals. *All* Spanish, 'even women and children', took delight in this 'national pleasure'. Italy came in for similar treatment, guilty of national cruelty of a different sort: an advanced form of 'indifference'. 'You may', he noted, 'frequently meet on the road an old man [*pater*] driving a gig [*odnokolka*] loudly reciting the Hail Mary and the Our Father, happily thumbing his rosary, yet paying absolutely no attention at all to the suffering of his thirsty, hungry, exhausted horse.' Discussing birds, Vil'kins condemned as a great cruelty the popular Italian practice 'during the time of the carnivals, held under the patronage of His Holiness the Pope' of throwing 'bouquets ... with birds tied to them'.[60]

The tendency to view 'southern Europeans' stereotypically as cruel to animals was not exclusive to Vil'kins, nor was it confined to the 1870s. Baron Lauden of the Russian Society for the Acclimatisation of Animals and Plants in 1913 blasted 'southern neighbours' who killed large numbers of small birds – representing 'capital' and 'wealth' – as they passed along migration routes toward Russia.[61] Others raised the issue too, often negatively contrasting the 'mediterraneans' – who ate small birds in significant numbers – with Russians (and others) who did so rarely.[62] Sometimes names were named, with Italy often criticised particularly for the destruction of migratory birds passing through.[63]

The sense of moral superiority some Russians may have felt over some southern Europeans on these issues did *not* translate into a broader indictment of the West, however. In fact, it appears as an exception to the more general conception among Russians that compared to western states Russia was far behind. It is hard to read very far into the primary source material of the period without encountering over and over the same refrain: that Russia needed to catch up. It is not difficult to suspect, even, that some Russians saw bird protection as an opportunity to distance themselves from 'cruel' southern Europe and claim a place instead among the more 'advanced' northern and western states. Thus, in virtually every relevant domain, the same few states provided the models and results to be studied, emulated and achieved: the RISPCA frequently cited the work of its British and American counterparts as the standards against which to judge its own activities; the British RSPB was the premier bird protection outfit; Germany's Organisation for the Protection of German Monuments of Nature, founded in 1906 by Hugo Conwentz, was the premier nature conservation organisation;[64] the best national parks and reserves were American[65] and German (especially Prussian).[66] As late as 1914, Sweden, the British Empire, Canada, Australia and New Zealand were also considered far ahead of Russia in this latter regard.[67]

Matters were much the same regarding bird *study*. Russians were still far behind British, American and West European achievements. Writing in 1912 on the state of Russian scientific ornithology, Baron G.V. Lauden pointed out that so far, 'the ornithologists of our great country ... can only follow with envy the biological successes of our western neighbours [... and we] can no longer delay in this cultural work, if we do not wish to deserve being reproached for being backward compared to Western Europe'.[68] Lauden went on to urge Russians to more fully adopt 'advanced' ornithological techniques such as bird-banding and the establishment of observation stations along migration routes. The same year, Johannes Thienemann, head of the Rossitten bird observatory in East Prussia, delivered a depressing report (for Russians) contrasting the advanced state of work in Germany, Hungary and elsewhere, where, increasingly, birds were being systematically caught, banded, and their migration routes studied, with the 'piles of dead birds' of Russian provenance he had been recently receiving, with all manner of bits of 'string, bands, [and] wires' tied to their legs and feet, rarely with any record of where they had been caught.[69] While lauding the recent proliferation in Russia of amateurs, public organisations and bird samples, the lack of uniform standards and professional procedures, he asserted, demanded quick attention. Russian ornithologists agreed. And the lack even of a comprehensive list of the birds of the Russian Empire was continually lamented through 1917.[70]

4. Romantic, Sentimental and Religious Impulses

Calls for bird protection couched in romantic, sentimental or religious tones were common throughout the West at this time, especially in Germany and the English-speaking countries, where advocates spoke of birds as adornments of nature or 'amiable' country companions, noted their pleasing songs, and pointed out one's Christian duty to be a good steward of nature. It seems obvious that at least some Russians would have felt similarly. And yet none of these impulses appears to have been especially developed or influential in Russia. One can certainly find suggestive anecdotes, however. In the area of romantic sentimentalism, for example, the Empresses Elizabeth (1741–62) and Catherine the Great (1762–96) both decreed protection for nightingales (only) in the woods and grounds around their royal residences, apparently out of appreciation for the beauty of the bird's song.[71] Similarly, birds were a recurrent motif in Russian landscape painting of the nineteenth century, suggesting at least that they held a place in intellectual imaginings of the ontology of Russian rural beauty. The hunting and fishing guides published by Sergei Aksakov in the 1840s–50s are generally credited by historians as having awoken sentimental interest among the educated Russian public in Russian nature and wildlife, perhaps comparable to the role played in Britain by the writings of Gilbert White;[72] and some late-nineteenth-century Russian novelists and playwrights touched on issues of animal cruelty (though rarely birds). But clear linkage between any such ideals and serious debate on bird protection in Russia remains highly elusive. No doubt there is room here for further research.

The same is true regarding the intersection of religion with calls for protection and against cruelty to animals and birds. The RISPCA did periodically link these ideas, claiming, for example, biblical support for the correctness of their basic aims and sometimes seeking out 'important figures of the Orthodox, Jewish and Muslim faiths' for help 'preaching to their congregations' about more humane treatment of animals and birds.[73] But again religious motivations and persons do not appear to have played a decisive role in shaping debates or moulding opinions.

5. Other Impulses Toward Bird Protection

Brief note should be made of hunters' calls for bird protection. Articulated since at least the 1870s in agricultural conferences and subsequently in hunting journals and elsewhere, these focused, understandably, on maintaining or increasing stocks of the commonly-hunted game species. A bird's usefulness here was usually framed in terms of how tasty it was, or how pleasurable it was to hunt. For this reason some hunting advocates saw no point in protecting smaller birds that Russians, unlike some mediterranean peoples, neither ate nor hunted for sport.[74]

Among academic naturalists, after about 1900, 'rarity' also became an increasingly common part of the lexicon of bird protection. The conservation advocate D.N. Aniutin, for example, spoke in 1914 of the need to protect 'rare, wonderful, interesting, intriguing things' including birds.[75] And two years earlier, Baron G.V. Lauden of the Russian Society for the Acclimatisation of Animals and Plants noted that 'protection must not be limited just to absolutely useful [bird] species, but must also cover harmful ones which, having already become rare, now constitute monuments of nature, and the disappearance of which would greatly impoverish nature'.[76] As well as the sympathy shown here for 'harmful' birds, note should also be made of the term 'monuments of nature' (*pamiatniki prirody*). The term more often connoted not individual species but much larger natural entities such as mountains, valleys, forests and estuaries – what we might now refer to whole ecosystems. Interest in this kind of protection took off rapidly among Russian academic naturalists during the last few years of the Russian Empire. Birds were certainly among the focuses of attention here too, worth preserving for their vital role in these larger ecological webs. It is precisely here, incidentally, that one sees most clearly the influence in Russia of Darwin's ideas about evolution and their connection to bird protection agendas. Birds, like all living organisms, were the product of a long history of natural selection and were integral to their environments. Anyone who cared about the well-being of whole 'natural monuments' and ecosystems had to be concerned also about the fate of the individual species and other component parts of the larger wholes. In general, Darwinism was popular among academic ornithologists, becoming more-or-less canonical by century's end, though not so much among the more varied and conservative sorts at the heart of the anti-cruelty movement.[77] The movement for protecting monuments of nature, best represented by F.E. Falts-Fein, I.P. Borodin, Andrei Semenov-tian-shanskii, G.A. Kozhevnikov and others, eventuated, mostly after the Bolshevik Revolution, in the creation of a major network of Russian and Soviet nature preserves, or *zapovedniki*, about which much has been written in recent years.[78]

'RUSSIANISING' THE DEBATE ON BIRDS

The Russians were still trying to catch up with foreign developments, but by late century, at least in one area, they had begun to forge their own trail. This concerns debate about birds being 'useful' or 'harmful' to agriculture, forestry and the human economy in general. Internationally, the notion seems to have remained fairly fixed well through century's end that each species could be properly and permanently placed either in one category or the other. Although significant debate existed about *which* 'side' a given species was on, and while some were occasionally reassigned (the aforementioned sparrows, for example), in general there does not seem to have been much doubt across and beyond Europe in the viability of the categories themselves. In the 1890s, however, Russians began to buck the trend, insisting against the weight of foreign opinion that birds did *not* always fit easily into such categories, at least not in the Russian Empire. Here, they argued, the size of the country, its diversity of climates, soils, flora and agriculture, and other factors meant that the same species could be useful *or* harmful at different times and places. The relative population density of a given species mattered and, it was proposed, Russian bird populations were more fluid, dynamic and ephemeral than those in, say, Britain. The notion found some support in comparisons of recent studies of Siberian avifauna which, combined, found great differences from one year to the next in the size and composition of bird populations on the lower Yenesei based on 'varying annual climatic changes'.[79] These circumstances necessitated more flexible legislation allowing for regional differences, annual changes in bird demography.

This kind of reasoning was presented to foreign colleagues at least as early as 1891 at the Second International Ornithological Congress held in Budapest. Thereafter, it became a more frequent and popular motif in Russian discourse.[80] It was a factor in Russian participation in the long-winded negotiations for the 1902 Paris Convention on cross-border bird protection (and in Russia's refusal to sign), and in the 1910s, it reappeared as the central theme in a draft for a major reform of the game laws. It is to these developments that we now turn.

For the 'Preservation of Friends' ...

RUSSIAN ORNITHOLOGY AND BIRD PROTECTION ON THE INTERNATIONAL STAGE: THE PARIS CONVENTION

In Europe, serious international interest in cross-border protection, focusing on migratory species, dates at least from the 1868 Agricultural and Forestry Convention held in Germany. At a session of the Convention the idea was mooted that since insectivorous birds beneficial to agriculture did not respect national boundaries, and in many cases were migratory, it was necessary to create an international legislative framework for protecting them.[81] The issue was revisited thereafter at a series of conferences and negotiations spread over the last quarter of the nineteenth century that regularly brought together representatives from many countries, including the Russian Empire.

At the International Agricultural Conference of September 1873, held in Vienna, representatives from Italy (a 'cruel' southern neighbour from some Russians' perspective) and Austria-Hungary agreed to cooperate in ending the mass destruction of birds within and moving between their countries.[82] Two years later the governments of the same two countries signed an agreement that would be lauded a generation later by a Russian ornithologist as a 'first-of-its-kind agreement unconditionally ban[ning] the destruction of nests, eggs and nestlings, certain methods of hunting birds, and establish[ing] a hunting season from 1 September to the end of February, and so on'.[83] It covered only 'agriculturally useful' species. Beyond these two states further similar activity was ongoing or already accomplished. Britain had already legislated protection for seabirds in 1869 and would do so for all wild birds by 1880. Laws on bird protection appeared in Bavaria in 1866, Saxony in 1876, and Prussia in 1880. There were many others besides.

Interested in catching up with events abroad, Russian ornithologists and anti-cruelty advocates met in 1882 at Russia's First Congress of Societies for the Prevention of Cruelty to Animals and discussed the need to protect migratory birds that flew over or visited the Russian Empire, especially in the ecologically important Caucasus and Black Sea regions. By 1884 *zemstvo*s (local rural governing bodies) in Odessa and some other areas of the Empire had also expressed interest in bird protection, again focusing primarily on useful insectivores.

The international movement, meanwhile, continued to burgeon. Expanding beyond their original home within agricultural conferences, advocates of cross-border bird protection organised the First International Ornithological Congress in Vienna in 1884. Chair Gustav F.R. Radde 'issued a statement arguing the desirability of creating an international convention covering the whole world and based on two legal principles: 1. The hunting of birds by any means other than firearms, and their capture or trade, [should be] conducted only by special permission during [a close season, covering] the first half of the year. 2. Mass capture of birds [should be] banned at all times of the year'. Progress, however, was slow. Seven years later, in 1891, the issue was discussed at least twice at the Second International Ornithological Conference in Budapest and also at an agricultural congress held in The Hague. In 1895 an International Commission on the Protection of Birds Useful to Agriculture met in Paris and drafted protection measures, subsequently signed by delegates from sixteen states. The resulting document was 'sent to governments all around the world' along with an invitation to join.[84] The issue came up that year also at the Second Ornithological Congress (eleven years after the first one) in Budapest.

The momentum thus achieved resulted in a major treaty issued 19 March 1902 in Paris under the title 'Convention for the Protection of Birds Useful to Agriculture', more often referred to simply as the Paris Convention. Setting out as an eventual goal the 'total protection' of all 'useful' birds, including their nests, eggs and fledglings, the Paris Convention offered a list of about forty entries – mixing species and families – subject to a close season from 1 March to 15 September. It also put curbs on trapping, transporting and selling listed birds. Several exemptions and loopholes were offered, however, including the right for landowners, tenants and others to apply for permission to kill birds or remove nests if they could be shown to interfere with agriculture. Signatory states had three years to come into compliance with the Convention, could 'make necessary changes to weaken' it, and could withdraw at one year's notice. Protected birds included most types of owls, all woodpeckers, all titmice, swifts, nightingales and others prized for their insectivorous or rodent-eating habits. A list of 'harmful birds' appended to the law included jays, magpies, crows, virtually all birds of prey (except owls), pelicans, herons, cormorants and other fish-eaters. The French government would serve as the nexus through which national governments would inform of existing laws or submit new ones under the Convention's umbrella.[85]

The Russian Empire, however, was not among the eleven states to sign on. Nor, conspicuously, were Britain (in other ways in the vanguard of bird protection), the Netherlands, Italy or Norway. Signatory states were Austria-Hungary, Germany, Belgium, Spain, France, Greece, Luxembourg, Monaco, Portugal, Sweden and Switzerland. Russia retained the right to sign on later if desired. But eight years on, with the number of signatory nations swollen by the entrance of Canada and the Netherlands, along with submission of national legislation as a sign of cooperation by Britain, India, China, New Zealand, the USA and many others, Russia (and Italy) remained holdouts, limiting themselves merely to 'acknowledging receipt of materials' from the Convention and retaining the right to join later.[86] In the event, however, the Russian Empire never did sign.

The question arises, why not? One reason put forward by Russian ornithologists of the time, or shortly thereafter, involved the state of Russian public taxonomic expertise. A.A. Silant'ev, for example, noted in 1915 that Russians were largely ignorant about birds, especially 'small' ones.[87] Even the Russian Hunting Code of 1892, which concerned relatively few and generally more well-known larger species, foundered on public inability to distinguish between protected and unprotected species.[88] He appears to have had in mind not just the public, but also gamekeepers, forest guards and others charged with enforcing game law! Even among Russian naturalists ornithological knowledge was not what it might be, with Russia still lacking a 'simple list of all of its bird species'.[89] The condition persisted. As late as 1927, the Russian ornithologist D.M. Rossinski still cited his countrymen's popular ignorance of birds as the main problem in the way of preventing the then-USSR from passing bird protection laws:

> Our ornithological fauna is extremely rich with different kinds of game birds, but the population, somehow focusing on the main hunting species, [is] completely unfamiliar with the mass of small birds. In Russia people have some knowledge of birds that are bright, and have coloured markings and outer appearance, but even these they don't know all that well. And everything else, so far as the ordinary masses are concerned, is just an unknown mass of birds.[90]

How, then, could Russians be expected to protect birds or be held accountable for breaking laws concerning species that they could not even recognise?[91]

Given Russia's lack of bird knowledge (especially at a popular level), Silant'ev suggested in 1915, the best way forward might *not* be laws at all, but popular education.[92] This was in fact a common thought among Russian conservationists of the late nineteenth and early twentieth centuries, some of whom looked askance at the average Russian peasant with his low regard for the opinions of scientists and technologists, his provincialism, and his abiding superstitions. The latter, for example, led many peasants to fear and kill all owls and eagle-owls, most of which were included in the Paris Convention as 'useful' species. In other cases, however, peasant traditions promoted bird conservation: for example, it was customary in southern Russia and Ukraine for peasants to put up nest-boxes, particularly for common and rosy starlings; and in Moscow it was an old practice to free caged birds in commemoration of the Annunciation on 25 March.[93] Overall, the number and diversity of Russian and Slavic superstitions about birds is great and has been well studied.[94]

In trying to explain Russia's refusal to sign the Paris Convention contemporaries such as Silant'ev (who supported this decision) also hinted at the economic fallout signing might have entailed. As the statistics for bird exports show, Russia had by the end of the nineteenth century developed a powerful vested interest in continuing to hunt and trap. Both the state and individuals benefited. On the other hand, while Russian bird-protection advocates applauded the growth of the Russian export economy generally, they were mostly unhappy with the manner in which this aspect of it was being done, judging the harvests unsustainable since they were based in large measure on illegal, out-of-season and 'predatory' methods of hunting. Parts of the government appear to have shared these concerns, if sporadically. For example, a general and 'growing decline' in the population of profitable Russian game had been noted by the Ministry of Internal Affairs as early as 1856, leading to discussion and even a draft re-script within that organ of game laws before 1860.⁹⁵ Nothing came of this, however. By the century's end, calls for abolition of the plumage trade and reform of the game laws continued much as before, but perhaps with an added undercurrent of resentment that European feather fashions, having already caused havoc among bird populations elsewhere, were now significantly focused on Russian birdlife. Silant'ev himself complained bitterly in 1915 that the trade and its depredations had 'bit by bit spread widely across European Russia and also ... appeared in Asiatic Russia, [causing] whole regions [the Caucasus and Caspian regions were a particular concern] to have been literally emptied of birds.'⁹⁶ Meanwhile, some Russians continued to focus attention on the putative inaction of some other countries, especially southern Europeans, who, it was sometimes asserted, had done little so far to legislate or otherwise act against the plumage trade.⁹⁷ (It should also be noted that the plumage trade had its own organised defenders and lobbies, though these were not primarily Russian.⁹⁸)

More speculatively, it is possible also that Russia did not sign the Paris Convention because its ornithologists and government faced less popular pressure to do so than did counterparts from other countries. This would also have derived in part from the relatively low level of interest in birds among the Russian public. (I have found no evidence in Russia, for example, of the kinds of petitions that literally poured into the British Parliament from ordinary citizens in support of bird protection from 1869 on.) Efforts to educate Russians on birds – including the creation from 1898 forward of 'May Unions', children's scouting groups whose leadership emphasised bird conservation and organised activities such as nest-box construction – were still extremely nascent at the time. (Pressure to sign does seem to have been applied by foreigners, however: inaction at Paris convinced 'some persons' that Russia 'is a wild country, in which there reigns a complete lawlessness and where there takes place a mass destruction of small birds'.)⁹⁹

Similarly, in the West, especially in Britain, bird protection and anti-cruelty were affairs pushed forward in large part by the middle and upper-middle classes, often urbanites, who pressured legislatures that were increasingly democratically elected. Almost everything was different in Russia. Through 1917 the country was overwhelmingly peasant; the first parliament was authorised only in 1905; and autocracy persisted – the RISPCA and other organisations had to seek official permission to organise and then worked within limits allowed by government censors. Overall, then, the all-important 'middling sorts' and the liberal environments in which they best thrived were mostly absent in the Russian Empire. Notably, a large proportion of those Russians who advocated for birds and animals were not middle but *upper* class. The membership of the RISPCA, for example, was heavily aristocratic (and compared to its American and British counterparts, also very male):¹⁰⁰ almost its entire roster of founding members were ranked nobles, mostly from the upper strata of the Civil Service; some 2 per cent were military officers, and the organisation was immediately sponsored by Grand Duke Nikolai Nikolaevich the Elder (hence the organisation's use of the word 'Imperial').[101]

Other, somewhat less aristocratic organisations that might have pushed for signing the Paris Convention do not appear to have taken up the issue (as institutions). Such was the case for the Kharkov Society of Nature Enthusiasts (founded 1869).[102] Still other relevant societies were founded too late to play a role, including the Russian Society for the Raising of Game and Other Useful Animals (*Rossiiskoe obshchestvo khoziaistvennogo razvedeniia promyslovykh zhivotnykh i predstavitelei poleznoi dichi*, founded 1905), the Khortitsa Society of Defenders of Nature (*Obshchestvo okhranitelei prirody v Khortitse*, founded 1911), and the Society for the Study and Reform of Hunting Affairs in Russia (*Obshchestvo izucheniia i uporiadocheniia okhotnich'ego dela v Rossii*).[103] Organisations dedicated specifically to birds, and which *were* explicitly interested in their protection, were only just beginning to appear around the time of the Paris Convention. These included the Circle of Enthusiasts of Song Birds and other Wild Birds (*Kruzhok liubetelei pevchei i drugoi vol'noi ptitsy*) founded in 1900 in Moscow by natural history professors V.V. Popov and D.M. Rossinskii and the K.F. Kessler Kiev Ornithological Society, founded in 1906 by V.M. Artobolevskii, a Kiev university professor, in honour of Kessler, a Russian ornithologist. These and other examples of a rapid upturn in the organisation of interest in bird conservation around the turn of the century had little time to achieve much before the onset of the First World War and the Bolshevik Revolution.

A final and more important factor to consider is the aforementioned growing Russian resistance to the cast-iron lists of good and bad birds which were fundamental to the Paris Convention. It is noticeable that after disengaging from Paris and from the search for an international agreement, the more flexible 'Russian approach' discussed above was quickly placed at the centre of a new effort at bird protection legislation, this time focused on game law reform.

Even before the era of the Paris Convention, amendments had been made to existing Russian game law on behalf of wild birds. So far, however, the more traditional categorisations had been used, at least where 'harmful' birds were concerned. Thus the 1886 'Established Ruling on Urban and Agricultural Economies' (*Ustanovlenie o gorodskom i sel'skom khoziaistve*), while quite specific about naming which species and their nests might be destroyed – those of hawks, falcons, crows and the like, sparrows and all northern seabirds – was more ambiguous on protected species, referring simply to a ban on capturing 'birds' by means of 'crossbows, nets, or snares, and also during the close season ... ' (Articles 1174–75). Article 1173 banned the destruction of 'bird nests' ('predatory' species excepted).[104] An updated hunting law of 3 February 1892 offered only minor changes.[105]

As the new century dawned, the issue was taken up by a Russian Ornithological Committee within the Russian Society for the Acclimatisation of Animals and Plants headed by ornithologist D.M. Rossinskii. Over the following years, this Committee, in association with other leading ornithologists including Silant'ev, worked up a whole series of proposals and legal drafts. Following a major congress of Russian ornithologists held in Moscow in 1914, much of this work was crystallised in the drafting of yet another law. This one, however, appeared set for implementation. Known as the 'Draft Hunting Law of 1915' it promised greater clarity and precision of terminology, expansion of the law's jurisdiction to the whole of the Russian Empire, the outlawing of several techniques or devices for catching birds not covered in previous laws, new licensing requirements, and a longer close season (1 February to July 15 as opposed to the current season of 1 March to 29 June) covering all birds (and other animals) not explicitly exempted.

Most significantly, in recognition of the concern for Russia's supposedly 'unique' size and natural diversity, the draft also envisioned local flexibility in implementation, species lists, and in other areas. Fundamentally, it finally and fully rejected the traditional binary of 'useful' and 'harmful' birds (and other animals). Instead, it offered a *three*-category system which split 'harmful' into 'always harmful' and 'conditionally' so. The former it was always permissible to kill. The fate of the latter – species considered sometimes useful and sometimes harmful to agriculture depending on local conditions, population density and other factors – would be decided on an ongoing basis by local hunting bodies composed of representatives from agriculture, forestry and other relevant backgrounds. Had they been able to read, Russian birds might have been pleased to learn that ornithologists' ongoing advocacy had earned them a modest promotion: the list of 'always harmful' species was dominated by various big cats, along with wolves, and (to at least one naturalist's dismay) badgers. Birds earlier deemed 'harmful' were now considered to be only 'conditionally harmful'.[106]

Silant'ev summed up his own thoughts on the draft at the time by calling it a 'big step forward in comparison with current laws' and more likely to promote the 'preservation of friends' and the 'destruction of enemies'.[107] The draft's main innovation – the refusal to separate all species into harmful and beneficial and the use of the flexible new third category – thus characterised what had by now emerged as a distinct Russian idiosyncrasy in bird protection. In the event, unfortunately, the innovations of the 1915 draft were of little immediate consequence. Despite being accepted the same year by a specially-appointed Hunting Commission within the State Duma (Russian Parliament), with enactment anticipated for the near future, the project was ultimately forgotten – yet another of the victims of the senseless destruction of the First World War.

CONCLUSIONS

Russian developments in ornithology and bird protection seem in many respects to have followed the same lines as their western counterparts and to have occurred in full communication with them. At the same time, and unlike events in, say, England or Germany, there is a clear undercurrent of international competition. Russians felt the need to catch up with their foreign peers – to be understood as anyone's equal. On the other hand, by the close of the nineteenth century many of them had become convinced and vocal about their own identity and of the uniqueness of their circumstances. They understood that their country was unlike any other, at least in Europe, especially in terms of its size and consequent geographical and biological diversity. They also knew well the special challenges inherent in working with a population that was relatively uneducated, isolated, rural and traditional. The strategies they pursued reflected these realities and were, consequently, 'Russian'. Though this left much room for international cooperation, in at least one venue – the Paris Convention – it proved an obstacle.

The outbreak of the First World War greatly set back Russian advances on both the ornithological and conservationist fronts – the destruction of Buturlin's manuscripts and the failure of the Draft Hunting Law of 1915 respectively are emblematic. The ensuing collapse of the monarchy in March and the Bolshevik Revolution of November 1917 only made matters worse. Yet ornithologists and conservationists would rebound surprisingly quickly – bringing into the early Soviet period much of the agenda, tools and work of the Imperial period. Echoes of the 1915 draft would see the light of day under the changed political and social environment of the Soviet Union. This, of course, is an entirely different story.

NOTES

[1] Research for this paper was conducted with support from Youngstown State University's Faculty Reimbursement for Advanced Studies program, from the Center for Slavic and East European Studies at Ohio State University, and in part by a grant from the International Research and Exchanges Board (IREX), with funds provided by the National Endowment for the Humanities, the US Department of State, and the US Information Agency. None of these organisations is responsible for the views expressed. I am grateful to them all. For their useful comments and criticisms I would also like to thank two anonymous reviewers for *Environment and History*.

[2] Good gateway sources, including bibliographies for further study, are John Sheail, *Nature Conservation in Britain: The Formative Years* (London: The Stationery Office, 1998); Jeremy Gaskell, *Who Killed the Great Auk?* (Oxford and New York: Oxford University Press, 2000); Robin W. Doughty, *Feather Fashions and Bird Preservation: A Study in Nature Protection* (Berkeley and Los Angeles: University of California Press, 1975); Hilda Kean, *Animal Rights: Political and Social Change in Britain since 1800* (London:

Reaktion Books, 1998); and Benjamin Kline, *First Along the River: A Brief History of the U.S. Environmental Movement* (San Francisco: Acada Books, 1997).

[3] Space considerations preclude the inclusion of significant biographical material on the many ornithologists and other individuals who appear in this essay. Many of the Russians can be located in the different editions of the *Great Soviet Encyclopedia* (*Bol'shaia Sovetskaia Entsiklopediia*).

[4] Christopher Ely, *This Meager Nature: Landscape and National Identity in Imperial Russia* (DeKalb: Northern Illinois University Press, 2002).

[5] Cited in Paul Lawrence Farber, *Discovering Birds: The Emergence of Ornithology as a Scientific Discipline, 1760–1850* (Baltimore and London: The Johns Hopkins University Press [1982], 1997), 103–4.

[6] The original German title is *Beyträge zur topographischen Kenntniss des russischen Reichs*. Cited from Jean Anker, *Bird Books and Bird Art: An Outline of the Literary History and Iconography of Descriptive Ornithology* (Copenhagen: Levin and Munksgaard, 1938), 26, 122.

[7] Ibid., 26.

[8] Quoted in Theed Pearse, *Birds of the Early Explorers in the Northern Pacific* (Comox, British Columbia: Theed Pearse, 1968), 70.

[9] His results were published in expedition secretary Martin Sauer's *An Account of a Geographical and Astronomical Expedition to the Northern Parts of Russia for Ascertaining the Degrees of Latitude and Longitude ... of the Whole Coast of the Toulski to East Cape and of the Islands of the Eastern Coast Stretching to the American Coast. Performed by Command of her Imperial Majesty Catherine the Second—by Commodore Joseph Billings in the Years 1785 to 1794, the Whole Narrated from the Original Papers by Martin Sauer, Secretary of the Expedition* (London: T. Cadell, 1802). Merck's own journal from 1787–92 is available as Carl Heinrich Merck, *Siberia and Northwestern America, 1788–1792: The Journal of Carl Heinrich Merck, Naturalist with the Russian Scientific Expedition Led by Captains Joseph Billings and Gavriil Sarychev*, trans. Fritz Jaensch (Kingston, ON: Limestone Press, 1980).

[10] Though the book appears to have been published first in Russian (3 vols., 1771–80; 4th vol. posthumously in 1805; all St. Petersburg), I have been able to find full bibliographical information only on a German edition published soon after as Herrn Iwan Lepechin, *Tagebuch der Reise durch verschiedene Provinzen des russischen Reiches ... von M. Christian Heinrich Hase*. It contains 'a fairly large amount of information about birds ... scattered throughout the volumes' (Anker, *Bird Books and Bird Art*, 26, 154).

[11] Güldenstädt's observations were published posthumously by co-expeditionist Peter Simon Pallas under the title *Reisen durch Russland und im Caucasischen Gebürge* (St. Petersburg 1787–91). Güldenstädt's descriptive writings of the Caucasus remain to this day 'the most authoritative on the birds of that area' according to Michael Walters, *A Concise History of Ornithology* (New Haven and London: Yale University Press, 2003), 71.

[12] *Reise durch Russland zur Untersuchung der drey Natur-Reiche. Gedruckt bey der Kayserl* (Academie der Wissenschaften. St. Petersburg. 4 vols. [the last published posthumously by Pallas], 1771–84).

[13] Peter Simon Pallas, *Reisen durch versch. Provinzen des Russ. Reichs in den Jahren 1768–74* (1770/71–1776). The book was quickly translated and published in Russian as *Puteshestvie po raznym provintsiiam Rossiiskoi imperii* (St. Petersburg: Imperatorskaia

For the 'Preservation of Friends' ...

Akademiia nauk, 1786–1809).

[14] Pearse, *Birds of the Early Explorers*, 11–12.

[15] The Great Northern Expedition was a huge undertaking, unparalleled in eighteenth-century exploration. It consisted of an eastward moving centre – under the command of the Dane Vitus Bering – from which numerous detachment expeditions were sent north to survey sections of the Arctic, and east and south to Pacific destinations including Kamchatka, the Kuriles, Japan and – the centrepiece of the whole venture – Alaska.

[16] Georg Wilhelm Steller, *Journal of a Voyage with Bering, 1741–1742*, ed., O.W. Frost (CA: Stanford University Press, 2002 [c.1988]), 18. This was preceded by Steller's first publication (also posthumous) of a 'Latin treatise on the zoology of the North Pacific ... published by the Russian Academy of Sciences in 1751' (Steller, *Steller's History of Kamchatka*. Trans. Margritt Engel and Karen Willmore. Rasmusson Library Translation Series [Fairbanks: University of Alaska Press, 2003], viii).

[17] *Steller's History of Kamchatka*, 145–7.

[18] Ibid., 4, 6–7. The 1758 paper on nests and eggs in Siberia was published in *Novi Commentarii* (the journal of the Imperial Academy of Sciences in St. Petersburg).

[19] As Stepan Petrovich Krasheninnikov, *Opisanie zemli Kamchatki*. A publication date of 1735 is cited in some sources.

[20] Pearse, *Birds of the Early Explorers*, 50, 53–68.

[21] Stepan Petrovich Krasheninnikov, *The History of Kamtschatka and Kurilski Islands with the Countries Adjacent; Illustrated with Maps and Cuts. Translated into English by James Grieve, M.D.* (Chicago: Quadrangle Books, 1962), 152–63. (Translation of source cited in n. 19).

[22] Other persons associated with Bering's expeditions whose (generally minor) bird-related observations have been published include Sven Waxell, A.I. Chirikov, J. von Stachlin and G.A. Sarychev.

[23] Outside of Russia Bellingshausen is better known as Fabian Gottlieb Thaddeus von Bellingshausen. His journal was not published until 1831 (and in only 600 copies). It was translated for the first time [into German] in 1902. The first English translation was made in 1945 by the Hakluyt Society.

[24] Cited in Anker, *Bird Books and Bird Art*, 165, as A.T. (using the German spelling of his middle name) von Middendorf, *Reise in den äussersten Norden und Osten Sibiriens ... 1843 und 1844. Mit allerhöchster Genehmigung auf Veranstaltung der Kaiserlichen Akademie der Wissenschaft zu St. Petersburg ausgeführt und in Verbindung mit vielen Gelehrten herausgegeben von A. Th. V. Middendorff*. St. Petersburg, 1853. The second volume (of four) treated 210 bird species and included 40 lithographic plates.

[25] Including Leopold von Schrenck *Vögel des Amur-Landes* (volume two of his four-volume work, *Reisen und Forschungen im Amur-Lande... 1854–56 im Auftrage der Kaiserl. Akademie der Wissenschaften zu St. Petersburg ausgeführt und in Verbindung mit mehreren Gelehrten herausgegeben von Leopold v. Schrenck* [1858–95]); G.F.R. Radde, *Reisen im Süden von Ost-Sibirien ... 1855–59 incl. Im Auftrage der Kaiserlichen Geographischen Gesellschaft ausgeführt von Gustav Radde. Vol. II Die Festlands-Ornis des sudostlichen Sibiriens* (Buchdruckerei von W. Besobrasoff & Co. St. Petersburg, 1863.)

[26] A basic overview of the ornithological aspects of several of these expeditions is in Walters, *A Concise History of Ornithology*, 145. I have drawn on this source for much of the basic information in this and the following paragraph.

[27] The species was first described in 1881. In the absence of a specimen of the common ancestor of the modern domestic horse and Przheval'skii's Wild Horse, experts variously classify the latter as either *Equus ferus przewalskii* (a distinct species apart from the modern horse) or *Equus caballus przewalskii* (a subspecies thereof). Designated during the 1960s as extinct in the wild, a small population has since been successfully reestablished in Mongolia.

[28] On Severtsov, see N.G. Dement'ev, *Nikolai Alekseevich Severtsov, zoolog i puteshestvennik (1827–1885)*, 2nd edn (Moscow, 1948); and R.L. Zolotniskaia, *N.A. Severtsov – geograf i puteshestvennik* (Moscow, 1953). The latter source includes a bibliography of Severtsov's relevant publications. For more on Menzbir (and other Russian ornithologists of the period), see K.A. Vorob'ev, *Zapiski ornitologa* (Moscow: Nauka, 1978); and *Moskovskie ornitologi* (Moscow: Moscow State University Press, 1999).

[29] *Ornitologicheskii vestnik*, vol. 3, no. 2 (1912): 191.

[30] M.A. Menzbir, *Ptitsy Rossii (Evropeiskaia Rossiia, Sibir', Turkestan, Zakapiiskaia Oblast' i Kavkaz*. Third Edition (Moscow, 1918), i, iv. Menzbir was particularly critical of Russian and foreign efforts to invent trinomial and quadronomial systems. He urged a 'cleansing' of the nomenclature and a return to Linnaean binomialism.

[31] Ibid., i-ii.

[32] See, for example, 'Obzor russkoi ornitologicheskoi literatury', *Ornitologicheskii vestnik* vol. 4, no. 1 (1913): 60–61.

[33] V.D. Il'ichev and G.N. Simkin, 'Mikhail Aleksandrovich Menzbir.' (No page numbers). Viewed online at Soiuz okhrany ptits Rossii http://www.rbcu.ru/information/personalia/menzbir.html (28 March, 2005).

[34] See *Buturlinskii sbornik. Materialy I Vserossiiskoi nauchno-prakticheskoi konferentsii, posviashchennoi pamiati S.A. Buturlina* Ul'ianovsk, 19.09.2002 – 22.09.2002 (Ul'ianovsk: Ul'ianovskii oblastnoi kraevedcheskii muzei 2003). This includes an extensive bibliography of his works (51–67). See also K.A. Vorob'ev, *Zapiski ornitologa* (Moscow: Nauka, 1978); and *Moskovskie ornitologi*.

[35] *Buturlinskii sbornik*. 5.

[36] It is unclear from the Russian sources exactly which species is referred to here. The term *Rosy Gull* seems to have been applied to at least three different species in various contexts (*Larus Philadelphia, Larus franklinii* and *Rhodostethia rosea*). *Rhodostethia rosea* seems most likely.

[37] Ia. A. Red'kin, 'Vklad S.A. Buturlina v kollektsionnoe delo v rossiiskoi ornitologii.' In *Buturlinskii sbornik*. 202–3. It is unclear whether or not the sale occurred.

[38] S.A. Buturlin (with G.P. Dementev), *Polnyi opredelitel' ptits SSSR*. 5 vols. (Moscow and Leningrad, 1934–41). Though too late to be of direct relevance here, it has been called 'the first comprehensive guidebook to the birds of the Soviet Union' (M.M. Kozlova, 'Literaturnoe nasledie S.A. Buturlina'. In *Buturlinskii sbornik*, 49).

[39] On the history of royal and aristocratic hunting in Russia, see V.E. Boreiko, *Tsarskoe okhoty: ot Vladimira Monomakha do Vladimira Shcherbitskogo*. Seriia: Istoriia okhrany prirody. Vypusk 3. Kiev: Ekologo-kul'turnyi tsentr, 1995.

[40] On British examples of the differences, tensions and interactions of game laws and nineteenth century bird protection laws, see Brian Bonhomme, 'Nested Interests: Assessing Britain's Wild Bird Protection Laws of 1869–1880', *Nineteenth Century Studies* 19 (2005): 47–68.

[41] Founded in 1765 in St. Petersburg by a group of wealthy landowners for the purpose of finding ways to improve agricultural productivity and efficiency. The group was relatively liberal and westernising, serving as a forum for debate on numerous social issues including the abolition of serfdom during the nineteenth century. It lasted until 1919.

[42] One comprising members of the RIFES only, the other adding representatives from the Society of Nature Enthusiasts (*Obshchestvo estestvoispitatelei*), the Russian Horticultural Society (*Rossiiskoe obshchestvo sadovodstva*), and the Russian Entomological Society (*Russkoe entomologicheskoe obshchestvo*). See V.E. Iverson, compiler, *Pervoe desiatiletie rossiiskogo obshchestva pokrovitel'stva zhivotnym: istoricheskii ocherk ego deiatel'nosti v 1865–1875 gg.* (St. Petersburg, 1875), 40.

[43] Iverson, *Pervoe desiatiletie*, 41–3.

[44] Ibid., 44–9.

[45] Bonhomme, 'Nested Interests', 55.

[46] 'Rapport sur les travaux de la Société.' *Bulletin de la Société Impériale Zoologique d'Acclimatation*, vol. 1 (1854): xlvii. A particularly good sense of the French debate can be taken from M.N. de Jonquières-Antonelle, 'Note sur la destruction par l'homme de quelques espèces animals qui lui sont utiles'. In ibid., vol. 4 (1857): 79–90.

[47] I am grateful for this information to J.F.M. Clark.

[48] The Russian title literally translates as 'Russian Society for the Patronage of Animals'. The same Russian wording was often used by Russians to translate the title of the British and American Societies. At other times they translated literally (*obshchestva predokhranenia zhivotnykh ot muchenii*). For the sake of simplicity I have chosen the translation that will allow more instant recognition among Anglophone readers. The RISPCA was based in St. Petersburg. Provincial counterparts, most of them independent of the RISPCA, quickly arose after 1865 in Odessa, Riga, Tiflis and elsewhere. Nearly 100 existed by 1900.

[49] Iverson, *Pervoe desiatiletie*, 3.

[50] These lacked the force of law, of course, although they were often adopted voluntarily by the St. Petersburg police and other organs.

[51] Iverson, *Pervoe desiatiletie*, 4. Laws protecting privately-owned animals from undue cruelty existed in the Russian Empire from at least 1864. They were generally considered by the RISPCA to be insufficient and improperly enforced.

[52] Ibid., 36.

[53] Ibid., 33–4.

[54] Rossiiskoe obshchestvo pokrovitel'stvo zhivotnym. *Istoricheskyi ocherk ego deiatel'nosti, 1865–1875* (St. Petersburg, 1878), 102. The talk, by Iverson, was published in the Society's bulletin the following year (ibid., 106).

[55] *Shestoi mezhdunarodnyi kongress obshchestv pokrovitel'stva zhivotnym v Londone* (1874). Doklad delegata rossiiskogo obshchestva pokrovitel'stva zhivotnym, N. Vil'kinsa (St. Petersburg, 1875), 98–9.

[56] 'O sokranshchenie vesennogo vyvoza dichi za granitsu', *Okhotnich'ia gazeta*, no. 33 (19 August, 1891), page no. missing, first page of issue. One *pud* equals approximately thirty-six pounds.

[57] A.A. Silant'ev, *Okhrana zverei i ptits, poleznykh v sel'skom khoziaiztve* (Petrograd, 1915), 37.

[58] The Ukrainian historian V.E. Boreiko confirms that as populations of plumage birds

were exhausted in western Europe, Russia came under increasing hunting pressures. He offers the following figures of birds taken for plumage during 1911 only and just from the Russian Caspian coast: 150,000 seagulls, 20,000 eider ducks, 3,500 swans. He also records 30,000 sparrows processed and exported in 1892 by a single Moscow establishment and in 1889, '11–42,000 *puds*' of bird hides sent to Paris along the Moscow-Brest route. The carnage seems to have moved farther and farther east, reaching western Siberia around 1890 – mirroring in some respects a pattern long-ago established by Russian fur-hunters who chased ever farther east in search of valuable furs. See Boreiko, *Belye piatna*, 63.

[59] *Shestoi mezhdunarodnyi kongress*, 70.

[60] Ibid., 71–2.

[61] Baron G.V. Lauden, Imperatorskoe Rossiiskoe Obshchestvo Akklimatizatsii Zhivotnykh i Rastenii, *Ptitsevedenie i Ptitsevodstvo*. God IV, Vypusk 1, no. 36 (1912: Moscow), 2.

[62] Silant'ev, *Okhrana zverei*, 15.

[63] See for example, Iverson, *Pervoe desiatiletie*, 48.

[64] In German, *Organisation der Naturdenkmalpflege in Deutschland*. See, for example, D.N. Aniutin, *Okhrana pamiatnikov prirody* (Moscow, 1914), 4. Published as a joint volume with G.A. Kozhevnikov, *Mezhdunarodnaia okhrana prirody* (see n. 66.)

[65] Ibid., 6–29, especially 28–9.

[66] G.A. Kozhevnikov, *Mezhdunarodnaia okhrana prirody* (Moscow 1914), 51. Published as a joint volume with D.N. Aniutin, *Okhrana pamiatnikov prirody*. (Second author and title appear first), 56.

[67] D.N. Aniutin, *Okhrana pamiatnikov prirody*, 6, 38.

[68] Baron G.V. Lauden, Imperatorskoe Rossiiskoe Obshchestvo Akklimatizatsii Zhivotnykh i Rastenii, *Ptitsevedenie i Ptitsevodstvo*. God IV, Vypusk 1, no. 36 (1912: Moscow), 1.

[69] Ibid., God III, Vypusk 1–2, no. 27 (1912: Moscow), 1. The Rossitten bird observatory in east Prussia was established in 1901. The town, now part of Russia, is currently called Rybachii.

[70] An outline of the situation, including the best but incomplete listings to date, is in 'Voprosy i otvety', *Ornitologicheskii vestnik*, vol. 2, no. 2 (1911): 209.

[71] Boreiko, *Belye piatna*, 164.

[72] Widely available in translation. See S.T. Aksakov, *Notes on Fishing*, trans. Thomas P. Hodge (Evanston, Il: Northwestern University Press, 1997); and *Notes of a Provincial Wildfowler*, trans. Kevin Windle (Evanston, Il: Northwestern University Press, 1998).

[73] Iverson, *Pervoe desiatiletie*, 7.

[74] Boreiko, *Belye piatna*, 164–5; D.M. Rossinskii, *Okhrana ptits*. Vserossiiskoe obshchestvo okhrany prirody. (Moscow: Izdanie obshchestva, 1927), 7.

[75] Aniutin, *Okhrana pamiatnikov prirody*, 1.

[76] Baron G.V. Lauden, Imperatorskoe Rossiiskoe Obshchestvo Akklimatizatsii Zhivotnykh i Rastenii, *Ptitsevedenie i Ptitsevodstvo*. God IV, Vypusk 1, no. 36 (1912: Moscow), 9.

[77] Darwinism was, however, the target of increasingly vocal and organised Russian criticism from philosophers, the church and elsewhere starting near the turn of the century. For more on the reception of Darwin in the Russian Empire, see Alexander Vucinich, *Darwin in Russian Thought* (Berkeley/Los Angeles: Univ. California Press, 1989); and three articles by James Allen Rogers: 'The Reception of Darwin's Origin of Species by Russian Scientists', *Isis*, 1973, 64: 484–50; 'Charles Darwin and Russian Scientists',

Russian Review, 1960, 13(4): 371–8; and 'Russian Opposition to Darwinism in the Nineteenth Century', *Isis* 1974, 65: 487–505.

[78] See Weiner. *Models of Nature*.

[79] D.C., 'Review of *A Summer on the Yenesei* by Maud D. Haviland.' In *The Geographical Journal* 45,6 (June 1915), 526.

[80] A.A. Silant'ev, *Okhrana zverei i ptits, poleznykh v sel'skom khoziaiztve* (Petrograd, 1915), 37.

[81] See Rossinskii, *Okhrana ptits*, 4.

[82] Ibid.; also, Silant'ev, *Okhrana zverei i ptits*, 27.

[83] Rossinskii, *Okhrana ptits*, 4.

[84] Ibid., 5.

[85] The Convention, including schedules of 'useful' and 'harmful' birds appears in full in Silant'ev, *Okhrana zverei*, 30–33. It is also available on-line through The American Society of International Law at http://www.internationalwildlifelaw.org/bird_1902.html

[86] Rossinskii, *Okhrana ptits*, 5. By 1910, 29 states were involved in one way or another with the Paris Convention: 13 as signatories, 10 reporting to the Convention on their own bird laws, 4 (including Russia) retaining the right to join the at a later date, and 2 which had entered into dealings or negotiations with the Convention.

[87] Silant'ev, *Okhrana zverei*, 12.

[88] Ibid., 6–7, 11.

[89] Ibid., 11, 13.

[90] Rossinskii, *Okhrana ptits*, 5. Russian popular knowledge of *non-avian* wildlife was also rated poorly by Russian experts. See, for example, 'The low level of zoological knowledge among Russian society [*Nizkii uroven' znanii zoologii v russkom obshchestve*]', in G. Norkskii, 'Brakonery i khishchniki. Sredstva bor'by s nimi na zapade' in *Okhotnich'ia gazeta. Illustrirovannoe ezhenedel'noe izdanie*, Vtoroe polugodie (1891), June-December, 428–59.

[91] This raises the question: did the publics of other countries, ones that *did* have such laws, also have better basic ornithological skills? The answer is probably yes. Certainly, several countries, Britain especially, had numerous relatively comprehensive field guides before the end of the nineteenth century. These, moreover, were consumed in significant numbers by an interested public that was also on average more literate than its Russian counterpart. It was in the West, moreover – and especially in Britain, Germany and the USA – that the nineteenth century popular craze for collecting and cataloguing wildlife specimens was most pronounced, and where bird-watching as a hobby was the best developed. Russia contrasts significantly with all of these developments.

[92] Silant'ev, *Okhrana zverei*, 14.

[93] Boreiko *Belye piatna*, 163.

[94] See, for example, Jack V. Haney, Trans., *The Complete Russian Folktale: Volume 2: Russian Animal Tales* (M.E. Sharpe, 2000); and A.S. Ermolov, *Narodnaia selskokhoziaistvennaia mudrost v poslovitsakh, pogovorkakh i primetakh*. 4 vols. (St. Petersburg : A.S. Suvorin, 1902–05).

[95] Iverson, *Pervoe desiatiletie*, 34–5.

[96] Silant'ev, *Okhrana zverei*, 16.

[97] Aniutin, *Okhrana pamiatnikov prirody*, 38.

[98] Representatives of the plumage trade attended many of the conferences noted throughout this paper. At one – the 1913 Berne Conference for the International Protection of Nature – they spoke of the '100,000s of workers, primarily women' who depended on the plumage trade. See, G.A. Kozhevnikov, *Mezhdunarodnaia okhrana prirody*, 51, 55.

[99] Silant'ev, *Okhrana zverei*, 42. This sense, says Silant'ev, was particularly present during later rounds of Paris negotiations and discussions, 1909–13.

[100] The Society counted very few women among its early members. In 1873 a debate on expanding women's activities in the RISPCA and establishing 'special women's committees' (the issue was raised by a few vocal female members) 'did not lead to a polite resolution of the issue. From everywhere there came only refusals.' At least through about 1890 the situation does not appear to have changed dramatically. Rossiiskoe obshchestvo pokrovitel'stvo zhivotnym. *Istoricheskyi ocherk ego deiatel'nosti, 1865–1875* (St. Petersburg, 1878), 118.

[101] The list of founding members and early officers is in *Istoricheskii otchet deiatel'nosti Rossiskogo obshchestva pokrovitel'stva zhivotnym so dnia ego osnovaniia* ... (St. Petersburg, 1891 [misprinted as 1890 on inside frontispiece), 9–13.

[102] Founded at Kharkov University. See *Ustav obshchestva ispitatelei prirody, pri imperatorskom kharkovskom universitete* (Kharkov: Universitetskaia tipografiia, 1869), 1.

[103] I have not been able to ascertain the date of the group's founding.

[104] Boreiko *Belye piatna*, 165–6.

[105] 'Pravila ob okhote.' *Polnoe sobranie zakonov rossiiskoi imperii*. Collection (sobranie) 3, vol. 12, 1892 (St. Petersburg, 1895), 81 (statute no. 8501).

[106] Silant'ev, *Okhrana zverei i ptits* 40–41.

[107] Ibid., 8.

Wolves in the Early Nineteenth-Century County of Jönköping, Sweden

Örjan Kardell and Anna Dahlström

INTRODUCTION

Ever since the wolf, *Canis lupus*, started to recolonise parts of Sweden in the early 1980s there has been a growing political concern about wolf management. This concern has culminated in Sweden currently facing the European Union Court on charges of not following the letter of the European Habitat Directive 92/43 of 21 May 1992, applicable since 1995 after the country entered the European Union. The Swedish government allowed quota-related culling under license for limited periods during the years 2010 and 2011. The culling has breathed new life into the scientific debate on the minimum number of wolves needed in order to ensure the long term genetic survival of the population, the current population (Figure 1) being based on a single pair from 1983 with an additional input of a long-distance dispersed male of eastern origin in 1991. Various signs of inbreeding deficiencies have been verified and have left the scientific community divided in its interpretations and apprehensions as to the future management of the wolf population.[1]

In addition to the scientific and political aspects of the struggle to attain a viable population status for the wolf, there is also a polarised and hostile debate in Swedish society, with different interest groups representing completely opposed opinions on the presence and number of wolves in the country. A longstanding conflict in wolf management is related to the loss of hunting dogs attacked by territorial wolves as intruders while hunting. To this specific problem is added a general concern where wolves are viewed as competitors for hoofed game, especially moose (*Alces alces*). Another area of conflict is related to livestock, reindeer (*Rangifer rangifer*) included, where wolves have become a threat to farming.[2]

The wolf is expected to increase in numbers and spread over larger areas, eventually colonising both the north and the south of Sweden. This scenario will probably entail an increased tension, as a growing number of people will have wolves in their backyard, and not only for the reasons mentioned above, but also out of personal fear. A poll carried out during 2009, showed that 25 per cent of respondents feared encountering wolves in the woods. Further, the poll indicated an acceptance among the public of culling large carnivores such as the brown bear (*Ursus arctos*) and the wolf under certain circumstances.[3]

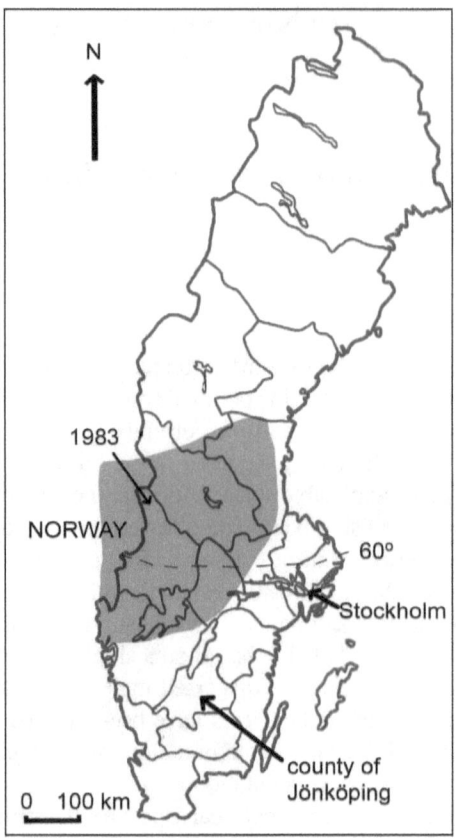

Figure 1. Sweden with the breeding area of the present shared wolf population of Sweden and Norway (in grey) and the location of the historical study area – the county of Jönköping. Source: *Sand et al.* 2010.

The Swedes' apprehensions concerning the wolf are not vindicated by historical records. The only thorough, but still limited, Swedish investigation of wolf–human encounters ever made builds on church records (for cause of death). A sample of twenty parishes in the county of Värmland – where the current Swedish wolf population was first established in 1983 (Figure 1) – and one parish from the neighbouring county of Dalarna were researched for the period 1749–1859. To supplement the general investigation, a special search was made where popular tradition held that fatal encounters between humans and wolves had occurred in the historic past. The general investigation yielded no cases, but the special investigation yielded two. During the winter of 1727–28 two children were killed by wolves, probably by the same animal and on different occasions in Värmland. To this should be added two substantiated cases from the county of Västra Götaland in 1731 and 1763, also involving children. The conclusion to be drawn is that yes, wolves have killed humans in Sweden, in all known cases children, but that this is exceptionally unusual behaviour for wolves. This is also verified from what we know about Swedish historic herding practices, which often involved unarmed children acting as herders (see below). Children would not have been employed as herders if carnivores had been conceived as a serious threat to their safety.[4]

Popular myths and legends are, however, forces to be reckoned with concerning apprehensions about wolves. Swedish ethnological records contain at least four different legends which are retold with different geographical settings: a sled-party pursued by a wolf pack during winter, where the driver saves himself by unhitching the horse and tipping a tub or vat from the cargo over himself; a small girl taken by wolves when visiting the privy one winter night; a soldier attacked and killed by wolves on his way home on a winter night, when his sword or cutlass had frozen in its scabbard; and, finally, the faithful watchdog attacked by wolves in a farmhouse vestibule, likewise on a winter night.[5]

These legends all build on some observed traits of wolf behaviour, such as their being inquisitive and usually being spotted by humans during wintertime, with occasional nocturnal visits to human habitations. However, while they are all peppered with content and action that the audience knows to be fictional, they are not entirely inconceivable. Thus, wolf legends made (and make) thrilling fireside stories, which were (and are) apprehended and understood in much the same way as the widely known European folktale of Little Red Riding Hood. These legends, handed down through the generations, are generally the only popular experience of the wolf available to the Swedish population, as most live in areas that have lacked wolves since the 1850s.[6]

On the one hand, the fact that since the 1880s the wolf population has been largely confined to the mountainous area between Norway and Sweden, along the border of the northern half of the country, and has therefore mainly been a concern for the reindeer herding Sami communities, might also explain why in current Swedish debates the wolf has not become such an icon of wilderness as it has in North America. And, on the other, the early twentieth century Swedish environmental movement did not enthusiastically embrace the idea of northern parts of the country as a wilderness area, devoid of people and traces of human activity, as was the case with its more established North American counterpart.[7]

The wolf's continuing ability to figure as a killer of livestock, both in the minds of farmers and the authorities, throughout the first half of the twentieth century, undoubtedly preserved negative attitudes and prevented the wolf from being treated as a sympathetic candidate for protection, in spite of its ever-dwindling numbers. Swedish environmentalists of the late 1920s and early

1930s had campaigned successfully to turn the brown bear into a protected species. But no similar attempts were made on behalf of the wolf. The wolf only became a protected species in Sweden in 1965, which is also the most likely date for its near extinction. All sightings thereafter were in all probability long distance dispersed individuals from Finland (see below), until 1983 when the first successful denning was recorded in the county of Värmland. Today, the most proactive organisation advocating carnivore rights in Sweden is the Svenska Rovdjursföreningen (the Swedish Carnivore Society) with about 3,500 registered members. Its views are most openly contested by the representatives of something like 200,000 organised hunters (out of a total of 262,000 registered Swedish hunters) from the Svenska Jägareförbundet (the Swedish Association for Hunting and Wildlife Management) and the Jägarnas Riksförbund (the National Federation of Hunters).[8]

The conflict between wolves and humans is as old as the advent of agriculture. This process simultaneously included the domestication of the ancestors of our farm animals, the dog (*Canis lupus familiaris*) excluded. Sedentary mixed farming communities and nomadic herding societies, which developed as a result of this initial domestication, have long seen wolves as fierce competitors for their livestock. In Europe Christian dogma has also branded the wolf as inherently evil, a fact which has made wolf control a worthy cause in its own right. In Swedish folklore one of several names that denoted the wolf was *hålehund* – dog of the devil. Hunters and gatherers, on the other hand, do not generally share these negative notions as far as is known to anthropology. Here the wolf might be regarded as an accomplished fellow hunter and even admired.[9]

In this article we argue that current and future debates concerning wolf management would benefit from a historical perspective rendered from a situation when wolves, livestock and people depending on their herds were far more numerous than today. The historical perspective will be informed by discussing aspects of available wolf food supply, territorial size and the distribution of wolves in early nineteenth century agrarian Sweden, focusing on the county of Jönköping as an example. In order to address the various issues profitably it is necessary, however, to first pay heed to some aspects of wolf biology and the region to be analysed in the paper, before examining the historical source materials and methodology employed here in more depth.[10]

WOLF BIOLOGY

The achievements of Swedish–Norwegian research cooperation on the SKANDULV project concerning the shared wolf population on the Scandinavian Peninsula, along with international research, has brought forth social ecology data on dispersal rates, size of packs and territories in relation to food supply and biomass. SKANDULV is an acronym derived from the words *Skandinavien*

Wolves in Jönköping, Sweden

(Scandinavia in both Norwegian and Swedish) and *ulv*. *Ulv* is the Norwegian word for wolf. In Swedish the term for wolf is *varg* (which meant 'assailant' or 'murderer' in archaic Middle Ages Swedish), but the original Viking-age word was *ulv*.[11]

There is a general relationship between food supply, the size of a pack and the size of territory. The wolf density in North American populations is chiefly accounted for by the density of prey biomass. In those same populations, the general dependency between territorial size and prey biomass is nearly as significant and is also mirrored in the strong link within the relationship between territory size and latitude: the higher the latitude, the larger the territory. Wolves are highly territorial and they will defend their home range, combining hunting and defence in their widespread and regular travels through their territory/home range. For instance, a territory as large as 1,600 square kilometres, with a diameter of 40 kilometres, could be covered within less than a day by a wolf hunting and marking as it goes.[12]

The location of dens is influenced by territoriality, not always by being centred in the middle of the territory, but by generally not being located in the one kilometre wide zone at the borders of territories where most encounters with neighbouring packs occur. Research shows that such encounters result in 56 per cent of wolf mortality caused by other wolves. A study of distances between active dens of neighbouring packs in south-central Alaska varied with territory size, but it showed a mean inter-den distance of 45 kilometres. A specific den can be used year after year or new dens excavated each year. Similarly litters/pups can be moved between several dens within the same territory and year. Usually there is just one litter per pack annually.[13]

In the current Swedish wolf population pups are usually born from late April to early May. There is, however, a certain variation which allows for some pups being born as late as the end of May. At seven months old they accompany their parents when hunting for the first time. They are physically mature and start to look like adults during the period of 7–12 months of age and are sexually mature after 22 months. The pups spend their first eight weeks of life in and around the den. During the following period, between 8–20 weeks, pups are stationary at the so-called rendezvous-site, an area situated a short distance from the den. Accordingly, a wolf pup born in May leads a rather sedentary life until November.[14]

Pups and the lactating she-wolf are cared for by all pack members. When rearing pups, pack members radiate from the home site (both den and rendezvous-site) to other areas of the territory, returning periodically to feed and care for the pups. Once the pups are developed enough to join the adults on their hunts, the pack becomes nomadic and moves as a unit through the territory.[15]

A wolf pack is generally built around a nucleus of a breeding pair, their annual litter of five to six pups and, to a varying degree, from litters reared two to three years previously. Thus a breeding pair must establish a territory far larger than they themselves need for their own support. When the pups are six months old, they eat as much as an adult wolf, which means that food supply, reflected in territory size, needs to be quadrupled. Taking the offspring of previous years into account, the territory required might have to be as much as 15 times larger than initially needed by a single pair. Pairs usually establish territories large enough for a full-sized pack from the beginning and these are maintained even if pack size declines or if one individual in the breeding pair for some reason dies.[16]

The wolf pack however does not expand limitlessly. There is a built-in dispersal mechanism in wolf biology which is triggered by both social competition and food competition. Pups remain with their parents for a period of 10–54 months. The natal pack in their turn, under certain conditions, can acquire additional members by accepting foreign dispersed adolescent wolves. The mean average dispersal range of wolves leaving their natal pack is 50–100 kilometres. There is, however, also a strategy of long-distance dispersal, where individual animals set off on far longer journeys, which bring them in contact with other wolf populations or to areas currently not occupied by breeding wolves. In North American studies the longest recorded documented dispersal distance measured 886 kilometres. In comparison, individuals from the present Swedish–Norwegian shared wolf population have been found, in August 2010, killing a large number of sheep 200 kilometres south-west of the nucleus showed in Figure 1.[17]

The wolf is a flexible and opportunistic predator, which usually relies on large ungulates for food. But its diet is highly variable and is as broad as its geographic range. In a Eurasian context moose, red deer (*Cervus ephalus*), boar (*Sus scrofa*) and roe deer (*Capreolus capreolus*) are important prey species. The wolf's choice of prey seems to be an equation between the relative size, abundance and vulnerability in local occurrences of different prey species. If suitable large game is lacking, wolves easily switch over to livestock. The Scandinavian population currently supports itself on natural prey, which accounts for more than 99 per cent of the wolves' diet, mainly moose. In the southern-most territories roe deer surpass moose as the mainstay in wolves' diet. The average number of moose consumed in Swedish wolves' territories is between 100–140 animals per year. Another way to put it is that the average pack kills a moose every fourth day, and during the summer months more often than this, since calves dominate in terms of their prey.[18]

Physiologically the wolf's constitution is geared either for starvation or gluttony. Wolves have been known to gorge themselves, consuming up to eight kilograms of meat on a single occasion. Three Swedish males, culled and autopsied during 2010, had a little less than four kilograms of roe deer or moose meat respectively in their stomachs. The amount of food required to meet nutritional needs, expressed as a daily average, is two kilograms of meat.[19]

Wolves in Jönköping, Sweden

THE COUNTY OF JÖNKÖPING

Situated in the southern third of Sweden, the county of Jönköping slightly exceeds ten thousand square kilometres (Figure 1). This upland region, resting mainly on granite bedrock, is covered with moraine deposited by the last glaciation, which ended about 10,000 years ago. Because of its elevation the region was never covered by seawater during the different stages of the Holocene Baltic, which left a mixture of fine and coarse material untouched by the waves. Thus productive soils are found at any altitude in the landscape, and not as alluvial sediments. Despite a human presence since the Neolithic period, land use has never centred on arable cultivation. Historically, livestock production has been the main branch of the region's agriculture and the rearing of oxen for export to mining areas of the country was still an important part of the economy in the nineteenth century. Forested land (outland) and pastures used to dominate the landscape with, however, important hay meadows and some arable land surrounding the numerous villages. [20]

The county of Jönköping was representative of a forested region in southern Sweden during the nineteenth century. It was populated by farmers who relied on traditional mixed farming techniques, but with a large dependence on livestock compared to a plains region. In addition, it must also be understood that Sweden industrialised quite late in comparison to central European countries. The first effects of industrialism were not felt until 1870, which stamps Sweden as overwhelmingly rural during the studied period. So, all in all, even though our source material (see below) dictated the county to be studied, it could hardly have been a better choice; it was densely settled by farmers, with livestock in abundance, and it contained large tracts of wooded land for wolves to roam in.[21]

Today the county is still characterised by forested land. More than 2,300 lakes are scattered throughout its forests, together with several large rivers and the largest bog in south Sweden, Store Mosse. The highest peak is situated 377 metres above sea level and the vegetation growth period stretches over six to seven months. Forestry is now of significant economic importance and agriculture is small scale, although livestock production, in combination with the conservation of grassland biodiversity, has a relatively strong hold.

The county of Jönköping has no established wolf population today, but their return is probably just a matter of time. During 2011 a she-wolf was traced via GPS on her way from Norway to the county of Kronoberg (immediately south of the county of Jönköping) where she seems to have decided to stay – making several attacks on livestock.[22]

WOLF POPULATIONS AND HISTORICAL SOURCES

As stated above, sedentary farming and transhumance have clashed with the wolf wherever they have met through history. Thus, across much of their natural range in Europe and North America there has been a gradual extinction of wolves. This is the result of a combination of a loss of habitat (loss of suitable core areas and of hoofed game through the agency of humans) and of direct human persecution. In the latter case persecution has been aided by incentives — bounties — from early on, both in Europe and North America. Despite recorded organised persecution since the Middle Ages in Europe, wolf populations seem to have persisted surprisingly well until the advent of strychnine use from the middle of the nineteenth century. Up until then human hunting methods and perseverance had only managed to clear limited parts of Europe and North America of wolves. In Europe densely settled and farmed plains areas or confined geographical spaces, like the British Isles, were the first places where wolves were wholly eradicated – with bounty hunting playing only a supporting role in events.[23]

However, since bounties were often used to cut wolf numbers, there exist both published and unpublished records from the organisations that administered their disbursement, showing the amounts paid out and the number of animals destroyed per annum, and by geographical area (either district, county or national level). This is true for both Europe and North America. These records, which also contain information on other animal and bird species categorised as 'vermin', are usually of great interest for wildlife biology. They can often be interpreted and used as markers over time for dwindling numbers of those endangered species listed. A diminishing bag over time usually signified a population decrease. The moment when disbursement of bounties ends is usually regarded as the nominal extinction date for the species concerned in the geographical area under scrutiny, at least if this occurs before the mid-twentieth century and the advent of environmental protection. What wildlife biology rarely does is to use these kinds of records in order to calculate and present historical population numbers, at least not without access to additional modern material for comparative purposes. This is because numbers in these records are impacted upon by unknown variables, such as changes over time in the intensity of persecution by humans as well as natural changes in population dynamics, the latter being independent of human activities. For example, it is generally agreed among wildlife biologists that political unrest, wars and epidemic diseases could impede organised persecution of species regarded as vermin. Similarly, an increase in bounties paid out by parishes and governments for the destruction of vermin could significantly increase the level of persecution.[24]

In Sweden bounties were introduced in 1647, in addition to contemporary legislation (dating from the Middle Ages), prescribing mandatory drives to eliminate wolves. From 1827 up until 1965 there exist records on the total number of wolves killed per annum and county, bagged either through such mandatory

Wolves in Jönköping, Sweden

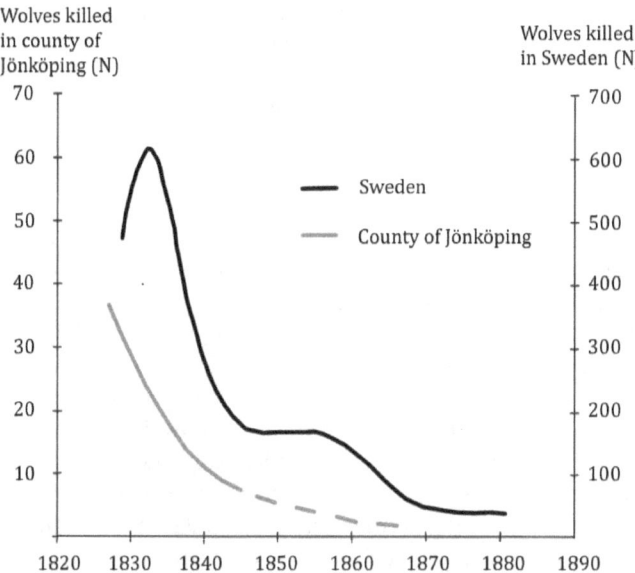

Figure 2. Wolf decline in Sweden and the county of Jönköping.
The graph shows two adjusted curves based on Lönnberg's material. The top curve gives the trend for all Swedish wolves destroyed through mandatory drives and bounty hunting. The bottom curve, as a comparison, gives the specific trend for the county of Jönköping (derived from figures presented in Table 1, below). Source: Lönnberg 1934.

drives or by individual hunting (for bounties). The time series 1827–1931 is presented and most thoroughly commented upon by the zoologist Einar Lönnberg (1934). Persson and Sand (1998) present a graph depicting the full time series (1827–1965) at the national level and provide further comments on developments after 1931 concerning the wolf's range as related to counties and geographical areas. These records are used by the authors to verify and show the decrease of the Swedish wolf population over time, but not in order to present historical densities of wolves.[25]

Figure 2 is based on Lönnberg's material and compares the national trend for wolves killed with the trend for wolves killed in the county of Jönköping. The decline in wolves killed illustrates the fall in their total numbers. The combined impression of both curves indicates that the Swedish wolf population was at its peak at the first quarter of the nineteenth century and then quite rapidly decreased in numbers thereafter. The diminishing trend for the county of Jönköping follows the national pattern, signifying a parallel decrease with no general discrepancies in either pace or time.

The decline in wolves killed illustrates the fall in total numbers of the wolf. The combined impression of both curves indicates that the Swedish wolf population was at its peak by the late 1820s and early 1830s, and then quite rapidly decreased in numbers thereafter. The trend for the county of Jönköping follows the national pattern.

However valuable Lönnberg's material may be, it needs to be complemented with data of a higher geographical resolution in order to paint a more detailed picture regarding the activities of early nineteenth-century wolves. Possibilities to do so have recently arisen through previously undetected source material located at the National Archives, *Riksarkivet*. This material is unique as far as we know. Similar data have not been detected in a randomised sample of contemporary accounts from other Swedish counties. The material consists of applications for the disbursement of bounties with attached testimonials from the parish where wolves and other carnivores were killed, and receipts for the bounties paid in Jönköping between the years 1822–1859 (Table 1), with the latter date being the final year any bounties were paid on wolves in the county. This new material gives information on species, age (adult or juvenile), the parish in which the carnivore was killed and usually the name and occupation of the claimant as well as the time of the year 'vermin' was destroyed; information that is lacking in Lönnberg's 1934 study, which just yields the number of wolves (without ages) killed per year and county.[26]

These two datasets can be compared, indicating trends in the number of wolves caught per annum, but they do not give a total number for the historical wolf population, nor do they provide a total number for wolf territories within the county of Jönköping. True, the new material furnishes data at a new level of resolution, the parish, but the drawback is, however, that wolves and other carnivores killed during mandatory drives (*skall*) were not eligible for bounties, which make them invisible in the Jönköping bounties material from the Riksarkivet.[27]

In the present study, to begin with we will concentrate on the years between 1823–1845, as this was the period when both adult and juvenile wolves were hunted for bounties. The last year that bounties were paid for wolf pups was 1845, probably signifying the end of regularly inhabited wolf territories in the county of Jönköping.

In the county of Jönköping during the years 1822–1845, the total number of wolves upon which bounties were disbursed was 144 (56 adults and 88 pups). This meant that nearly two-thirds (61 per cent) of the total consisted of juveniles. Some 80 per cent of the total number of pups shown in Table 1 derived from parish testimonials dated from May – October, with 53 per cent from testimonials dated May, June and July and 27 per cent September and October. Bounties paid on 33 per cent of the total number of destroyed pups included

Wolves in Jönköping, Sweden

Table 1. Wolves killed between the years 1822–1845, Jönköping.

Year	Adult No	Pups No	Pups per application	Total number from bounties	Total number from mandatory drives and bounties, 1827–1845 (Lönnberg's material)
1822	2	-	-	2	-
1823	1	6	6	7	-
1824	4	9	1+1+7	13	-
1825	3	10	6+4	13	-
1826	3	15	3+5+7	18	-
1827	9	-	-	9	40
1828	2	6	1+5	8	35
1829	3	2	2	5	18
1830	1	9	5+4	10	33
1831	6	1	1	7	27
1832	3	7	3+4	10	18
1833	6	2	1+1	8	40
1834	1	6	6	7	12
1835	2	2	1+1	4	18
1836	2	-	-	2	19
1837	2	-	-	2	7
1838	1	-	-	1	21
1839	2	6	1+5	8	36
1840	3	-	-	3	*
1841	-	-	-	-	*
1842	-	-	-	-	*
1843	-	3	1+2	3	*
1844	-	-	-	-	12
1845	-	5	5	5	17
Total	**56**	**88**	**88**	**144**	

The table shows the individual number of wolves which bounties were paid for in the county of Jönköping 1822–1845 (column 2–5). Totals are given for each year and likewise the number of adults and juveniles (pups). The column 'Pups per application' gives both the number of applications and pup numbers for individual applications. The combination 3+5+7 (1826) should be interpreted as 3 applications containing 3, 5 and 7 pups respectively. In the last column, Lönnberg's statistics for all wolves killed (mandatory drives and bounties) in the county of Jönköping 1827–1845 are listed. These figures have been used when constructing the adjusted curve for Jönköping in Figure 2 above. Please note that the symbol * denotes a missing report in Lönnberg's material, a fact which explains why a total is not given in this column. Sources: Verifikationer, Länsräkenskaper för Jönköpings län 1822–1845, Riksarkivet and Lönnberg 1934.

parish testimonials that expressly stated that the pups were caught in dens. Pups are clearly pointed out in the material, as their bounties were disbursed at a lower rate than for adult wolves.[28]

Concerning bounties and wolf pups, Lönnberg discussed the possibility of hunters substituting counterfeits, that is, presenting the authorities with the ears or pelts of animals other than the target species. There are some comparatively modern rumours that pelts from arctic fox pups (*Alopex lagopus*) have been passed off as those of wolf pups from the northern part of Sweden. Since the arctic fox pups have similar colouring to wolves, and are lacking the silvery tip tail carried by the red fox (*Vulpes vulpes*), this might be conceivable. But for the present investigation it is not a concern, as the county of Jönköping is far beyond the reach of the present or historical range of the arctic fox.[29]

There is however another possible 'counterfeit' species to ponder– the dog. As long as the dog pups had the right colouring and erect ears it might have been possible to collect bounties on them. However, the opportunity for counterfeiting was probably checked by the arduous administrative procedure used for obtaining bounties in the county of Jönköping at the time. Money for bounties was collected as a tax, calculated at the ratable value (*mantal*) of an individual farmer's property, by the county authorities. This meant that a would-be fraudster would not only have deceived the authorities but also his immediate neighbours, who had to be present at the parish council (*sockenstämma*) when the initial claims for bounties were made, resulting in the production of parish testimonials. It is likely that any such cases were few in number.[30]

The next step was to bring the parish testimonial to the Hundred-court (*häradsrätten*) in order to procure an additional testimonial during one of the three annual sessions the court held. These testimonials, together with a written application, had then to be sent to the county governor's office (*landshövding*). The application was passed by the county administration to the forest administration (*jägeristaten*), which in turn had to scrutinise the documentation for both adherence to formal procedures and information given on the success of the hunts. The logic for this process derived in part from the fact that the forest administration had, among its other duties, the responsibility for organising mandatory drives to eradicate large carnivores. If nothing was found to be amiss, the bounties were then paid out.

In this investigation the combined source material on wolves is interpreted as follows: the two adjusted curves for numbers of wolves killed, based on Lönnberg's material, show the same downward trend when compared. More important is that the Jönköping curve shows the same peak in wolf numbers at the start as the national curve, implying a situation where most territories are inhabited, at least during the 1820s and early 1830s. The almost unbroken chain of one or more dens harvested for pups each year, shown in the Jönköping bounties material during the period of 1823–1835, strengthens this interpretation of the data. Bounties paid for wolf pups signified a territory with at least one breeding pair which had raised a litter in a den situated in the parish during the same year and season that the parish testimonial was produced and signed.

THE PRESENCE OF WILD GAME AND LIVESTOCK

If the wolf population was at its peak in the early nineteenth century, all historical data on moose, roe deer and red deer show that by 1820 they were no longer present in the county of Jönköping. This was largely due to the introduction of unrestricted hunting after 1789, when a law allowed peasant proprietors (freeholders) – and not only the Crown and gentry as before – to take hoofed game. Modern investigations on the interplay between livestock and hoofed game in a given grazing area show competition and competitive displacement as active factors in the decline of the latter, but it is hard to estimate their relative impact versus hunting. But, whatever the reason for the absence of wild game, we can safely assume that the only large prey present in early nineteenth century Jönköping was domestic livestock.[31]

Historical livestock-numbers have not previously been used in this kind of investigation due to the shortcomings of nineteenth century Swedish agricultural statistics, but it is now possible to do so by using the methodology developed by Dahlström. She has thoroughly studied changes in livestock numbers for the parish of Alseda in Jönköping. Based on her methodology, our calculations show that in 1850 there were about 900–1,300 horses, 23,000–25,000 oxen, 55,000–58,000 cows, 33,000–36,000 young cattle, 88,000–100,000 sheep and 3,400–7,000 goats in the county of Jönköping. To estimate the livestock numbers during our study period we use the trends calculated in Alseda parish, situated in the studied county. Between 1800 and 1850, livestock numbers only changed slightly. Around 1800 the numbers of horses, cattle and sheep were lower (15, 12 and 25 per cent respectively) compared to 1850, while there were twice as many goats in 1800 as in 1850. A similar development can be assumed for the entire county, thus reducing the number of livestock slightly during the studied period compared to our calculation for 1850.[32]

If the livestock is transformed into potential carnivore feed, as kilograms of meat (live weight), then the evolution of livestock sizes must also be taken into account. Historical information about livestock sizes is very scarce and must be seen in a longer time perspective. The changes between 1500 and the mid-nineteenth century were very small. The size evolution of cows can be used as an example. In the sixteenth century, on average a Swedish cow weighed somewhere between 100 and 130 kilograms; by the mid-seventeenth century it was around 120 to 165 kilograms; in 1800 the average was circa 150 kilograms; and at the end of the nineteenth century there is a dramatic increase to circa 320 kilograms. Swedish research is unanimous that livestock breeding and significant increases in sizes only started after 1870. This was the first occasion when fodder resources and agricultural conditions were good enough to achieve successful breeding results. Therefore, it is a safe assumption that on average cows weighed around 150 kilograms throughout the first half of the nineteenth century in the county of Jönköping. The same context is also valid for other types of livestock. During the period under discussion a horse weighed on average around 250 kilograms; oxen about 200 kilograms; and sheep and goats an average of 35 kilograms. From this we can calculate that in 1800 the county of Jönköping kept livestock that taken together weighed about 22,000 tons and in 1850 somewhere around 24,500 tons.[33]

LIVESTOCK AS WOLF FEED? THE IMPLICATIONS OF GRAZING AND HERDING

Livestock were kept indoors all winter fed with hay, straw and leaves. During the summer period they were let out to graze. The start of the grazing season could differ between regions and it took place from the emergence of the first green grass through the beginning of June. Sheep, goats and young cattle were generally let out before herds of cows. In village bylaws, from the nineteenth century and earlier, the official date given for the start of the grazing season is the first of May.[34]

The grazing season was considered to come to an end at the beginning of November, but in years with late snowfall livestock could be kept outdoors until Christmas. Therefore, livestock were present in the landscape from early May until the end of October, and sometimes for longer periods. Furthermore, all types of land – arable, hay meadows and outland – were utilised for grazing livestock during the full, or just a part of, the grazing season.[35]

For our purposes, livestock is mainly seen as potential wolf feed and therefore its availability as carnivore prey must be discussed. As long as humans have kept livestock, one must assume that they have tried to protect them from competing carnivores – mainly by means of herding. Herding, in a Swedish historical context, has some traits that are peculiar when compared to the general picture in Western Europe, north of the Alps and west of the river Elbe. Apart from the southernmost tip of Sweden, herding was not generally carried out by an adult male herder. Rather, herding was a job for women or children, from at least the sixteenth century. Herding was the responsibility of individual farmers, and not organised collectively in villages and hamlets.[36]

Roughly above the 60th parallel (Figure 1), Sweden had summer farms (*fäbod*) where herding on outland pastures was differently organised (transhumance), but it was still a task considered suitable for both women and children. In the case of women they often doubled as milkmaids and herders. South of the 60th parallel, large parts of the pastures on the outland were enclosed (*hage*) by fences, and increasingly so during the eighteenth and nineteenth centuries.

Arable land was always enclosed by a mandatory fence, from medieval times right up until 1857; likewise most hay meadows south of the 60th parallel. Prior to 1857, the Fencing Act prescribed that fences be constructed around all arable land. The new Act of 1857, however, ensured that fences were constructed along property boundaries instead.[37]

Therefore, it is clear that livestock were more or less closely watched by people at all times, whether grazing took place on outland pastures or on arable land after haymaking and harvest. Likewise, herders were present whether the pastureland in question was enclosed or not. Herding was good general practice for farmers and it had multiple purposes. Livestock were to be protected from carnivores and thieves, growing crops had to be protected from livestock and the herd had to be directed to the right grazing grounds in order to maximise the feeding potential of what was a limited resource.[38]

Despite the different measures employed to protect livestock, animals were occasionally taken by carnivores and this was noted by contemporaries both in written records and in the form of statistics. From 1827, for example, Israel Adolf af Ström logged figures on the number of livestock killed by carnivores for the whole country. At the time, and in our bounties material, lynx (*Lynx lynx*) and red fox are present as well as the wolf. There were, however, no traces found of brown bear, which is substantiated by the historical records discussed in Lönnberg (1929). He did not mention a precise final date for bears being shot in the county of Jönköping, but Lönnberg gave the year 1830 as the final year when bears were killed in the two neighboring counties of Östergötland and Kronoberg, north and south respectively of Jönköping. In the county of Jönköping, in 1827 af Ström claimed that 9 horses, 315 cattle, 2,151 sheep and goats and 47 pigs were taken, which represented some 0.1 per cent of all horses, 0.3 per cent of all cattle and swine and 2.5 per cent of all sheep and goats. In terms of overall weight of meat, this represented around 125 tons. In the 1850s, livestock losses due to predation could still be a problem, as was noted in the five-year reports from the county governor to the state.[39]

A present day comparison is possible from Norway, based on statistics regarding compensation paid for sheep killed by predators. During the 2010 grazing season, 1.7 per cent of the sheep feeding on outland pasture were killed by carnivores. The corresponding figure for sheep killed by wolves is only 0.09 per cent, or 1,800 sheep. Moreover, Norwegian sheep today are not herded and closely protected in comparison with historical livestock, making them more vulnerable to attacks by predators. This comparatively low figure is, however, understandable, since most of the sheep-grazed areas do not have a stable wolf population (Figure 1) and are only exposed to dispersing individuals.[40]

HISTORICAL (AND FUTURE) WOLF TERRITORIES

If we now try to summarise the description of the county of Jönköping by the early nineteenth century, with regard to the historical context in combination with wolf biology, the following picture can be discerned. As wolf territory it was lacking in large prey during six months of the year, from November to April. The stabling of livestock also coincided with the time of the year when food requirements peaked in the territory, since wolf pups consumed as much as adults when six months old. Livestock constituted the only large-sized prey available during the summer months, but their acquisition as potential wolf feed was again rendered difficult due to Swedish herding practices.

One hypothesis to be drawn from the historical context is that the early nineteenth century wolf territory was probably larger in size when compared to a current territory. At present, there is no wolf population in the county of Jönköping to draw a comparison with, which means other ways of testing the hypothesis must be found. We can come to some tentative conclusions by drawing on the historical records in combination with present day research on wolf biology.

What we do know is the dates and spatial distribution of dens in parishes where pups had been destroyed. We also know that there is a general relationship between food supply, the size of a pack and the size of territory, and a strong link between territory size and latitude: the higher the latitude, the larger the territory (see above). The present Scandinavian (Sweden and Norway) wolf population lives in territories with a mean average size of 900–1,200 square kilometres. These are all situated at a higher latitude than the county of Jönköping, but in areas not yet fully saturated with wolves, which means that there is room for additional wolf territories within the area of general distribution.[41]

This information can be compared to the distribution of dens where wolf pups were caught in the county of Jönköping between the years 1823–1845, (Figure 3). The historical record contains two years, 1824 and 1826, where three dens were harvested respectively, interpreted as being located within three simultaneously active territories. The map, however, may not show all possible dens used during this period. But we suggest that the spatial distribution and clustering of the dens on the map is indicative of a historical wolf territory with a radius of 20 kilometres. This represents a territory of 1,600 square kilometres; a size that could easily be covered by a fleet-footed wolf within the course of a day. Such an exercise is at least a pointer towards the historical circumstances, but of course cannot be verified with any certainty.

There are, however, further means of comparison at hand. The spatial distribution of dens can be compared with the map (Figure 4) showing areas most favoured by wolves when colonising the southern parts of Sweden, presented by Karlsson *et al*. The map builds on distinctive topographical traits in the current Swedish wolf territories compared to as yet uncolonised areas. The proportion of open land within the current territory was the single best variable limiting the

Wolves in Jönköping, Sweden

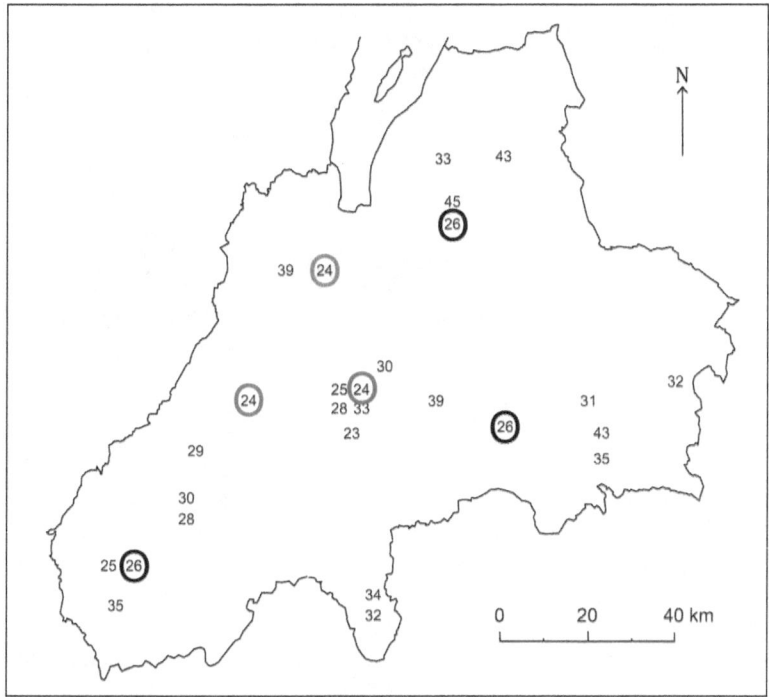

Figure 3. Wolf dens 1823–1845.
The map shows parishes where wolf pups had been caught in dens in the county of Jönköping 1823–1845. The figures on the map denotes the year, 18XX.
Source: Verifikationer. Länsräkenskaper för Jönköpings län 1823–1845, Riksarkivet.

occurrence of wolf territories, followed by local road density, total road density and built-up areas. In other words, the more open, arable land and the higher density of roads, the less likelihood there is of wolves colonising an area.[42]

Concerning the county of Jönköping, it is interesting to note that the northeastern part of the historical map (Figure 4) shows an area devoid of dens. The same area is shown by Karlsson *et al.* as being the least attractive to a future wolf population. The area contains a rather large proportion of open land, as well as some larger lakes. It is likely that the concentration of several large lakes in the region might to some extent explain why there are no reports of wolves being killed here in the past, and why it is deemed by Karlsson *et al.* as being less preferable for establishing wolf territories today. In North American studies, lakeshores have been found to be effective territorial borders, even though the lakes are covered with ice during the winter. In the present historical case it is fairly safe to assume that the series of lakes in the area acted as a deterrent to

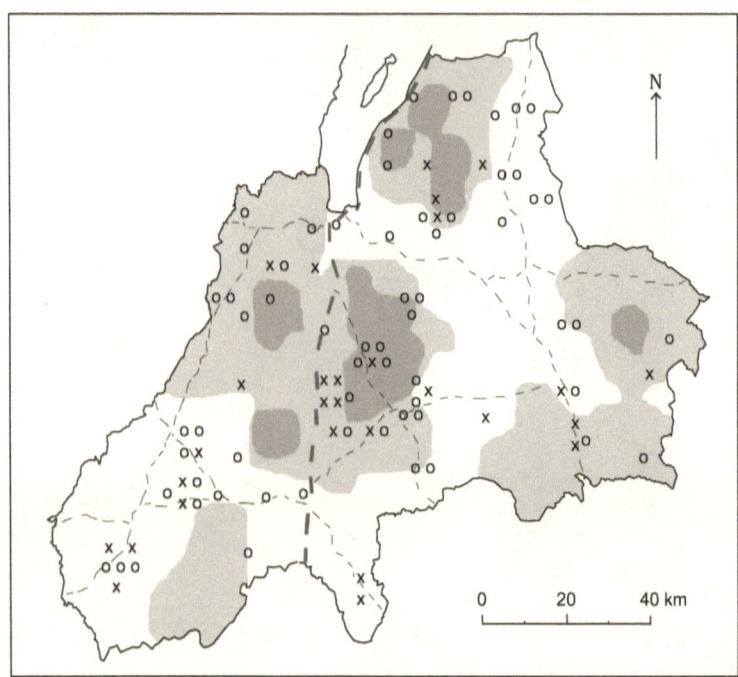

Figure 4. Historical and predicted wolf distribution.
The map contains a combination of historical and predicted future distribution of wolves in the county of Jönköping. Letters show locations where pups (x) and adult wolves (o) were caught on single occasions between 1822 and 1859. Future predicted establishment is in grey (probable establishment) and dark grey (higher probability of establishment), after a map published by Karlsson et al. European Highway No 4 crosses in a north–south direction (heavy broken line) and the county is crossed by several country roads (light broken lines). Sources: Verifikationer. Länsräkenskaper för Jönköpings län 1822–1859, Riksarkivet and Karlsson et al. 2007.

colonisation by wolves, thus strengthening the effect that open land had – and has – on wolf habitat preferences.[43]

It should also be noted that the south-western corner of the county of Jönköping is also deemed to be less favoured by Karlsson et al. – an area which in our map is covered with dens (shown with an x in Figure 4). This discrepancy between historical and predicted distribution patterns invites several interpretations. Firstly, it could indicate historical conditions that attracted (or forced) wolves to colonise an area that today is unfavourable for wolf dens. Another interpretation could be that the prediction-model of Karlsson et al. exaggerates the hostility of the present landscape in this case – for example, due to an overestimation of its openness. The wolves caught in the nineteenth century were all found in a region with both forests and wetland (among these the large bog Store Mosse) that Karlsson *et al.* might have classified as being too small to hold wolf territories today. The presence of historical dens in this area, during a time when its forests were not as dense, indicates that it may actually be appropriate for the future establishment of wolf territories.[44]

A third difference between wolf activity in the past and predictions for the future can also be noted. The far north-eastern corner of the map has a high concentration of open land and has been viewed as an unlikely area for future wolf colonisation. However, wolves were caught in this area between 1822–59, although they were exclusively adults (denoted as o in Figure 4). No dens (x) were detected here in the source material. One straightforward interpretation is that wolves, in this otherwise uninhabited part of the county, were dispersed adults, detected and killed while making long journeys. Another possible interpretation, perhaps more complex but still of historical interest, is as follows: between 1822–1859 some 74 adult wolves were destroyed and bounties disbursed in Jönköping. Following scrutiny of the parish testimonials regarding the time of each kill a pattern could be discerned: 52 adult wolves were killed during winter (November–March), four were destroyed during other seasons, while the dates of 18 kills were not recorded (see note 28). Expressed as a percentage, this means that 70 per cent of all adult wolves killed met their end in winter, when prey was difficult to locate. Information gleaned from the parish testimonials suggests that a fair proportion of the destroyed adult wolves were shot during the nighttime, close to human settlements, often after being lured with bait (carrion) placed outside a cowshed or barn. This fits nicely with the picture that the Swedish ethnological material has left us. Two thirds of all wolf encounters or sightings reported in this material occur during winter, when wolves roamed their food-scarce territories in search of large prey.[45]

Our notion is therefore that wolves were drawn towards human habitations, which during the winter emitted promising smells from both livestock and waste; very much in the same manner that some modern European wolves now feed on human refuse during nighttime in built-up areas. The dunghill, in all probability, was the final destination for kitchen wastes that could not be digested by pigs, like larger sized bones. (Bones were vital in the wolf's diet as the major source of calcium and phosphorus and were readily consumed; in fact, all parts of a prey carcass were consumed, except for the plants in the digestive system of herbivore prey). Snow conditions, in the Swedish historical case, left revealing tracks and made it possible for human would-be hunters to prepare for their next visit. Therefore at least some of the adult wolves shown in Figure 4 were likely to have been food-scavenging wolves, making nighttime visits to human settlements from the core areas of their territories during the winter. It is, however, impossible to tell if the wolves killed came from more favoured areas of the county of Jönköping or were visitors from the neighbouring county of Östergötland.[46]

Örjan Kardell and Anna Dahlström

WHAT DID WOLVES EAT IN JÖNKÖPING DURING THE NINETEENTH CENTURY?

A more intriguing comparison between current and historic conditions concerns the complex issues of what wolves ate, the availability of large prey and the carrying capacity of the outland (forested land).

Table 2. Total number of grazing animals in the county of Jönköping in 1800 and 2009.

	Animal species	Number of animals	Weight (tons)
Around 1800	Horses	8 000	2 000
	Cattle	100 000	17 000
	Sheep and goats	87 000	3 000
	Swine*	15 000	2 250
	Total 1800	**210 000**	**24 250**
Year 2009	Moose	13 000	5 070
	Roe deer	64 000	1 600
	Wild boar	7 800	1 326
	Total 2009	**85 000**	**8 000**

*In the absence of historical data on historical swine, we used the average weight of a sow (150 kilograms) from the only old swine species present in Sweden today – the Linderöd-pig. Source: www.nordensark.se

As shown above, the early nineteenth century county of Jönköping held no large prey potentially available to wolves except for livestock – and then only for part of the year. The modern-day county (2009) holds a summer population – before hunting in the autumn – of 13,000 moose, 64,000 roe deer and 7,800 wild boar (Table 2). An immediate and obvious reflection is that the number of livestock (210,000) in the early nineteenth century by far exceeded the current number of hoofed game (85,000). Expressed as possible wolf feed, livestock numbers were equal to 24,250 tons in weight as compared to just 8,000 tons for hoofed game today. However, we should bear in mind that livestock were generally well protected in the past and the number of livestock reported as killed by carnivores in 1827 only represented 125 tons of meat in terms of their combined weight.[47]

A comparison concerning wolf feed between the current context and the historical one encounters several obstacles, since there are many variables that cannot be accurately determined. To begin with, we assume that all sheep and goats killed by carnivores in 1827 were eaten by wolves. Expressed in terms of weight (75 tons), and transformed into the average requirements for an adult wolf

Wolves in Jönköping, Sweden

(two kilograms of meat per day), these sheep and goats could have sustained 103 wolves per annum in the early nineteenth century. If we include the figures for cattle and pigs in our calculations (125 tons), then there was enough meat to support around 170 wolves. But, on the one hand, we must keep in mind that there were other large carnivores that preyed upon sheep, goats and cattle, which reduces the possible number of wolves. On the other, livestock must have been complemented with other wolf feed, especially during the winter months, which acts in the other direction and increases the prospects of a bigger possible wolf population in Jönköping.

For the present situation, we know that the possible large prey in 2009 (moose, roe deer and wild boar) together weighed approximately only one third of what the livestock in the early nineteenth century did. But, as we have shown, at this time livestock were closely watched and efficiently protected by farmers and herders against carnivores. Wild game today is not protected in the same ways and we can therefore assume that a larger proportion of the population would end up as wolf feed if the county was recolonised by *Canis lupus*. Given the complex relationship between wild game, wolves and human hunters (of both wolves and their prey), though, we cannot foresee a substantial proportion ending up as wolf feed. But we can calculate how a large population of wolves could be sustained, were they to be the beneficiaries of the present human bag of game. Through hunting, some 9,600 roe deer and 3,900 moose are killed annually in the county of Jönköping, which is equal to 918 tons of meat, or enough to feed as many as 1,258 wolves. To this could be added a proportion of wild boar; however we currently lack reliable information on wolf predation on wild boar in Sweden. These estimated numbers are undoubtedly on the generous side and could easily be contested, but they nevertheless point to a suggested link between past and present wolf feed supply – that is, the past and present carrying capacity of forested land.[48]

An obvious question that arises from the discussion above, and the fact that larger prey was basically absent during winter in early nineteenth century Jönköping, is what did wolves actually feed on between the months of October and May? We know today that wolves can survive on smaller prey. In the study area, the most important prey in the nineteenth century was likely to have been the hare (*Lepus timidus*) and perhaps also the black grouse (*Tetrao tetrix*). The former litters from two to three times per season with an average yield of one to seven young and it is known that the snowshoe hare (*Lepus americanus*) plays an important seasonal role in the diets of wolves in parts of North America. Polish–Russian investigations point at the brown hare (*Lepus europæus*) as a significant prey species for European wolves. During the nineteenth century, the black grouse was in all probability more numerous than it is today, attracted by the well-grazed and comparatively open forests that existed at the time, with heather (*Calluna vulgaris*) dominating the forest floors of southern Sweden. The black grouse has a habit of spending the night on the ground, in winter buried in the snow, which recommends it as a possible prey species. An additional and perhaps surprising prey species is the badger (*Meles meles*). It turned out to be the third most important prey species for large carnivores in a study carried out in the county of Värmland, Sweden. The badger, however, spends winter underground in long stretches of hibernation-like sleep, which makes its availability seasonal. However, wolf–prey interaction in history is an open field for new research and the issues arising cannot be covered comprehensively in this paper.[49]

CONCLUSIONS

By drawing on new data, this study provides an important historical context for present discussions on wolf management in Sweden. These data are used to create a unique picture of the distribution of historical wolf dens in a regional setting, the county of Jönköping. The study also offers an insight into the natural preconditions for future wolf establishment. Furthermore, the spatial distribution of dens, and the scarcity of large prey as wolf feed, both independently support our notion that historic wolf territories in early nineteenth century agrarian Sweden were likely to have been larger in size than their equivalents today; resulting in a past wolf population which was rather sparse when compared to territorial densities reached in present populations.

We have also gained several insights into wolf–human interactions. Seasonal encounters are important in this respect: the killing of wolf pups in their dens during the summer months; and the attraction of adult wolves to human settlements during late winter. The main and most obvious conclusion to be drawn from the recreation of the historical context, however, is just how effective herding practices seem to have been as a livestock protection method. The percentages given for different kinds of livestock lost to carnivores in 1827 are almost negligible when compared to total numbers of livestock – a conclusion that might be the most useful one for those concerned with modern wolf management to ponder over. An interesting question, combining social and environmental history, deriving from this is how the presence of wolves and other carnivores affected day-to-day human livestock-keeping practices and the use of pastures.[50]

Finally, our investigation of the historical context has only touched lightly upon the important question of what was the mainstay of wolves' diets during the early nineteenth century in Jönköping, especially during winter-time when all livestock were stabled. If neither wild nor domestic ungulates were available, the choice of prey for wolves is not so easy to identify. In the case of the past wolf population in Sweden, the most likely prey species that comes to mind is the hare. As historians, we sincerely hope that this study will inspire new research on wolf biology that delves into this complex but still open question.

ACKNOWLEDGEMENTS

We wish to express our sincere gratitude to a number of people and organisations. First of all, a vital grant from Sven och Dagmar Saléns Stiftelse made the initial research work in the National Archive possible. Dr. Jonas Kindberg, at the Svenska Jägareförbundet, helped with wildlife statistics and guidelines for calculations. Different stages of the manuscript were read and commented upon by professor Kjell Danell, SLU (Swedish University of Agricultural Sciences), Roger Bergström, senior researcher at Skogforsk, and Per Espen Fjeld, senior adviser at Statens Naturoppsyn (Norwegian Directorate for Nature Management). We also warmly thank three anonymous reviewers for their constructive comments on the manuscript.

NOTES

[1] The recolonisation of wolves in Sweden was not a planned process. It came about spontaneously, in the same way that wolves entered France from Italy (1992) and Germany from Poland (2000), and even earlier in the United States where wolves from Canada arrived into Montana (1979). This inspired projected re-introductions of wolves in Wyoming and Idaho (1995): see Ekman 2010, 224–235. See also McNamee 1998; and Boitani 2003, 317–340. For details on Swedish wolf management, see the homepage of Naturvårdsverket, the Swedish Environmental Protection Agency, www.naturvardsverket.se, which carries information in English. For the overall picture of Swedish wildlife management, see: Danell and Bergström 2010; Bergström and Danell 2011; Ekman 2010, 66–69, 142–145; and Sand et al. 2010, 16–20.

[2] Sand et al. 2010, 30–36; and Ekman 2010, 288–291.

[3] Karlsson et al. 2007; and Ericsson et al. 2010. All counties situated in the northern two-thirds of Sweden were polled and compared against the county of Stockholm (Fig. 1). Subsamples were made in each municipality of the individual counties. All in all 15,317 persons were polled. The fear of wolves was higher in counties which currently have a wolf population. Hunting was considered acceptable firstly, if large carnivores enter densely populated areas and secondly, in order to minimise the risk to domesticated animals and thirdly, to some extent, because people are scared. Around a third of the polled group thought that it was acceptable to hunt large carnivores in order to reduce competition for game.

[4] Eles 1986. The above stated does not apply to the semi-tamed wolf which, purposely released from captivity, turned into a man-eater. The animal – the Gysinge wolf – killed nine children and one adult in Sweden between 1820–1821: see Pousette 1986. Several Finnish nineteenth century confirmed cases of man-eating wolves exist, see: Godenhjelm 1891; and Teperi 1977. The backgrounds of these animals are not as fully known as that of the Gysinge wolf, but it is evident that the cases concern wolves turned specialist hunters. However, one of the perpetrators was a she-wolf, nearly toothless with old age, which turns the train of thought towards the most likely causes: old age or a poorly healed injury impeding the animal from pursuing its natural prey.

[5] Strand 1986; and Kardell 2008. For an international overview, see Lopez 1978 (North America) and Fritts et al. 2003, 289–294.

[6] Eles 2008; and Lönnberg 1934.

[7] Lönnberg 1934, 19–25; Persson and Sand 1998, 11–13. On the North American develop-

ment of the wolf as an icon, compare Jones 2011 with the specific concept of wilderness as described in Nash 1982 and discussed further in Cronon 1996. See Anshelm 2004 on the Swedish environmental movement.

[8] Persson and Sand 1998, 11; Anshelm 2004, 11–25. The Swedish Carnivore Society (Svenska Rovdjursföreningen) www.rovdjur.se. The largest and oldest (1830) hunter's organisation in Sweden, the Svenska Jägareförbundet (the Swedish Association for Hunting and Wildlife Management), has currently about 180–90,000 members. The association is partly state funded since it is still responsible for Game Statistics and for certain research funds, www.jagareforbundet.se. The Jägarnas Riksförbund (the National Federation of Hunters) has about 30,000 members and was founded in 1940. The federation is strictly opposed to free ranging wolves in the country, www.jagarnasriksforbund.se.

[9] Khazanov 1994,85–118; presentation by Dr. Karin Dirke (Stockholm University, Sweden) at the 6th ESEH Conference in Turku, Finland, 2011; Fredman and Kardell 2007, 221; and Lopez 1978. See also Kaiser-Guyot 1974; Brunefaud 1984; Lucas 1989; Lalanne 2000; Pluskowski 2006 and Walker 2004.

[10] In 1805 10% of the Swedish population lived in urban conditions. In 1850 the percentage was unaltered whereas in 1900 21% lived in cities. Atlas över Sverige, map-page 53–54, which is bilingual in Swedish and English.

[11] Sand et al. 2010; and Mech and Boitani 2003.

[12] Fuller, Mech and Cochrane 2003, 170, 172–175 and Mech and Boitani 2003, 19–20, 22, 30. For a full and comprehensive discussion on statistical methods and dependencies, see Fuller, Mech and Cochrane 2003, 161–191.

[13] Packard 2003, 45; and Mech and Boitani 2003, 31. There is statistical evidence for wolves denning in the central 60% of their territories, that the larger the territory, the closer to the centre the wolves denned.

[14] Sand et al. 2010, 8; Mech and Boitani 2003, 7, 9–10; Fuller, Mech and Cochrane 2003, 175; and Packard 2003, 46.

[15] Mech and Boitani 2003, 31; and Packard 2003, 46.

[16] Mech and Boitani 2003, 21, 28; and Fuller, Mech and Cochrane 2003, 163.

[17] Mech and Boitani 2003, 2, 5–6 and 12–17. Fuller, Mech and Cochrane 2003, 181; Persson and Sand 1998, 48–50; and www.rovviltportalen.no

[18] Peterson and Ciucci 2003, 104–111; Sand et al. 2010, 30–32; and Ekman 2010, 58, 285. Some 80% of the moose taken during a year as wolf prey were calves (64%) and yearlings (16%). During the summer months of June–September, moose calves dominate (90%) as vulnerable prey. The remaining 10% were yearlings. Older age classes (2–11 years and above) are mainly taken during the winter when cows, older than 11 years and above, dominated (11%). The remaining 9% were distributed evenly in age classes 2–10 years. It must be borne in mind that these figures derive from moose populations also harvested by humans.

[19] Ekman 2010, 60.

[20] In the early nineteenth century everything that was not arable and hay meadows counted as outland (*utmark*). Outland did not necessarily have to be covered with trees to be recognised as outland. Open pasture was also part of the *utmark*. Today, nineteenth century outland corresponds to forested land. See Myrdal 1999, 255–258, for details on animal husbandry, especially oxen.

[21] Myrdal and Morell 2011.

[22] From August to mid-October 2011 she killed twenty sheep during her attacks on eight different flocks. On the 14 October the Swedish Environmental Protection Agency

decided to allow her to be hunted. www.naturvardsverket.se

[23] Boitani 2003, 318–321 and Fuller, Mech and Cochrane 2003, 162–163.

[24] See for instance Figure 6.1. (including the adjoining text) in Fuller, Mech and Cochrane 2003, 162; for a comparison of how bounty records have been used see Swenson et al. 1995 and Elgmork 2000.

[25] Lönnberg 1934 and Persson and Sand 1998, 11–12

[26] Verifikationer, Länsräkenskaper för Jönköpings län 1822–1860, Riksarkivet.

[27] Lönnberg used his statistics to map the time of the extinction of the wolf in individual counties. A decline in the numbers of destroyed wolves was thought to reflect the situation in the total population. This approach has also been used in more recent Scandinavian works on bears and wolves which are based on bounties materials: see Swenson et al. 1995; and Elgmork 2000.

[28] The parish testimonials, covering the remaining number of pups, cannot be scrutinised for a specific date, since they all cover a mixed bag of carnivores caught during more than one hunting trip, usually during the passing of a whole season.

[29] Lönnberg 1934, 12–13.

[30] Lönnberg 1934, 12–13.

[31] Cederlund and Liberg 1995, 21–22 (on roe deer); Björklöf 1994, 91–96 (on moose); and Ahlén 1965 (on red deer). See also: Stewart et al. 2002; and Jenks and Leslie 2003.

[32] Dahlström 2006. Her methodology is described in an English summary, 246–247, and she uses scattered information on livestock from individual farmers to extrapolate livestock numbers for larger administrative units. Two complementary sources have been used here, parish maps and five year reports. Parish maps including animal statistics were produced for 13 parishes in the county of Jönköping around 1850. These made up around 11% of the total area in the county (based on agricultural statistics from the 1910s; *Statistiska centralbyrån*). The total number of livestock has been calculated from the assumption that these parishes also kept 11% of their livestock. The complementary source is five-year reports on agricultural statistics, delivered by the county governor to the state. The figures from the five-year reports support the calculation from parish maps.

[33] Calculations made in Dahlström 2006 from information about cattle: see also, Myrdal 1999, 252–258; Gadd 1983, 138; Gadd 2000, 166–168. About sheep: Myrdal 1999, 258; www.gutefar.se 2004, 54; Hannerberg 1971, 107. On goats: Hallander 1989, 346–367; and horses, Hallander 1989, 55–56 and 64; Gadd 2000, 166.

[34] Cserhalmi 2004, 142–146; Israelsson 2005, 189–202; Dahlström et al. 2008, Table 2; and Ehn 1991. This is also supported in the discussion on the timetable for annual enclosure maintenance in Kardell 2004, 161–165.

[35] Israelsson 2005, 189–202; Dahlström et al. 2008, Table 2.

[36] Myrdal 1999, 132.

[37] Kardell 2004; Kardell 2006; Larsson 2009; and Larsson 2011.

[38] Kardell 2006.

[39] Ström, af 1832, 22; Länsräkenskaper för Jönköpings län 1822–1860; and Lönnberg 1929, 3. Kronofogden i Östra härads fögderi. E.V.c. vol: 50. Information on carnivore-killed livestock, in this material, is too sparse to be used for estimating total numbers at a county level. From the early 1820s, the county governors had to deliver a five-year progress report to the government on behalf of their county. Details and statistics were passed to the county governor through his local administrations in the Hundreds.

[40] Compensation was paid for 32,882 sheep. This includes both sheep that were verified as killed by carnivores by examination, plus those that were lost and supposedly killed

by carnivores but without any verification. The difference is calculated from the total number of missing sheep reduced by the estimated loss due to other reasons (accidents, diseases, and the like). The total number of outland grazing sheep was 1,985,000 in the year of 2009. This includes both sheep verified as killed by wolves by examination, plus those that were lost and supposedly killed by wolves, but without verified cause of death. To this have also been added 300 sheep, which is 4.56% of the sheep killed by carnivores, but without the possibility of establishing by which type of animal. The figure is based on the proportion of cases when wolves are the known cause of the killings. Sources: www.rovviltportalen.no and oral information from Per Espen Fjeld.

[41] Sand *et al.* 2010, 24 and 73. The size of territories differs slightly depending on the method used for calculation.

[42] Karlsson *et al.* 2007. This map is also reproduced in Sand *et al.* 2010.

[43] Mech and Boitani 2003, 22–23.

[44] Compare the discussion on topographical traits for wolf territory borders in Karlsson *et al.* 2007 with Mech and Boitani 2003. The openness of forest/outland has been studied in Dahlström 2006, 217.

[45] See above for dispersal ranges in present day conditions. If the 18 wolves with no discernible date of death are excluded, then the figure reaches 93%. Similar percentages are found in Norwegian bounties material on wolves: see, Elgmork 2000, 5–6. Fredman and Kardell 2007, 221.

[46] Linda Qvistrom, (Archeologist at Upplandsmuseet, Uppsala, Sweden), related that bones found in historic archeological rural sites usually carried animal gnaw marks, suggesting outdoor final deposition. Personal communication, 10 February 2012. See also: Peterson and Ciucci 2003, 104–109,122–125.

[47] The figures for hoofed game populations are based on the harvested numbers of each species through hunting during 2009. All hunting is undertaken during the fall. Jonas Kindberg at the Svenska Jägareförbundet (the Swedish Association for Hunting and Wildlife Management) has kindly supplied us with the relevant figures and models for calculation.

[48] The current distributions of wolves and wild boar in Sweden do not coincide geographically, as yet. For wolf and wild boar interaction outside Sweden, see: Jedrzejewska and Jedrezewski 1998, 199–208; and Peterson and Ciucci 2003, 107–108.

[49] Peterson and Cuicci 2003, 108–111; Table 4.8 in Jedrezejewska and Jedrezewski 1998, 199–200; Dahlström 2006, 17; Jägarskolan 1983, 52 (hare), 62 (badger) and 72 (black grouse); and Persson and Sand 1998, 67 (badger).

[50] Compare with Mosley 2006.

BIBLIOGRAPHY

Archival and primary sources

Kronofogden i Östra härads fögderi. E.V.c. vol: 50, Landsarkivet in Vadstena. Riksarkivet. The National Archive.

Lönnberg, Einar 1929. *Björnen i Sverige*. Almqvist & Wiksells Boktryckeri AB: Stockholm and Uppsala.

Lönnberg, Einar 1934. *Bidrag till vargens historia i Sverige*. 'K. Svenska

Wolves in Jönköping, Sweden

Vetenskapsakademiens skrifter i Naturskyddsärenden. N:r 26': Stockholm.
Parish maps from the parishes of: Alseda, Dannäs, Forsheda, Hjelmseryd, Kulltorp, Kållerstad, Kävsjö, Ramkvilla, Rogberga, Skirö, Tofteryd, Värnamo, Ökna. Lantmäteriverkets Forskningsarkiv in Riksarkivet in Arninge. The National Archive.
Statistiska centralbyrån. 1916. Jordbruk och boskapsskötsel: År 1913. Sveriges officiella statistik: Jordbruk med binäringar: Stockholm.
Statistiska centralbyrån. 1918. Jordbruk och boskapsskötsel: År 1916. Sveriges officiella statistik: Jordbruk med binäringar: Stockholm.
Statistiska centralbyrån. 1920. Jordbruk och boskapsskötsel: År 1917. Sveriges officiella statistik: Jordbruk med binäringar: Stockholm.
Statistiska centralbyrån. 1920. Jordbruk och boskapsskötsel: År 1918. Sveriges officiella statistik: Jordbruk med binäringar: Stockholm.
Statistiska centralbyrån. 1921. Jordbruk och boskapsskötsel: År 1919. Sveriges officiella statistik: Jordbruk med binäringar: Stockholm.
Statistiska centralbyrån. 1923. Jordbruk och boskapsskötsel: År 1920. Sveriges officiella statistik: Jordbruk med binäringar: Stockholm.
Verifikationer. Länsräkenskaper för Jönköpings län 1822–1860. Riksarkivet in Marieberg. The National Archive.

Secondary sources

The Agrarian History of Sweden: From 4000 BC to AD 2000. 2011. J. Myrdal and M. Morell (eds.) Nordic Academic Press: Lund.
Agriculture and forestry in Sweden since 1900: Geographical and historical studies. 2011. H. Antonson and U. Jansson (eds). 'Skogs- och lantbrukshistoriska meddelanden No 54.' Stockholm: KSLA.
Ahlén, Ingmar. 1965. *Studies on the red deer, Cervus elaphus L., in Scandinavia.* 'Swedish Wildlife. Volume 3. Number 1'. Stockholm: Svenska Jägareförbundet.
Anshelm, Jonas. 2004. *Det vilda, det vackra och det ekologiskt hållbara: Om opinionsbildningen i Svenska Naturskyddsföreningens tidskrift 'Sveriges Natur' 1943–2002.* 'Skrifter från Forskningsprogrammet Landskapet som Arena Nr 8.' Umeå: Umeå University.
Atlas över Sverige. 1953–1971. M. Lundqvist (ed). Svenska Sällskapet för Antropologi och Geografi. Stockholm: Generalstabens Litografiska Anstalts Förlag.
Bergström, Roger and Kjell Danell. 2011. 'Game management: a period of organization and conservation', in H. Antonson and U. Jansson (eds.) *Agriculture and forestry in Sweden since 1900: Geographical and historical studies.* Stockholm: KSLA.
Björklöf, Sune. 1994. *Älgen i vår historia och vardag.* Stockholm: Tiden.
Boitani, Luigi 2003. 'Wolf conservation and recovery', in L. D. Mech and L. Boitani (eds.) *Wolves: Behavior, Ecology, and Conservation.* Chicago and London: The University of Chicago Press.
Brunefaud, Michel Pierre. 1984. *Le loup. Mythes et réalités.* 'École Nationale Vétérinaire de Toulouse 1984:12'. Toulouse.
Cederlund, Göran and Olof Liberg. 1995. *Rådjuret. Viltet, ekologin och jakten.* Spånga: Svenska Jägareförbundet.

Cronon, William. 1996. 'The Trouble with Wilderness, or, Getting Back to the Wrong Nature'. *Environmental History* 1(1) (January 1996): 7–55. **CrossRef**

Cserhalmi, Niklas. 2004. *Djuromsorg och djurmisshandel 1860–1925: Synen på lantbrukets djur och djurplågeri i övergången mellan bonde- och industrisamhälle.* 'Acta Universitatis Agriculturae Sueciae. Agraria.' *ISSN 1401–6249:498.* Hedemora: Gidlunds förlag.

Dahlström, Anna. 2006. *Betesmarker, djurantal och betestryck 1620–1850: Naturvårdsaspekter på historisk beteshävd i Syd- och Mellansverige.* 'CBM:s skriftserie nr 13/ Acta Universitatis Agriculturae Sueciae nr 2006:95'. Uppsala.

Dahlström, A., T. Lennartsson, J. Wissman and I. Frycklund. 2008. 'Biodiversity and traditional land use in south-central Sweden'. *Environment and History* 14(3) (August 2008): 385–403. **CrossRef**

Danell, K. and R. Bergström (eds.) 2010. *Vilt, människa, samhälle.* Stockholm: Liber.

Ehn, Wolter. 1991. *Mötet mellan centralt och lokalt: Studier i uppländska byordningar.* 'Skrifter utgivna genom dialekt- och folkminnesarkivet i Uppsala. Ser. B21'. Uppsala.

Ekman, Henrik. 2010. *Vargen den jagade jägaren.* Stockholm: Nordstedt.

Eles, Håkan. 1986. 'Vargen i kyrkböckerna', in H. Eles (ed.) *Vargen. Värmland förr och nu.* Årsbok från Värmlands museum. Årgång 84. Karlstad: Stiftelsen Värmlands museum och Värmlands fornminnes- och museiförening.

Eles, Håkan. 2008. 'Ihiälrefwenaf en glubisk ulf'. *RIG NR 2 2008. Kulturhistorisk tidskrift grundad 1918*: 94–97.

Elgmork, Kåre 2000. 'Abundance of brown bears and wolves in central south Norway after 1733 as revealed by bounty records'. *Fauna Norvegica* 20 (2000): 1–8.

Ericsson, Göran, Camilla Sandström, Jonas Kindberg and Ole-Gunnar Støen. 2010. *Om svenskarnas rädsla för stora rovdjur, älg och vildsvin.* Umeå: Institutionen för vilt, fisk och miljö. Rapport 2010:1. SLU.

Fuller, Todd K., L. David Mech and Jean Fitts Cochrane. 2003. 'Wolf population Dynamics', in L. D. Mech and L. Boitani (eds.) *Wolves: Behavior, Ecology, and Conservation* Chicago and London: The University of Chicago Press.

Fredman, Per-Olof and Örjan Kardell. 2007. 'Vargjakt förr', in H. Tunón, M. Iwarsson and S. Manktelow (eds.) *Människan och Faunan: Etnobiologi i Sverige 3.* Stockholm: Wahlström & Widstrand förlag.

Fritts, Steven H., Robert O. Stephenson, Robert D. Hayes and Luigi Boitani. 2003. 'Wolves and Humans', in L. D. Mech and L. Boitani (eds.) *Wolves: Behavior, Ecology, and Conservation.* Chicago and London: The university of Chicago Press.

Gadd C-J. 1983. *Järn och potatis: jordbruk, teknik och social omvandling i Skaraborgs län 1750–1860.* Ekonomisk-historiska institutionen, Göteborgs universitet: Göteborg.

Gadd C-J. 2000. *Den agrara revolutionen: 1700–1870.* Stockholm: Natur och kultur/ LTs förlag.

Godenhjelm, Uno. 1891. *Minnen från vargåren i Åbo län 1880–1882.* Helsingfors.

Hallander, H. 1989. *Svenska lantraser: deras betydelse förr och nu.* Veberöd: Blå ankan.

Hannerberg, D. 1971. *Svenskt agrarsamhälle under 1200 år: gård och åker, skörd och boskap.* Stockholm: Läromedelsförlaget.

Israelsson, Carin. 2005. *Kor och människor: Nötkreatursskötsel och besättningsstorlekar på torp och herrgårdar 1850–1914.* 'Agraria 2005:102'. Hedemora: Gidlunds förlag.

Jägarskolan. 1983. N. Hermansson, J. Boëthius and M. Ekman (eds.) Stockholm: Proprius förlag.

Jansson, U. (ed.) *Agriculture and forestry in Sweden since 1900: Geographical and historical studies*. Stockholm: KSLA.

Jedrzejewska, B. and W. Jedrzejewski. 1998. *Predation in vertebrate communities: The Bialowieza Primeval Forest as a case study*. 'Ecological studies 135'. Berlin: Springer.

Jenks, J. A. and D.M. Leslie Jr. 2003. 'Effect of domestic cattle on the condition of female white-tailed deer in southern pine-bluestem forests, USA'. *Acta Theriologica* **48**: 131–144. CrossRef

Jones, Karen. 2011. 'Writing the Wolf: Canine Tales and North American Environmental-Literary Tradition'. *Environment and History* **17**: 201–228. CrossRef

Kardell, Örjan. 2004. *Hägnadernas roll för jordbruket och byalaget 1640–1900*. 'Acta Universitatis Agriculturae Sueciae. Agraria. 445/Skogs- och lantbrukshistoriska meddelanden nr 31'. Stockholm: KSLA.

Kardell, Örjan. 2006. 'Vallning, bete och hägnader kring sekelskiftet 1900'. *Svenska landsmål och svenskt folkliv 2006*: 49–77.

Kardell, Örjan. 2008. 'Om Rödluvan och vargen och den svenska vargdebatten'. *RIG NR 1 2008. Kulturhistorisk tidskrift grundad 1918*: 1–10.

Karlsson, J., H. Brøseth, H. Sand, H. and H. Andrén. 2007. 'Predicting occurrence of wolf territories in Scandinavia'. *Journal of Zoology* **272**(3) (July 2007): 276–283. CrossRef

Kaiser-Guyot, Marie-Thèrèse. 1974. *Le berger en France aux XIVe et XVe siècles*. Paris: Éditions Klincksieck.

Khazanov, Anatoly M. 1994. (2nd ed). *Nomads and the Outside World*. Madison and London: The University of Wisconsin Press.

Lalanne, Christine. 2000. 'Le loup dans l'histoire'. *Histoire Medievale. Premier mensuel sur la vie au Moyen Age*. **10** (October 2000): 20–35.

Larsson, Jesper. 2009. *Fäbodväsendet 1550–1920*. 'Universitatis Agriculturae Sueciae. Agraria, 1652–6880;2009:51'. Uppsala and Östersund.

Larsson, Jesper. 2011. 'The transformation of the summer farm: from backbone of North Swedish animal husbandry to experience tourism and branded products', in H. Antonson and U. Jansson (eds.) *Agriculture and forestry in Sweden since 1900: Geographical and historical studies*. Stockholm: KSLA.

Lopez, Barry Holstun.1978. *Of Wolves and Men*. New York.

Lucas, A. T. 1989. *Cattle in Ancient Ireland*. 'Studies in Irish Archaeology and History'. Kilkenny: Boethius.

Människan och Faunan: Etnobiologi i Sverige 3. 2007. H. Tunón, M. Iwarsson and S. Manktelow (eds.) Stockholm: Wahlström & Widstrand förlag.

McNamee, Thomas. 1998. *The Return of the Wolf to Yellowstone*. New York: Henry Holt & Co.

Mech, L. David and Luigi Boitani. 2003. 'Wolf social ecology', in L. D. Mech and L. Boitani (eds.) *Wolves: Behavior, Ecology, and Conservation*. Chicago and London: The University of Chicago Press.

Mosley, Stephen 2006. 'Common Ground: Integrating Social and Environmental History', *Journal of Social History* **39**(3) (Spring 2006): 915–33. CrossRef

Myrdal J. 1999. *Jordbruket under feodalismen: 1000–1700.* Stockholm: Natur och kultur/LTs förlag.

Nash, Rodrick .1982. *Wilderness and the American Mind.* New Haven: Yale University Press.

Packard, Jane M. 2003. 'Wolf behavior: Reproductive, social, and intelligent' in L. D. Mech and L. Boitani (eds.) *Wolves: Behavior, Ecology, and Conservation.* Chicago and London: The University of Chicago Press.

Persson, Jens and Håkan Sand. 1998. *Vargen: Viltet, ekologin och människan.* R. Brittas, G. Glöersen, H. Huldt and O. Liberg (eds). Spånga: Svenska Jägareförbundet.

Peterson, Rolf O. and Paolo Ciucci. 2003. 'The wolf as a carnivore', in L. D. Mech and L. Boitani (eds). *Wolves: Behavior, Ecology and Conservation.* Chicago and London: The University of Chicago Press.

Pousette, Evert 1986. *De människoätande vargarna.* Gamleby: ARKEO-Förlaget.

Pluskowski, Aleksander 2006. *Wolves and the Wilderness in the Middle Ages.* Woodbridge: Boydell.

Sand, H., O. Liberg, Å. Aronson, P. Forslund, H. Chr. Pedersen, P. Wabakken, S. Brainerd, S. Bensch, M. Åkesson, J. Karlsson and P. Ahlqvist. 2010. *Den Skandinaviska Vargen: En sammanställning av kunskapsläget från det skandinaviska vargforskningsprojektet SKANDULV 1998–2010.* Rapport till Direktoratet for Naturforvaltning i Norge. Uppsala: Grimsö forskningsstation, SLU.

Stewart, K. M., R.T. Bowyer, J.G. Kie, N.J. Cimon and B.K. Johnson. 2002. 'Temperospatial distributions of elk, mule deer and cattle. Resource partitioning and competitive displacement'. *Journal of Mammalogy* **83**: 229–244.

Strand, Ante. 1986. 'Folkliga föreställningar om vargen', in H. Eles (ed.) *Vargen. Värmland förr och nu.* Årsbok från Värmlands museum. Årgång 84. Karlstad: Stiftelsen Värmlands museum och Värmlands fornminnes- och museiförening.

Ström, Israel A. af 1832. *Skogs- och jagt-arkiv för Sverge.* Stockholm: Norstedts.

Swenson, Jon E., Petter Wabakken, Finn Sandegren, Anders Bjärvall, Robert Franzén, and Arne Söderberg. 1995. 'The near extinction and recovery of brown bears in Scandinavia in relation to the bear management policies of Norway and Sweden'. *Wildlife Biology* **1**(1) (1995): 11–25.

Teperi, Jouko. 1977. 'Sudet. Suomen rintamaiden ihmisten uhkana 1800-luvulla'. *Historiallisia tutkimusa, 0073; 101:* Helsinki. (With a German summary).

Walker, Brett L. 2004. 'Meiji Modernization, Scientific Agriculture, and the Destruction of Japan's Hokkaido Wolf'. *Environmental History.* **9**(2) (April 2004):248–274. **CrossRef**

Internet sources

All internet links were live at 1 April 2013.

www.gutefar.se/handboken.htm (Föreningen gutefåret. Gutefårägarens handbok 2004).

www.jagareforbundet.se

www.jagarnasriksforbund.se

www.naturvardsverket.se

www.nordensark.se

www.rovdjur.se

www.rovviltportalen.no

De-Domestication: Ethics at the Intersection of Landscape Restoration and Animal Welfare

Christian Gamborg, Bart Gremmen, Stine B. Christiansen, and Peter Sandøe

INTRODUCTION

In Holland, thirty miles from Amsterdam, a nature reserve of about 5,600 hectares of reclaimed land called Oostvaardersplassen has been turned into one of Europe's largest and most ecologically ambitious – and controversial – nature restoration experiments. The aim is to develop a natural and dynamic ecosystem resembling those of the estuaries of the major European rivers prior to human disturbance. Of particular importance in this landscape-scale exercise in natural habitat restoration are large grazing animals such as horse, elk, wisent and wild boar. Currently, deer as well as special breeds of horse (Konik) and cattle (Heck) are the large herbivores. The Konik and Heck are derived from domestic horses and cattle. However, they occupy an ecological niche similar to that of the Aurochs (wild ancestors of our domestic cattle) and Tarpans (predecessors of today's horses) that once roamed the open meadows and forests of Europe; and they are therefore used as functional equivalents of these ancient grazers. The self-sustaining populations, with no supplemental feeding, remain out in the open all year and should as such be under selective pressures similar to those of the wild cattle and horses that once lived in this area. 'Re-wilding' or de-domestication has allegedly begun.

However, in the absence of sufficient feed in winter time, mortality rates of 30–60 per cent are recorded (Meissner, 2008). Its opponents look upon de-domestication as cruelty: the lack of complementary feeding and withdrawal of veterinary care results in starvation, stress and exposure to parasites. In essence, it is argued, the whole practice sacrifices 'the health and welfare of individual animals to … restore primeval nature' (Keulartz, 1999: 168). According to advocates of de-domestication, by contrast, the mortality rates are (in a sense that needs to be clarified, clearly) 'natural'; they are an expression of population dynamics and not unlike those in comparable wild populations (Vera et al., 2007).

De-domestication is a process, undertaken over generations, of trying to turn domestic animals (or plants: here we are concerned with animals) into self-sustainable wild or semi-wild animals. It can be viewed as an end in itself: as a sort of species restoration, a way of getting populations of animals to resemble their wild ancestors not only in appearance but also in terms of behaviour. But it is most often advocated as means to an end: as part of a complex process of ecological restoration aiming to increase the so-called wildness and naturalness of an area in a long-term nature management strategy (Vera et al., 2007). The Oostvaardersplassen restoration project pursues both goals. It seeks to manage the landscape using an advanced breeding scheme sometimes referred to as 'breeding back'. This is a process in which the genome of an extinct subspecies is, in effect, re-assembled from genes that are still present in the gene pool (Koene and Gremmen, 2001). This can happen naturally. For example, back-breeding is thought to occur in the wild in feral populations, where, for example, domestic pigs seem to revert to 'wild boar' status in their appearance, behaviour and hardiness (ibid.).

The Oostvaardersplassen de-domestication project steers right into a long-standing debate among ecologists about how former landscapes, such as European lowland wilderness, looked and functioned, and what the role of natural grazing was in maintaining such landscapes – and, especially, which animals occupied which ecological niches (Vuure, 2005). One line of thought, advocated by the Dutch ecologist Frans Vera, is that European lowland wilderness was not just one dense forest, but more of a half-open park-like landscape created by the grazing and browsing of large herbivores such as the Tarpan, Aurochs, deer and possibly European bison (Vera et al., 2007). Thus, restoration efforts should take these characteristics into account. This has been done in the Netherlands where Heck and Konik are used as 'tools' of nature restoration – as substitutes, or rather, proxies, for their extinct wild cousins. Lately, management resembling the practice of de-domestication has also taken place in other European countries, notably in the UK and Denmark.

Evidently, this new practice gives rise to various problems and questions of a technical or scientific nature. It may be asked, for example, whether the large herbivores undergoing the process of de-domestication will be able to match the ecological role of their ancestors, to what extent different species of large herbivore can live together, and in what ways the environment in which the Aurochs once lived has changed. Questions like these obviously must be tackled, but the practice also raises some important ethical questions. These concern (i) the moral status of the de-domesticated animals, and issues about how they should be treated; and (ii) the value of nature and what kind of nature management is wanted. A special problem here is that the animals and the habitats in which they live, develop between 'boxes'. In the beginning there are domesticated animals on pasture; by the end of the process there should be wild animals living in open land. However, the familiar norms covering domestic animals and agricultural land are very different from the norms regarding our treatment of wildlife and wild nature.

First, think of livestock, i.e. animals domesticated for food (or other products, such as leather) or work. Here, today, the main norm in most parts of the western world requires us to look after the welfare of the individual animal; whereas

De-Domestication

when it comes to wildlife the focus is much more on protection operating at the level of species and population (Sandøe and Christiansen, 2008). At present, we lack clear ethical guidance on how to reconcile these concerns; and as Koene and Gremmen (2002) point out, individually focused norms of animal treatment may well conflict with herd-level norms.

Secondly, and turning to the value of nature and desirable kinds of nature protection, two recognisable trends follow the more traditional approach to wilderness preservation: trying to look after whatever is left of original nature, and the more recent ecological restoration approach, which '... initiates or accelerates the recovery of an ecosystem with respect to its health, integrity and sustainability' (SER, 2004). The latter includes reforestation, lake restoration, elimination of non-native species and weeds, and reintroduction of native species. In Europe and North America examples of such projects are plentiful. These include salt marsh restoration in the Wadden Sea, lowland heath restoration in the UK (Madgwick and Jones, 2002) and the gigantic wetland restoration being undertaken across the US under the North American Wetland Conservation Act (Wali et al., 2002).

Assessment of the merits of these approaches involves not only sorting out their ecological consequences but, equally, discussion of the level of human involvement acceptable in areas designated as nature *reserves* or the like (Turnhout et al., 2004; Young et al., 2005). What makes de-domestication different from other forms of nature restoration is that it involves deliberate intervention at the genetic level as well as conventional landscape management. Is populating the landscape with animals through de-domestication too much intervention? Is it merely a reasonable way to make the landscape and nature suit us? And if we restore, do we get a second-rate imitation of the real thing, fake nature (Elliot, 1982), or wildness by proxy?

The aim of this paper is to identify the conflicting ethical concerns about de-domestication. We also consider the impact of the current compartmentalisation of ethical enquiry, and especially the apparent division, roughly speaking, between animal and environmental ethics: here we ask if these categories are adequate to guide contemporary landscape restoration and the specific practice of de-domestication. First, de-domestication and domestication are characterised. We describe how the animals involved are foreseeably changed during this process. Secondly, the question how such animals should be treated is analysed with reference to influential norms and ideas in animal ethics. Thirdly, de-domestication is examined in relation to issues of naturalness and wildness, and it is asked if de-domestication should be viewed as a legitimate form of nature management. Finally, the possibility and theoretical basis of a more unified view of de-domestication is discussed.

DE-DOMESTICATION: THE *RE*-CREATION OF NATURE'S PAST?

De-domestication is by no means an uncontroversial practice (Keulartz, 1999). One concern is whether it is, in fact, possible to achieve backward-change in behavioural and genetic characteristics, and whether it is accurate to talk about de-domesticated animals being 'wilder' than their recent progenitors. In other words, is this practice a case of *re*-creation or merely new creation? Rather than being the conservation of existing nature or the restoration of 'old' nature, is de-domestication just another exciting way to form nature, to develop 'new nature'? (cf. van der Heijden, 2005) Consideration of this question entails among other things an examination of the concepts of domestication and de-domestication.

For thousands of years animals have been domesticated for food production, fur and leather, companionship, entertainment, experimentation and so on; varying degrees of dependence on humans for survival have resulted from this. It is not uncommon for domestic animals to escape or be released from a farm or home and live independently, breeding in the wild. Thus, for example, in Northern Europe substantial feral populations of farmed mink have become established in recent times. We even have a name for the outcome of this process: we call the escapees 'feral' (Koene and Gremmen, 2002). Clearly, the practice of de-domestication differs from this inasmuch as, in it, the animals' return to the wild is part of a wider nature restoration project, and there is an expectation, or hope, that genetic changes will come about which reverse the earlier changes through which the animals were domesticated. Furthermore, de-domestication will normally involve species which, unlike mink in Europe, once lived in the relevant area.

Domestication itself is a highly contested concept (Clarke, 2007; Russell, 2002). By some it is regarded as an imposition of 'efficiency' seeking to exclude links in the food chain that run between '... consumers and those living things they wish to consume' (De Landa, 1997: 108). As compared with their wild relatives, domesticated species are considerably altered in appearance and behaviour; following many generations of breeding, they become accustomed to human control and provision. According to one definition 'domestication' can be defined as '... a process by which a population of animals becomes adapted to man and the captive environment, by some combination of genetic changes occurring over generations and environmentally induced developmental events recurring during each generation' (Price, 1984: 3). The reverse process, by which a population of animals become de-adapted to man and captivity, and adapted (to a degree) to the wild environment from which they came, by a combination of genetic changes taking place over generations and environmentally induced events experienced in each generation, is known as *de-domestication* (ibid.). De-domestication is a process that often begins with the *intentional* introduction of animals to an area with the aim of de-adapting the animals to captivity; it involves more or less premeditated genetic change (breeding back) which,

De-Domestication

over generations at any rate, is expected to turn the domestic animals into self-sustainable wild or semi-wild animals (Klaver et al., 2002). In both practical and theoretical terms, de-domestication is very much a 'work in progress'. Because the exact definition and actual practice are open to interpretation (Meissner and Limpens, 2001), we may ask whether the practice of re-wilding is really possible, or whether it is just a matter of changed breeding goals and methods which, ultimately, represent a novel variety of domestication.

In the European context, human-initiated breeding back has been of particular interest, since most, if not all, of the original wilderness has now gone. Besides bred back 'wolves' such as the Tamaskan wolfdog (not involving cross-breeding with wolves) and the so-called Quagga project, which seeks to bring back an extinct subspecies of a Zebra called Quagga, the most prominent and best examples of breeding back schemes are probably the Heck cattle – a hardy breed of cattle developed in the early twentieth century in an effort to breed back modern cattle to a presumed ancestral form, the Aurochs, and the Konik – a horse breed from the mid-twentieth century resembling the extinct wild European equine the Tarpan. The key assumption is that '... the wild horse and the Auroch live on in the genes of their domestic off-spring' (Stichting Ark, 1999: 29).

In Europe the last Aurochs were recorded at the beginning of the seventeenth century; in some places, like in Britain, evidence of their use dates back to the tenth century. These animals were able to survive on nutrient-poor plants and endure harsh winters; they were much more robust than many present-day breeds, which are adapted to indoor, high-productivity environments. Such robustness is sought after in the various kinds of nature management in which overgrowth by shrubs and trees is prevented so as to create, or maintain, habitats rich in meadow plants and animals. It is possible to obtain robust contemporary breeds, such as Scottish Highlanders, but they look little like the original wild cattle of Europe. Only recently have information and data been compiled and analysed to build a picture of the physical appearance, behaviour and habitat of Aurochs, and of their supposed impact on the forest structure and habitats in which they lived, as well as the accumulated changes of domestication. The resulting picture has made it possible to compare Aurochs with bred-back Heck cattle and thus initiate a process of de-domestication (Vuure, 2005). It would seem, therefore, that what is particular about de-domestication is the search, over time and through the alteration of genotypes, for an increased degree of wildness and naturalness *within* a given species population.

Wildness might easily be thought of as a quality, in specific individual animals, of being wild or un-wild. But it may also be conceived as a broader concept and equated with parts of nature that are not controlled by humans. The lifecycles of animals that are wild in this latter way are wholly free of deliberate human intervention; the animals are in this sense autonomous (Evanoff, 2005). Consequently, this kind of wildness cannot be preserved in human-run, artificial environments (Jamieson, 1995). Clearly, difficulties arise with de-domestication

Christian Gamborg et al.

in landscapes heavily influenced by human activities: in such environments, what is artificial and what is natural? More fundamentally, it appears to be an underlying assumption of this anti-interventionist conception of wildness that humans are in some sense 'unnatural' – an assumption that can certainly be queried (Callicott, 1994).

The related concept of 'naturalness' – an equally debated term (e.g. Elliot, 1994) that is much used in connection with restoration ecology – is often defined, correspondingly, as a quality or state of ecosystems without human interference (Peterken, 1996). Somewhat paradoxically, the creation of naturalness is thought to be possible through planned 'natural' disturbances (ibid.). We shall return to this notion later in the section on environmental ethics and nature management.

As Figure 1 shows, many generations are considered necessary to accomplish real (or as real as possible) de-domestication through changes in genotype at population level. The process of de-domestication initially involves the development of distinct, more fully adapted behaviour (in terms of natural group formation, leadership and rutting period, and so on) and selection pressure to initiate genetic changes over generations.

In the Dutch attempts at de-domestication – like those involving the reintroduced Przewalski horse (a descendant of the Asiatic wild horse known as the Taki), the Konik horse, and Heck cattle – only phases up to III or at most IV have been achieved. Here, then, the animals have become feral in a new environment. A population of feralised, self-sustainable animals can be discerned,

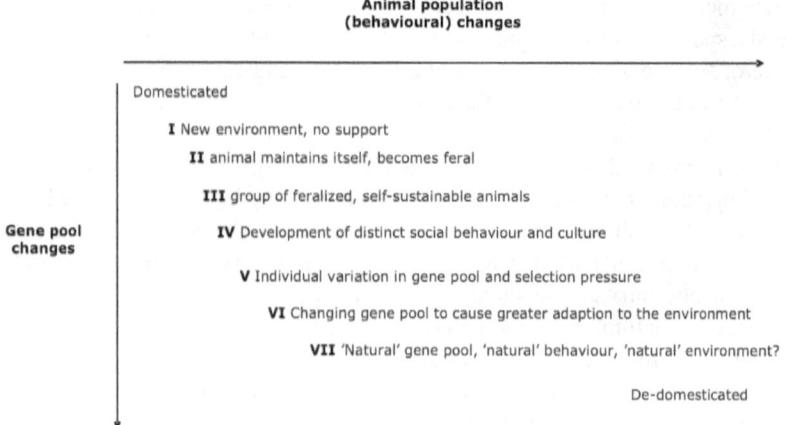

FIGURE 1. An idealised process of de-domestication in terms of changes in behaviour and in the gene pool. Based on Koene and Gremmen (2002).

De-Domestication

and changes in behaviour and the development of a culture are recognisable. However, significant *genetic* change has yet to occur. The Ark Foundation in the Netherlands is trying to achieve phases V–VII through a series of genetic management activities, i.e. breeding back schemes (Meissner and Limpens, 2001; Koene and Gremmen, 2002).

Ark Foundation specialists believe that a genetically healthy minimum population requires 50 fertile animals capable of reproducing. They calculate that the minimum area needed for genetic autonomy is 1,000 Hectares. However, they do not have an area of this size yet, and hence they are obliged to consider their 40 small herds as a single virtual herd. Inbreeding can be prevented by removing animals and adding non-relatives to a group. Ark selects its animals by (what they call) 'looking through the eyes of a wolf', a method designed to counter the risk that selection will be anthropocentric. The last phase of de-domestication automatically sets a problem, however, because the animal population will only behave like their ancestors if the genes responsible for their natural behaviour are intact and have not been lost during the previous process of domestication.

De-domestication, as here described, shares certain characteristics with ecological restoration: suitable reference points must be found, valid data must be used to flesh the scheme out, and the present state of the environment must be compared with the conditions prevailing when the environment originally existed. De-domestication is therefore an exercise in approximation with an unpredictable result and an end-point that is hard to define.

During these stages of obtaining increased wildness or naturalness, how should the animals undergoing de-domestication be conceived: as wild or unwild animals? In the early stages of de-domestication, the animals still bear a strong resemblance to domestic animals. On the other hand, they will gradually become more fully adapted to different environmental conditions, and thus, as a population, be more like wildlife; yet they may still not be considered wild animals in the full sense. When, if at all, should we cease to regard the animals, individually, as domestic animals (with the associated right to be treated in accordance with the welfare legislation covering animals in our care)? When should we begin to regard the populations of which those same animals are members as wild populations?

ANIMAL ETHICS: HOW SHOULD DE-DOMESTICATED ANIMALS BE TREATED?

Looking at actual practices and existing legislation, the animals undergoing de-domestication, such as the Heck cattle and Konik horses in pastoral landscapes in the Netherlands, seem to fall into a sort of grey zone so far as regulations protecting animal welfare and health are concerned. The animals are not covered by wildlife legislation. However, they resemble wild animals in their behaviour (such as less individual and more social herd members, synchronised births and new skills such as swimming), and in being year-round in herds with males and females of all ages, with no supplementary feeding. The animals seem to continue to fall under regulations covering farm animals, requiring the identification of individual animals, the killing of animals in slaughterhouses, the protection of animal welfare and the monitoring of animal disease. In practice, of course, this regulation tends to be adapted to circumstances. Thus on reserves it is common to remove animals, where necessary, by shooting them, if they are too wild to catch or considered dangerous (Meissner, 2008). When it comes to diseases, in practice, there are no vaccination programmes. Reportedly, herders try to find a balance between treatment and natural recovery, evidently thereby jeopardising the health and welfare of individual animals (ibid.). Lately, practitioners working with de-domesticated animals have asked for a new official status to be given to the de-domesticated horses and cattle. But what should this status be? How should these animals be regarded, ethically speaking? How ought they be treated?

In the mainstream literature on animal welfare and ethics it is difficult to find clear, unanimous answers to these questions. Unanimity is elusive because, when it comes to animals, we live in a pluralist world where different ethical views compete; and clarity is limited by the fact that, in one way or another, most writers draw a distinction between the duties to domestic animals and the duties to wild animals. In the following we will take as our starting point the dominant view expressed in recent European animal welfare legislation. After that we will consider alternative views.

Since the 1950s there have been considerable developments in animal protection in the western world. On the one hand, human wealth in this region has reached unprecedented heights; on the other, the way animals are bred and raised has been hugely intensified. The wealth, which involves products becoming (in both relative and absolute terms) cheaper and cheaper, has been achieved partly at a cost to animal welfare.

Particularly in Europe a perceived need for legislation at EU and national level, and other initiatives which place limits on the use of animals for purposes to which most people agree, has emerged. Such initiatives fall under the heading of 'animal welfare'; they may be viewed as an add-on to the traditional, much older, 'anti-cruelty' legislation. The point of the newer legislation is to prevent farmers from doing what is, economically speaking, the most rational thing to do. Farmers are required by it to ensure high standards of animal welfare during the life of any animal in human care, even if this entails inefficiencies, and hence less profit.

In *animal husbandry*, depending upon the species, there are in practice different degrees of focus on the individual animal, even in countries with elaborate animal welfare legislation. For example, in broiler chicken production the main focus is on the flock, whereas sometimes in cattle it might be on the individual. Despite failures to conform with the intentions of regulation, what is

De-Domestication

worth noting is that the rationale behind animal welfare legislation is to secure a decent minimum of animal welfare for each individual animal; and this includes looking after the physiological as well as the behavioural needs of the animals (Sandøe and Christiansen, 2008).

Let us turn to *game animals* such as pheasants and partridges, which are raised or bred – but not domesticated – for hunting purposes. These animals are, to an extent, in human care before they are released. Periodically responsibility may be assumed by the keeper by, for instance, feeding wildlife in severe winter conditions or culling when epidemics occur. But most of the time the focus is on the *population dynamics* of a certain animal species group in an *ecosystem*. Much the same goes for other kinds of game animal, such as deer, which are in places raised or 'assisted' by humans, but controlled through intensive culling. In many European countries, deer populations have grown substantially over the last 50 years, and it is well known that the ecological pressure exerted by high concentrations of them hinders natural regeneration of forest trees – one of the key measures of the now increasingly sought 'close-to-nature forestry' (Gamborg and Larsen, 2003). In consequence, deer culling in many parts of Europe has increased. More generally, conservation practices revolving around such wildlife have the aim, not necessarily of sustaining a certain population, but simply of keeping a habitat, such as a forest or meadow, in a certain state.

With *other kinds of wildlife* the case is clearly less hedged around by moral demands. Here the moral requirements that do apply are usually aimed at the entire population. In the past wild animals were used as hunting animals, or as game, or were killed as pests or vermin. Attitudes were far more straightforward in their ethical anthropocentricity than they generally are today, as can be seen in the following credo (Wesenberg-Lund, 1939: 198, our translation):

> The law of all fauna in our strictly economically managed forests is as follows. If you can be of benefit – which in most cases means: can you bring us the joy of hunting – we will protect you. If you do damage – that is to say, if you harm our [other] game animals – or if you damage the forest as we want it, we will eradicate you for as long as possible, and a bit more. And if you are of no immediate value to us, then hang on if you can! However the demands you have for life will always have to give way to whatever serves our purposes.

Today, increasingly, wild animals are objects of fascination and grave concern. This is, of course, closely related to general concern about man's destruction of nature and the environment. Efforts are being made all over the world to protect wild animals and their habitats. Here, humans are not instrumental or active in bringing the relevant animals into the world, nor is there any direct involvement in their upbringing. Thus, as reflected in legislation, less direct responsibility than we have for domestic animals is assumed. Any measures here are indirect and operate at the level of the population. Consequently, conflicts are prone to arise between considerations of wildlife management and considerations of individual animal welfare (Jamieson, 1995). Incidental care for the wildlife, while often anticipated, is secondary, or integrated with the larger purpose of nature conservation (Norton, 1995).

The current European regulatory apparatus governing animal use is bound to create problems for de-domesticated animals like the Konik horses and the Heck cattle in Oostvaardersplassen. They fall between two thoughts: about *animal welfare*, with a focus on the well-being of each individual animal, and about *wildlife management*, with a focus on the well-being of population and/ or species. To deal with the issues here, it may help to draw upon some of the better-worked out moral views presented by philosophers interested in animal ethics. Here we will briefly consider three such views: utilitarianism, rights views, and contextual views.

According to the utilitarian, what matters in our dealings with animals is our impact on their well-being. We should always aim to act so as to achieve the largest total sum of well-being (Singer 1991). Leaving out complications following from the fact that what we do may affect the number of animals which will come to exist, a utilitarian view may consider de-domestication as an opportunity to develop varieties of animal which, in effect, foster overall animal welfare.

From a utilitarian perspective there is no clear divide in principle between the way we are required to treat domestic animals and the way we are required to treat wild animals. As effectively as possible, we should look after the well-being of animals, whether domestic or wild. The only difference is a pragmatic one: in practice, it may be more difficult to look after the well-being of wild animals than it is to look after the well-being of animals our direct care. Thus from a utilitarian perspective one is morally obliged to look after de-domesticated animals as well as possible; for example, one might be required to cull weak individuals rather than allowing them to die on their own.

According to animal rights advocates (Regan, 1984; 2007) many animals, including all vertebrates, have an *inherent value* of their own, based on their nature and capacities. They are not to be treated as instruments for someone else's use and benefit. Inherent value cannot be traded off, factored into calculations about consequences, or replaced. Creatures that possess it have basic moral rights, including the right to life and to liberty. On this view animal production should simply be stopped because it is bound to violate animal rights. When it comes to wild animals we may not kill these animals for our own purposes; and it seems that the main policy call coming out of a rights view is a 'hands-off' recommendation. According to the rights view we are responsible for what we do to animals in our care, but it is less clear that we have any duty to look after individual wild animals. Therefore even though a defender of rights view may well object to the starting point of de-domestication, it is much less clear how he or she would consider later stages of the process.

De-Domestication

Finally we shall here consider one form of the so-called contextual view[1] focusing on *relations* between humans and animals. On this approach, humans have quite different relations – and hence moral obligations – to wild animals than they have to domestic ones. This is not, primarily, due to differing human emotional responses (though these may be a consideration). Rather, it is because humans are responsible for the very existence of domestic animals (unlike wild ones), and, additionally, through selective breeding, for their natures; and because the latter often render the relevant animals dependent and vulnerable in ways wild animals are not. This kind of special obligation is not owed to animals struggling as the result (say) of natural drought or heavy snowfall.

This relational approach takes into account a variety of factors – in particular, however, human interactions with, and causal responsibility for, the situations of particular animals – before coming to a judgment about what obligations might arise in any particular context. It is well placed to deal with animals falling in the boxes 'domestic' and 'wild'. However it seems rather useless when it comes to awkward contexts between these boxes such as the context of de-domestication.

Recently, a more integrated perspective on domesticated and wild animals has been described (Swart, 2005). In this 'care-based' view, which is really another form of a contextual view, care for domestic animals is dubbed 'specific care' because it is directed primarily towards the individual animal's needs. However, the main focus here is not on care and what it consists of, but on the distinction between having taken human responsibility for certain animals once and for all and a sense of optional responsibility towards an animal group. In connection with wild animals, Swart uses the label 'non-specific care', because this kind of care involves attending to the animal's relationship to the natural environment.

This raises issues about the natural environment in which the animals being de-domesticated are placed, the level of human involvement acceptable in such areas, our conceptions of nature. In other words, it prompts discussion of environmental ethics. What kinds of management practice are acceptable – the active restoration type or only the more passive wilderness preservation type?

ENVIRONMENTAL ETHICS: SHOULD DE-DOMESTICATION BE VIEWED AS A LEGITIMATE FORM OF NATURE MANAGEMENT?

In the Dutch example of de-domestication, the Konik horses and Heck cattle were brought in not only to ensure the long-term 'survival' of a past species, but also as *agents* promoting variation in the natural environment, and, allegedly, fostering biodiversity and naturalness. An interesting feature of the discussion is that appeals to biodiversity are made by both the advocates and opponents of de-domestication practices. However, they are made on the basis of different background assumptions and entail very different conceptions of the kinds of practice that are ethically acceptable. Thus de-domestication moves us into a discussion, running within environmental ethics, about the way nature is looked upon and how nature should be treated. In particular, one is drawn into a long-standing restoration *versus* faking nature debate. This debate originated with Elliot (1982) and was subsequently revived, and expanded upon, by among others, Katz (1991; 1992; 1996), Elliot (1994; 1997), Light (2000) and Chapman (2006).

The fakery discussion can be framed within two paradigmatic views of nature and biodiversity: the *historical* view and an *end-state*, or *consequentialist*, view (Gamborg and Sandøe, 2004). To say what is good and right judged by end-state principles, we do not need any information about the way this state of affairs was brought about. On historical principles, by contrast, legitimacy or acceptability depends entirely on past developments. Here information about events of the past is not merely relevant, or interesting, but essential to the determination of moral value (ibid.).

Model advocates of the historical view would take naturalness to be a goal in itself, or end value. They would attach no value to restoration schemes involving de-domestication – at least, as long as there were 'true' preservation initiatives to support. By contrast, a straightforward consequentialist would judge end-state principles sufficient and would welcome restoration practices as an instrument to create more genetic and landscape-related diversity. The elaboration of this simple distinction between historical and consequentialist views allows us to define a number of hybrid positions on the value of de-domestication (see Figure 2).

In Figure 2, the first question is: *what is nature?* Vis-à-vis de-domestication the figure shows that once there is agreement about the desirability of more naturalness and wildness, the underlying conception of nature, and of naturalness,

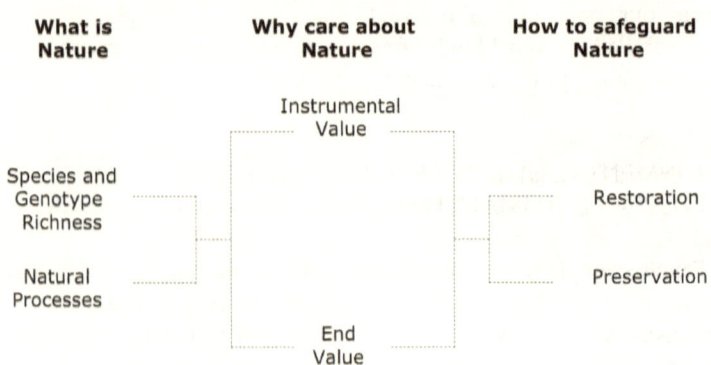

FIGURE 2. Key questions about conceptions of nature and biodiversity allowing for the definition of a number of hybrid views between judging nature from purely end-state principles and from a historical view

De-Domestication

has to be specified. Do we see nature as an (eco)system with elements, structures and functions – something indirectly or directly represented through species and genotype richness? Or should we emphasise natural processes, in a way entailing that human interference cannot add to naturalness, regardless of its observable effects (e.g. overgrown meadows or lack of rare species)?

In the consequentialist perspective, it is still necessary to specify what is meant by the idea that there is more or less nature. Many attempts have been made to categorise and operationalise the notably slippery notion of naturalness (Siipi, 2008). Peterken (1996) describes five degrees of naturalness. These include 'original-naturalness' (i.e. the state that existed before people became a significant ecological factor) and 'future-naturalness' (i.e. the state that would eventually develop if if human interference were to cease). Granted that it is possible to quantify degrees of naturalness, different characteristics still have to be balanced here (Gamborg and Rune, 2004). Anderson (1991) describes naturalness as 'conservation potential'. A determination of the degree to which a system would change if humans were removed from it could be used to assess this potential. Alternatively, and from a management point of view, one could try to determine the amount of cultural work that would be needed to fulfil the potential. In a similar vein, and somewhat paradoxically, the creation of wildness requires intervention management.

Secondly, *why care about nature*? Closely related to the first issue – i.e. the question what nature is – are the reasons for our interest in nature and connected explanations of what we find valuable. The value of diversity and naturalness may be predominantly instrumental, in the sense that we promote certain elements in nature, such as 'wild' horses, because they help us to achieve other goals, like the maintenance of tall-grass meadows. In a contrasting attitude, the emphasis is placed on greater diversity, wildness or naturalness in its own right, as an end value regardless of where it takes us (cf. the view of Rolston (1989) on intrinsic value).

Finally, there is the issue of *how we should safeguard nature*. The methods used to safeguard what is held valuable in nature must be carefully considered. Given that it is possible to find a suitable benchmark against which to set targets and measure progress, practices such as de-domestication can be seen as commendable tools for gaining greater stability, resilience or functionality in nature. (This is true, at any rate, if we disregard breaks in historical continuity of the sort occurring when we try to de-domesticate, say, a certain cattle species after a gap of 6,000 years without the original, wild ancestor.)

In contrast with this, preservationists hold that regardless of the qualitative success of the 'copy' – that is, independently of whether certain genotypes can be recreated, whether a certain type of behaviour can be brought back, and whether the physical environment resembles its past condition – *authenticity* is always missing. Evaluation and appreciation of natural areas, and of the biodiversity they contain, depends on knowledge '... that can be acquired through education and experience, just as one learns the history of art' (Katz, 1991: 92, cf. Elliot, 1982). The only way authenticity can be secured, it is argued, is to retain continuity, and to try to preserve what is here now.

So how do the two conceptions of nature and biodiversity with which we are concerned here – the end-state view and historical view – connect with questions about the way nature should be regarded and treated in relation to de-domestication? The invocation of end-state principles to judge certain types of nature, or certain practices, is compatible with the idea that man is an integral part of nature and the view that restoration efforts like de-domestication make sense as an element in nature management. By contrast, the historical view seems to go hand in hand with a notion of nature that excludes de-domestication as part of nature protection. Between these two extremes lie various hybrid views, each of which is defined by a distinctive combination of answers to the three questions presented above.

A UNIFIED VIEW OF DE-DOMESTICATION?

So, is it possible to distinguish between the authentic and the fake when it comes to de-domestication? Does it make sense to talk about a general view of our duties to animals and nature? Is it reasonable to try to differentiate wild animals and animals in our care? And to what extent, and in what ways, can animal and environmental ethical concerns fruitfully be combined to answer such questions?

In Figure 3 some of the key issues raised by the setting, management and value questions relating to de-domestication are listed. De-domestication itself is placed somewhere between agriculture and nature protection with regard to its objectives, management intensity and interests.

The preceding discussion, as Figure 3 brings out, suggests that three potentially unified views need to be considered. The first view says that, at the end of the day, what matters are human and animal interests only. Thus the focus, in de-domestication projects, should be on high standards for each individual animal's health and well-being; and this will remain the focus until we are satisfied that the de-domestication process is completed (assuming that can be satisfactorily determined). The value of the landscape, and of nature as an abstract ideal, is secondary to the concern for the welfare of animals in our care.

The second view sees the key concern in ethics as that of maintaining species, ecosystems, habitats, and so on – not individuals or herds. Hence animals undergoing de-domestication should be treated exactly as other wild fauna are treated. It should, for example, as is already practice in the Oostvaardersplassen, contemplate the possibility of leaving sick or dying horses and cattle to cope naturally, without human assistance. The priority should be a semi-natural landscape with a high degree of habitat/nature quality.

De-Domestication

		Agriculture	Dedomestication	Traditional nature protection
SETTING	Sub group	Animal husbandry	-	Wildlife management
	Animal species	Domesticated animals (e.g. cattle, horse, sheep, goat)	Extinct, bred-back species (e.g. Heck cattle, Konik horse)	Wild animals (e.g. deer, wild boar, hare)
	Where	Agricultural, productive land	Marginal, abandoned agricultural land, existing or new nature reserves	Protected areas, nature reserves
	Socio-economic context	Subsidies for environmentally friendly managed farms	New type of management (e.g. grazing herds where agriculture is too intensive or where agriculture is disappearing)	Natural foraging
	Aim	Value production	Nature management	Nature protection
MANAGEMENT	Interests	(Short term) economic interests	Sustainable ecosystem?	(Long term) ecological interests
	Key issues	Veterinary Animal health Animal welfare	Veterinary *and* ecological Animal welfare Wildness Authenticity	Ecological Biodiversity Habitat/nature quality
	Action status	Active	Active, then passive?	Passive
	Degree of management	Managed	Human intervention and natural processes	(Un)managed
	Management type	Production Creation	Restoration, re-creation	Conservation/ preservation
VALUES	Animal's role	Element of production	Sustainable management tool	Ecosystem component
	Value of nature and landscape	Cultural landscape Richness	Value judged by end-state principles or by historical view?	Semi-natural landscape Natural dynamics
	Type of nature considered valuable	Productive nature	Authentic nature?	Untouched, unspoiled nature
	Focus is on the	Human responsibility for care for individual or herd of animals	Human responsibility for care for individuals and populations?	No, or only optional, human responsibility for care
	Norms found within	Animal/agricultural ethics (e.g. ethics of care)	Elements from animal ethics/agricultural ethics or environmental ethics?	Environmental ethics (e.g. respect for nature)

FIGURE 3. Comparison of setting, practices/management and values associated with the new practice of de-domestication against agriculture and traditional nature protection.

Finally, there seems to be room for a kind of pluralism in which different standards exist for, on the one hand, dealing with humans and domestic animals and, on the other hand, nature management, as suggested by Klaver, et al. (2002). However, this kind of pluralism would mean that certain kinds of view about animals – particularly those cast in biological and moral terms – need to be reconsidered, and that the seemingly key value of animal welfare must be revisited. Moreover, a discussion and clarification of conflicting views of nature, of the ways in which the 'wild' and the 'natural' are conceived, and of the kind of protection this entails, must be pursued. In furthering such discussion, we can deploy two archetypical perspectives on nature and biodiversity productively: the historical and the end-state views.

CONCLUSIONS

De-domestication is a practice caught between two sets of norms governing animals and nature. As such, it shakes up a range of commonly made assumptions about current nature conservation practice and our treatment of animals within it. Besides the more technical problems and the scientific challenges of identifying traits that should be altered, of saying when the process of 're-wilding' is complete, and of determining what the natural behaviour of Heck cattle and Konik horses is, a number of ethical questions arise. These concern human responsibilities to animals and the specifically human conception of nature's value. To these questions no simple answers can be given.

As an ethically assessable practice, de-domestication does not comfortably engage established principles of nature conservation or contextual standards of animal treatment. De-domestication animals are generally handled in a way to serve the needs of nature management. The management is a very active form of *nature* protection in terms of human involvement; it not only attempts to increase the level of biodiversity, but also seeks to increase wildness and naturalness.

In practical terms, consideration of these ethical issues ought to improve discussion in this difficult area, and, eventually, inform any subsequent decisions. It hardly needs saying that, whatever one's views, it is important to get clear about whether, to what extent, and why, it is acceptable for de-domestication to bring about reduced animal welfare for the domestic animals in nature reserves. We also require principled answers to questions about when, in the de-domestication process, animals move from domestic to wild status, and what kinds of duty are owed to wild animals. Consideration of the ethical issues will promote proper debate about whether constant human involvement in nature reserves and other wild areas is desirable, and about where to draw the line between 'good' and 'bad' nature.

De-domestication challenges the current division of nature ethics into the neat, bipolar categories of 'animal ethics' and 'environmental ethics'. In the

De-Domestication

long term, it will be necessary to consider whether that division hampers the resolution of issues raised by contemporary practices, and whether the boxes into which the issues are currently placed are adequate. A bit more 'thinking outside the box' with regard to animal and environmental ethical frameworks might well prove valuable.

NOTES

[1] Thanks to Clare Palmer for guidance at this point; the text draws on material currently being prepared by her and Peter Sandøe.

REFERENCES

Anderson, J.E. 1991. 'A conceptual framework for evaluating and quantifying naturalness'. *Conservation Biology* **5**: 347–352.
Callicott, J.B. 1994. 'A critique of and an alternative to the wilderness idea'. *Wild Earth* **4**: 54–59.
Chapman, R.L. 2006. 'Ecological restoration restored'. *Environmental Values* **15**: 463–478.
Clarke, N. 2007. 'Animal interface: The generosity of domestication', in R. Cassidy (ed.), *Where the Wild Things Are Now: Domestication Reconsidered* (Oxford: Berg Publishers), pp. 49–70.
De Landa, M. 1997. *A Thousand Years of Nonlinear History*. New York: Swerve Editions.
Elliot, R. 1982. 'Faking nature'. *Inquiry* 25: 81–93.
Elliot, R. 1994. 'Extinction, restoration, naturalness'. *Environmental Ethics* 16: 74–144.
Elliot, R. 1997. *Faking Nature. The Ethics of Environmental Restoration*. London and New York: Routledge.
Evanoff, R.J. 2005. 'Reconciling realism and constructivism in environmental ethics'. *Environmental Values* **14**: 61–81.
Gamborg, C. and J.B. Larsen 2003. '"Back to nature" – a sustainable future for forestry?' *Forest Ecology and Management* **179**: 559–571.
Gamborg, C. and F. Rune. 2004. 'Economic and ecological approaches to assessing forest value in managed forests – ethical perspectives'. *Society and Natural Resources* **17**(8): 799–815.
Gamborg, C. and P. Sandøe. 2004. 'Beavers and biodiversity: The ethics of ecological restoration', in M. Oksanen and J. Pietarinen (eds.), *Philosophy and Biodiversity* (New York: Cambridge University Press), pp. 217–237.
Jamieson, D. 1995. 'Wildlife conservation and individual animal welfare', in B.G. Norton, M. Hutchins, E.F. Stevens and T.L. Maple (eds.), *Ethics on the Ark. Zoos, Animal Welfare and Wildlife Conservation* (Washington and London: Smithsonian Institution Press), pp. 69–73.
Katz, E. 1991. 'The ethical significance of human intervention in nature'. *Restoration & Management Notes* **9**: 90–96.

Katz, E. 1992. 'The big lie: human restoration of nature'. *Research in Philosophy and Technology* **12**: 231–241.
Katz, E. 1996. 'The problem of ecological restoration'. *Environmental Ethics* **18**: 222–224.
Keulartz, J. 1999. *Struggle for Nature: A Critique of Environmental Philosophy*. Florence, KY: Routledge.
Klaver, I., J. Keulartz, H.v.d. Belt and B. Gremmen. 2002. 'Born to be wild: a pluralistic ethics concerning introduced large herbivores'. *Environmental Ethics* **24**(1): 3–21.
Koene, P. and B. Gremmen 2001. 'Genetics of dedomestication in large herbivores', in 35th ISAE Conference, Davis, California.
Koene, P. and B. Gremmen 2002. *Gewogen wildheid: samenspel van ethologie en ethiek bij de-domesticatie van grote grazers*. Wageningen: Wageningen University.
Light, A. 2000. 'Ecological restoration and the culture of nature: a pragmatic perspective', in P.H. Gobster and R.B. Hull (eds.), *Restoring Nature: Perspectives from the Social Sciences and Humanities* (Washington, DC: Island Press), pp. 49–70.
Madgwick, J. and T. Jones. 2002. 'Europe', in M.R. Perrow and A.J. Davy (eds.). *Handbook of Ecological Restoration: Restoration in Practice* (Cambridge: Cambridge University Press), pp. 32–56.
Meissner, R. 2008. *Practical Experiences with Welfare and Ethics*. Symposium, Lüneburg, 25–27 September 2008. Bundesamt für Naturschutz, http://www.bfn.de/fileadmin/MDB/documents/themen/landschaftsundbiotopschutz/Tagung_2008/Meissner_Lueneburg_2008_Text.pdf (accessed 17 May 2009).
Meissner, R. and H. Limpens. 2001. 'Dedomestikation – Wilde Herden zwischen den Menschen. Praktisches, veterinärmedizinisches, genetisches und soziales Management wildlebender Herden von Konikpferden und Gallowarindern in den Niederlanden'. *Natur- und Kulturlandschaft* **4**: 112–122.
Norton, B.G. 1995. 'Caring for nature: A broader look at animal stewardship', in B.G. Norton, M. Hutchins, E.F. Stevens and T.L. Maple (eds.), *Ethics on the Ark. Zoos, Animal Welfare and Wildlife Conservation* (Washington and London: Smithsonian Institution Press), pp. 102–121.
Peterken, G.F. 1996. *Natural Woodland*. Cambridge: Cambridge University Press.
Price, E.O. 1984. 'Behavioural aspects of animal domestication'. *Quarterly Review of Biology* **59**: 1–32.
Regan, T. 1984. *The Case for Animal Rights*. London: Routledge.
Regan, T. 2007. 'The case for animal rights', in H. Lafollette (ed.), *Ethics in Practice*, third edition (Maldon MA and Oxford: Blackwell), pp. 205–211.
Rolston, H. 1989. *Environmental Ethics: Duties to and Values in the Natural World*. Philadelphia: Temple University Press.
Russell, N. 2002. 'The wild side of animal domestication'. *Society and Animals* **10**: 285–302.
Sandøe, P. and S.B. Christiansen. 2008. *Ethics of Animal Use*. Oxford: Blackwell.
SER (Society for Ecological Restoration) 2004. *The SER Primer on Ecological Restoration, Version 2*. Society for Ecological Restoration Science and Policy Working Group.
Siipi, H. 2008. 'Dimensions of naturalness'. *Ethics and the Environment* **13**(1): 71–103.
Singer, P. 1991. *Animal Liberation*. Second edition. London: Thorsons.

De-Domestication

Stichting Ark 1999. *Natural Grazing*. Stichting Ark Hoog Keppel, http://www.ark.eu/ (accessed 17 May 2009).

Swart, J.A.A. 2005. 'Care for the wild: An integrative view on wild and domesticated animals'. *Environmental Values* 14(2): 251–263.

Turnhout, E., M. Hisschemöller and H. Eijsackers. 2004. 'The role of views of nature in Dutch nature conservation: The case of the creation of drift sand area in the Hoge Veluwe National Park'. *Environmental Values* 13: 187–198.

Van der Heijden, H.A. 2005. 'Ecological restoration, environmentalism and the Dutch politics of "new nature"'. *Environmental Values* 14: 427–446.

Vera, F., F. Buissink and J. Weidema. 2007. *Wilderness in Europe – What Really Goes on between the Trees and the Beasts*. Driebergen: Tirion B.V. Baarn, Staatsbosbeheer.

Vuure, C. van 2005. *Retracing the Aurochs: History, Morphology and Ecology of an Extinct Wild Ox*. Sofia: Pensoft Publishers.

Wali, M.K., N.M. Safaya and F. Everendilek. 2002. 'The Americas: with special reference to North America', in M.R. Perrow and A.J. Davy (eds.), *Handbook of Ecological Restoration: Restoration in Practice*. (Cambridge: Cambridge University Press), pp. 3–31.

Wesenberg-Lund, C. 1939. 'Kulturskov, Fauna og Aesthetik' [Managed forest, fauna and aesthetics]. *Dansk Skovforenings Tidsskrift* 24: 181–206.

Young, T.P., D.A. Petersen and J.J. Clary. 2005. 'The ecology of restoration: historical links, emerging issues and unexplored realms'. *Ecology Letters* 8: 662–673.

Where Culture Meets Creature

'The Common Cormorant or Shag Lays Eggs Inside a Paper Bag'.[1] A Cultural Ecology of Fish-eating Birds in Western Australia

Joanna Sassoon

A line of street-lamps with a distinctive water-bird design decorates one of Perth's main roads near the corner of Barrack Street and Riverside Drive. They are intended to create a visual identity and a night-time attraction for part of the foreshore.[2] With their silhouette mimicking the head of a pelican and the hoop neck of a swan and cormorant, their design incorporates metaphors for the water-birds known to have once frequented the area. While serving an illumination function and indicating a relationship between the waterfront and the river, the street-lamps become citations, referencing something that is now held in our memories. They are therefore part of a strategy of creating memorials – of using an absence of water-birds to invoke a sense of nostalgia for something 'that is no longer'.[3]

FIGURE 1. 'Swan lights', The Esplanade, Perth.
Courtesy Lighting Images

The Swan River, on whose banks Perth is built, holds a place in the cultural imagination of those living in the city. The place of water-birds within this frame has been represented through art and photography.[4] A long series of visual representations of the view from Mt Eliza shows the development of the city, its impact on the landscape and its encroachment into the river as land reclamation swallowed the river shallows.[5] To some, these reclaimed areas have cleansed the river environment, but to those operating at water level these littoral shallows became understood as essential to the fauna of the river. What the view from the Park now shows, as many lament, is that 'the foreshore boatsheds and the old pier and bathing facility at the foot of Barrack Street have been replaced by the freeway complex and parking areas'.[6] While Dominic Serventy describes how his sense of loss is visualised, as a Perth based CSIRO scientist[7] he played an integral part in constructing ecological understandings that formed the foundation for arguments for the river's preservation.

The street-lamps memorialise the loss of water-birds from the river through creating echoes of their form. Placed, perhaps ironically, on the site of their former feeding grounds they stimulate a history of the rise in ecological awareness of the Swan River system. As will be discussed, while there has been a long-standing cultural perception in Western Australia that fish-eating birds were the cause of the loss of fish from the river, over time and with increased scientific understanding, reclamation of the river shallows has become understood to be a major contributing factor. What emerges from this intimate case study of the perceptions of fish-eating birds on the Swan River is, in contrast to the case study of the wheat-belt in Western Australia, how scientific ideas infiltrated public policy development.[8] Through such a study it is possible to track the ebb and flow of the political acceptance of scientific advice, albeit for a short window of time, and the ultimate dominance of an ideology of development that blinded decision makers to other forms of advice.[9] Through combining design, function and location, these street-lamps become part of a history of substitution for the 'real thing'. They also become a way of entering a cultural ecology of the attitude towards fish-eating birds in Western Australia.

PRESENCE

Early arrivals from Europe to Western Australia brought with them a sense of natural history and were keen observers and describers of fauna and flora.[10] On most occasions it was the difference between the fauna that they knew from other parts of the world that was documented, rather than the similarities with what was already known.[11] Water-birds were often specifically noted by explorers along the Western Australian coastline prior to settlement. For example in 1688 Dampier noted pelicans in Shark Bay, which is now known to be the nearest substantial breeding ground to Perth.[12] More locally, along with all forms of

FIGURE 2. Archibald Bertram Webb. c.1922. *Shags* [colour woodcut]. Courtesy The Holmes à Court Collection, Heytesbury.

bird life surrounding the Swan River, fish-eating birds attracted the attention of early visitors. In 1801 de Freycinet noted 'a prodigious multitude' of pelicans at the entrance to the Swan River, and in 1827 Fraser noted the abundance of waterfowl, in particular the black swan. In 1829 Captain Fremantle expressed his amazement at the big flocks of little black cormorants, and noted that for all the species he saw, this was of most interest because of 'the spectacular community fishing technique it has adopted when feeding'.[13] In giving some sense of the volume of bird life on the Swan River, Mrs Jane Roberts reported in 1833 that a friend said he would

> never forget the sight of thousands and tens of thousands of black swans, which as his party coasted the shore, rose and darkened the air to the distance of eight or ten miles.[14]

The process of naming enabled early explorers and settlers to take an active part in re-inscribing the landscape to make it familiar to their own ways of seeing and referencing place.[15] While the act of naming becomes a form of colonisation and silencing through displacing Aboriginal ways of knowing, European names around the Swan River provide evidence of a prior abundance of bird life. The Swan River was named by Vlamingh in 1697 and later, land features around the river were named including Cormorant Rocks and Pelican Point. These naming practices may at once seem to have been a failure of imagination on the part of the explorers to invent new names, but they cemented the fish-eating birds in their place of special cultural significance in the imagination of Western Australians.

The early explorers and settlers to the Swan River did not limit their interaction with the bird life on the Swan to passive acts such as naming and observation. They were also keen shooters for both sport and food.[16] The effects of this level of shooting activity did not escape observation, though it remained unregulated for some time.[17] In 1833 it was noted that the bird life on the Swan was 'rapidly decreasing, the constant warfare kept up against them on the part of the colonists being so active that scarcely one of the feathered race could escape them'.[18] It is likely that some of the assault on bird life was related to the need for a variety of food – with advertisements appearing in newspapers describing such species as duck, teal and swan for sale as food.[19] The effect of this shooting on the wildlife began to be noticed in official circles. In 1892 it was mentioned in Parliament that 'a general wish has long been expressed that all shooting on Perth Water should be stopped, so that native game might settle there, as it used to do years ago before it was driven away by shooting'.[20] Legislative attempts to reduce the impact of shooting on wildlife were limited to the preservation of species to retain stocks for hunting.

CULTURE

A genealogy of an emerging idea of preservation is clear from the names and intent of the early acts relating to the preservation of fauna in Western Australia. As Spencer Roberts reflected in 1930,

> Game laws are in some respects selfish, for they are sometimes the result of the desire to have a set of conditions which will ensure a supply of material for sport and food. They are not concerned with where the birds breed or their habits.[21]

The intent of the first Preservation of Game Act of 1872 in Western Australia was to 'provide for the preservation of imported Game, and (during the breeding season) of Native Game'.[22] This was achieved through gun control and the introduction of closed seasons to allow game to breed.[23] With similar intent to attitudes expressed across the Australian colonies and in New Zealand, the Game Act of 1892 enshrined the valuing of imported over indigenous species.

It achieved this through penalties for killing game out of season being greater for imported than for indigenous fauna.[24] Indicative of the local hunting habits, John Forrest described 'At present, if a duck or a swan happens to show itself on these waters, many persons start off at once with a gun determined to kill it'.[25] Aiming to preserve both imported and native game through closed seasons and game reserves, this act appears to be a laudable attempt at habitat preservation. However, this equally implied 'open season' on game for the rest of the year, thus legislating a culture of hunting. While it was in the schedule to this act that the emu, black swan and pelican first became protected species, all four species of cormorant still lay outside official protection.[26]

Debates around the passage of the Game bill in 1891/2 provide insights into the contemporary culture of preservation. One member provided articulation of popular prejudice surrounding specific native species of birds perceived as pests for which little scientific foundation was evident at this time. He said that 'among the birds proposed to be protected is the cormorant or shag. Now, considering that this bird destroys a large quantity of fish, I think it is absurd to protect it. ... It is of neither use nor ornament.' Likewise he described the pelican as

> another bird that destroys a lot of fish. The pelican is certainly an ornamental bird, and probably it may be necessary to protect it; still, at the same time, the fact remains that the quantity of fish destroyed on the river by pelicans and shags must be something enormous, and in placing these birds on the schedule, the question is whether it will not do a great deal more harm than good.[27]

While there was a predilection for shooting fauna for sport or food, the way Acts designed to protect native fish and fauna related to each other was at best ambivalent. So, while the Game Acts provided protection for certain declared native species, the Fisheries Acts provided for preservation of fish for their value as an economic resource rather than as a native species. While certain species of birds were protected under the 1892 Game Act, the Fisheries Acts of 1899 and 1905 enabled permission to be granted to declare a scale of rewards for 'the destruction of cormorants, pelicans and such other birds as by proclamation may be declared hostile to fish life'.[28] Moreover, the Vermin Act of 1919 enabled the declaration of species as vermin that were protected under the Game Act. Thus, through the way the specific purposes of the Acts were framed, fish-eating birds sit with some ambivalence between their status as native species considered worthy of preservation and a pest seen as competition for fish resources.

Parliamentary debates surrounding fisheries legislation rest on anecdotal evidence that fish-eating birds were seen as competition for and potentially depleting the fish resources at a time when the price of fish was seen as being too high.[29] They also reveal a lack of understanding as to which fish species are being eaten by the birds, and whether these are the same fish as those preferred for human consumption. Thus, one member saw it as 'more important to save the fish in the river than to save the birds. Shags and pelicans are the great enemies of the fish in the Swan River'.[30] Another, showing some ambivalence towards the status of pest versus their aesthetic appeal, stated that

> We want to destroy the shags and pelicans, although I must say the pelicans look very nice swimming on the river. It is a pleasure to see them, but according to my experience they destroy a tremendous lot of fish. I have watched them, and have seen one pelican swallow as many as 20 herrings.[31]

While this member bought into the 'war on nature' he also mused that 'It requires a great deal of consideration as to how we are first to protect the fish from ourselves, and then from these destructive birds and larger fish'.[32] This was a challenge whose complexity would only emerge several decades later.

PREJUDICE

From the scant details which survive, records of commercial fish catches on the Swan River show a pattern of decline. For example, in 1899 the average weight of fish caught per boat was 7,704kg, and in 1906 this had reduced to 2,349kg per boat.[33] In the late nineteenth century, the removal of fish-eating birds was seen as a way of protecting declining fish resources, despite their fish-eating habits being poorly understood. The official campaign against fish-eating birds as pests in Western Australia began in 1898 with a bounty of threepence a head offered for destruction of cormorants.[34] The Fisheries Act of 1899 formalised this vendetta and raised the bounty to sixpence a head[35] as it was 'not worth the powder and shot to shoot them at that price'.[36] While the number of birds destroyed under the 1899 act was not recorded, Abjornsson, a Fisheries Inspector, wryly noted that the reward did not affect the number of cormorants killed 'for it is only when the ducks are on the river that anyone pretends to be shooting cormorants'.[37] Seven years later in 1906, a bounty on the head of pelicans was introduced.[38] Indicative of the scale of shooting, during this year Abjornsson noted that 'Pelicans have been very numerous on the river throughout the whole year, and although I have shot about 100, and wounded a great number of them, they do not seem scared away'.[39]

Ideas about fish-eating birds enshrined in nineteenth- and early twentieth-century legislation were borne from anecdotal evidence rather than from scientific understandings of ecological relationships. However, meetings of the Australian Association for the Advancement of Science were concerned with the place of science in the national interest, and they invariably discussed the protection of native fauna and flora.[40] In one report on the protection of native fauna, they recognised the binary divide between economic and scientific value of species, and sought resolution to this.[41] In Western Australia, an understanding of the zoology of the State was emerging through interests at the Western Australian Museum, the Royal Society, and community groups.[42] However the rise of professional zoology came too late for scientific knowledge to infiltrate the political imagination sufficiently to be incorporated into the 1912 Game Act.

By the time the Game Act of 1912 was being framed, analyses of relationships between fish-eating birds and their food supply had been published. In 1908 the ornithologist Mattingley argued that the reduction in the supply of fish noted by anglers and fishermen was not due to the cormorant competing for the same fish species as humans.[43] Rather, he argued that cormorants ate fish and crustacea that were predators on commercial species, and that eradicating the cormorants served ultimately to reduce fish stocks as one element in the food chain had been removed. However, while a description of ecological relationships surrounding fish-eating birds was in the public domain, there simply were not enough scientific voices to balance prejudice or influence public policy formation in any meaningful way.

The Select Committee inquiring into the Game Bill sought expert opinion about specific birds, indicating concern at their status as both native species and pests.[44] Opinions solicited about the pelican range from 'I do not think it does much harm', to the oft repeated anecdote that it was 'an unmitigated nuisance. He destroys enormous quantities of fish'. It was Bernard Woodward, director of the Western Australian Museum, and J.G. Hay who introduced ecological information into the debate.[45] Woodward stated 'the pelican is a handsome bird and very attractive, and feeds largely on the cobblers and other fish that live in the shallow water and eat the spawn and young of useful fish'. He specifically noted the effects of removing cormorants on the economically valuable fish species, and showed his awareness of Mattingley's work when he said that 'if you shoot them all off the cobblers will increase and the mullet decrease'. When pressed for his personal opinion about the pelican he responded 'I do not think it does much harm, and it is a thing of beauty'.[46]

Drafted after comparison with acts in Australia and New Zealand, the 1912 Game Act reveals a desire to preserve species for their scientific and economic value, and thus a nascent transition from a hunting to a conservation culture.[47] As one member noted, the resources of the State were gradually being understood as finite and there was an emerging desire to protect native fauna for the longer term. He saw the harm done to native game by 'shooting them out of season and by killing them by most unsportsmanlike methods, [and] it must be recognised that it is time that some step was taken to put an end to such an undesirable state of affairs'.[48] While the Act introduced equal penalties for killing introduced and native fauna, its approach to creating schedules of protected species led to considerable confusion.[49] This failure to grasp the complexity of the issues being addressed may have been a consequence of a failure to listen to the scientific information presented. Triumph of prejudice over science rests with the evidence that the pelican and all species of cormorants were explicitly left off the schedule and thus could be shot when seen as competition for fish or as pests.[50] Scientific answers to whether the fish consumed by cormorants were economically valuable species were not to be provided in Western Australia until 1936.

MYTH

Between the 1912 Game Act and the 1950 Fauna Protection Act[51] there was a marked increase in ecological knowledge of the inter-relationships between fish and birds, and the nature of the Swan River ecosystem. Over time, newspapers played a role in shifting the tension between prejudice and science around the perceived evil of the fish-eating birds with rhetorical flourish. Perth's inefficient system for distributing and marketing fish was of concern,[52] and in 1919 the intensity of the river fishing industry is noted with 130 professional fishermen in eight miles of the Swan River.[53] Despite these factors being seen as possible contributors to the high price of fish and stock reduction, fish-eating birds continued to be the focus of public discontent. Thus, one letter in 1919 concluded that 'fish should be one of our cheapest foods, but unless the Pelicans, Shags and Swans are driven out of the Perth waters fish will never be plentiful'.[54] The most common solution offered was to shoot cormorants, but this met with a consistent official Fisheries Department response. Typical of these are that shooting is 'likely to result in serious consequences', and that 'the little shooting at cormorants permitted under authority quite recently, led to several complaints'.[55]

There was consistent public pressure to rid the river of the cormorants.[56] Under one headline 'Shags or fish? We cannot have both', the rhetoric was restated. It proffered its case that

> so long as the shags are allowed to thrive and multiply and deplete the river, so long will the people yearn and hunger for food which should be part of the daily diet. ... The shags should be hunted off the Swan to give the fish a chance. War should be declared on them.[57]

Gradually, information arising from studies by ornithologists, including White into the dietary consumption of cormorants and Mattingley's ecologically based arguments relating the removal of cormorants to the reduction of fish stocks, became evident in Fisheries Department policy and public responses.[58] Official policy shifted from granting permits to shoot the birds, to arguing that the cormorant is not 'an unmixed evil' as it eats fish that are seen as inedible such as cobblers.[59] Alongside this gradual change in official attitude that cormorants did more harm than good, and while war was declared on the enemy of fish, the interdependence of aquatic life was also being discussed.[60] In response to a flurry of correspondence, the Chief Inspector of Fisheries wrote that 'to my mind, a man should get at the facts of the web of life before, not after, he advocates drastic destructive measures'.[61] However, systematic scientific work on bird and fish life on the Swan River began in 1936.

SCIENCE

As scientific studies stimulated by perceptions of fish-eating habits of the birds began to challenge their popular image internationally, new prejudices against cormorants emerged from a more powerful class of wealthy leisure boat owners on the Swan River. Agitation in regard to boat damage by cormorants was first mooted in Parliament in 1892, and its re-iteration in 1928 represents a shift in the focus of prejudice. This time, ironically, the debate led to a significant advance in understanding the fish-eating habits of the cormorants.

In 1928 a parliamentarian echoed the interests of his yacht-owning constituents, stating that cormorants 'eat tremendous quantities of fish and ruined yachts anchored in the river'.[62] While the Fisheries Department reiterated that cormorants did more good than harm, they acknowledged that 'by using sailing boats, launches etc, as resting places, they cause a considerable amount of annoyance'. Indicative of the political influence that the yacht owners enjoyed, a deputation to the Minister resulted in the issue of specific permits to shoot cormorants. During this time the Chief Harbour Master reported that 'serious damage has been done to navigation lights on the Swan River', intimating this may have been done by those with permission to shoot cormorants either by direct firing or by ricocheting.[63]

During this time, the newspapers began to introduce a more informed debate, which itself reveals the speed at which information published internationally infiltrated public debate in Western Australia.[64] That natural history and ecological relationships were gradually creeping into discussions about the role of cormorants in maintaining fish stocks in Western Australia followed a similar trend in England on the same issue. In 1932 a report in the Perth *Sunday Times* described the volte-face by the Cornish fishermen. When it was shown cormorants did not compete for fish with fishermen the birds were placed on protected lists at their request.[65] From this point, the newspapers began publishing articles from a range of naturalists in an attempt to raise public understanding of the ecological roles of fish-eating birds.

As scientific debate began to quell the cacophony of public outrage against cormorants, there was a new entrant into the politics of food and sporting resources in Western Australia. With their letterhead depicting partridge, trout and pheasant, the Fish and Game Protection Society were clearly on the side of human control over the environment.[66] They took up the public cause for creating a resource for sporting shooting and fishing, and while concerned with the depletion of fish stocks in the Swan River, they were keen to be seen as more than a mouthpiece for the Yacht Clubs. As their minutes of meetings show, they were rigorous in their pursuit of scientific answers. Thus,

> the question of the menace or otherwise of the shag or cormorant on the Swan River was discussed. Dr Serventy should be requested to investigate thoroughly

the desirability or otherwise of an onslaught of these birds, which in the popular opinion, are destroying large quantities of fish in our rivers.[67]

Following international trends where the diets of cormorants have been studied specifically because they were perceived as competitors with humans for food,[68] Serventy's study of the fish-eating habits of cormorants in Western Australia was undertaken at the request of the Fish and Game Protection Society in 1936.[69] Similar studies had been undertaken by Abjornsson in Western Australia,[70] nationally[71] and internationally.[72] In analysing whether cormorants ate economically valuable fish or those considered unfit for human consumption, these studies addressed whether the cormorant was a pest or an ornamental occupant.

By the 1930s the Fisheries Department in Western Australia incorporated the 1908 argument that removing cormorants may lead to a diminution rather than an improvement in fish stocks.[73] They also began to explain the ecology to complainants – that some fish leave their ova in the rushes where they are eaten by crustacea which form the diet of cormorants. More informed correspondents showed the extent to which these ecological studies were known. One wrote that 'Clearly it is not the shags but the methods of the white man that have so badly deteriorated the fishing ... to save our fisheries it is necessary to leave the shag alone. ... They eat the destroyers of the marketable fish spawn'.[74] Thus, Serventy's study in Western Australia was based on established methods, and had an informed national constituency to greet it. It had an equally established set of local prejudices against which to measure his scientific observations.

Serventy analysed the stomachs of 441 birds and concluded that the cormorant did not prey upon the commercially valuable estuarine fish. He attributes this to the fact that most edible and sporting fish are too agile to be caught by the cormorant. He noted that interactions between the fish and birds could operate either as competition for the fish food supply, or as a check on their predators. He discussed briefly that, while cormorants ate some species of fish which were also food for marketable fish, he thought it unlikely that the cormorant was a limiting factor on the food of the commercial fish. In concluding that these relationships require much more study to be fully understood, he was cognisant of the complexity of the ecological relationships of fish-eating birds and their food source.

Serventy's results concurred with international studies of the fish-eating habits of cormorants. These also concluded that popular perceptions that cormorants compete with fishermen for edible species tend to be without foundation.[75] Of particular note are results of studies in England which were decisive in shifting public and commercial attitudes towards the fish-eating habits of the birds.[76] However, Serventy's paper did not have the desired effect on public policy in Western Australia, and the strength of his conclusions was not enough to counter the depth of local prejudice against the fish-eating birds.

CONSERVATION

That new fauna protection legislation was needed in Western Australia was acknowledged at the Australian and New Zealand Association for the Advancement of Science conference held in Perth in 1926. Against the post 1945 backdrop of an increasing population, extensive clearing for agriculture, and recognition of the need for industrial development, there was concomitant recognition by some individuals of the need for some kind of environmental protection. Specialist scientific advice about the conservation of native game, and the introduction of game from outside the State was eventually provided to government by the Fauna Advisory Committee.[77] Amongst its more routine duties of assessing requests for permits to shoot native fauna, one task of this Committee was to frame new fauna protection legislation.

Much work in shaping the new fauna protection legislation was undertaken by the ornithologist, and good friend of Serventy, Major Whittell. He wrote of the profound cultural shifts in ecological thinking that should be reflected in new legislation. Thus he argued that

> All legislation to date has stressed as the titles thereto indicate, the aspect of fauna as 'game', a word which denotes something available for hunting and killing. Modern lines of thought discard the word game, preferring 'Fauna'. ... That legislation is necessary is obvious if we are to retain our native fauna in its natural habitat and the principle such legislation should apply is *Conservation* rather than *Game Protection*. ... The peculiar and interesting native fauna is an integral part of the Australian environment and should be conserved for its own sake.[78]

Scientific influence, in particular from the Fauna Advisory Committee, is clear in this legislation. The Fauna Protection Act 1950 ensured that all terrestrial vertebrate native fauna were protected unless otherwise declared vermin or scheduled to be unprotected. It contained provisions relating to habitat preservation first mooted in debate in the 1912 act.[79] Thus, this legislation reflected the shift evident in the naturalists' literature for some time – from species protection to habitat protection.

Advice given by Whittell and the Fauna Advisory Committee was evident in the debates surrounding this act. In introducing the Bill, the Minister for Fisheries stated that 'The basis of this measure is not to preserve wildlife to enable it to be shot or otherwise hunted, but for the value and interest it will have to the people of Western Australia.'[80] Likewise, another member said that 'In the past many species of birds and animals have been slaughtered indiscriminately because they were thought to be pests, but time and experience have shown that they were friends of man, in that they kept other pests down'.[81] While saying this, much of the debate revealed concern at the possible protection of species seen as a pest to farmers – grasshoppers and the emu in particular.

FIGURE 3. 'Over Heirrisson Island'. Perthfume, 1989.
Created by Michael Collins and Mark Calligan.
Reproduced with permission from Michael Collins, Black Splash, Western Australia.

Even with the decline in the fishing industry the cormorant remained the focus of prejudice for the river-based Yacht clubs.[82] However the birds' role in the removal of fish paled into insignificance in the eyes of the leisured yacht owners compared to the emphasis on the damage to their boats. In 1953 a meeting with the Minister for Fisheries enabled the yachtsmen to present their case. They stated that

> The damage to our marine craft is absolutely terrific. For instance it costs £30 to £150 to cover a boat, which lasts about three years. ... It is a terrific business on a Saturday afternoon to get on one's boat. It meant going at least an hour earlier to make it clean enough to take anyone on board.[83]

In response to these complaints the Minister noted to the meeting that 'I know it will get a strong abuse from birdlovers and various other societies, but we will just have to put up with that'.[84]

The Fauna Advisory Committee refused a related application by the Yacht Racing Association to shoot cormorants in the vicinity of the Club premises.[85] Serventy explained that the little pied cormorant, the species causing most of the fouling of the boats, was protected precisely because it is the sole producer of guano, and that with 'the shortage of super-phosphate, destruction is short-sighted'.[86] The Minister accepted the advice from his Advisory Committee that cormorants are 'valuable natural control of such commercially useless shoal fish as hardyheads. ... Any upsetting of the natural balance may have a serious permanent effect on the aquatic life of the Swan River'.[87] He suggested that the Yacht Clubs continue to experiment with measures to protect their craft from roosting birds.

This divergence of opinion resulted in a meeting between the yachtsmen, the Fauna Protection Advisory Committee and politicians, grandly entitled a 'Conference on cormorants'.[88] With the yachtsmen unwilling to believe his 1936 survey results, Serventy undertook another analysis of bird diets and like his published results concluded that 'none of the stomachs contained fishes of commercial value'.[89] With his scientific status at the meeting, Serventy introduced the idea of the cultural role of the cormorant in the Western Australian imagination. He expressed the opinion that a large section of the public sought protection for the cormorants 'on aesthetic grounds, and considered that they were a picturesque part of the attractions of the Swan River which could be a bare stretch of water without them'.[90] The outcome of this 'Conference' finally showed the primacy of science over prejudice. While it was acknowledged that cormorants cause inconvenience and expense to boat owners, the Minister considered that 'the views of all sections of the community had to be considered'.[91]

HABITAT

Disputes over the fish-eating birds fed popular prejudice against individual species and stimulated scientific and ecological studies, but their conclusions were not always respected. In response to requests for permits to shoot cormorants in 1941, Serventy wrote in a forthright manner that the

> cormorant is not an important predator. The danger of fisherman and fishermen's organisations focussing their attention on such factors as cormorants is that they may overlook the real causes making for diminution and hence neglect to take the requisite remedial measures in time. Such causes as like as not, are over-fishing.[92]

In pointing out potential threats to bird life beyond immediate prejudice, he may have been thinking another threat was the lack of scientific understanding of the ecology of fish-eating birds.

In 1903 Abjornsson showed contemporary understandings of cause and effect when he wrote that he 'visited the rookeries and destroyed eggs, nests and young shags. This method of destruction is proving effective'.[93] Serventy showed that relationships between the decline in birds and fish stocks on the river were much more complex than such anecdotal evidence suggested. In 1940 he wrote that the reduction in bird life is as likely to be related to 'changes which settlement has made in the bird's normal environment' as the targeted shooting or egg collecting from individual species.[94] As understandings of the relationships between species on the river developed, the focus of study shifted from the fish-eating habits of birds to the habitats of the fish. What emerged from these studies was that the most biologically productive parts of the Swan River were the shallows, and therefore the reduction in fish and birds from the river was likely to be related to the loss of these areas of the river.[95] However, as these ecological relationships were being investigated, a greater ideological threat to the River emerged – that of government-sponsored development.

CULTURAL ECOLOGY

Inland from where the street-lamps now stand, Jesse Hammond noted Aboriginal people in the 1860's spearing cobblers in the shallows between Barrack and William Street.[96] These fertile shallows were removed during reclamation projects which have continued at regular intervals since the middle of the nineteenth century.[97] The advantages of reclamation were seen to include the removal of mosquitoes and smells from rotting algae, a desire to have easier access to the water, and the creation of additional land. By the 1950's what was once seen as an important clean-up technique was to become an environmental contest. As knowledge of the role of the shallows of the river increased, so did concern for proposals for major reclamation works in the 1960's that were to engulf them.

Once a marine environment, the Swan River is now a seasonally fluctuating estuarine environment.[98] The salinity of the river in summer is similar to that of the ocean, whereas in winter the water can become practically fresh after a heavy downfall.[99] In winter the lowering of the water temperature and the freshwater plume overlying the salt water wedge resulting in deoxygenation have a profound influence on the fauna of the river.[100] Studies into the effects of this seasonal variation on the river show that the deeper portions of the estuary become untenable for animal life in winter.[101] As a consequence, it is understood that the biologically productive parts of the river are areas less than ten feet deep where the fauna is less affected by seasonal variation in the temperature and salinity of the water.[102] With this increasing ecological understanding of the river, Serventy wrote that it is 'becoming apparent that the reclamation of the shallows has greater deteriorative effect on the fauna than its occasional overexploitation by over-fishing, amateur or professional'.[103] He argued that the loss of the shallows reduced suitable feeding areas in the estuary and in part led to the reduction in bird life that so impressed early visitors. Thus, while the shallow areas were designated 'foul ground' and were thus the focus of reclamation, they were 'equally important feeding grounds for commercially valuable fish as well as waterfowl'.[104]

In the 1950s, when there was a growing understanding of the ecological value of the river shallows, the stage was being set for public conflict with 100 acres of shallows earmarked for reclamation for a freeway interchange near the newly opened Narrows Bridge. Successive Western Australian governments showed a preference to defer to political ideologies over scientific advice, as seen in the area of land clearance for agriculture.[105] While previous threats to the river ecology from fishermen and yachtsmen had been fairly benign and thus scientific advice had a window of attention from politicians, in the 1960s the threat was the Brand Government's development imperative.[106] While ecological knowledge of the river was harnessed by a coalition of naturalist and scientific groups in opposition to the proposed developments, the battle against private transport policies and the development of the river for roads could not be won on arguments about the river shallows being important faunal habitats. Even arguments about sustainable transport rang hollow against Brand's populist rhetoric. He reported the progress of reclaiming shallows for

> beautifying the Swan and Canning Rivers, and making them more accessible to the people of Perth. ... New beaches have been created, unsightly tidal flats have been filled to provide clean access to the water, and a long term programme to turn swampy marshlands into useful foreshore is well advanced.[107]

On the heels of the freeway reclamation came a 1965 proposal to fill in some areas of shallows around the western suburb of Nedlands – from Pelican Point to the Nedlands Jetty. This proposal hit the heartland and homeland of many of those active in the protests and raised (yet unrealised) fears that this would lead to another freeway across the river. It was proposed to fill in shallows close to the bird habitat on Pelican Point where prior work filled in some of the marshes in 1936. This area was noted and named in 1827 and was the site of Serventy's bird observations, as he lived very close by.[108]

The Naturalists Club argued these shallow areas of the river were critical to the life in the river, and that the flats proposed for reclamation between Pelican Point and Nedlands Jetty were known feeding grounds for commercial species of fish.[109] As Serventy explained clearly on behalf of the Club 'The flats are important *feeding* grounds for the birds which *roost* at Pelican Point bird sanctuary. It seems pointless to leave birds a roosting place but not a feeding place'.[110] However, once again, the battle against reclamation of river shallows was lost. While the multiple long-term effects of this reclamation have yet to be fully studied, recent bird counts at the sanctuary show that overall, the bird life has returned to the area at levels higher than noted by Serventy in the area in 1936.[111] There are several likely reasons for this. Serventy undertook his survey during a time of widespread river reclamation which led to the local loss of the samphire marshes on Pelican Point, and thus a likely low point in bird numbers.[112] The more recent closure of the Point to public access in 1976, a nearby jetty which altered the water flow on one side of the point causing dune stabilisation, and the changes in vegetation over time are considered to have assisted in the increase in bird life.

Since the 1960s, the effects of foreshore development on bird life have faded from public consciousness. Contemporary debates relating to the Swan River concentrate on conflicting uses, for example the appropriateness of jet-skis, and the speed of river craft.[113] The Gallop Government has publicly recognised the need to protect the river landscape – including natural elements and the built form – so as to 'sustain the environmental, cultural, economic and social values' of the river.[114] Political concern for the biological diversity of the river rests with electoral promises to return the symbolic black swan to its former habitat.[115]

The fish-eating birds recede both from view on the river, and from public debate from the 1960's as pressing ideologies of development over-rode emerging ecological understanding, while community based management of the Swan River has tried to address conflicting concerns.[116] Thus, the appearance of the street-lamps as some kind of memorial is all the more apposite. Situated on land reclaimed from what was once biologically rich shallows that formed their predecessors' feeding grounds, they stand as mute and immobile monuments to a range of once dynamic ecological, political and cultural contexts. As an integral part of a new foreshore development, their stark poles and metaphoric design represent a set of displacements. They are reminders of the emergence of development ideology over science, and situated on a sterile, reclaimed environment they rest as a reference to a rich, fertile and diverse biotic past. In using art as a substitute for a natural environment, they serve to aestheticise the memory of a site that was once decorated by fish-eating birds.

NOTES

[1] First two lines of an anonymous rhyme. Work on this paper was funded as part of an Australian Research Council Linkage Grant with the National Trust of Australia (W.A.).

[2] 'Swan lighting concept' passed by City of Perth 9.6.98. Email from Roger Blackburn, Senior Urban Designer, City of Perth 9.4.2002.

[3] Malcolm Chase and Christopher Shaw, 'The dimensions of nostalgia', in *The Imagined Past: History and Nostalgia*, ed. C. Shaw and M. Chase (Manchester: Manchester University Press, 1989), 1–17.

[4] See for example A.B. Webb. c1922. *Shags* [colour woodcut], reproduced in Roderick Anderson, *Early Western Australian Art from the Robert Holmes à Court Collection* (Perth, W.A.: Heytesbury Holdings, 1983).

[5] Many of the key photographs and artworks showing views from the Park over the City are reproduced in George Seddon and David Ravine, *A City and its Setting: Images of Perth, Western Australia* (Fremantle, W.A.: Fremantle Arts Centre Press, 1986).

[6] Dominic Louis Serventy, 'The Swan River – a history of natural history discovery' (undated), Dominic Serventy papers, Battye Library 4893A/272.

[7] Commonwealth Scientific and Industrial Organisation.

[8] Quentin Beresford, 'Developmentalism and its environmental legacy: the Western Australian wheatbelt, 1900–1990's', *Australian Journal of Politics and History* 47(3) (2001): 403–14. For a slightly later example of an in-depth case study of the rise in ecological consciousness in Victoria, see Libby Robin, *Defending the Little Desert: The Rise of Ecological Consciousness in Australia* (Carlton, Vic: Melbourne University Press, 1998).

[9] For discussions of development ideology in Western Australia see Lenore Layman, 'Developmental ideology in Western Australia, 1933–1965', *Historical Studies* 40 (1982): 234–60.

[10] Tom Griffiths, *Hunters and Collectors: The Antiquarian Imagination in Australia* (Cambridge: Cambridge University Press, 1996).

[11] In 1696, Vlamingh took several Black Swans, which were entirely different to those seen in Europe, alive to Batavia. Details of them were published by the Royal Society of London in *Philosophical Transactions*, 1698.

[12] M. Blakers, S.J.J.F. Davies and P.N. Reilly, *The Atlas of Australian Birds* (Melbourne: Royal Australian Ornithological Union, 1984).

[13] Serventy, 'The Swan River – a history of natural history discovery'.

[14] W.B. Alexander, 'History of zoology in Western Australia. Part III 1829–1840', *Journal and Proceedings of the Royal Society of Western Australia* 3 (1917): 39–40.

[15] Tim Bonyhady and Tom Griffiths, *Words for Country: Landscape and Language in Australia* (Sydney, N.S.W.: University of New South Wales, 2002).

[16] For an ethnographic study of the Swan River, and resource competition between Aboriginal people and Europeans see Paul Weaver, 'An ethnohistorical study of the Swan-Canning fishery in Western Australia: 1697-1837' (BA(Hons) diss., Edith Cowan University, 1991) and Sylvia Hallam, 'Aboriginal resource usage along the Swan River', in *The Swan River Estuary Ecology and Management: Proceedings of a Symposium on the Swan–Canning Estuarine System, Western Australia, 1986*, ed. J. John (Curtin University Environmental Studies Group report no. 1. 1987): 21–33.

[17] In Western Australia the earliest regulation relating to fauna preservation was the 1853 Kangaroo Ordinance. For a discussion as to the experience in New South Wales, see Tim Bonyhady, *The Colonial Earth* (Melbourne: The Meigunyah Press, 2002).

[18] Lieutenant H.W. Breton quoted in Alexander, 'History of zoology in Western Australia. Part III 1829–1840', 38.

[19] *Perth Gazette and West Australian Journal*, 23.11.1833

[20] Western Australia. *Parliamentary Debates* 1892, 194

[21] Spencer Roberts, 'The preservation of our birds', *Emu* 30 (1930), 196.

[22] Preamble to the *Preservation of Game Act*, 38 Vict no, 4.

[23] With the emerging knowledge that recognisable breeding cycles were different across Australia, the 1878 amendment to the *Preservation of Game Act* acknowledged the impossibility of creating a single closed season for native game across the State. For a discussion of attitudes to native fauna in other Australian colonies, see Bonyhady, *The Colonial Earth*.

[24] Western Australia. *Game Act* 55 Vict no. 36.

[25] Western Australia. *Parliamentary Debates* 1891, 83.

[26] The Emu was preserved under the *Game Act* 28.9.1894 thus beginning a history of its status as native fauna but its place in the cultural psyche as a pest. In the late 1940s its status was equally declared vermin and protected species.

[27] Western Australia. *Parliamentary Debates* 1891/2, 84.

[28] *Vermin Act*, no. 39 of 1919, *Fisheries Act*, no. 47 of 1899, *Fisheries Act*, no. 18 of 1905.

[29] Western Australia. Fisheries Department. *Report on the Fishing Industry for the Year ... 1900–1915*.

[30] Western Australia. *Parliamentary Debates*, 1899, 2382.

[31] Western Australia. *Parliamentary Debates*, 1899, 2376.

[32] Western Australia. *Parliamentary Debates*, 1899, 2377.

[33] Based on figures compiled in R.C.J. Lenanton, 'The commercial fisheries of temperate Western Australian estuaries: early settlement to 1995', *Western Australian Fisheries Department Report* 62 (1984): 44.

[34] Western Australia. *Government Gazette* 19.1.1898.

[35] Western Australia. *Government gazette* 10.11.1899.

[36] Western Australia. Fisheries Department, *Report on the Fishing Industry for the Year 1900 by the Chief Inspector of Fisheries* (Votes and proceedings of the Legislative Council Paper 5/1901).

[37] Western Australia. Fisheries Department, *Report on the Fishing industry for the Year 1900 by the Chief Inspector of Fisheries*. The 1913–14 year was the only period in which records survive of the total bounty paid on the heads of shags (albeit excluding the Swan River). The total payment of £42.7/6 represented rewards on about 2000 heads. Fisheries Protection Act. Cormorants and Black Shags – General file, 1914–1962, Fisheries Dept file 170/23, State Records Office of Western Australia (hereafter SROWA) Acc 477.

[38] Western Australia. *Government gazette* 23.3.1906. The system of rewards ceased in 1914 due to financial constraints.

[39] Western Australia. Fisheries Department, *Report to the Chief Inspector of Fisheries 1906*, (Votes and proceedings of the Legislative Council Paper 4/1907).

[40] Libby Robin, *The flight of the Emu. A hundred years of Australian ornithology, 1901–2001* (Melbourne: Melbourne University Press, 2001), 14.

[41] Australian Association for the Advancement of Science, *Report on the protection of native fauna*, Colonial Secretary's Office file 1609/94, SROWA Cons 652.

[42] W.B. Alexander was appointed as zoologist at the Western Australian Museum in 1912, and in 1913 Dakin was appointed as the first professor of biology at University of Western Australia.

[43] A.H.E. Mattingley, 'Cormorants in relation to fishes', *Emu* 8 (1908): 18–23.

[44] Select Committee of the Legislative Council of Western Australia, *Report of the Select Committee of the Legislative Council on the Game Bill 1911* (Votes and proceedings of the Legislative Council Paper A4/1911).

[45] J.G. Hay was involved in the Gould League in Western Australia after its foundation in 1939.

[46] Select Committee of the Legislative Council of Western Australia, *Report of the Select Committee of the Legislative Council on the Game Bill 1911*.

[47] Western Australia. *Game Act*, no. 72 of 1912.

[48] Western Australia. *Parliamentary debates*, 1911, 310.

[49] J.R. Kinghorn, 'Bird protection in Australia', *Emu* 29 (1929): 263–71.

[50] The black swan appeared on the schedule of protected species in 1912, the pelican in 1914, and all species of cormorant in 1917.

[51] Western Australia. *Fauna Protection Act*, no. 77 of 1950.

[52] Lenanton, 'The commercial fisheries of temperate Western Australian estuaries: early settlement to 1995', 9.

[53] R.C.J. Lenanton, 'Fish and exploited crustaceans of the Swan-Canning estuary', *Western Australian Department of Fisheries and Wildlife Report* 35 (1978), 14.

[54] Letter from Anderson's Saddlery Works, *West Australian* 12.6.1919.

[55] Chief Inspector of Fisheries 21.6.1919. Fisheries Protection Act. Cormorants and Black Shags – General file, 1914–1962.

[56] See for example, *West Australian* 21.5.1924, *Sunday Times* 3.5.1925, *Sunday Times* 26.6.1927.

[57] *Sunday Times* 26.6.1927.

[58] Mattingley, 'Cormorants in relation to fishes', S.A. White, 'An investigation con-

cerning the food of cormorants', *Emu* 16 (1916): 77–80, S.A. White, 'Further notes on cormorants, other foods, temperatures etc', *Emu* 17 (1918): 214–15.

[59] Chief Inspector of Fisheries 21.6.1919. Fisheries Protection Act. Cormorants and Black Shags, 1914–1962.

[60] Paper read by E.J. Prout at the Naturalists Club. *West Australian* 6.4.1937.

[61] *West Australian* 18.6.1936.

[62] *West Australian* 22.8.1928.

[63] Chief Harbour Master to Chief Inspector of Fisheries 5.2.1929. Fisheries Protection Act. Cormorants and Black Shags, 1914–1962.

[64] For example A.H.E. Mattingley, 'Cormorants in relation to fisheries', *Condor* 29 (1927): 187–7 was quoted in the *West Australian* 9.1.1928.

[65] *Sunday Times* 8.5.1932.

[66] This group was active between 1935 and 1946. Fish and Game Propagation Acclimatisation and Protection Society, 1934–1946, Fisheries Department file 47/35, SROWA Acc 477.

[67] Minutes 11.6.1936, Fish and Game Propagation Acclimatisation and Protection Society, 1934–1946.

[68] Ralph W. Schreiber and Roger B. Clapp, 'Pelicaniform feeding ecology', in *Seabirds: Feeding Ecology and Role in Marine Ecosystems*, ed. J.P. Croxall (Cambridge: Cambridge University Press, 1987): 173–88.

[69] Dominic Serventy, 'The feeding habits of cormorants in South-Western Australia', *Emu* 38 (1938): 293–316.

[70] This work is mentioned in *Daily News* 13.7.1932. Serventy also notes this work though was unable to find evidence of this study.

[71] White, 'An investigation concerning the food of cormorants', White, 'Further notes on cormorants, other foods, temperatures etc', W.T. Forster, 'Cormorants: are they pests or otherwise?', *Emu* 18 (1918): 103–5.

[72] C.H. Hartley and J. Fisher, 'Marine food of birds in an inland fjord region in West Spitzbergen, Part II', *Journal of Animal Ecology* 5 (1936): 370–89, G.A. Steven, 'The food consumed by shags and cormorants around the shores of Cornwall (England)', *Journal of the Marine Biology Association* XIX (1933): 277–92, A. Wetmore, 'The amount of food consumed by Cormorants', *Condor* 28 (1927): 273–4.

[73] Chief Inspector of Fisheries 27.5.1932, Fisheries Protection Act. Cormorants and Black Shags, 1914–1962.

[74] Mr Clarke, Kulin to Chief Inspector of Fisheries 6.5.1936, Fisheries Protection Act. Cormorants and Black Shags, 1914–1962. The Department followed up on his information and collected data relating to cormorants in South Australia.

[75] Schreiber and Clapp, 'Pelicaniform feeding ecology', 178.

[76] Steven, 'The food consumed by shags and cormorants around the shores of Cornwall (England)'.

[77] The Committee, initiated in 1944, comprised of A.J. Fraser (Chief Inspector of Fisheries), L. Glauert (Director of the W.A. Museum), D.L. Serventy (CSIRO), and H.M. Whittell (Ornithologist).

[78] Hubert Massey Whittell, Western Australia. Fauna Advisory Committee, (1944–1950), H.M. Whittell papers, Battye Library 559A/3.

[79] Western Australia. *Parliamentary Debates* 1912, 1009.
[80] Western Australia. *Parliamentary Debates* 1950, 796.
[81] Western Australia. *Parliamentary Debates* 1950, 939.
[82] In 1953 there were 18 professional fisherman removing total of 66885lbs of fish at an average of 3715lbs per boat. At the 1948 conference of Western Australian Fisheries Inspectors, it was noted that the 'fishing industry in the Swan River is practically finished. Almost 10 years ago there were about 25 men operating full-time'.
[83] 1.7.1953, Fisheries Protection Act. Cormorants and Black Shags, 1914–1962.
[84] 1.7.1953, Fisheries Protection Act. Cormorants and Black Shags, 1914–1962.
[85] 20.6.1953, Fisheries Protection Act. Cormorants and Black Shags, 1914–1962.
[86] 20.6.1953, Fisheries Protection Act. Cormorants and Black Shags, 1914–1962.
[87] 31.7.1953, Fisheries Protection Act. Cormorants and Black Shags, 1914–1962.
[88] 13.8.1953, Fisheries Protection Act. Cormorants and Black Shags, 1914–1962.
[89] Western Australia. Fisheries Department. Conference of Fisheries Inspectors, *Report* (Perth, W.A. Government Print, 1943–1953). 1953 report, 24.
[90] 13.8.1953, Fisheries Protection Act. Cormorants and Black Shags, 1914–1962.
[91] 13.8.1953, Fisheries Protection Act. Cormorants and Black Shags, 1914–1962. On file on top of this debate is a pamphlet for recipes for the shag published by the Piscatorial Club of South Australia
[92] Serventy to Chief Inspector of Fisheries 14.8.1941, Fisheries Protection Act. Cormorants and Black Shags, 1914–1962.
[93] Western Australia. Fisheries Department. *Report to the Chief Inspector of Fisheries 1903* (Votes and proceedings of the Legislative Council Paper 5/1905).
[94] Dominic Serventy, 'Reflections on bird protection – the neglect of habitat protection', *Emu* 40 (1940): 153–8.
[95] Western Australia. Swan River Reference Committee, *Report by Sub-Committee on Pollution of Swan River* (Perth, W.A.: Government Print, 1955).
[96] Jesse Hammond quoted in Hallam, 'Aboriginal resource usage along the Swan River'.
[97] Seddon and Ravine. *A City and its Setting: Images of Perth, Western Australia*, 121.
[98] D.M. Churchill, 'Late quaternary eustatic changes in the Swan River district', *Journal and Proceedings of the Royal Society of Western Australia* 42 (2) (1959): 53–55.
[99] J.M. Thomson, 'New crustaceae from the Swan River estuary', *Journal and proceedings of the Royal Society of Western Australia* 30 (1946): 35–53.
[100] Dominic Serventy, 'The fauna of the Swan River estuary', in Western Australia. Swan River Reference Committee, *Report by Sub-Committee on pollution of Swan River* (Perth, W.A.: Government Print, 1955): 70–77.
[101] Western Australia. Swan River Reference Committee, *Report by Sub-Committee on pollution of Swan River*.
[102] Dominic Louis Serventy, 'Reclamation of the Swan River', (undated), Dominic Serventy papers, Battye Library 4893/115.
[103] Serventy, 'The Swan River – a history of natural history discovery'.
[104] Serventy, 'Reclamation of the Swan River'.
[105] For example see Beresford, 'Developmentalism and its environmental legacy: the Western Australian wheatbelt, 1900–1990', and for a broad discussion of development

ideology see Layman, 'Development ideology in Western Australia, 1933–1965'.

[106] David Brand was Liberal (Conservative) Premier of Western Australia between 2.4.1959 and 3.3.1971.

[107] Serventy, 'Reclamation of the Swan River'.

[108] Dominic Louis Serventy, 'Waders and other aquatic birds on the Swan River estuary, Western Australia', *Emu* 38 (1938): 18–29.

[109] Letter from WA Naturalists Club to Charles Court 2.11.1965, Serventy papers.

[110] Serventy, 'Reclamation of the Swan River'.

[111] Max Bailey and Kate Creed, 'Observations of bird species at Pelican Point, Perth, Western Australia', *Western Australian Naturalist* 17(8) (1989): 229–32.

[112] Dominic Louis Serventy, *The Birds of the Swan River District Western Australia* (Melbourne: Brown, Prior, Anderson, Pty. Ltd, 1948), 15.

[113] Environmental Resources Management Australia, *Review of Speed Limits on the Swan and Canning Rivers: Final Report* (Perth, W.A.: Department of Transport, 2000).

[114] Swan River Trust, *Introducing the Swan and Canning Rivers Precinct Planning Project* (Perth, W.A.: Swan River Trust, 2002). The Labour government of Geoffrey Gallop came to office on 16.2.2001.

[115] ATA Environmental, Bamford Consulting Ecologists and MP Rogers and Associates, *Bringing Back the Swans* (Perth, W.A.: Waters and Rivers Commission, 2000 report no. 63).

[116] Max Shean, 'The Swan River Management Authority and its functions', in *The Swan River Estuary Ecology and Management: Proceedings of a Symposium on the Swan-Canning Estuarine System, Western Australia, 1986*, ed. J. John (Curtin University Environmental Studies Group report no. 1. 1987): 314–17.

A Cultural History of Crocodiles in the Philippines: Towards a New Peace Pact?

Jan van der Ploeg, Merlijn van Weerd and Gerard A. Persoon

In March 2004, we conducted a crocodile survey along the coast of the Northern Sierra Madre Natural Park in Isabela Province, Northeast Luzon.[1] We counted crocodiles and interviewed people on human–crocodile conflicts. Hunters explained the importance of treating crocodiles with respect and farmers told anecdotes about enchanted crocodiles. We heard stories about spirits changing into vengeful crocodiles. Some people told us that they were afraid of crocodiles. Others mentioned that they had recently found a crocodile nest and had eaten the eggs. But none of the respondents expressed a fundamental objection to living with crocodiles. On our way back, waiting for the aeroplane, we had a conversation with a senior government official who reassured us that there were no more dangerous crocodiles in the protected area: Moro hunters and the military had killed and eaten them all to protect the people. Jokingly he added that if we were looking for crocodiles we had better go to the halls of Congress in Quezon City. We had heard this joke many times before but never in such contrast to the perceptions of hunters, farmers and fishermen as on that day in Palanan.

INTRODUCTION

Two crocodile species occur in the Philippines: the Indo-Pacific crocodile *Crocodylus porosus* and the Philippine crocodile *Crocodylus mindorensis*. The Indo-Pacific crocodile, or estuarine crocodile, is widely distributed throughout South-east Asia and Northern Australia. The species is threatened with extinction in the Philippines but, as viable Indo-Pacific crocodile populations still exist in Papua New Guinea and Australia, the species is not globally threatened.[2] In the Philippines, the Indo-Pacific crocodile was common on all major islands. At present, it is restricted to a few localities on Palawan, Mindanao and Northeast Luzon. Large individuals can pose a significant risk to humans, as the species can grow up to 6 m.[3]

The Philippine crocodile, in contrast, is a relatively small, palustrine crocodile species: the largest individual recorded in the wild was 2.7 m. This endemic species was widely distributed throughout the archipelago but is now restricted to a few upland localities in North Luzon and Mindanao.[4] The species is classified as critically endangered.⁵ It is difficult for laymen to distinguish a Philippine crocodile from an Indo-Pacific crocodile, especially in wild conditions.⁶

Commercial hunting to serve the international trade in crocodile skins decimated crocodile populations in the Philippines.⁷ *Crocodylus porosus* is a premium species for the crocodile leather industry and the species has been hunted intensively in the Philippines since the 1940s. As the Indo-Pacific crocodile became rare, hunters shifted their attention to the Philippine crocodile. The Convention on International Trade in Endangered Species of Wild Fauna and Flora (CITES) banned the international trade in *Crocodylus mindorensis* skins on 1 July 1975. Ten years later, on 1 August 1985, the Philippines' Indo-Pacific crocodile population was also placed on CITES Appendix 1.

Since 2004, both crocodile species have been officially protected under Philippine law (by virtue of the Wildlife Act: Republic Act 9147). However, in the socio-political context of the Philippines, environmental legislation is seldom enforced: crocodiles continue to be killed for food or fun and out of fear.⁸ The conversion and degradation of wetland habitat pose significant threats to crocodiles in the Philippines and might prevent a recovery of the species.⁹ The widespread use of dynamite, electricity and pesticides to maximise fish catches also poses a heavy toll on the remaining crocodile populations. As a result the Indo-Pacific crocodile and the Philippine crocodile have become rare in the wild: both species face a high risk of extinction in the Philippines in the near future.

In mainstream Filipino culture, crocodiles are seen as vermin and considered a severe threat to children and livestock.¹⁰ Crocodiles are stereotyped as ferocious monsters or bloodthirsty man-eaters and are associated with greed and deceit: corrupt government officials, selfish athletes, landlords and moneylenders are often called *buwaya*, Filipino for crocodile. In the media, politicians are often portrayed as crocodiles (Figure 1).

It is argued that these negative attitudes of the Filipino public form a major obstacle to *in-situ* crocodile conservation. Since the 1980s, government policy has been based on the idea that in order to secure the survival of crocodiles in the Philippines, animals have to be removed from the wild and bred in captivity:

> Filipinos have a strong dislike for the reptiles, especially crocodiles, due to the reputation of the estuarine crocodile as a man-eater, causing fear for all crocodiles. This has pushed the [Philippine crocodile] to the verge of extinction ... There is little future for Philippine crocodiles in the existing (and proposed) wildlife sanctuaries, and ... captive breeding is the only hope for survival for the species until public sentiment and awareness permit effective protection.¹¹

In this paper we contest this view. Attitudes towards crocodiles are indefinitely more complex and diverse than policy-makers, conservationists and the media suggest.

In earlier times crocodiles were feared *and* revered: specific rules regulated the relationship with crocodiles and enabled people to share the landscape with

FIGURE 1. In Philippine media crocodiles are associated with corruption and nepotism. Left: A congressman portrayed as a hungry crocodile (Philippine Star, 14 December 2006). Right: President Gloria Macapagal-Arroyo can't get rid of her corrupt image (Philippine Star, 13 December 2007)

potentially dangerous carnivores. The Spanish friars recorded these primordial sentiments towards crocodiles in detail. Moreover such beliefs did not disappear: in the uplands of the Philippines indigenous communities still associate crocodiles with ancestors, fertility and mystic power. This veneration is expressed in material art, architecture, music and oral tradition. More importantly, it has played a role in the survival of the crocodiles in the Philippines. On Luzon the Kalinga sing ballads about the relationship between chiefs and crocodiles.[12] On Palawan the Tagbanwa believe their ancestors made a blood pact with the crocodiles to prevent attacks. And on Mindanao the T'boli weave cloth with delicate crocodile motifs[13] and the Magindanaon believe they descend from crocodiles.[14] Not surprisingly these are also areas where crocodiles still survive in the wild.

In this paper we look through W.H. Scott's proverbial 'cracks in the parchment curtain' in order to get a better understanding of the relations between crocodiles and people in the pre-colonial Philippines and the changes that occurred in this relationship over time.[15] We present a literature overview of historical sources on perceptions of crocodiles in the Philippines, complemented with information from the ethnographic literature. For contemporary attitudes towards crocodiles we mainly rely on fieldwork in the northern Sierra Madre between 2001 and 2008. We adopt a historical and comparative perspective, explicitly showing the cultural continuity of perceptions of crocodiles in both space and time.

A Cultural History of Crocodiles

The Kalinga in the northern Sierra Madre, for example, make rice cakes in the form of a crocodile during healing ceremonies. Gatmaytan (2004) and Maceda (1984) report similar healing rituals among the Manobo and the Magindanaon, respectively. This seems remarkably akin to the offerings of rice cakes in the form of crocodiles (*binuwaya*) in pre-colonial Visayas, reported by W.H. Scott (1994). This transcends academic curiosity: the Kalinga ancestral lands in the northern Sierra Madre form the last stronghold for the Philippine crocodile in the wild. Here, the species survived as an unintended result of traditional values, beliefs and practices.

Our aim in this paper is to document the views, feelings and imaginings of the inhabitants of the Philippine Islands toward crocodiles through time and to counter the simplistic assumption that culture hinders crocodile conservation.[16] Filipino culture in all its diversity and flux is not a barrier for coexistence with crocodiles. On the contrary, an assessment of indigenous cosmology and contemporary marginalised perceptions of crocodiles might offer clues for conserving crocodiles in the Philippines in the wild in the twenty-first century.

THE PRE-COLONIAL HERITAGE

A reconstruction of primordial sentiments towards crocodiles in the Philippines inevitably has to cope with the bias of the Spanish *conquistadores* and friars. Obviously, notes on the biology of the Philippine Islands and the cosmology of the *indios*, as the native Filipinos were called, were primarily made for effective exploitation and conversion. But despite the racism and religious dogma, the Spanish archives provide detailed information about everyday life in the archipelago and surprisingly often mention crocodiles.[17]

One of the first and best-known written accounts of crocodiles in the Philippines was made by Antonio de Morga (1609: 93–94) a high-ranking colonial officer in Manila:

> There are … a great number of crocodiles [in the rivers and creeks], which are very bloodthirsty and cruel. They quite commonly pull from their *bancas* the natives who go in those boats, and cause many injuries among the horned cattle and the horses of the stock-farms, when they go to drink. And although the people fish for them often and kill them, they are never diminished in number. For that reason, the natives set closely-rated divisions and enclosures in the rivers and creeks of their settlements, where they bathe, secure from those monsters, which they fear so greatly that they venerate and adore them, as if they were beings superior to themselves. All their oaths and execrations, and those which are of any weight with them (even among the Christians) are, thus expressed: 'So may the crocodile kill him!' They call the crocodile *buhaya* in their language. It has happened when someone has sworn falsely, or when he has broken his word, that then, some accident has occurred to him with the crocodile, which God, whom

he offends, has so permitted for the sake of the authority and purity of the truth, and the promise of it.

As the Spanish settled in the coastal lowlands or along major river systems, in de Morga's case Laguna de Bay and the estuary of Pasig River, the historical accounts most likely refer to the Indo-Pacific crocodile. Throughout the Philippine archipelago, and indeed most of the Malay world, the Indo-Pacific crocodile was called *buwaya*.[18] In most parts of the Philippines, people distinguished between the two crocodile species (Table 1). This is reflected in seventeenth-century Spanish vocabularies where a distinction was often made between *cocodrilo* and *caimán*; a nuance that was later lost in English dictionaries.[19] But local taxonomy was indefinitely more complex than this: it included ancestor-crocodiles, spirit-crocodiles and witch-crocodiles.

Taxonomy and cosmology

De Morga's words exemplify the paradoxical relationship between crocodiles and men in pre-colonial Philippines. On the one hand, crocodiles posed a significant danger to people and livestock. Man-eating crocodiles are a recurrent theme in the Spanish archives. The historiographer of Aragon, Bartolomé Leonardo de Argensola (1708: 235), for example, wrote:

> In the rivers and lakes are many monstrous caimans, or crocodiles; these kill the Indians very easily, and especially the children, who happen unadvisedly to come where they are, as well as the cattle when they go to drink. It often happens that they lay hold of their snouts, or noses, and draw them under water, where they are drowned, without being able to defend themselves.

On the other hand, crocodiles were venerated. The best illustration of this fact comes from the book *Labor Evangelica* written in 1663 by Francisco Colin:

> [The Tagalogs] held the crocodile in the greatest veneration; and, when they made any statement about it, when they saw it in the water cried out, in all subjection, '*Nono*', signifying Grandfather. They asked it pleasantly and tenderly not to harm them; and for that purpose offered it a portion what they carried in their boats, by throwing it into the water.

People prayed and made offerings to edifices of crocodiles.[20] The *buwaya* was a benign symbol of physical strength, sexuality, fierceness and power. In legends and myths, heroes and chiefs were depicted as crocodiles or thought to have personal bonds with crocodiles.[21] Warrior chiefs traced their ancestry to crocodiles and wore necklaces made of crocodile teeth, *boaia*, as symbols of their power. Crocodile teeth were also widely used as omens and as amulets to protect the bearer from evil spirits and sickness.[22] Crocodile motifs were woven into funeral cloths and carved into coffins to protect the deceased from evil spirits.[23] Throughout insular Southeast Asia crocodiles were associated with water

A Cultural History of Crocodiles

and rain and thus with agricultural fertility and rice culture.[24] In the pre-colonial Philippines crocodiles were symbols of danger as well as protection, a benevolent and malevolent power at once.[25] The functional interpretation of Antonio de Morga that crocodiles were worshipped because of the danger they posed – 'monsters, which they fear so greatly that they venerate and adore them' – does not, however, do justice to the complexity of pre-colonial Philippine cosmology.

The *indios* in fact worshipped a variety of ancestor spirits, nature gods and mythical creatures, which could take the form of a crocodile. First, it was thought that the ancestors could reincarnate in crocodile form: 'They believe that after a certain cycle of years, the souls of their forefathers were turned into crocodiles.'[26] These benevolent ancestor spirits, called *anito*, were venerated as personal guardians and secured good harvests. But they could also cause death and destruction if not given due respect.[27] Second, crocodiles could be the embodiment of nature-gods, generally called *diwata*. Negrito peoples in the Philippines, for example, believed that a large crocodile called *Lahua* inhabited the earth and caused earthquakes.[28] In several origin myths from the Philippines the creator-god takes the form of a crocodile.[29] These crocodile-gods were seen as the guardians of the underworld: they were invoked to secure a safe passage for the dead to the next life.[30] Miguel de Loarca (1582: 129), an influential member of the Catholic clergy in Manila, wrote:

> It is said that the souls of those who [are] eaten by crocodiles ... which is considered a very honourable death, go to heaven by way of the arch which is formed when it rains, and become gods. The souls of the drowned remain in the sea forever.

These crocodile-gods lived in a parallel world, often literally interpreted as an underwater village. Third, people believed in malevolent spirits and witches, most often called *aswang*, which could take the form of a crocodile.[31] Father Antonio Mozo (1673: 16), for example related that:

> [I]n two islands, called Zebu and Panay ... dwell a people who are called the Mundos; they have the same barbarian characteristics of fierceness and barbarism ... but they have besides this a peculiarity which renders them intractable, for they have among them some fearful wizards. ... Instructed and misled by the demon, those barbarians do fearful things, especially to revenge themselves, to the continual terror of those about them. The natives say that these wizards, change into crocodiles, follow them when in their canoes, and do not stop until they seize some person whom they hate; also that they change themselves into other animals, in order to commit other wicked acts – as likewise that, availing themselves of various enchantments, they commit horrible murders, with a thousand other diabolic acts.

These *aswang* ate people and disinterred corpses. But simple precautions, such as making noise or avoiding being alone, could be taken against these creatures.[32]

TABLE 1. Local terminology for crocodiles in the Philippines

Area	Language	C. porosus	C. mindorensis	Reference
North Luzon	Ilocano (Iloko)	buaya	Bokkarut	Vanoverbergh 1928: 11
Cagayan Valley	Itawis	?	lamag	pers. obs.
	Ibanag	binuaya/buaya/bubuaya	bukarut/lamag	pers. obs.
	Yogad	bwaya	bukarot/lamág	pers. obs.
	Gaddang	-	lamig	Reid 1971: 65
	Isneg	buwaya	bokarót	Vanoverbergh 1972
	Bugkalot (Ilongot)	-	buwaya	Aquino 2004: 290
Sierra Madre	Agta (Dupaninan)	?	bukahot/lamag	Headland 2007 pers. comm.
	Kasiguranin	buwaya	?	
	Dumagat	buya	?	
	Umirey	mangato (?)	?	
	Kalinga	-	lamag	pers. obs.
Cordillera	Bontoc	-	buaya/bo'waya	Reid 1971: 65
Zambales	Sambal	buaya	?	Reid 1971: 65
Central Luzon	Kapampangan	dapo	?	Forman 1971
South Luzon	Tagalog	mamuaya/manbuaya/namumuaya	tigbin	de San Antonio 1624
Bikol	Bikol	bu'aya	barangitaw	de Lisboa 1865
Masbate	Masbatenyo	buwaya/bwaya	?	Wolfenden 2001
Mindoro	Mangyan	buaya	barangitaw/burrangás/burranggaris	Barbian 1977
Central Visayas	Sebuano	boàya/balanghítao/balangĭta	?	de la Encarnacion 1885
East Visayas	Waray (Samar-Leyte)	binuaya	barangitáw*	Tramp 1995
Surigao	Mamanwa	buaja/bowaza	?	Reid 1971: 65
Agusan	Manobo (Agusan)	búaya/bu'ada	ngusó (?)	Elkins 1968
Bukidnon	Binukid (Manobo)	bu'qaya/vuaya	?	Polenda 1989: 275
Davao del Norte	Mandaya (Mansaka)	bowaya	sapding	Svelmoe & Svelmoe 1990
Lanao	Maranao	boaia/lotoi	balangitao/dagoroqan	McKaughan & Macaraya 1967
Ligauasan	Maguindanao (Moro)	buhaya/bohaya	?	Juanmartí 1892
Cotabato	T'boli	bwenghel	?	Paterno et al. 2001
Zamboanga	Subanon	buaya	?	Reid 1971: 65
Sulu	Tausug	buaya/buqayah	?	Reid 1971: 65
Basilan	Yakan	buwaye	-	Behrens 2002
Calamian Islands	Kalamianon	bukayaq	?	Reid 1971: 65
North Palawan	Batak	buaya	bungut	Eder 2006 pers. comm.
South Palawan†	Tagbanwa	buaya	bungot	Reid 1971: 65

* One is tempted to conclude that *barangitaw* is a common name for the Philippine crocodile in the Visayas. Marcos de Lisboa, for example, defined *barangitaw* in his *Vocabulario de la lengue Bicol* (1865) as a 'type of crocodile found in fast flowing rivers'. However, Juan Felipe de la Encarnacion (1885) defines the Cebuano word *balanghítao* as an '*especie de caiman muy maligno*': a very malicious caiman species. And here one would conclude that *balanghítao* refers to the Indo-Pacific crocodile. To make matters more complicated, the Cebuano word

A Cultural History of Crocodiles

It is important to note that not all crocodiles were seen as the personification of the ancestors, gods or witches. Enchanted crocodiles could be distinguished from normal crocodiles by having extraordinary traits, such as being very large, docile, strangely coloured, crippled or having a necklace or four toes instead of five.[33] The Franciscan priest Juan Francisco de San Antonio (1738: 154) wrote:

> It is definite that crocodiles do not have a tongue. However, I am told that a crocodile who had swallowed a man whole and was later followed and killed, the man being found complete in its stomach, had a large black tongue. It is not known whether this is because it was of a special type ... It was the strangest one seen by my informant during his whole life. This happened in 1736 in the Macabebe River in Pampanga. The man who was thus swallowed was Captain Culango who owned a tavern in the village called Manlauay, well known by the natives.[34]

Conversely, not all spirits were crocodiles. The *anito*, *diwata* and *aswang* could manifest themselves in many possible ways, not necessarily in the form of a potentially dangerous animal. They could also take the form of harmless animals such as nightjars, owls, or kingfishers, which were feared as much as crocodiles.[35]

The peace pact

A drawing by the Tagalog artist Francisco Suárez provides a rare glimpse of daily life in the early eighteenth century (Figure 2). Crocodiles were common throughout the Philippine archipelago and people often lived in close proximity to them. The Spanish colonisers were puzzled by the apparently indifferent attitude of the *indios* towards crocodiles. This can be best illustrated by a quote of the Augustinian friar Casimiro Diaz (1890: 212–213) who lived in Pampanga in 1717:

> In another way they exhibit other rash actions, by which it is seen that their rashness is rather the daughter of ignorance and barbarity than of valour ... The same thing happens in the rivers where there are crocodiles, although they see them swimming about; for they say the same as do the Moros (i.e. Mahometans), that if it is from on high it must happen, even though they avoid it ... The world is just so. If it is written on the forehead that one is to live, than he will live; but if not, then he will die here.

---

barang means 'witch'. Thus *balanghítao* could best be translated as a witch-crocodile. This shows the limitations of using ethnographic and linguistic sources for determining the historical distribution of the two crocodile species in the Philippines.

† The fact that two separate names are used for crocodiles in Batak and Tagbanwa suggests that two crocodile species occurred in Palawan. However, there are no records of Philippine crocodiles on Palawan (but see Schultze 1914).

FIGURE 2. Fragment from Murillo Velarde's *Carta hydrographica y chronographica de las Islas Filipinas* by F. Suárez (1734). Note the caption: '1. Caiman or crocodile of which the rivers of these isles are full'.

In some areas people built bamboo fences as precaution against man-eaters: the *patiwa* described by Antonio de Morga.[36] But in general people seemed to take not much notice of the danger posed by crocodiles and adopted no rigid safety measures.[37] During a visit to Leyte, the German ethnologist Fedor Jagor (1875: 269) described the almost submissive attitude of the natives:

> The principal employment of our hosts appeared to be fishing, which is so productive that the roughest apparatus is sufficient. There was not a single boat, but only loosely-bound rafts of bamboo, on which the fishers, sinking, as we ourselves did on our raft, half a foot deep, moved about amongst the crocodiles, which I never beheld in such number and of so large a size as in this lake. Some swam about on the surface with their backs projecting out of the water. It was striking to see the complete indifference with which even two little girls waded in the water in the face of these great monsters. Fortunately the latter appeared to be satisfied with their ample rations of fish.

Here, the prejudice of the Europeans obstructed a comprehensive analysis. A comparative South-east Asian perspective enables us to contextualise these

A Cultural History of Crocodiles

anecdotes and better understand the relationship between people and crocodiles in pre-Hispanic Philippine cultures.[38]

In Malay cosmology crocodiles never arbitrarily attacked people. On the contrary, crocodile attacks were seen as a selective punishment of the *anitos* that followed socially unacceptable behaviour. Man-eating crocodiles were seen as divine arbiters: '*alguazil* of the water'.[39] Crocodiles guarded the social order and avenged the transgression of taboos. Crocodile attacks were considered the victims' own mistake. In this perspective it was futile to be afraid of, or to take precautions against, crocodiles.

It was believed that crocodiles personally knew and were closely related to the local community.[40] People constructed personal relationships with crocodiles through reincarnation, descent, marriage, friendship or blood pacts. In the marshes of Mindanao the *datus* traced their ancestral lineage to mythical crocodiles.[41] In the Cordillera Mountain Range on Luzon the Kalinga called themselves *buwaya*.[42] And in the Visayan Islands it was believed that women could give birth to crocodiles. In 1668 the Jesuit Francisco Alcina wrote:

> One of [the] parishioners gave birth to a crocodile twin. She was the wife of Pakotolini of Tubig, who had been raised in a Jesuit house as a church boy, and the little creature was delivered together with a normal child. The parents moved away to get rid of it, but it not only followed them but regularly brought them a wild hog or deer, or large fish.[43]

These personal alliances have been extensively documented in the ethnographic literature from insular South-east Asia. The Dutch ethnologist George Wilken wrote that the Bugis believed that the deceased changed into crocodiles: they placed offerings in the water for those who had become crocodiles.[44] The Kanyah, Kenyah and Iban in Sarawak believed that they were related to crocodiles.[45] The Batak in Sumatra also thought they descended from crocodiles and therefore could not eat crocodile meat.[46] And in Nusa Tenggara people traced their origins to a powerful crocodile that had married a girl from the village.[47]

Consequently there were strict taboos on killing crocodiles or eating their meat. Doing so was also considered an unwise provocation: crocodiles were known to take revenge.[48] There was one clear exception: when a crocodile attacked a human, that specific animal was killed, irrespective of the fact that it might have acted as an instrument of the gods.[49] Obviously the killing of the man-eater had to be justified. People searched the stomach of the crocodile for stones and pebbles, which proved its guilt. It was thought that each stone represented the soul of a victim.[50] When the man-eater was killed, offerings were made to restore the peace between crocodiles and people.[51] People and crocodiles could again live together in peace.

These personal bonds in effect included crocodiles into the moral order. The laws and logic that regulated social life also applied to the relationship between people and crocodiles. To make sure that crocodiles and people could peacefully co-exist, there were specific rules and obligations for both parties.[52] The wellbeing of the community depended on its harmonious relations with crocodiles. People's attitudes towards crocodiles were respectful, tolerant and non-aggressive. Violations on either side were punished. When a crocodile attack took place, people sought a logical explanation and killed the man-eater in retaliation. This 'peace-pact' gave meaning to a dangerous and unpredictable world and enabled people to co-exist with crocodiles.[53]

THREE-HUNDRED YEARS IN THE CONVENT, ONE-HUNDRED YEARS IN HOLLYWOOD

When the *datu* Soliman, Ache, and Lakandula surrendered to Miguel López de Legazpi in 1571, crocodiles were still invoked:

> The oaths of these nations were all execrations in the form of awful curses. *Matay*, 'may I die!' *Cagtin nang buaya*, 'may I be eaten by the crocodile!' ... When the chiefs of Manila and Tondo swore allegiance to our Catholic sovereigns ... they confirmed the peace agreements and the subjection with an oath, asking the sun to pierce them through the middle, the crocodiles to eat them, and the women not to show them any favor or wish them well, if they broke their word.[54]

Four hundred years later the bond between crocodiles and people has been broken. Crocodiles are exterminated in most parts of the Philippines. Catholicism and a surging global demand for crocodile leather transformed Filipino perceptions of crocodiles and redefined the moral order.[55] Crocodiles are no longer seen as guardians but as dangerous pests. But the fear of the beast paradoxically increased as crocodiles disappeared from the landscape.

In the medieval perception of the Spanish friars crocodiles were the personification of the devil.[56] They brought with them Biblical notions of the Leviathan, an image that suited the Indo-Pacific crocodile well.[57] In the eyes of the friars, crocodiles not only posed a physical threat to communities but a challenge to the faith itself. The adulation of crocodiles in the Philippines reinforced the evangelical notion of an epic struggle against paganism. The slaying of the dragon and the subsequent conversion of the infidels are recurring themes in medieval Christian mythology, for example in the legends of St. Martha, St. George and the dragon and Philip the Evangelist.[58] These tropes perfectly fitted the Philippine context, where people made offerings to statues of crocodiles. The religious orders actively tried to destroy these pagan idols and liberate the *indios* from the evil crocodiles.[59] Conversion could save people from the danger posed by crocodiles:

> In this same year occurred a miraculous conversion of an infidel. This latter was crossing the river of Manila in one of those small boats so numerous in the islands, which do not extend more than two dedos out of the water. As there are

A Cultural History of Crocodiles

many caimans in this river (which in that respect is another Nile), one of them happened to cross his course, and, seizing him, dragged him to the bottom with a rapidity which is their mode, by a natural instinct of killing and securing their prey. The infidel, like another Jonas, beneath the water called with all his heart upon the God of the Christians; and instantly beheld two persons clad in white, who snatched him from the claws of the caiman; and drew him to the bank safe and sound; and as a result of this miracle he was baptized, with his two sons, and became a Christian. The very opposite befell another Christian, who forgot of God, passed every night to the other side of the river to commit evil deeds. God, wearied of waiting for him, sent his 'alguazil of the water' – which is the name of the cayman – who, seizing him executed upon his person the divine chastisement for his wickedness.[60]

During the Spanish occupation crocodiles became symbols of evil and danger. The dragon captured at the feet of a Saint became an icon in art and literature.[61] Figure 3, a painting from the parish church of San Mariano, is exemplary: a Saint saves his congregation by trampling a crocodile.

The novels of Jose P. Rizal, the Filipino novelist and nationalist whose execution set off the Philippine revolution, provide another illustration of the changes that occurred in peoples' perceptions of crocodiles. Rizal used the Spanish chronicles as a source of inspiration to 'awaken [the] consciousness of our past ... and to rectify what has been falsified and slandered'.[62] There are numerous references to 'caymans' in the works of Rizal, who apparently did not know that there were two species of crocodiles in the Philippines. One of the most famous is a passage in *Noli Me Tangere* when a crocodile is encountered, and killed, during a fishing trip on Laguna de Bay:

> 'All because we didn't hear mass', sighed one. 'But what accident has befallen us, ladies?' asked Ibarra. 'The cayman seems to have been the only unlucky one.' 'All of which proves', concluded the ex-student of theology, 'that in all its sinful life this unfortunate reptile has never attended mass – at least I've never seen him among the many other caymans that frequent the church. ... The body of the cayman writhed about, sometimes showing its torn white belly and again its speckled greenish back, while man, Nature's favourite, went on his way undisturbed by what the Brahmin and vegetarians would call so many cases of fratricide.[63]

Clearly, the association of crocodiles with greed and egoism was already commonly accepted in the nineteenth century Philippines. In his book *El Filibusterismo*, Rizal took things a step further: crocodiles became symbols of nepotism and colonial suppression:

> But when they began to harvest their first crop a religious corporation, which owned land in the neighboring town laid claim to the fields ... The administrator of the religious order left to them, for humanity's sake, the usufruct of the land on condition that they pay a small sum annually – a mere bagatelle, twenty or

FIGURE 3. Painting in the parish church in San Mariano by C. Domelod (1999)

thirty pesos ... Tandang Selo said to him, 'Patience! You would spend more in one year of litigation than in ten years of paying what the white padres demand. And perhaps they'll pay you back in masses. Pretend that those thirty pesos had been lost in gambling or had fallen into the water and been swallowed by a cayman.' ... Another year passed, bringing another good crop, and for this reason the friars raised the rent to fifty pesos, which Tales paid in order not to quarrel and because he expected to sell his sugar at a good price. 'Patience! Pretend that the cayman has grown some.'[64]

Rizal portrayed the Spanish friars as crocodiles, and paid with his life.[65]

The conversion of marshes and the clearance of riparian forests fuelled by a growing human population must have had an impact on crocodile populations during the Spanish occupation, particularly in Luzon and the Visayas.[66] But it was the frontier mentality of the American imperialists that fundamentally altered the relationship between crocodiles and people in the Philippines: for the Americans crocodiles were not only dangerous pests but also valuable resources.[67] After the Philippine Revolution and the treaty of Paris of 1898 that ended the Spanish–American War, the United States started to explore and exploit its newly acquired colony. The Taft Commission, tasked to investigate the conditions in the Philippine Islands, stereotyped crocodiles as dangerous man-eaters:

> Crocodiles are extremely abundant in many of the streams and freshwater lakes, and are sometimes met with in the sea along the coast. They frequently attain a very large size ... In certain parts of the archipelago they occasion no little loss of life, while in other regions the natives may be seen bathing with apparent impunity in streams where they are known to abound. The natives explain this by saying that the taste for human flesh is acquired, and that having once tasted it by accident a crocodile is content with nothing else and becomes a man-eater.[68]

The early explorers and naturalists often exaggerated the dangers of the Orient for their overseas readers (Figure 4). Even the zoologist Joseph Steere, who collected the paratype specimen of the Philippine crocodile in Mindoro in 1888, coloured his story with 'a violent bite from the captive crocodile'.[69] More empirically-oriented observers however, such as W. Cameron Forbes, the US Governor-General of the Philippines from 1908 to 1913, wrote that crocodile attacks on humans were in fact 'comparatively rare'.[70]

Commercial crocodile hunting in the Philippines started in the 1920s and intensified after World War Two.[71] Crocodile hunters were widely admired and rewarded for their 'exemplary service to the community'.[72] No reliable quantitative records exist of the trade in crocodile leather. But a figure published by the American geographer Frederick Wernstedt gives an indication of the scale of the slaughter: in 1953 five tons of crocodile skins were exported from the port of Cebu.[73] By the end of the 1960s, crocodile populations were depleted to the point where commercial hunting was no longer considered a 'remunerative occupation'.[74] In the 1970s and 1980s, skins, specimens, teeth and organs were

FIGURE 4. Cover illustration of the book *Twenty years in the Philippines (1819–1839)* by H. Valentin (de la Gironière 1854).

sold on markets in Manila as tourist curios.[75] The reclamation of 'crocodile infested swampland'[76] further contributed to the disappearance of crocodiles in most parts of the archipelago.

As early as 1977, the Philippine Government played with the idea of establishing crocodile farms 'to minimise the dangers being posed by these dangerous reptiles to men as well as to animals and to turn to a more productive purpose instead'.[77] It took another ten years and Japanese funding before these ideas were put in practice. Responding to the decline of crocodiles in the Philippines, a captive breeding programme for the species was established in 1987 in Palawan: the Crocodile Farming Institute (CFI). The underlying idea was to develop a crocodile leather industry to 'instil in trappers/catchers the relative economic importance of a ferocious, living crocodile relative to a harmless dead one'.[78] CFI succeeded in breeding both crocodile species in captivity. But captive-bred crocodiles were never reintroduced to the wild as policy makers assumed that rural communities would resist such an intervention:

> People's attitudes would have to be changed by challenging old and accepted, even if unscientific, notions about the crocodile ... so that people in the rural areas would come to appreciate the crocodile as a viable wildlife species in our environment that needs to be appreciated and conserved.[79]

A Cultural History of Crocodiles

However, no efforts were made to mobilise support and engage rural communities in *in situ* crocodile conservation.[80]

A remarkable transformation has taken place in the way people regard crocodiles in the Philippines: from divine guardian to devil, from symbol of social injustice to commodity and from obstacle to economic development to 'endangered pest'.[81] Nowadays crocodiles are the 'most maligned, unfairly-treated and misunderstood species in the country'.[82] Mainstream Filipino society has become increasingly alienated from crocodiles. Most people now only see crocodiles on TV or in commercial advertisements. Hollywood horror movies such as *Lake Placid* and Discovery Channel documentaries such as *Crocodile Hunter* have entrenched an image of the crocodile as dangerous monster in contemporary mainstream Philippine culture.[83] But in the remote rural areas people often have very different perceptions of crocodiles.

CROCODILES IN THE NORTHERN SIERRA MADRE

We interviewed Marcella Impiel in April 2003 in Cadsalan, a village in the municipality of San Mariano in the uplands of the northern Sierra Madre (Figure 5).[84] Her words are illustrative of indigenous people's attitudes towards crocodiles in the remote rural areas of the Philippines:

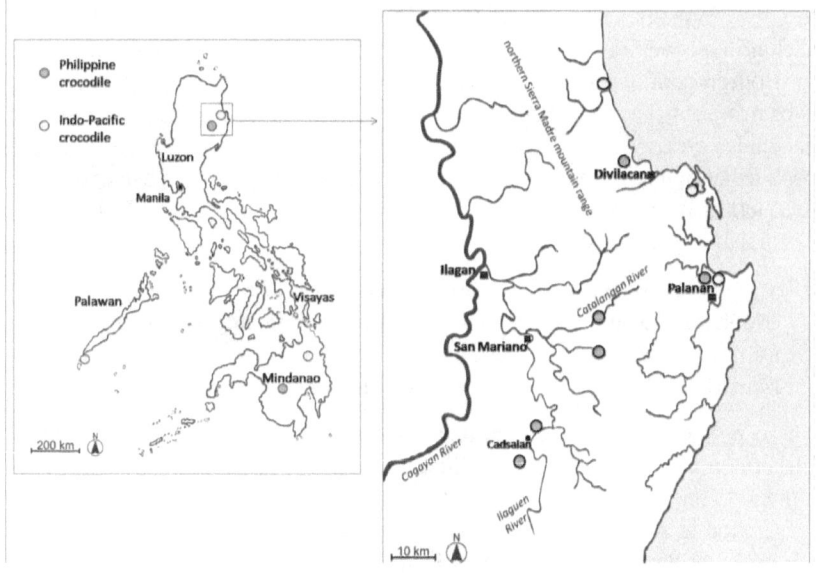

FIGURE 5. Map of the northern Sierra Madre showing remaining crocodile populations

> We're afraid of the crocodile. I do not allow my children to swim alone in the river. If a crocodile faces you it will blow at you and you will get beriberi. Crocodiles are very powerful. They have a fifth sense. Therefore you should not say bad things about the crocodile. My grandmother said: if you kill a crocodile you will get sick. The crocodile always takes revenge. Even if you cut your hair the crocodile will recognise you. Even on land it will strike you. But the crocodile will not bite innocent people. If you do not harm the crocodile, the crocodile will not harm you.[85]

In the northern Sierra Madre crocodiles have survived in the ancestral lands of the Agta and the Kalinga. Here, a delicate mix of respect, fear and indifference characterises the relationship between people and crocodiles.

The Agta

The Agta are a Negrito forest-dwelling people inhabiting the Sierra Madre mountain range on Luzon.[86] Fishing, hunting and gathering are important livelihood strategies. Settlements are located along forest streams or in the coastal area near river estuaries: the habitat of Philippine crocodiles and Indo-Pacific crocodiles respectively. The Agta differentiate between *bukarot* and *buwaya* and often have detailed knowledge of the occurrence and behaviour of crocodiles in their ancestral domains. They respectfully call large crocodiles *Apo* (Sir) or *Lakay* (old man). The Agta sometimes find half-eaten sea-turtles on the beach: 'a gift from the old crocodile'.[87] If people see an Indo-Pacific crocodile taking shelter in a cove, it is interpreted as a sign of an approaching typhoon.

Both crocodile species are feared but the Agta do not take specific precautions, even in areas where Indo-Pacific crocodiles occur. Agta fishermen occasionally encounter crocodiles underwater but are unconcerned about the risks. In the past, fishermen requested permission of the crocodiles to catch fish and asked to be left alone in the water, but this practice has largely disappeared. Fishermen claim that crocodiles will not attack them:

> My father knew an underwater cave in Dipagsangan. There was always a large crocodile in the cave. The crocodile allowed my father to enter the cave and spear fish. They were friends and blood brothers. My father asked the crocodile not to harm his family. When my father died, the crocodile was also gone.[88]

These personal bonds are common throughout the northern Sierra Madre. Fishermen know individual crocodiles and say that these animals do not pose a threat to them.

Crocodile attacks on humans are rare in the northern Sierra Madre. In 1996 a boy, Arnel de la Peña, was bitten in the leg by an Indo-Pacific crocodile in Dibulos Creek in Divilacan; he luckily survived the attack. Several respondents said it was his mistake:

> Crocodiles never forget and always take revenge. Arnel cut the tail of a small crocodile and threw stones at it. After a few years he was bitten in his legs by the same crocodile. A crocodile will always remember you.[89]

The moral of stories like this is that people should respect crocodiles: 'if you harm a crocodile, the crocodile will harm you'.[90] Killing a crocodile is considered an unwise provocation. Not so much because of the physical danger posed by crocodiles, but because of the risk that 'an evil spirit will bite your soul'.[91] The Agta think that some crocodiles are guarded by spirits; these *enkantado* crocodiles are considered dangerous. Some respondents say that these enchanted crocodiles are very large, wear a necklace, have two tails or are completely black.

The hunter-gatherer lifestyle of the Agta has relatively little impact on crocodiles and wetlands. People do not eat crocodile meat but when a nest is found the eggs are collected and eaten. In general the Agta are indifferent towards the crocodiles that inhabit their ancestral domain. When we observed an adult estuarine crocodile in Palanan in 2004 our Agta guide reassured us that he knew the animal and that it did not pose a risk: 'never mind the crocodile...'[92]

The Kalinga

The Kalinga are shifting cultivators in the forest frontier of the northern Sierra Madre. They inhabit two remote watersheds in San Mariano: Catalangan and Ilaguen.[93] A remnant Philippine crocodile population survives in these river systems. It is said that in the past the Kalinga and crocodiles peacefully coexisted: 'people used to cross the river on the back of crocodiles'.[94] The Kalinga say that crocodiles are dangerous animals but claim that those that live in their ancestral domains are an exception: they are 'friendly'.[95] Killing crocodiles is a taboo and can cause sickness: 'you cannot kill something that is stronger than you'.[96] If people become sick because of a crocodile, they can be cured by placing a cross with chalk on their forehead and performing a ritual.

Crocodiles play an important role in Kalinga culture. During festivities and healing rituals (*patunnuk*) the Kalinga make rice cakes in the form of a crocodile: offerings to the ancestors. Transmogrification and metempsychosis are recurrent themes in Kalinga society. The Kalinga believe that crocodiles are the embodiment of the ancestors, and sometimes make a small food offering to the ancestor crocodiles when crossing a river.[97] People tell that their chiefs can change at will into fierce crocodiles; and they joke that today's *punong barangay* (the elected village leader) has luckily lost that ability. The Kalinga believe that the *bugeyan*, the traditional healer, still has the ability to change into a crocodile. In a trance she risks becoming a crocodile.[98] Faith healers can also command crocodiles to attack people as a punishment for anti-social behaviour. People tell stories of other remarkable transformations:

> A girl never wanted to share her betel nut with her family. She was possessed by

a spirit and became sick. Her parents cooked nice food, but she did not want to eat. Every night she went to the river to swim. One night she said to her parents: 'you can eat my betel nut, I am a crocodile now'. She cried and said goodbye. Then she went to the river and became a crocodile.[99]

In another popular Kalinga folktale, a woman hit her children too hard and subsequently turned into a crocodile. As it is widely thought that crocodiles eat their own offspring, people consider this a logical punishment.[100]

Traditional beliefs and practices prove to be surprisingly resilient. Three hundred and fifty years after Father Alcina wrote about women giving birth to crocodiles in the Visayas, the Kalinga in the northern Sierra Madre think that some people are born with a spiritual crocodile-twin:

> The girl and the crocodile grew up together. But one day the father got angry with the crocodile and tried to kill it. The crocodile escaped but his tail was chopped off. You can still see this twin crocodile without tail in the river. We call him *putol*. The crocodile regularly visits and protects his sister.[101]

Different versions of this story are told throughout the Sierra Madre. Some narrators claim the enchanted crocodile was released by its human parents with a necklace. Others say it killed its human brother. Poldo Velasco recited another version of the crocodile-twin story:

> A woman gave birth to twins: one was a girl and the other a crocodile. They grew up together, although the crocodile was mostly in the water. His sister talked to him and said: 'please do not eat dogs or humans. Otherwise I will kill you.' But one day a dog went missing, and she suspected it was her sibling who did this. She went to the river and called: 'all of you crocodiles, related to my sibling, come to me!' Many crocodiles came, really a lot. The river was full of them. Then she said: 'there is still one missing!' So she asked them to look for her sister crocodile. A few moments later her sister crocodile came. 'So you were the one who ate the dog' she said. And she killed her sister crocodile.[102]

The Kalinga try to find a logical explanation for crocodile behaviour. In Cadsalan crocodiles are often observed in the creek near the traditional cemetery. People concluded that these crocodiles were the personification of the ancestors and therefore would not disturb these animals. Aggressive behaviour of individual crocodiles is justified: 'even a chicken protects its chicks'.[103] In 2003 a boy, Marlon Robles, was attacked by an adult Philippine crocodile in Dinang Creek in San Mariano; luckily he escaped unharmed. People explained that the father of the boy had tried to kill a crocodile and that the crocodile attacked in retaliation:

> There is a spell on the crocodiles. Nobody can kill them. Boy Robles has tried to kill the crocodiles but he did not succeed. Now the crocodiles are taking revenge and are attacking his family.[104]

A Cultural History of Crocodiles

But the Kalinga don't see a fundamental problem in living in close proximity to crocodiles: the peace pact is still honoured.

Social change

The historical continuity of people's attitudes towards crocodiles in the northern Sierra Madre is remarkable (Figure 6). But it also masks fundamental changes. In the 1960s commercial logging companies started operating in the forests of the Sierra Madre. Commercial crocodile hunters systematically killed crocodiles for the leather trade. Some older respondents remember how 'Moro hunters' killed crocodiles by luring the animals with a prayer and stabbing them underwater: 'their magic made them invulnerable to the wrath of the spirits'.[105] In several areas, the army shot crocodiles to 'protect the local populace'.[106] Immigrant farmers settled in the forest frontier and organised hunting parties to 'clean the river from crocodiles because they posed a threat to our children and pigs'.[107] These Ilocano and Ibanag immigrants generally see crocodiles as vermin. They believe that crocodile meat is an excellent medicine against asthma, that crocodile scales have magical power during cockfighting and that a crocodile penis is an aphrodisiac.

FIGURE 6. Historical continuity and change: a compilation of photos from the northern Sierra Madre. From left: Kalinga traditional healer; Ilocano boys on a carabao; juvenile Philippine crocodile; Agta girl pounding rice; Ibanag boy with plough; Kalinga house.

Nowadays, the Agta and Kalinga form minorities in the northern Sierra Madre. Immigrants have dispossessed the indigenous people of most of their ancestral lands. The Agta have maintained their cultural distinctiveness to a large degree, but are generally excluded from social and economic life. The Kalinga, in contrast, have undergone a rapid process of 'Ilocanization'.[108] Most Kalinga have been converted to Christianity and have adopted the production and consumption patterns of their Ilocano and Ibanag neighbours. The Agta and the Kalinga are marginalised groups, often stigmatised by lowland communities. As a result people are reluctant to talk about their traditions and beliefs, afraid of being labelled as 'stupid, 'backward' or 'superstitious'. During interviews people explain that only enchanted crocodiles attack people but add that they personally 'no longer believe in these stories'.[109] Traditional values and practices are changing as markets, schools, chainsaws and televisions become more accessible.

In the remote villages one finds a mix of often contradictory stories and anecdotes. Some people claim that enchanted crocodiles attack people whereas normal crocodiles are harmless, others say that normal crocodiles attack people and that enchanted crocodiles are 'friendly' and carry people across rivers. Indigenous people and immigrant farmers in the northern Sierra Madre creatively fuse Malay beliefs, European fairytales and Hollywood movies into one contemporary reality. In June 2001, for example, a Philippine crocodile was killed in the municipality of Divilacan. The animal was buried. When it started raining intermittently for several days, people made a link between the rains and the dead crocodile: the crocodile needed water. As a result the crocodile was exhumed and thrown into the sea to appease the crocodile-spirit and prevent a flood. Another example comes from the municipality of Palanan where treasure-hunters were draining an underwater cave in 2004. They were convinced that a Japanese plane loaded with gold had crashed in the cave during World War Two. The fact that crocodiles were observed in the area strengthened this idea: 'everybody knows that crocodiles protect treasures'.[110] This chaotic and often inconsistent mix is in our view not a sign of deculturation but a characteristic element of oral history. Folktales, myths and movies form the logical framework wherein new experiences and observations are flexibly incorporated. People in Divilacan for example say that there used to be an Indo-Pacific crocodile that was so large that bamboo grew on its back. Seeing this animal was an omen for a good harvest. But this is no longer the case: 'the bamboo died because of the use of pesticides'.[111]

The argument that crocodiles survived in the ancestral domains of the Agta and the Kalinga because of low population densities, rudimentary technology and the absence of markets can easily be refuted. Indigenous people in the northern Sierra Madre tolerated crocodiles; they could have exterminated the crocodiles had they wished to. Indifference, respect and fear of the spirits assured that crocodiles were not purposely killed. Conversely the Kalinga and Agta have not

A Cultural History of Crocodiles

actively protected crocodiles or critical wetland habitat in their ancestral lands. There is, in essence, no need to protect ancestors, spirits or witches. Obviously immigration and acculturation have had profound impacts on the traditional belief and knowledge systems that structured people's relations with crocodiles. But that does not make these indigenous experiences less relevant. Agta and Kalinga culture provide a valuable counterweight to the commonly held view that negative attitudes of rural communities form a major obstruction for *in situ* crocodile conservation in the Philippines. As such the perceptions of the Agta and the Kalinga are more than relics from a distant past: they are proof that people and crocodiles can coexist in intensively-used landscapes in the Philippines of the twenty first century. The experiences of the Kalinga and the Agta provide very practical solutions for specific problems: when a crocodile attacked Marcella Impiel's livestock in Cadsalan in 2001 she did not kill the crocodile but decided to relocate her house a little further from the creek and to prevent her pigs from roaming freely at night. It solved the problem.

DISCUSSION

In a speech in January 2007 the undersecretary of the Department of Environment and Natural Resource Management, Jose Ferrer, laid out the rationale for crocodile conservation in the Philippines:

> If there are any creatures that are capable of provoking a range of emotions from us, they are crocodiles ... When we see crooks in government, we call them crocodiles, when we see fat-bellied policemen on the streets, we call them crocodiles ... Hunters were all too happy to relieve the reviled Indo-Pacific crocodile of its profitable skin and uncontrolled harvests reduced the wild population dramatically. Not that many people cared. To most, the only good crocodile was a dead one ... Several years after we first implemented the Philippines' crocodile recovery program, Indo-Pacific crocodile numbers (although in captivity) are now approaching densities not seen before. Tourism has become a major force with crocodiles as a star attraction. Even those who still dislike crocodiles acknowledge their economic importance and would never want to see them vanish. Such is the importance of linking conservation with people ... Local people must see that their crocodiles are important, not only to the environment, but to themselves ... Those of us who admire crocodiles need only to know that they exist, but this opinion is very much the exception for the people who have to share their habitat with crocodiles. When animals threaten your livelihood, or even your life, it influences your opinion about those animals.[112]

Ferrer's speech is exemplary of how policymakers and conservationists in the Philippines think about crocodiles and 'the opinion of local people'. It is argued that negative attitudes of rural communities form a major obstruction for *in situ* crocodile conservation. In this view removing crocodiles from the wild and breeding them in captivity is considered the only solution to safeguard crocodile populations in the Philippines.[113]

There are several flawed assumptions in this reasoning. As this paper has shown, people who live in close proximity to crocodiles do not necessarily consider crocodiles a pest. In fact, indigenous peoples in the northern Sierra Madre tolerate crocodiles. Here, as well as in the mangrove forests of Palawan and the marshes of Mindanao, rural communities have a tradition of co-existence with crocodiles that goes back more than four hundred years. As a result crocodiles have survived in the ancestral domains of these peoples. Ignoring this fact not only inhibits the design of effective conservation interventions but also adds to the marginalisation and disenfranchisement of indigenous peoples. Paradoxically, people who have no actual experiences of crocodiles are more afraid of and hostile towards crocodiles. When people are 'disengaged', incoherent representations and irrational fears of crocodiles prevail.[114]

A narrow focus on the utilitarian value of crocodiles does not seem to be a practical conservation strategy in the Philippines. There are no undisturbed wetlands and too few crocodiles left in the wild for a community-based sustainable harvesting and ranching programme in the Philippines. Crocodile farming certainly has economic potential but requires large capital investment. At present, the crocodile leather industry in the Philippines is dominated by six wealthy hog and poultry farmers, who operate closed-cycle crocodile farms.[115] Crocodile farming has not so far generated economic benefits for rural communities living in crocodile habitat and it is highly unlikely it will do so in the near future. In most areas where crocodiles occur, tourism is not a viable option: civil insurgency and the lack of infrastructure make travelling to the northern Sierra Madre, the Balabac Islands in Palawan and the Ligauasan and Agusan marshes in Mindanao difficult. The exclusive focus on sustainable use and captive breeding diverts scarce resources from *in situ* conservation efforts. Removing crocodiles from the wild contributes to local extinctions and reinforces the idea among policy-makers and the public that cohabitation is impossible. Moreover it ignores the fact that people have found ways to co-exist with crocodiles in human-dominated landscapes. But the sustainable use model has, despite Ferrer's optimism, failed to conserve crocodiles and improve the wellbeing of people in the Philippines.

The pre-colonial heritage and the practical knowledge and experiences of indigenous people offer an alternative perspective for the modernist and utilitarian views of policy makers and conservationists.[116] Philippine history and culture provide a conservation ethic entrenched in society and history and adaptive to local circumstances. In areas where crocodiles survive in the wild, indigenous beliefs and practices towards the species often prevail. Here people know crocodiles from their own experience and treat them with respect. These are not archaic remnants of a forgotten past, irrelevant to modern life. On the contrary, the worldviews and ecological knowledge of the Kalinga and Agta offer

A Cultural History of Crocodiles

pragmatic solutions for living with crocodiles. With common-sense precautionary measures, such as tying livestock at night and avoiding areas where crocodiles are known to occur, human–crocodile conflicts are minimised. These experiences provide a different narrative: one that stresses cohabitation and wellbeing instead of 'threats to livelihood' and 'economic importance'. It enables the design of a conservation strategy that positively enhances the capacity and knowledge of rural communities to conserve the resources they value.

Our experiences in the northern Sierra Madre suggest that crocodiles can effectively be conserved in human-dominated landscapes.[117] Setting aside cultural prejudice, the municipal government of San Mariano proclaimed the Philippine crocodile as the flagship species of the municipality. Village councils prohibited the use of destructive fishing methods, established crocodile sanctuaries and maintain riparian buffer zones. A public awareness campaign engages people in crocodile conservation: posters are distributed, community dialogues are organised to address peoples' questions and concerns, and schoolchildren are brought into the field to see the Philippine crocodile in the wild.[118] Farmers and fishermen now know that the Philippine crocodile is protected by law.[119] More important perhaps is that people take pride in the occurrence of a rare and iconic species in their village; that fishermen enjoy talking about crocodile ecology and behaviour; and that children become excited about seeing a crocodile in the wild. For many people in San Mariano these immaterial values seem to be an important motivational factor to tolerate the species in their midst.

There is broad support for these conservation interventions at the grassroots level. Confronted with declining fish stocks and the effects of flooding, people want authorities to ban fishing with dynamite and to act against destructive land use practices such as the conversion of creeks and ponds and logging along river banks. In this view the wellbeing of the community depends on the conservation of watersheds, wetlands and crocodiles. For rural communities who 'share their habitat with crocodiles' the conservation of crocodiles in the wild is not an externally imposed alien concept, but builds on existing cultural values.

In 1890 Jose P. Rizal published an annotated version of Antonio de Morga's *Sucesos de las Islas Filipinas* (1609):

> [O]ther nations have great esteem for the lion or the bear, putting them on the shields and giving them honourable epithets. The mysterious life of the crocodile, the enormous size that it sometimes reaches, its fatidic aspect, without counting anymore its voraciousness, must have influenced greatly the imagination of the Malayan Filipinos.[120]

Crocodiles still capture the imagination of many Filipinos. This forms a strong foundation to conserve the species in the wild, for poor rural communities in remote areas too.

NOTES

[1] Over the past eight years we have conducted fieldwork in the northern Sierra Madre in the context of a research and conservation project for the Philippine crocodile (van der Ploeg *et al.* 2008b).

[2] IUCN 2006.

[3] Webb and Manolis 1989, p. 125.

[4] van Weerd and van der Ploeg 2004.

[5] IUCN 2006.

[6] There are several morphological differences that distinguish the two crocodile species. In addition, there are differences in habitat preference: the Indo-Pacific crocodile is generally restricted to mangroves, lakes and marshes in the lowlands, whereas the Philippine crocodile occurs mainly in upland river systems.

[7] Wernstedt and Spencer 1967.

[8] van der Ploeg and van Weerd 2004.

[9] Ross and Alcala 1983; Thorbjarnarson 1999.

[10] Ortega 1998; Banks 2005.

[11] WCSP 1997, pp. 76–79. See also Ross 1982; Ortega *et al.* 1993.

[12] Menez 2004.

[13] Paterno *et al.* 2001.

[14] Mangansakan 2008.

[15] Scott 1982.

[16] While acknowledging our moral engagement and active involvement with crocodile conservation in the Philippines, we do not advocate a romantic view of indigenous people living in harmony with nature since time immemorial or aim to construct a 'usable past' for contemporary political gains (McNeill 2003: 15). Nor do we suggest a linear evolution from primitive to modern ideas about wildlife.

[17] We mainly relied on the 55 volumes of the *Philippine Islands, 1493–1898* edited by Emma Blair and James Robertson (1907). Unless otherwise indicated, we have used their translation of the Spanish archives. For clarity we opted to refer in the text to the date and author of the original publication. In the literature search we have not limited ourselves to the Philippines but have included references and historical anecdotes from insular Southeast Asia. The article *De krokodil in het leven van de Posoërs* [The crocodile in the life of the Poso] of Albert Kruyt (1906), a Dutch missionary in Sulawesi, is perhaps the most interesting primary source on the relation between crocodiles and people in Southeast Asia. Charles Hose and William McDougall (1901) also provide valuable insights on the relations between crocodiles and people in the Malay world.

[18] *Buwaya* or a derivate thereof is the common name for crocodile throughout Southeast Asia (Table 1). In areas where both crocodile species occur, such as in the northern Sierra Madre, *buwaya* refers to *C. porosus* and other names are used for *C. mindorensis*, such as *lamag* in Ibanag or *bukarot* in Ilocano. However, in upland areas where only *C. mindorensis* occurs, such as the Central Cordillera on Luzon, people have adopted the generic name for crocodile for *C. mindorensis*: *buwaya*.

[19] See, for example, Long 1843, p. 88. Most of the Spanish lexicographers had spent years in Mexico and probably knew the spectacled caiman (*Caiman crocodilus*) and the

A Cultural History of Crocodiles

American crocodile (*Crocodylus acutus*) which occupy similar ecological niches to the Philippine crocodile and the Indo-Pacific crocodile respectively.

[20] Blumentritt 1882, p. 12; Jagor 1875, p. 207; Cole 1913, p. 114.

[21] Crocodiles are a popular character in Filipino folktales (Eugenio 2002, p. 19). In folktales the crocodile is generally the dupe who is tricked by a monkey or a turtle (Fansler 1921, pp. 374–79; Hart and Hart 1966: 323; Eugenio 1985, p. 161; Eugenio 1994, p. 144).

[22] de Loarca 1582, p. 130; Bowring 1859, p.157; Scott 1994, p. 82.

[23] Maxwell 1990, p. 98; Benedict 1916, p. 42.

[24] Schulte Nordholt 1971; Middelkoop 1971: 437; Hose and McDougall: 198.

[25] Maxwell 1990, p. 133.

[26] Pablo de Jesus cited in Nocheseda 2002: 104.

[27] Scott 1994.

[28] Schebesta 1957, p. 276; Garvan 1963, p. 204.

[29] Gray 1979.

[30] Maxwell 1990, p. 98.

[31] Gardner 1906, p. 195.

[32] Alejandro 2002; Scott 1994, p. 81.

[33] Wilken 1885; Kruyt 1935. Crocodiles have five toes on the front limb without webbing between them. On the hind limb crocodiles have four toes, of which three are clawed and have webbing between them. The hind limb also has a small rudiment of a fifth toe.

[34] The reason why crocodiles have no tongue is a popular theme in Philippine folktales (Ratcliff 1949: 282). In fact, the tongue of all crocodile species is attached along its entire length to the floor of the mouth, and cannot be protruded.

[35] Colin 1663, p. 77; Gardner 1906, p. 193.

[36] Nocheseda 2002: 71. Albert Kruyt, a Dutch missionary, photographed these bamboo fences in Central Sulawesi (1906: 6).

[37] See Bowring 1859, pp. 130–131; Worcester 1898, p. 514.

[38] It is tempting to provide an ecological explanation for the indifference of people towards crocodiles. It seems plausible that in areas where the Indo-Pacific crocodile occurred, people feared crocodiles and took precautions; whereas in the habitat of the much smaller Philippine crocodile people would be indifferent to crocodiles. On closer inspection, however, this lowland–upland dichotomy does not hold. In several areas in the Philippines, for example on the Pacific coast of Sierra Madre, both crocodile species occur. In these areas people differentiate between the species but do not take specific precautions against *Crocodylus porosus*. Although there are no records of fatal attacks on humans, the Philippine crocodile poses a risk to humans, particularly during breeding season.

[39] Chirino 1604, p. 201; Kruyt 1935, p. 14; Adams 1979, p. 93; Bakels 2000, pp. 366–367; Nocheseda 2002: 65. In the Spanish Empire an *alguazil*, a derivation from the Arabic *visir*, was a municipal judge.

[40] Hose and McDougall 1901, pp. 186; Boomgaard 2007: 17.

[41] Polenda 1989.

[42] de Raedt 1993.

[43] cited in Scott 1994, pp. 114–115.

[44] Wilken 1885, p. 70.

45 Hose and McDougall 1901, pp. 190–99. In Borneo, people engraved crocodile images on rocks, and constructed life-size outlines of crocodiles with clay, wood and stones. These crocodile images were ritually killed during a ceremony (*ulung buaya*). After the ceremony, the crocodile image continued to serve as a symbol of leadership, as platform for juridical sessions, a ritual site for offerings, or as boundary marker between warring groups (Hose and McDougall 1901; Harrison 1958; Datan 2006). In the Philippines, however, such large megalithic relics were never recorded.

46 Wilken 1885, p. 69.

47 Schulte Nordholt 1971: 323; Middelkoop 1971: 436–440; Adams 1979, p. 92.

48 Boomgaard 2007: 19.

49 Hose and McDougall 1901, p. 186.

50 de la Gironière 1854, p. 221; Skeat 1900, pp. 292–293. Large crocodiles often have several stones, gastroliths, in their stomach to aid digestion.

51 Kruyt 1935, p. 9; Nocheseda 2002: 93; Gavin 2003, p. 98.

52 Kruyt 1935, pp. 12–13; Bakels 2000.

53 Kruyt 1935, p. 10.

54 Colin 1663, pp. 78–79.

55 The pre-colonial Philippines were subject to Indian, Chinese and Islamic influences, which obviously left traces in material and oral culture. The *naga* and the dragon, for example, are symbols that are closely associated with crocodiles and that have been adopted throughout the archipelago (Maxwell 1990). The popular folktale about the crocodile and the monkey probably originates from Indian literature (Francisco 1964). These influences are, however, now so thoroughly mixed up that it is almost impossible to disentangle them (Skeat 1900, pp. xii–xiii). Nevertheless it is important to highlight one aspect: Muslims generally consider crocodile meat *haram* and will thus not kill crocodiles for food. Persoon and de Iongh (2004) have already pointed to the differences between Islamic and Christian communities in Southeast Asia and the implications for wildlife conservation, a point of particular relevance for the conservation of crocodiles in Mindanao and Luzon.

56 Cohen 1994.

57 Kiessling 1970

58 Hédard and Fréchet 2005, p. 96.

59 Bankoff 1999: 40.

60 Chirino 1604, p. 201.

61 Nevertheless some remarkable transformations took place in this image: St. Martha the Patron Saint of housewives in Europe, became in the Philippines the Patron Saint of the duck egg (*balut*) industry after driving crocodiles out of Pasig River (Nocheseda 2002). Her victory over the crocodiles is still celebrated every year in the municipality of Pateros. A similar fiesta is held in the municipality of Gattaran to celebrate the disappearance of crocodiles from Cagayan River.

62 Rizal 1889, cited in Hall 1999.

63 Rizal 1886, pp. 156–160

64 Rizal 1891, pp. 34–43.

65 A bronze sculpture made by Rizal of a dog attacking a crocodile to save her pup represents the Filipino people and the Spanish rulers, respectively. The association between

crocodiles and landlords is still a popular theme in Filipino literature (see for example: Hernandez 1983).

[66] Bankoff 2007.

[67] See Bankoff 2009 on the origin of the utilitarian conservation ethic in the Philippines.

[68] Philippine Commission 1901, pp. 318–19.

[69] Schmidt 1938: 89.

[70] Forbes 1945, p. 17. In the Dutch Indies, the colonial government created a premium system to eradicate crocodiles. The system officially started in 1935 but was terminated because most people refused to kill crocodiles! (Knapen 2001) To our knowledge no systematic pest eradication system was set up in the Philippines.

[71] Jenkins and Broad 1994; Thorbjarnarson 1999.

[72] Ortega 1998, p. 102.

[73] Wernstedt 1956: 346.

[74] Wernstedt and Spencer 1967, p. 108.

[75] Ross 1982.

[76] DBP 1979: 2.

[77] PCARR 1977: 1130.

[78] Ortega *et al.* 1993: 126.

[79] Palawan State College 1991: 11.

[80] Since 1992 there has been growing awareness of the plight of the country's endemic wildlife. Since 2004 crocodiles have been protected by law. However, most people are simply not aware of environmental legislation.

[81] The term endangered pest was coined by John Knight (2000, p. 13).

[82] Malayang 2007: 1.

[83] Vivanco 2004.

[84] This paragraph is based on around 150 unstructured interviews with Agta, Kalinga and immigrant farmers (mainly Ilocano, Ibanag and Ifugao) in the northern Sierra Madre between 2002 and 2008. Most interviews were conducted in Ilocano, the lingua franca in north Luzon, with the help of an interpreter. Specific quotes were selected if they were considered representative for a general theme. The name of the respondent and the year when the interview was conducted are provided for each quote.

[85] *Beriberi* is a nervous system ailment caused by vitamin B1 deficiency. Symptoms include weakness, pain, weight loss, emotional disturbances and swelling of limbs.

[86] There are approximately 10,000 Agta in the Sierra Madre on Luzon (Early and Headland 1998). The Northern Sierra Madre Natural Park in the province of Isabela, where we conducted most of our fieldwork, is home to 1,700 Agta, distributed over more than 80 settlements (Minter 2009).

[87] Pers. comm. D. Gonzales 2004.

[88] Pers. comm. E. Prado 2006.

[89] Pers. comm. R. Gonzalez 2005.

[90] Pers. comm. W. Cabaldo 2004.

[91] Pers. comm. M. Molina 2005.

[92] Pers. comm. B. Mijares 2004.

[93] It is important to differentiate the Kalinga of the Sierra Madre from the Kalinga of

the Central Cordillera: these are two different ethno-linguistic groups. In Ibanag the word 'kalinga' means enemy. The Christian communities in the Cagayan Valley called all infidel mountaineers Kalinga which might explain why these separate groups are both called Kalinga. The Kalinga of the Sierra Madre, also known as Irraya, Kalibugan or Catalangan, were first described by a German explorer, Carl Semper, in 1861 (Scott 1979). Felix Keesing (1962) postulated that the Sierra Madre Kalinga are Ibanag and Gaddang who rebelled against Spanish rule and retreated to the foothills of the Sierra Madre. The local government of San Mariano estimates that there are approximately 2,500 Kalinga living in the municipality. This is most likely an underestimate: many Kalinga nowadays identify themselves as Ilocano. At present there are also several Cordillera Kalinga migrant communities in the northern Sierra Madre, particularly in the municipality of Divilacan.

[94] Pers. comm. A. Fransisco 2004.
[95] Pers. comm. W. Languido 2003.
[96] Pers. comm. Baliwag 2004.
[97] Knibbe and Angnged 2005, p. 71.
[98] Pers. comm. M. Espiritu 2005.
[99] Pers. comm. T. Catalunia 2003.
[100] This myth is widely known throughout the Philippines and insular Southeast Asia. It probably finds its origin in the maternal care of crocodilians: several crocodile species crack the eggs to assist the young in hatching and carry the hatchlings to the water in their jaws. See: Navarette 1676, p. 305; Skeat 1900, p. 286; Alvina 2007.
[101] Pers. comm. B. Robles 2003.
[102] Cited in Knibbe and Angnged 2005, p. 72.
[103] Pers. comm. Robles 2006.
[104] Pers. comm. F. Languido 2003.
[105] Pers. comm. T. Francisco. Throughout northern Luzon people narrate how in the 1960s and 1970s professional hunters searched the rivers and creeks at night, killed crocodiles, dried the skin and distributed the meat to local people. It is generally assumed that these hunters were from Mindanao: hence people refer to them as 'Moro.' In fact it is probable that these professional crocodile hunters were Orang Bugis from Sulawesi, who controlled the crocodile leather networks in insular Southeast Asia. Most crocodile skins from the Philippines were exported to tanneries in Singapore (Hemley and Caldwell 1986).
[106] Pers. comm. J. Arburo 2004
[107] Pers. comm. R. Corpus 2004.
[108] Keesing 1962, p. 326.
[109] Pers. comm. P. Maneia 2003. Interestingly, this ambivalence has been a recurrent element in the anthropological literature on human–wildlife relations for more than 100 years. See: Hose and McDougall 1901, p. 190; Martin 1978, pp. 155–156.
[110] Pers. comm. L. Salazar 2004.
[111] Pers. comm. J. Centeno 2004.
[112] Ferrer 2008: 7–9.
[113] Ross 1982, p. 27; WCSP 1999, pp. 76–9.
[114] Ingold 1994, p. 19.
[115] Mercado 2008: 29.

A Cultural History of Crocodiles

[116] Schama 1995; Scott 1998; Maffi and Woodley 2010.
[117] van der Ploeg and van Weerd 2004a; van der Ploeg et al. 2008b.
[118] van der Ploeg et al. 2008a; van der Ploeg et al. 2009.
[119] As a result the Philippine crocodile population in San Mariano is slowly recovering from 12 individuals in the wild in 2000 to 64 in 2009.
[120] Rizal cited in Nocheseda 2002: 75.

BIBLIOGRAPHY

Adams, M.J. 1979. 'The Crocodile Couple and the Snake Encounter in the Tellantry of East Sumba', in A.L. Becker and A.A. Yengoyan (eds.) *The Imagination of Reality. Essays in Southeast Asian Coherence Systems* (Norwood: Ablex Pub. Corp) pp. 87–104.

Alejandro, R.G. 2002. *Laguna de Bay; the Living Lake* (Manila: Unilever Philippines).

Alvina, C. 2007. 'Philippine Crocodile Chronicles', *Crocodile Specialist Group Newsletter* **26**, 1: 16–17

Antonio, F. de san. 1624 [2000]. 'Vocabulario Tagalo', in A. Postma (ed.) *Tagalog-Spanish dictionary* (Quezon City: Ateneo de Manila University).

Antonio, J.F. de san. 1738 [1977]. *The Philippine Chronicles of Fray San Antonio*. (Manila: Casalinda and Historical Conservation Society).

Aquino, D.M. 2004. *Resource Management in Ancestral Lands; the Bugkalots in Northeastern Luzon*. PhD. thesis, Leiden University, Leiden.

Argensola, B.L. de. 1708 [1909]. 'Conquest of the Malucas Islands', in E.H. Blair and J.A. Robertson (eds.) *The Philippine Islands, 1493–1898* (Cleveland: Arthur H. Clark).

Bakels, J. 2000. *Het verbond met de tijger; visies op mensenetende dieren in Kerinci, Sumatra*. PhD. thesis, Leiden University, Leiden.

Bankoff, G. 1999. 'Devils, Familiars and Spaniards: Spheres of Power and the Supernatural in the World of Seberina Candelaria and her Village in the Early 19th Century Philippines', *Journal of Social History* **33**,1: 37–55.

Bankoff, G. 2007. 'One Island Too Many: Reappraising the Extent of Deforestation in the Philippines Prior to 1946', *Journal of Historical Geography* **33**: 314–334.

Bankoff, G. 2009. 'Breaking New Ground? Gifford Pinchot and the Birth of 'Empire Forestry' in the Philippines 1900–1905'. *Environment and History* **15**, 3: 369–393.

Banks, C. (comp). 2005. *National Recovery Plan for the Philippine Crocodile, Crocodylus mindorensis. 2005–2008*, 2nd edition (Quezon City: DENR and RMZG).

Barbian, K.J. 1977. *The Mangyan Languages of Mindoro: a Comparative Study on Vocabulary, Phonology, and Morphology* (Cebu: University of San Carlos Library).

Behrens, D. 2002. *Yakan-English Dictionary* (Manila: Linguistic Society of the Philippines).

Benedict, L.W. 1916. *A Study of Bagobo Ceremonial Magic and Myth*, Annals of the New Academy of Sciences, Vol. XXV (New York).

Blumentritt, F. 1882. 'Der Ahnencultus und die religiösen Auschauungen der Malaien des Philippinen-Archipels'. *Mittheilungen der K.-K. Geographischen Gesellschaft in Wien* (Vienna).

Boomgaard, P. 2007. 'Crocodiles and Humans in Southeast Asia: Four Centuries of Co-existence and Confrontation.' Keynote address for the symposium on environmental challenges across Asia. Center for International Studies, University of Chicago, 2 March 2007.

Bowring, J. 1859. *A Visit to the Philippines Islands* (London: Smith, Elder & Co.).

Chirino, P.S.J. 1604. [1909] 'Relacion de las Islas Filipinas', in E.H. Blair and J.A. Robertson (eds.) *The Philippine Islands, 1493–1898*, Vol. XII (Cleveland: Arthur H. Clark).

Cohen, E. 1994. 'Animals in Medieval Perceptions: the Image of the Ubiquitous Other', in A. Manning and J. Serpell (eds.) *Animals and Humans in Society; Changing Perspectives* (London: Routledge), pp. 59–80.

Cole, F.C. 1913 [2006]. *The Wild Tribes of Davao District, Mindanao* (Chicago: Field Museum of Natural History).

Colin, F. 1663 [1909] 'Labor Evangelica', in *The Philippine Islands, 1493–1898* E.H. Blair and J.A. Robertson (eds.) *The Philippine Islands, 1493–1898*, Vol. XL (Cleveland: Arthur H. Clark).

Datan, I. 2006 'Crocodile Images of Highlands Borneo', Paper presented at the 8th biennial international conference of the Borneo Research Council in Kuching, Sarawak.

DBP (Development Bank of the Philippines). 1979 'Success Story: from a Crocodile Infested Swampland into an Integrated Farm Paradise', *DBP Bulletin* **XI**, 8: 2

Diaz, C. 1890 [1909] 'Conquistas de las Islas Philipinas' in E.H. Blair and J.A. Robertson (eds.) *The Philippine Islands, 1493–1898*, Vol. XL (Cleveland: Arthur H. Clark).

Early, J.D. and T.N. Headland. 1998. *Population Dynamics of a Philippine Rain Forest People: the San Idelfonso Agta*, (Gainesville: University Press Florida).

Elkins, R.E. 1968. *Manobo-English Dictionary*, (Pacific and Asian Linguistic Institute. Honolulu: University of Hawaii Press).

Encarnacion, J.F. de la (comp). 1885. *Dicconario bisaya-español*, 3rd edition (Manila: Tipografia de amigos del pais).

Eugenio, D.L. 1985. 'Philippine Folktales: an Introduction', *Asian Folklore Studies* **44**: 155–177.

Eugenio, D.L.1994. *Philippine Folk Literature: the Myths*, Philippine Folk Literature Series Vol. II (Quezon City: University of the Philippines Press).

Eugenio, D.L. 2002. *Philippine Folk Literature: the Legends*, Philippine Folk Literature Series Vol. III (Quezon City: University of the Philippines Press).

Fansler, D.S. 1921 [1965]. *Filipino Popular Tales* (Hatboro: Folklore Associates, Inc.).

Ferrer, J.N. Jr. 2008. 'Welcome Message', *National Museum Papers* **14**: 7–9.

Forbes, W.C. 1945. *The Philippine Islands* (Boston: Harvard University Press).

Forman, M.L. 1971. *Kapampangan Dictionary* (Honolulu: University of Hawaii).

Francisco, J.R. 1964. *Indian Influences in the Philippines; with Special Reference to Language and Literature* (Quezon City: University of the Philippines, Diliman).

Gardner, F. 1906. 'Philippine (Tagalog) Superstitions', *The Journal of American Folklore* **19**, 74: 191–204.

Garvan, J.M. 1963. *The Negritos of the Philippines* (Vienna: Verslag Ferdinand Berger Horn).

Gatmaytan, A.B. 2004. 'The Hakyadan of Froilan Havana: Ritual Obligation in Manobo Religion', *Philippine Studies* **52**, 3: 383–426.

Gavin, T. 2003. *Iban Ritual Textiles* (Leiden: KITLV Press).
Gironière, P.P. de la. 1854. *Twenty Years in the Philippines* (New York: Harper and Brothers Pub.).
Gray, J.P. 1979. 'Filipino Myths of Death and Speciation: Content and Structure', *Asian Folklore Studies* **38**, 2: 11–72.
Hall, J.Q. 1999. *The First Philippine History Book*. Filipino American Journal. http://www.univie.ac.at/Voelkerkunde/apsis/aufi/rizal/hall03.htm Downloaded 18 March 2008.
Harrison, T. 1958. 'A Living Megalith in Upland Borneo', *Sarawak Museum Journal* **8**, 12: 694–702.
Hart, D.V. and H.C. Hart. 1966. 'Cinderella in the Eastern Bisayas: with a Summary of the Philippine Folktale', *The Journal of American Folklore* **79**, 312: 307–337.
Hédard, M. and G. Fréchet. 2005. 'Dragons et saints enluminés', in Z. Gourarier, P. Hoch and P. Absalon (eds.) *Dragons; au jardin zoologique des mythologies* (Metz: Éditions Serpenoise) pp. 91–111
Hemley, G., and J. Caldwell. 1986. 'The Crocodile Skin Trade since 1979', in *Crocodiles*, Proceedings of the 7th Working Meeting of the IUCN/SSC Crocodile Specialist Group (Gland: IUCN), pp. 398–412.
Hernandez, A.V. 1983. *Luha ng buwaya* (Quezon City: Ateneo de Manila Univ. Press).
Hose, C. and W. McDougall. 1901. 'The Relations between Men and Animals in Sarawak', *The Journal of the Anthropological Institute of Great Britain and Ireland* **31**: 173–213.
Ingold, T. 1994. 'From Trust to Domination. An Alternative History of Human–Animal Relations', in A. Manning and J. Serpell (eds.) *Animals and Humans in Society; Changing Perspectives* (London: Routledge) pp. 1–22.
IUCN (World Conservation Union). 2006. *2006 IUCN Red List of Threatened Species*. www.iucnredlist.org. Downloaded on 20 November 2006.
Jagor, F. 1875 [2004]. *The Former Philippines Thru Foreign Eyes*. The Project Gutenberg EBook. Downloaded on 23 November 2006.
Jenkins, M. and S. Broad. 1994. *International Trade in Reptile Skins: A Review and Analysis of the Main Consumer Markets, 1983*–1991 (Cambridge: TRAFFIC International).
Juanmartí, J. 1892. *Diccionario moro-maguindanao-español* (Manila).
Keesing, F.M. 1962. *The Ethnohistory of Northern Luzon* (Stanford: Stanford University Press).
Kiessling, N.K. 1970. 'Antecedents of the Medieval Dragon in Sacred History', *Journal of Biblical Literature* **89**, 2: 167–177.
Knapen, H. 2001. *Forests of Fortune? The Environmental History of Southeast Borneo, 1600–1880* (Leiden: KITLV Press).
Knibbe, K.E. and A.J. Angnged. 2005. *Cultural Change Among the Kalinga and Catalangan in the Foothills of the Sierra Madre* (Cabagan: CVPED).
Knight, J. 2000. 'Introduction', in J. Knight (ed.) *Natural Enemies; People–Wildlife Conflicts in Anthropological Perspective* (New York: Routledge) pp. 1–35.
Kruyt, A.C. 1935. *De krokodil in het leven van de Posoërs* (Oegstgeest: Zendingsbureau).
Lisboa, M. de. 1865 [2004]. 'Vocabulario de la lengue Bicol', in M.W. Mintz (ed.) *Bikol-English Dictionary* (Quezon City: New Day Publishers).
Loarca, M. de. 1582 [1909]. 'Relacion de las Islas Filipinas', in E.H. Blair and J.A. Robertson (eds.) *The Philippine Islands, 1493–1898*, Vol. V (Cleveland: Arthur H. Clark).

Long, G. (ed). 1843. *The Penny Cyclopaedia*, Vol. XVIII-B (Oxford: Society for the Diffusion of Useful Knowledge).

Maceda, J. 1984. 'A Cure of the Sick Bpagipat in Dulawan, Cotabato (Philippines)', *Acta Musicologica* **56**, 1: 92–105.

Maffi, L. and E. Woodley. 2010. *Biocultural Diversity Conservation; a Global Sourcebook* (London: Earthscan).

Malayang III, B.S. 2007. 'Philippine Crocodile Conservation in the Philippines', Keynote address during the Forum on Crocodiles in the Philippines, 31 January 2007, Manila. www.su.edu.ph/pres_speaks/bsm_croc_phils.html Downloaded on 26 March 2008.

Mangansakan II, D.G. 2008. 'Crocodile Symbolism in Maguindanaon Culture', *National Museum Papers* **14**: 133–39.

Martin, C. 1978. *Keepers of the Game: Indian–Animal Relationships and the Fur Trade* (Berkeley: University of California Press).

Maxwell, R. 1990. *Textiles of Southeast Asia; Traditions, Trade and Transformation* (Australian National Gallery. Melbourne: Oxford University Press).

McKaughan, H.P. and B.A. Macaraya. 1967. *A Maranao Dictionary* (Honolulu: University of Hawaii Press).

McNeill, J.R. 2003. 'Observations on the Nature and Culture of Environmental History', *History and Theory* **42**, 4: 5–43

Menez, H. 2004. *Talisman, Leadership, and Power; the Belief in Magical Potency Continues to pervade Filipino Life* (Manila: National Commission for Culture and the Arts).

Mercado, V.P. 2008. 'Current Status of the Crocodile Industry in the Republic of the Philippines', *National Museum Papers* **14**: 26–34.

Middelkoop, P. 1971. 'Nai Tirans and Nai Besis in kosmische huwelijksrelatie met de krokodil', *Bijdragen tot de Taal-, Land-, en Volkenkunde* **127**, 4: 434–451.

Minter, T. 2009. 'Contemporary Relations between the Agta and their Farming Neighbours in the Northern Sierra Madre, the Philippines', in K. Ikeya, H. Ogawa and P. Mitchell (eds.) *Interactions between Hunter-gatherers and Farmers from Prehistory to Present*, Senri Ethnological Studies 73 (Osaka: SENRI) pp. 205–228.

Morga, A. de. 1609 [1909]. 'Sucesos de las Filipinas', in E.H. Blair and J.A. Robertson (eds.) *The Philippine Islands, 1493–1898*, Vol. XVI (Cleveland: Arthur H. Clark).

Mozo, A. 1673 [1909]. 'Missiones de Philippinas de la Orden de nuestro Padre San Augustin: noticia historico naturel', in E.H. Blair and J.A. Robertson (eds.) *The Philippine Islands, 1493–1898*, Vol. XLVIII (Cleveland: Arthur H. Clark).

Navarette, D.F. 1676 [1909]. 'Tratados Historicos, Politicos, Ethicos y Religiosos de la Monarchia de China', in E.H. Blair and J.A. Robertson (eds.) *The Philippine Islands, 1493–1898*, Vol. XXXVII (Cleveland: Arthur H. Clark).

Nocheseda, E.I. 2002. 'Ecological and Ritual Change in the Devotion to Santa Marta of Pateros', *Philippine Quarterly of Culture and Society* **30**, 1/2: 65–110.

Ortega, G.V. 1998. 'Philippine Crocodile Conservation', *Crocodiles*, Proceedings of the 14th meeting of the Crocodile Specialist Group (Gland: IUCN) pp. 101–133.

Ortega, G.V., P.A. Regoniel and M.L.M. Jamerlan. 1993. 'Philippine Crocodiles: Their Conservation, Management and Future Sustainable Use', *The Asian International Journal of Life Sciences* **2**: 121–139.

Palawan State College. 1991. 'Survey of Lake Manguao Residents on Level of Awareness

and Acceptance of Crocodile Conservation and the CFI project', *CFI News* **4**, 2: 4–11.
Paterno, M.E.P., S.B. Castro, R.B. Javellana and C.S. Alvina. 2001. *Dreamweavers* (Makati: Bookmark Inc.).
PCARR (Philippines Council for Agriculture and Resources Research). 1977. 'Crocodile Meat: Another Delicacy?' *PCARR Farm News* 4 July, Los Baños: 1130.
Philippine Commission. 1901. *Report of the Philippine Commission to the President*, Vol. III (Washington).
Persoon, G.A. and H.H. de Iongh. 2004. 'Pigs Across Ethnic Boundaries; Examples from Indonesia and the Philippines', in J. Knight (ed.) *Wildlife in Asia; Cultural Perspectives* (London: Routledge) pp. 165–184.
Ploeg, J. van der and M. van Weerd. 2004. 'Devolution of Natural Resource Management and Philippine Crocodile Conservation in San Mariano, Isabela', *Philippine Studies* **52**, 3: 346–383.
Ploeg, J. van der, M.C. Cureg and M. van Weerd. 2008a. 'Mobilising Public Support for In-situ Conservation of the Philippine Crocodile in the Northern Sierra Madre: Something to be Proud Of!' *National Museum Papers* **14**: 68–94
Ploeg, J. van der, D. Rodriguez, B. Tarun, J. Guerrero, M. Balbas, S. Telan, A. Masipiqueña, M.C. Cureg and M. van Weerd. 2008b. 'Crocodile Rehabilitation, Observance and Conservation (CROC) Project: the Conservation of the Critically Endangered Philippine Crocodile (Crocodylus mindorensis) in Northeast Luzon, the Philippines', Final report BP Conservation Program Consolidation Award (Cabagan: Mabuwaya Foundation).
Ploeg, J. van der, M.G. Balbas and M. van Weerd. 2009. 'Do Crocodiles Have Rabies? Initiating a Dialogue on In-situ Crocodile Conservation', *Crocodile Specialist Group Newsletter* **28**, 3: 8–10
Polenda, F.C. 1989 [2002]. *A Voice from the Hills: Essays on the Culture and World View of the Western Bukidnon Manobo People* (Manila: Summer Institute of Linguistics).
Raedt, J. de. 1993. *Buaya Society*, Cordillera Study Center Monograph 5 (Baguio City: UP Baguio).
Ratcliff, L.K. 1949. 'Filipino Folklore', *The Journal of American Folklore* **62**, 245: 259–289.
Reid, L.A. (ed.). 1971. *Philippine Minor Languages: Word lists and Phonologies* (Honolulu: University of Hawaii Press).
Rizal, J. 1886 [1996]. *Noli Me Tangere* [The Social Cancer] (Quezon City: Giraffe Books).
Rizal, J. 1891 [1997]. *El Filibusterismo* [The Reign of Greed] (Quezon City: Giraffe Books).
Ross, C.A. 1982. 'Philippine Crocodile Crocodylus mindorensis', Final report, Smithsonian Institution/World Wildlife Fund Philippine crocodile project (Washington).
Ross, C.A. and A.C. Alcala. 1983. 'Distribution and Status of the Philippine Crocodile (Crocodylus mindorensis)', *Kalikasan: The Philippine Journal of Biology* **12**: 169–173.
Schama, S. 1995. *Landscape and Memory* (London: Harper Collins).
Schebesta, P. 1957. *Die Negrito Asiens*, Studia Instituti Anthropos, Vol. 13, Band II.2 (Vienna: St. Gabriel-Verlag).
Schmidt, K.P. 1938. 'History of a Paratype of Crocodylus Mindorensis', *Copeia* **2**: 89.
Schulte Nordholt, H.G. 1971. *The Political System of the Atoni of Timor*, Verhandelingen

van het Instituut voor Taal-, Land- en Volkenkunde (The Hague: Martinus Nijhoff).

Schultze, W. 1914. 'Notes on a Nesting Place of Crocodilus palustris', *Philippine Journal of Science* **IX**, Sec. D, 3: 313

Scott, J.C. 1998. *Seeing like a State: How Certain Schemes to Improve the Human Condition Have Failed* (New Haven: Yale University Press).

Scott, W.H. 1979. 'Semper's "Kalingas" 120 Years Later', *Philippines Sociological Review* **27**: 93–101.

Scott, W.H. 1982. *Cracks in the Parchment Curtain and Other Essays in Philippine History* (Quezon City: New Day Publishers).

Scott, W.H. 1994. *Barangay; Sixteenth Century Philippine Culture and Society* (Quezon City: Ateneo de Manila Univ. Press).

Skeat, W.W. 1900 [1984]. *Malay Magic; Being an Introduction to the Folklore and Popular Religion of the Malay Peninsula* (Singapore: Oxford Univ. Press).

Svelmoe, G. and T. Svelmoe. 1990. *Mansaka Dictionary*, Language data Asian-Pacific series 16 (Dallas: Summer Institute of Linguistics).

Thorbjarnarson, J. 1999. 'Crocodile Tears and Skins: International Trade, Economic Constraints, and Limits to the Sustainable use of Crocodilians', *Conservation Biology*. **13**, 3: 465–470.

Tramp, G.D. 1995. *Waray-English Dictionary* (Kensington: Dunwoody Press).

Vanoverbergh, M. 1928. 'Animal Names in Iloko', *Journal of American Oriental Society* **48**: 1–33.

Vanoverbergh, M. 1972. *Isneg-English Vocabulary*, Oceanic linguistics special publication 11 (Honolulu: University Press of Hawaii).

Vivanco, L.A. 2004. 'The Work of Environmentalism in an Age of Televisual Adventures', *Cultural Dynamics* **16**, 1: 5–27.

WCSP (Wildlife Conservation Society of the Philippines). 1997. *Philippine Red Data Book* (Makati: Bookmark).

Webb, G.J.W. and S.C. Manolis. 1989. *Australian Crocodiles; a Natural History* (Sydney: New Holland).

Weerd, M. van and J. van der Ploeg. 2004. 'A New Future for the Philippine Crocodile', *Sylvatrop* **13**, 1/2: 31–50.

Wernstedt, F.L. 1956. 'Cebu: Focus of Philippine Interisland Trade', *Economic Geography* **32**, 4: 336–346.

Wernstedt, F.L. and J.E. Spencer. 1967. *The Philippine Island World: a Physical, Cultural and Regional Geography* (Berkeley: University of California Press).

Wilken, G.A. 1885. *Het animisme bij den volken van den Indischen Archipel* (Leiden: E.J. Brill).

Wolfenden, E.P. (comp). 2001. *A Masbatenyo-English Dictionary* (Manila: Linguistic Society of the Philippines).

Worcester, D.C. 1898 [2005]. *The Philippine Islands and Their People; a Record of Personal Observation and Experience, with a Short Summary of the More Important Facts in the History of the Archipelago* (New York: Macmillan Company).

Demonstration Wildlife: Negotiating the Animal Landscape of Vancouver's Stanley Park, 1888–1996

Sean Kheraj

From the portrait of a beaver on the five-cent coin to the inflatable moose that whimsically hovered over the audience in BC Place during the closing ceremonies of the 2010 Winter Olympic Games in Vancouver, wildlife has come to represent a significant aspect of Canada's national identity. Canadian historians often look to the study of wildlife in national parks and wilderness areas outside of cities to better understand the relationship between Canadians and the rest of nature because, in many ways, wildlife has become emblematic of the country.[1] Some of the earliest Canadian wildlife conservationists, including Ernest Thompson Seton, Charles Gordon Hewitt and Grey Owl were principally concerned with safeguarding the most prominent mammals of the northwest that were representative of a particular wilderness ideal.[2] Yet most Canadians in the past century encountered wild animals in cities rather than distant wilderness areas. Since 1931, Canada has been a majority urban society with most of its population concentrated in a handful of southern cities. Given the urban character of Canadian society in the twentieth century, histories of large city parks, such as Stanley Park in Vancouver, BC, illustrate the changing relationship between people and wild animals in Canada because they represent local, regular encounters with a diverse range of animal species. Studies of urban parks, then, can help historians better understand and situate attitudes toward wildlife in predominantly urban countries around the world where people are more likely to encounter wild animals on a regular basis in cities than in wilderness areas.[3]

The histories of local and regional parks in Canada reveal that human relations with wildlife were not limited to occasional, and sometimes fleeting, encounters in large national parks, distant from major population centres. As this article argues, the everyday interactions between people and animals within shared urban environments also influenced Canadian perceptions of wildlife and the management of park animals in the nineteenth and twentieth centuries. Shifts in popular perceptions of wildlife were, of course, influenced by broader changes in environmental thought in North America but they were also the product of the quotidian experiences of urban park visitors with animals and the position of places like Stanley Park within an urban environment. This, in turn, influenced changes in park policies that aimed to satisfy tourist demand. Therefore, this case study illustrates that park animal management policies and attitudes toward the place of animals in parks were not always informed by imagined, idealised concepts about wildlife from a distance but were shaped and changed over time according to local concerns and regular interactions between people and animals living in a shared environment.

Nigel Rothfels accurately conveys the problem of trying to understand animals historically through human-produced sources, recognising, however, that 'even if animals are always only what we think they are, we should not be deterred from exploring their historical record'. That record, in the case of Stanley Park, shows that human ideas and perceptions of animals are shaped in part by the autonomous behaviour of the animals themselves over time as well as their interactions within a common environment.[4] Furthermore, that autonomous animal behaviour placed limits on human control of animals in this park. This particular history illustrates numerous unforeseen consequences of the introduction of new species to this environment. Human modifications to the park environment opened niches for opportunist animal species to exert their autonomy and occupy the park. Animals found ways to elude park policy and operate beyond the purview of human control. At times, animals exercised autonomy by attacking one another (or human bystanders), escaping and destroying park property. There were also environmental limits to human control over animals in Stanley Park. This was especially true for the exotic zoo animals, many of which suffered shortened lives due to captivity in alien environments.

While Vancouver Park Board animal management policies changed over the course of the twentieth century, the consequences and legacies of the board's ecological modifications to Stanley Park endured beyond the vacillating perceptions of human-animal relations. Those legacies placed further constraints on human agency and reshaped policy options regarding the animal population of Stanley Park. Early twentieth-century decisions to introduce new species to the park, such as grey squirrels or trout, were intended to be long-term programmes yet these policies were short-lived. The impermanence of such animal management programs contrasts with the endurance of their ecological consequences.[5]

Stanley Park is one of the oldest and largest urban parks in Canada. Created in 1887, the park was one of Canada's most ostentatious examples of the North American urban parks movement, which ushered in the creation of Central Park in New York City (1853), Fairmount Park in Philadelphia (1855), Golden Gate Park in San Francisco (1870) and Mount Royal Park in Montreal (1876). Like the origins of Canada's national parks, Stanley Park was created toward the end of the nineteenth century within the current of a parks movement influenced by events and ideas across the border in the United States.[6]

A 1909 *Vancouver Daily Province* magazine article described Stanley Park as 'a symphony in green' and proclaimed that the park was the 'pride of Vancouver and jewel of British Columbia and as long as its beauties are left unspoiled by the rude hand of commercialism or so-called "improvement" it will always remain one of the most unique playgrounds in the world'. But, of course, the rude hand of 'commercialism' and 'improvement' had in fact already done much to construct the internationally renowned beauty of Stanley Park.

Demonstration Wildlife

This active human intervention included significant modifications to the animal population of the peninsula. By 1909, Stanley Park was home to a more diverse range of animal species than any other time in its history, including squirrels, swans, ducks, beaver, bears, monkeys and even bison.[7] From the late nineteenth century to the end of the twentieth century, the Vancouver Park Board used Stanley Park to display samples of animal species from across Canada and around the world for non-consumptive recreational purposes to urban tourists and other park visitors who might not have had the opportunity to engage with such animals otherwise.[8]

Over the course of the late nineteenth and twentieth centuries, human–animal relations on the Stanley Park peninsula shifted according to prevailing notions of 'improvement' and landscape modification current in the North American parks and later environmental movements. Prior to 1945, Park Board animal management policies embodied the perception that human modification of the animal composition of the park was a necessary improvement for the pleasure of tourists and other park visitors. The board actively introduced new free-roaming and captive species to the peninsula in order to achieve a particular landscape effect and nature experience consistent with the expectations of a public that wanted to regularly encounter such creatures as they rambled through the forest. After 1945, the Park Board moved away from such interventionist policies and began instead to foster habitat to establish sanctuaries for wildlife observation. These policies represented changing perceptions of park environments, popular understandings of ecology and altered sentiments toward non-human animals among urban dwellers by the late twentieth-century. By 1994, Vancouverites voted to remove the zoo facilities from Stanley Park, eliminating one of the last remnants of the artificial introduction of new animal species to the peninsula, a practice no longer considered appropriate for an urban park.

THE ANIMALS OF THE STANLEY PARK PENINSULA TO 1900

Vancouver was cut out of the forest along the shores of Burrard Inlet in the 1880s. When the Canadian Pacific Railway Company announced that Coal Harbour would be the terminus for the long-anticipated transcontinental railway, what began in the mid-1860s as a small lumber settlement of just a few hundred non-Aboriginal colonists surrounding one of two sawmills on the inlet, suddenly grew into a city with a population of more than 13,000 people by 1891. Vancouver was nestled within a dense coniferous forest along the Northwest Coast with an array of both terrestrial and marine wildlife. As the city grew and the forest was cut back to make room for roads and buildings, the peninsular tip of the Burrard uplands, which became Stanley Park in 1887, stood adjacent to the emerging urban environment as a lone island of forest (Figure 1).[9]

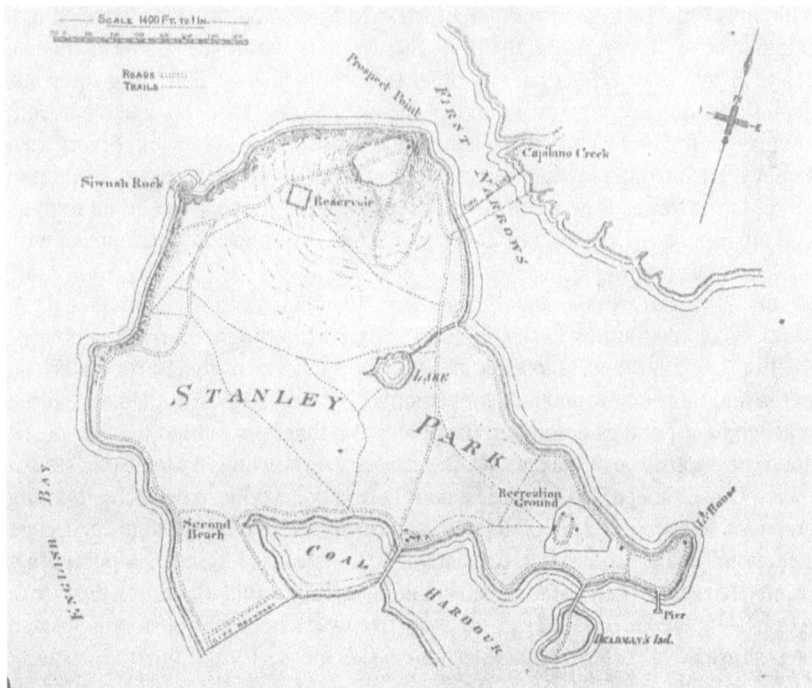

Figure 1. 1911 Map of Stanley Park. Source: City of Vancouver Archives (hereafter CVA), Map 368.

By 1888, the year Stanley Park first opened to the public, urbanisation had transformed wildlife habitats on the Burrard uplands, leaving Stanley Park an isolated forest for a significantly reduced population of wild animals. The Great Fire of 1886 and clear-cut logging drove larger animals like deer (*Cervidae*), bears (*Ursidae*), cougars (*Puma concolor*) and wolves (*Canis lupus*) to the suburban fringes of the city in South Vancouver, Burnaby and across Burrard Inlet to the North Shore. Early Vancouver settlers exhibited hostility toward wild animals that transgressed the emerging perceived boundary between wilderness and the city, illustrating Patricia Partnow's argument that the urban view of wildlife is rooted in a territorial separation of humans and wild animals. Settlers showed little tolerance for these 'intruders'. One pioneer settler named George Cary recalled the presence of deer in the West End of Vancouver in the 1880s as loggers cleared the land. He said that the deer 'got so used to the men slashing that they became quite tame; they would come around, you could see them any day; everyone knew about them. On one occasion, a few of those unfortunate deer trod too close to the city. Cary said he 'heard those deer go by on that board walk, tap, tap, tap, as they walked along the boards', before two men shot the deer that dared to mix the wild with the urban. As people cut away the forest in

Demonstration Wildlife

order to carve out a new urban environment for human settlers, they did so at the expense of habitat that had previously sustained wild animal populations.[10]

At just under one thousand acres, Stanley Park was too small to sustain significant numbers of large wild animals in its early years but it was home to many small animals, including raccoons (*Procyon lotor*), beaver (*Castor canadensis*), skunks (*Mephitis mephitis*), red squirrels (*Tamiasciurus hudsonicus*), Douglas squirrels (*Tamiasciurus douglasii*) and a variety of wild birds. The largest animals that lived in the park prior to 1888 were, in fact, not wild but instead domestic livestock animals. In its early years, the park hosted the domestic animals of the settlers and Coast Salish peoples who lived on the peninsula. Prior to the creation of Stanley Park, the peninsula – once the site of a large Aboriginal village called Whoi Whoi – was inhabited by Aboriginal, European and Asian peoples and their domestic animals, including cattle (*Bos primigenius*), horses (*Equus ferus caballus*), pigs (*Sus*) and chickens (*Gallus gallus domesticus*).[11] August Jack Khahtsalano, a former Squamish resident of Whoi Whoi, described how his family raised cattle on the Stanley Park peninsula long before its designation as a public park:

> The cows, at night, were put in the stable; in the day they ran loose in the park; or along the beach; they got wild grass mostly – along the beach – but there was some English grass, not much, some, enough to carry us over the winter, and if there was not enough, Father bought hay from Black's and Maxie's. Mother milked the six cows in the morning – the other six were dry – and put the milk in big high milk cans – about five gallons – and took it to Hastings Mill in the canoe.[12]

The 1876 Indian Reserve Commission census recorded two horses, seven cows and 151 fowl living on the peninsula that would later become Stanley Park. When the Park Board took charge of the peninsula in 1888, it evicted or destroyed the remaining domestic animals tended by the park inhabitants. Sarah Avison, the daughter of the first park ranger, recalled the fate of some of these animals when the city evicted the Chinese settlers who lived at Anderson Point in Stanley Park in 1889:

> The Park Board ordered the Chinamen to leave the park; they were trespassers; but the Chinamen would not go, so the Park Board told my father to set fire to the buildings. I saw them burn; there were five of us children, and you know what children are like when there is a fire. So father set fire to the shacks; what happened to the Chinese I do not know, but the pigs were set loose and the bull untied, and they got lost in the forest of Stanley Park, and they could not track them down until the snow fell. Then my Dad tracked them down, and they shot them in the bushes, and the bull's head was cut off, and my father had it stuffed and set up in our hallway in our house, the 'Park Cottage'.[13]

By the end of the 1920s, the Vancouver Park Board drove out all of the domestic livestock animals that lived on the Stanley Park peninsula, along with most of their human owners. Domestic animals did not conform to the broader objectives of the Park Board to transform the peninsula into a public park for leisure and recreation. Cows, pigs and other domestic animals represented consumptive uses of nature, which contradicted the prevailing attitude of nineteenth-century urban park advocates and Park Board members who strove to construct Stanley Park as public space for non-consumptive uses of nature. By the end of the nineteenth century, with most of the large wildlife driven out of the area and most of the original settler livestock destroyed, the Vancouver Park Board set out to remake the animal landscape of Stanley Park.

ANIMAL LANDSCAPE ART

The creation of Stanley Park in 1887 marked a turning point in human attitudes toward non-human animals on the peninsula. Whereas in the mid-nineteenth-century both Aboriginal and non-Aboriginal inhabitants of the park kept domestic livestock animals and regularly hunted, fished and trapped wild animals living on and around the peninsula as a source of food, the designation of that space as a public park led to significant changes in human–animal relations. As environmental historian Karl Jacoby found in the context of the American conservation movement of the late nineteenth-century, previous legitimate uses of animals through hunting, trapping, and fishing were suddenly outlawed with the creation of national parks and reserves. Similarly, the designation of large landscape urban parks in North America also transformed these subsistence practices into delinquent behaviour. Park authorities in Vancouver attempted to eliminate traditional consumptive uses of animals on the Stanley Park peninsula and promote recreational uses instead.[14]

The Park Board explicitly prohibited hunting and grazing within the boundaries of Stanley Park, beginning with the passage of the first comprehensive park by-law regulating the use of Stanley Park in 1896. No longer was it permissible for Vancouver residents to set their cattle free to roam and graze within the forest of Stanley Park, a practice that had previously been common for some adjacent residents of the West End and the inhabitants of the peninsula itself. Furthermore, the board relied on the watchful eyes of its park ranger and local police to ensure that park-goers did not hunt or trap the numerous small animals within the park. All fishing off the shores of the peninsula and within Beaver Lake in Stanley Park was also strictly prohibited without special licenses issued by the Park Board.[15]

Of course, ordinary Vancouverites continued to exploit the natural resources of the peninsula for consumptive use in contradiction to the will of the Park Board. One early Vancouver resident recalled how common it was for people to haul wood from the park to make split shingles and hunt grouse within the forest of the peninsula. Another settler recounted hunting wild ducks in the park

Demonstration Wildlife

where he 'used to shoot them down in Coal Harbour'. Even in 1904, the Park Board was alarmed to find that people were 'robbing ... the swan and geese nests in the park'. In 1908, E. Miller Small requested permission to cut four slabs of wood off stumps or fallen timber in Stanley Park. Later that same year, Superintendent George Eldon reported that someone was covertly removing sand from Second Beach at night.[16]

Perhaps the most audacious case of delinquent park use occurred in 1910 when an unknown trapper was found to have been living within the forest undetected for weeks before the Park Superintendent discovered him. The trapper evaded detection until park employees discovered a raccoon and a dog caught in two traps within the park. Eventually, by following the trap lines, the superintendent stumbled upon two small shack dwellings buried within the forest. The mysterious trapper managed to construct a relatively comfortable living space within Stanley Park. Even today, Stanley Park is home to an anonymous, shifting population of homeless people who find comfort, shelter and freedom from police surveillance within the protective forest of the peninsula. It was common to discover such individuals living inside the park throughout the twentieth century, sometimes even under such tragic circumstances as when, in October 1911, park employees uncovered the body of a deceased man from Vancouver's 'floating population', according to a newspaper report.[17]

While some urban residents of Vancouver continued to see the animals and natural resources in Stanley Park as a valued source of food and shelter, many more shared the Park Board's new vision for the peninsula which positioned the animals as aesthetic components of landscape design and the leisure experience of Stanley Park. Many park visitors expected to see free-roaming animals in Stanley Park as part of their nature experiences and the Park Board set out to satisfy those expectations by altering the composition of free-roaming animals on the peninsula. Early park visitors often complained that Stanley Park lacked these animals. They expected the forest to be teeming with wildlife throughout the woods. One Vancouver resident wrote to the Park Board, wondering why '[t]he province is full of wild game [but] none in Stanley Park plenty of feed there and hiding places'.[18] Beginning in the early years of the 1900s, the board selectively stocked Stanley Park with animals of a gentle demeanour and pleasant appearance that would entertain park visitors and produce a sanitised and tamed wilderness effect. The swans and squirrels in Stanley Park best illustrate the Park Board's deliberate efforts to produce a rationalised modern urban wildlife experience for park-goers through the construction of new habitat and the introduction of novel animal species to the peninsula.[19]

The majestic mute swans (*Cygnus olor*) that cruise the waters of Lost Lagoon today owe a debt to early park officials who strove to maintain a vibrant swan population in Stanley Park. In 1900, Chairman Robert Tatlow successfully procured exotic black swans (*Cygnus atratus*) from the Zoological Gardens in Sydney, Australia to stock a series of seven ornamental ponds constructed along the broad promenade from Coal Harbour to Lumberman's Arch. The Public Parks Board for the City of Victoria also donated mute swans from Beacon Hill Park in the provincial capital. The Park Board stocked the ponds with the popular birds, to the delight of visitors, adding to the already abundant wildfowl population of the park.[20]

It was also common for park authorities across North America to stock urban parks with eastern grey squirrels (*Sciurus carolinensis*), which were admired for their charcoaled coats and charming appearance – Stanley Park was no exception (Figure 2). While Stanley Park was home to the dark brown Douglas squirrel

Figure 2. A young boy watching a squirrel climb a tree in Stanley Park, 190[?]. Source: CVA. Vancouver Museums and Planetarium Association fonds. Add MSS. 336 Item 677-664.

Demonstration Wildlife

(*Tamiasciurus douglasii*), native to coastal British Columbia, it lacked the more popular grey squirrels found in eastern North American parks, like New York City's Central Park. In 1909, Vancouver Park Board Chairman Charles Tisdall attempted to purchase a set of grey squirrels from the New York City parks commission and the City of Baltimore Department of Parks and Squares but was informed that these squirrels could be easily purchased through a third-party company that trapped and distributed park animals throughout the continent. After consulting with Park Commissioners in other cities, the board ordered 24 grey squirrels from a game preserve company in Yardley, Pennsylvania called Wenz and Mackensen. The company was originally unable to fill the order and instead sent eight fox squirrels (*Sciurus niger*) until they could forward a shipment of twelve grey squirrels to Vancouver in 1911. Grey squirrels have since co-existed with the native Douglas squirrels in Stanley Park for decades since this original introduction in the early twentieth century. The swans and squirrels of Stanley Park were just two examples of how the Park Board sought to remake the animal landscape through the introduction of new species.[21]

HUNTING AND THE AUTONOMY OF WILDLIFE

Such manipulations of the animal composition of the Stanley Park peninsula, of course, produced unforeseen consequences for the Vancouver Park Board. Introducing free-roaming species, like swans and squirrels, to the park only offered new opportunities for conflict with the existing wild animals on the peninsula. The tenacity of opportunist species, including raccoons (*Procyon lotor*), Northwestern crows (*Corvus caurinus*) and even Great horned owls (*Bubo virginianus*), challenged the Park Board's efforts to manipulate animal populations in Stanley Park. When the board stocked the park with grey squirrels, it ignored warnings from William Manning, General Superintendent for the Department of Public Parks and Squares in Baltimore, who shared his experiences at Druid Hill Park: 'The raccoons in the less frequented places of the Park kill the squirrels during the night, and we are unable to kill all of the raccoons as they come from adjacent woodlands'. The much-admired swans of Stanley Park were equally vulnerable to predator attacks. One newspaper report described a gruesome scene at the birth of a nest of cygnets: 'Shortly after the young ones were hatched, an immense flock of crows attacked the nest in an unguarded moment and killed three of the little ones by picking their eyes out before the old birds could hasten to the rescue'. Marauding raccoons regularly pillaged the ponds, further challenging the fate of the swans in Stanley Park. Park visitors and their accompanying dogs also commonly clashed with swans, a problem that persists to this day. In his 1916 annual report, the park superintendent disturbingly noted that '[o]ur water fowl suffered very severely from the depredations of the great horned owl, which driven from the North in search of food, invaded Stanley Park and worked havoc around the Duck ponds'. The pleasure species provided new opportunities for predators, like crows, owls and raccoons, that took advantage of the open niche, prompting the Park Board to seek out new methods of predator control.[22]

In the first half of the twentieth century, crows were the main objects of attention for the Vancouver Park Board's predator control policies. The board's reaction to the crows vividly illustrates Anne Whiston Spirn's observation that '[i]n the city, humans subsist in an uneasy cohabitation with other animals', especially those we cannot control. Many observers demonised the crows in Stanley Park, describing them in sharply unfavourable terms. M.W. Woods, a Vancouver resident and self-proclaimed 'student of nature', offered one such perspective on the state of the crow 'problem' in 1908. Woods believed that '[t]here is possibly no bird more rapacious and distructive [sic] than the common black crow'. He blamed the crow for the lack of small songbirds in the park. M.G. Johnson, another park observer called the crow, 'the worst of all winged vermin'. Yet another park user complained that the park was full of 'nothing but nest robbing crows'. It was clear that in the early twentieth century, a significant constituency of Vancouverites disliked the presence of crows in Stanley Park. In 1910, in an effort to spare their investment in the swans and other pleasure animals, the Park Board approved a motion to allow members of the Vancouver Gun Club to shoot crows in Stanley Park on Saturday mornings – a policy that was renewed every year until 1961. The gun club regularly lobbied the Park Board to permit its members to shoot in Stanley Park but it failed to get such approval until the club leadership made the case that crows were a particularly troublesome nuisance that warranted this modest form of hunting.[23]

The crow question became more urgent in 1914 when forestry experts blamed the crows for an insect outbreak that threatened the trees of Stanley Park. Thomas Hawkes, a park commissioner from Portland, first raised the problem after experts in Oregon reviewed the forest conditions in Stanley Park and concluded that the insect outbreak was a result of a lack of insectivorous birds. Hawkes claimed 'that they have been driven away from their habitat by the large number of crows'. He encouraged the Park Board to expand the crow hunt and suggested that 'when the balance of nature is again restored the depredations of the insects will be checked'. Federal entomologists also suggested that the board should construct bird boxes throughout the park to attract smaller insectivorous birds.[24]

The Stanley Park crow hunt did not occur without dissent. Some Vancouver residents questioned the scientific wisdom and class interests that lay behind the Vancouver Gun Club's hunting privileges. Ronald C. Campbell Johnson wrote to the *Daily News-Advertiser* to complain about the legality of the crow hunt, stating: 'these commissioners cannot condone such offences and grant class privileges to any particular men'. He pointed to the yacht and rowing clubs in Stanley Park as further evidence of unfairly granted class privileges in the people's park. Campbell Johnson was also opposed to what he considered 'bad taste and wanton cruelty to destroy our crows'. He was not alone in this opinion. The *Sun* echoed Campbell Johnson's sentiments in its editorial pages, referring to the hunt as a 'slaughterfest'. It questioned the scientific rationale behind the crow hunt, arguing that 'there is much reason to believe that the depredations of the crow family have been much exaggerated'. Furthermore, the newspaper editor suggested that the crow played a useful role in the urban environment, claiming that crows 'perform an immense service in the destruction of injurious insects of almost every description and in performing duty as scavengers'. Rather than protecting songbirds, some nearby residents believed that the sound of firearms in the early hours of the morning was, in fact, 'scaring the timid songsters from the park'.[25]

The Stanley Park crow hunt, however, continued until 1961 in spite of local opposition from some residents of the nearby West End neighbourhood. Members of the Vancouver Gun Club were the instruments of a Park Board predator control policy but it was clear that shooting crows on a weekend morning in Stanley Park was also a recreational activity for club members. Hunting opportunities abounded in the rural hinterland of BC, but Stanley Park offered a rare opportunity for city dwellers to engage in this form of recreation closer to home. George Colpitts's study of human attitudes toward wildlife in Western Canada prior to 1940 argues that local fish and game societies, such as the Vancouver Gun Club, played a significant role in promoting early wildlife conservation and animal control efforts outside of urban areas in the west but the Stanley Park crow hunt reveals that these organisations were also active in promoting similar efforts within western cities. In the first half of the twentieth century, Stanley Park brought hunting, a traditionally non-urban wilderness recreation activity, into the urban environment.[26]

The case of the crows also demonstrates some of the difficulties the Park Board faced in its attempt to reshape the animal landscape of Stanley Park in the early twentieth century. Despite its best efforts to introduce new species for the pleasure of visitors, opportunist species took advantage of the swans, ducks and squirrels as new sources of food. Park officials were unable to exert complete control over the free-roaming animals in Stanley Park, even the ones they introduced.

The autonomy of the wild animals of Stanley Park took an extraordinary turn in the autumn of 1911 when a cougar from the North Shore took up residence in the depths of the park forest. In the middle of October, the Stanley Park zookeeper awoke to find five of his animals killed – two deer and three goats. The remains were strewn about the animal paddocks, evidence of a brutal attack. The Stanley Park zoo, with its vast collection of animals, was a veritable feeding ground for wild cougar. The Park Board hired three game hunters from Cloverdale to scour the forests and kill the miscreant cougar. For two weeks, the creature eluded the hunters and devoured another deer until a team of hounds tracked it down. The hunters eventually shot and killed the animal, finally ending the 'terror' of Stanley Park.[27]

The cougar episode revealed the limits of the human relationship with park wildlife in the city in the early twentieth century. While the Park Board was happy to introduce to the environment of Stanley Park novel animals that could be enjoyed like an ornament on the landscape – squirrels and swans, for example – it did not tolerate larger free-roaming species that acted beyond human control and threatened human life. Many considered the cougar to be a threat because it had transgressed the boundary between wilderness and the urban environment. Newspapers portrayed the cougar as 'a very crafty animal'. One newspaper report headline pondered whether the Park Board was dealing with a 'Cougar or the Devil[?]' Some saw the Stanley Park cougar as an intruding, murderous villain, threatening human life and safety. After viewing the body of the animal, one reporter said that 'one could not help thinking how terrible it would have been if it had crept up behind one of the little ones in the park and given it one stroke with its mighty paw'. Cartoons published in the *Sun* further underlined the perspective that the cougar was a cunning, shrewd threat to human enjoyment of nature in Stanley Park (Figure 3). This attitude toward cougars was common across the province and was rooted in a long-standing tradition of cougar hunting in BC.[28]

Figure 3. Cartoon depicting the Stanley Park cougar hunt. Source: *Vancouver Daily Province*, 27 October 1911: 1.

The portrayal of the cougar as an immoral killer helped justify its extermination, but some Vancouverites were sympathetic toward the creature. A.H. Peters, a local Vancouver resident and park-goer, was a lone voice that autumn calling on others to see the cougar as 'a noble beast'. Peters sarcastically blamed human intervention to explain the presence of the cougar in Stanley Park. He claimed that the animal was '[l]ured from the mountain fastnesses by the persistent boosting of the Vancouver Tourist Association ... of Stanley Park's wild and prehistoric tangle', where it found, '[d]eer and goats that had, in its native home, often taken days, nay weeks, of unremitting toil to capture, were here provided free of charge or toil'. Peters's remarks, however, were drowned out by the excitement of a cougar hunt on the doorstep of the city.[29]

Observers were enthralled and exhilarated by the discovery of big game in the heart of the urban environment. Cougar hunting in BC was a popular recreational activity. The provincial government and tourist promoters carefully

Figure 4. The Stanley Park cougar, slain and presented at the office of the *Vancouver Daily Province*, 1911. Source: CVA. Major Matthews Photograph Collection. Add. MSS. 54. Item St Pk P271.2.

managed the image of BC as a wildlife frontier and a hunter's paradise. The *Province* followed the hunt daily with such fervour that its owners even offered a reward for the cougar's capture. When the hunters finally killed the beast, they delivered the corpse to the offices of the *Province* newspaper to be photographed and displayed (Figure 4). The Park Board later mounted the pelt in the Stanley Park Pavilion where it remained for many years. One reporter claimed that '[t]his cougar hunt has been so remarkable as to be almost without parallel in the annals of Canada'. He was amazed by the thrill of 'hunting absolutely wild big game within the limits of a big city'. The story of the cougar in Stanley Park captured the imaginations of Vancouverites and remained part of the lore of the park for many years. In his 1929 recollections of Stanley Park, Robert Allison Hood colourfully recounted the story, informing tourists that 'looking savage and cruel just as she was in life, the animal is to be seen stuffed, in a case above the mantelpiece, in the Park Pavilion. Thus were the deer avenged.' The presentation of the skin in Stanley Park both symbolically affirmed the wildness of the park and human dominion over nature and its creatures. Hunting in Stanley Park represented this popular desire to control animals on the peninsula in the early twentieth century as a mode of recreation.[30]

Sean Kheraj

FISHING AND THE TRANSFORMATION OF BEAVER LAKE AND LOST LAGOON

While the Vancouver Gun Club assiduously lobbied the Park Board to license its weekend crow hunting expeditions in Stanley Park, the Vancouver Angling and Game Association also viewed the park as an opportunity to create a local recreational fishery in the early decades of the twentieth century. Beginning in the summer of 1916, the Park Board received requests from the local angling society to stock Beaver Lake with trout. The anglers argued that the introduction of a recreational fishery in Stanley Park 'would not only add to the inducements in Stanley Park for the residents, but would be of interest to tourists who stay here on their way to fishing in other parts of B.C.' The park would provide a sample of the great fishing opportunities to be found throughout the province. Over the course of the next two decades, the efforts to establish a recreational fishery on Beaver Lake, and later on Lost Lagoon, would entirely transform the environments of these two lakes.[31]

For years the Park Board had tried to improve Beaver Lake to attract more park visitors further into the depths of the peninsula, so as to avoid overcrowding at the park entrances at Beach Avenue and Georgia Street. While Beaver Lake had been a moderately popular site for nature walks, it was a relatively isolated part of the park in its early years. The first topographical survey of Stanley Park

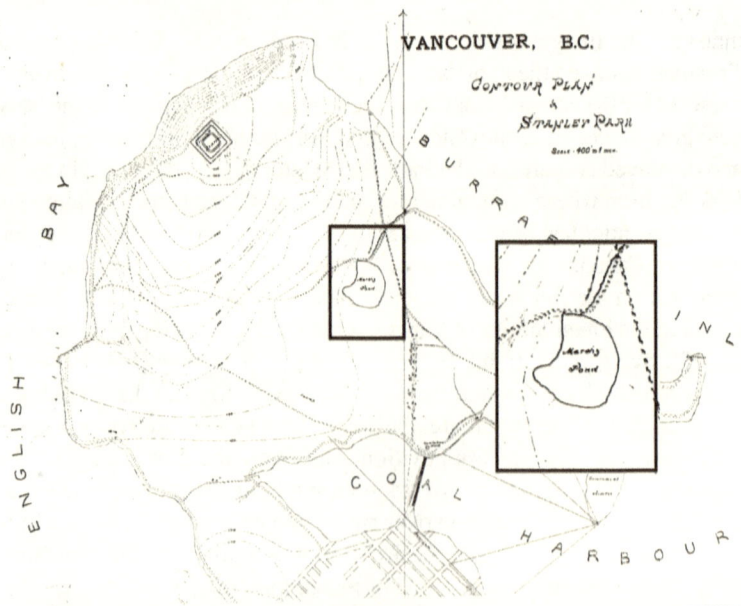

Figure 5. 1890 Contour Plan of Stanley Park with body of water labelled 'Marshy Pond'. Source: CVA Maps Collection Map 721.

Demonstration Wildlife

from 1890 marked the lake as 'Marshy Pond', suggesting that the area was a low-lying marsh that occasionally filled with water to form a small pond (Figure 5). Without adequate drainage and trails, the area remained cut-off to most park visitors and was home to a small beaver colony in the early decades after the opening of the park in 1888. Prior to 1915, when the Park Board initiated rudimentary forest management activity in Stanley Park, the forest surrounding Beaver Lake suffered greatly from insect and fungus infestations, which left many dead trees lying about the woods.[32]

In 1911, the Park Board set out to improve the visual appearance of the lake and make it more accessible for visitors. In order to eliminate its marshy character, the board had the lake deepened and the underbrush in the surrounding area cleared away. To prevent the area from becoming waterlogged, as a result of flooding from the construction of beaver dams, the board encircled the lake with an earthen embankment and path and drove the beaver away from the area. While the improvements made the lake more accessible and eliminated most of its swamp-like appearance, some park-goers lamented the transformation of the little lake in Stanley Park. G.A. Jen, a Vancouver resident, wrote to the *Daily News-Advertiser*, protesting that the changes to 'the lake of the beavers' in 1911 had disturbed one of the most unique wildlife sites in the park. Jen was concerned that the modification of Beaver Lake would destroy both the flora and fauna of the area. 'I think for all these reasons', Jen said, 'a plea may be made to leave the little lake alone'. But the improvements of 1911 were just the beginning of an effort to alter the plant and animal life at Beaver Lake for recreational purposes.[33]

In 1916, convinced that Beaver Lake could be made more useful for active recreation, the Park Board agreed to pursue a proposal from the Vancouver Angling and Game Association to establish a trout fishery in Stanley Park. Following a presentation by representatives from the angling association, the board established a committee to investigate the best means to establish such a fishery. By August 1916, the board contracted the local Dominion Inspector of Fisheries, F.H. Cunningham, to investigate the best means to build a fishery on Beaver Lake, hoping to enlarge the creek running from the lake to encourage deep-sea fish to travel up the creek from Burrard Inlet. Cunningham instead suggested that the Park Board invest in the construction of new ponds and a trout hatchery to artificially stock the lake with new species of fish.[34]

Work on the trout hatchery began in the spring of 1917 with support from the federal Department of Fisheries (Figure 6). Cunningham ordered park and fisheries engineers to deepen the creek running out from Beaver Lake and instal screens at the mouth of the creek to prevent fry from escaping from the lake. In preparation for the introduction of the young trout, the Park Board also arranged for all of the existing fish stock in Beaver Lake to be removed, including an introduced catfish species of brown bullhead (*Ameiurus nebulosus*) and the indigenous eulachon (*Thaleichthys pacificus*). The Department of Fisheries

Figure 6. Trout hatchery on Beaver Lake, 1925. Source: CVA. Major Matthews Photograph Collection 466-20. Add. MSS. 54 Item 466-20.

then constructed a series of small still-water pools adjacent to the lake for the introduction of about 300 to 400 trout fingerlings of a variety of species.[35]

In order to legitimate this proposed new recreational activity, the board amended the park by-laws to permit licensed fishing on Beaver Lake and commissioned the local angling society to draft a set of specific guidelines to regulate the fishery. The board proposed to charge 25 cents per license and restrict the lake to fly-fishing. The purpose of the fishery was explicitly recreational and therefore it was not intended to be a food fishery for local Vancouver residents. The angling society sought to make the regulations even stricter than those adopted by the Park Board in order to ensure that fishers could only catch a maximum of ten fish per day and limited themselves to artificial fly as bait. Such

Demonstration Wildlife

restrictions were not only meant to ensure that Beaver Lake would remain an exclusively recreational fishery, but also reflected particular class perceptions of the middle-class membership of the Vancouver Angling and Game Association. Beaver Lake provides an urban example of the role of angling societies in determining and controlling the regulation of fisheries in Canada, a phenomenon that historians have documented in fisheries outside urban centres.[36]

The original crop of trout struggled to survive and propagate in the first year of the Beaver Lake hatchery programme. The flow from the main body of water through the adjacent ponds proved too strong, limiting the efficacy of the ponds for development of the fingerlings. In the spring and early summer of 1918, park engineers constructed a new channel to divert water from the main body of the lake away from the hatchery ponds. Cunningham also expanded the project by providing 100,000 new fingerlings, which were installed in the ponds by July 1918, including cutthroat trout (*Oncorhynchus clarkia*), steelhead salmon (*Oncorhynchus mykiss*) and Atlantic salmon (*Salmo salar*). For the next three years, the Park Board continued to struggle with establishing a thriving trout population on Beaver Lake, annually requesting that the Department of Fisheries provide new fingerlings. By August 1921, a deputation from the Vancouver Angling and Game Association made a new proposal to the Park Board to further dredge Beaver Lake and redistribute the sediment throughout the remaining marshy areas surrounding the lake. The association believed that the depth of Beaver Lake was not yet suitably adapted for a quality recreational fishery.[37]

Plans to dredge Beaver Lake and continue stocking the hatchery ponds, however, were cancelled due to budget constraints in 1921, leaving the fishery project on hold. The Vancouver Angling and Game Association made another abortive attempt to convince the Park Board to spend its limited funds on clearing out Beaver Lake and re-stocking the failed hatchery ponds with new trout fingerlings. The following year, the British Columbia Angling Association attempted to persuade the Park Board to re-attempt its recreational fishery program instead on Lost Lagoon, the artificial lake that had been formed from the western basin of Coal Harbour during the construction of the Stanley Park causeway in 1916. The association promised to subsidise this project with its own membership funds. The board rejected this plan upon the advice of the park superintendent who found the brackish water of Lost Lagoon to have salt-levels too high to sustain a freshwater fishery.[38]

In 1929, P.A.O. Sankey and a group of other delegates from the BC Fish and Game Protective Association finally won the approval of the Vancouver Park Board to form an organisation called the Stanley Park Fly-Fishing Society in order to raise funds through memberships to finance the establishment of hatchery facilities on both Beaver Lake and Lost Lagoon, including plans to desalinate the latter. They proposed to clear out and deepen Beaver Lake and construct a six-inch main to the Prospect Point reservoir in order to feed the overflow of fresh water into the lagoon. Sankey and his cohorts agreed to provide all the necessary funds to the Park Board and to support all maintenance of these facilities.[39]

By September 1929, Sankey had attracted over one hundred members to the newly formed Stanley Park Fly-Fishing Society. With the funds raised, the Park Board was able to adjust the outflow of Lost Lagoon to drain its brackish water and redirect the fresh water flow from the reservoir at Prospect Point into the lagoon. Sankey reported that over 100,000 trout fingerlings were placed in hatcheries on both lakes over the summer. After three years of work, Sankey recommended that the board finally open Lost Lagoon and Beaver Lake to fly-fishing for one month in April 1932 to test the fishery. The fishery opened that year and continued annually in the late spring and early summer until the end of the 1930s, when the outbreak of the Second World War led the Park Board to close both lakes to fishing once again. Lost Lagoon was turned over to the Air Raid Precautions programme for fire-fighting purposes and the construction of a water pump for home defence, which remained in Lost Lagoon until 1947.[40]

In the aftermath of the Second World War, the Vancouver Park Board reassessed its fisheries management efforts on Beaver Lake and Lost Lagoon and opted to abandon prior strategies to introduce novel fish species to Stanley Park for recreational purposes. Instead, the board decided to focus its efforts on fostering the habitat on both lakes to support wildfowl populations. In his 1947 annual report, the park superintendent identified the lakes as 'the main sanctuaries for wild life in the park and every effort has been made to give the waterfowl and other birds a fair chance for survival'. In that same year, the board hired a game warden to monitor wildlife on both lakes and to ensure that other recreational activities, like boating, did not interfere with the animals. This new focus on the protection of wildlife on Beaver Lake and Lost Lagoon stood in sharp contrast to earlier efforts in the 1920s and 1930s to establish a recreational fishery, signalling broader changes in Park Board animal management policies. The fly-fishing society continued to offer lessons in fly-fishing on Lost Lagoon into the 1950s but, for the most part, the two lakes were maintained as urban wildlife sanctuaries. By the 1950s, after years of human modifications and adjustments, the board saw greater value in fostering the two lakes in Stanley Park for nature observation and admiration of plants and birds. As the park superintendent found in 1952, Beaver Lake 'is very much prized by those who are interested in natural history'. This transformation in the management of animals on the lakes in Stanley Park marked an end to the efforts of the Vancouver Park Board to introduce new free-roaming animal species to Stanley Park. The board limited its acquisition and introduction of novel animals to those held in captivity in the Stanley Park Zoo.[41]

Demonstration Wildlife

NATURE ON DISPLAY

The Stanley Park zoo was one of the earliest and most popular attractions in the park. The zoo was the animal environment most controlled and modified by human intervention in Stanley Park because, as Rothfels notes, 'at their most basic level zoos are for people and not for animals'. But that environment was never entirely under human control and it was never entirely divorced from the surrounding environment of the park, including its climate, geology, hydrology and other natural characteristics. John Berger's contention that '[t]he zoo is a demonstration of the relations between man and animals; nothing else' ignores the material presence of the zoo itself as habitat for people and animals. The history of the Stanley Park zoo, in fact, demonstrates the relations between humans, animals and the environment of an urban park.[42]

As the Stanley Park zoo grew its collection and expanded its facilities over the course of the nineteenth and twentieth centuries, the Park Board's management policies shifted in response to both the material conditions and behaviours of the animals and the prevailing popular human perceptions of what constituted the appropriate exploitation of captive animals within the environment of an urban park. In the 1890s, the first park ranger's wife started the Stanley Park

Figure 7. The Stanley Park zoo, 1898. Source: CVA. Major Matthews Photograph Collection. Add. MSS. 54. Item St Pk P288.3.

zoo collection by tending to a captive bear and a few other small local animals just outside the ranger's residence at the Coal Harbour entrance. This modest collection eventually grew into a more elaborate assemblage of animals, which drew the attention of thousands of visitors every year (Figure 7). BC residents donated animals from across the province to display the wealth of the region's wildlife. For instance, in 1904 a man named Lee Kee offered to donate a black bear (*Ursus americanus*) to the Stanley Park zoo. Another man named Mr. Corrigan from Hope, BC offered a marmot (*Marmota caligata*) to the Park Board for inclusion in its growing collection of regional animals. In 1907, W.G. Murphy from Bute Inlet sent a pair of Canada Geese (*Branta Canadensis*) to Stanley Park.[43]

The Park Board sought more exotic creatures from zoological societies and governments from across Canada and around the world to meet the demand of park-goers who flocked to the growing zoo facilities in the thousands in the early twentieth century. Eventually, the park zoo featured a diverse assemblage of animals, including bears, elk (*Cervus elaphus*), kangaroos (*Macropodidae*), plains bison (*Bison bison bison*), coyotes (*Canis latrans*), raccoons, seals (*Phocidae*) and a very popular collection of monkeys (*Cercopithecoidea*). The animals in the Stanley Park zoo were the most rigidly controlled wildlife in the park, intended to entertain and delight tourists and other park visitors, but, even within this closed area, the zoo was vulnerable to natural forces beyond human control and the autonomy of the captive animals.

Not all the animal species in zoo were suited to the climate of the Northwest Coast, nor did their keepers always manage the captive conditions of the animals with proper care. The Park Board kept very rough early zoo facilities, constructed *ad hoc* to accommodate the great variety of animals. For instance, the quality of the cages did not always provide adequate protection against harsh winter weather. Although Vancouver's climate was milder than other parts of Canada, temperatures dropped well below tolerable levels for some of the exotic animals. One report from 1907 noted that not 'only with the monkeys, but with many other inhabitants of the zoo which are natives of more tropical climates than this, has the present period of cold weather been particularly hard'. The park ranger had to board up the enclosures and light fires for the vulnerable animals during snowfalls and cold snaps. He had to shelter the swans indoors in the winter before their ponds froze over. Despite these efforts there were always winter casualties.[44]

Park visitors also posed a threat to the animals in the zoo. In October 1905, a fire broke out in the zoo, killing several of the animals inside. The fire killed an opossum (*Didelphidae*), twelve rabbits (*Leporidae*) and several birds. After investigation, the park ranger found that the likely culprit was a careless visitor who dropped a cigar or cigarette stub, causing the tragic blaze. The zoo animals were equally capable of literally biting back at the crowds of human spectators. On more than one occasion, mothers wrote to the Park Board, seek-

Demonstration Wildlife

ing compensation after their poorly behaved sons lost fingertips to frustrated monkeys. The condition of their captivity was ultimately the greatest threat to the animals in the Stanley Park zoo. Year after year, annual reports recorded the deaths of different animals from various causes. In one year alone a falling tree crushed an antelope, someone stole a black swan, a bull elk was killed in a fight with another elk, a bear died from a mysterious disease, a dog killed a pea hen, a cougar cub was found strangled in a fence and several animals died from 'natural causes'. Recording those deaths as 'natural' was most likely a case of unintended irony given the most unnatural conditions of the zoo.[45]

By the mid-1940s, a growing constituency of animal advocates and park-goers became increasingly vocal about the conditions of the animals in the Stanley Park zoo. Editorials in the press lamented the fact that 'Vancouver has nothing to be proud of in its accommodation for wild life in Stanley Park'. Others referred to the zoo as 'a harrowing sight for animal lovers'. The general public opinion was that either the zoo had to be abolished or it had to be improved. Even Superintendent Phillip Stroyan begrudgingly admitted, '[t]he accommodation leaves much to be desired'. He hoped that, when the funding became available, the board would construct new modern zoo facilities. The Stanley Park zoo was still one of the most valuable tourist attractions in the Lower Mainland.[46]

In 1949, the Park Board secured additional funds to improve the existing enclosures, but major renovations and expansion did not commence until 1950, when the city's ten-year civic plan allocated funds for entirely new zoo facilities. The board started with the renovation of the bear cages and the construction of a new monkey house to replace the older building. In 1952, the Park Board received a shipment of twelve penguins for the newly constructed penguin pool. The expansion continued to 1955 with the completion of a new bear pit, otter pool, pheasant display and aviary building.[47]

At the same time that the Park Board was upgrading its zoo facilities, it was also engaged in replacing the aquarium at English Bay with a new facility in Stanley Park. As early as 1946, the park commissioners declared their intention to build a new aquarium because the old building at English Bay was no longer adequate. From 1939, a private operator leased the bathhouse at English Bay to use as an aquarium but, by the mid-1940s, it was apparent that the building was in disrepair and a new organisation called the Public Aquarium Society formed to raise money to build a new aquarium at Coal Harbour near the Vancouver Yacht Club. The society garnered support from all levels of government to contribute a total of $300,000 toward the construction of this new park attraction. Because construction at Coal Harbour was too expensive, the board decided instead to build the new aquarium adjacent to the expanded zoo area. The new aquarium opened to the public in May 1956.[48]

The Stanley Park zoo and aquarium remained popular tourist attractions, drawing millions of visitors and providing much-needed revenue for the Park Board into the 1990s when, once again, the degrading condition of the animals in the zoo attracted negative public attention. The Park Board proposed to implement a new $9.1 million 'interpretation and wildlife plan' to yet again modernise the zoo facilities with a new conservation centre focused on the protection and rehabilitation of endangered, indigenous species. At a public meeting on the proposal, several Vancouverites voiced their opposition to the plan. Joe Arnaud, a West End resident, suggested that the board should '[l]eave the park in its natural state. Stanley Park is not an appropriate place for a zoo.' Arnaud's remarks captured the spirit of a new public attitude toward the management of animals in the park and the interrelationship between the 'natural' conditions of the peninsula and its animal population. In spite of the very vocal opposition, the Park Board approved the plans in 1993 by a five to two margin. The chair of the board, Nancy Chiavario argued that what the Park Board was 'trying to do is make Stanley Park a place where people can learn about the wilds of the province and the habitats of animals who live there'. The project, she contended, would modernise the Stanley Park zoo, eliminating previous animal capture programmes and instead focusing on rescue and rehabilitation.[49]

The controversy over the Park Board decision to upgrade the zoo facilities in Stanley Park led City Council to put the matter to a vote in a public referendum. Vancouverites were asked whether or not they supported 'the first phase of replacing the existing animal exhibits around the miniature railway with British Columbia animal habitats focusing on endangered species, conservation and education'. In the November 1993 referendum, 54.13% of Vancouver voters rejected the proposal to upgrade the Stanley Park zoo and instead called upon the Park Board to eliminate its zoo facilities. In accordance with the results of the referendum, a newly elected Park Board set out to dismantle the Stanley Park zoo. By 1996, the Park Board had removed most of the animals from the defunct zoo in Stanley Park, leaving only Tuck, the thirty-five year old polar bear (*Ursus maritimus*) as the final resident of an urban zoo that had once housed animals from across Canada and around the world.[50]

Clearly, by the 1990s public attitudes toward the management of animal life in Stanley Park had shifted. Even the Park Board's proposed conservation and wildlife centre focused instead on fostering habitat and supporting native species in the park. The most significant exception to this move away from animal captivity in Stanley Park is the continued operation of the Vancouver Aquarium but, for the terrestrial animals of the peninsula, the board, in conjunction with the Stanley Park Ecology Society, has instead diverted its efforts toward fostering habitat for urban wildlife, including raccoons, wild fowl, skunks and even encouraging the return of beaver to Beaver Lake and Lost Lagoon. The ecology society formed out of the former Stanley Park Zoological Society in the wake of the closure of the zoo in the 1990s and shifted its efforts toward conservation and wilderness education programmes. The management of animals in Stanley Park today, however, continues to be directed toward recreational, non-consumptive uses of nature.[51]

CONCLUSION

This history of animal management in a major Canadian city park underscores the need for further sustained studies of human–animal relations in urban environments. The trials of the Vancouver Park Board in its efforts to modify and manage the animal composition of Stanley Park since 1888 illustrate the complexity of the interrelationship between people and non-human animals within a major urban centre. Ordinary Vancouverites encountered the animals of Stanley Park on a more regular and intimate basis than the wildlife of Canada's national parks. The management of wild animals in Stanley Park reflected shifting popular attitudes and ideas about the relationship between people and nature within a local, shared space. Debates over the annual crow hunt, the establishment of a recreational fishery and the modernisation of the zoo were influenced by issues of proximity between perceived human space and animal space as well as popular perceptions of the appropriate uses of an urban park. This case study, therefore, illustrates that Canadians' attitudes toward the management of wildlife in the nineteenth and twentieth centuries were not exclusively shaped by occasional, and often fleeting, experiences in national parks outside major population centres. Urban dwellers, such as those in Vancouver, also encountered wild animals on a regular basis in large city parks and zoos.

In the early twentieth century, the Park Board deliberately set out to alter the animal landscape of Stanley Park in order to produce a particular nature experience for urban park goers. The introduction of new species, including squirrels and swans, and the modification of habitat to accommodate those species, were substantial interventions. Of course, these animal management policies produced feedback effects and unintended consequences for the Park Board and park visitors, as each new species and habitat modification generated ecological niches for opportunist species, such as crows and cougars. For decades, the Park Board resisted the autonomy of animals that contradicted its broader animal management policy objectives. In this sense, animals placed material limits on the ability of park officials to control the composition of wildlife in Stanley Park. Furthermore, early animal species introductions and habitat modifications have had enduring ecological consequences that have placed further constraints on park policy, even as attitudes toward such practices changed over the course of the twentieth century.

By the mid-twentieth century, animal management policy for Stanley Park moved away from artificial introductions of free-roaming animals and eventually toward the near elimination of animal captivity. The Park Board shifted its attention toward fostering wildlife habitat for the protection of the existing animal population of the peninsula. This new policy represented changing public perceptions of nature in Stanley Park and changing understandings of the relationship between people and animals. No longer did park visitors wish to see artificially propagated species and altered habitat. Nature observation as a non-consumptive recreational activity instead focused on indigenous species of free-roaming, wild animals. This shift in popular perceptions was, of course, influenced by broader changes in environmental thought in North America but it was also the product of the everyday experiences of park visitors with wild animals within a shared environment.

This new approach to animal management, however, has become more complicated in recent years in the case of Beaver Lake, where the cessation of dredging and other modifications to sustain this artificial lake have led to increased sedimentation and a decline in the depth of the lake.[52] The surrounding forest now threatens to reclaim Beaver Lake, eliminating this beloved site for wildlife observation. In response, the Vancouver Park Board in early 2011 agreed to resume its long-abandoned policy of dredging the lake and clearing its surface of invasive plants. Ironically, these proposed modifications will once again disrupt the resident beaver population, which recently returned to Beaver Lake in 2008, after nearly a century of exile. The beaver have, to the frustration of park staff, been busily blocking the drainage for Beaver Lake, causing flooding of the surrounding paths and forest as they once did nearly a hundred years ago. Aesthetics and the demands of a public with an interest in observing the wildfowl and other animals that have come to inhabit the lake seem now to have placed pressure on the Park Board to 'restore' Beaver Lake in a similar manner to the first 'improvements' applied in 1911. Beaver Lake will not be permitted to regress into the 'Marshy Pond' it was deemed to be in the first topographical survey of Stanley Park in 1890. Instead, the demands of park-goers, who have become accustomed to the recreational benefits of earlier lake modifications (originally intended to facilitate the establishment of a trout fishery), have led the Park Board to intervene in order to cease the new threat of sedimentation.[53]

Finally, what remained consistent over this history were the class-based assumptions about the non-consumptive use of animals for recreation and leisure in Stanley Park. The creation of the park eliminated past consumptive uses of animals, including the raising of domestic livestock as well as fishing and hunting for subsistence or trade. The by-laws and regulations that govern the use of Stanley Park fundamentally changed human-animal relations by creating a new legal space that forbade such practices. While some Vancouver residents still exploit the animals on the peninsula for subsistence (including the resident homeless population within the park as well as the net fishers who illicitly harvest herring off the shores), legally sanctioned uses of animals in Stanley Park remain limited to recreation and leisure. As Canadian cities grow and more people come into regular contact with animals within urban areas, local city parks will continue to embody the changing interrelationship between species within a common environment.

Demonstration Wildlife

ACKNOWLEDGMENTS

I would like to acknowledge the financial support of the Social Sciences and Humanities Research Council of Canada. An early draft of this paper benefitted from the remarks of participants at the 'Historical and Global Perspectives on Provincial and Local/Regional Parks in Canada Symposium' held at the University of Saskatchewan. In particular, I would like to acknowledge the help and assistance of critical reviewers of this article, including Sterling Evans, Jonathan Clapperton, Keith Carlson, Joe Anderson, Andrea Gill and the anonymous reviewers for *Environment and History*.

NOTES

[1] Tina Loo, *States of Nature: Conserving Canada's Wildlife in the Twentieth Century* (Vancouver: University of British Columbia Press, 2006) p. 1. Prominent studies of wildlife in national parks and other wilderness areas in Canada include Janet Foster, *Working for Wildlife: The Beginning of Preservation in Canada* (Toronto: University of Toronto Press, 1998); Karen Jones, *Wolf Mountains: A History of Wolves Along the Great Divide* (Calgary: University of Calgary Press, 2002); John Sandlos 'Federal Spaces, Local Conflicts: National Parks and the Exclusionary Politics of the Conservation Movement in Ontario, 1900–1935', *Journal of the Canadian Historical Association* **16** (2005): 293–318. Jean L. Manore and Dale G. Miner (eds.) *The Culture of Hunting in Canada* (Vancouver: UBC Press, 2006); John Sandlos *Hunters at the Margin: Native People and Wildlife Conservation in the Northwest Territories* (Vancouver: UBC Press, 2007); Greg Gillespie, *Hunting for Empire: Narratives of Sport in Rupert's Land, 1840–70* (Vancouver: UBC Press, 2007); George Colpitt's *Game in the Garden: A Human History of Wildlife in Western Canada to 1940* (Vancouver: UBC Press, 2002), while primarily focused on wildlife in wilderness areas, devotes considerable attention to the influence of urban-based hunting and game associations that played a prominent role in early twentieth-century conservation efforts in Western Canada. Canadian historiography also has a well-established body of literature on Atlantic, Pacific and freshwater fisheries, including Dianne Newell, *Tangled Webs of History: Indians and the Law in Canada's Pacific Coast Fisheries.* (Toronto: University of Toronto Press, 1997); Diane Newell and Rosemary Ommer (eds.) *Fishing Places, Fishing People: Traditions and Issues in Canadian Small-Scale Fisheries* (Toronto: University of Toronto Press, 1998); Margaret Beattie Boghue, *Fishing the Great Lakes: An Environmental History, 1783–1933* (Madison: University of Wisconsin Press, 2000); Matthew Evenden, *Fish Versus Power: An Environmental History of the Fraser River* (New York: Cambridge, 2004); Dean Bavington, *Managed Annihilation: An Unnatural History of the Newfoundland Cod Collapse* (Vancouver: UBC Press, 2010); Liza Piper, 'Parasites from "Alien Shores": The Decline of Canada's Freshwater Fishing Industry', *Canadian Historical Review* **91**/1 (2010): 87–114.

[2] Ernest Thompson Seton, *Wild Animals I Have Known* (New York: C. Scribner & Sons, 1898); Charles Gordon Hewitt, *Conservation of Wild Life of Canada* (New York: C. Scribner & Sons, 1921); Grey Owl, *The Men of the Last Frontier* (London: Country Life, 1931).

[3] Statistics Canada, *Census of Population, 1851–2006*, http://www40.statcan.gc.ca/l01/

cst01/demo62a-eng.htm Accessed 9 January 2011.

[4] Nigel Rothfels, *Savages and Beasts: The Birth of the Modern Zoo* (Baltimore: Johns Hopkins University Press, 2002) p. 5.

[5] For more on the agency of animals, see Jason Hribal, '"Animals are Part of the Working Class": A Challenge to Labor History', *Labor History* **44**/4 (2003): 435–453; Jason Hribal, 'Animals, Agency, and Class: Writing the History of Animals from Below', *Human Ecology Review* **14**/1 (2007): 101–112.

[6] In 1887, the federal government permitted the City of Vancouver to use the peninsular tip of the Burrard uplands as a public park. Previously the peninsula was a military reserve under the authority of the Government of Canada. Stanley Park opened to the public in 1888, named for then Governor General of Canada, Lord Stanley of Preston. For more on the history of Canadian urban parks, see A.L. Murray, 'Frederic Law Olmsted and the Design of Mount Royal Park', *Journal of the Society of Architectural Historians* **26** (1967): 163–71; W. Nus Van, 'The Fate of the City Beautiful Movement Thought in Canada, 1893–1930', *Canadian Historical Association Historical Papers* (1975): 191–210; Alan Metcalfe, 'The Evolution of Organized Physical Recreation in Montreal, 1840–1895', *Histoire Sociale/Social History* **11**/21 (1978): 144–166; Gene Howard Homel, 'Sliders and Backsliders: Toronto's Sunday Tobogganing Controversy of 1912', *Urban History Review* **10**/2 (1981): 25–34; W.C. McKee, 'The Vancouver Park System, 1886–1929: A Product of Local Businessmen', in *Recreational Land Use: Perspectives on Its Evolution in Canada*, ed. by Geoffrey Wall and John Marsh (Ottawa: Carleton University Press, 1982); Robert A.J. McDonald, 'Stanley Park: Vancouver's Forest Playground', *British Columbia Historical News* **15** (1982): 6–13; George Woodcock, 'Savage and Domestic: The Parks of Vancouver', *Journal of Garden History* **3**/3 (1983): 26–53; Robert A.J. McDonald, '"Holy Retreat" or "Practical Breathing Spot"?: Class Perceptions of Vancouver's Stanley Park, 1910–1913', *Canadian Historical Review* **45**/2 (1984): 127–53; Bruce Curtis, 'The Playground in Nineteenth-Century Ontario: Theory and Practise', *Material History Bulletin* **22** (1985): 21–29; William Brennan, 'Visions of a City Beautiful: The Origin and Impact of the Mawson Plans for Regina', *Saskatchewan History* **46** (1994): 19–33; Susan Mather, 'One of Many Homes: Stories of Dispossession from "Stanley Park"' (Master of Arts Thesis, Simon Fraser University, 1998); Barbara Schrodt, 'Control of Sports Facilities in Early Vancouver: The Brockton Point Athletic Association at Stanley Park, 1880 to 1913', *Canadian Journal of History of Sport* **23**/2 (1992): 26–53; John Selwood, John C. Lehr and Mary Cavett, '"The Most Lovely and Picturesque City in All of Canada": The Origins of Winnipeg's Public Park System', *Manitoba History* **31** (1996): 21–29; David Bain, 'The Early Pleasure Grounds of Toronto', *Ontario History* **91**/2 (1999): 165–82; Lyle Dick, 'Commemorative Integrity and Cultural Landscapes: Two National Historic Sites in British Columbia', *Association for Preservation Technology Bulletin* **31**/4 (2000): 29–36; Ken Kruikshank and Nancy B. Bouchier. '"The Heritage of the People Closed against Them": Class, Environment, and the Shaping of Burlington Beach', *Urban History Review* **30**/1 (2001): 40–55; Michèle Dagenais, 'Entre Tradition Et Modernité : Espaces Et Temps De Loisirs À Montréal Et Toronto Au Xxe Siècle', *Canadian Historical Review* **82**/2 (2001): 307–30; David Bain, 'The Queen's Park and Its Avenues: Canada's First Public Park', *Ontario History* **95**/2 (2003): 192–215; Jean Barman, *Stanley Park's Secret: The Forgotten Families of Whoi Whoi, Kanaka Ranch and Brockton Point* (Vancouver: Harbour, 2005); H.V. Nelles, 'How Did Calgary Get Its River Parks?' *Urban History Review* **34**/1 (2005): 28–45; Sean Kheraj, 'Restoring Nature: Ecology, Memory, and the Storm History of Vancouver's

Demonstration Wildlife

Stanley Park', *Canadian Historical Review* **88**/4 (2007): 577–612.

[7] This includes the period prior to European colonisation when the peninsula was inhabited by Coast Salish peoples.

[8] *Vancouver Daily Province*, 10 April 1909: 1 [magazine section]; for more on park improvements in the late nineteenth and early twentieth centuries see Sean Kheraj, 'Improving Nature: Remaking Stanley Park's Forest, 1888–1931', *BC Studies* **158** (2008): 63–90.

[9] *Census of Canada, 1890–91*, Vol. 1 (Ottawa, 1893) p. 370.

[10] Anne Whiston Spirn argues that the urban environment offers new habitats for alien wildlife species, but usually in smaller numbers due to the reduced green spaces in cities: 'Scattered, fragmented remnants of woodland, meadow, and marsh embedded within the urban fabric are islands surrounded by a sea of buildings and pavement.' Anne Spirn, *The Granite Garden: Urban Nature and Human Design* (New York: Basic Books, 1984) p. 207; Patricia H. Partnow, 'Ursine Urges and Urban Ungulates: Anchorage Asserts Its Alaskaness', *Western Folklore* **58**/1 (1999): 39; Major J.S. Matthews, *Early Vancouver: Narratives of Pioneers of Vancouver* Vol. 2 (Vancouver: 1933) p. 182.

[11] For more on the former inhabitants of Stanley Park, see Jean Barman, *Stanley Park's Secret*, and Susan Mather, 'One of Many Homes'.

[12] Major J.S. Matthews, *Conversations with Khahtsalano, 1932–1954* (Vancouver: City Archives, 1955) p. 114.

[13] City of Vancouver Archives (hereafter CVA). Major Matthews Collection. Topical and Categorical Files. Henry Avison. AM0054.013.00126.

[14] Karl Jacoby, *Crimes against Nature: Squatters, Poachers, Thieves, and the Hidden History of American Conservation* (Berkeley: University of California Press, 2001) p. 2. Roy Rosenzweig and Elizabeth Blackmar discuss the ways in which early park regulations prevented urban working class residents of Manhattan from hunting and trapping small animals in New York City's Central Park in *The Park and the People: A History of Central Park* (Ithaca: Cornell University Press, 1992) p. 239. For further reading on the prohibition of hunting, trapping and fishing within national parks in Canada and the US see Louis S. Warren, *The Hunter's Game: Poachers and Conservationists in Twentieth-Century America* (New Haven: Yale University Press, 1997); Theodore Catton, *Inhabited Wilderness: Indians, Eskimos, and National Parks in Alaska* (Albuquerque: University of New Mexico Press, 1997); I.S. MacLaren, 'Cultured Wilderness in Jasper National Park', *Journal of Canadian Studies* **34**/3 (1999): 7–58; Theodore Binnema and Melanie Niemi, '"Let the Line Be Drawn Now": Wilderness, Conservation, and the Exclusion of Aboriginal People from Banff National Park in Canada', *Environmental History* **11**/4 (2006): 724–50; John Sandlos, *Hunters at the Margin*.

[15] CVA. Board of Parks and Public Recreation. Board Minutes. MCR 47-1. 8 August 1896.

[16] Major J.S. Matthews, *Early Vancouver: Narratives of Pioneers of Vancouver* Vol. 2 (Vancouver: 1933) p. 177; CVA. Major Matthews Collection. Topical and Categorical Files. Animals – Beaver. AM0054.013.06014; CVA. Board of Parks and Public Recreation. Board Minutes. MCR 47-1. 11 May 1904.

[17] *Vancouver Daily Province*, 4 April 4 1910: 1; 26 October 1911: 1.

[18] CVA. Board of Parks and Recreation fonds. Correspondence. Stanley Park. 1916-1919. 49-A-5. File 2, Letter from 'An Observer' to the Board of Park Commissioners.

[19] Tina Loo argues that the wildlife policies adopted in provinces across Canada were intended to produce a 'modernized wilderness' where principles of practical sciences

were applied to the breeding of certain species and the construction of new habitats for game preserves. Tina Loo, 'Making Modern Wilderness: Conserving Wildlife in Twentieth-Century Canada', *Canadian Historical Review* **82** (2001): 91–120.

[20] *The Province*, 19 May 1900: 2; 1 August 1901: 8; CVA. Board of Parks and Recreation Fonds. Correspondence January-December, 1908. 48-C-1. File 2, Letter from the Secretary of Public Parks Board for Victoria to Charles Tisdall, Chairman of the Board of Park Commissioners, 26 August 1908; the wetlands of Stanley Park are part of the Pacific Flyway and host different seasonal populations of wildfowl including various species of ducks, geese, and herons. The park is home to one of North America's largest urban heronries. The park's coastline has also been designated an Important Bird Area (IBA) of Canada according to Stanley Park Ecology Society, *State of the Park Report for the Ecological Integrity of Stanley Park* (Vancouver: Stanley Park Ecology Society, 2010) p. 96.

[21] CVA. Board of Parks and Recreation fonds. Correspondence. Stanley Park. 1916-1919. 49-A-5. File 2, Letter from 'An Observer' to the Board of Park Commissioners; 48-C-1 File 3, Letter from Henry Smith, Commissioner of Parks, Boroughs of Manhattan and Richmond, to Charles E. Tisdall, Chairman of the Board of Park Commissioners, Vancouver, BC 29 March 1909; Letter from William S. Manning, General Superintendent, Department of Public Parks and Squares, City of Baltimore, to Charles E. Tisdall, Chairman of the Board of Park Commissioners, Vancouver, BC 23 April 1909; Invoice from Wenz & Mackensen, Naturalists, Yardley, Pa., proprietors of the Pennsylvania Pheasantry and Game Park, to Charles Tisdall, Vancouver, BC 3 January 1910; Letter from Wenz & Mackensen, Naturalists, Yardley, PA., to Mr. A. Hauchet, 22 June 1910; in 1951, Donald Joseph Robison, zoology graduate student from the University of British Columbia, conducted a study of the interrelationship between grey squirrels and Douglas squirrels in Stanley Park. He found that the grey squirrels had successfully established a stable population in Stanley Park by the 1920s and were able to cohabit with Douglas squirrels because they occupied different habitats within the park, reducing competition. For more, read Donald Joseph Robinson, 'The Inter-Relations of the Introduced Gray Squirrel (*Sciurus carolinensis*) with the Ecological Conditions in Stanley Park', M.A. Thesis, Department of Zoology, University of British Columbia, 1951.

[22] CVA. Board of Parks and Recreation fonds. Correspondence January–December 1909. 48-C-1 File 3, Letter from William S. Manning, General Superintendent, Department of Public Parks and Squares, City of Baltimore, to Charles E. Tisdall, Chairman of the Board of Park Commissioners, Vancouver, BC 23 April 1909; *The Province*, 1 August 1901: 8; CVA. Major Matthews Collection. Topical and Categorical Files. Henry Avison. AM0054.013.00126, 10 January 1912; CVA. Board of Parks and Recreation Fonds. Annual Reports. 1916. PDS 12.

[23] Spirn, *The Granite Garden*, p. 208; CVA. Board of Parks and Recreation Fonds. Correspondence January–December, 1908. 48-C-1. File 2, Letter from Mr. M.W. Woods to the Chairman of the Board of Park Commissioners. 2 July 1908; Letter from M.G. Johnson to the Board of Park Commissioners, 12 February 1909; 49-A-5. File 2, Letter from 'An Observer' to the Board of Park Commissioners. CVA. Board of Parks and Public Recreation. Board Minutes. MCR-47-1, 9 March 1910; *The Sun*, 28 December 1916: 10; One year, the Park Board invited the Vancouver Gun Club to shoot horned owls in Stanley Park.

[24] CVA. Board of Parks and Recreation fonds. Correspondence. Entomological Dept re

insect pests. 48-C-5, file 3, Letter from Thomas Hawkes to W.S. Rawlings, 26 May 1914; 49-A-5. File 5, Letter from Gordon Hewitt, Dominion Entomologist, to W.S. Rawlings, Superintendent of Parks, 8 November 1916; for more on the role of insects in the development of a forest management plan for Stanley Park see Sean Kheraj, 'Improving Nature'.

[25] *Daily News-Advertiser*, 19 March 1914: 10; *The Sun*, 20 March 1914: 6; 25 March 1914: 6.

[26] *The Province*, 31 May 1961: 2; Colpitts, *Game in the Garden*.

[27] *Vancouver Daily Province*, 20 October 1911: 1; 23 October 1911; 26 October 1911; *Daily News Advertiser*, 27 October 1911: 15; see also Richard Mackie, 'Cougars, Colonists, and the Rural Settlement of Vancouver Island', in *Beyond the City Limits: Rural History in British Columbia*, ed. by Ruth Sandwell (Vancouver: UBC Press, 1999).

[28] *Vancouver Daily Province*, 28 October 1911: 6; 26 October 1911: 1.

[29] *Vancouver World*, 31 October 1911: 5.

[30] See Tina Loo, 'Of Moose and Men: Hunting for Masculinities in British Columbia', *Western Historical Quarterly* **32**/3(2001): 296–319 and George Colpitts, *Game in the Garden: A Human History of Wildlife in Western Canada to 1940* (Vancouver: UBC Press, 2002); *Vancouver Daily Province*, 27 October 1911: 7; Robert A. Hood, *By Shore and Trail in Stanley Park*. (Toronto: McClelland and Stewart, 1929), p. 147.

[31] CVA. Board of Parks and Public Recreation. Board Minutes. MCR 47-2, 12 July 1916; CVA. Board of Parks and Recreation Fonds. Correspondence. Stanley Park. 1911–1920. 49-A-5. File 9, Undated Report by the Vancouver Angling Club regarding the stocking of Beaver Lake in Stanley Park.

[32] CVA. Maps Collection. Map 721 'Contour Map of Stanley Park' 1890; CVA. Board of Parks and Recreation Fonds. Annual Reports. 1915. PDS 12.

[33] *Vancouver Daily Province*, 16 December 1911: 28; *Daily News-Advertiser*, 27 October 1911: 4.

[34] CVA. Board of Parks and Public Recreation. Board Minutes. MCR-47-1, 26 July 1916; 23 August 1916; CVA. Board of Parks and Recreation Fonds. Correspondence. Stanley Park. 1914–1919. 49-A-5. File 3, Letter from F.H. Cunningham, Chief Inspector of Fisheries, to the Superintendent of Parks, 13 December 1916; CVA. Board of Parks and Recreation Fonds. Annual Reports. 1916. PDS 12.

[35] CVA. Board of Parks and Public Recreation. Board Minutes. MCR-47-1, 14 February 1917; 21 July 1917 CVA. Board of Parks and Recreation Fonds. Correspondence. Stanley Park, 1916–1919. 49-A-5. File 2, Letter from J.E. Hugh, Fisheries Engineer, Dominion Fisheries, to A.S. Wootton, Park Engineer, 19 March 1917; *The Sun*, 1 March 1917: 4; CVA. Board of Parks and Recreation Fonds. Correspondence. Stanley Park. 1914–1919. 49-A-5. File 3, Letter from the Superintendent of Parks to F.H. Cunningham, Dominion Fisheries, 17 July 1917; CVA. Board of Parks and Recreation Fonds. Annual Reports. 1917. PDS 12.

[36] *The Sun*, 1 March 1917: 4; 29 March 1917: 2; CVA. Board of Parks and Recreation Fonds. Correspondence. Stanley Park. 1911–1920. 49-A-5. File 9, Letter from the Secretary of the Vancouver Angling and Game Association to the Board of Park Commissioners, 15 November 1916; Bill Parenteau, 'A "very determined opposition to the law": Conservation, Angling Leases, and Social Conflict in the Canadian Atlantic Salmon Fishery, 1867–1914', *Environmental History* **9**/3 (2004): 436–463.

[37] CVA. Board of Parks and Recreation Fonds. Annual Reports. 1918. PDS 12; CVA.

Board of Parks and Public Recreation. Board Minutes. MCR 47-4, 23 July 1919; 12 May 1920; 9 August 1921.

[38] CVA. Board of Parks and Public Recreation. Board Minutes. MCR 47-5, 13 February 1923; 8 January 1924; 12 February 1924.

[39] CVA. Board of Parks and Public Recreation. Board Minutes. MCR 47-5, 28 March 1929; 11 April 1929; *Vancouver Daily Province*, 15 February 1929: 16; 15 March 1929.

[40] CVA. Board of Parks and Public Recreation. Board Minutes. MCR 47-5, 12 September 1929; 14 April 1932; 13 June 1935; *Vancouver Daily Province*, 13 September 1929: 23; CVA. Board of Parks and Recreation Fonds. Annual Reports. 1947. PDS 12.

[41] CVA. Board of Parks and Recreation Fonds. Annual Reports. 1947. PDS 12.

[42] Rothfels, *Savages and Beasts*, p. 7; John Berger, 'Why Look at Animals', in *About Looking* (New York: Pantheon, 1980) p. 24.

[43] CVA. Board of Parks and Public Recreation. Board Minutes. MCR-47-1, 10 August 1904; 13 December 1905; 9 October 1907.

[44] *Vancouver Daily Province*, 15 January 1907: 6.

[45] *The Province*, 14 October 1905: 1; CVA. Board of Parks and Public Recreation. Board Minutes. MCR 47-2, 28 May 1913; 10 January 1917; 14 February 1917; CVA. Board of Parks and Recreation Fonds. Annual Reports. 1920–21. PDS 12.

[46] *News-Herald*, 23 March 1946: 4; *Province*, 8 July 1947: 4; CVA. Board of Parks and Recreation fonds. Annual Reports. 1947. PDS 12.

[47] *Province*, 24 January 1950: 24; *Sun*, 24 July 1952: 18; CVA. Board of Parks and Recreation fonds. Annual Reports. 1950. PDS 12; 1952; 1955.

[48] CVA. Board of Parks and Recreation fonds. Annual Reports. 1946. PDS 12; 1954; 1955; 1956.

[49] *Vancouver Sun*, 2 June 1993: B1; 7 July 1993: B1.

[50] *Vancouver Sun*, 5 October 1993: A.1; 22 November 1993; Bill Burns, 'Retiring Polar Bear', *Beautiful British Columbia* **38**/3 (1996): 47.

[51] Stanley Park Ecology Society, *State of the Park Report for the Ecological Integrity of Stanley Park* (Vancouver: SPES, 2010), p. 21.

[52] The increased sedimentation has been falsely attributed to the construction of the causeway connecter in the 1930s, which forms part of Highway 99, running through the middle of the park. Recent debate over the fate of Beaver Lake has either ignored or forgotten past dredging and modifications from the 1910s and 1920s, during the period when the Park Board attempted to establish a recreational trout fishery in Stanley Park. This small body of water, once known as 'Marshy Pond', only achieved a more lake-like character following substantial human alteration.

[53] 'Beavering Away to Save a Condemned Lake', *Globe and Mail*, 15 January 2011: S4; 'Commissioner Calls for Beaver Lake Conservation', *Vancouver Courier*, 14 January 2011: 15.

Hunting Narratives of the Age of Empire:
A Gender Reading of Their Iconography

Karen Wonders

INTRODUCTION: GAME TROPHY REPRESENTATIONS

The display practices relating to game trophies can be subdivided into two different categories. Primary displays involve the objects themselves, often prepared by means of taxidermy, and put on show at special trophy exhibitions, in museums of natural history, and as part of private collections on the walls of hunting lodges and country estates. These practices and the meaning of their visual language have been discussed in previously published studies.[1] Secondary displays occur in the form of illustrations of the objects. The subject matter of the paintings, wood cut engravings and photographs can cover the entire range of trophy objects, from living animals in nature, across various stages of the hunting practices, to the individual trophy items as well as their primary display, for example in the form of a pair of antlers above the fireplace in a hunter's den.

The richest sources of such illustrations are the many hunting narratives written by the sportsmen. Their account of the chase depended on illustrations to elucidate and authenticate the text. Illustrated hunting narratives were published in the form of articles in the popular press, of monographs, and of edited compilations. Often they were republished in literature that had other primary functions such as tourist guides, or the illustrations were recycled with a different text. During the Age of Empire (1875–1914), the veritable frenzy of collecting antlers, horns, skulls and animal hides from various parts of the British Empire – in particular in Africa and India – also reached the Canadian part of the Rocky Mountains and the Pacific Northwest.

This paper deals with the hunting-and-collecting mania by examining the iconography of trophy display, found in British Columbia (BC) hunting narratives, written by the in many instances prominent and wealthy foreign sportsmen. The reason for taking BC as the geographical unit of analysis is that it produced a rich body of illustrated hunting literature. This in turn was due to the fact that the province was home to much of the last remaining wilderness on the North American continent, 'a Sportsman's Eden'.[2] To analyse the iconography of BC trophy display, some 25 hunting narrative monographs as well as several illustrated weeklies that contain visual representations of BC big game and BC hunting have been selected as sources.[3] Typical examples include the following four books by prominent sportsmen, three American and one European: *Cruising in the Cascades* (1889) with 47 wood engravings, by George O. Shields (1846–1925), the founder of the American magazine *Recreation*, one of the earliest game law advocates and the head of the Camp Fire Club; *Sport and Life* (1900) with 77 photographs and wood engravings, by William A. Baillie-Grohman (1851–1921), a English-Austrian aristocrat, mountaineer and part-time BC resident; *Camp-Fires in the Canadian Rockies* (1906) with 61 photographs, by William Hornaday (1854–1921), a passionate American wildlife campaigner and the first director of the New York Zoological Garden; *Wilderness of the North Pacific Islands* (1912) with 63 photographs and five photogravures, by Charles Sheldon (1867–1928), an American industrialist and one of the first wilderness advocates. None of the 25 sources were published in Canada, but rather in London (13), New York (9), Philadelphia (1), Berlin (1), and Vienna (1). Some books were reprinted with additional illustrations, such as Paul Niedieck's *Mit der Büchse in fünf Weltteilen* (1905). The first edition had 32 full-page photographs by the author, while subsequent editions included an extra 174 illustrations in the text.[4]

Baillie-Grohman, a distant relative of the Duke of Wellington and the owner of a castle in the Austrian Alps, was probably the best-known and most influential of the foreign sportsmen to write about big game hunting in BC, having earlier published a narrative of wilderness hunting in the American West, *Camps in the Rockies* (1882) that was often reprinted in both America and Britain.[5] Described as 'an ardent nature-lover and a keen sportsman', his bag of over 1,100 Rocky Mountain big game trophies was considered one of the best ever obtained by European sportsmen.[6] Baillie-Grohman published illustrated accounts of his hunting adventures in BC in journals such as *The Field, Wide World Magazine, The Century* and the *Fortnightly Review*, and repeated these in his *Sport and Life*, providing photographic representations of 'the best trophies of North American big game killed by English and American sportsmen'.[7]

Gender is a useful category of analysis for hunting, in particular also when applied to the trophy iconography of the hunting narratives, because it helps answer the question of why well-heeled and in some instances aristocratic or politically powerful hunter-naturalists travelled long distances to climb the mountains, and to struggle through the thick underbrush and forests in pursuit of 'big-heads' and trophy specimens. The representational conventions that developed around the trophies, in verbal representations as well as in non-verbal, visual ones, contributed to defining the sportsmen and hunter-naturalists in terms of their essential masculinity. Thus the gender approach to the illustrations provides detail and specifics about the strategy of self-enactment of the hunters in the public sphere, as these showed to the public at large the ways in which the act of hunting confirmed masculinity.[8]

ICONOGRAPHIC MOTIFS

As a collective source of historical information on hunting, the narratives have as yet failed to attract scholarly attention, and their illustrations as well – only a few titles have entered the recycling process of secondary citation. This study contributes to opening up the genre of hunting accounts to the social history of hunting by focusing on its iconography. What can the illustrations tell us about the driving forces of the fervent passion for collecting antlers, horns, skulls and animal hides? At a mundane level, the visual representations of game trophies and trophy game served to authenticate the account and enliven the autobiographical story. Yet there exists a variety of other, more trenchant ways of 'reading' the illustrations. One of these relates to the process of production, by considering who the artists or photographers were, where and how the illustrations were produced and printed. The early hunter-naturalists made their own sketches in the field, which allowed them to make a claim to veracity – 'drawn from nature' – even though the illustrations were later transcribed for printing by professional draftsmen and engravers. In his path-breaking *Picturing Empire* (1997), James Ryan observes that already from the late 1850s 'explorers, soldiers, administrators and professional hunters began to employ the camera to record images of dead animals.'[9] During the 1870s, a technological transition began whereby the artist-produced trophy illustration was increasingly replaced by photo-mechanical methods of mass-reproduction, and after 1900 the trophy genre was dominated by photographic representations.

Another way of 'reading' the illustrations considers the extent to which these reflect contemporaneous representational conventions. The game animals were portrayed according to a variety of customs of visualisation: as hunting trophies known from a long tradition of European aristocratic-royal painting, as staffage in landscape scenes showing similarities with the primary, taxidermic displays of dioramas, as zoological specimens, or as scientific documentation of the natural history of game species and their habitats. The Austrian industrialist and sportsman Philipp von Oberländer (dates unknown), for example, depicted in some detail the embryo of *Ursus americanus*, while Hornaday illustrated the details of the feet of a mountain goat.[10]

A representational convention that grew increasingly popular with the advent of photography was that of hunters posing with their accoutrements and trophies. Such 'posing' of hunters with their game animals had symbolic cultural dimensions, and this brings us to a further, third 'reading'. Harriet Ritvo added to her by now classic *The Animal Estate* (1987) a section on 'Animals and Empire', densely packed with a miscellany of interpretations, seeing symbolic meaning invested in the game species, the hunters, the trophies, and the trophy displays (see below).[11]

What idea or quality did the trophy iconography communicate? This approach to analysing the illustrations is followed here. The recent literature in the history of science on 'visual representation' is showing, among other things, that iconography, even when entirely accurate in the representation of its object, may communicate an ideological message and in many instances has functioned as a vehicle of information that is not or only partially expressed in accompanying texts.[12] As David Livingstone argues in his *Putting Science in Its Place* (2003), the iconography of geographical regions – how we choose to represent places, peoples, animals, plants and scenery – to ourselves and to others 'is of immense moral and political significance.'[13] Visual representation has contributed to the construction in human consciousness of different global regions, and this capacity of representation 'has been fundamental to the practices of political supremacy.'[14] Photography was a particularly powerful medium used to 'picture place'.[15]

Given the large number of illustrations and the multiplicity of their topics, there is a danger of arbitrary or selective use in support of special pleading. In order to move beyond the arbitrariness of such 'anecdotal' use of illustrations, a systematic – that is, non-selective – documentation of the hundreds of illustrations in the above-mentioned sources has been carried out. Furthermore, by means of an analysis of the principal iconographic motifs – of distinctive, dominant elements in the composition of the illustrations – an attempt has been made to probe what messages were being transmitted.

Some five specific iconographic motifs of trophy animals and animal trophies have been identified in the hunting narratives of the period. The first of these is that of the dangerous inaccessibility of the home or habitat of a particular game species (Figure 1). The hunter is shown climbing precipitous rock faces in arduous pursuit of his quarry, risking life and limb to hunt down a nimble, strong animal. Most commonly depicted in such scenes are either the bighorn mountain sheep or the mountain goat, both elusive species found only on the highest and most isolated rocky peaks. Baillie-Grohman, an Alpine climber and a connoisseur of horns, poetically expressed those qualities that made the bighorn so desirable as a trophy:

> The bold and majestic ram, standing motionless on yonder giddy shelf, showing in perfect repose the classic outline of his noble head against the blue of the Rocky Mountain sky, as if cut in cameo fashion by the deft hand of a Grecian sculptor. With his sturdy, massive body, his thick-set limbs firmly planted on the ledge, his small head carried light, as if the heavy horns were a mere feather's weight, he looks the emblem, not of agility, as does the chamois, but of strength. Of all game that calls the Rocky Mountains its home, he is the truest type of their grand solitude and barren vastness.[16]

The bighorn was considered the equivalent of the European ibex, a *Hochwild* species reserved for royal and privileged sportsmen. The mountain goat had a more ambivalent status as a grotesque oddity, virtually unknown even to science until the end of the century and without an Old World hunting *etiquette*.

Hunting Narratives of the Age of Empire

THE WHITE GOAT IS AN AGILE CLIMBER

FIGURE 1. 'The White Goat is an Agile Climber', illustration by Carl Rungius in George Bird Grinnell and Casper Whitney, eds. *Musk-ox, Bison, Sheep and Goat* (1904).

Baillie-Grohman made several trips in vain to the American West to kill a mountain goat. Finally in 1882, determined 'to find goat or perish in the attempt',[17] he travelled to the Selkirk Range of the Kootenay district of south-eastern BC. Here he discovered that 'British Columbia, that very beautiful but hitherto singularly isolated corner of America, is the true home of this rare animal'.[18] His 1884 account of hunting the mountain goat included six wood engravings by George Inness Jr. (1854–1926), an accomplished artist trained under his father of the same name, who was a founding member of the Hudson River school of American landscape painting. Inness depicted Baillie-Grohman as a 'wilderness' hunter struggling to overcome the harsh conditions of the mountain goat habitat.[19] Another early description of the mountain goat was published in

FIGURE 2. 'The First Shot at a Grizzly Bear', wood engraving in William Francis Ainsworth's *All Round the World* (1873).

1890 by John Fannin (1837–1904), an expatriate Briton and early BC settler who provided guiding and outfitting services to visiting foreign sportsmen.[20] Prominent New Yorkers who came to BC to hunt the mountain goat included the Harvard-educated western writer Owen Wister (1860 – 1938). His hunting narrative was illustrated by none other than Carl Rungius (1869–1959), an artist trained in the German tradition of trophy representation and hunting art whose American patrons included Hornaday and Roosevelt.[21] Rungius was himself an avid big game hunter, especially of mountain sheep and goats, and his work has been linked to the birth of wildlife art.[22] His illustration, 'The White Goat is an Agile Climber', emphasised the mountaineering qualities of the species that made it so difficult to hunt in the high often perpendicular alpine peaks.

The second motif is that of the confrontation of a hunter with a dangerous and difficult-to-shoot animal (Figure 2). Most commonly included in this category are predators such as cougars, black bears, and especially grizzlies. As Shields explained in *Cruising in the Cascades* (1889), 'the decidedly hazardous character of the sport [of grizzly hunting] is what gives it its greatest zest and renders it the most fascinating of pursuits ... no man ever felt his heart swell with pride, his nerves tingle with animation, his whole system glow with wild, uncontrollable enthusiasm ... as does the man who stands over the prostrate form of a monster grizzly that he has slain.'[23] In North America, from the early days of exploration, grizzlies were closely associated with 'wilderness'. In his 1834 western exploration narrative, Prince Maximillian of Wied (1782–1867) pictured a ferocious, attacking grizzly, and this visual 'first' inspired a representational convention when later on hunters and adventurers such as George Catlin (1796–1872) and John Palliser (1807–1887) produced their dramatic grizzly illustrations.[24] In an ambitious four-volume narrative of travel around the world, the grizzly engraving from Palliser's hunting account of the American West was incorrectly 'recycled', being included in the section on Vancouver Island, which has no grizzlies.[25] The vicious nature of the colossal beast and the acute danger posed by the surprise attack is shown in the form of fright and panic of the hunter's horse. More variations on the grizzly attack theme can be cited, one of these entitled 'He had given me enough chances', printed in Warburton Pike's acclaimed narrative *Through the Subarctic Forest* (1896) and drawn by the London-based animal illustrator Charles Whymper (1853–1941).

The third motif is formed by various representations of a 'large bag', that is a miscellany of decapitated heads, horned skulls, antlers as well as skins. Such miscellanies might be temporarily put together in the hunting ground – a hunter's campsite; a pack-train, a collection site for further transport – for the purpose of taking a photograph (Figure 3). Or they might be displayed permanently at home, on the walls of a hunter's den, above his fire-place or elsewhere in his country home (Figure 4). During the Age of Empire, many of the best BC trophies were shipped back to Europe for private display. In the words of Baillie-Grohman: 'American millionaires have for years past, it is well known, ransacked the picture galleries of Europe, where they garnered many of the masterpieces that once adorned the walls of England's mansions or the marble-flagged galleries of continental palaces. Europe has revenged itself by sending to the Western hunting grounds her sportsmen, who have succeeded in capturing there quite as many, and probably quite as irreplaceable, *chefs d'oeuvre*, not of man's but of Nature's choiciest handiwork'.[26]

An iconographic motif that became more dominant with photography was the sportsman himself, posed in 'victory-over-vanquished' portraits (Figure 5). This constitutes a fourth distinct category of representation, showing the hunter standing next to a slain game animal's body, rifle in hand, and victor's foot on vanquished's body. Large species are common, such as – once more – the grizzly, here shown in the case of John M. Phillips (1861–1953), hunting companion to Hornaday and a dedicated American conservationist, credited with having persuaded Canadian authorities to allocate Canada's first game reserve in 1906 in the Kootenays.[27]

The motif of manly victory over the native game had similarities with the flag planting of mountaineers and other explorers of foreign parts. 'Monarch of

Trophäen der Expedition.
(Nach einer Aufnahme des Postmeisters in Wrangell.)

FIGURE 3. 'Trophäen der Expedition', photograph in Paul Niedieck's *Jagdfahrten in Nord Amerika* (1911).

the wilderness! Lord of the mountain! King of the plain!' began Shields' tribute to 'the elk' (as most Americans called the wapiti), 'What hunter, has sought thee in thy pine-embowered home, whose heart-beat does not quicken and who's eye does not brighten at the mention of thy name! For with it comes the recollection of boundless prairies, grass-robed and flower-decked; of pine-clad, snow-capped mountains; of sweet breezes, gentle melodies, grand trophies'.[28] The wapiti closely resembled the venerated 'royal' stag of the Old World, a semi-domestic species bred and guarded for centuries by the aristocracy on private game reserves. The fact that the wapiti was the largest deer in the world made it irresistible to sportsmen such as Baillie-Grohman, the sole aim of whose many hunting expeditions to the North American West was, as he put it, 'to bag big heads'.[29] An illustration for an article written by Baillie-Grohman, 'Wapiti Hunting in North America', published in 1886 on the front page of *The Illustrated London News*, shows the author as a wilderness hunter, dressed in a fringed buckskin jacket and accompanied by an Indian guide. He has just shot 'a master stag whose

Hunting Narratives of the Age of Empire

When the light wanes

FIGURE 4. 'When the light wanes', illustration by Charles Whymper in Clive Phillipps-Wolley's *Big Game Shooting* (1894).

branching antlers need fear but few, if any, rivals, in the great collections made by the ardent sportsmen of Europe.' The inset illustration shows the prostrate stag lying under the rifle of Baillie-Grohman, his huge trophy head carefully delineated; the author noting that 'his antlers alone, on their arrival in Europe, turned the scales at 44 lb.'[30]

A final and fifth motif is that of horns and antlers of exceptional size. Commonly exhibited were the horns of mountain sheep and the antlers of wapiti,

FIGURE 5. 'Mr. Phillips Regrets the Impending Extinction of the Grizzly Bear', photograph by John M. Phillips in William Hornaday's *Campfires in the Canadian Rockies* (1906).

Hunting Narratives of the Age of Empire

FIGURE 6. 'Largest Bighorn on Record,' uncredited photograph in William Baillie-Grohman's *Sport and Life* (1900).

moose and caribou (Figure 6). A photograph entitled 'My favourite Wapiti Head' was printed as the frontispiece to Baillie-Grohman's book *Sport and Life* and he described the trophy as his most cherished souvenir of the Rockies, 'a grand old fellow' who peered down with authority from his place of honour and 'stately exclusiveness' on the tapestried wall.[31] The author was shown seated beneath another esteemed trophy, a bighorn sheep head. The book included a photograph of the largest bighorn on record, shot in the winter of 1892–93 in the Rocky Mountains near Fort Steele in the East Kootenay. Trophy mountain sheep were also sought in the Cassiar district, where in 1896 an American collector from New York discovered a new species, *Ovis stonei*. The Stikine River and Cassiar became known as the best big game hunting grounds on the North American continent; in a period from 1906 to 1931, of 40 trophy heads of the Stone sheep noted for their record dimensions, all but three (from the Yukon), were bagged in the Cassiar.[32] Edward House noted that when he sailed from Vancouver in 1907, on a shooting trip to the Cassiar Mountains, there were 21 sportsmen from various parts of the world on board the steamer *Princess May*.[33]

CONFLATING VICTOR AND VANQUISHED

To repeat: in addition to entertainment and instruction, trophy illustrations had symbolic value. The iconography of game trophies contributed to a celebration of conquest by Europeans and Euro-Americans. The main meaning that the secondary literature has read into hunting, its practices and its display culture is that of the connection with 'empire'. Big game hunting was an expression of domination, an emblem of the conquest of territories and, increasingly toward the end of the nineteenth century, a form of administration when big game hunting became connected to preservation. Hunting was, Ritvo says, the emblem of the style 'in which the English dominated the natural and the human world'.[34] A number of historians have made the connection between hunting and British imperialism in Africa and Asia.[35] With the rise of global imperialism at the end of the century, the collecting of exotic trophies from colonial possessions and far-off corners of the earth claimed by imperial powers became a passionate and unbridled activity spurred on by the international hunting competitions and trophy exhibitions held in European state capitals. Wealthy sportsmen, some of noble birth, were joined by members of the high-ranking military as well as the new capitalist élite in their aspiration to collect the most diverse and greatest numbers of record-breaking heads and horns, or 'big heads' as they were called. The sportsmen were celebrated as an empire builders, and exhibitions of trophies and diorama displays became symbols of imperial power with territorial possession.[36]

The connection with empire is apparent for the British American West, too, as recently described by Greg Gillespie for the mid-nineteenth century, and by F. G. Moyles and Douglas Owram in their earlier study of British views of Canada around the turn of the twentieth century, *Imperial Dreams and Colonial Realities* (1988).[37] From the beginning, the native big game species of BC, as of every other colony, were conceived as 'empire big game.'[38] Gillespie argues that hunting narratives were part of the larger work of empire, that the travel writings by big game hunters were a form of cultural appropriation and belonged to the broader cultural discourse of imperialism through which the British fashioned, maintained, and extended their empire. Moreover, the task of empire hunting evolved from territorial conquest to 'administration',[39] and hunting and wildlife conservation became causally related.[40]

Focusing on the trophy display culture, this, too, was an integral part of the work of empire, which is particularly evident in the case of the primary trophy shows of exhibitions, museums and private collections.[41] A recent work by George Colpitts, *Game in the Garden* (2003), shows how trophies were used to create an image of superabundant wild animals in western Canada to stimulate immigration.[42] Yet in the case of secondary displays – the illustrations in hunting narratives – the empire connection, although not wholly absent, is weak and another one dominates. My interpretation of the iconographic mo-

Hunting Narratives of the Age of Empire

tifs is that they contributed to defining the hunters in terms of their masculine virtues. Others already have taken the meaning of big game hunting beyond the 'spoils of empire' reading to that of 'sexual politics', arguing that big game hunting was to its practitioners an affirmation of masculinity.[43] With respect to BC one author concludes that big game hunting 'constituted its practitioners as masculine and bourgeois, while simultaneously racializing and sexualizing them' – a conclusion, which is based primarily on a study of the social identity of the men who came to BC to hunt its big game and on their relationships to the aboriginal guides.[44]

The analysis of the hunting iconography of this study corroborates but also amplifies the gender interpretation. As stated in the introduction, the illustrations provide detail and specifics about the strategy of self-enactment of the hunters in the public sphere. They documented for the benefit of the public at large the various ways in which the act of hunting was a test of masculinity. Trophy iconography– I should like to argue – functioned as a major means of masculinity enhancement by giving content to the hunter's activities: picturing him in reference to particular animals, parts of animals and field situations. The iconography celebrates the sportsman hunter and his masculine qualities.[45] The trophy representations were instances of conflation of 'victor and vanquished' – and thus a means by which the hunter could appropriate some of the qualities associated with the trophy and its habitat.[46] The five motifs show that more was involved than physical appropriation of the specimens – that too, but '[a]long with the hide and the horns, the victorious sportsman assumed the admirable moral qualities of his vanquished foe'.[47] The depicted animal species are worthy adversaries, as indicated by their size, strength, agility or also ferocity. The five most frequently depicted genera of BC big game were: the wapiti, the mountain sheep, the mountain goat, the caribou and the grizzly bear. The wapiti – Shield wrote – was 'the noblest, the grandest, the stateliest ... in size ... in sagacity, caution, cunning and wariness ... He is always on the alert, his keen scent, his piercing eye, his acute sense of hearing ... His great size and powerful muscular construction give him almost unbounded endurance'.[48] Male moose and deer were also included as desirable ungulates.

Where sexual dimorphism is distinct and the males stand out because of size, large horns or massive antlers, these are the specimens that were thought to merit depiction. The game species most valued were represented as having those qualities most admired as exhibiting human male virtues such as aggressive displays of dominance and courage in battle, determined upon victory or death. The horns of a wapiti are at their best during the fall season when the animal is in rut and the desire for copulation drives the mature males to become ardent, restless and fierce. Wapiti stags are polygamous and fight mighty contests for the dominant possession of harems of up to twenty females. Likewise, mountain sheep rams are determined to defeat any competitors to become the undisputed master of the field. They have large bands of ewes and are territorial and combative, head butting each other with their massive horns during the rut. Both horns and antlers are important for mating behaviour, without them the male cannot keep the females in his harem nor protect his territory from rivals. Baillie-Grohman explained that during rutting season, 'The proud stag, filled with the dominant instinct of the season – love and war – exhibits at this time the full virile vigour of his prime. His neck swells, and he steps with a consciousness of power ...'.[49] In contrast were the females, the 'coy hinds, ever watchfully guarding their lovesick masters, who are now careless of danger, and bent only upon gaining and keeping the mastership over their respective female bands'.[50]

The five motifs speak to the reader with a single refrain, namely the glorification of the hunter in terms of the masculinity of game and landscape. The dangerous inaccessibility of a game species' habitat requires matching agility on the part of the hunter. A large, aggressive and dangerous animal demands a fearless man to conquer it in combat. The larger the sportsman's cache of slain adversaries, the greater a latter-day Nimrod he is. How great a victor he really can be, is symbolised by a juxtaposition of the hunter to the largest and most ferocious of his slain objects of pursuit. And the more spectacular and record-breaking the horns, antlers and hides are that a hunter has amassed, the more he can measure up to other great hunters, in his own and other countries. The secondary trophy display, in the form of illustrations in hunting narratives, were a superlative self-affirmation of the hunters, of their masculine character traits, as valued in a society that honoured those who went out to conquer and dominate.

The contextuality of the landscape in which the game species were depicted further confirms this reading. The big game animals of BC were used to reinforce the gendered perception of landscapes constructed as wilderness territories where exploration and adventure could take place and manhood could be tested. The landscape was portrayed as dangerous and a place for male challenge.[51] Daily diaries or journals were carefully kept to record the chronological instances especially of the pleasures, excitements and dangers of the stalking of wild and fierce big animals. Personal sacrifice, hardship in extreme weather, miraculous escapes, severe cold, unceasing exertion, steep declivities of tremendous mountains, penetration of unknown canyons, fording swirling torrents, scaling perilous cliffs, descending precipitous slopes, wading treacherous torrents – these and more were the subject matter of the verbal and non-verbal communication of the gaming adventures. Scenes in which hunters confront their quarry are examples of how landscapes were made into settings for a celebration of masculinity and conquest. To stalk a big horn sheep ram on the loftiest summits of the Rockies or to track an elk bull through the deep forests of the lower mountain slopes involved manly solitude in rough and savage terrains of wild nature far away from the confines of the domestic world of women. These were uncivilised primeval places where only men with great physical strength, perseverance and courage dared to go. Thus the physiography of the landscape conveyed the idea of men as conquerors of unclaimed territory and the presence of big game or hunters in the landscape represents nature as a wilderness playground for males. Big game trophies were not only symbols of imperial conquest but also of confirmation of the essential masculinity of European civilisation – confirmed in the remoteness of the BC wilderness.

As such, part of the hunting lore was mountaineering. In 1802, the German scientific explorer Alexander von Humboldt (1769–1859) had tried but failed to scale Chimborazo; not until 1880 was this Andean peak 'conquered', a feat performed by Edward Whymper (1840–1911), the London artist (and brother to Charles) and mountaineering hero who had earlier ascended the Matterhorn. Late in his life, at the invitation of the newly completed Canadian Pacific Railroad, he visited the Canadian Rockies (to the disappointment of his hosts, he did not write about his mountaineering feats – being too old and in ill health). The idea of the male conquest of nature communicated by the representing of big game trophies in a context of mountain iconography, was the leading theme of the visual representation of hunting adventures. This was clearly displayed in Hornaday's Kootenay hunting narrative which includes many photographs of big game trophies with mountain landscape backdrops. A photograph entitled 'Phillips Peak' shows Hornaday and Phillips posed with their hunting rifles while surveying the panoramic vista of the Selkirk mountains. Again, by killing and exhibiting a particular species, the hunter conflated his abilities with those of the animal he had shot and killed. For example, the representation of species such as the mountain sheep and mountain goat celebrated the mountaineering skills of the person who had succeeded in slaying these adroit climbers, the denizens of the rocky wastes.

The Irish-born surveyor and sportsman Arthur O. Wheeler (1860–1945) was the first to introduce mountain climbing as recreation in North America. He played a leading role in founding the Alpine Club of Canada in 1906 and was its first president. His book, *The Selkirk Range* (1906), contained a chapter by Baillie-Grohman, a member of the prestigious British Alpine Club, who had written extensively of the sporting and mountaineering traditions of the Tyrolean alps.[52] *The Selkirk Range* was illustrated by many photographs of mountain peaks and the mountaineers who conquered them and in addition there were photographs of big game trophies. Like Baillie-Grohman, Wheeler was an avid hunter who stalked the big game he encountered in the high altitudes of the Selkirks, including grizzlies: 'The Selkirk Range in British Columbia offers a greater diversity of Big Game than anywhere else in the great dominion,' wrote Wheeler 'and hundreds of big game hunters from all parts of the world visit that district yearly, in order to add a few more specimens to their collection of trophies of the chase'.[53]

A further instance of the fusing of trophy, landscape and hunter was formulated by Baillie-Grohman who described how his favourite wapiti head reminded him that there were 'few more inspiring sights than a fine stag in his true home, the beautiful Alpine retreats high up on certain of the great ranges of the Rocky Mountains. Scenery, grand as it may be, receives fresh charm when framed in by a noble pair of branching antlers; and I know no trophy of days spent in the far-off wilds that will recall stirring memories in more lifelike and warmer colours, or fill your soul with such longing desire to return speedily to the well-known glade in the forest, where in a fair struggle the bearer of yonder head found in you his master'.[54] Sheldon, too, blended his trophy with the landscape:

'Among the delights of a wilderness hunter are those of skinning and dressing the game high on the mountains. The supreme moments of joy comes immediately after the success of a difficult stalk. Then, while this state of exaltation continues, intensifying the beauty of the landscape, comes the fascination of examining the prize. Intense satisfaction merged with feelings of elation sustains one during the labor of taking off the skin to complete the possession of a scientific specimen or trophy'.[55]

CONCLUSION

Thus the representational conventions that developed around the trophies, in verbal representations as well as in non-verbal, visual ones, contributed to defining the sportsmen and hunter-naturalists in terms of their essential masculinity. There existed a certain scientific interest in these animals, their antlers, horns, and dimensions. The connection with the work of empire was present, too. Yet the meaning of the secondary trophy representations went well beyond the parameters of science or empire. The restricted number of approximately half a dozen principal game species can not be explained in terms of the scientific value of just these kinds of animals, but only by reference to their subjective conflation value to the hunters. The picture of a heavy and well-palmated head of horns indicated expeditionary sway; a pair of large multi-tined antlers denoted masculine vigour; a stuffed rock-climber alluded to manly prowess in mastering precipitous terrain. In a naked instance of conflation, Phillips was shown in 'a most dangerous position' on a rock face in the Selkirk Mountains, in a situation of bilateral symmetry, the hunter matching the mountain goat opposite in fearless climbing agility (Figure 7). In another instance of undisguised conflation, Phillipps-Wolley depicted himself on the title page to his *Big Game Shooting* (1894) not standing next to, and lording over, a slain game specimen, but merging with a trophy wapiti by covering himself with the animals enormous antlers: the victor fused with the vanquished, the sheer magnitude of the trophy conferring greatness on the human hunter (Fig. 8).

FIGURE 7. 'Mr. Phillip's Most Dangerous Position,' illustration by Charles Hudson in William Hornaday's *Campfires in the Canadian Rockies* (1906).

FIGURE 8. Title page illustration by Charles Whymper in Clive Phillipp-Wolley's *Big Game Shooting*, vol. I (1894).

NOTES

[1] On mounted animals as cultural icons, see Donna Haraway's deconstruction of the Akeley Hall, 'Teddy Bear Patriarchy: Taxidermy in the Garden of Eden, New York City, 1908–36', in *Primate Visions: Gender, Race and Nature in the World of Modern Science* (New York: Routledge, 1989), 26–58. On the art history of dioramas, see Karen Wonders, *Habitat Dioramas: Illusions of Wilderness in Museums of Natural History* (Stockholm: Almquist & Wiksell, 1993). On wild animal representation in general, including trophies, see John Dorst, *Framing the Wild: Animals on Display* (Laramie: University of Wyoming Art Museum, 2002).

[2] Karen Wonders, 'Sportsman's Eden: A Wilderness Besieged', *The Beaver* (Dec. 1999/Jan. 2000), 30–37, 'A Sportsman's Eden: A Wilderness Beckons', *The Beaver* (Oct./Nov. 1999), 26–32.

[3] William Francis. Ainsworth, ed. *All Round the World: An Illustrated Record of Voyages, Travels and Adventures in All Parts of the Globe*, 4 vols. (London: W. Kent, 1860–62); William A. Baillie-Grohman, *Fifteen Years' Sport and Life in the Hunting Grounds of Western America and British Columbia* (London: Horace Cox, 1900, 1907); J. R. Bradley, *Hunting Big Game in Far Northwest British Columbia* (New York: Mail & Express, 1904); William T. Hornaday, *Camp-Fires in the Canadian Rockies* (New York: Scribners,

1906); Edward J. House, *A Hunter's Camp-Fire* (New York, Harper, 1909); Horace G. Hutchinson, ed. *Big Game Shooting*, 2 vols. (London: Country Life, 1905); A. E. Leatham, *Sport in Five Continents* (London: Blackwood, 1912); Thomas Martindale, *Sport Royal* (Philadelphia: Shaw, 1897); Thomas Martindale, *Sport Indeed* (London: Everett, 1907); Thomas Martindale, *With Gun and Guide* (Philadelphia: Jacobs, 1910); Paul Niedieck, *Mit der Büchse in fünf Weltteilen* (Berlin: Parey, 1905); Philipp von Oberländer, *Jagdfahrten in Nordamerika* (Wien: Hubert & Lahme, 1911); Clive Phillipps-Wolley, ed. *Big Game Shooting*, 2 vols. (London: Longmans, 1894); Warburton Pike, *Through the Subarctic Forest* (London: Edward Arnold, 1896); John Rogers, *Sport in Vancouver and Newfoundland* (London: Chapman & Hall, 1912); Heywood W. Seton-Karr, *Bear-hunting in the White Mountains* (London: Chapman & Hall, 1891); Charles Sheldon, *The Wilderness of the North Pacific Coast Islands* (New York, Scribners, 1912); George O. Shields, *Cruisings in the Cascades* (New York and Chicago: Rand, McNally, 1889); George O. Shields, ed. *The Big Game of North America* (New York and Chicago: Rand, McNally, 1890); Mrs. Algernon St. Maur [The Duchess of Somerset], *Impressions of a Tenderfoot* (London: John Murray, 1890); William S. Thomas, *Hunting Big Game with Gun and with Kodak* (New York: Putman's, 1906); J. Turner-Turner, *Three Years Hunting and Trapping in America and the Great North-West* (London: Maclure, 1888); *Life in the Backwoods* (London: Stereoscopic, 1888); Harold F. Wallace, *Stalks Abroad* (London: Longmans, 1908); George Bird Grinnell, Casper Whitney, eds. *Musk-Ox, Bison, Sheep and Goat* (New York: Macmillan, 1904).

[4] Paul Niedieck, *Mit der Büchse in fünf Weltteilen; Beschreibung von 14 Jagdexpeditionen* (Berlin: Parey, 1905). 2nd edition 1905. Reprints 1906, 1907, 1909. 3rd. edition 1922. French translation 1907. English translation by H. B. Stanwell, *With Rifle in Five Continents* (London: Rowland Ward, 1908; New York: Scribners, 1909).

[5] William. A. Baillie-Grohman, *Camps in the Rockies: Being a Narrative of Life on the Frontier, and Sport in the Rocky Mountains* (London: Sampson Low, 1882), reprint 1883. (New York: Scribners, 1882), reprints 1884, 1896, 1898, 1905, 1910). By 1900, Baillie-Grohman could report in *Sport and Life*, that his books had received over 57 reviews in the English and American press.

[6] *British Sports and Sportsmen Past & Present*, 13 vols (London: Sportsman, 1908–38).

[7] Baillie-Grohman, *Sport and Life*, frontispiece.

[8] The animal-man symbolism of big game hunting as a celebration of masculinity is explored in my 'Caccia grossa nel XIX secolo: un trionfo della mascolinita', in Georgio Verzotti, ed. *Il Bello e le bestie: Metamorfosi, artifici e ibridi dal mito all'immaginario scientifico* (Milano: Skira, 2004), 199–208.

[9] James Ryan, *Picturing Empire: Photography and the Visualization of the British Empire* (London: Reaktion, 1997), especially chapter 4, 'Hunting with the Camera', 99–138.

[10] Oberländer, 59. Hornaday, 103.

[11] Harriet Ritvo, *The Animal Estate: the English and other Creatures in the Victorian Age* (Cambridge MA: Harvard UP, 1987), chapters 5 and 6, 205–88. See also Ritvo's recent overview of the role played by animals in environmental history, 'Animal Planet', in *Environmental History* vol. 9, no. 2, (April 2004), 204–20.

[12] Michael Lynch and S. Woolgar, eds. *Representation in Scientific Practice* (Cambridge MA: MIT Press, 1990); Renato Mazzolini, ed. *Non-Verbal Communication in Science Prior to 1900* (Florence: Olshki, 1993); Stephanie Moses, *Ancestral Images. The Iconography of Human Origins* (Ithaca: Cornell UP, 1998).

[13] David Livingstone, *Putting Science in Its Place: Geographies of Scientific Knowledge* (Chicago: Chicago UP, 2003), 8.

[14] Livingstone, 10.

[15] Joan M. Schwartz and James R. Ryan, eds. *Picturing Place: Photography and the Geographical Imagination* (London: Tauris, 2003).

[16] Baillie-Grohman, *Sport and Life*, 142–3.

[17] Ibid., 88.

[18] William Baillie-Grohman, 'Hunting the Rocky Mountain Goat', *The Century* (Dec. 1884), 193–203; 199.

[19] Ibid. Another account by Baillie-Grohman is 'Stalking the Haplocerus in the Selkirks', *World Wide Magazine* (May, 1895), 127–33.

[20] John Fannin, 'The Rocky Mountain Goat', in G. O. Shields, *The Big Game of North America* (New York: Rand, McNally, 1890), 343–61. Fannin was a knowledgeable self-trained naturalist and in 1896 was appointed provincial taxidermist and curator of the new Provincial Museum.

[21] Owen Wister, 'The White Goat and his Ways', George Bird Grinnell and Casper Whitney, eds. *Musk-Ox, Bison, Sheep and Goat* (New York: Macmillan, 1904), 227–76.

[22] Karen Wonders, 'Big Game Hunting and the Birth of Wildlife Art', in *Carl Rungius: Sportsman Artist,* ed. M. Kjorlien (Toronto: Warwick, 2001), 17–38.

[23] Shields, *Cruising in the Cascades*, 180.

[24] Maximilian zu Wied, *Reise in das Innere Nord-Amerika in den Jahren 1832 bis 1834* (Koblenz: Hoelscher, 1839–41), 2 vols. and Atlas. Palliser published an illustrated hunting narrative of his expedition to the American West, *Solitary Rambles and Adventures of a Hunter in the Prairies* (London: Murray, 1853). Catlin's *Life Among the Indians* (London: Gall & Inglis, 1874) included an illustration of a grizzly bear attack, 'Grizzly bears overhauling us'.

[25] Ainsworth, *All Round the World.*

[26] Baillie-Grohman, *Sport and Life*, 43.

[27] *National Cyclopaedia of American Biography*. Phillips' large trophy collection was donated to the Carnegie Institute in Pittsburgh. In 1923 he received the gold medal from the Permanent Wildlife Protection Fund.

[28] Shields, *Cruising in the Cascades*, 181.

[29] Baillie-Grohman, *Sport and Life*, 44.

[30] William A. Baillie-Grohman, 'Wapiti Hunting in North America', *The Illustrated London News,* 6 Nov. 1886, n.p. The engraving is by Richard Caton Woodville, a London-based artist whose father was the American artist of the name, a well-known illustrator of western scenes.

[31] Baillie-Grohman, *Camps in the Rockies*, p. 122.

[32] Prentiss Gray, ed. *Records of North American Big Game* (New York: Derrydale Press, 1932), 73.

[33] House, 307.

[34] Ritvo, 287–88.

[35] John M. MacKenzie, *The Empire of Nature: Hunting, Conservation and British Imperialism* (Manchester: Manchester UP, 1988); Peter Boomgaard, *Frontiers of Fear: Tigers and People in the Malay World, 1600–1950* (New Haven: Yale University Press,

2001); William Storey, 'Big Cats and Imperialism: Lion and Tiger Hunting in Kenya and Northern India, 1898–1930', *Journal of World History* 2, no. 2 (1991): 135–73; and William Beinart, 'Empire, Hunting and Ecological Change in Southern and Central Africa', *Past and Present* 128 (1990): 162–86.

[36] For an example of how the notion of biological nativeness became invested with political meaning in the Swedish context, see my 'Habitat Dioramas and the Issue of Nativeness', *Landscape Research*, vol. 28, no. 1, (2003), 89–100.

[37] Greg Gillespie, '"I Was Well Pleased with Our Sport among the Buffalo": Big-Game Hunters, Travel Writing, and Cultural Imperialism in the British North American West, 1847–72', *The Canadian Historical Review* 83, 4, (2002): 555–84; and F. G. Moyles and Doug Owram, '"Hunter's Paradise": Imperial-Minded Sportsmen in Canada', in *Imperial Dreams and Colonial Realities, British Views of Canada 1880–1914* (Toronto: University of Toronto Press, 1988), 61–85.

[38] This view persisted well into the twentieth century and included Canada, Australia, Malaysia, New Zealand, India and East Africa. See Hugh Gunn, 'The Sportsman as an Empire Builder', in Hugh Gunn, ed. *Empire Big Game* (London: Simpkin, 1925): 1–26. An essay by Charles Hose, 'Big Game and Fur Animals of British Columbia', ends with a quote from Kipling to express the English hunter's longing for 'the wilder parts of our glorious Empire', 56.

[39] Ritvo, 287.

[40] Tina Loo, 'Making a Modern Wilderness: Conserving Wildlife in Twentieth-Century Canada', *The Canadian Historical Review* (2000), 92–121.

[41] See Sharon Macdonald, 'Exhibitions of Power and Powers of Exhibition: An Introduction to the Politics of Display', in Sharon Macdonald, ed. *The Politics of Display: Museums, Science, Culture* (London: Routledge, 1998), and Annie Coombes, *Reinventing Africa: Museums, Material Culture and Popular Imagination* (New Haven: Yale UP, 1994).

[42] George Colpitts, *Game in the Garden: A Human History of Wildlife in Western Canada to 1940* (Vancouver: University of British Columbia Press, 2003).

[43] Michael Kimmel, *Manhood in America: a Cultural History* (New York: Free Press, 1996), 136; MacKenzie, *The Empire of Nature*; Tina Loo, 'Of Moose and Men: Hunting for Masculinities in British Columbia, 1880–1939', *Western Historical Quarterly* 32 (Autumn 2002), 296–319.

[44] Loo, 'Of Moose and Men', 296.

[45] This conclusion is supported by *trompe l'oeil* paintings of hunting trophies, a genre practiced by the influential American artist William M. Harnett (1848–1898). See David M. Lubin, A Manly Art: American *Trompe L'Oeil* Painting and the Manufacture of Masculinity,' in *The Material Culture of Gender: The Gender of Material Culture* (Hanover: University Press of New England, 1997), eds. Katharine Martinez and Kenneth L. Ames, 365–89. A broader study in the same volume further supports the centrality of gender to hunting iconography: Ruth Irwin Weidner, 'Gifts of Wild Game: Masculine and Feminine in Nineteenth-Century Hunting Imagery,' 337–64.

[46] The caption 'Victor and Vanquished' appears on an photogravure of a wilderness hunter dressed in buckskins and posed beside his massive grizzly trophy which is spread out so as to clearly show the sharp weaponry of claws and teeth possessed by the beast. This is one of many trophy representations in *Game of British Columbia, Official Bulletin No. 17*, Legislative Assembly, Bureau of Provincial Information (1906).

[47] Ritvo, 267.
[48] Shields, *Cruising in the Cascades*, 181.
[49] Baillie-Grohman, *Camps in the Rockies*, 123.
[50] Baillie-Grohman, 'Wapiti Hunting in North America' (1886), n.p.
[51] 'Landscape and Gender: the Visual Representations of Alexander von Humboldt's "Views of Nature"', a paper presented by Karen Wonders at the European Society for Environmental History conference, St. Andrews University, Scotland, 2001.
[52] A. O. Wheeler, *The Selkirk Range* (Ottawa: Government Printing Office, 1905). Chapter 5, 'Notes on the Upper and Lower Kootenay Valleys and Kootenay Lake' by Baillie-Grohman, was taken from an account published first in *The Field* (25 April and 29 May, 1885). See William A. Baillie-Grohman. *Sport in the Alps in the Past and Present* (London: A. & C. Black, 1896) (New York: Scribners, 1896).
[53] Wheeler, 47. Archival photographs taken in 1906, for example, show Wheeler proudly posed on a mountainside with three grizzlies lying at his feet as trophies (in the Wheeler papers at the Whyte Museum and Archives of the Canadian Rockies).
[54] Baillie-Grohman, *Camps in the Rockies*, 121–22.
[55] Charles Sheldon, *The Wilderness of Denali; Explorations of a Hunter-Naturalist in Northern Alaska* (New York: Scribners, 1930), 159.

Index

A

agriculture *see also* crops; farming; livestock ix, 21, 25, 32, 48, 49, 50, 79, 139, 163–5, 170–2, 176, 188, 191, 197, 198, 216, 228–9, 247, 250, 263
Age of Reason *see* Enlightenment
Agta people 264, 274–80
Aitken, Gill vi, ix–xi, xiii, 115–30
Alaska 60, 62, 158, 189
Alps 50, 198, 324, 337
Alpes Maritimes 42–3
America 93, 96
    North 74, 88, 96, 145, 149, 158, 167, 174, 187, 189, 190, 192, 201, 205, 217, 271, 293, 294, 295, 298, 300, 301, 316, 323, 324, 327–30, 333, 334, 337
    South 93
amusement *see* entertainment
angling 80, 136, 243, 306–10
Antarctica 66
anthropocentrism x, xvii, 5, 10, 28, 221, 223
anthropology 83, 188
anthropomorphism v, xviii, 50
ape 7, 11, 147
aquarium 313–14
archaeology viii, 44, 58, 60, 67, 69, 93, 101
archives 22, 24, 25, 43, 94–5, 131, 194, 261–2
Arctic viii, 58–73, 158
aristocracy xvi, 45, 80, 162, 174, 175, 324, 325, 330
Atlantic Ocean 62, 69, 149
Audubon Society 156
auk, little viii, 66–9

Aurochs 215–16, 219
Australia 167, 258
    South-East viii, 74–92
    Western xiii, 237–57
authenticity 227–9
autonomy (of animals) xvi, 219, 221, 294, 301–03, 312, 315
avifauna *see also* birds ix, 60, 62, 157, 159–61, 170

B

badger 141, 176, 206
    culling 141
Bankoff, Greg vii, 21–41, 287
Barnard, Chris 126–7
bear v, xvi, 281, 295, 296, 312, 313
    black 312, 328
    brown 185, 188, 199
    grizzly 332, 335
    polar 314
beaver xvii, 293, 295, 297, 307, 314, 316
behaviour, animal 9, 13, 64, 117, 132, 146, 148, 160, 187, 215–16, 218–221, 223, 227, 230, 267, 274, 276, 281, 294, 311, 336
Bentham, Jeremy 7
Berger, John 311
Bering Sea 60, 62
biocentrism 1
biodiversity; biological diversity 11, 12, 15, 42, 124, 177, 191, 225–30, 251
biology; biological research 1, 2, 3, 12, 60, 62, 64, 69, 132, 139, 146, 148, 149, 161, 177, 188, 190, 192, 200, 206, 230, 261
    conservation 11
    evolutionary 122

Index

birds *see also* avifauna and individual species names v, vi, viii, ix, x, xiii, 2, 4, 6, 7, 8, 10, 28, 62, 66–9, 74–92, 115–16, 123, 135, 146, 148, 156–84, 192, 237–57, 297, 300, 302–03, 310, 312,

bison 215, 216, 295, 312
   European 215, 216
   plains 312

blackbird 164

boar, wild 45, 190, 204, 205, 214, 216, 229

bones viii, 58–62, 67–9, 203,

Bonhomme, Brian ix–x, xvi, 156–84

botany 2, 83, 160

bounty (for hunting) xii, xiii, 81, 132, 192–3, 242

breeding *see also* inbreeding; interbreeding vii, xiii, 13, 79, 80, 86–7, 132–3, 136, 138, 141–3, 146, 189–90, 197, 198, 218, 225, 238, 240
   'breeding back' 216, 218, 219, 221
   captive 9–11, 15, 17, 259, 272, 280

Britain *see* UK

British Columbia 293–322, 323–44

C

camel 4

Canada 138, 143, 144, 148, 167, 172, 293–322, 323–44

capercaillie 120, 124

captivity *see also* breeding, captive xvii, 5, 9–11, 15, 17, 218, 259, 271–2, 279, 280, 294, 295, 310–15

carabao 21, 25, 26, 27, 29, 30, 31, 33, 277

Caribbean vii, 93–111

carnivore 185, 187, 188, 194, 196–9, 204–06, 260

catch (in fishing and whaling) viii, 60, 61, 65, 69, 99, 104, 136, 142, 148, 242, 259, 308

cats *see also* individual species names v, 4, 5, 9, 11, 86, 176

cattle v, xii, 4, 9, 21, 26, 29, 30, 32, 33, 44, 45, 197, 198, 199, 204, 205, 215, 219, 222, 227, 228, 261, 262, 297, 298
   Heck 215, 219, 220, 221, 224, 225, 230

charisma v, ix, 3–5, 10, 11

chauvinism, human 8

cheetah v, 13, 14

chicken *see also* poultry v, 4, 21, 28, 30, 222, 276, 297

child v, 4, 10, 46, 167, 187, 198, 259, 262, 267, 274, 276, 277, 281, 297

chimpanzee xvii, 7, 8

China 32, 159, 160, 172

Christianity xii, 48, 49, 163, 168, 188, 261, 268–9, 278

Christiansen, Stine B. 215–33

city *see* urban

class, social xvi, 8, 29, 51, 77, 82, 97, 141, 174, 245, 302, 309, 316

classification 2, 3, 13, 16, 17, 51

cod, polar 66

co-existence 268, 280, 301

colonial; colony (historical / political term) viii, ix, xv, xvii, 22, 74–7, 79, 80, 82, 88, 97, 101, 240, 261, 265, 269, 295, 334

colony (of animals / birds) viii, xi, 62, 65, 67, 69, 132, 138, 249

colonising (by animals / plants) xii, 12, 14, 185, 200–03, 205

conflict
   of people and animals xiii, 45, 148, 185, 188, 258, 281, 301

Index

socio-political xvi, 45, 147, 149, 250, 252
values 147, 217, 223
conservation vi, ix–xii, xiv–xvi, 94, 115–130, 131–55, 160, 174–5, 191, 218, 223, 224, 227, 230, 243, 247, 259, 261, 273, 279–81, 298, 303, 314, 334
conservationist ix, xii, 42, 116, 120–7, 132, 149, 160, 173, 177, 293, 329
cormorant xiii, 81, 147, 172, 237–57
cougar xvi, 296, 303–5, 313, 315, 328
cow *see* cattle
coyote 312
crocodile xiv–xv, 258–92
   farming 272, 280
   Indo-Pacific 258, 259, 262, 268, 274, 278–9
   Philippine 258, 259, 261, 264, 271, 274–7, 278, 281
   leather / skin 259, 268, 271, 272, 277, 279, 280
crocodile-god xiv, 261, 263, 265, 267
crop x, 21, 27, 32, 33, 46, 52, 148, 163, 159, 269
crossbill, Scottish 124
crow xvi, 115, 120, 172, 175, 301–03, 306, 315
cruelty (to animals) xi, xiii, xvii, 6, 7, 156, 163, 165–9, 171, 174, 215, 223, 303
crustacean xiii, 8, 64, 243, 246
culling ix–xi, xii, xvi, 15, 120–7, 131–2, 137, 139–49, 185, 190, 223–4
culture vi, viii, xi, xiv–xv, xvii, 4, 28, 33, 47–52, 75, 80, 82–5, 88, 103, 104, 146–8, 156–7, 166, 168, 221, 227, 238, 240–3, 247, 249–52, 258–92, 325, 334

D

Dahlström, Anna xi–xiii, 185–214
Darling, Frank Fraser 135, 145–7
Darwin/ Darwinian 3, 12, 117, 119, 162, 169
Deakin, Roger x, 122
de-domestication xii, xiii, 214–33
deer 11, 45, 215, 216, 223, 267, 296, 303, 305, 330, 335
   muntjac 148
   red ix–xi, 115, 120–7, 148, 190, 197
   roe 148, 190, 197, 204, 205
Denmark 216
development, economic / infrastructure x, 42, 238, 247, 249, 250–2, 273
destruction 15, 22, 24–5, 28, 29, 31, 33, 263, 268, 294
   of animal / birds 79, 86, 87, 137, 164–5, 167, 171, 174, 175, 176, 192, 194, 200, 203, 241, 242, 248, 249, 297
   of habitat / environment xv, 15, 44, 79, 86, 104, 118, 123, 223, 281
disaster vii, 21–41, 50,
disease 21, 26, 27, 29, 32, 117, 122, 123, 164, 192, 222, 313
distribution (of animal populations) 60–1, 94, 101, 160, 161, 188, 200, 202, 206, 258, 265
dog v, vi, xii, 4, 5, 9, 11, 74, 76, 78, 80, 185, 187, 188, 196, 219, 276, 299, 301, 313
dolphin 11, 93, 100–01, 103–04
domestic; domestication *see also* de-domestication vii, xii, xiii, xvi, 4–5, 9–10, 15, 21–41, 50, 75, 76, 118, 165, 188, 197, 206, 215–33, 297–8, 316, 330
Dow, Coral viii–ix, x, 74–92
drought 21, 32, 46, 50, 225

duck 4, 21, 28, 30, 76, 78, 80–6, 88, 240, 241, 242, 295, 298, 303
  eider viii, 66, 69
  Pacific black 75, 79
  ruddy 115
  teal 75, 78, 82, 85, 88, 240
  white-eyed 86
  white-headed 115
dugong 11
duty xii, 5–6, 163, 168, 224, 230

E

eagle
  bald 4
  golden 124
  Steller's sea 158
earthquake 21–2, 27–8, 263
ecocentrism 1, 3
ecology; ecologist vi, ix, 3, 12, 14, 42, 60, 69, 84, 87, 93, 139, 188, 216, 238, 246, 250, 295, 314
economy; economic vi, vii, ix, x, xiv, 4, 32, 33, 42, 44–6, 49–51, 61, 143, 144, 147, 149, 161, 170, 173, 191, 223, 241, 242–4, 246, 251, 272–3, 278–81
ecosystem vi, viii, ix, x, xiii, xv, xvii, 13–17, 58–73, 92, 115, 120, 142, 169, 215, 217, 220, 223, 228, 244
education 8–10, 14, 17, 149, 162, 164, 166, 173, 174, 227, 314
egg vii, 76, 79, 82, 86, 135, 158, 161, 164, 171, 172, 249, 258, 275
elephant v, 10, 11, 126, 127
  African 148
elk 145, 215, 312, 313, 330, 336
empire 271, 325, 334, 337, 338
  British 323, 75
  Russian 156–84
empiricism 6, 12, 271
endangered species 8–10, 12, 15, 17, 18, 192, 259, 314

England xvi, 76–8, 83, 133, 140–6, 148, 149, 166, 177, 245, 246,
Enlightenment 6, 46–7
entertainment 6–10, 17, 121, 218, 299, 312, 334
ethics *see also* moral v, xi, xii, xv, 145, 166, 215–33, 280
European Union 144, 148, 185, 222, 224
Europe; European ix, xii, 22, 46, 51, 58, 75, 83–5, 87–8, 93, 96, 149, 156, 157, 162, 170, 171, 174, 177, 187, 188, 192, 203, 205, 215, 216, 217, 219, 223, 238, 240, 266, 278, 324, 325, 329, 331, 334, 337
  Central 191
  Eastern 160
  Northern 218
  Southern 42, 166, 167, 174
  Western 44, 49, 61, 156, 157, 160, 162, 166, 167, 168, 198
evolution vi, 3, 5, 8, 11, 12, 14–17, 79, 116–19, 122, 126–7, 169, 197,
exotic xvii, 3, 4, 5, 9, 10, 83, 294, 299, 312, 334
extinction vi, viii, xii, xvii, 4, 8, 9, 11, 15, 17, 69, 84, 86, 87, 93, 99, 102, 104, 188, 192, 216, 219, 258–9, 280

F

farming; farmer *see also* agriculture; crops; livestock v, xiv, 21, 27, 31, 32, 42, 43, 45, 48, 52, 122, 148, 165, 185, 187, 188, 191, 192, 196, 198, 199, 205, 218, 22, 247, 258, 261, 272, 277, 278, 280, 281
Farne Islands, UK 130–46
fear v, xi, xiv, xvii, 24, 47–52, 173, 185, 259, 261, 263, 265, 268, 274, 278, 280,
feral 29, 216, 218, 220

Index

film *see* movie
finch 164
Finland 188
fire 42, 52, 296, 297, 312,
fish *see also* individual species names xiii, 2, 4, 5, 28, 31, 66, 67, 69, 238, 239, 241–51, 266, 267, 274, 281, 307–08, 310
fishing; fisher; fishery *see also* angling xi, xiii, xvi, 31, 58, 80, 86, 93, 95, 97, 99, 100–05, 131–2, 136–49, 168, 241–51, 258, 261, 266, 269, 274, 281, 298, 306–10, 315, 316
fitness, evolutionary 115–20, 127
flood vii, 21, 23–33, 50, 74, 88, 123, 278, 281, 306, 316
folklore xii, 49, 131, 147, 187, 188, 276
forest xv 44, 48, 49, 123, 124, 166, 169, 191, 196, 203, 204, 216, 219, 223, 271, 274, 275, 277, 280, 295, 296–9, 302, 303, 307, 316, 324, 336, 338
forestry 170, 176, 223, 302
Forbes, H.A. 44
Foucault, Michel 46–7
fox xvi, 11, 115, 116, 120, 141, 196, 199 arctic 196
France 43, 160, 164, 165, 172
Franz Josef Land 58, 64
Frith, H.J. 84–5
fulmar 67, 69

G

Gamborg, Christian vi, xii–xiii, 215–36
game viii, ix, x, xii, xv, xvi, xvii, 45, 75, 76, 78–82, 115, 162–4, 169, 170, 173–5, 185, 190, 192, 197, 204–05, 223, 240–1, 243, 247, 299, 301, 303–05, 310, 323–5, 328–40

gender xvii, 29, 232–44
genetics; genes v, 2, 3, 9, 12, 14, 15, 185, 216–21, 226
Germany; German 98, 157, 159, 164, 167, 168, 171, 177, 328, 337
Gippsland Lakes, Australia viii, 74–92
global warming 43
goat vii, xv–xvi, 4, 21, 30, 42–57, 197, 198, 199, 204, 205, 305
mountain 325–8, 337–8
goose 67, 86, 149
barnacle 148
Cape Barren 87
Greenland white-fronted 148
magpie 76
government xi, xiv, 100, 132, 133, 135, 140, 141, 142, 144, 146, 148, 149, 158, 164, 171–4, 184, 247, 249–51, 259, 272, 304, 312, 313
grazing xii, xvii, 33, 42, 43, 45, 46, 49, 85, 123–6, 197–9, 204–05, 215, 216, 298,
Greece 42, 48
Greenpeace 132, 144
Gremmen, Bart 215–33
Grenada 99, 104–05
grouse 75, 115, 149, 162, 298
black 205
Severtsov's 159
guillemot
black 67, 68
Brünnich's 68, 69
common 67, 68
gull 69, 142,
glaucous 67, 68
rosy 161

H

habitat vi, ix, x, xii, xiii, xv, 9, 13–17, 45, 60, 86, 88, 102, 104, 115, 120, 122–5, 145, 146, 185, 187, 192, 202, 203, 216, 219, 223, 228, 241, 247, 249, 251, 279, 280, 281, 295–7, 299, 302, 310, 314, 315, 325, 326, 327, 335, 336

Hacquebord, Louwrens vii–viii, 58–73

Hancock, Keith 84

hare 124, 205, 206

Hawaii 12, 14

hazard vii, 21–35, 118–19, 328

hen harrier 149

herd; herding xii, xv, 27, 45, 187–8, 198–9, 205, 206, 221–2, 228,

heron 81, 172

Highlands, Scottish xi, 124

holism vi, xii, 1, 13, 16, 17, 115, 120, 121

Holland *see* Netherlands

horse 4, 11, 21, 27, 29, 30, 32, 33, 167, 197, 198, 199, 204, 215, 222, 227, 228, 261, 297,
    Konik xii, 215, 219, 220, 221, 224, 225, 230
    Przewalski 159, 220
    Taki 220

humaneness xi, 126, 165, 166, 169

humans v–vii, xi, xii, xiii, xiv, xvi, xvii, 4–8, 11, 13–15, 21, 32–4, 119–21, 147, 149, 186–7, 192, 203, 206, 218–20, 223, 225, 227, 230, 271, 276, 294–8, 302, 304, 311

hunting; hunter vii–ix, x–xii, xv–xvii, 4, 5, 6, 45, 52, 58–73, 74–92, 93–114, 127, 131, 132, 138, 141, 143, 148, 161–4, 169, 171–7, 188–9, 192–4, 196–7, 203–05, 223, 240–1, 243, 247, 259, 271, 277, 298, 302–06, 315, 316, 323–44

husbandry xii, 222

I

iconography xv, xvii, 42, 47, 49, 50, 51, 147, 156, 169, 187, 269, 323–44,

imperialism *see* empire

inbreeding 185, 221

indigenous
    people and culture *see also* names of specific peoples xiv, 74, 101, 260, 261, 266, 271, 273, 278–80
    species 75, 76, 80, 81, 82, 86, 217, 240, 241–3, 247, 301, 304, 307, 314, 316

individualism v–vi, ix–x, xii, xiii, 1, 3, 12–17, 115–30, 145, 147, 222–5, 228,

insect x, 10, 163, 165, 302–03, 307

insectivore 153–5, 171, 302

interbreeding 13, 115

interdependence 162, 244

invertebrate 3, 12

Ireland 148

Italy 167, 171, 172,

IUCN 144, 146

J

Jacoby, Karl xvi, 298

jay 172

Index

K

Kalinga people xiv, xv, 260–1, 274–80,
Kamchatka 158
kangaroo 80, 84, 86, 312
Kant, Immanuel 6
Kardell, Örjan 185–214, vi, xi, xii, xiii
Kheraj, Sean xiii, xvi–xvii, 293–322
Kiley-Worthington, Marthe 126
Kirkwood, J. 116–19
kittiwake 67, 68
Kolars, J. 44
krill 66

L

Lambert, Robert vi, xi, xiii, xvii, 131–55,
landscape x, xiv, 31, 42, 77, 191, 215, 216–17, 221, 228, 238, 240, 251, 259, 268, 279, 281, 295, 298, 299, 304, 336–8
    painting 156, 168, 325, 327
law *see* legislation
Lee, Keekok v–vi, ix, xi, xiii, xvii, 1–18
legend *see also* folklore; myth xii, 187, 262
legislation ix, xiii, xvi, 26, 43, 45, 75, 81–2, 84, 102, 138, 146, 148–9, 156, 161, 162–6, 170–7, 197, 221–3, 240–2, 247, 259, 298, 316
lemur 11
leopard 10
Leopold, Aldo 145
lion 4, 14, 281,
literature 48, 147, 269, 323
livestock *see also* names of specific types of livestock xii, 21–41, 188–91, 197–200, 203–06, 259, 281, 297, 298
Livingstone, David 326

Luzon, Philippines 21, 22, 26, 29, 32, 258, 260, 267, 270, 274

M

Mabey, Richard 122, 147
magpie 75, 172
Mak Mak people 87
mammal v, vi, 4–8, 10, 11, 13, 15, 84, 293
    sea vii, viii, 67, 93–111, 143, 147
management (of habitat or species) vi, xi, xiii, xvi, 44, 52, 119, 122, 131, 132, 141, 144, 146, 148, 149, 185, 206, 215–33, 252
manatee 11, 93, 95, 101–05
Manila, Philippines 22, 24, 27, 31, 261, 263, 268, 272
marine environment 58, 69,
masculinity xvii, 324, 335–8
meat vii,
medieval *see* Middle Ages
Mediterranean vii, 42–5, 167, 169
Melbourne, Australia 74–86
midden viii, 60, 62, 67, 69
Middle Ages xv, 43, 51, 199, 268
Middle East 42–3
migration; migrant 60, 62, 64, 87, 158, 167, 168, 171
milk vii, 4, 44, 297
Mindanao, Philippines 25, 32, 258, 260, 267, 280
mink 218
monkey xvi, 11, 295, 312, 313
monsoon 24
moorland 115, 124, 149
moose 185, 190, 197, 204, 205
morality; moral *see also* ethics xi, xiv, 6–8, 13, 144, 166, 167, 216, 223–6, 230, 267, 335
Moscow 157, 173, 175, 176

mountain 12, 14, 28, 48, 49, 50, 83, 169, 304, 324, 336–8
mountain goat *see* goat
mouse 5
movie 273, 278
museum 75, 82, 83, 160, 164, 323, 334,
myth v, xii, xiv, xv, 47, 48, 52, 141, 187, 262, 263, 267

N

national park 145, 167, 293, 294, 298
National Trust 130, 135, 136, 141, 146
nationalism x, 4, 122, 156, 166
native *see* indigenous
natural history 74, 141, 156, 169, 245, 310, 323, 325,
natural selection *see also* fitness 3, 12, 115, 116–20, 169
Netherlands xii, 172, 216, 215, 221
New South Wales 84, 85
New Zealand 148, 167, 172, 240, 243, 247
nightingale 164, 168
Norway 138, 147, 172, 191, 199, 200

O

oil 115, 118
    seal 147
    whale viii, 58, 97–8, 101, 104
Orkney, UK 142–4
ornithology 76, 78, 84, 86, 87, 156–64, 168–77, 244
owl 172, 302
    eagle 173
    great horned 301
    short-eared 124

P

Pacific Northwest, USA 157, 323

Palawan
paleoecology 93
panda 4
Paris Convention x, 157, 170–7
pastoralism 48, 50, 78, 85
pelican 85, 172, 237, 238, 240, 242–3
penguin 66
Persoon, Gerard A. 258–92
Perth, Australia xiii, 237–57
pest xi, 5, 139, 148, 223, 242, 243, 246, 247, 271, 273
pet 4–5, 30
pheasant 75, 79, 162, 223, 313
Philippines vii, xiv, xv, 21–41, 258–92
philosophy v–vi, xi, 1, 3, 5–8, 11, 13, 15, 17, 120–1, 224
photography 95, 134, 142, 238, 305, 323–6, 329, 333, 337
pig 4, 21, 30, 31, 199, 205, 216, 277, 279, 297, 298
pigeon 75, 78, 81, 86, 88
plankton 60
Plato 48
plumage xi, 80, 166, 174
pluralism 222, 230
politics; political 8, 29, 33, 143, 144, 147, 149, 162, 177, 185, 192, 245, 251, 252, 259, 324, 326, 335
population
    animal vii, viii, ix, x, xi–xiii, 9, 12–15, 29, 30, 31, 42–5, 64, 66, 74, 84, 87, 93, 95, 98, 99, 104, 115, 120–6, 133, 135–9, 141–9, 164, 166, 170, 173, 176, 185, 187–94, 197, 200–01, 204–06, 215–24, 259, 271, 275, 280, 294, 295, 297, 299, 300, 301, 310, 314, 315, 316

Index

human vii, xiv, 15, 21, 29, 32, 43,
    45–50, 97, 247, 271, 278,
    293
Port of Spain, Trinidad 97, 98
poultry 21, 29, 30, 31, 35, 165, 280
power xiv, xvii, 15, 45, 47–9, 132, 142,
    148, 245, 260, 262–3, 324, 334
pre-Columbian era 93, 96, 105
predator viii, xii, xiii, 115, 127, 139, 146,
    147, 175, 199, 243, 301, 302,
    303
prejudice xv, 46, 47, 49–51, 242, 244–5,
    248–9, 266
prey viii, 79, 80, 189, 190, 197, 198,
    200, 203–06,
protection x, xi–xii, xiii, 80–2, 86, 99,
    101–02, 115, 120–5, 131–2, 135,
    136, 138–40, 143–9, 156–84,
    187–8, 192, 198–9, 204–06, 217,
    221–3, 228, 230, 241–3, 247–9,
    251, 259, 263, 277, 279, 303,
    310, 315
ptarmigan 124
public, the xi–xii, xvi, xvii, 9, 10, 17, 81,
    131, 132, 141–44, 148–9, 157,
    172–4, 185, 244–5, 249, 295,
    314–16, 324
Pyrenees 50

Q

quail 28, 75, 76, 78–81, 86, 87

R

rabbit 142, 312
Rachels, James 12
raccoon xvi, 297, 299, 301–02, 312, 314
reclamation, land 238, 250–1, 272
reconstruction, historical xii, 60, 62, 69,
    74, 93, 261
redpoll 124

Regan, Tom 5–8, 13
regeneration, of habitat 123–5, 223
rehabilitation, of animals ix–x, 115–120,
    125–7, 314
reindeer 185, 187
relationship
    ecological and interspecies 205, 225,
        245, 249, 316
    human with the natural world vii,
        xiii, 28, 34, 131, 259–60,
        267, 271, 274, 293, 304, 315
religion vi, x, xv, 4, 32, 47, 168–9, 261,
    268, 269
representation vi, xv, xvii, 48, 49, 52,
    238, 252, 280, 323–44
restoration, ecological xii, 215–33, 316
Revolution
    Bolshevik 162, 170, 175, 177
    French 46
    Philippine 269, 271
re-wilding xiii, 215, 219
rhinoceros 4, 10, 11
rights
    animal v, vi, ix, x, xi, 6–8, 11, 12, 15,
        17, 141, 147, 148, 188, 224
    human 45, 147
risk 21–2, 29, 31, 33–4, 274, 326
Ritvo, Harriet 325, 334
RISPCA xi, 165–6, 169, 174
rivers 24, 25, 30, 74, 77, 88, 101, 136,
    145, 191, 198, 215, 237–57, 261,
    262, 265, 269, 274–7, 281, 327,
    333
Rizal, Jose P. 269, 271, 281
Rocky Mountains xvii, 333, 336, 337
romantic x, 168
Romero, Aldemaro 93–114
rookery *see* colony
Rothfels, Nigel xvii, 294, 311
RSPCA 131, 141, 149, 165
RSPB 120, 131, 148, 163
Russia ix, x, xi, 61, 156–84, 205

Index

S

Sainsbury, A.W. 117–19
salmon 132, 136, 138, 142, 147, 309,
sanctuary, wildlife 135, 139, 140, 145, 251
Sandøe, Peter 215–34
Sarawak 267
Sassoon, Joanna ix, xiii, 237–57
Scotland ix, xi, 120–5, 131–2, 138, 140–9, 219
Scott, W.H. 260, 261
seal x, xii, xvii, 312
   Antarctic fur 66
   bearded 66
   common 132, 136
   crabeater 66
   Greenland 66
   grey 131–55
sentience 6–8, 13
sentiment x, xi, 144, 145, 165, 168, 259, 295
shag 237–57
shark 98, 100
Sheail, John 131
sheep 4, 21, 30, 32, 42–5, 49, 124, 190, 197–9, 204–05
   bighorn mountain 326, 333
   mountain 326, 328, 331, 335, 337
shooting *see also* hunting viii, xvi, xvii, 77–88, 119–21, 127, 132, 222, 240–9, 299, 302–03
Siberia 158, 159, 161, 170
Siddle, David vii, x, xv–xvi, 42–57
Sierra Madre, Philippines xiv, xvii, 258, 260–1, 273–81
Singer, Peter xi, 5–8, 13, 224
skunk 297, 314
snake 4, 27
snipe viii, 75–6, 78–81, 87–8
Soviet Union 144, 161, 173, 177
Spain 166
sparrow ix, 165, 170, 175
species v–vi, viii–x, xi, xii, xiii, 3, 5, 8–17, 29, 62, 75, 79–88, 115, 118–24, 133, 145–6, 148–9, 164, 169–71, 173, 175, 176, 188, 190, 192, 196, 206, 215–28, 240–4, 247, 249, 258–9, 294–5, 301, 314–16
Spitsbergen 58, 60, 63–5, 67, 69,
sport viii–ix, xvii, 74–90?, 131, 136, 169, 240, 241, 245, 323–4, 326, 329, 330–8
squirrel 295, 299, 301
   Douglas 301
   fox 301
   grey 115, 294, 300, 301
   red 119, 124, 297
SSSI 122
state, the 47, 157, 173, 243
stoat 115
subsistence vii, xvi, 42–6, 49, 132, 298, 316
suffering vi, xi, 3, 7, 21, 24, 126–7, 163, 167, 294, 301,
Sumatra 267
Svalbard vii, 58–73
swallow 164
swan 80, 81, 83, 85–6, 237, 240, 295, 299, 301–04, 312
   black 76, 81, 85–7, 239, 251, 299, 313
   mute 299, 300
Swan River, Australia 237–57
Sweden xi, 167, 185–214
swift 116, 172

T

tarpan 215
Tagbanwa people 260, 264, 265
Tatungalung people 85
taxation 196

Index

taxidermy 323, 325
taxonomy 88, 172, 262
T'boli people 260
teal *see* duck
television v, 132, 141, 178
territory xii, xvi, 189–90, 194–6, 200–03, 206. 296, 336
tiger 1, 4, 10, 15, 148
tree 2, 25, 32, 123–4, 145, 164, 219, 223, 302, 307, 313
Trinidad and Tobago vii, 93–111
trophy 131, 323–8, 333–8
trout 136, 245, 294, 306–07, 309
Tudge, Colin 10
turkey 4, 86
Turkey 44
typhoon 21–2, 24, 26, 29–30, 274

U

UK *see also* England; Scotland; Wales xi, viii, 74–6, 79–80, 97, 123, 127, 131–55, 157, 160, 162–7, 171, 172, 174, 216, 324, 334
Ukraine 173
ungulate 11, 190, 206, 335
urban xvi, 147, 238, 293–322
USA *see also* America 138, 162, 172, 271, 294
USSR *see* Soviet Union
utilitarianism x, 6, 7, 145, 147, 162, 224, 280

V

values (non-economic) ix, x, xiv, xvii, 80, 115–16, 120–4, 217, 224, 226–30, 251, 261, 278, 281
Vancouver, Canada xiv, xvi–xvii, 293–322, 329, 333
van der Ploeg, Jan xiv, xvii, 258–92

van Weerd, Merlijn 258–92
vegetation x, 42–4, 60, 191, 251
Venezuela 94, 103–04
Vera, Frans xii, 215, 216
vermin *see also* pest 77, 147–8, 192, 223, 241, 247, 277, 302
vertebrate 3, 11, 12, 224, 247
Vines, G. 126–7
volcano vii, 27–9
vulnerability vii, x, 21, 28–9, 31–4, 45, 126, 190, 225, 301

W

Wales 122
walrus, Atlantic vii–viii, 58–73
wasp 12, 14
waterfowl *see also* individual species names 74–92, 250, 310
welfare, animal xi, xiii, 15, 17, 125–7, 131, 141, 144–7, 163, 165, 215–33
whale vii–ix, xi, xvii, 4, 11, 58, 60, 62–7, 69, 96–111, 147
  bowhead, 58
  Greenland right viii, 58, 60, 62, 66, 69
  humpback 98, 99
  minke 66
  pilot 98
  sperm 98
whaling vii–viii, 58–73, 96–111
Wigan, M. 121–2, 124–6
wild xii, xiii, xvi, 3, 5, 9, 15, 16, 29, 48, 79, 115–20, 174, 215–33, 258–61, 272, 280–1, 296, 316, 336
wilderness 42, 187, 217, 219, 225, 293, 296, 299, 303, 304, 314, 323, 324, 327, 330, 336–8
Wilson, E.O. 12–13
wisent *see* bison

witch; witchcraft xv, 47, 50, 51, 262, 263, 265, 279
wolf vi, xii, 11, 127, 176, 185–214, 219, 221, 296
Wonders, Karen xvii, 323–44
woodland; woods *see also* forest xv, 42–3, 45, 48, 51, 119, 123–5, 168, 299, 301, 307
woodpecker 172
wool xv, 43, 45, 49, 52

World War I 177
World War II 99, 278, 310

Z

zoo vi, xvi, xvii, 4, 8–11, 15, 141, 294, 295, 311–15
zoologist v, vi, 1–5, 11, 16, 88, 126, 193, 271

www.ingramcontent.com/pod-product-compliance
Lightning Source LLC
Chambersburg PA
CBHW021134230426
43667CB00005B/106